CRIMINAL JUDICIAL REVIEW

This is a comprehensive guide to challenging decisions of criminal courts and public bodies in the criminal justice system using judicial review. Written by a team of criminal and public law practitioners, it considers claims for judicial review arising in the criminal justice system, which now represent a distinct area of public law. These claims are set apart by special considerations and rules; for example, on the limits of the High Court's jurisdiction or the availability of relief during ongoing proceedings.

Criminal practitioners may lack the background to spot public law points. Equally, public law specialists may be unfamiliar with criminal law and types of issues that arise. *Criminal Judicial Review* is intended as a resource for both.

The book deals with the principles, case law, remedies and, the practice and procedure for obtaining legal aid and costs. It will be of assistance to any practitioner preparing or responding to judicial review claims involving the following:

— The Police and the Crown Prosecution Service.
— Magistrates' courts, the Crown Court and Coroners.
— Prisons and the Parole Board.
— Statutory bodies such as the Independent Police Complaints Commission and the Legal Aid Agency.
— Claimants who are children, young persons or have mental disorders.
— The international dimension including extradition proceedings and European Union law.
— Practical considerations such as CPR Part 54, remedies, legal aid and costs.

Criminal Judicial Review

A Practitioner's Guide to Judicial Review in the
Criminal Justice System and Related Areas

General Editor
Piers von Berg

Foreword by
The Rt Hon Lord Judge

·HART·
PUBLISHING
OXFORD AND PORTLAND, OREGON
2014

Published in the United Kingdom by Hart Publishing Ltd
16C Worcester Place, Oxford, OX1 2JW
Telephone: +44 (0)1865 517530
Fax: +44 (0)1865 510710
E-mail: mail@hartpub.co.uk
Website: http://www.hartpub.co.uk

Published in North America (US and Canada) by
Hart Publishing
c/o International Specialized Book Services
920 NE 58th Avenue, Suite 300
Portland, OR 97213-3786
USA
Tel: +1 503 287 3093 or toll-free: (1) 800 944 6190
Fax: +1 503 280 8832
E-mail: orders@isbs.com
Website: http://www.isbs.com

Hart Publishing is an imprint of Bloomsbury Publishing plc.

British Library Cataloguing in Publication Data
Data Available

ISBN: 978-1-84946-537-3

Typeset by Compuscript Ltd, Shannon
Printed and bound in Great Britain by
CPI Group (UK) Ltd, Croydon CR0 4YY

Foreword

The scope of judicial review as a remedy against decisions by the executive or public authorities which have misunderstood or misapplied the relevant legal principles has escalated far beyond the narrow confines of the ancient prerogative writs which it came to replace. There are occasions when issues of cardinal significance to the rule of law itself are examined in the course of proceedings for judicial review and, much more frequently, the court grapples with problems of less shattering significance to the public at large which none the less may be of life changing importance to the individual citizen seeking the remedy. What perhaps has been less apparent, as this book demonstrates, is that judicial review has steadily widened its ambit within the system for the administration of criminal justice.

I have to confess that when I was invited to write this foreword I questioned what a book about criminal judicial review might add to the understanding of what I believe to be a very circumscribed aspect of this process. However, while carefully addressing the availability of judicial review to question decisions which may impact on whether or not there should be a prosecution in the Crown Court or the Magistrates Court, this book examines far wider aspects of the judicial review process in the context of criminal justice. For example, it considers the extent of the availability of judicial review of investigative decisions by the police; decisions by coronial officers and the Criminal Cases Review Commission; cases which involve vulnerable individuals as the criminal justice system impinges on them, and the way in which judicial review may operate in proceedings for extradition as well as the impact of the Convention on them all. During the last few years, the topic of judicial review in the criminal justice system has developed increased momentum. The writers seek to identify the current place of judicial review in the broad system of criminal justice, identifying areas of uncertainty where the development of the law awaits the decisions of the court, and noting the decisions which have already expanded or alternatively limited the availability of judicial review.

The book is offered in clear and simple style, focussing less on esoteric theoretical considerations and more on the practical needs of the practitioner. It brings together materials relating to public law about which a criminal specialist may be less well informed, and material relevant to the criminal justice processes which may not be immediately apparent to the public law specialist. It will assist with the preparation of arguments, and also enable submissions which are unarguable to be discarded. It will therefore provide valuable guidance in this broad and developing area of practice.

The Rt Hon Lord Judge

Preface

A person's interaction with the criminal justice system can raise many issues of administrative law. A knowledge and grasp of the relevant principles can inform correspondence and submissions in court, and ultimately form the basis for a claim for judicial review. Many books touch on parts of this subject, but this work aims to deal with it as a whole, as follows:

   i.   The opening and closing chapters provide practical guidance to the key principles, procedure, remedies, funding and costs.

   ii.   It considers the range of potential defendants and claims from a pre-charge stage through to miscarriages of justice post-conviction.

   iii.   Potential claims are looked at not only from the perspective of the prosecution or defence, but also from that of a complainant, prisoner or witness.

   iv.   It explores judicial reviews concerning those who are more vulnerable by reason of either youth or mental infirmity.

We describe the field as 'criminal judicial review'. The authors find that it is a distinctive area with its own idiosyncrasies, that deserves to be treated as a subject area in its own right. The more well-known aspect is the special rules limiting the scope of the High Court's jurisdiction over ongoing proceedings, particularly in the Crown Court. Perhaps less well charted are the rich seams of case law on judicial review against the lower courts, the increasing authorities on personal data and the police, and the emergence of distinctive principles involving children and young persons.

The contributors have attempted to sketch out this well-established yet still dynamic field. We have tried to categorise, record and interpret the case law and enable practitioners to find the lead authorities quickly. This is not straightforward, as criminal judicial review can be an elusive subject. In some areas it is an exceptional as opposed to commonplace remedy. Our purpose is to assist those who spend their working lives in police stations, Magistrates' courts, Crown Courts or prisons to perceive principles of administrative law that may be relied on in an otherwise criminal practice. It is also intended to benefit public law specialists, with a guide to how the courts have applied well-trodden principles to a perhaps unfamiliar statutory framework and context.

The book aims to be accessible for criminal practitioners, both in being structured around the subject matter, including factual examples from criminal cases, and in simplifying the sections on procedure and remedies, without omitting the relevant law. It also includes two sections which are often misunderstood—legal aid for criminal judicial reviews, and costs.

The structure of the book is explained below.

The Structure of the Book

The structure of the book is intended as a step-by-step guide allowing a reader to progress from general principles and practical issues (Part I) to considering detailed grounds and specialist law (Parts II and III), and then questions of funding and costs (Part IV). Readers will find the rules for pre-action conduct, the 'Pre-Action Protocol', and forms for issuing and responding to a claim at the end of the book.

Part I (Chapters 1–3)

— The principles applied in judicial review with examples from criminal cases.

— The procedure and types of remedies.

Part II (Chapters 4–10)

Identification of particular unlawful actions by specific public bodies in the criminal justice system and related areas that may be subject to judicial review claims.

Part III (Chapters 11–14)

Specialist areas of law in cases of vulnerable individuals or with an international dimension.

Part IV (Chapters 15–16)

— How to secure public funding.

— The law on costs in judicial review claims.

Annexes

— Rules for pre-action conduct, court forms and the Convention rights incorporated into domestic law.

Note on the Law

The law is as stated on 1 May 2014.

References to the Civil Procedure Rules include the 72nd update contained in the *Civil Procedure (Amendment No 4) Rules* 2014 (SI 2014/867), which came into force on 22 April 2014.

References to the Criminal Procedure Rules are to the *Criminal Procedure Rules* 2013 (SI 2013/1554), which came into force on 7 October 2013 as amended by the *Criminal Procedure (Amendment) Rules* 2013 (SI 2013/2525), and the *Criminal Procedure (Amendment No 2) Rules* 2013 (SI 2013/3183).

References to the *Practice Direction (Criminal Proceedings)* [2013] EWCA Crim 1631, [2013] 1 WLR 3164 incorporate subsequent changes made by the *Practice Direction (Criminal Proceedings: Various Changes)* [2013] EWCA Crim 2328, [2014] 1 WLR 35.

The Criminal Justice and Courts Bill 2014 was laid before Parliament on 5 February 2014. Although it is unknown to what extent the current text will be passed into law, if at all, it contains important potential changes: cl 14 (police cautions in Chapter 4 at n 516), cl 20 (youth cautions, conditional cautions and the presence of an appropriate adult at 11-51), cl 50 (grant of relief in Chapter 3 at n 4) and cll 51–56 (changes to the rules on provision of financial information, costs in respect of interveners and protective costs orders in Chapter 16 at n 5).

As always a number of important judgments were handed down after our cut off date for the law (1 May 2014). Several contributors have elected to footnote these to alert the reader but this is by no means a comprehensive treatment of that case law and this work must be treated as up to date to 1 May 2014.

Aside from the ever-growing body of case law, the book may have to be read in light of any other reforms to the procedure for judicial review or changes to public funding, which may be subsequently enacted (see *Judicial Review—proposals for further reform: the Government response*, February 2014, Cm 8811). One important pending reform to public funding, the residence test, is mentioned below at 15-7.

Piers von Berg
36 Bedford Row
1 July 2014
criminaljr@36bedfordrow.co.uk

Acknowledgements

There have been a large number of people—possibly due to the number of writers involved—who have given up their free time to help in various ways, to whom we are enormously grateful.

Lana Adamou, Andrew Arthur, Renata Burns, Miriam Carrion-Benitez, James Collins, Rebecca Crane, Georgina Gibbs, Kate Gooch, Karma Hickman, Saoirse Kerrigan, John Lloyd-Jones QC, Malcolm MacDonald, Hannah Markham, Declan O'Callaghan, Nadia Silver, Gus Silverman, Allison Summers, Christine Taylor and Phil Taylor commented on the drafts. Pranjal Shrotri checked parts of the law in Chapter 6.

Material written by Sian Cutter, Emilie Pottle, and Martha Spurrier in earlier drafts was used in some of the chapters. James Packer, Rachel Taylor and Richard Wilson QC commented on the layout of the book and early drafts.

The staff at Gray's Inn Library were very helpful in tracking down old texts and judgments.

William Harbage QC and Richard Wilson QC, joint Heads of Chambers at 36 Bedford Row, have been very supportive in this endeavour, as have Michelle Simpson and Chris Lane, and the clerking team in Chambers.

The editor thanks Richard Hart, Rachel Turner, Mel Hamill, Tom Adams and the team at Hart Publishing for their support and patience with the writing team. The writing team is indebted to Christopher Long for copy-editing the manuscript.

The editor thanks Emma Grower, who listened to the latest developments and insisted on the occasional break during writing.

Finally, the book was finished at a time when the editor lost an incredible person, who had supported him all the way and would have placed it on her mantelpiece.

Any mistakes in the text are our own.

Summary Contents

Part IV: Public Funding and Costs

Annexes

Detailed Contents

Part III: Specialist Areas—Youths, Mental Health, Extradition and European Union Law

List of Contributors

David Ball is a barrister at 36 Bedford Row. He has a broad administrative law practice. He is on the panel of preferred counsel for the Equality and Human Rights Commission.

Kathryn Howarth is a barrister at 36 Bedford Row. She practises in domestic and international criminal law, extradition, immigration and public law. She is listed in the Legal 500 for criminal law.

Florence Iveson is a barrister at 36 Bedford Row. She co-founded and sits on the board of Vocalise, which teaches parliamentary debate to prisoners. She is currently seconded to the CPS Extradition Unit.

Justin Leslie is a barrister at 42 Bedford Row specialising in public law, with an interest in mental health issues. He contributes to Jordans Public Law Online service and co-convenes the ALBA Public Law Forum.

Liam Loughlin is a barrister at Church Court Chambers with a common law practice. He specialises predominantly in criminal law including large drugs conspiracies, fraud, terrorism and violent offences.

James McLernon is a barrister at 36 Bedford Row. He practises in criminal law with a focus on serious offences of violence, multi-handed drugs conspiracies, fraud, money laundering and the confiscation of the proceeds of crime.

Gráinne Mellon is a barrister at Garden Court Chambers where she practises in public law, human rights and discrimination. She teaches international human rights law at the London School of Economics.

James Packer is a solicitor and Public Law Director and Joint Head of Department at Duncan Lewis. He has conducted many costs cases of general importance, including *Bahta*. He provides training and writes regularly on judicial review.

Sarah Parkes is a barrister at 36 Bedford Row. She specialises in public and employment law, with a particular focus on the rights of women and families.

Geoffrey Sullivan is a barrister at 36 Bedford Row and is an Assistant Coroner for North London.

Rachel Taylor is a solicitor at Fisher Meredith, where she specialises in actions against the Police. Rachel is a committed and active campaigner for StopWatch and is a member of the Police Action Lawyers' Group.

Saoirse Townshend is a barrister at 36 Bedford Row. She acts for requesting judicial authorities and governments in extradition proceedings and individuals being requested at first instance hearings and appeals in the High Court.

Piers von Berg is a barrister at 36 Bedford Row. He specialises in criminal judicial review. He acts in claims against a wide range of public authorities, often on behalf of youths. He writes on children's rights.

Richard Wilson QC is a barrister and joint Head of Chambers at 36 Bedford Row. He is a public law specialist, who has appeared in leading cases on EU law, Article 8 and costs in judicial review, including *ZO Somalia, Negassi,* and *Bahta.* He has delivered papers on proportionality analysis and commercial judicial review at annual conferences for the profession.

Part I
Key Principles, Procedural Steps and Remedies

1

Judicial Review
An Introduction to the Key Principles
(with illustrations from criminal judicial review cases)

RICHARD WILSON QC

A. What is Judicial Review?

(1) Introduction

1-1   This book is about judicial review claims made against public authorities operating within the criminal justice system. A claim for judicial review is a claim issued in the Administrative Court of the Queen's Bench Division of the High Court against a public authority, where it is alleged that a decision or action (or inaction) of the public authority is 'unlawful'. In respect of such claims, what is or is not 'unlawful' is to be ascertained by consideration of the principles of public and administrative law, as developed by case law. If the decision, action (or inaction) is found to be unlawful, the court may grant relief, for example, by quashing the decision, and in some circumstances also awarding damages.

    'A public authority' may be part of, or connected to, the criminal justice system. For example, a criminal court is 'part of' the criminal justice system; whereas the Independent Police Complaints Commission (IPCC), whose function it is to investigate complaints against the police, may properly be considered to be 'connected to' the criminal justice system. A defendant in a criminal case, a suspect, prisoner, witness, relative or other sufficiently interested person may bring a claim for judicial review against a public authority. Moreover, one public authority may seek judicial review of a decision by another public authority; for instance, where the Crown Prosecution Service (CPS) challenges a decision of a criminal court. Provided a person or public authority has 'legal standing' (ie, a sufficient interest in the decision impugned), that person or public authority may be entitled to bring a claim for judicial review against a public authority.

    Judicial review is governed by principles of public and administrative law. Just how these principles operate in a criminal justice context is an important, but somewhat neglected subject. This book aims to assist those who are familiar with the criminal law, but less familiar with the way judicial review operates or might operate in criminal cases and within the wider criminal justice system. Similarly, public and administrative lawyers unfamiliar with the criminal justice system may derive benefit from topics covered in this work.

    A principal objective of the authors is to provide factual illustrations from the case law showing how principles of administrative law apply to decisions of public authorities operating within the criminal justice system. Illustrations showing the precise context of an impugned decision tend to better illuminate the principle applied by a court, than a more textured theoretical analysis. For as has been frequently said: 'in public law, context is all'.[1]

    In terms of an outline of this introductory chapter:

    i.   Section A defines 'judicial review'.
    ii.   Section B explains what may be understood as the field of 'criminal judicial review' and the subject of this book.

---

[1] For example: see *R (Daly) v Secretary of State for the Home Department* [2001] UKHL 26, [2001] 2 AC 532 [28] (Lord Steyn): 'In law context is everything'; *R (Sharaf) v General Medical Council* [2013] EWHC 3332 (Admin) [39] (Carr J): 'Indeed in public law it has been said that "context is all"'; and De Smith *Judicial Review*, 7th edn (London, Sweet and Maxwell, 2013) para 11-086: 'Indeed the intensity of review will differ, for the reason that in public law, context is all'.

               Richard Wilson QC

iii.   Section C considers the special rules affecting the scope of the High Court's jurisdiction over police investigations and the criminal courts.

iv.   Section D looks at the rules governing the operation of the Divisional Court, which hears many criminal judicial reviews.

v.   The chapter then proceeds to give step-by-step guidance to practitioners as to what and who can be challenged by a claim for judicial review, and who can bring such claims (Sections E and F).

vi.   Section G examines in detail the potential grounds for judicial review and provides illustrations of how these function in criminal judicial review cases. There is emphasis on making the principles accessible to criminal practitioners with illustrations of the facts of cases involving a variety of defendants in the criminal justice system.

vii.   The later sections (H, I, J and K) set out more practical matters such as the timing of a claim and an outline of the procedure in the High Court, including the rules governing appeals from the High Court in a 'criminal cause or matter'. There is a summary of the types of remedies a claimant may obtain in Section K.

viii.   Finally, Section L gives examples of how criminal judicial review has contributed to both public and administrative law and criminal law.

Readers may find it helpful to cross-refer to other chapters by using references in the text or footnotes in order to consider points provided in more detail or in a particular context.[2]

(2) Supervisory Jurisdiction of the High Court

Judicial review is the means by which the High Court exercises supervisory jurisdiction and control over the administrative decisions of ministers of State, public bodies, or private individuals or entities exercising public functions (collectively referred to in this book as 'public authorities').[3] Public authorities are bodies exercising a power or performing a duty that involves a 'public element'.[4]   1-2

By judicial review the High Court enforces the rule of law,[5] and protects the rights and legitimate interests of those affected by the (abusive) exercise of power by public authorities.[6] Judicial review is available only against public authorities.

A claim for judicial review is a claim to review the lawfulness of: (i) an enactment or (ii) a decision, action or failure to act in relation to the exercise of a public function.[7]

---

[2] For a description of how the entire structure of the book operates, readers should refer to the Preface.

[3] A court or tribunal is a 'public authority' for the purposes of the Human Rights Act 1998, s 6(3), and they are also described as public authorities throughout this book. It is considered that the High Court retains its supervisory jurisdiction over the Criminal Injuries Compensation Authority (CICA), notwithstanding the creation of the First Tier Tribunal and the Upper Tribunal. See below at 9-39.

[4] *R v Panel on Takeover and Mergers, ex parte Datafin Plc* [1987] QB 815, 838E (Sir John Donaldson MR).

[5] Dicey gave three meanings to 'the rule of law', the second sense being 'not only that with us no man is above the law, but (which is a different thing) that here, every man, whatever be his rank or condition, is subject to the ordinary law of the realm and amenable to the jurisdiction of the ordinary tribunals' (Professor AV Dicey, *An Introduction to the Study of the Law of the Constitution* 9th edn (London, MacMillan and Co, 1945)). This sense of the expression is captured in Lord Bingham's own working definition: 'The core of the existing principle is, I suggest, that all persons and authorities within the state, whether public or private, should be bound by and entitled to the benefit of laws publicly made, taking effect (generally) in the future and publicly administered by the courts' (Tom Bingham, *The Rule of Law* (London, Penguin Books, 2011) 7.

[6] See De Smith, *Judicial Review* (n 1) paras 1-001 to 1-011; and Fordham, *Judicial Review Handbook*, 6th edn (Oxford, Hart, 2012) paras 1.1 to 1.2.

[7] CPR 54.1(2).

The procedural rules governing claims for judicial review are contained in Part 8 of the Civil Procedure Rules (CPR), as modified by Part 54. These rules govern the way the Administrative Court of the High Court Queen's Bench Division exercises its supervisory jurisdiction over public authorities.

(3) Decision-Making

1-3   The subject matter of every claim for judicial review is a decision made by a public authority or a refusal (or failure) by the public authority to make a decision:

> To qualify as a subject for judicial review the decision must have consequences which affect some person (or body of persons) other than the decision-maker, although it may affect him too. It must affect such other person either:
>
> (a)   by altering rights or obligations of that person which are enforceable by or against him in private law; or
>
> (b)   by depriving him of some benefit or advantage which either:
>
>> (i)   he had in the past been permitted by the decision-maker to enjoy and which he can legitimately expect to be permitted to continue to do until there has been communicated to him some rational grounds for withdrawing it on which he has been given an opportunity to comment; or
>>
>> (ii)   he has received assurance from the decision-maker will not be withdrawn without giving him first an opportunity of advancing reasons for contending that they should not be withdrawn. (I prefer to continue to call the kind of expectation that qualifies a decision for inclusion in class (b) a 'legitimate expectation' rather than a 'reasonable expectation', in order thereby to indicate that it has consequences to which effect will be given in public law, whereas an expectation or hope that some benefit or advantage would continue to be enjoyed, although it might well be entertained by a 'reasonable' man, would not necessarily have such consequences...).[8]

The purpose of judicial review is to ensure that an individual receives fair treatment. Its purpose is not to ensure that the relevant decision-maker, after according fair treatment, reaches—on a matter that the decision-maker is authorised by law to decide for itself—a conclusion which is correct in the eyes of the court.[9]

(4) Judicial Review: Sources of Law

1-4   In terms of sources of law, five basic categories of judicial review have been identified:

   i.   a ground of review in domestic law (other than a fundamental right);
   ii.   a fundamental right recognised by the common law;
   iii.   an ECHR ('Convention') right;
   iv.   a directly effective European Union right; and
   v.   a 'devolution' issue.[10]

---

[8] *Council of Civil Service Unions v Minister for the Civil Service* [1985] AC 374, [1984] 3 WLR 1174, 408E–409A (Lord Diplock).
[9] *Chief Constable of The North Wales Police v Evans* [1982] 1 WLR 1155, 1161A (Lord Hailsham).
[10] De Smith, *Judicial Review* (n 1) para 1-108.

Richard Wilson QC

B. What is Criminal Judicial Review?

(1) Criminal Judicial Review: A Description

The expression 'criminal judicial review' is used in this book to refer to that area of **1-5** judicial review concerned with the decisions of public authorities (including the magistrates' courts and the Crown Court) that operate within, or are connected to, the criminal justice system.

Judicial Review, Public Authorities and the Criminal Justice System

Traditionally, legal commentators dealing with criminal judicial review have tended to focus on criminal court proceedings.[11] However, criminal proceedings are but one part, albeit an important one, of the wider criminal justice system.[12] A diagram setting out the relationship between the High Court and the main public authorities in the criminal justice system and related public authorities can be found above, p 9.

(2) The Criminal Justice System

1-6 The criminal justice system, overseen by the Home Office, the Ministry of Justice and the Attorney General's Office, operates primarily to reduce crime, protect the public and punish offenders. It encompasses (amongst others) the functions of the police, prosecution, courts and judiciary, prisons, youth justice services and probation. It involves the detection of crime, bringing criminals to justice, and carrying out the orders of the court, such as collecting fines, providing rehabilitation, supervising community orders and providing custodial sentences.[13]

The core agencies within the criminal justice system are:

i.   The Ministry of Justice, which oversees the magistrates' courts, the Crown Court, the higher appeal courts, the Legal Aid Agency and the National Offender Management Service (including prisons and probation).

ii.   The Home Office, which oversees the police.

iii. The Attorney General's Office, which oversees the Crown Prosecution Service, the Serious Fraud Office and the Revenue and Customs Prosecution Office.

(3) Decision-Making

1-7 Decisions made by public authorities operating within the criminal justice system as a whole, may be subject to judicial review. It is the unlawful decision-making by such public authorities that falls within the description 'criminal judicial review', and the scope of this book.

Grounds for judicial review may occur at any stage of a person's interaction with, or transit through, the criminal justice system, for example:

i.   Before arrest—a decision to issue a search warrant.

ii.   A decision to administer a police caution.

iii. A decision to charge and prosecute; or not to charge or prosecute.[14]

iv.   Decisions relating to detention in custody.

---

[11] For instance, see Horder, 'Rationalising Judicial Review in Criminal Proceedings' 2008 13(4) *Judicial Review* 207; and Spencer, 'Judicial Review of Criminal Proceedings' [1991] *Criminal Law Review* 259.

[12] For the distinction between the 'criminal process' and the wider 'criminal justice system', see Ashworth and Redmayne, *The Criminal Process*, 4th edn (Oxford, Oxford University Press, 2010) 1–2.

[13] The National Audit Office Report on 'The Criminal Justice System' (2010), www.nao.org.uk/wp-content/uploads/2010/11/Criminal_Justice_Review.pdf, 1.

[14] *Mohit v DPP of Mauritius* [2006] 1 WLR 3343 [18].

Richard Wilson QC

v.   Certain decisions by magistrates' courts and/or the Crown Court that fall within the supervisory jurisdiction of the High Court[15] (for example bail, extension of custody time limits, lifting a reporting restriction, a local practice direction requiring defendants to sign defence case statements, and forfeiture in relation to an accused's parent).[16]

vi.   Decisions by prison authorities.

vii.   Decisions by other statutory bodies in a variety of circumstances (for example the Legal Aid Agency, the Criminal Cases Review Commission, the Independent Police Commission and the Criminal Injuries Compensation Authority).

viii. Decisions made in extradition proceedings.

(4) Scope of Criminal Judicial Review

The scope of criminal judicial review extends to any material interaction with the crim-   **1-8**
inal justice system. It is not restricted only to persons at risk of punishment by the state as defendants undergoing criminal process. Accordingly, victims of crime, witnesses, third persons whose premises are searched or whose property or personal data is seized without prosecution, those seeking a proper inquest into an unexplained or sudden death, a prisoner challenging his categorisation, a suspect objecting to certain bail conditions, relatives of an accused or deceased person, and generally persons or bodies with sufficient legal standing or interest in the relevant decision may all, where appropriate, seek permission from the Administrative Court to bring a claim for judicial review.

(5) Serious Abuse of Power

The judiciary has a constitutional duty in the field of criminal law to oversee executive   **1-9**
action and refuse to countenance decisions by public authorities that threaten either fundamental human rights or the rule of law. In *R v Horseferry Road Magistrates' Court, ex parte Bennett (No 1)*,[17] Lord Griffiths, having considered 'abuse of process' in the narrow sense of whether an accused could have a fair trial, extended and applied the application of administrative law concepts of abuse of power to criminal law:

> Your Lordships are now invited to extend the concept of abuse of process a stage further. In the present case there is no suggestion that the appellant cannot have a fair trial, nor could it be suggested that it would have been unfair to try him if he had been returned to this country through extradition procedures. If the court is to have the power to interfere with the prosecution in the present circumstances it must be because the judiciary accept a responsibility for the maintenance of the rule of law that embraces a willingness to oversee executive action and to refuse to countenance behaviour that threatens either basic human rights or the rule of law.

---

[15] Generally, see Fordham, *Judicial Review Handbook* (n 6) para 32.1.4(B), 363.

[16] In the magistrates' courts decisions to stay proceedings as an abuse of process and dismissal of charges are decisions that could be subject to judicial review. In contrast, such decisions by the Crown Court would not fall within the jurisdiction of the High Court, as they would be considered 'matters relating to trial on indictment' (see discussion below at 1-25 and at 7-2).

[17] *R v Horseferry Road Magistrates' Court, ex parte Bennett (No 1)* [1993] UKHL 10, [1994] 1 AC 42.

My Lords, I have no doubt that the judiciary should accept this responsibility in the field of criminal law. The great growth of administrative law during the latter half of this century has occurred because of the recognition by the judiciary and Parliament alike that it is the function of the High Court to ensure that executive action is exercised responsibly and as Parliament intended. So also should it be in the field of criminal law and if it comes to the attention of the court that there has been a serious abuse of power it should, in my view, express its disapproval by refusing to act upon it.[18]

1-10   The case law tends to suggest that the key over-arching concept in criminal judicial review is that of 'serious abuse of power'. Unless such abuse by a public authority can be demonstrated, the High Court is unlikely to express disapproval by quashing or otherwise interfering with the decision in question or by requiring the public authority concerned to give a (reasoned) decision.

The expression 'abuse of process' tends to be used in a narrow sense in criminal court proceedings. That description is not to be confused with the administrative law concept of 'serious abuse of power'. In *Ex p Bennett (No 1)*, Lord Griffiths explained that although it might to be convenient to label the wider supervisory jurisdiction with which they were concerned in that appeal under the head of abuse of process, that expression in an administrative law context referred to 'a horse of a very different colour from the narrower issues that arise when considering domestic criminal trial procedures'.[19]

1-11   Basically, as held in *Ex p Bennett (No 1)*, the jurisdiction exercised by magistrates, whether sitting as committing justices or exercising their summary jurisdiction, to protect the court's process from abuse was confined to matters directly affecting the fairness of the trial of the particular accused with whom they were dealing, and did not extend to the wider supervisory jurisdiction for upholding the rule of law. That wider responsibility was vested in the High Court. So, for instance, where a question arose as to the deliberate abuse of extradition procedures, the magistrates should adjourn the matter so that an application could be made to the Divisional Court, which was the proper forum for deciding the matter.

C. The Scope of the High Court's Jurisdiction

(1) Introduction

1-12   The High Court has a general supervisory jurisdiction over the decisions of public authorities. The court's supervisory jurisdiction will be outlined in relation to decision-making by public authorities in four principal areas of the criminal justice system, namely: over police investigations, prosecutorial decisions, the magistrates' courts and the Crown Court.

---

[18] ibid 62. Discussed below in context of judicial review of the magistrates' courts at 6-16, 6-35, and 6-43
[19] ibid 64C (Lord Griffiths).

(2) Police Investigations

Whilst in principle it was open to the High Court by way of judicial review to order a   **1-13**
police investigation be discontinued where there was no prospect of an eventual prosecution, such relief would only be granted in 'the most exceptional cases'.[20] Where there
were unquestionably reasonable grounds initially to suspect a person under investigation, the court would be very slow to second-guess the police in deciding at what point
the suspect could be dismissed from the inquiry.[21]

(3) Prosecutorial Decisions

(i) Judicial Restraint

The High Court exercises a high degree of restraint over the judicial review of decisions   **1-14**
to commence or continue a prosecution. Although the decision of a prosecutor is susceptible to judicial review, the courts have traditionally been most reluctant to interfere
with prosecutorial discretion.[22] There is a substantial body of authority on judicial
review of decisions not to prosecute.[23]

The general approach of the courts is not to disturb a decision of an indepen-   **1-15**
dent prosecutor save in highly exceptional cases. In *Sharma v Brown-Antoine*,[24] Lord
Bingham explained that the courts have given a number of reasons for their extreme
reluctance to disturb decisions to prosecute by way of judicial review. First, that the
powers in question are entrusted to the officers identified and to no one else, and no
other authority may exercise the powers or make the judgments on which such exercise
must depend; secondly, that the courts have recognised the polycentric character of official decision-making in such matters including policy and public interest considerations
that are not susceptible to judicial review; and, thirdly, that the powers are conferred in
very broad and non-prescriptive terms.[25]

Where there is a remedy within the criminal process, and absent any claim of dishonesty, bad faith or other exceptional circumstance, the decision of the DPP to consent
to a prosecution is not amenable to judicial review.[26] In summary, judicial review of a
prosecutorial decision is possible but it is a highly exceptional remedy.

---

[20] *R (C) v Chief Constable of A* [2006] EWHC 2352 (Admin)—discussed below at 4-14. The sort of circumstances that would qualify as exceptional are addressed by Underhill J, ibid [33]. In *R (Bermingham) v Director
of the Serious Fraud Office* [2007] QB 727, Laws LJ said it would 'take a wholly exceptional case on its legal
merits to justify a judicial review' of the Director's decision to investigate or not, ibid [64].

[21] *R (C)* (n 20) [33].

[22] See citation of authority in *Sharma v Brown-Antoine* [2007] 1 WLR 780, 788 B–C.

[23] See *R v DPP, ex parte Manning* [2001] QB 330 (see 5-29 below); *R (Da Silva) v DPP* [2006] Police LR 176
(see 5-30 below); *Sharma v Brown-Antoine* (n 22) and *Marshall v DPP* [2007] UKPC 4.

[24] *Sharma v Brown-Antoine* (n 22).

[25] For these and other reasons cited, see *Sharma v Brown-Antoine* (n 22) 788E–H.

[26] *R v DPP* [1999] 3 WLR 972, [2000] 2 AC 326. In principle, a decision to prosecute is ordinarily susceptible to judicial review; and the surrender of what should be an independent prosecutorial discretion to
political instruction, persuasion or pressure is a recognised ground of review: *Matalulu v DPP of Fiji* [2003] 4
LRC 712, 735–36; *Mohit* (n 14) [17], [21]—see below at 5-8.

(ii) Decisions not to Prosecute

1-16   The exercise of the court's power of judicial review is less rare in the case of a decision not to prosecute than it is where a decision to prosecute has been taken. This is because a decision not to prosecute is final, subject to judicial review, whereas a decision to prosecute leaves the defendant free to challenge the prosecution's case in the usual way through the criminal court. But it is still exceptional.[27] In *R v DPP, ex parte Manning*,[28] Lord Bingham explained the reasons for the difference in approach to the two situations:

> In most cases the decision will turn not on an analysis of the relevant legal principles but on the exercise of an informed judgment of how a case against a particular defendant, if brought, would be likely to fare in the context of a criminal trial before (in a serious case such as this) a jury. This exercise of judgment involves an assessment of the strength, by the end of the trial, of the evidence against the defendant and of the likely defences. It will often be impossible to stigmatise a judgment on such matters as wrong even if one disagrees with it. So the courts will not easily find that a decision not to prosecute is bad in law, on which basis alone the court is entitled to interfere. At the same time, the standard of review should not be set too high, since judicial review is the only means by which the citizen can seek redress against a decision not to prosecute and if the tests were too exacting an effective remedy would be denied.[29]

1-17   In *R (F) v Director of Public Prosecutions*[30] Lord Judge LCJ explained that by contrast with a flawed decision to prosecute, where the individual facing trial is provided with ample alternative remedies in the Crown Court (or magistrates' court), by definition when it is contended that the decision that there should be no prosecution itself constitutes a miscarriage of justice, the only judicial remedy would be a judicial review.[31] He went on to emphasise that:

> 5. ... the court examining the decision not to prosecute is not vested with a broad jurisdiction to exercise its own judgment, and second guess the Director's decision, and direct reconsideration of the decision simply because the court itself would have reached a different conclusion. The remedy is carefully circumscribed. In the decided cases different epithets have been applied to highlight how sparingly this jurisdiction should be exercised. The remedy is 'highly exceptional', 'rare in the extreme', and 'very rare indeed'.
>
> 6. Without suggesting a comprehensive list, the decision not to prosecute may be shown to follow a perverse decision to disregard compelling evidence or inexplicably to ignore the relevant prosecutorial policy or policies, or a combination of both. It may, although as far as we know there have never been any such examples, follow some impropriety or abuse of power by those entrusted by the Director with the relevant responsibility. It may also be based on an error of law. If so it would be open to this court to require the decision to be reconsidered and the law correctly applied.

---

[27] *R (B) v DPP* [2009] EWHC 106 (Admin), [2009] 1 WLR 2072, [52]. See discussion below at 5-31.
[28] *Ex p Manning* (n 23). See below at 1-87, 1-121 and 5-29.
[29] ibid, [23].
[30] *R (F) v DPP* [2013] EWHC 945 (Admin), [2014] 2 WLR 190. See below at 5-27.
[31] ibid, [3].

Richard Wilson QC

In *L v DPP*,[32] the Divisional Court of Sir John Thomas P and Simon J held that a challenge could be brought against a CPS decision on the following narrow grounds:

    i.   there had been some unlawful policy;

    ii. the Director of Public Prosecutions had failed to act in accordance with his own set policy; or,

    iii. the decision was perverse.[33]

1-18

Judicial review proceedings should not be brought until the CPS had had an opportunity to conduct a further review under its new victim right of review procedure. The court also pointed out that in the ordinary case if a challenge was brought before that right of review had been taken up it should not be entertained by the court.

(4) Supervision of the Magistrates' Courts

(i) Challenges to Magistrates' Courts Decisions

Decisions by the magistrates' courts can be challenged by way of:

1-19

    i.   appeal to the Crown Court (against conviction or sentence);[34]

    ii. case stated to the High Court on the ground that the conviction, order, determination or other proceeding of the court is 'wrong in law or is in excess of jurisdiction';[35] and

    iii. a claim for judicial review.

The ordinary route of challenge where a defendant complains that a magistrates' court has reached a wrong decision of fact, or a wrong decision of mixed fact and law, is to appeal to the Crown Court.

The ordinary route of challenge where a defendant contends that a magistrates' court erred in law is to appeal by way of case stated to the High Court, where the question posed for the opinion of the High Court is whether on the facts they found, the magistrates were entitled to convict the defendant (see below at 6-9). However, sometimes the question is whether there was any evidence upon which the magistrates could properly convict a defendant; and this has also traditionally been regarded as an issue of law.[36]

Judicial review is the appropriate means of 'pursuing challenges based on fairness, bias or procedural irregularity in magistrates' courts'.[37] The High Court has a general supervisory jurisdiction over the magistrates' courts (an inferior court of record) to make mandatory, prohibitory and quashing orders by way of judicial review.[38]

---

[32] *L v DPP* [2013] EWHC 1752 (Admin). See below at 5-28.

[33] These propositions were applied in *R v DPP, ex parte Chaudhary* [1995] 1 Cr App R 136. To these 'narrow grounds', must be added the broader grounds of impropriety or abuse of power mentioned by Lord Judge LCJ in *R (F) v DPP* (n 30).

[34] Magistrates' Courts Act 1980, s 108.

[35] ibid, s 111.

[36] See *R v Hereford Magistrates' Court, ex parte Rowlands* [1998] QB 110, 118. See below at 6-7, 6-8, 6-12 and 6-16.

[37] Ibid, p 120B-C (per Lord Bingham LCJ).

[38] Senior Courts Act (SCA) 1981, s 29(1A)(4).

(ii) No Alternative Remedy

1-20   Judicial review of a magistrates' court's decision on general administrative law principles is generally permissible only where no alternative remedies are available (ie, by way of appeal to the Crown Court against conviction or sentence or by way of case stated to the Divisional Court of the High Court and see below at 6-6 and 6-9). Any party with sufficient standing is able to challenge a magistrates' court's decision by making a claim for judicial review. Typically, that will be either the accused or the prosecutor, but subject to being able to establish sufficient standing to bring a claim for judicial review, other persons may also be entitled to make a claim of judicial review against a magistrates' court's decision.

1-21   The unavailability of any alternative remedy to that of judicial review is a general principle; it is not an absolute rule. Accordingly, where an accused seeks to challenge his conviction by claiming judicial review on grounds of procedural impropriety, unfairness or bias, an application for judicial review is permissible notwithstanding the existence of a subsisting right of appeal against conviction by way of re-trial in the Crown Court.[39] The rationale is that were a party to be prevented from being able to make complaint of procedural unfairness or bias within the magistrates' courts in such circumstances, the supervisory jurisdiction for the High Court would be severely undermined (see also below at 7-2):

> So to hold [ie, prevent the judicial review claim from being brought] would be to emasculate the long-established supervisory jurisdiction of this court over Magistrates' Courts, which has over the years proved an invaluable guarantee of the integrity of proceedings in those courts. The crucial role of the Magistrates' Courts, mentioned above, makes it the more important that that jurisdiction should be retained with a view to ensuring that high standards of procedural fairness and impartiality are maintained.[40]

1-22   Similarly, where a magistrate was acting not as an examining magistrate, but deciding a preliminary issue as to jurisdiction, his ruling upon that was final and could properly be challenged by way of case stated or judicial review. The more expeditious procedure in such circumstances could be to determine by way of judicial review the questions on which the case would have been stated.[41] Expedition is a key consideration for the High Court in determining the appropriate procedure where a potential claimant has a choice of procedure.

(iii) Committal Proceedings

1-23   Committal proceedings were in principle susceptible to judicial review.[42] In *R v Highbury Magistrates' Court, ex parte Boyce*[43] it was explained that the High Court

---

[39] *Ex p Rowlands* (n 36). See below at 6-16.

[40] ibid, 125 (Lord Bingham LCJ).

[41] *R (Donnachie) v Cardiff Magistrates' Court* [2007] EWHC 1846 (Admin), [2007] 1 WLR 3085 (DC) [6], [34]. Note discussion on challenging interlocutory decisions at 6-17 below.

[42] Committal proceedings were substantially reformed and removed as of 28 May 2013 in all parts of England and Wales (they were abolished progressively in specified areas before that date)—see below at 6-58.

[43] *R v Highbury Magistrates' Court, ex parte Boyce* (1984) 79 Cr App R 132.

Richard Wilson QC

would quash a committal where, in breach of rule 4(10) of the Magistrates' Courts Rules 1968 (now rule 6(2) of the Magistrates' Courts Rules 1981), the accused was not given the opportunity to give evidence himself before the justices considered whether or not he should be committed for trial.

Similarly, a committal was quashed where, in breach of section 6(1) of the Children and Young Persons Act 1969, a person under the age of 17 was committed for trial without the justices having considered the evidence and having asked themselves whether they were of the opinion that there was sufficient evidence to put him on trial.[44]

These are examples of cases where the justices have not acted in accordance with the jurisdiction conferred on them by statute or, as it has sometimes been said, where there has been a denial of jurisdiction. The distinction between acting within and acting beyond (or outside, or in denial of) jurisdiction is well recognised. The court will not interfere in the former situation; it will (or may) in the latter.[45]

(iv) Fairness

A party's right to 'fairness' is stronger in criminal proceedings in the magistrates' courts   **1-24**
than in administrative or domestic tribunals.[46] Where a defendant had not received a fair trial before a magistrates' court, he could apply for judicial review even though he had a right of appeal to the Crown Court.[47]

However, permission to apply for judicial review should not be granted unless the claimant advances an apparently plausible complaint, which if made good might arguably be held to vitiate the proceedings in the magistrates' courts. Immaterial or minor deviations from best practice would not have that effect, as the High Court should be respectful of discretionary decisions of magistrates' courts, as of all other courts.[48]

(5) Supervision of the Crown Court

(i) The Crown Court's Jurisdiction

The Crown Court sits in several different capacities: as a criminal trial court; as an   **1-25**
appeal court on appeals from the magistrates' courts against conviction or sentence (by way of rehearing); as a sentencing court, following conviction at a trial on indictment or committal for sentence from the magistrates' courts; and, as a civil court.

---

[44] *R v Coleshill Justices, ex parte Davies* [1971] 1 WLR 1684.
[45] See, for example, *R v Wells Street Magistrates' Court, ex parte Seillon* [1978] 3 All ER 257, [1978] 1 WLR 1002.
[46] *Ex p Rowlands* (n 36) 124E (Lord Bingham LCJ).
[47] *R v Bradford Justices, ex parte Wilkinson* [1990] 1 WLR 692, 696 (Rose J); *Ex p Rowlands* (n 36) 125C–D (Lord Bingham LCJ). Unfairness in an appeal before the Crown Court may also found a ground of review. For example, non-disclosure of a witness's previous conviction for dishonesty where that witness's credibility was in issue. *R v Harrow Crown Court, ex parte Dave* [1994] 1 WLR 98.
[48] ibid, 125D–E (Lord Bingham LCJ).

(ii) Challenging Decisions of the Crown Court

1-26 Decisions of the Crown Court can be challenged by appeal to the Court of Appeal (Criminal Division), by appeal to the High Court by way of case stated, and by application to the High Court for judicial review. Section 29(3) of the SCA 1981 gives jurisdiction to the High Court over certain criminal matters in the Crown Court:

> In relation to the jurisdiction of the Crown Court, other than its jurisdiction in matters relating to trial on indictment, the High Court shall have all such jurisdiction to make mandatory, prohibiting or quashing orders as the High Court possesses in relation to the jurisdiction of an inferior court.

The supervisory jurisdiction of the High Court over the Crown Court is therefore excluded by statute only 'in matters relating to trial on indictment' (see also below at 7-2).[49]

(iii) 'Matters Relating to Trial on Indictment'—Imprecise Meaning

1-27 This ouster of jurisdiction for judicial review for all 'matters relating to trial on indictment' ('the exclusionary clause') has created difficulties of interpretation, as the phrase is not defined in the Act. Lord Browne-Wilkinson described the exclusionary clause as 'extremely imprecise';[50] in another case, Lord Bridge said that it might be impossible to lay down any precise test to determine what is and what is not excluded.[51]

Despite the difficulties, the courts have attempted to provide an answer as to the meaning and scope of the exclusionary clause, on a case-by-case basis. There has been considerable litigation, which has led to decisions that are not always readily reconcilable.[52]

1-28 The case law has provided pointers as to the interpretation of the exclusionary clause. Two tests have been put forward as pointers towards a true construction. The first pointer is that of Lord Bridge in *Re Smalley*[53] in which he said that the correct approach construing section 29(3) is to ask whether the order sought to be reviewed is an order 'affecting the conduct of a trial on indictment'. The second pointer is the suggestion of Lord Browne-Wilkinson in *R v Manchester Crown Court, ex parte DPP*[54] where he proposed this test: 'is the decision sought to be reviewed one arising in the issue between the Crown and the defendant formulated by the indictment (including the costs of such issue)?' If 'yes', it was excluded from review; if 'no', the decision of the Crown Court was truly collateral to the indictment of the defendant, and judicial review would not delay the trial. Delay to the trial appears to be a key factor, one way or the other.

---

[49] The reason for this restriction appears to be that it is in the interests of justice for trials to proceed without being delayed by appeals and applications to the High Court; see Law Commission, *High Court's Jurisdiction in Relation to Criminal Proceedings* (Law Com No 324, 2010).

[50] *R v Manchester Crown Court, ex parte DPP* [1993] 1 WLR 1524, [1993] 4 All ER 928, HL, 1528C.

[51] *Re Smalley* [1985] AC 622, [1985] 2 WLR 538, HL, 643H.

[52] For a substantial list of cases where matters have been held to relate to trial on indictment and are therefore not judicially reviewable, and the case law where judicial review has been held to be available see: Law Commission, *High Court's Jurisdiction in Relation to Criminal Proceedings* (n 48) paras 2.51–2.52; and Fordham, *Judicial Review Handbook* (n 6), para 32.1.4.

[53] *Re Smalley* (n 51).

[54] *Ex p DPP* (n 50).

Richard Wilson QC

In *R (Lipinski) v Wolverhampton Crown Court*[55] Stanley Burnton J opined that the Lord Bridge formulation in *Re Smalley* (ie, did the decision affect the conduct of the trial on indictment) seemed to indicate that matters of procedure as well as substance fell within that formulation; whereas the Lord Browne-Wilkinson formulation in *Manchester Crown Court* seemed to indicate that procedural matters might be outside the exclusion. It seemed to Stanley Burnton J that 'to a significant extent both pointers take one in different directions'.[56]

1-29

(iv) Matters Held to Relate to Trial on Indictment (Judicial Review not Available)[57]

The case law indicates that the following matters 'relate' to a trial on indictment, and that accordingly the High Court had no jurisdiction to judicially review a decision of the Crown Court that:

1-30

i.   affected the conduct of the trial in any way;[58]
ii. was an integral part of the trial process;[59] this would include first instance decisions to stay (or not) proceedings, [60] or to grant (or not) extensions of time;[61]
iii. was an issue arising between the Crown and defendant formulated by the indictment;[62]
iv. was not truly collateral to the trial;[63] or
v.   is in substance the answer to some issue between the prosecution and the defence arising during a trial on indictment.[64]

(v) Matters Held not to Relate to Trial on Indictment (Judicial Review Available)

Decisions in the Crown Court that do not relate to trial on indictment (or that have been deemed not to relate to relate to trial on indictment), and are therefore subject to judicial review, have been held to include: (i) decisions on appeals against conviction or sentence, (ii) sentences on committal from the magistrates courts, and (iii) bail (see below, section B in Chapter 7).

1-31

---

[55] *R (Lipinski) v Wolverhampton Crown Court* [2005] EWHC 1950 (Admin).
[56] ibid [12]. There have been calls for Parliament to introduce clarifying legislation which addresses the problems arising from s 29(3) and its relationship with other legislation. For instance, see *R v Crown Court (Manchester), ex parte H* [2000] 1 WLR 760, 766C, 765H–766B.
[57] See also below at 7-2 – 7-3.
[58] *Re Smalley* (n 51) 642–43 (Lord Bridge); and *Re Ashton* [1994] 1 AC 9, 20 (Lord Slynn).
[59] *Re Sampson* [1987] 1 WLR 194, 196–98 (Lord Bridge).
[60] *Re Ashton* and *R (Salubi) v Bow Street Magistrates' Court* [2002] EWHC 919, (Admin) [2002] 1 WLR 3073.
[61] *R v Isleworth Crown Court, ex parte King* [1992] COD 298.
[62] *Ex p DPP* (n 50) 1530 (Lord Browne-Wilkinson).
[63] ibid, 1530 (Lord Browne-Wilkinson).
[64] *R v DPP, ex parte Kebilene* [2000] 2 AC 326, [1999] 3 WLR 972, 394 (Lord Hobhouse). Generally, see Law Commission, *High Court's Jurisdiction in Relation to Criminal Proceedings* (n 49).

(vi) Challenging Crown Court Decisions Made in its Appellate Jurisdiction[65]

1-32 Both the prosecution and defendants can challenge a decision of the Crown Court made in its appellate jurisdiction by applying to the High Court for judicial review pursuant to section 29(3) of SCA 1981. There is no appeal to the Court of Appeal available to either party in respect of decisions made by the Crown Court when sitting in an appellate capacity.[66]

It was wholly inappropriate to bring what was effectively an appeal against the Court's conclusions in relation to the evidence, by way of judicial review proceedings. The appropriate way to challenge the Crown Court's decision, in such circumstances, was the normal statutory prescribed method of appeal, namely by way of case stated. That is opposed to a situation where the challenge is based, for example, on an allegation of unfairness, bias or procedural irregularity, when judicial review may be an appropriate procedure.[67]

Where the proper route of appeal from the Crown Court was by case stated, the Court did have power to consider an application brought by way of judicial review in certain circumstances, but that power should be exercised sparingly.[68]

(vii) Challenging Decisions of the Crown Court Made in its Committal for Sentence Jurisdiction

1-33 A defendant may appeal against sentence to the Court of Appeal with leave,[69] but may apply to the High Court for judicial review in respect of any rulings by the Crown Court made prior to sentence, as such a decision would not be one relating to trial on indictment. For instance, any failure to disclose a prosecution witness's previous conviction goes to the fairness of the hearing at the Crown Court, and as such, judicial review is the appropriate avenue by which to seek relief.[70]

(viii) Bail

1-34 Pre-trial and post-trial decisions in the Crown Court concerning bail are amenable to challenge by judicial review (see below, section B in Chapter 7).[71] However, a decision concerning bail during a criminal trial cannot be challenged by judicial review as the

---

[65] See also below section F in Chapter 7.

[66] The rationale for this appears to be that by the conclusion of the appeal in the Crown Court there have already been two hearings of the facts: see Law Commission, *High Court's Jurisdiction in Relation to Criminal Proceedings* (n 49), para 2.18.

[67] *R (Clarke) v Ipswich Crown Court* [2013] EWHC 1129 (Admin) (DC) [17] (Moses LJ).

[68] *B v Carlisle Crown Court* [2009] EWHC 3540 (Admin) applying *Ex p Dave* (n 47).

[69] Criminal Appeal Act 1968 ss 10–11.

[70] *Ex p Dave* (n 47) 102D–H.

[71] *R (M) v Isleworth Crown Court* [2005] EWHC 363 (Admin) [7]–[11] (Maurice Kay LJ). It is now settled law that the appropriate remedy for refusal of bail is by judicial review, in the light of the abolition of the right of appeal from the magistrates' court and the Crown Court to a High Court judge in chambers, as a result of the provisions of the Criminal Justice Act 2003, s 17: see *R (Fergus) v Southampton Crown Court* [2008] EWHC 3273 (Admin) (AC) [9] (Silber J). See s B in Chapter 7 below.

decision falls within the exclusionary clause in section 29(3) of SCA 1981, as a matter 'relating to trial on indictment'.[72]

(ix) Delay

When the High Court has found that a judicial decision does not to 'relate to trial on indictment', it is almost invariably in circumstances where a review of that decision can be considered without delay or interruption to the hearing before the jury.[73] Satellite litigation in criminal proceedings is generally regarded as undesirable.[74] The policy underlying section 29(3) appears to be that criminal proceedings should not be subjected to delay by collateral challenges, and as a general rule the courts would, in accordance with that policy, refuse to entertain a judicial review application where the complaint could be raised within the criminal trial and appeal process.[75]

1-35

D. The Administrative Court and the 'Divisional Court'

(1) The Administrative Court of the High Court

The High Court's supervisory jurisdiction over the magistrates' courts and (to a more restricted extent) the Crown Court is, in fact, exercised either by the Administrative Court or by a Divisional Court of the Queen's Bench Division of the High Court, which is conventionally called 'the Divisional Court'.

The Administrative Court has an administrative law jurisdiction for England and Wales, as well as supervisory jurisdiction over inferior courts and tribunals.

The Administrative Court deals with all claims for judicial review in respect of magistrates' court and Crown Court decisions, but in the case of the Crown Court only in respect of matters that do not relate to trial on indictment.

1-36

(2) The Divisional Court

The work of the Administrative Court is divided between single judge courts and Divisional Courts (which consist of at least two judges, one of whom is normally a Lord Justice of Appeal and the other a judge of the High Court).

Divisional Courts may be held for the transaction of any business in the High Court which is, by virtue of rules of court or any other statutory provision, required to be

1-37

1-38

---

[72] *R (Uddin) v Leeds Crown Crown* [2013] EWHC 2752 (Admin), [35]—see below at 7-8-7-9; and Commentary in Criminal Law Review 2014, vol 4, 305Z–09. See also *M*, ibid.

[73] Horder, 'Rationalising judicial review in criminal proceedings' (2008) 13(4) *Judicial Review* 207 [17]; Law Commission, *High Court's Jurisdiction in Relation to Criminal Proceedings* (n 49); *R (CPS) v Sedgemoor Justices* (2007) EWHC 1803 (Admin).

[74] *Ex p Kebilene* (n 64) 371.

[75] ibid.

heard by a Divisional Court.[76] Any number of Divisional Courts may sit at the same time.[77] A Divisional Court shall be constituted of not less than two judges.[78] Every judge of the High Court shall be qualified to sit in any Divisional Court.[79]

The 'Divisional Court' is, in fact, simply a division constituted of not less than two judges of the High Court, and as Goff LJ explained:

> In considering this question, it is not to be forgotten that there is no court known as 'the Divisional Court'. We are not here concerned with a court such as the Court of Appeal, which is one court, though it usually sits in a number of divisions: see *Young v. Bristol Aeroplane Co. Ltd.* [1944] K.B. 718, 725, *per* Lord Greene M.R. A divisional court of a particular division, for example of the Queen's Bench Division, is not *the* divisional court of that division. Whatever their historical background, the status of divisional courts today is to be found in the relevant provisions of the [Senior Courts Act 1981].[80]

The effect of the relevant provisions of the SCA 1981[81] is that:

> [E]very divisional court is simply a court, constituted of not less than two judges, held for the transaction of business of the High Court, which is (by rules of court or by statute) required to be heard by a divisional court.[82]

1-39   Some notable features of Divisional Court practice are:

    i.   A larger Divisional Court may sit to hear cases of particular importance.[83]

    ii.   A Divisional Court is bound by its own previous decisions in the same way and subject to the same exceptions as the Court of Appeal.[84]

    iii.   In later cases, it has been held that although a Divisional Court sitting in its supervisory jurisdiction would follow a decision of another High Court judge sitting at first instance as a matter of judicial comity unless convinced that the decision is wrong, it was not bound to do so, and could depart from a decision of a court of equal jurisdiction.[85] It would only be 'in rare cases that a divisional court will think it fit to depart from a decision of another divisional court exercising this jurisdiction'.[86]

    iv.   Where two judges of a two-judge Divisional Court disagree on an appeal to it, the judges will consider the possibility of not delivering judgment and arranging

---

[76] SCA 1981, s 66(1).

[77] ibid, s 66(2).

[78] ibid, s 66(3).

[79] ibid, s 66(4).

[80] *R v Greater Manchester Coroner, ex parte Tal* [1985] QB 67, 69 (Goff LJ).

[81] SCA 1981, ss 19, 66 and 151(4).

[82] ibid.

[83] In *Wilcock v Muckle* [1951] 2 KB 844, [1951] All ER 367 there was a five-judge court which included the Lord Chief Justice, the Master of the Rolls, another Lord Justice and two High Court judges. The issue in that case was whether a wartime measure, the National Registration Act 1939, which prescribed the production of identity cards to police officers on demand, was still in force. The issue was 'one of very great public importance' (Lord Goddard LCJ).

[84] *Huddersfield Police Authority v Watson* [1947] KB 842, which followed *Young v Bristol Aeroplane Co* [1944] KB 718; see Lord Greene's summary of the three exceptions, ibid 729–30.

[85] *R (Dyer) v Watford Magistrates' Court* [2013] EWHC 547 (Admin); applied *ex p Tal* (n 80), 79E–F and 81C–D.

[86] ibid, *ex p Tal* (n 80). See above at 1-38. The principle was re-affirmed in *JC and RT v The Central Criminal and others* [2014] EWHC 1041 (Admin), [22]–[23], discussed below at 11-7 and 11-42.

for the matter to be re-argued before three judges.[87] In deciding whether to take that course, the judges will have regard to whether the importance of the subject matter is such as to justify the extra cost that would involve. In *Cambridgeshire County Council v Associated Lead Mills Ltd*[88] the two-judge Divisional Court decided that the subject matter was not sufficiently important to warrant re-consideration by a three-judge court. Accordingly, owing to lack of agreement the appeal in that case failed and was dismissed.[89]

v.   What is less clear is what would happen in the event of evenly split disagreement on a claim for judicial review. It is suggested that in those circumstances, an equally divided Divisional Court is likely to direct that the matter be reconsidered by a three-judge court. This is because the High Court's exercise of its supervisory jurisdiction for the purposes of enforcing the rule of law is likely to merit a definitive ruling by the Divisional Court.

(3) Jurisdiction to Award Costs out of 'Central Funds': a Distinction

There is an important distinction between the Administrative Court and a Divisional Court in terms of the jurisdiction to award costs out of 'central funds' (see also below, at 16-15).   **1-40**

Under section 16(5)–(6) of the Prosecution of Offences Act 1985, where any proceedings in 'a criminal cause or matter' are determined before a Divisional Court of the Queen's Bench Division, that Court may make a defendant's costs order in favour of the accused for payment out of central funds:[90]

An order for costs from central funds can include costs below. This power may be particularly important if the primary defendant in the judicial review is, for example, a lower court (against whom a costs order cannot generally be obtained).[91]

Section 51(1)(b) of SCA 1981 provides that all costs of and incidental to all proceedings in the civil division of the Court of Appeal, High Court and any county court shall be in the discretion of the court.

There is no jurisdiction to make an order for payment of costs out of central funds unless there is specific statutory provision to allow it. No such jurisdiction could be implied in either section 51(1) of the SCA 1981 or section 50 of the Solicitors Act 1974.[92] Accordingly, a Divisional Court of the Queen's Bench Division may make an award out   **1-41**

---

[87] *Cambridgeshire County Council v Associated Lead Mills Ltd* [2005] EWHC 1627 (Admin).

[88] ibid.

[89] See also *Metropolitan Water Board v Johnson & Co* [1913] 3 KB 900, 904: 'I think it is the proper result, wherever there is an appeal to two judges who differ, that the judgment appealed from should stand, and not that the junior judge should withdraw his judgment' (Chanel J); and also *Bradford Corp v Myers* [1916] 1 AC 242, 245, 253.

[90] 'Central funds' in an enactment means 'money provided by Parliament': Sch 1 to the Interpretation Act 1978. Note Sch 7 of LASPO 2012 came into force in October 2012. This inserted s 16A, which emasculates defendant's costs orders made in the Divisional Court. These are renamed 'Recovery of Defence Costs Orders' (RCDOs). For further discussion, see below at 16-15.

[91] Bailin QC and Craven, 'Judicial Review in Criminal Cases: Tigers in Africa?' (2011) 16(4) *Judicial Review* 411, 413.

[92] *Holden & Co v CPS (No 2)* [1994] 1 AC 22.

of central funds by reason of express statutory provision, whereas the Administrative Court and the Court of Appeal (Civil Division) may not.[93]

E. Who and What can be Challenged by Way of Judicial Review?

(1) Public Authorities and the Criminal Justice System

1-42   Judicial review is available only against public authorities. Public authorities are bodies or individuals exercising a power or performing a duty that involves a 'public element'.[94]

In terms of criminal judicial review, where the challenge is as to the lawfulness of (i) an enactment; or (ii) a decision, action or failure to act,[95] defendants may include any of those set out below:

   i.   Chief Constables of Police;
   ii.   Criminal Cases Review Commission (CCRC);
   iii.   First Tier Tribunal or the Criminal Injuries Compensation Authority (CICA) in respect of decisions by the CICA;
   iv.   The Crown Court;
   v.   Crown Prosecution Service (CPS);
   vi.   Director of Public Prosecutions (DPP);
   vii.   Director of the Serious Fraud Office (SFO);
   viii. Independent Police Complaints Commission (IPCC);
   ix.   Legal Aid Agency (LAA);
   x.   A magistrates' court;
   xi.   National Probation Service;
   xii.   Prison governors;
   xiii. Parole Board;
   xiv.   Secretary of State for the Home Department;
   xv.   Secretary of State for Justice (including the ministers with responsibility in this field); and,
   xvi.   Serious Organised Crime Agency (SOCA).

The above list is non-exhaustive.

(2) Test for Determining Susceptibility to Judicial Review

1-43   The test for determining who may be subject to a challenge for judicial review is not a matter of simply ascertaining the office held or the status of the body or person concerned, or even the general description of the body. Rather, the question of jurisdiction

---

[93] Jurisdiction to make an award of costs out of central funds is conferred on magistrates' courts, the Crown Court, the Criminal Division of the Court of Appeal and the Supreme Court by the Prosecution of Offences Act 1985, s 16.

[94] See *Ex p Datafin* (n 4) 838E (Sir John Donaldson MR).

[95] CPR 54(2)(a).

for a claim of judicial review has to be resolved by looking at the function being performed by the public authority.[96]

Accordingly, private companies undertaking public functions (such as managing custody services to and from and at court, or elsewhere) may, in terms of the exercise of their public functions, be subjected to judicial review.[97]

(3) What Can Be Challenged?

The range of decisions, acts (and inaction) of public authorities that a claimant may seek to impugn has been classified as follows:[98]   1-44

i.   decisions;[99]
ii. primary legislation/EU legislation;
iii. regulation/rule/order/standing order;
iv. ordinance/byelaw/practice/scheme/resolution;
v.   proposal/draft;
vi. direction/directive/instruction;
vii. notice/declaration/circular;
viii. guidance;
ix. advice/recommendation/opinion/comment/publication;
x.   action/failure/refusal.

F. Who Can Make a Claim for Judicial Review?

(1) Rules on Standing

(i) Introduction

No application for judicial review can be made unless permission of the High Court has been obtained in accordance with rules of court; and the court shall not grant permission to make such an application unless it considers that the applicant has a sufficient interest in the matter to which the application relates.[100] A 'sufficient interest' has been explained in these terms: 1-45

(a) The threshold at the point of the application for [permission] is set only at the height necessary to prevent abuse.

---

[96] *R v Supreme Court Taxing Office, ex parte Singh & Co* (1995) 7 Admin LR 849, 853E (Latham J); *Leech v Deputy Governor of Parkhurst Prison* [1988] AC 533, 583B–C; and see Fordham *Judicial Review Handbook* (n 6) paras 34.2.3–34.2.8.

[97] See also HRA 1998, s 6(3)(b) which defines 'public authority' as including 'any person certain of whose functions are of a public nature' but that 'in relation to a particular act, a person is not a public authority by virtue only of subsection (3)(b) if the nature of the act is private'.

[98] See Fordham *Judicial Review Handbook* (n 6), para 5.2, and of particular relevance to criminal judicial review see the cases cited at para 5.2.11.

[99] For the avoidance of doubt, 'decisions' include convictions or acquittals in the magistrates' courts, or the Crown Court acting in its appellate capacity. See below at 7-25.

[100] SCA 1981, s 31(3).

(b) To have 'no interest whatsoever' is not the same as having no pecuniary or special personal interest. It is to interfere in something with which one has no legitimate concern at all; to be, in other words, a busybody.

(c) Beyond this point, the question of standing has no materiality at the [permission] stage.[101]

Establishing 'sufficient interest' in criminal judicial review cases tends not to be a difficulty often encountered, as the claimants are usually those who are defendants or potential defendants in criminal proceedings, or conversely public authorities involved in the criminal justice system, all of whom can readily establish a sufficient interest in an application for permission for judicial review.

1-46   The threshold for standing for judicial review has generally been set by the courts at a low level. This is so, because of the importance in public law that someone should be able to call decision-makers to account, 'lest the rule of law break down and private rights be denied by public bodies'.[102] But where the traditional and invariable parties to criminal proceedings, namely the Crown and the defendant are both able to, and do, challenge judicial decisions which are susceptible to judicial review, there is generally no need in criminal cases for a third party to seek to intervene to uphold the rule of law.[103]

Nonetheless, outside actual criminal court proceedings, there are circumstances where members of the general public or a section of the public may be able to establish a sufficient interest, such as, for instance, where judicial review of a policy decision is sought.[104]

(ii) Standing under the Human Rights Act 1998

1-47   Different rules for standing are provided for claims brought under the Human Rights Act (HRA) 1998. Section 7 of HRA 1998 provides for a 'victim test'. Accordingly, a person who claims that a public authority has acted (or proposes to act) in a way which is made unlawful by section 6(1) of HRA 1998, may bring proceedings against the public authority only if he is (or would be) a victim of the unlawful act. Moreover, if the proceedings are brought on an application for judicial review, the applicant is to be taken to have a sufficient interest in relation to the unlawful act only if he is, or would be, a victim of that act.[105]

A person is a victim of an unlawful act only if he would be a victim for the purposes of Article 34 of the ECHR were proceedings brought in the European Court of Human Rights (ECtHR).[106] Article 34 of the ECHR provides that the ECtHR may

---

[101] *R v Somerset County Council, ex parte Dixon* [1998] Env LR 111, 117 (Sedley J).

[102] *R v Secretary of State for the Home Department, ex parte Bulger* [2001] EWHC Admin 119 [20].

[103] ibid. In *Ex p Bulger*, the father of a murdered child had applied for permission to move for judicial review of a decision of the Lord Chief Justice in relation to the tariff that the two juveniles convicted of the murder should serve. The application for judicial review was refused, as it was open to the Crown or a defendant to challenge any judicial decision that was susceptible to judicial review and it was held therefore neither necessary or desirable that a third party should seek to intervene.

[104] For instance, see *R v Commissioner of Police of the Metropolis, ex parte Blackburn (No 1)* [1968] 2 QB 18 (CA), [1968] 2 WLR 893, where the applicant sought judicial review of a policy decision by police not to enforce the law on gambling in gaming clubs in London. See below at 4-11.

[105] HRA 1998, s 7(3).

[106] ibid, s 7(7).

receive applications from any person, non-governmental organisation or group of individuals claiming to be 'the victim' of a violation by one of the Contracting States to the ECHR. ECtHR case law treats a person as a victim within the meaning of Article 34 if they run the risk of being directly affected by a law or other act of state interference that violates their Convention rights.[107]

The following are domestic examples of 'victims' within the meaning of the HRA **1-48** 1998 and Article 34 of the Convention, who were not defendants in a criminal trial:

i.   Family members in relation to a substantive violation of Article 2 of the Convention.[108]

ii.   An organisation campaigning on rural issues and a number of individuals adversely affected by the passing of the Hunting Act 2004, as their fear was that the Hunting Act created the risk that their Convention rights might be violated in that it might be given effect to in a way which would be incompatible with their Convention rights.[109]

iii.   A person serving a life sentence in England for murder in relation to the failure of the Secretary of State for Justice and the local authority to permit him to vote in parliamentary and European Union elections.[110]

iv.   A parent complaining of breach of a child's rights.[111]

v.   A deceased's widow and father claiming that with a better policy for handling cases of detention by customs officers and with better care, the deceased's life could have been saved and there had thus been a breach by the defendant Revenue and Customs Commissioners of the deceased's rights under Articles 2 (right to life) and 3 (prohibition of torture) of the ECHR.[112]

vi.   A family member as distant as a nephew can bring a claim under the HRA as a 'victim'; so too can a partner of the deceased, in particular if that person is also the parent of a child of the deceased; and a fiancée of the deceased; but if a claimant was 'merely in a relationship with the deceased' whether that would suffice would have to be determined on the particular facts of the case, as would a situation where a claimant was not the biological daughter of the deceased but had been brought up on the understanding that she was his daughter.[113]

---

[107] *R (Countryside Alliance) v Attorney General* [2006] EWCA Civ 817, [2007] QB 305 (CA) 305 [65]; see *Marckz v Belgium* (1979) 2 EHRR 330 and *Institut de Pretres Francais v Turkey* (1998) 92-A DR 15.

[108] *Rabone v Pennine Care NHS Trust* [2012] UKSC 2 [46].

[109] *Countryside Alliance* (n 107) [65]–[66]. In fact, in those proceedings there was no suggestion that the claimants did not have standing to seek a declaration of incompatibility

[110] *R (Chester) v Secretary of State for Justice and McGeoch v Lord President of the Council* [2013] UKSC 63, [2013] 3 WLR 1076.

[111] *R (Holub) v Secretary of State for the Home Department* [2001] 1 WLR 1359 [14].

[112] *Al Hassan v Revenue and Customs Commissioners (JUSTICE intervening)* [2010] EWCA Civ 1443, [2011] QB 866.

[113] See *Christina Morgan (on her own behalf and as administratrix of the estate of Karl Lewis), Courtney Morgan (by her mother and litigation friend Christina Morgan) v Ministry of Justice, The Crown* [2010] EWHC 2248, QB where the decisions of the ECtHR were considered, and the law summarised ibid [70].

(iii) Special Cases: Children and Protected Parties

1-49   Certain claimants, children and others lacking capacity (such as those suffering from mental disorders) generally cannot bring a claim for judicial review themselves but must have a litigation friend to conduct proceedings for them.[114]

   In the case of a child, the court may make an order permitting the child to conduct proceedings without a litigation friend.[115] For the purposes of Part 21 of the CPR, a 'child' means a person under the age of 18 years.[116] A protected person, on the other hand, must always have a litigation friend to conduct the proceedings on his or her behalf.[117] Any step taken before a child or protected party has a litigation friend, shall be of no effect, unless the court otherwise orders (see discussion below, at 11-11).[118]

   A 'protected party' means a party, or an intended party, who lacks capacity (within the meaning of the Mental Capacity Act 2005) to conduct the proceedings. A person lacks capacity in relation to a matter if at the material time he is unable to make a decision for himself in relation to the matter because of an impairment of, or a disturbance in the functioning of, the mind or brain.[119]

   Rules for the appointment of a litigation friend for a child or a protected party are contained in the Part 24 of the CPR.[120]

G. Grounds for Judicial Review

(1) Introduction

1-50   Claims for judicial review may be brought to review a decision, action or failure to act in relation to the exercise of a public function, on several grounds.

   The traditional grounds upon which administrative action by public authorities is subject to control by judicial review have been classified under three heads: (i) illegality (error of law); (ii) irrationality; and (iii) procedural impropriety (unfairness).[121] More recently, grounds such as proportionality and the principle of equality or consistency have been developed or are in the process of development. Other grounds include bad faith and improper motive. Decisions in relation to policy guidance (or its absence), is an area of criminal judicial review that has been subjected to some scrutiny by the courts, and is addressed in this section.

---

[114] CPR 21.2(1)–(2). See below at 11-11 and at 12.2.

[115] CPR 21.2(3).

[116] *Cf* for criminal sentencing purposes a 'child' means a person under the age of 14 years, whereas a 'young person' means a person who has attained the age of 14 years and is under the age of 18 years, see Children and Young Persons Act 1933, s 107(1). See table below at 11-14.

[117] CPR 21.2(1).

[118] CPR 21.3(4).

[119] Mental Capacity Act 2005, s 2. See s 3 of the 2005 Act for the meaning and scope of an 'inability to make decisions'. See also below at 12-15.

[120] See below at 12-2 and 11-11.

[121] *Council of Civil Service Unions* (n 8) 410D (Lord Diplock).

The various grounds are not exhaustive, and are not necessarily mutually exclusive.[122] Future development on a case-by-case basis may add further grounds.[123]

(2) Illegality (Error of Law)

In *Council of Civil Service Unions v Minister for the Civil Service*,[124] Lord Diplock set out his classic formulation of the three traditional grounds upon which administrative action by public authorities is subject to control by judicial review. The first of these grounds was what he called 'illegality'. He went on to explain: **1-51**

> By 'illegality' as a ground for judicial review I mean that the decision-maker must understand correctly the law that regulates his decision-making power and must give effect to it. Whether he has or not is par excellence a justiciable question to be decided, in the event of dispute, by those persons, the judges, by whom the judicial power of the state is exercisable.[125]

The High Court may judicially review the decisions, actions (and inaction) of a public authority for error of law, and is competent to correct any error of law, whether or not it goes to jurisdiction.[126] A public authority 'must understand correctly the law that regulates his decision-making power and must give effect to it'.[127] **1-52**

Consideration will be given to errors of law in four situations: (i) domestic (non-ECHR) law; (ii) ECHR law; (iii) European union law; and generally, (iv) errors of fact, as errors of law.

(3) Errors of Domestic Law: Illustrations

(i) Search Warrants[128]

Where a search warrant was drawn too widely, so that what had been seized ought not to have been seized, there was a consequential failure to identify so far as practicable the articles sought; and in that event, a failure to comply with section 15(2)(c) of the Police and Criminal Evidence Act 1984 Act. The warrant was the authority for officers to go on the premises searched. Given the defect of being drawn too wide, the whole warrant was invalidated and was accordingly quashed by the Divisional Court.[129] **1-53**

---

[122] Lord Roskill in *Wheeler v Leicester City Council* [1985] AC 1054, 1078B–C, reflecting on the traditional three heads of illegality, irrationality and procedural impropriety. Those observations remain true at the present time in respect of grounds generally.

[123] *Council of Civil Service Unions* (n 8) 410D (Lord Diplock).

[124] *Council of Civil Service Unions* (n 8).

[125] ibid 410F.

[126] *Anisminic Ltd v Foreign Compensation Commission* [1969] 2 AC 147, [1969] 2 WLR 163.

[127] *Council of Civil Service Unions* (n 8) 410F (Lord Diplock).

[128] Discussed below in detail in section D in Chapter 4.

[129] *R (F) v Blackfriars Crown Court* [2014] EWHC 1541 (Admin) (Elias LJ, Kenneth Parker J). See also below at 4-41.

(ii) Committals[130]

1-54   On a consideration of where to commit a young person for trial in the Crown Court, it was not open to a Youth Court to ignore either section 24(1) of the Magistrates' Courts Act 1980 or section 51A of the Crime and Disorder Act 1998. Wherever possible, the policy of the legislature is that those under 18 should be tried in a Youth Court, which is best designed for their specific needs.[131]

In *R (G) v Llanelli Magistrates' Court*[132] the accused was aged 13 years old when he appeared before the magistrates' court on a charge of robbery. The justices decided to refuse jurisdiction and commit the accused to stand trial in the Crown Court. The committal amounted to an error of law as the court was required to determine whether pursuant to section 24 of the Magistrates' Courts Act 1980, it was appropriate to commit the accused for trial in Crown Court; either because a custodial sentence of over two years in length was a realistic prospect, or because the offence had other unusual features that made a trial in the Crown Court appropriate.

(iii) Vacation of Plea

1-55   A magistrates' court is required to invite a defendant to indicate how he would plead if the case were to proceed to trial and to explain the consequences of indicating a guilty plea.[133] In *R (Rahmdezfouli) v Wood Green Crown Court*,[134] the magistrates' court had taken a guilty plea for an offence triable either way without having followed the required statutory procedure. The claimant was committed to the Crown Court for sentence, where the judge refused his application to vacate his guilty plea. The effect of having not followed the statutory requirements was that the magistrates' court had thereafter acted without jurisdiction, in convicting the claimant on his plea and committing him to the Crown Court. Accordingly, the subsequent proceedings in the Crown Court had been invalid and a nullity. The conviction was quashed.[135]

(iv) Prosecution Out of Time

1-56   In *R (Donnachie) v Cardiff Magistrates' Court*[136] the claimant was prosecuted by a local authority in the exercise of its duty to enforce the provisions of the Trade Description

---

[130] See discussion from 6-58 below.

[131] *R (DPP) v South East Surrey Youth Court* [2005] EWHC 2929 (Admin), [2006] 1 WLR 2543, and see below at 6-65. The CPS' claim for judicial review was dismissed because although the Youth Court's approach in so far as they declined to consider the provisions of the Crime and Disorder Act 1998, s 51A(3)(d) was flawed, the conclusion that summary jurisdiction should be accepted for the purposes of trial was unimpeachable ([15]–[18]). See also *R (H, A and O) v Southampton Youth Court* [2004] EWHC 2912 (Admin) (see 6-64 below), approved by the Divisional Court in *R (Crown Prosecution Service) v Redbridge Youth Court* [2005] EWHC 1390 and *R (T) v Bromley Youth Court* [2014] EWHC 577 (Admin) (Moses LJ, Silber J).

[132] *R (G) v Llanelli Magistrates' Court* [2006] EWHC 1413 (Admin) (DC).

[133] Section 17A of the Magistrates' Courts Act 1980.

[134] *R (Rahmdezfouli) v Wood Green Crown Court* [2013] EWHC 2998 (Admin), [2014] 1 WLR 1793 (Moses LJ, Mackay J).

[135] ibid, at [16]–[17].

[136] *R (Donnachie) v Cardiff Magistrates' Court* [2007] EWHC (1846) Admin, [2007] 1 WLR 3085.

Richard Wilson QC

Act 1968, for altering odometer readings of a number of vehicles and thereby applying false descriptions to the vehicles, in contravention of the Act. The district judge's decision to reject the claimant's submission that the prosecution was out of time was an error of law. The judge had erred in concluding both that at the time the odometers had been altered no offence had been committed, and that the local authority employee with authority to institute proceedings was the prosecutor. His decision that the information had been laid in time was quashed and the matter was remitted to him for redetermination.[137]

(v) Secure Remand (Young Person)

In *R (A) v Lewisham Youth Court*[138] the claimant was 15 years old when he was arrested   **1-57**
and charged with an offence of murder. He applied for judicial review of the Youth Court's decision to remand him in custody in prison, rather than in secure accommodation (see also below, at 11-21). The judge's ruling that the statutory power to order a secure remand did not apply in the case of a child or young person who appeared before a Youth Court charged with murder, was held to be wrong in law.[139]

(vi) No Liability to Prosecution

In *R (Hampstead Heath Winter Swimming Club) v Corporation of London*,[140] the   **1-58**
Corporation of London, defendant in the judicial review proceedings, had responsibility for the management of Hampstead Heath and its three bathing ponds and lido. The Corporation by a resolution refused to allow members of a winter swimming club to swim early in the morning in one of its ponds without lifeguards in attendance, notwithstanding the provision of appropriate indemnities by the club and its members. This was because the corporation considered that it would be vulnerable to prosecution under the Health and Safety at Work Act 1974 (section 3) if any harm befell swimmers. Allowing the club's claim for judicial review, it was held that the Corporation's resolution was 'based on legal error', as any grant to the club of permission to swim unsupervised in the mixed pond would not of itself render the Corporation liable to prosecution under the 1974 Act.[141]

(vii) Burden of Proof

The issue of whether or not a person in receipt of housing benefit and council tax   **1-59**
benefit had failed to notify a change of circumstances promptly and within a reasonable period depended on the circumstances of the individual benefit claimant. The Crown Court had been wrong in law to dismiss an appeal from the magistrates' court (by re-hearing) on the basis that the appellant had not provided the information

---

[137] ibid [25]–[31], [34]: see also *RSPCA v Johnson* [2009] EWHC 2702 (Admin) (DC); *Burwell v DPP* [2010] EWHC 1953 (Admin) (DC).
[138] *R (A) v Lewisham Youth Court* [2011] EWHC 1193 (Admin) (DC), [2012] 1 WLR 34. See below Chapter 11 at nn 10, 131 and 226.
[139] ibid [17]–[20], [22].
[140] *R (Hampstead Heath Winter Swimming Club) v Corporation of London* [2005] EWHC 713 (Admin), [2005] 1 WLR 2930. See also below at 5-41.
[141] ibid [63], [69].

promptly and within a reasonable period as required by section 112(1A) of the Social Security Act 1992. The date and time that the claimant had notified the local authority should have been established by evidence, and the prosecution bore the burden of proof on the issue.[142]

(viii) Policy Decision

1-60   In *R (A) v Secretary of State for the Home Department*[143] the claimant was found not guilty by reason of insanity of kidnap and assault occasioning actual bodily harm. An order was made for the claimant's admission to hospital, and that order was treated for the purposes of the Mental Health Act 1983 as if the claimant had been admitted in pursuance of a hospital order. Subsequently, a mental health review tribunal decided to order the claimant's conditional discharge. A suitable hostel was identified which agreed to accept the claimant on condition that he completed a six-week trial period. The Secretary of State refused his consent to the claimant's 'leave of absence' for the six-week period, since in his opinion he could not attach conditions for the leave of absence under section 17 of the 1983 Act. He decided instead that he should direct the claimant's conditional discharge under section 42 of the 1983 Act. This was a course of action which allowed the Secretary of State to attach conditions to the claimant's leave of absence, including a condition that the Secretary of State be provided with reports. The Divisional Court held that the policy, or at least the settled practice, of the Secretary of State not to give consent to leave under section 17 for overnight stays to restricted patients granted deferred conditional discharge (other than in exceptional circumstances), was 'mistaken' in law. The giving of leave under section 17 should be the normal method under the 1983 Act.[144]

(ix) Criminal Cases Review Commission[145]

1-61   The claimant was convicted of murdering a neighbour. His defence at trial had been that by reason of diminished responsibility he was guilty only of manslaughter. He challenged a decision of the Criminal Cases Review Commission (CCRC) not to refer his case to the Court of Appeal (Criminal Division), the CCRC having concluded that there was no 'real possibility' that the Court of Appeal would not uphold the conviction. The Divisional Court allowed the application and quashed the CCRC's decision because of error of law. The CCRC had failed to identify properly the inadequacies in the trial judge's directions on the issue of provocation and the significance of the claimant's depressive illness, which was undoubtedly a characteristic relevant to the issue of provocation. He had also misunderstood the Court of Appeal's appellate role in evaluating fresh psychiatric evidence relating to provocation by assuming that the Court of Appeal would consider the fresh evidence and resolve the issue of provocation pursuant to section 3 of the Homicide Act 1957, as a jury would.[146]

---

[142] *Taffs v Chelmsford Crown Court* [2014] EWHC 899 (Admin) (Laws LJ, Foskett J).
[143] *R (A) v Secretary of State for the Home Department* [2002] EWHC 1618 (Admin), [2003] 1 WLR 330.
[144] ibid [49].
[145] See section C of Chapter 9 below.
[146] *R (Farnell) v Criminal Cases Review Commission* [2003] EWHC 835 (Admin) [35]–[38]; and see below at 9-22.

(x) Independent Police Complaints Commission[147]

As a result of an incident involving police officers, the claimant had sustained partial **1-62** paralysis, with significant cognitive impairment thereafter. He made a complaint to the defendant Commission (IPCC). The IPCC decided that it did not have power to investigate potentially criminal conduct which might have arisen before the police became involved, and so arranged for the Sussex police to conduct the investigations relating to the period before the police became involved. The IPCC restricted its own investigations to events following the claimant's contact with the police.

The Court of Appeal held that the IPCC's decision was based on an error of law. Since there had been a serious injury which manifested itself while the claimant was in police custody and the claimant had made a formal complaint to the IPCC about the matter, the IPCC pursuant to statute had both a power and a duty to investigate in order to determine whether there had been misconduct on the part of the police. In determining that question the IPCC was required as part of its investigation to consider, evaluate and test any evidence pointing to a competing cause of injury, even one occurring before contact with the police.[148]

(xi) Coroner[149]

In 1997 the Princess of Wales and Dodi Al Fayed died following a road accident in Paris **1-63** when the car in which they were being driven was being pursued by paparazzi. Their bodies were repatriated to the coronial district of West London. The coroner, a recently retired judge of the High Court, decided not to summon an inquest jury. A three-judge Divisional Court (Smith LJ, Collins and Silber JJ) held that the coroner's decision was wrong in law, as the provisions of the Coroners Act 1988, properly construed, required the summoning of a jury.[150]

(4) The ECHR and Errors of Law

Under the HRA 1998, errors of law can now include failures by the state to act com- **1-64** patibly with the Convention.[151] The HRA 1998 incorporated Convention rights into UK law.[152] Infringement of Convention rights by a public authority is a ground of illegality,[153] and subject to judicial review.[154]

---

[147] See section D of Chapter 9 below.
[148] *R (Reynolds) v IPCC* [2008] EWCA Civ 1160, [2009] 3 All ER 237 [16]–[17]. See also *R (Chief Constable of West Yorkshire) v Independent Police Complaints Commission* [2013] EWHC 2698 (AC) where the Court set out 12 propositions on the law concerning the Commission's functions at [47] (appeal to Court of Appeal pending at time of writing); and see below at 9-32.
[149] See Chapter 10 below.
[150] *R (Paul) v Coroner of the Queen's Household* [2007] EWHC 408 (Admin), [2008] QB 172 [40]; *R (O'Connor) v Avon Coroner* [2009] EWHC 854 (Admin), [2011] QB 106, (DC) [13]–[14] (coroner's material misdirection of law, verdict quashed).
[151] *R(Q) v Secretary of State for the Home Department* [2003] EWCA Civ 364, [2004] QB 36, [112] (Lord Philips MR).
[152] HRA 1998, ss 1(1)–(2), 3, 4, 6 and 7. See Annex 1 for a list of the Articles contained in ibid, Sch 1.
[153] ibid, s 6(1).
[154] ibid, s 7(1), (3).

Some Convention rights are absolute and unqualified, in the sense that a Contracting State cannot derogate from them, even in an emergency.[155] Other Convention rights are qualified rights, which require a court to determine whether or not the decision of the public authority was in accordance with or prescribed by the law and justified in terms of the proportionality principle.[156]

As a general principle, where the question before a court concerns whether a decision interferes with a right under the ECHR and, if so, whether it is proportionate and therefore justified, it is necessary for the court to conduct a high-intensity review of the decision. The court must make its own assessment of the factors considered by the decision-maker. The need to do this involves considering the appropriate weight to give them and thus the relative weight accorded to the interests and considerations by the decision-maker. The scope of review thus goes further than the traditional grounds of judicial review.[157] Although cases involving rights under the ECHR involve 'a more exacting standard of review', there has been no shift to a merits review.[158] It remains the case that the judge is not the primary decision-maker. In *Axa General Insurance Ltd v HM Advocate*, Lord Reed stated:

> Although the courts must decide, whether in their judgment the requirement of proportionality is satisfied, there is at the same time nothing in the Convention, or in domestic legislation giving effect to Convention rights, which requires the courts to substitute their own views for those of other public authorities on all matters of policy, judgment and discretion.[159]

Errors of reasoning in cases concerned with interference of a Convention right did not automatically render a decision disproportionate if the right result was achieved; substance not procedure was the key concern.[160] However where substance and procedure were heavily entwined, adherence to some form of process would help not only determine whether a decision was wrong, but would also provide guidance to the primary decision-maker in future cases and achieve a better quality of decision.[161]

Illustrations of the most relevant Convention rights for criminal judicial review are set out below.

(i) Article 2 (Right to Life)

1-65   The state is under a substantive obligation not to take human life without justification.[162]

---

[155] Unqualified Convention rights include Art 2 (right to life), Art 3 (prohibition of torture, inhuman and degrading treatment), Art 4 (prohibition of slavery and forced labour), Art 6 (right to a fair trial), Art 7 (no punishment without law), and Art 14 (prohibition of discrimination).

[156] Qualified Convention rights include Art 8 (right to respect for family and private life), Art 9 (freedom of thought, conscience and religion), Art 10 (freedom of expression) and Art 11 (freedom of assembly and association), Art 1 of the First Protocol (protection of property).

[157] See, for example, *Daly* (n 1) [27]; *R (A) v Chief Constable of Kent* [2013] EWCA Civ 1706, [36].

[158] *Huang v Secretary of State for the Home Department* [2007] UKHL 11, [2007] 2 AC 167, [13], per Lord Bingham.

[159] *Axa General Insurance Ltd v HM Advocate* [2011] UKSC, [2012] 1 AC 868; applied in *R (A) v Chief Constable of Kent* (n 157).

[160] *DS v Her Majesty's Advocate* [2007] UKPC D1, [2007] SC (PC) 1; *R (A) v Chief Constable of Kent* (n 157) [46].

[161] See *R (A) v Chief Constable of Kent* (n 157) and cases cited at [48]–[52].

[162] *R (Middleton) v West Somerset Coroner* [2004] UKHL 10, [2004] 2 AC 182 [2]–[3]. See below at 10-12.

Richard Wilson QC

(ii) Article 3 (Prohibition of Torture, Inhuman and Degrading Treatment)[163]

Under Article 3, the police have a duty to conduct effective investigations into particularly   **1-66**
severe crimes prepetrated by private parties, and to do so in a timely and efficient manner.
In *DSD v Commissioner of Police for the Metropolis*.[163a] It was held that the police were liable for systemic failings in investigating a large number of rapes and sexual assaults perpetrated by the so-called 'black cab rapist' over a six-year period. The 'systemic' failings
could be accounted in five areas: (i) failure properly to provide training; (ii) failure properly to supervise and manage; (iii) failure properly to use available intelligence sources;
(iv) failure to have in place proper systems to ensure victim confidence; and (v) failure to
allocate adequate resources. The failure to have in place proper systems to ensure victim
confidence; and (v) failure to allocate adequate resources. The failure to conduct an effective investigation amounted to a breach of the victims' rights under Article 3.

A decision by the Crown Prosecution Service to discontinue a prosecution on the
basis that the victim (a person suffering from mental health problems) was not a credible witness was a violation of the victim's rights under Article 3.[164] A prisoner's solitary
confinement was not incompatible with Article 3.[165] But limiting a prisoner to one meal
per day was a violation of the prisoner's Article 3 rights.[166]

(iii) Article 5 (Right to Liberty and Security)[167]

Confining a person to a flat for 18 hours a day was a violation of Article 5,[168] as was a   **1-67**
16-hour curfew and social isolation.[169]

(iv) Article 6 (Right to a Fair Trial)[170]

A late withdrawal of legal aid that effectively denied access to the court was a breach   **1-68**
of Article 6;[171] as was a prison disciplinary finding where the prisoner had not been
afforded legal representation.[172]

A suspect at a police station was unlawfully denied right of access to a solicitor of his
choosing when interviewed, in breach of his rights under Article 6(3)(c).[173]

---

[163] See also discussion on police custody below in section G of Chapter 4.
[163a] *DSD v Commissioner of Police for the Metropolis* [2014] EWHC 436 (QB), discussed in detail below at 4-13.
[164] B (n 27). See also below at 5-31.
[165] *R (N) v Secretary of State for Justice* [2009] EWHC 1921 (Admin).
[166] *R v Governor of Frankland Prison, ex parte Russell* [2000] 1 WLR 2027.
[167] See also Chapter 4 below – stop and search at section E and 'kettling' at 4-67.
[168] *Secretary of State for the Home Department v JJ* [2007] UKHL 45, [2008] 1 AC 385.
[169] *Secretary of State for the Home Department v AP (No 1)* [2010] UKSC 24, [2011] 2 AC 1.
[170] See also stop and search at 4-33 police bail at 4-84, court bail at 6-47 and abuse of process at 6-39.
[171] *R (Alliss) v Legal Services Commission* [2002] EWHC 2079 (Admin) [44]. See also below at 9-11.
[172] *R (Greenfield) v Secretary of State for the Home Department* [2005] UKHL 14, [2005] 1 WLR 673. See
also below at 3-29.
[173] Article 6(3)(c): 'Everyone charged with a criminal offence has the following minimum rights … (c) to
defend himself in person or through legal assistance of his own choosing …'. See *Beeres v Crown Prosecution
Service West Midlands* [2014] EWHC 283 (Admin) and Chapter 4, n 464.

(v) Article 8 (Right to Respect for Private and Family Life)[174]

1-69   The statutory regime for enhanced criminal record certificates under section 113B of the Police Act 1997, requiring mandatory disclosure of all convictions and cautions relating to recordable offences held on national computer against an individual, was disproportionate and incompatible with Article 8.[175] Similarly, the disclosure of a witness's health records to an accused lacked sufficient procedural safeguards;[176] and a sex offender's life-long notification requirements absent any provision for individual review were violations of Article 8.[177] But the notification requirements under sections 47–52 of the Counter-Terrorism Act 2008 imposed for 10 years on an offender on conviction of a terrorism offence, were not incompatible with the offender's rights under Article 8 even though there was no right of review.[178]

(vi) Article 10 (Right to Freedom of Expression)[179]

1-70   A blanket ban on prisoner contact with the media by telephone was a breach of Article 10, as it was not necessary in a democratic society.[180] But the powers granted to the police under Schedule 7 of the Terrorism Act 2000 to stop and detain individuals had the necessary quality of law to satisfy the requirements of articles 8 and 10 (see 4-20 below on Schedule 7). It was applicable to only a limited category of persons, existed only in the narrow context of port and border controls, and is subject to cumulative statutory limitations. ECtHR jurisprudence did not require prior judicial scrutiny as a necessary safeguard in all cases, and the safeguards identified were sufficient to comply with Article 10.[181]

(vii) Article 14 (Prohibition of Discrimination)

1-71   Detention without trial was found to be a violation of Article 14 (taken together with Article 5) because the detention policy targeted non-nationals only, and so amounted to unjustified discrimination on nationality grounds.[182]

---

[174] See also stop and search at 4-25 prisoners' correspondence at 8-12 (and 8-15), appropriate adults and youths at 11-16 and decisions to charge at 5-34 and 11-35

[175] *R (T & others) v Chief Constable of Greater Manchester & others* [2013] EWCA Civ 25. [2013] 1 WLR 2515 (judgment was handed down, subsequent to the completion of this chapter, in *R (T and another) v Secretary of State for the Home Department and another* [2014] UKSC 35). See below at 4-112.

[176] *R (B) v Stafford Combined Court* [2006] EWHC 1645 (Admin), [2007] 1 WLR 1524.

[177] *R (F (A Child)) v Secretary of State for the Home Department (Lord Advocate and another intervening)* [2010] UKSC 17, [2011] 1 AC 331, [51], [57]–[58]. See below at 1-130.

[178] *R (Irfan) v Secretary of State for the Home Department* [2012] EWCA Civ 1471, [2013] QB 885.

[179] See also reporting restrictions at 11-44.

[180] *R (Hirst) v Secretary of State for the Home Department* [2002] EWHC 602 (Admin), [2002] 1 WLR 2929. See also below at 8-13.

[181] *Miranda v Secretary of State for the Home Department* [2014] EWHC 255 (Admin)—see below at 4-22.

[182] *A v Secretary of State for the Home Department* [2004] UKHL 56, [2005] 2 AC 68.

Richard Wilson QC

(5) European Union law and Errors of Law

Pursuant to the principle of the primacy of EU law,[183] any national measure (including   **1-72**
primary and secondary legislation), rules or decision-making that falls within the scope
of competence of EU law may be subject to challenge before domestic courts on the
grounds of incompatibility with EU law. National courts are required to give effect to
EU law when applicable, and any applicable norm of EU law will take precedence over
any (inconsistent) provision of national law.[184]

The Charter of Fundamental Rights of the EU is the principal basis on which the
Court of Justice of the European Union (CJEU) will ensure that EU human rights
are observed.[185] The Charter is applicable whenever a member state is implementing
EU law.[186] This means that a challenge by judicial review can be made not only to
implementing UK legislation, but also to regulations, directives and other measures by
EU institutions (see Chapter 14 below).

(i) Illustrations: Extradition and the Framework Decision 2002/584[187]

In *R (Spain) v City of Westminster Magistrates' Court*,[188] the Issuing Judicial Authority   **1-73**
(IJA), the Central Examining Court of Madrid, issued European Arrest Warrants against
each of five interested parties. The CPS provided the IJA with drafting assistance in the
preparation of a European Arrest Warrant. The district judge held that such assistance
was capable in law of constituting an abuse of process. The IJA made an application for
judicial review of the district judge's decision. The Divisional Court held that the decision was an error of law, as such simple assistance did not amount to an abuse of process.

> The simple provision of drafting assistance to the IJA is not, in law, capable of constituting an
> abuse. It impacts neither on the principle of equality of arms, nor on the visible independence
> and impartiality of the Spanish Judicial Authority.[189]

There was no objection to an IJA using services such as those given the CPS (drafting an   **1-74**
entire European Arrest Warrant), so long as it was done entirely on the IJA's instructions
and was adopted, and not merely rubber-stamped by the IJA. Where there is reason
to suspect departure from these principles, but not otherwise, the Examining Judicial
Authority in England could seek further information with a view to satisfying itself that
there had not been an abuse of process.[190]

In *R (Szklanny) v City of Westminster Magistrates' Court*[191] the claimant applied for   **1-75**
judicial review of a district judge's decision to extend the time for his extradition to

---

[183] *Costa v ENEL* [1964] ECR 585, 593.
[184] *A v Chief Constable of West Yorkshire* [2004] UKHL 21 [2004] ICR 806 [9].
[185] *Kadi v Council and Commission ('Kadi I')* (Joined Cases C-402/05P and C-415/05P) [2009] 1 AC 1225,
[2009] 3 WLR 872 [308]. See below at 14-19.
[186] Charter of Fundamental Rights of the European Union, Art 51.
[187] See Chapter 13 below.
[188] *R (Spain) v City of Westminster Magistrates' Court* [2007] EWHC 2059 (Admin) (DC).
[189] ibid [35].
[190] ibid [24]–[25].
[191] *R (Szklanny) v City of Westminster Magistrates' Court* [2007] EWHC 2646 (Admin), [2008] 1 WLR 789.
See 13-22 below.

Poland by seven days, arguing that an extension should only be granted where the surrender of the requested person was prevented by circumstances beyond the control of the Member States. The judicial review application was refused. It was held that the discretion conferred by section 35(4)(b) of the Extradition Act 2003 was in broad terms, and was in accordance with the Framework Decision:

> The obligation to interpret national law, so far as possible, in the light of the wording and purpose of the Framework Decision should not require the discretion to be cut down in the way suggested by the claimant, so as to be exercisable only if it is shown that extradition within the normal period has been prevented by circumstances beyond the control of the member states concerned.[192]

If informed that there was a judicial review pending, it would be quite wrong for the Serious Organised Crime Agency to take steps to remove a person who had been subjected to an order by the magistrates' court ordering his extradition to the requesting country. This would be so, even in the absence of an injunction restraining removal.[193]

(ii) Fundamental Rights: Legality and Proportionality

1-76   Article 49 of the Charter of Fundamental Rights of the European Union deals with principles of legality and proportionality in relation to criminal offences and penalties. Article 49(3) provides that 'The severity of penalties must not be disproportionate to the criminal offence', and as such may be a ground for non-execution of a European Arrest Warrant if the penalty sought by the issuing Member State would be intolerably severe.[194]

(iii) Fundamental Rights: Rule of Law Based on Judicial Review

1-77   In *Kadi v Council and Commission*,[195] the claimant was a resident of Saudi Arabia, and was designated by the Sanctions Committee of the United Nations Security Council as being associated with the Al-Qaeda network. His name was placed on a list annexed to Regulation 881/2002, so that his funds and other economic resources in the European Union were frozen. The claimant sought annulment of the Regulation as it related to him, on the grounds that the EU lacked competence to adopt the Regulation. It was argued that this was because the Regulation breached certain of his fundamental rights enjoyed under EU law, in particular: (i) the right to a fair hearing, on the basis that none of the evidence relied on against him had been disclosed to him, nor even the reasons for his name being placed on the prohibited persons list, and (ii) the right to property.

The Grand Chamber of the CJEU held that the European Union was based on the rule of law by judicial review, and that the lawfulness of all EU measures had to be considered in the light of fundamental rights guaranteed by the European Union, even where the EU measure implemented an international law (Security Council) measure.[196]

---

[192] ibid [18] (Richards LJ). For judicial review relating to extradition matters see Ch 13.

[193] *Sokolovs v Office of the Public Prosecutor General (Latvia)* [2013] EWHC 929 (Admin) [5].

[194] This was the conclusion reached by the Higher Regional Court in Stuttgart, Germany in *General Public Prosecution Service v C* (2010) 1 Ausl (24) 1246/09, translated judgment in *Criminal Law Review* 2010, 474. For arrest warrants generally, see below at 4-51 below.

[195] *Kadi I* (n 185). See below at 14-19.

[196] ibid.

Subsequent to the CJEU decision, the European Commission disclosed to the claim-   **1-78**
ant a summary of reasons for the listing provided by the UN Sanctions Committee.
The claimant provided his comments on the list. The European Commission then
decided, by means of a further regulation, to maintain the claimant's name on the EU
list relating to persons subject to restrictive measures. The claimant complained once
more to the CJEU, arguing that the new regulation was also unlawful ('*Kadi II*').[197]
The CJEU agreed, holding that none of the allegations presented against the claimant were such as to justify the adoption, at EU level, of restrictive measures against
him. This was because the statement of reasons was insufficient, and/or because the
information or evidence which might have substantiated the reasons concerned, was
lacking.[198]

(6) Errors of Fact—as an Error of Law

The High Court in its supervisory jurisdiction does not have the power to substitute its   **1-79**
own view of the primary facts for the view reasonably adopted by the body to whom
the fact-finding process has been entrusted;[199] or to interfere where the decision-maker
has preferred one version of the facts to another when it could reasonably have accepted
either version.[200]

However, some factual errors may amount to an error of law. Whether there is any   **1-80**
evidence to support findings of fact is always a question of law, as is the question
'whether the inferences drawn are possible inferences from the facts as found'.[201]

As a practical matter, criminal judicial review for errors of fact will only lie in the
very clearest of cases,[202] such as where committal from the magistrates' court to the
Crown Court is based solely on inadmissible evidence or evidence not reasonably
capable of supporting the committal;[203] or where a magistrate had erred in concluding at the end of a preliminary enquiry that there was no prima facie case that any
indictable offence had been committed and then dismissed a private prosecution;[204] or
where the decision of the police to caution a defendant for an offence of assault rather
than charge him was made on an incorrect basis of fact, on the material then available
to the police.[205]

---

[197] Joined Cases C-584/10 P, C-593/10 P and C-595/10 P *Commission, Council, United Kingdom v Yassin Abdullah Kadi* ('*Kadi II*'). See also 14-19 below.
[198] ibid.
[199] *Adan v Newham London Borough Council* [2001] EWCA Civ 1916, [2002] 1 WLR 2120 [41].
[200] ibid [35]–[36].
[201] *Hemns v Wheeler* [1948] 2 KB 61, 66 (Tucker LJ).
[202] *R v Whitehaven Justices, ex parte Thompson* [1999] COD 15.
[203] *R v Bedwellty Justices, ex parte Williams* [1997] AC 225, 237C–E.
[204] *Nicholas v Rambachan* [2009] UKPC 1 [34].
[205] *R (Omar) v Chief Constable of Bedfordshire Constabulary* [2002] EWHC 3060 (Admin) (DC) [40]; and *R (Alconbury Developments Ltd) v Secretary of State for the Environment, Transport and the Regions* [2001] UKHL 23, [2003] 2 AC 295 [53] (Lord Slynn).

(7) Irrationality

1-81   Irrationality is an established ground for judicial review of a decision by a public authority. Lord Diplock explained his use of the term:

> By 'irrationality' I mean what can by now be succinctly referred to as '*Wednesbury* unreasonableness' … It applies to a decision which is so outrageous in its defiance of logic or of accepted moral standards that no sensible person who had applied his mind to the question to be decided could have arrived at it … 'Irrationality' by now can stand upon its own feet as an accepted ground on which a decision may be attacked by judicial review.[206]

1-82   In the *Wednesbury* case,[207] Lord Greene MR had summarised the relevant principles:

> The court is entitled to investigate the action of the local authority with a view to seeing whether they have taken into account matters which they ought not to take into account, or, conversely, have refused to take into account or neglected to take into account matters which they ought to take into account.

> Once that question is answered in favour of the local authority, it may be still possible to say that, although the local authority have kept within the four corners of the matters which they ought to consider, they have nevertheless come to a conclusion so unreasonable that no reasonable authority could ever have come to it. In such a case, again, I think the court can interfere.

> The power of the court to interfere in each case is not as an appellate authority to override a decision of the local authority, but as a judicial authority which is concerned, and concerned only, to see whether the local authority have contravened the law by acting in excess of the powers which Parliament has confided in them.[208]

1-83   There are, therefore, two traditional aspects to '*Wednesbury* unreasonableness'. The first is whether a public authority has failed to take into account relevant considerations or has taken into account irrelevant ones (the relevancy/irrelevancy principle); the second is whether a public authority has acted in a way that was not reasonably open to it (the unreasonableness principle).[209]

1-84   A common modern formulation is that the decision must be outside the range of reasonable responses open to the decision-maker.[210] This is a high threshold test. One way in which a decision may pass the threshold is if it is irrational in the proper sense of the word; that is, if the reasoning is not logically capable of supporting the conclusion.[211]

(8) Irrationality: the Relevancy/Irrelevancy Principle

1-85   It is a basic principle of judicial review that the High Court will exercise its supervisory jurisdiction to ascertain whether a public authority has taken into account matters

---

[206] *Council of Civil Service Unions* (n 8) 410G (Lord Diplock). See above at 1-3 and 1-50.
[207] *Associated Provincial Picture Houses Ltd v Wednesbury Corporation* [1948] 1 KB 223. See above at 1-81.
[208] ibid 233–34.
[209] See Fordham *Judicial Review Handbook* (n 6) para 56.1.
[210] See, for example, *Boddington v British Transport Police* [1992] 2 AC 143, 175H per Lord Steyn.
[211] *R v Parliamentary Commissioner for Administration ex parte Balchin* [1998] 1 PLR 1, 13E-F per Sedley J; and *R (Norwich and Peterborough Building Society) v Financial Ombudsman Service Ltd* [2002] EWHC 2379, [59], Ouseley J.

which it ought not to take into account, or, conversely, has refused to take into account or neglected to take into account matters which it ought to take into account.[212] Illustrations from the case law on each limb of the relevancy/irrelevancy principle are provided below.

(i) Illustrations (Limb 1)—Failing to Take a Relevant Matter into Account

a. Decisions not to Prosecute[213]

With regards to prosecutorial decisions not to prosecute, the remedy is carefully circum- **1-86** scribed (see below at 5-8 and 5-12). Generally, in order to bring a successful claim for judicial review of such prosecutorial decisions, the claimant will need to demonstrate that the decision not to prosecute is based on a perverse decision to disregard compelling evidence or, inexplicably, ignores the relevant prosecutorial policy or policies, or a combination of both.[214]

In *Ex p Manning* (see above at 1-16 and below at 5-27 and 5-29) the sisters of the **1-87** deceased, who had died of asphyxia whilst being restrained by prison officers, applied for judicial review of the DPP's decision not to prosecute any of the officers involved. A coroner's inquest, having found that the asphyxia had been attributable to the way in which the deceased had been held by one of the officers, returned a verdict of unlawful killing. Police investigations into the incident followed. The CPS concluded that there was insufficient evidence to support a criminal prosecution, and that the case did not have a realistic prospect of success. The Divisional Court allowed the application for judicial review holding (inter alia) that there were five points that the relevant police officer would have to overcome in dealing with the prima facie case against him, but that the CPS caseworker (inadvertently) had not addressed or resolved these points.[215]

In *Re MacMahon's Application for Judicial Review*[216] the Public Prosecution Service **1-88** in Northern Ireland had failed to follow its own policy, by accepting pleas of guilty to several offences and discontinuing the trial without first explaining its decision to the deceased victim's family. A declaration was granted to reflect the finding that by failing to explain its decision to the deceased's family, the PPS had breached its own policy:

> There is little point in having such a policy if it is not conscientiously adhered to … The PPS should ensure that those involved in making decisions governed by the Code of Practice and Victims policy are reminded of its requirements.[217]

---

[212] *Wednesbury Corporation* (n 189) 233–34; *R v Secretary of State for Trade and Industry, ex parte Lonrho Plc* [1989] 1 WLR 525, 533D (Lord Keith); *Alconbury Developments Ltd* (n 205) [50] (Lord Slynn); *R (FDA) v Secretary of State for Work and Pensions* [2012] EWCA Civ 332, [2012] 3 All ER 301 [67]–[68], [81] (Lord Neuberger MR).
[213] See below in section C of Chapter 5.
[214] *R (F) v DPP* (n 30) [6] (Lord Judge LCJ) (see above at 5-24).
[215] *Ex p Manning* (n 23), 42 (Lord Bingham LCJ) (see above at 1-15 and below 1-121 and 5-29); see *R (Da Silva) v DPP* [2006] EWHC 3204 (Admin). See also below at 5-30.
[216] *Re MacMahon's Application for Judicial Review* [2012] NIQB 60, [2013] NI 154. See below at 5-33.
[217] ibid [107] (Treacy J).

b. Prison[218]

1-89 In *R (Kristic) v Secretary of State for Justice*[219] the claimant applied for judicial review of the Secretary of State's decision that he should remain a Category A (standard escape risk)[220] prisoner. An International Criminal Tribunal had convicted him of war crimes and genocide. The decision of the Secretary of State refusing to re-categorise the claimant was held to be irrational, he having failed to take into account relevant matters. The Secretary of State had failed to consider, or consider with the necessary degree of scrutiny, the matters relied on by the claimant in support of his representations that he ought to be considered for de-categorisation:

> It is not for me to substitute my decision for that of the Defendant [Secretary of State for Justice]. It is however my function to quash decisions which fail to take proper account of the material representations and evidence available. In my judgment the reality is that the Defendant failed to look beyond the gravity of the offence and ask himself the right question—which was whether the Claimant was highly dangerous at the date of the relevant decision—or answer it by a proper consideration of all the material facts and matters relevant to the determination of that issue bearing in mind the policy that every prisoner is to be placed in the lowest security Category consistent with the needs of security and control.[221]

(ii) Illustrations (Limb 2)—Wrongly Taking into Account an Irrelevancy

a. Basic Principles

1-90 In *R (FDA) v Secretary of State for Work and Pensions*[222] Lord Neuberger MR set out the basic principles which pertain with regards to legally irrelevant factors; namely, that where a decision-maker has taken a legally irrelevant factor into account when making his decision, the normal principle is that the decision is liable to be held to be invalid unless the factor played no significant part in the decision-making exercise. A decision would not be set aside where the irrelevant factor was 'insignificant or insubstantial', as opposed to a case where the irrelevant factor's 'influence was substantial'. However, even where the irrelevant factor played a significant or substantial part in the decision-maker's thinking, the decision may, exceptionally, still be upheld, provided that the court is satisfied that it is clear that, even without the irrelevant factor, the decision-maker would have reached the same conclusion.[223]

---

[218] See generally Chapter 8 below.

[219] *R (Kristic) v Secretary of State for Justice* [2010] EWHC 2125 (Admin).

[220] 'Prisoners whose escape would be highly dangerous to the public or the police or the security of the state, no matter how unlikely that escape might be, and for whom the aim must be to make escape impossible.' See PSO 0900, Ch 1, para 1.1.1.

[221] *R (Kristic)* (n 219) [25] (HHJ Pelling QC).

[222] *R (FDA) v Secretary of State for Work and Pensions* [2012] EWCA Civ 332, [2012] 3 All ER 301.

[223] ibid [67]–[68].

Richard Wilson QC

b. Magistrates' Courts[224]

In *R (Stace) v Milton Keynes Magistrates' Court*[225] the claimant applied for judicial review   **1-91**
of the magistrates' dismissal of his appeal against the decision of a traffic commissioner
revoking his bus passenger-carrying vehicle licence. Following three convictions of
assault against his wife, in respect of which he had been subjected to a community
rehabilitation order, the Secretary of State transferred the question of his fitness to hold
the licence to the traffic commissioner. The traffic commissioner revoked the claimant's licence and disqualified him indefinitely, following the claimant's failure to attend
hearings on two occasions. The magistrates dismissed the appeal. The Administrative
Court found that the magistrates' decision was flawed because (inter alia) they had
taken into account an irrelevant consideration, namely the fact that the community
rehabilitation order was still in place: 'The fact that the community rehabilitation order
was still in place was not a relevant factor. It was not open to the magistrates to say that
[the claimant] was not a fit person to hold a PCV driver's licence because, to use a col-
loquialism, "he was still on probation"'[226]

c. The Crown Court[227]

In *R v Portsmouth Crown Court, ex parte Thomas*[228] the claimant had been found guilty   **1-92**
of common assault by the Crown Court, which had taken into account his previous
convictions, and was conditionally discharged. The Crown Court judge refused to state
a case for the opinion of the High Court. The High Court held that the judge in refusing
to state a case had erred because the mere fact that a defendant had previous convictions did not make it frivolous, as the judge thought, for him to seek to avoid a further
conviction, especially where the conviction was unwarranted. Accordingly, it appeared
that the judge had been influenced by irrelevant factors.

d. Criminal Injuries Compensation Authority (CICA)[229]

In *R (M) v Criminal Injuries Compensation Authority*[230] M was a child, who brought a   **1-93**
claim by his litigation friend against the CICA's delay and failure to determine his claim
for compensation for injuries arising from non-accidental shaking by one of his parents.
The CICA had indicated from the outset of the claim that it required an assessment of
M and a schedule of care costs. This information was provided. There then followed a
delay of several months for which there was no 'rational' explanation.[231] The CICA then
began to request information on the loss of earnings and benefits which had until that
point been considered irrelevant to the claim. McCombe J said: 'After the passage of a

---

[224] See generally Chapter 6 below.
[225] *R (Stace) v Milton Keynes Magistrates' Court* [2006] EWHC 1049 (Admin).
[226] ibid [17] (Keith J).
[227] See generally Chapter 7 below.
[228] *R v Portsmouth Crown Court, ex parte Thomas* [1994] COD 373.
[229] See generally section E of Chapter 9.
[230] *R (M) v Criminal Injuries Compensation Authority* [2002] EWHC 2646 (Admin). See also at 9-39 below.
[231] ibid [35].

year, it cannot be reasonable for the Authority to try to assess the claim on an entirely different basis'.[232] The claimant submitted that there was unreasonable and irrational delay by the defendant authority coming to a decision and, in fact, failing to determine the claimant's case at all. The court agreed. It held that the delays were irrational and unreasonable in a *Wednesbury* sense. It also found it 'instructive' that the CICA's own guidance for its scheme indicated that it would reach a decision within four weeks of a submission of a claim.[233] Furthermore, the CICA 'has had for a long time, all the information it needs to assess this claim, and its failure to do so over many months was "Wednesbury" unreasonable'.[234]

M is an example of a judicial review of a CICA decision (or inaction) for which the appeals process might not provide an adequate alternative remedy (see 9-39 below).

e. Coroners[235]

1-94   A coroner's direction to an inquisitorial jury had included a reference to 'manslaughter due to recklessness and gross negligence'. That type of manslaughter was irrelevant to the considerations that the jury had to consider, but in other respects the summing up was satisfactory. The reference to manslaughter was not a misdirection that affected the outcome in any way, and that being so the application for judicial review was held by the Court of Appeal to have been rightly dismissed by the Divisional Court.[236]

f. Relevancy and Weight

1-95   Where a public authority does take into account relevant factors, then the weight to be given to any particular factor is a matter for the public authority – subject only to a challenge for irrationality.[237] In *C v Winchester Crown Court*,[238] a young offender was tried on charges of kidnap and sexual assault on a child. An order had been made under section 39 of the Children and Young Persons Act 1933, banning publication of any details relating to him. Following his conviction, the Recorder varied an earlier order so that the young offender's name could be made public. It was held that the Recorder

---

[232] ibid [36].

[233] ibid [39].

[234] ibid [34].

[235] See generally Chapter 10 below.

[236] *R v HM Wolverhampton Coroner, ex parte McCurbin* [1990] 1 WLR 719 (CA) 730–31, [1990] 2 All ER 759.

[237] *Secretary of State for the Home Department v AP (No 1)* [2010] UKSC 24, [2011] 2 AC 1; *R v Mid-Herefordshire Justices, ex parte Cox* (1996) 8 Admin LR 409, 413H (magistrates failed to give any weight to the evidence of the claimant's changed circumstances); *R v Manchester Crown Court, ex parte McDonald* [1999] 1 WLR 841, 846E ('any application for extension of custody time limits will call for careful consideration and many will call for rigorous scrutiny'; the Crown Court had to take care to give full weight to the overriding purposes of the statutory provisions relating to custody time limits). See also Fordham, *Judicial Review Handbook* (n 6), para 56.3. For other cases on custody time limits see *R (Raeside) v Luton Crown Court* [2012] EWHC (Admin), [2012] 1 WLR 2777 and *R (McAuley) Coventry Crown Court* [2012] EWHC 680 (Admin), [2012] 1 WLR 2766 (decisions of judges to extend custody time limits quashed). See section C of Chapter 7 below.

[238] [2014] EWCA Crim 339 (Jackson LJ, Griffith Williams J). Note that despite the report that suggests this was heard by the Court of Appeal, it was in fact a Divisional Court. See also discussion below of reporting restrictions at 11-44.

had given insufficient consideration to the overwhelming need for rehabilitation in the instant case:

> The Recorder proceeded on an erroneous assumption as to the small amount of harm which the claimant would suffer if his identity was made public. In addition to that, the sole reason advanced by the Recorder which stands as a relevant consideration is in our view of only modest weight. The public know that the prosecution had been successful. The public know that a young man has been convicted of these two very serious offences. The benefit of knowing the identity of the young man who has been so convicted is modest. In our view those factors in favour of publication are outweighed by the other powerful considerations to which we have referred.[239]

(9) Irrationality—the Unreasonableness Principle

To make a successful judicial review claim on the unreasonableness principle, it will generally be necessary to show that the decision in question was not within the range of reasonable responses open to a decision-maker; or was one which no reasonable public authority could have made if properly directing itself in law; or one which a reasonable person in the position of the public authority could not have made.[240]   **1-96**

The court's standard of review for unreasonableness will vary according to the subject matter of the impugned act or decision. Where the decision involves a fundamental human right, the court will subject such decisions to 'anxious scrutiny'.[241] This approach is often characterised as a 'high intensity' review by the court.

At the other end of the scale, in cases involving political, economic, market, and similar judgments by public authorities better placed than the courts to make the relevant assessments, the court tends to adopt a 'low intensity' review. In such situations, the court will not interfere with the impugned decision unless a claimant is able to show 'unreasonableness' in the sense of an absurd or perverse decision, bad faith or improper motive.[242]

---

[239] ibid, at [12], per Jackson LJ.

[240] *Wednesbury* unreasonableness has been heavily criticised by some judges and legal commentators: eg Lord Cooke in *Daly* (n 1) 549 described it as 'an unfortunately retrogressive decision in English administrative law insofar as it suggested that there are degrees of unreasonableness and that only a very extreme degree can bring an administrative decision within the legitimate scope of judicial invalidation'. See also: Lord Lester and Jeffrey Jowell, 'Beyond Wednesbury: Substantive Principles of Administrative Law' [1987] *Public Law* 368; 'Unreasonableness and Proportionality in UK Law' in Evelyn Ellis (ed), *The Principle of Proportionality in the Laws of Europe* (Oxford, Hart, 1999) 95. Others have mounted a strong defence of the principle, eg see Lord Irvine, 'Judges and Decision-makers: the Theory and Practice of Wednesbury Review' [1996] *Public Law* 59. See also Mark Elliott, 'The Human Rights Act 1998 and the Standard of Substantive Review' (2001) 60 *Cambridge Law Journal* 301.

[241] *Bugdaycay v Secretary of State for the Home Department* [1987] AC 514, 531F–G (Lord Bridge); *R (MN (Tanzania)) v Secretary of State for the Home Department* [2011] EWCA Civ 193, [2011] 1 WLR 3200.

[242] *R v Secretary of State for the Environment, ex parte Nottinghamshire County Council* [1986] AC 240, 247G.

(i) Illustrations—Irrationality (the Unreasonableness Principle)

a. Refusal of an Adjournment[243]

1-97 Where a witness for the prosecution failed to attend a criminal trial and neither the Crown nor the witness was at fault, a decision by the magistrates to refuse the Crown's application for an adjournment could fairly be characterised as irrational and perverse.[244]

> Delays are of course important, but the ultimate issue is, as the magistrates themselves recognised, the interests of justice. They did not, however, properly apply their minds to that question and, in my judgment, reached a conclusion that no justices properly directing themselves could reach. Their decision was therefore irrational and perverse and should therefore be quashed, along with the decision to dismiss the case.[245]

b. Reasons for an Adjournment

1-98 Although it is necessary and appropriate for justices to give reasons for refusing an adjournment, the circumstances have to be considered. In *R (Crown Prosecution Service) v Reading and West Berkshire Magistrates' Court*[246] the prosecution had made an application to adjourn a trial date at 7.40 pm and the justices gave their decision dismissing the application and the informations laid against an offender for motoring offences, at 8.00 pm. The Crown Prosecution Service applied for judicial review to quash the decision dismissing the informations, arguing that the magistrates had not sufficiently referred in their reasoning to the factors relied on for refusing the application to adjourn. The Divisional Court (Pill LJ, Roderick Evans J) dismissed the Crown Prosecution Service's application holding that a detailed exposition could not reasonably be expected from the magistrates at the late hour at which the application was made, but that in any event the magistrates had covered the substance of the points made by the prosecution, with the exception of one matter. The court concluded:

> It may be that other justices on the same material would have given pre-eminence to the court error and, notwithstanding other factors, would have allowed the application for an adjournment. I am, however, far from satisfied that the decision reached by the justices was so unreasonable that no reasonable bench of magistrates in like circumstances could have come to it.[247]

c. Dismissal of Prosecution

1-99 A magistrates' court had acted unreasonably in exercising their powers to dismiss informations laid against the accused, as a means of punishing the Crown Prosecution Service for perceived inefficiency (ie, non-appearance of the prosecutor). On the facts of

---

[243] For challenges to adjournments in the magistrates' courts see below at 6-69.
[244] *R (DPP) v North and East Hertfordshire Justices* [2008] EWHC 103 (Admin).
[245] ibid [30] (Cooke J).
[246] *R (Crown Prosecution Service) v Reading and West Berkshire Magistrates' Court* [2010] EWHC 3260 (Admin).
[247] *R (Crown Prosecution Service) v Reading and West Berkshire Magistrates' Court* [2010] EWHC 3260 (Admin) [27].

Richard Wilson QC

the case, no reasonable bench could have come to that decision which was outside their statutory powers, and the decision was accordingly a nullity.[248]

d. Expert Witness

In *R (Doughty) v Ely Magistrates' Court*[249] the claimant was the managing director of a **1-100** company that specialised in the giving of expert opinions and evidence in road traffic matters. One of the company's clients was charged with a speeding offence, based on evidence captured on a police camera. The claimant, who was a former transport police officer, produced a report raising doubts about the procedures adopted in the use of the speed detection device and the reliability of its readings. When the claimant appeared at the trial ready to give evidence in an expert capacity on behalf of the accused, the magistrates ruled that the claimant was not an expert on the matters before the court, and that his evidence was therefore inadmissible. The claimant applied for judicial review, claiming that the magistrates' ruling as regards his status as an expert witness was wrong in law. Although the Divisional Court considered the claim for judicial review an unusual one, it saw no reason in principle why the claim should not be entertained by the court. The application was allowed:

> It seems to me that the matters relied on by the magistrates for ruling that the claimant was not entitled to give expert opinion do not provide a reasonable basis for that conclusion. In my judgment, what the magistrates have done is to rely on matters that go to the weight of the claimant's evidence, if given, as a reason for preventing him from giving evidence as an expert at all. I do not think that there was a reasonable basis here for ruling him out as an expert witness altogether.[250]

e. Independent Police Complaints Commission[251]

Whilst it was not right to expect or look for, in an appeal decision of the IPCC, the **1-101** sort of tightly argued judgment that might be expected of a professional judge, it was nonetheless important and necessary that the conclusions of the IPCC should be clear. The reasons for an appeal decision should be readily understood by the relevant parties, namely the complainant, the police officers concerned and the relevant police authority who might need to review internal procedures in the light of the appeal decision. Accordingly, in *R (Dennis) v Independent Police Complaints Commission*[252] the Administrative Court quashed an appeal decision of the IPCC that it found to be fatally flawed and irrational, in that it was based on a misunderstanding of the facts, 'a lack of clarity in reasoning' that rendered the decision difficult to understand, and also made unjustified criticisms of a police officer.[253]

---

[248] *R v Hendon Justices, ex parte DPP* [1994] QB 167, [1993] 2 WLR 862.
[249] *R (Doughty) v Ely Magistrates' Court* [2008] EWHC 522 (Admin) (DC).
[250] ibid [20] (Richards LJ).
[251] See generally section D of Chapter 9.
[252] *R (Dennis) v Independent Police Complaints Commission* [2008] EWHC 1158 (Admin).
[253] ibid [32] (Saunders J). See Chapter 9 below.

f. Bail[254]

1-102 It was an irrational decision by a Crown Court judge (in the sense that no reasonable judge could have made the decision) to withdraw bail that had been granted to an accused awaiting trial, given that the accused had been on bail for more than four months, had complied with all reporting and residence conditions of bail, and had surrendered to bail when so required.[255] Silber J, in quashing the decision of the Crown Court withdrawing bail, stated that:

> First, it is not reasonable for a court to withdraw bail unless it is necessary to do so especially as any decision to withdraw bail engages rights under Article 5 [ECHR]. Second, any such reason justifying the decision to withdraw bail must be stated by the decision maker explaining why bail should be withdrawn and that reason must relate to the facts. Such a reason must be more than merely reciting that one of the statutory grounds has been made out. The underlying facts have to be put forward.

> In this case no good reason has been put forward by the judge nor by the Crown Prosecution Service to establish one of the statutory grounds as to why bail should be refused.[256]

g. Discontinuance of Prosecution[257]

1-103 In *R (B) v DPP*[258] the claimant had suffered an assault in which part of his ear was bitten off. He gave a coherent and credible account identifying the accused as the perpetrator, but had a history of psychotic illness in which at times he held paranoid beliefs about certain people, and also suffered hallucinations. On the basis of a medical report which concluded that the claimant's mental condition might affect his perception and recollection of events, the Crown Prosecution Service decided that it could not put the claimant before the jury as a reliable witness and that there was no realistic prospect of a conviction, and offered no evidence. The claimant sought judicial review by way of a declaration that the CPS's decision to discontinue was irrational under domestic public law principles, and unlawful on other grounds. The Divisional Court allowed the claim, stating that:

> The reasoning process ... for concluding that the [the claimant] could not be placed before the jury as a credible witness was irrational in the true sense of the term. It did not follow from Dr C's report that the jury could not properly be invited to regard [the claimant] as a true witness when he described the assault which he undoubtedly suffered. The conclusion that he could not be put forward as a credible witness, despite the apparent factual credibility of his account, suggests either a misreading of Dr C's report (as though it had said that [the claimant] was incapable of being regarded as a credible witness) or an unfounded stereotyping of [the claimant] as someone who was not to be regarded as credible on any matter because of his history of mental problems.[259]

1-104 In *R (Crown Prosecution Service) v Norwich Magistrates' Court*[260] the magistrates upheld a submission of no case to answer, based in part on the prosecution's failure to

---

254 See also below at 4-83, 6-47 and section B of Chapter 7.
255 *Fergus* (n 71)See also below at 7-8 and 7-15.
256 ibid [21]–[22].
257 See below in section C in Chapter 5.
258 *R(B) v DPP* (n 27). See below at 5-31.
259 ibid [55].
260 *R (Crown Prosecution Service) v Norwich Magistrates' Court* [2011] EWHC 82 (Admin). See below at 6-82.

Richard Wilson QC

prove identification, namely that the accused was the man seen throwing the punch on the CCTV footage. The prosecution complained that it had been taken by surprise that identity was an issue, and sought leave to re-open its case and call a police officer to deal with the point. It was ascertained that the police officer was available and could attend court. The magistrates refused the prosecution application to re-open its case, and held that there was no case to answer. The decision to refuse the prosecution application to re-open its case ran counter to the overriding objective of the Criminal Procedure Rules, was plainly contrary to the interests of justice and lacked any reasonable basis.[261]

h. Parole Board[262]

In *R (Houchin) v Secretary of State for Justice*[263] the decision of the Secretary of State for Justice refusing to accept the advice of the Parole Board that a prisoner should be transferred to an open prison was *Wednesbury* unreasonable, given the superficial consideration the Secretary of State had paid to the views expressed by the Parole Board:

1-105

> In my judgment, the way in which the Secretary of State has stated his disagreement with the main conclusions of the Parole Board is so cursory and lacking any supporting argument that it is evidence of only the most superficial consideration of the decision. In light of that I am driven to the conclusion that the views expressed by the Parole Board have scarcely been given any consideration at all.[264]

In *R (Hindawi) v Secretary of State for Justice*[265] the Secretary of State had acted unfairly by basing his decision to refuse the release of a prisoner on a document prepared by his department officials setting out the reasons for refusing parole, but not the reasons for granting it. Fairness required that the Secretary of State's officials put the issues to him in a balanced way so he that he could arrive at a decision that had a rational basis: 'He could not rely, if he was to follow what a fair procedure dictated, upon a document which set out only the case for rejection of the panel's decision.'[266] The Secretary of State's rejection of the Parole Board's findings was held to have no rational basis.

1-106

i. Coroner[267]

In *Litvinenko v Secretary of State for the Home Department*,[268] the claimant was the widow of a Russian national killed in London as a result of radiation poisoning in suspicious circumstances. The Secretary of State had been asked to set up an inquiry under section 1(1) of the Inquiries Act 2005 by Sir Robert Owen, the judge appointed to conduct the inquest into the death. The widow brought a claim for judicial review of the refusal by the Secretary of State to order the setting up of a statutory inquiry. The Divisional Court held that the Secretary of State's decision was irrational. The

1-107

---

[261] ibid [25] (Richards LJ).
[262] See below at section D of Chapter 8.
[263] *R (Houchin) v Secretary of State for Justice* [2010] EWHC 454 (Admin). See below at 6.82.
[264] ibid [84] (Wilkie J).
[265] *R (Hindawi) v Secretary of State for Justice* [2011] EWHC 830 (QB) (DC).
[266] ibid [73], [75].
[267] See generally Chapter 10 below.
[268] [2014] EWHC 194 (Admin), [2014] HRLR 6 (Richards, LJ, Treacy LJ, Mitting J).

possible involvement of Russian state agencies in the death was an important issue that the Coroner had been unable to address within the scope of the inquest owing to the Foreign Secretary's PII claim in respect of much of the relevant material. The case for setting up an immediate statutory inquiry as requested by the Coroner was found to be a strong one. The Secretary of State was ordered to give 'fresh consideration' to the exercise of her discretion under section 1(1) of the 2005 Act, and to take into account the points made in the judgment.[269]

j. Police Contractor[270]

1-108   A chief constable's decision to disallow a contractor from being able to work on police vehicles on the basis of his alleged association with people involved in criminality was irrational, there being insufficient information to support the conclusion reached:[271]

> the key contention, that there was or could reasonably be thought to have been, a criminal association on the part of [the claimant], simply does not bear scrutiny from the perspective of rationality. The conclusion ... simply cannot stand.[272]

(10) Procedural Impropriety

1-109   The third traditional ground for a claim for judicial review is procedural impropriety:

> I have described the third head as 'procedural impropriety' rather than failure to observe basic rules of natural justice or failure to act with procedural fairness towards the person who will be affected by the decision. This is because susceptibility to judicial review under this head covers also failure by an administrative tribunal to observe procedural rules that are expressly laid down in the legislative instrument by which its jurisdiction is conferred, even where such failure does not involve any denial of natural justice. But the instant case is not concerned with the proceedings of an administrative tribunal at all.[273]

(i) Procedural Unfairness

1-110   Two principal characteristics of the duty to act fairly (or natural justice) are the two fundamental rights accorded by that duty; namely, the right to be heard and the rule against bias on the part of the person upon whom the decision falls to be made.[274]

---

[269] ibid [73]–[76].
[270] See below at 4-7 and n 31.
[271] *R (Sands) v Chief Constable of Merseyside* [2010] EWHC 2698 (Admin).
[272] ibid [48] (HHJ Waksman QC).
[273] *Council of Civil Service Unions* (n 8) 411A-B (Lord Diplock).
[274] *O'Reilly v Mackman* [1983] 2 AC 237, 279F–G (Lord Diplock).

Richard Wilson QC

(ii) Illustrations of Procedural Unfairness

a. Secret Evidence

In *Al Rawi v Security Service (JUSTICE intervening)*,[274a] the Supreme Court by a major-   **1-111**
ity affirmed the general principle that in a civil trial—just as in a criminal trial[274b]—the
use of a closed material procedure was so alien to the right of a party to know the case
advanced by the opposing party and to have a fair opportunity to respond to it, as to be
permissible only by Act of Parliament.[274c]

b. Material Irregularity

Committal proceedings are susceptible to judicial review[275] and a quashing order would   **1-112**
lie if the procedural irregularity were a serious one leading to a demonstrable injustice
to the accused. A magistrate's decision to allow witness statements to be read when the
witnesses had refused to give oral evidence (they asserted out of fear) went beyond the
mere receipt of inadmissible evidence, because the accused had lost the opportunity to
have the eye-witnesses' mental state, or their substantive testimony, or both, subjected
to scrutiny (by cross-examination).[276]

On an appeal against conviction, the judge intervened whilst two defence witnesses
were giving evidence to ask them whether they had any, and if so what, previous convictions but did not ask similar witnesses of the prosecution witnesses. This was an irregularity that was material to the proceedings, and required the Divisional Court to quash
the appeal proceedings before the Crown Court because: 'to do as the judge did in this
case was in effect to give the appearance of usurping the role of the prosecution'.[277]

c. Unfairness and Propriety

A public authority may act with complete propriety, yet still have its decision quashed   **1-113**
for unfairness: 'it is sufficient if objectively there is unfairness'.[278] It was objectively
unfair for a forfeiture order to have been made by a magistrates' court, without the
claimant having received notice.[279]

[274a] *Al Rawi v Security Service (JUSTICE intervening)* [2011] UKSC 34, [2012] 1 AC 531.
[274b] *R v Davis* [2008] UKHL 36, [2008] AC 1128.
[274c] Observation made by Lord Toulson JSC at [23], in *R (British Sky Broadcasting Ltd) v Central Criminal Court* [2014] UKSC 17, [2014] 2 WLR 558 (discussed below at 7-22). There were certain classes of case where a departure from the general rule might be justified for special reasons in the interests of justice, eg child welfare proceedings, and intellectual property proceedings (see Lord Dyson JSC in *Al Rawi*, at [63]–[65]).
[275] *Colchester Stipendiary Magistrate, ex parte Beck* [1979] QB 674, (1979) 69 Cr App R 128, 686D and 135 (Robert Goff J); *R v Horseferry Road Stipendiary Magistrate, ex parte Adams* [1977] 1 WLR 1197; *R v Coleshill Justices, ex parte Davies* [1971] 1 WLR 1684; *Highbury Corner Magistrates' Court, ex parte Boyce* (1984) 79 Cr App R 132, 134. See Chapter 6, n 248 below.
[276] *Neill v North Antrim Magistrates' Court* [1992] 1 WLR 1220; (1993) 97 Cr App R 121.
[277] *B v Carlisle Crown Court* [2009] EWHC 3540 (Admin) (DC) [24] (Langstaff J).
[278] *R v Criminal Injuries Compensation Board, ex parte A* [1999] 2 AC 330, 335C–D (Lord Slynn).
[279] *R (Harrison) v Birmingham Magistrates' Court* [2011] EWCA Civ 332 [44] and [54].

d. Search Warrants[280]

1-114   A copy of a search warrant issued under section 8 of the Police and Criminal Evidence Act 1984 was statutorily required to record the address being searched, so that the occupier served with the copy would know for certain that the warrant as issued covered his premises. The police practice of filling in the address by hand as the warrant was executed and after the warrant had been signed, would leave the occupier in doubt as to the scope of authority of the police to search the premises. Such an approach by the police was in breach of the procedure laid down in section 16(5) of the 1984 Act and rendered any entry, search or seizure illegal pursuant to section 15(1). In the circumstances, the occupier was entitled to the return of his seized property.[281]

e. The Right to be Heard

1-115   It was unfair to deny a contemnor the opportunity to apologise in contempt proceedings;[282] or to deny a contemnor the opportunity to be represented or to deny or admit his involvement in the relevant incident;[283] or to not allow a dog-owner the opportunity to be heard before making a court order for the destruction of the dog under the Dangerous Dogs Act 1991.[284]

1-116   A female prisoner sought judicial review of a decision to exclude her from the prison's mother and baby unit and separate her from her son. The Divisional Court quashed the decision to exclude and separate, partly on the procedural ground that the prisoner had not been afforded the opportunity to respond to allegations made against her about her conduct, and that accordingly the procedure fell short of what fairness required.[285]

1-117   Where a chief constable is minded to include material in an Enhanced Criminal Records Certificate on the basis that he or she inclines to the view that it satisfies the statutory requirements, the officer is obliged to contact the person concerned and seek their views, taking into account anything that person says, before reaching a final conclusion.[286]

f. The Right to Have Sufficient Time to Prepare

1-118   A magistrate's refusal of an adjournment amounted to both a breach of common law principles of natural justice and Article 6 of the ECHR because in view of the lengthy default term of imprisonment for non-compliance with a confiscation order (five

---

[280] See section D in Chapter 4 below.

[281] *R (Bhatti) v Croydon Magistrates' Court* [2010] EWHC 522 (Admin), [2011] 1 WLR 948; applied in *R (Global Cash & Carry Ltd) v Birmingham Magistrates' Court* [2013] EWHC 528 (Admin) [DC] – discussed below at 4-40; and in *Poonam v Secretary of State for the Home Department* [2013] EWHC 2059 (Admin) (QB). In *R (Redknapp) v Commissioner of the City of London Police (Practice Note)* [2009] 1 WLR 2091, the failure to identify any property at all in the search warrant, was struck down as unlawful. See 4-41 below.

[282] *R v Pateley Bridge Justices, ex parte Percy* [1994] COD 453; and see *R v Moran* (1985) 81 Cr App R 51.

[283] *R v Selby Justices, ex parte Frame* [1991] 2 WLR 965, [1992] QB 72 (DC).

[284] *R v Trafford Magistrates' Court, ex parte Riley (Robertina)* (1996) 160 JP 418.

[285] *R (CD) v Secretary of State for the Home Department* [2003] EWHC 155 (Admin), [2003] 1 FLR 979.

[286] *R (L) v Commissioner of Police for the Metropolis* [2009] UKSC 3, [2010] 1 AC 410 [46] (Lord Hope) and [82] (Lord Neuberger). See below at 4-114.

years), the defendant had been entitled to an adjournment so that his case could be properly prepared and presented by his solicitor.[287]

g. Legitimate Expectations (of Procedural Fairness)

Legitimate expectations are a subset of the wider concept of fairness. For a legitimate expectation to arise in public law, a public authority had to make a clear and unequivocal representation.[288] Where a public authority charged with the duty of making a decision promised to follow a certain procedure before reaching that decision, good administration required it should act fairly and implement its promise, provided the implementation did not conflict with the public authority's statutory duty.[289]   **1-119**

(iii) Reasons (as an Aspect of Procedural Fairness)

Judges are subject to a general duty to give reasons for their decisions.[290] Article 6 of the ECHR also requires that 'adequate and intelligible reasons are given for judicial decisions'.[291]   **1-120**

Historically, the position at common law was that a public authority was not under a general duty to give reasons for an administrative decision.[292] The position has now changed. As a general proposition it appears that a public body should give reasons: 'fairness or procedural fairness usually will require a decision-maker to give reasons for its decision',[293] and 'the duty to give reasons is a facet of the obligation to deal fairly with the parties'. [294]

(iv) Illustrations—Duty to Give Reasons

a. Decision not to Prosecute[295]

Whilst no absolute obligation was imposed on the DPP to give reasons for a decision not to prosecute, the right to life was the most fundamental of all human rights (with limited powers of derogation under the ECHR). The DPP would be expected, in the absence of compelling grounds to the contrary, to give reasons for a decision not to prosecute where it related to a death in custody, or in respect of which an inquest jury had returned a verdict of unlawful killing that implicated an identifiable person, against whom there was prima facie evidence.[296]   **1-121**

---

[287] *R (Agogo) v North Somerset Magistrates' Court* [2011] EWHC 518 (Admin) (DC). See below at 6-69.
[288] *R (Royal Brompton and Harefield NHS Foundation Trust) v Joint Committee of Primary Care Trusts* [2012] EWCA Civ 472 [104].
[289] *Attorney-General of Hong Kong v Ng Yuen Shiu* [1983] 2 AC 629, [1983] 2 WLR 735.
[290] *Flannery v Halifax Estate Agencies Ltd (t/a Colleys Professional Services)* [2000] 1 WLR 377, 381B (Henry LJ).
[291] *Anya v University of Oxford* [2001] EWCA Civ 405, [2001] ICR 847 [12].
[292] *R v Secretary of State for the Home Department, ex parte Doody* [1994] 1 AC 531, [1993] 3 WLR 154, 564 (Lord Mustill).
[293] De Smith, *Judicial Review* (n 1) 444.
[294] *Mubarak v General Medical Council* [2008] EWHC 2830 (Admin) [36].
[295] See below section B of Chapter 5.
[296] *Ex p Manning* (n 23). See above at 1-15, 1-87 and below at 5-29.

b. Crown Court[297]

1-122   A Crown Court in its appellate jurisdiction was obliged to give reasons. Basically, the court had to say enough to demonstrate that it had identified the main contentious issues in the case, and state how they were resolved. In some cases a bald statement that the evidence of a particular witness was accepted would be sufficient. What was necessary for the court to say depended on the circumstances.[298]

Where the Crown Court had failed to give any reasons for its decision, then no application should be made to the Administrative Court unless reasons had been asked for and refused.[299]

However, where the Crown Court had given some reasons for its decision, but a party considered that the reasons were legally inadequate, there was no obligation on the party to request further and better reasons before applying to the High Court on the basis of inadequacy of reasons. Indeed, to do so would usually be entirely inappropriate.[300]

c. Criminal Injuries Compensation Authority (CICA)[301]

1-123   The CICA should have given reasons for concluding that an applicant's conduct had 'caused or contributed to the incident'.[302] Failure to give any reasons for its departure from guidelines, proved fatal to the Authority's refusal to make an award of criminal injuries compensation.[303]

d. Prisoners[304]

1-124   The common law duty of procedural fairness is engaged wherever the function being carried out affects the liberty and/or status of persons affected by it.[305]

A decision as to a high security prisoner's escape classification was amenable to the common law rules of fairness. The prisoner had to be given the reasons for the decision in sufficient detail to enable him to decide whether a worthwhile challenge could be made, and he had to be given the opportunity of making representations with a view to modifying the decision.[306] A prisoner deemed unsuitable for release on home detention curfew had to be informed of the reasons.[307]

e. Coroners[308]

1-125   A coroner was obliged to leave to the jury inquisition only those verdicts which were properly open to them to reach on the evidence, and that required an exercise of

[297] See generally Chapter 7 below.
[298] *Ex p Dave* (n 47).
[299] *R v Crown Court of Southwark, ex parte Samuel* [1995] COD 249.
[300] *R (Aitchison) v Sheffield Crown Court* [2012] EWHC (Admin).
[301] See section E in Chapter 9 below.
[302] *R v Criminal Injuries Compensation Authority, ex parte Leatherland* [2001] ACD 13.
[303] *R (Mahmood) v Criminal Injuries Compensation Appeal Panel* [2005] EWHC 2919 (Admin).
[304] See generally Chapter 8 below.
[305] *R v Secretary of State for the Home Department, ex parte P Duggan* [1994] 3 All ER 277, 287G–288A.
[306] *R (Mohammed Ali) v Director of High Security Prisons* [2009] EWHC 1732 (Admin), [2010] 2 All ER 82.
[307] *R (Rowen) v Governor of Kirkham Prison* [2009] EWHC 3756 (Admin).
[308] See generally Chapter 10 below.

judgment.[309] Failure by a coroner to give reasons as to her conclusion that there was no evidence on which the jury could return an unlawful killing verdict, rendered the proceedings procedurally unfair.[310]

(11) Fettering of Discretion

A public authority on which a power is conferred cannot fetter the future exercise of its discretion by committing itself now as to the way in which it will exercise the power in future, or alternatively by ruling out of consideration on the future exercise of that power factors which might then be relevant to such exercise.[311]   **1-126**

For example, the Police Complaints Board,[312] as an independent body with a duty to receive complaints, should not fetter its duty to consider instituting proceedings by accepting that it was bound by a decision of the Director of Public Prosecutions not to prosecute.[313]

In another case, the Isle of Wight prison service operated a points system that applied equally to any sex offender with a sexual offences training programme as a target but who was also 'in denial'. The policy excluded any element of discretion in the decision-making process as to whether an 'Unready Denier' should be denied Enhanced status, and was therefore held to be unlawful.[314]

(12) Proportionality

(i) Overview

Speaking extra-judicially on the developing importance of the proportionality principle and proportionality analysis, the Rt Hon Lady Justice Arden DBE advised the legal profession that: **1-127**

> Today lawyers and judges in England and Wales have to understand proportionality primarily because it is part and parcel of the jurisprudence of the European Court of Human Rights (the Strasbourg court) and of the jurisprudence of the Court of Justice of the European Union (the Luxembourg court).[315]

---

[309] *R v Inner South London Coroner, ex parte Douglas-Williams* [1999] 1 All ER 344, 349A (Lord Woolf). See Ch 10 below.

[310] *R (Cash) v HM Coroner for Northamptonshire* [2007] EWHC 1354 (Admin).

[311] *R v Secretary of State for the Home Department, ex parte Venables* [1998] AC 407, 496G–497C (Lord Browne-Wilkinson).

[312] The Board was replaced by the Police Complaints Authority, which in turn was succeeded by the IPCC.

[313] *R v Police Complaints Board, ex parte Madden* [1983] 1 WLR 447; *R v Chief Constable Thames Valley Police, ex parte Police Complaints Authority* [1996] COD 324; and generally see De Smith, *Judicial Review* (n 1) Ch 9 'Procedural Fairness: Fettering of Discretion', and Fordham, *Judicial Review Handbook*, (n 6), P50 (pp 517–25).

[314] *R (Shutt) v Secretary of State for Justice* [2012] EWHC 851 (Admin) [25].

[315] The Rt Hon Lady Justice Arden DBE in a speech given on 12 November 2012 at King's College London as the Annual Address of the UK Association for European Law and published as 'Proportionality: the way ahead' [2013] *Public Law* 498.

The proportionality principle is a strong part of the jurisprudence in Europe, and is increasingly showing signs of development within the common law, even when the courts are not addressing a question of ECHR or EU law. The proportionality principle will be briefly considered below in each context: (i) ECHR law, (ii) EU law and (iii) within the common law (non-ECHR/EU laws).

(ii) ECHR and Proportionality

1-128   Proportionality involves the weighing of ends against means. The concept has its origins in the administrative law of nineteenth-century Prussia, then a powerful independent German state. It was adopted as an evaluative exercise by judges of the ECtHR, as a practical and (politically sensitive) means of addressing the delicate question of what is, in fact, 'necessary in a democratic society'? This is the very question posed in those articles of the ECHR concerned with 'qualified' rights.[316]

The words 'proportionate' or 'proportionality' are not mentioned anywhere in the ECHR. Yet, the sophisticated methodology provided by the proportionality evaluative is arguably the most valuable contribution made by the HRA 1998 to the jurisprudence of England and Wales.[317]

Properly applied, proportionality is about a structured inquiry. It is a sophisticated methodological exercise that should produce structured, transparent decisions clearly showing how the judge or public authority has got from 'A to B'.

1-129   In considering whether a measure is proportionate, these general principles are to be derived from *Huang v Secretary of State for the Home Department*:[318]

> (i) the legitimate aim in question must be sufficiently important to justify the interference, (ii) the measures taken to achieve the legitimate aim must be rationally connected to it, (iii) the means used to impair the right must be no more than is necessary to accomplish the objective, and (iv) a fair balance must be struck between the rights of the individual and the interests of the community; this requires a careful assessment of the severity and consequences of the interference.[319]

1-130   It is now recognised that 'a basic principle of human rights law is the principle of proportionality'.[320] Accordingly, a public authority may be required to justify interference with a qualified Convention right[321] by demonstrating that the decision is proportionate within the meaning of the relevant Article. For instance, in *R (Irfan) v Secretary of State for the Home Department*,[322] the Court of Appeal considered the proportionality under Article 8 of a 10-year notification period for an offender convicted of a terrorism offence. The court distinguished the case of *R (F (a Child)) v Secretary of State for the Home Department*,[323] where the Supreme Court had held that a sex offender's life-long notification requirements absent any provision for individual review were violations of Article 8. Notwithstanding the

---

[316] Arts 8, 9, 10 and 11 and Art 1 of Protocol 1 of the ECHR.
[317] The Rt Hon Lord Justice Sedley speaking extra-judicially—opening remarks at the workshop 'Courts and the making of public policy', Oxford University, 25 June 2006.
[318] *Huang* (n 158).
[319] *R (H) v A City Council* [2011] EWCA Civ 403 [2011] UKHRR 599 [38] (Munby LJ).
[320] *Attorney General's Reference (No 2 of 2001)* [2003] UKHL 68, [2004] 2 AC 72 [120] (Lord Hobhouse).
[321] Arts 8, 9, 10, 11 and Art 1 of the first Protocol (protection of property).
[322] [2012] EWCA Civ 1471, [2013] QB 885; see above at 1-69.
[323] N 177 and see above at 1-69.

seriousness of sex offending, terrorism offences had unique features which compounded concern. A single act could cause untold damage, including loss of life, to a large number of people by someone motivated by extreme political or religious fanaticism. If anything called for a precautionary approach it was counter-terrorism, but even here the approach must be disproportionate. However, even in the absence of a right to a review, there was nothing disproportionate about the 10-year notification period in the instant case.[324]

(iii) EU Law and Proportionality

The proportionality principle is also one of the general principles of EU law. It has been given express effect in the Treaty on European Union,[325] and the Charter of Fundamental Rights of the EU.[326] The Court of Justice of the EU applies the principle of proportionality when examining executive acts, and national judges must apply the same principle when dealing with EU law issues.[327]   **1-131**

(iv) The Common Law and Proportionality

Proportionality is not a common law concept: 'the common law tends to like bright line rules whereas proportionality requires evaluation'.[328]   **1-132**

In the *Council of Civil Service Unions* case, Lord Diplock when summarising the three traditional heads of judicial review had in mind the possible adoption in future of the principle of proportionality ('which is recognised in the administrative law of several of fellow members of the European Economic Community').[329]

Since the 1980s, developments in the case law suggest that the proportionality principle may now have become part of ordinary English administrative law even when the impugned decision does not involve EU law or Convention law, at least that is when fundamental rights are being considered at common law [330] or when the court is dealing with penalties, sanctions or costs.[331]   **1-133**

I consider that even without reference to the Human Rights Act 1998 the time has come to recognise that [the proportionality] principle is part of English administrative law, not only when judges are dealing with Community acts but also when they are dealing with acts subject to domestic law.[332]

---

[324] *Irfan* (n 178), [12]–[13].
[325] TEU, Art 5(1), (3)–(4).
[326] Art 52(1).
[327] *Alconbury Developments Ltd* (n 205) [51] (Lord Slynn).
[328] The Rt Hon Lady Justice Arden DBE (n 273).
[329] *Council of Civil Service Unions* (n 8) 410E.
[330] *Alconbury Developments Ltd* (n 205) 320H, 321A–B (Lord Slynn); *Daly* (n 1) 547 (Lord Steyn), 549 (Lord Cooke). For a detailed consideration see Fordham, *Judicial Review Handbook* (n 6) para 58.3 ('Common law proportionality') pp 579–83.
[331] *R (Middleton) v Cambridge Magistrates' Court* [2012] EWHC (Admin) (costs); *R (Electoral Commission) v City of Westminster Magistrates' Court* [2009] EWHC 78 (Admin) [45] (penalty); *R v Highbury Corner Justices, ex parte Uchendu*, The Times 1994, 28 January 1994, (penalty); *R v Ramsgate Magistrates' Court and Thanet District Council, ex parte Haddow* (1993) 5 Admin LR 359, 363B; CPR 1.1 'at proportionate cost' and CPR 44.3(2) 'only allow costs which are proportionate to the matters issue'.
[332] *Alconbury Developments Ltd* (n 205) [51] (Lord Slynn).

However, in *Somerville v Scottish Ministers*[333] the House of Lords expressly left open the question whether proportionality was an independent ground for judicial review at common law, in addition to *Wednesbury* unreasonableness.[334]

(13) The Principle of Equality (Consistency)

1-134 The principle of equality or consistency underpins the High Court's supervision of public authorities at common law, under the European Convention and when applying EU Law.

(i) The Common Law and the Principle of Equality (Consistency)

1-135 In principle, the law should seek to treat like cases alike; a similar principle applies to the exercise of administrative discretions.[335] Accepting the common law principle of equality simply means that distinctions between different groups must be drawn on a rational basis. It is thus no more than an example of the application of *Wednesbury* rationality.[336]

1-136 In *R v Cheshire Justices, ex parte Sinnott*[337] the claimants had pleaded guilty to offences of driving with excess alcohol in the blood, and were disqualified from driving for periods of 12 months to three years. The claimants sought to challenge their convictions, by way of judicial review, on the basis that the police in obtaining the relevant specimens had failed to follow the statutory procedure. The Divisional Court held that the magistrates should not have accepted guilty pleas from the defendants when the police had not observed the 'Warren procedures'[338] and that in the circumstances, fairness required the convictions to be quashed as three separate (other) defendants had already been acquitted on materially similar facts. It was a question of fairness between one applicant and another.[339]

The approach in *Ex p Sinnott* on this point, did not commend itself to a subsequent Divisional Court which also dealt with the Warren procedures and drink-drive offences. In *R v Dolgellau Justices, ex parte Cartledge*,[340] a three-judge Divisional Court, Stuart-Smith LJ stated:

> we do not consider that this is a case where discretion should be exercised so as to quash the convictions. We are not persuaded by the argument that impressed McCowan LJ and Gage J in *Sinnott's* case [1955] RTR 281, namely, that since some people had their convictions quashed without opposition by the Crown Prosecution Service, it would be unfair to deny similar relief to the applicants. The fact that some people have been very fortunate to obtain an undeserved benefit does not mean that those who are not so lucky should have any justifiable sense of

---

[333] *Somerville v Scottish Ministers* [2007] UKHL 44, [2007] 1 WLR 2734.

[334] ibid [55]–[56] (Lord Hope) and [82], [147].

[335] *N v Secretary of State for the Home Department* [2005] 2 AC 296 [9] (Lord Bingham).

[336] *R (E) v Nottinghamshire Healthcare NHS Trust* [2009] EWCA Civ 795 [90].

[337] *R v Cheshire Justices, ex parte Sinnott* [1995] RTR 281.

[338] *DPP v Warren* [1993] AC 319.

[339] *R v Cheshire Justices, ex parte Sinnott* [1995] RTR 281, 286 (McCowan LJ).

[340] *R v Dolgellau Justices, ex parte Cartledge* [1996] RTR 207.

Richard Wilson QC

grievance or unfairness, in our judgment, for the reasons we have already given, we do not consider that these applicants have suffered any injustice.[341]

The common law principle of equality (or consistency) is applicable to adjournments. **1-137** Where a bench of magistrates refused an application to postpone a trial, a second bench should not reverse that ruling in the absence of a change of circumstances. In *R v Acton Youth Court, ex parte DPP*[342] the DPP claimed judicial review in respect of a decision by magistrates in a Youth Court to set aside an order made by a different bench, that the 13-year-old victim could give her evidence-in-chief by video recording and the remainder of her evidence by television link. When the case came on for trial before a differently constituted bench, the accused made a successful application to have the order of the first bench set aside. The decision of the second bench was quashed, the Divisional Court holding that there had been no relevant change of circumstances that justified the decision of the second bench to set aside the order originally made by the first bench of magistrates.[343]

But where there was a material change of circumstances, between the first hearing **1-138** and a subsequent hearing, it may be in the interests of justice for the magistrates' court to revisit its earlier decision and make a different decision.[344]

Further illustrations of the equality or consistency principle at common law can be found where a public body departs from policy guidance,[345] from its earlier action in a similar case, or its earlier decision in the same case.[346]

(ii) ECHR and the Principle of Non-Discrimination

Article 14 of the ECHR prohibits discrimination (or inequality of treatment) in terms **1-139** of the enjoyment of any ECHR right or freedom, on grounds such as sex, race, colour, language, religion, political or other opinion, national or social origin, association with a national minority, property, birth or other status. In *Ghaidan v Godin-Mendoza*[347] Lord Nicholls emphasised the importance of Article 14 in the context of the principle of non-discrimination:

It goes without saying that article 14 is an important article of the Convention. Discrimination is an insidious practice. Discriminatory law undermines the rule of law because it is the antithesis of fairness. It brings the law into disrepute. It breeds resentment. It fosters an inequality of outlook which is demeaning alike to those unfairly benefited and those unfairly prejudiced. Of course all law, civil and criminal, has to draw distinctions. One type of conduct, or one factual situation, attracts one legal consequence, another type of conduct or situation attracts a different legal consequence. To be acceptable these distinctions should have a rational and fair basis. Like cases should be treated alike, unlike cases

---

[341] ibid 215–16 (Stuart-Smith LJ).
[342] *R v Acton Youth Court, ex parte DPP* [2002] Crim LR 75.
[343] ibid (Laws LJ, Longmore J). See also *R (Watson) v Dartford Magistrates' Court* [2005] EWHC 905 (DC); *R (F) v Knowsley Magistrates' Court* [2006] EWHC 695 (Admin); and *R v Din* [2011] EWCA Crim 1475.
[344] *R (Jones) v South East Surrey Local Justice Area* [2010] EWHC 916 (Admin) (DC) [21]–[25] (Cranston J). See also below at 6-57.
[345] *R (A) v National Probation Service* [2003] EWHC 2910 (Admin) (probation service not bound to accept decision of Parole Board in terms of risk assessment; judicial review allowed on other grounds).
[346] *R (C) v Sunderland Youth Court* [2003] EWHC 2385 (Admin) (Youth Court's anti-social behaviour order unlawful, as it had previously refused to make one).
[347] *Ghaidan v Godin-Mendoza* [2004] UKHL 30 [2004] 2 AC 557.

should not be treated alike. The circumstances which justify two cases being regarded as unlike, and therefore requiring or susceptible of different treatment, are infinite. In many circumstances opinions can differ on whether a suggested ground of distinction justifies a difference in legal treatment. But there are certain grounds of factual difference which by common accord are not acceptable, without more, as a basis for different legal treatment. Differences of race or sex or religion are obvious examples. Sexual orientation is another ... Unless some good reason can be shown, differences such as these do not justify differences in treatment. Unless good reason exists, differences in legal treatment based on grounds such as these are properly stigmatised as discriminatory.[348]

1-140 So, in *A v Secretary of State for the Home Department*[349] it was declared that certain anti-terrorism legislation was incompatible with the HRA 1998 and Articles 5 and 14 of the ECHR. This was because the impugned legislation, which permitted the detention of suspected international terrorists, did so in a way that discriminated against individuals on the ground of their nationality or immigration status. Such treatment was inconsistent with the United Kingdom's international human rights treaty obligations to afford equality before the law, and to protect the human rights of all individuals within its territory.

(iii) EU Law and the Principle of Equality and Non-Discrimination

1-141 Equal treatment is a general principle of EU law. Identical or comparable situations must not be treated differently, and different situations should not be treated alike unless such treatment is objectively justified.[350]

The principle of equal treatment is breached when two categories of persons, whose factual and legal circumstances disclose no essential difference, are treated differently, or where situations which are different are treated in an identical manner.[351] Whether the treatment in question is objectively justified depends on the particular circumstances of each case.

When construing the meaning of domestic legislation that implements a provision of EU law, such as Council Framework Decision of 13 June 2002 on the European Arrest Warrant, regard must be had to the need for the uniform application of EU law and for the principle of equality. This means that the terms of a provision of EU law which makes no express reference to the law of the Member States for the purpose of determining its meaning and scope, must normally be given an autonomous and uniform interpretation throughout the European Union, having regard to the context of the provision and the objective pursued by the legislation in question.[352]

In *Advocaten voor de Wereld VZW v Leden van de Ministerraad*[353] the CJEU rejected an argument that the Council Framework Decision of 13 June 2002 on the European Arrest Warrant infringed the principle of equality and non-discrimination.

---

[348] ibid.

[349] *A v Secretary of State for the Home Department* [2004] UKHL 56, [2005] 2 AC 68.

[350] Case C-2/92 *R (Bostock) v Ministry of Agriculture, Fisheries and Food* [1994] ECR I-00955 [23]; Case C-292/97 *Karlsson v Sweden* [2000] ECR I-02737 [35]–[39]; Case 203/86 *Spain v Council* [1988] ECR 4563 [25]; Case C-15/95 *EARL de Kerlast* [1997] ECR I-1961 [35].

[351] Case T-10/93 *A v Commission* [1994] ECR II-179 [42].

[352] Case C-66/08 *Kozlowski* [2008] ECR I-604, [2009] QB 307 [42]; Case C-261/09 *Mantello* [2010] ECR I-11477, [2013] All ER (EC) 312 [38].

[353] Case C-303/05 *Advocaten voor de Wereld VZW v Leden van de Ministerraad* [2007] 3 CMLR 1 [55]–[60].

Richard Wilson QC

(14) Bad Faith and Improper Motive

(i) Bad Faith

Judicial review will be granted where a decision-maker is shown to have made an impugned decision in bad faith or dishonestly. Decisions made in such circumstances are an abuse of power and not in the public good.[354] Fully particularised pleadings[355] and cogent evidence will be required to prove bad faith or dishonesty on the part of a decision-maker.   **1-142**

(ii) Improper Motive

Judicial review will also be granted where an improper motive on the part of the decision-maker can be established.   **1-143**

In *R v Southwark Crown Court, ex parte Bowles*[356] there was a police investigation into complaints that the owners of a business had misappropriated clients' money for personal use, and the police wished to ascertain whether information supplied to an accountant for the preparation of the business's accounts had been false and misleading. The accountant refused to produce the relevant documentation, on grounds of confidentiality. The police then sought and obtained an order for their production under section 93H of Criminal Justice Act 1998 that fell within a part of the Act concerned with the confiscation of proceeds of crime. The Divisional Court quashed the order on the ground that the predominant reason for the application had been to further the investigation into the alleged criminality of the business's owners and that such purpose fell outside the ambit of section 93H. The House of Lords upheld that decision. On the subject of 'dominant purpose', Lord Hutton in giving the reasoned speech of the House, said:

> I consider that if the true and dominant purpose of an application under section 93H is to enable an investigation to be made into the proceeds of criminal conduct, the application should be granted even if an incidental consequence may be that the police will obtain evidence relating to the commission of an offence. But if the true and dominant purpose of the application is to carry out an investigation whether a criminal offence has been committed and to obtain evidence to bring a prosecution, the application should be refused.[357]

---

[354] *R v Derbyshire County Council, ex parte Times Supplements Ltd* (1991) 3 Admin LR 241.

[355] CPR, Practice Direction para 8.2 requires the claimant to specifically set out in their particulars of claim any allegation of fraud. The Queen's Bench Guide requires that full particulars of any allegation of dishonesty or malice and, where any inference of fraud or dishonesty is alleged, the basis on which the inference is alleged should also be included (para 5.6.3). Counsel could make pleaded allegations of 'fraud' if the material before counsel was of such a character as to lead responsible counsel exercising an objective professional judgment to conclude that serious allegations could properly be based upon it: *Medcalf v Mardell* [2002] UKHL 27, [2003] 1 AC 120.

[356] *R v Southwark Crown Court, ex parte Bowles* [1998] AC 641.

[357] ibid 651B-G; also see *R (Hicks) v Commissioner of the Police of the Metropolis* [2012] EWHC 1947 (Admin) [231], affirmed in the Court of Appeal in *R (Pearce) Commissioner of the Police of the Metropolis* [2013] EWCA Civ 866 and note the appeal in *Hicks* mentioned below—see Chapter 4, n 190.

1-144   Other examples where the motive was improper:

    i.   To adjourn a case because of an imminent change in the law which the magistrates regarded as more just ('It is the duty of the court to apply the existing law').[358]

    ii.   For a prosecutor to decide not to call witnesses, being partly motivated by her desire to finish the case and get to the next court.[359]

    iii.   For a judge of the Companies Court to prevent the Serious Fraud Office using transcripts obtained from an examination by liquidators of a company, in criminal proceedings ('it was an improper exercise of that discretion by a judge of the Companies' Court to seek to prevent the use by the SFO of those transcripts in the criminal proceedings Parliament having made the transcripts admissible, it is for the judge at the criminal trial alone to decide, in the light of all the circumstances known to him but not to the judge of the Companies' Court, whether the admission of the transcripts will prejudice a fair criminal trial').[360]

    iv.   To artificially create an arraignment situation with the deliberate intention of denying a defendant the right to bail because of the failure by the prosecution to obey the custody time limits.[361]

(15) Policy Guidance and Judicial Review

1-145   A public authority may be under a duty: (i) to have a policy, or (ii) to publish a policy,[362] or (iii) to follow the policy.[363]

(i) Illustrations—Policy Guidance

a. Prosecutorial Decisions[364]

1-146   A judicial review challenge could be brought against a CPS decision not to prosecute on the following narrow grounds: (i) there had been some unlawful policy; (ii) the Director of Public Prosecutions had failed to act in accordance with his own set policy; or (iii) the decision was perverse.[365]

---

[358] *R v Walsall Justices, ex parte W* [1989] 3 WLR 1311, [1990] 1 QB 253, 260E–H.

[359] *R v Wellingborough Justices, ex parte Francois* (1994) 158 JP 813. In such a case the Divisional Court held that the justices had a right to call a witness who had not been called by either party in circumstances where the liberty of the defendant was at stake. Approved in *R v Haringey Justices, ex parte DPP* [1996] 2 WLR 114, [1996] QB 351, 360. See below at 6-81.

[360] *Re Arrows Ltd (No 4)* [1995] 2 AC 75, 105F and 107E.

[361] *R v Maidstone Crown Court, ex parte Hollstein* [1995] 3 All ER 503; but see *R v Leeds Crown Court, ex parte Hussain* [1995] 1 WLR 1329 where *Ex parte Hollstein* not followed on the basis that it adopted a traditional view of arraignment but might not have taken into account 'all those other considerations which are intended as a matter of modern practice, to be dealt with at a plea and directions hearing', 1333A-C (Leggatt LJ). Also arraignment of a person who is subject to a trial on indictment was held to be a matter relating to trial on indictment within the meaning of SCA 1981, s 29(3) and therefore the High Court did not have jurisdiction to judicially review.

[362] *R (Roberts) v Secretary of State for Justice* [2009] EWHC 2321 (Admin); *R v Chief Constable of the North Wales Police, ex parte AB* [1999] QB 396, 429H.

[363] See Fordham, *Judicial Review Handbook* (n 6) para 6.2 and cases referred to there.

[364] See generally Chapter 5 below.

[365] *L v DPP* [2013] EWHC 1752 (Admin). See also *R v DPP, ex parte Chaudhary* [1995] 1 Cr App R 136, (1995) 7 Admin LR 385, where a decision not to prosecute husband was held to be unlawful, as the issue

Generally, the courts are reluctant to intervene regarding decisions to prosecute or to administer cautions, and would only do so where it was suggested that there was a breach of a prosecuting authority's clear and settled policy, and the breach itself was established.[366]

In respect of juveniles, the discretion of the Crown Prosecution Service to continue or discontinue criminal proceedings was subject to judicial review, but only where it could be demonstrated that the decision was made regardless of, or clearly contrary to, a settled policy of the DPP evolved in the public interest such as the policy of cautioning juveniles, a policy the CPS was bound to apply, where appropriate, to the exercise of their discretion to continue or discontinue proceedings.[367]

b. Prison Policy[368]

Two mandatory life sentence prisoners challenged a governor's decision (acting by his appointed representative) whereby he refused the claimants permission to undertake distance learning courses in human anatomy and physiology. It was held that the decision was unlawful as it was arrived at by giving effect to the governor's own protocol which derogated improperly from the mandatory terms of the Secretary of State's national policy on distance learning which were applicable under the Prison Rules.[369]   **1-147**

c. Published Policy

A decision-maker must follow his published policy unless there are good reasons for not doing so.[370]   **1-148**

H. When Should a Claim be Brought?

(1) Existence of an Alternative Remedy

Judicial review is discretionary and should not be granted where there was an equally effective and convenient remedy.[371] Generally, it is expected that alternative remedies will be exhausted before a claim for judicial review is made.[372] Typically, judicial review   **1-149**

---

had not been approached in accordance with the settled policy of the DPP as set out in the Code for Crown Prosecutions. See below at 5-10.

[366] *R (Mondelly) v Commissioner of Police of the Metropolis* [2006] EWHC 2370 (Admin) [42] (Moses LJ, Ouseley and Walker JJ). See below at 4.87.

[367] *R v Chief Constable of Kent, ex parte L* [1993] 1 All ER 756, (1991) 93 Cr App R 416, 428. See below at 5-22.

[368] See generally Chapter 8 below.

[369] *R (Campbell) v Governor of HMP Wakefield* [2011] EWHC 2596 (Admin).

[370] *R (Lumba) v Secretary of State for the Home Department* [2011] UKSC 12, [2012] 1 AC 245 [26] (Lord Dyson).

[371] *R v Peterborough Magistrates' Court ex parte Dowler* [1997] QB 911, [1997] 2 WLR 843 where judicial review was refused where statutory appeal procedure not exhausted. Note Chapter 6 n 22 below.

[372] *R v Inland Revenue Commissioners, ex parte Preston* [1985] AC 835, 852: 'a remedy by way of judicial review is not to be made available where an alternative remedy exists. This is a proposition of great importance. Judicial review is a collateral challenge; it is not an appeal' (Lord Scarman); and *R v Birmingham City Council, ex parte Ferrero Ltd* [1993] 1 All ER 530, 537: 'where Parliament has provided a statutory appeal procedure it is only exceptionally that judicial review should be granted' (Taylor LJ).

is used where there is no right of appeal or where all avenues of appeal have been exhausted. However, the existence of an alternative remedy would not of itself oust the jurisdiction of the High Court to determine, in the exercise its discretion, whether or not judicial review should be granted in a particular case. But it is only in exceptional circumstances that the court would exercise its discretion to grant judicial review where an adequate alternative remedy existed and had not been used.[373]

(2) Discretion and Relevant Factors

1-150   Where an alternative remedy does exist, some of the factors that a court should take into account when deciding whether to grant relief by way of judicial review are:[374]

    i.   whether the alternative statutory remedy will resolve the question at issue fully and directly;

    ii.   whether the statutory procedure would be quicker, or slower, than procedure by way of judicial review;

    iii.   whether the matter depends on some particular or technical knowledge which is more readily available to the alternative appellate body.

I. Judicial Review Procedure: an Outline

(1) CPR Part 54

1-151   Part 54 of the CPR contains the procedural rules on judicial review.[375] There is a Pre-Action Protocol for judicial review which must be complied with (discussed below at 2-11 and see Annex 1).[376] Failure to do so may result in adverse costs consequences (see at 16-19).[377]

(2) Judicial Review Procedure: Mandatory and Discretionary Use

1-152   Part 54 must be used in a claim for judicial review where the claimant is seeking: (i) a mandatory order; (ii) a prohibitory order; or (iii) an injunction under section 30 of the SCA 1981 (restraining a person from acting in any office in which he is not entitled to act).[378]

---

[373] *R v Epping and Harlow General Commissioner ex parte Goldstraw* [1983] 3 All ER 257 (CA), 262 (Sir John Donaldson MR); *R v Chief Constable of the Merseyside Police, ex parte Calveley* [1986] QB 424 (CA), 433 (Sir John Donaldson MR), and *R v High Peak Magistrates' Court, ex parte B* [1995] 1 FLR 568.

[374] *Ex p Waldron* [1986] QB 824, 852 (Glidewell LJ).

[375] Generally, see Chapter 2 on procedure below.

[376] See CPR 42.2(5) on costs ('the conduct of the parties include (a) … the extent to which the parties followed the Practice Direction—Pre-Action Conduct or any relevant pre-action protocol'); and the White Book Service para C8-001 et seq.

[377] See *R (Bahta) v Secretary of State for the Home Department* [2011] EWCA Civ 895 [59], [64]. See below at 16-10.

[378] CPR 54.2. See Chapter 3 on remedies below.

The judicial review procedure may be used in a claim for judicial review where the claimant is seeking: (i) a declaration; or (ii) an injunction.[379] A claim for judicial review may include a claim for damages, restitution or the recovery of a sum due but may not seek such a remedy alone.[380]

(3) Promptness

A claim form must be filed promptly; and in any event not later than three months after the grounds to make the claim first arose.[381] It is not open to the parties to extend the time limits.[382] But specific enactments may specify a shorter time for making a claim for judicial review.[383] A court may grant an extension of time for filing, pursuant to its general powers.[384]
    1-153

The court is likely to require a good reason or adequate explanation for the delay, and may refuse to grant (i) permission for the making of the claim for judicial review, or (ii) any relief on the claim, if it considers that the granting of the relief sought would be likely to cause substantial hardship to, or substantially prejudice the rights of any person, or be detrimental to good administration.[385]

So, even where a decision of the magistrates' court not to commit two offenders to the Crown Court for sentence following their convictions for converting criminal property was a decision that no reasonable magistrates' court would have made, the decision was not quashed owing to the Prosecution's undue delay in making a claim for judicial review.[386] The 3-month period allowed by the Civil Procedure Rules,[387] did not give unbridled liberty to delay to the end of that period, and the claim had been brought only days before the end of that period. The delay had been detrimental to the good administration of justice.[388]
    1-154

In *Uniplex (UK) Ltd v NHS Business Services Authority*[389] the CJEU held that the discretionary time limit ('promptly') was not compatible with EU law, in that doing something 'promptly' was contrary to the principle of legal certainty. This was because such a provision empowered a national court to dismiss an action as being out of time even before the expiry of the three-month time period if it took the view that the claim had not been made 'promptly'. National courts were under a duty to interpret national law consistently with EU directives. Therefore, national law was to be disapplied where
    1-155

---

[379] CPR 54.3; and see SCA 1981, s 31(2), which sets out the circumstances in which the court may grant a declaration or injunction in a claim for judicial review.

[380] CPR 54.3(2); and see SCA 1981, s 31(4), which sets out the circumstances in which the court may award damages, restitution or the recovery of a sum of money due on a claim for judicial review. See Chapter 3 below.

[381] CPR 54.5(1)(a)–(b). See below at 2-4 below.

[382] CPR 54.5(2).

[383] CPR 54.5(3).

[384] CPR 3.1(2)(a).

[385] SCA 1981, s 31(6).

[386] *R (DPP) v Swindon Magistrates' Court* [2013] EWHC 4237 (Admin).

[387] CPR 54.5.

[388] At time of writing a similar issue was before the court in *R (Craig Paolo) v City of London Magistrates Court*—judgment handed down on 20 June 2014.

[389] Case C-406/08 *Uniplex (UK) Ltd v NHS Business Services Authority* [2010] PTSR 1377.

it was incompatible with EU law. However, the *Uniplex* principle only applied when the domestic courts were dealing with the implementation of EU law. There was no reason why domestic and EU law challenges should not be subject to different time limits.[390]

(4) The Claim Form

1-156   The Claim Form (N461) for judicial review must include a request for permission to proceed with a claim for judicial review and state the remedy being claimed.[391] The claim form must be served on the defendant, and any person the claimant considers to be an interested party, within seven days of the date of issue of the Claim Form.[392] This is discussed in more detail below at 2-12.

(5) Acknowledgment of Service and 'Summary Grounds'

1-157   Any person served with the Claim Form who wishes to take part in the judicial review must file an Acknowledgment of Service (N462).[393] The Acknowledgment of Service must, where the person filing it intends to contest the claim, set out a summary of the grounds for doing so.[394] The purpose of the summary grounds is not to provide the basis for full argument of the substantive merits, but rather to assist the judge in deciding whether to grant permission, and if so, on what terms.[395] This is explained in more detail below at 2-30.

(6) 'Detailed Grounds' and Evidence

1-158   A defendant to a claim for judicial review or any other person served with a Claim Form who wishes to contest the claim or support it on additional grounds must file and serve: (i) detailed grounds for contesting the claim or supporting it on additional grounds; and (ii) any written evidence within 35 days after service of the order giving permission.[396] The court's permission is required if a claimant seeks to rely on grounds other than those for which he has been given permission to proceed.[397]

---

[390] *R (Berky) v Newport City Council* [2012] EWCA Civ 378 [35], confirmed in Case C-456/08 *European Commission v Ireland* [2010] 2 CMLR 47.
[391] CPR 54.6. See Annex 1.
[392] CPR 54.7.
[393] CPR 54.8. See below in section E in Chapter 2. Failure to file an acknowledgment of service will prevent a person from being able to take part in a hearing to decide whether permission should be given unless the court allows that person to do so (CPR 54.9). See Annex 4.
[394] CPR 54.8(4)(a).
[395] *R (Ewing) v Office of the Deputy Prime Minister* EWCA Civ 1583, [2006] 1 WLR 1260 [43].
[396] CPR 54.14.
[397] CPR 54.15.

Richard Wilson QC

(7) No Hearing

The court may decide a claim for judicial review without a hearing where all the parties   **1-159**
agree.[398] Where relief is granted by consent, CPR 54.18 provides a procedure whereby
the court may decide the claim for judicial review without a hearing. That procedure
should be followed wherever possible. It requires the filing of a document signed by all
the parties 'setting out the terms of the proposed agreed order together with a short
statement of the matters relied on as justifying the proposed agreed order and copies
of any authorities or statutory provisions relied on' (CPR PD 54A paragraph 17.1).[399]

(8) Permission Decision

The Administrative Court's permission is required to proceed with a claim for judicial   **1-160**
review.[400] Before making an application for permission, a claimant should normally
have complied with the Pre-Action Protocol for judicial review (see also at 2-9–2-10).

(i) Filtering out Weak Claims

The purpose of the requirement for the court's permission is to eliminate at an early   **1-161**
stage claims that might be frivolous, vexatious or without substance. The ordinary rule is
that the court will refuse permission to claim judicial review unless satisfied that there is
an arguable case that a ground for seeking judicial review exists which merits full investigation at a full oral hearing with all the parties and all the relevant evidence; and which
is not subject to a discretionary bar such as delay or an alternative remedy.[401] But argu-
ability has to be judged by reference to the nature and gravity of the issue to be argued.[402]

(ii) Decision on the Papers

Where the court determines an application for permission without a hearing, and   **1-162**
permission has been refused or subject to conditions or on certain grounds only, the
claimant cannot appeal but may request the decision to be reconsidered at a hearing.[403]
The court may give directions requiring the proceedings to be heard by a Divisional
Court.[404]

---

[398] CPR 54.18. See *Bahta* (n 377) [64] 'what needs to be underlined is the starting point in the CPR that a
successful claimant is entitled to his costs and the now recognised importance of complying with Pre-Action
Protocols' (Pill LJ).
[399] *Bahta* (n 377) [69].
[400] CPR 54.4.
[401] *R v Legal Aid Board, ex parte Hughes* (1992) 5 Admin LR 623, 628.
[402] *R (N) v Mental Health Review Tribunal (Northern Region)* [2006] QB 468 [62]; *Sharma* (n 22) [14(4)]
see above at 1-15, and Fordham, *Judicial Review Handbook* (n 6) (2012).
[403] CPR 54.12(1). A request for a reconsideration must be filed within seven days of after service of the
judge's reasons (CPR 54.12(2)).
[404] CPR 54.12(6).

(iii) Costs

1-163   The court will generally order an unsuccessful claimant to pay the costs associated with filing the Acknowledgment of Service.[405] But this general rule did not apply where the defendant filed the Acknowledgment of Service out of time.[406] A challenge to an order for costs made on an application for permission to seek judicial review or the quantum of such an order should be made by written submissions in accordance with the procedure set out in *Ewing v Office of the Deputy Prime Minister*.[407]

(9) Substantive Hearing

1-164   Certain aspects of the substantive hearing should be noted. The court will hear oral argument. It will not ordinarily order disclosure, further information or permit cross-examination owing to the duty of candour placed on all the parties (claimant, defendant and interested third parties) to a judicial review case.[408]

   Cross-examination on an application for judicial review, although not excluded, was in practice rarely permitted.[409] However, the modern position is that cross-examination, disclosure and orders for further information will be allowed whenever the justice of the particular case so requires,[410] or it is necessary for the fair and just disposal of the claim.[411]

(10) Appeals

(i) Court of Appeal (Civil Division)

1-165   CPR 52.15 governs the procedure for judicial review appeals to the Court of Appeal (Civil Division) in all cases other than those in respect of a 'criminal cause or matter' as that term has been interpreted in the case law.[412]

   Where permission has been refused in a civil (ie, non-criminal cause or matter) case after a hearing in the High Court, the person seeking that permission may apply to the Court of Appeal for permission to appeal within seven days of the decision of the High Court to refuse to give permission to apply for judicial review.[413]

---

[405] *R (Mount Cook Land Ltd) v Westminster City Council* [2003] EWCA Civ 1346; *Leach, Re* [2001] EWHC Admin 455; *Ewing* (n 395). See Ch 16 below.

[406] *Riniker v Employment Tribunals and Regional Chairman* [2009] EWCA Civ 1450.

[407] *Ewing* (n 395).

[408] Further, see Fordham, *Judicial Review Handbook* (n 6) para 10.3 (claimant's duty of candour).

[409] *O'Reilly v Mackman* [1983] 2 AC 237, 282D–283A.

[410] ibid. Fordham, *Judicial Review Handbook* (n 6), para 17.4; and *Cullen v Chief Constable of the Royal Ulster Constabulary* [2003] UKHL 39, [2003] 1 WLR 1763 [5]. See further below at 4-82.

[411] *R v (Bancoult) v Secretary of State for Foreign and Commonwealth Affairs* [2012] EWHC 2115 (Admin) [17].

[412] See 1-168 below, for meaning of 'criminal cause or matter' as used in SCA 1981, s 18(1)(a) and interpreted in the case law. For appeals see below at 2-44.

[413] CPR 52.15(1)–(2)

The Court of Appeal may, instead of giving permission to appeal, give permission to apply for judicial review, in which event the case will proceed in the High Court unless the Court of Appeal orders otherwise.[414]

(ii) Supreme Court

The House of Lords (now Supreme Court) had no jurisdiction to entertain an appeal against the Court of Appeal's refusal of permission to apply for judicial review.[415] However, where the Court of Appeal grants permission to appeal, but then refuses to grant permission to apply for judicial review (because of the alleged delay in filing the claim), the House of Lords (now Supreme Court) has jurisdiction to hear an appeal against the refusal to grant permission to apply.[416]   **1-166**

(iii) 'Criminal Cause or Matter'

Except as provided by the Administration of Justice Act 1960, no appeal lies to the Court of Appeal from any judgment of the High Court in 'any criminal cause or matter'.[417] The position in relation to what constitutes a 'criminal cause or matter' is not straightforward and is dealt with below at 1-168.   **1-167**

This means that decisions of the High Court in 'any criminal cause or matter' can only be appealed by a direct appeal ('leapfrog') to the Supreme Court.[418]

J. Appeals from the High Court: 'Criminal Cause or Matter'

(1) What is a 'Criminal Cause or Matter'?

The case law on what is or is not to be considered 'a criminal cause or matter' has a long history.[419] In the House of Lords in *Amand v Home Secretary and Minister of Defence of the Royal Netherlands Government*[420] it was stated that: **1-168**

> It is the nature and character of the proceeding … which provide the test. If the matter is one the direct outcome of which may be trial of the applicant and his possible punishment for an alleged offence by a court claiming jurisdiction to do so, the matter is criminal.[421]

---

[414] CPR 52.15(3)–(4).

[415] *R v Secretary of State for Trade and Industry, ex parte Eastaway* [2000] 1 WLR 2222.

[416] *R v Hammersmith and Fulham LBC ex parte Burkett* [2002] 1 WLR 1593. On permission-stage appeals and appeals after substantive hearings on a judicial review claims generally, see Fordham, *Judicial Review Handbook* (n 6), 257–65.

[417] SCA 1981, s 18(1)(a).

[418] Administration of Justice Act 1960, s 1(1) (as amended the Access to Justice Act 1999, s 63).

[419] Eg, see *Ex p Woodhall* (1888) LR 20 QBD 832 (CA), where the Queen's Bench Division of the High Court refused an application for a writ of habeas corpus on behalf of a fugitive accused of an extradition crime and it was held that the decision of the QBD was given in a 'criminal cause or matter' and that therefore no appeal lay to the Court of Appeal.

[420] *Amand v Home Secretary and Minister of Defence of the Royal Netherlands Government* [1943] AC 147, [1942] 2 All ER 381.

[421] ibid 156 (Viscount Simon LC).

...

The principle which I deduce from the authorities I have cited and the other relevant authorities which I have considered, is that if the cause or matter is one which, if carried to its conclusion, might result in the conviction of the person charged and in a sentence of some punishment, such as imprisonment or fine, it is a 'criminal cause or matter'. The person charged is thus put in jeopardy. Every order made in such a cause or matter by an English court, is an order in a criminal cause or matter, even though the order, taken by itself, is neutral in character and might equally have been made in a cause or matter which is not criminal.

The order may not involve punishment by the law of this country, but if the effect of the order is to subject by means of the operation of English law the persons charged to the criminal jurisdiction of a foreign country, the order is, in the eyes of English law for the purposes being considered, an order in a criminal cause or matter, as is shown by *Ex parte Woodhall* (1888) LR 20 QBD 832 and *R v. Brixton Prison (Governor of) ex p Savakar* [1910] 2 KB 1056.[422]

1-169 *Amand* has been followed in a number of the more recent authorities. In *R (Aru) v Chief Constable of Merseyside*[423] it was held that an official caution was a 'criminal cause or matter' within the meaning of section 18(1)(a) of the SCA 1981, and that accordingly the Court of Appeal had no jurisdiction to entertain an appeal in judicial review proceedings challenging the lawfulness of such a caution. The court did, however, consider the situation where the judgment in the High Court might be afflicted by legal error, but was not an error raising a point of law of public importance. In such circumstances, Maurice Kay LJ in giving the judgment of the court, opined that: 'perhaps the better course would be for amending legislation to provide an appellate route from a criminal cause or matter in the Administrative Court to the Court of Appeal (Criminal Division) rather than to the House of Lords or to this court' – but noted that this was for others to decide.

1-170 In *R (South West Yorkshire Mental Health NHS Trust) v Bradford Crown Court*[424] a defendant was charged with murder but was found unfit to stand trial, and a second jury found that he had committed the act as charged. The Crown Court made orders relating to the defendant's detention that were not appropriate under the provisions of the Criminal Procedure (Insanity) Act 1964 (as amended). The NHS Trust brought judicial review proceedings to quash the orders. The High Court judge set aside the orders and remitted the matter to the Crown Court for a judge of that court to make a proper order under the 1964 Act as amended. On an appeal by the defendant to the Court of Appeal, the Court of Appeal dismissed the appeal holding that where proceedings were initiated in the Crown Court following an allegation of breach of the criminal law, it was appropriate to view the proceedings overall and not analyse them order by order. Orders made in the Crown Court did not cease to be orders in a criminal cause or matter merely because the court was empowered by statute to make a custodial order in the absence of a conviction; and also circumstances might arise where a person in the defendant's position, if properly detained, might be remitted for a conventional criminal trial.

1-171 A decision by a public authority operating within or connected to the criminal justice system may be regarded as a civil matter, rather than a criminal cause or matter,

---

[422] ibid 162 (Lord Wright).
[423] *R (Aru) v Chief Constable of Merseyside* [2004] EWCA Civ 199, [2004] 1 WLR 1697.
[424] *R (South West Yorkshire Mental Health NHS Trust) v Bradford Crown Court* [2003] EWCA Civ 1857, [2004] 1 WLR 1664.

Richard Wilson QC

where the decision in question relates to policy. In *R v Commissioner of Police of the Metropolis, ex parte Blackburn (No 1)*[425] (discussed below at 4-11) the Commissioner of Police made a policy decision not to enforce a provision of the Betting, Gaming and Lotteries Act 1963 in gaming clubs in London. The applicant, a private citizen, applied to the Divisional Court for an order of mandamus (mandatory order) directing the respondent Commissioner to reverse the policy decision. The application was refused and the applicant appealed to the Court of Appeal. The Court of Appeal dismissed the Commissioner's argument that it was without jurisdiction because the decision by Divisional Court had been made in a 'criminal cause or matter'. The Court of Appeal explained that where an application was made to compel the reversal of a policy directive regarding the enforcement of a statute:

> Such an application has no reference to any particular criminal cause or matter, and is not even a remote step in relation to a criminal cause or matter, but is designed simply and solely to ensure that the police do not abdicate, in consequence of a policy decision, their functions as law enforcement officers. I therefore agree with my lords in holding that this court has jurisdiction to hear and determine the present appeal.[426]

K. What can the Claimant Achieve?

(1) Remedies

There is a range of remedies for judicial review available, but at the discretion of the court, namely: quashing orders; prohibitory orders; mandatory orders; declarations and injunctions; damages, restitution or payment of a sum due (debt). These remedies are addressed in Chapter 3, below.

1-172

(2) Discretionary

The first principle is that the court has an overall discretion as to whether to grant a remedy or not. In considering how that discretion should be exercised the court is entitled to have regard to matters such as: (i) the nature and importance of the 'flaw' in the decision challenged; (ii) the conduct of the claimant; and (iii) the effect on administration in granting the remedy (see below at 3-8).[427]

1-173

(3) Eventual Outcomes

A successful outcome may typically result in the impugned decision being quashed and the matter being remitted to the decision-maker for fresh consideration.

1-174

---

[425] *Ex p Blackburn (No 1)* (n 104).
[426] ibid 147F–G (Edmund Davies LJ).
[427] *Nichol v Gateshead Metropolitan Borough Council* (1988) 87 LGR 435, 460.

Where the court does make a quashing order in respect of the impugned decision, the court may remit the matter to the decision-maker and direct it to reconsider the matter and reach a decision in accordance with the judgment of the court; or in so far as any enactment permits, substitute its own decision for the decision to which the claim relates.[428] The circumstances in which the court having quashed the decision of a public authority is permitted to substitute its own decision for the decision in question, is strictly circumscribed. The court's power to substitute its own decision, is exercisable only if: (i) the decision in question was made by a court or tribunal; (ii) the decision is quashed on the ground that there had been an error of law; and (iii) without the error, there would have been only one decision which the court or tribunal could have reached.[429a]

However, when the matter is remitted for reconsideration, the eventual outcome upon proper re-consideration might produce the same or a similar decision to the one impugned; or it might produce a different outcome.

L. Criminal Judicial Review: Contributions to Administrative and Criminal Law

(1) Introduction

1-175 Criminal judicial review cases have made material contributions to the general development of administrative law principles, and to the content of the criminal law in terms of procedure, evidence and substantive law. Some examples are considered below.

(2) Administrative Law and Criminal Judicial Review

(i) Deference to Decision-Making Body

1-176 In *R v DPP ex parte Kebilene*[429] the House of Lords was concerned with the decision of the Director of Public Prosecutions to consent to the prosecution of persons under the Prevention of Terrorism (Temporary Provisions) Act 1989. It was held that although the doctrine of margin of appreciation is an integral part of the supervisory jurisdiction of the ECtHR and is not available to national courts when considering Convention issues within their own countries, there are nonetheless circumstances:

> [W]here it will be appropriate for the courts to recognise that there is an area of judgment within which the judiciary will defer, on democratic grounds, to the considered opinion of the elected body or person whose act or decision is said to be incompatible with the Convention.[430]

---

[428] CPR 54.19. SCA 1981, s 31 enables the High Court, subject to certain conditions, to substitute its own decision for the decision in question.

[429a] SCA 1981, ss 31(5), (5A)(a)-(c); and see *R(O'Connor) v Avon Coroner* [2009] EWHC 854, [2011] QB 106 (Admin) at [15], [32].

[429] *Ex p Kebilene* (n 64). See below at 5-12.

[430] ibid, 81B-D (per Lord Hope).

Richard Wilson QC

(ii) Extension of the Concept of Abuse of Power

The High Court has power to interfere with a prosecution not because the applicant could **1-177** not have a fair trial, but because the judiciary accept a responsibility for the maintenance of the rule of law that embraces a willingness to oversee executive action and to refuse to countenance behaviour that threatens either basic human rights or the rule of law.

> It is the function of the High Court to ensure that executive action is exercised responsibly and as Parliament intended. So also should it be in the field of criminal law and if it comes to the attention of the court that there has been a serious abuse of power it should ... express disapproval by refusing to act upon it.[431]

(iii) Greater Intensity of Review: Proportionality

In *R (Daly) v Home Secretary*[432] a prisoner sought permission to apply for judicial **1-178** review of the Home Secretary's decision (set out in the Security Manual) to require examination of prisoners' legally privileged correspondence in their absence. In considering whether the Home Secretary had violated the claimant's Article 8 rights under the ECHR, Lord Steyn made three observations of general application:

> First, the doctrine of proportionality may require the reviewing court to assess the balance which the decision maker has struck, not merely whether it is within the range of rational or reasonable decisions. Secondly, the proportionality test may go further than the traditional grounds of review inasmuch as it may require attention to be directed to the relative weight accorded to interests and considerations. Thirdly, even the heightened scrutiny test developed in *R v Ministry of Defence, Ex p Smith* [1996] QB 517, 554 is not necessarily appropriate to the protection of human rights.[433]

His Lordship then said that the differences in approach between the traditional grounds of review and the proportionality approach might therefore sometimes yield different results. He observed that it was important that cases involving Convention rights were analysed in the correct way, and that as Laws LJ emphasised in *R (Mahmood) v Secretary of State for the Home Department*[434] 'that the intensity of review in a public law case will depend on the subject matter in hand'.[435]

(3) The Criminal Law and Criminal Judicial Review

(i) Loss or Destruction of Evidence

The loss or destruction of evidence may amount to an abuse of process if the police or **1-179** prosecutor had been under a duty to obtain and/or retain the relevant material.[436]

---

[431] *Ex p Bennett (No 1)* (n 17), 62A-D.
[432] *Daly* (n 1). See below at 8-2.
[433] ibid [27].
[434] *R (Mahmood) v Secretary of State for the Home Department* [2001] 1 WLR 840.
[435] ibid 847 [18].
[436] *R (Ebrahim) v Feltham Magistrates' Court,* also known as *Mouat v Director of Public Prosecutions* [2001] EWHC (Admin) 130, [2001] 1 WLR 1293. See below at 6-45.

(ii) Special Measures

1-180   The fairness of proceedings that were challenged by reference to Article 6 of ECHR could only be judged retrospectively by reference to the trial and any appeal, but not prospectively before trial had taken place.[437]

(iii) Treating Children as Adults

1-181   It was a violation of Article 8 of ECHR for 17-year-old detainees to be treated as if they were adults. In *R (HC) v Secretary of State for the Home Department*[438] the claimant applied for judicial review of the Home Secretary's refusal to revise Code C of the Code of Practice under the Police and Criminal Evidence Act 1984 so as to distinguish procedures applicable to a 17-year-old detainee in police custody from those applicable to adults. The principle that the best interests of a child must be a primary consideration for public authorities making decisions in relation to a child, applies to decision-making in respect of 17-year-olds. For the Home Secretary to treat 17-year-olds as adults when in custody was to disregard:

> the definition of a child in the UNCRC, in all other international instruments to which the Strasbourg Court and the Supreme Court have referred, and the preponderance of legislation affecting children and justice which include within their scope those who are under 18. The Secretary of State's failure to amend Code C is in breach of her obligation under the Human Rights Act 1998, and unlawful.[439]

---

[437] *R (D) v Camberwell Green Youth Court* [2005] UKHL 4, [2005] 1 WLR 393. See below at 6-68.
[438] *R (HC) v Secretary of State for the Home Department* [2013] EWHC 982 (Admin). See below at 11-16.
[439] ibid [89].

Richard Wilson QC

2

Procedure

GRÁINNE MELLON

A. General Principles

(1) Introduction

2-1   Judicial review procedure is distinct from criminal, and indeed other civil claims in a number of ways.

    i.   A claimant needs permission to bring a claim (see below 2-30);

    ii.   All claims for judicial review against public bodies covered in this work must be issued in the Administrative Court (save for claims for judicial review of decisions of the First Tier Tribunal relating to appeals relating to the Criminal Injuries Compensation Authority – see below at 9-39);

    iii.   The procedure is 'front-loaded', in that pre-issue preparation incorporates much of the work that in other proceedings normally comes later. In order to obtain permission, a claimant will need to provide the court[1] with a well-argued claim supported by a bundle;

    iv.   Claims are often settled through pre-trial correspondence or after a claimant has received permission to bring a claim (see below at 2-46);

    v.   There is a procedure for considering and potentially resolving claims on an urgent basis (see below at 2-21);

    vi.   While in non-urgent cases, it can take some months before a case comes to trial, there are usually very few interim or directions hearings, and a full hearing in a straightforward case usually takes up to half a day (see below at 2-37);

    vii.   The court decides the matter on the basis of submissions and very rarely hears live evidence (see below at 2-37);

    viii.   The High Court can refuse relief or impose costs sanctions if important procedural steps are not followed—claimants must be aware that remedies are discretionary (see next chapter at 3-5);

    ix.   Criminal causes and matters[2] are usually heard by two judges sitting together, called a Divisional Court (see below at 2-40);

    x.   A claimant in a criminal cause or matter cannot appeal a decision of the High Court to the Court of Appeal, but only to the Supreme Court.

---

[1] References to 'the court' in this chapter are to the High Court.
[2] These are defined at section J in Chapter 1 above.

        Gráinne Mellon

The following documents can be found at Annexes 1-4 and are discussed at various points in this chapter:

i.   Annex 1: The Pre-Action Protocol;
ii. Annex 2: The Claim Form (Form N461);
iii. Annex 3: Application for Urgent Consideration (Form N463);
iv. Annex 4: Acknowledgement of Service (Form N462).

(2) Legal Framework

The procedure for judicial review claims is governed by:[3]   2-2

i.   Part 54 of the Civil Procedure Rules (CPR)[4] read alongside sections 29, 31 and 43 of the Senior Courts Act 1981 and Order 53 of the Rules of the Supreme Court;
ii. CPR Practice Directions 54A on Judicial Review and 54D on Administrative Court (Venue); and[5]
iii. the Pre-Action Protocol for Judicial Review.

The Criminal Procedure Rules 2013 (SI 2013/1554) do not contain any provisions for judicial review.

B. When to Make a Claim

(1) The Rule—Promptly and Within Three Months

In order to make a claim, a potential claimant must apply for and obtain permission to   2-3
bring the claim. An application for permission for judicial review must be filed:

i.   promptly; and
ii. in any event, not later than three months after the grounds to make the claim first arose.[6]

In certain criminal judicial reviews the Administrative Court has encouraged urgent action. This may mean acting within days or weeks of the decision, depending on the type of decision and claimant: for example, for judicial reviews of decisions on bail in

---

[3] Note the mandatory and discretionary use of CPR Pt 54 depending on the remedy sought—see section I in Chapter 1 above.

[4] Note that Pt 8 of the CPR may also apply. The CPR can be accessed online via the Ministry of Justice's website at www.justice.gov.uk/courts/procedure-rules/civil.

[5] Note there is a third Practice Direction under Pt 54, PD 54C, References by the Legal Services Commission (LSC). This deals with references by the LSC (although now replaced by the Legal Aid Agency) of a question that arises on a review of a decision by the LSC to the Court regarding financial eligibility for a representation order in criminal proceedings under the Criminal Defence Service (Financial Eligibility) Regulations 2006 (SI 2006/2492). These are not claims for judicial review. See Chapter 15, n 43.

[6] See discussion above at 1-149 regarding CPR 54.5(1). As of 1 July 2013, a shorter time limit was imposed for planning cases, procurement cases and challenges to decisions under the Inquiries Act 2005. See CPR 54.5(A1)(5), 54.5(A1)(6) and the Inquiries Act 2005, s 36.

the Crown Court (see below at 7-7), for judicial reviews where the claimant is under 18 (see below note 93 in Chapter 6), or for judicial reviews of adjournments in the magistrates' courts (see below at 6-71). The procedure for urgent applications is covered in this chapter below at 2-21.

(i) Promptness

2-4   A claimant has a duty to act promptly, and not simply wait until just before the three-month limit before making a claim. A claim can be refused even if it is made within the three-month period, if it is not made promptly.[7]

An assessment of whether a claim has been made promptly or not is based on the features and circumstances of the particular case.[8] The obligation to proceed promptly is of particular importance where the interests of third parties are involved.[9] When calculating time limits, the day on which a time period starts is not included in calculating that period.[10]

Compliance with the Pre-Action Protocol (see Annex 1) does not absolve the claimant from lodging a claim promptly.[11] The Administrative Court may require evidence to show that steps were taken promptly after the grounds first arose. It may be worth keeping a note of the dates of legal aid applications, briefs to counsel, attempts to exhaust alternative remedies and any other information relevant to timing.

In cases involving points of European Union (EU) law (see Chapter 14 below), the requirement of promptness will not apply: instead the only issue is whether proceedings were brought within three months.[12]

(ii) The Running of Time

2-5   Time starts running from when grounds for the application first arose. Time stops once the application for permission is lodged with (and stamped by) the Administrative Court Office.[13] It is important to lodge the application in the correct form, otherwise it may be rejected and time will continue to run.

Where the claim is for a quashing order in respect of a judgment, order or conviction, the date when the grounds to make the application first arose is the date of the judgment, order or conviction.[14]

---

[7] See *R v Independent Television Commission, ex parte TV NI Ltd* The Times, 30 December 1991 (CA); *R v Tunbridge Wells Justices, ex parte Tunbridge Wells Borough Council* [1996] JPN 514 (DC); *R (Crown Prosecution Service) v City of London Magistrates Court* [2007] EWHC 1924 (Admin); *R (Crown Prosecution Service) v Newcastle upon Tyne Youth Court* [2010] EWHC 2773 (Admin).

[8] *R v Chief Constable of Devon and Cornwall, ex parte Hay* [1996] 2 All ER 711, 732a (Sedley J).

[9] *R v Secretary of State for Health, ex parte Furneaux* [1994] 2 All ER 652, 658e.

[10] CPR r 2(8)(3).

[11] *R (Finn-Kelcey) v Milton Keynes Council* [2009] Env LR 17.

[12] In *Uniplex (UK) Ltd v NHS Business Services Authority* [2010] 2 CMLR 47, the Court of Justice of the European Union held that in the context of public procurement the requirement of promptness is in breach of EU law on grounds of legal certainty and effectiveness. See discussion above at 1-155.

[13] *R v Secretary of State for the Home Department, ex parte Chetta* [1996] COD 463.

[14] CPR 54.5.1(b).

There are no provisions identifying when time commences in other judicial review claims, but it will typically be the date of the decision or action by the public authority.[15] The fact that a breach is continuing does not mean the Court will not take into account the date that the breach began in assessing whether or not there has been a delay.[16]

Time runs from when the grounds arose—not the claimant's knowledge of when the grounds arose. The claimant's lack of knowledge that grounds for judicial review existed may, however, be relevant in considering whether or not to extend time.[17]

In cases involving points of EU law, time will only start to run from the date on which the claimant knew or ought to have known of that infringement.[18]

(2) Delay and Extensions of Time

Where there has been delay, the Administrative Court has a discretion to extend the time limit for bringing a claim, if there is good reason to do so.[19]   **2-6**

An application for an extension should be made in the Claim Form.[20] Grounds in support of the application must be filed and verified by a witness statement or affidavit.[21] The decision as to whether time should be extended is made at the hearing of the application for permission to apply for judicial review.

While there is no particular legislative guidance for determining whether or not to extend time for the bringing of an application for judicial review, the Court of Appeal has approved CPR 3.9 as a 'checklist' in the context of an extension of time for appeal.[22] The Administrative Court is likely to be particularly concerned with the strengths of the application[23] as well as the importance of the issues raised, the length of the delay, the explanation for the delay and the extent of any prejudice caused by the delay.[24]

It has been held that problems obtaining legal aid,[25] mistakes by legal advisors[26] and attempts to resolve the claim without litigation[27] are good reasons for extending the

---

[15] In *R v London Borough of Hammersmith and Fulham and others, ex parte Burkett and another* [2002] 1 WLR 1593, the House of Lords held that time runs from the occurrence of an act that gives rise to the real substance of the challenge, if that decision is taken before a final decision that has legal effect.

[16] *R v Essex County Council, ex parte C* [1993] COD 398 (Jowitt J).

[17] *R v Department of Transport, ex parte Presvac Engineering Ltd* (1992) 4 Admin LR 121, 133D–H; *R v Cotswold DC, ex parte Barrington Parish Council* [1998] 75 P&CR 515.

[18] Case C-406/08 *Uniplex (UK) Ltd v NHS Business Services Authority* [2010] PTSR 1377 [35]; *Sita UK Ltd v Greater Manchester Waste Disposal Authority* [2011] EWCA Civ 156 [2012] PTSR 645.

[19] CPR 3.1(2)(a); PD54A, para 5.6(3) per *R v Criminal Injuries Compensation Board, ex parte A* [1999] 2 WLR 974 (HL).

[20] CPR 54.5.

[21] *R v Warwickshire County Council, ex parte Collymore* [1995] ELR 217, 228F.

[22] *Sayers v Clarke Walker (a firm)* [2002] EWCA Civ 645, [2002] 1 WLR 3095.

[23] *R v Warwickshire County Council, ex parte Collymore* [1995] ELR 217; *R v Rochdale Metropolitan Borough Council, ex parte Schemet* [1994] ELR 89.

[24] See *R v Secretary of State for the Home Department, ex parte Ruddock* [1987] 1 WLR 1482; *R (Law Society of England and Wales) v Legal Services Commission* [2010] EWHC 2550 (Admin).

[25] *R v Stratford on Avon District Council, ex parte Jackson* [1985] 3 All ER 769 (CA). However, it is fact-dependent; see *R v Metropolitan Borough of Sandwell, ex parte Cashmore* [1993] 25 HLR 544. In urgent matters it is not appropriate to wait for an appeal against funding to take its course rather than take all possible steps to expedite a decision: *R (Patel) v Lord Chancellor* [2010] EWHC 2220 (Admin).

[26] *R v Secretary of State for the Home Department, ex parte Oyeleye* [1994] Imm AR 268 and *R v Tavistock General Commissioners, ex parte Worth* [1985] STC 564.

[27] *R (Independent Schools Council) v Charity Commission for England and Wales* [2010] EWHC 2604 (Admin).

time for bringing judicial review. Likewise, while the claimant's lack of knowledge as to when the grounds for the application arose does not affect when time starts to run, it may be a relevant factor in an application to extend time.[28]

If it is anticipated that there will be any delay in commencing proceedings, the claimant should put the defendant on notice of the contemplated proceedings at the earliest opportunity.[29] Claimants have a duty to disclose any issues arising as to delay and reasons for delay, including within the three-month time period, and these should be properly explained in the Claim Form.[30]

In the event that an application for extension is required, it may be worth seeking the consent of the defendant to proceedings being brought out of time. While the CPR is clear that the time limit for judicial review cannot be extended by agreement between the parties,[31] the consent of the defendant may indicate a lack of prejudice and therefore be a factor the Court considers relevant in assessing whether or not an extension should be granted.

In criminal judicial reviews during ongoing proceedings claimants should note that, the Crown Prosecution Service (or other prosecuting agency and any other parties to the proceedings) should be named by a claimant in their Claim Form as interested parties (see below at 2-9).

(i) Delay and the Substantive Hearing

2-7   If at the permission stage the Court considers there to be good reason to extend time, that decision should not generally be reviewed subsequently at the full hearing.[32]

If the Court extends time, permission or relief on the substantive application can still be refused, if granting it would 'be likely to cause substantial hardship to, or substantially prejudice the rights of, any person or would be detrimental to good administration'.[33] The criteria—substantial hardship, substantial prejudice and good administration—are to be read disjunctively.[34] In most cases, the Court should postpone consideration of these criteria until the full hearing.[35] If a claim is made within the context of criminal proceedings, the avoidance of delay and disruption to those proceedings is likely to be a significant factor (for example, see judicial reviews of decisions to prosecute at 5-12 and of decisions by the magistrates' courts at 6-16).

(3) Premature Applications

2-8   In addition to rejecting claims that have not been made promptly, the Administrative Court can reject an application if it is made prematurely. Claims may be premature for

---

[28] *R v Secretary of State for the Home Department, ex parte Ruddock* [1987] 1 WLR 1482, 1485F.
[29] *R v Swale BC, ex parte Royal Society for the Protection of Birds* (1990) 2 Ad LR 790.
[30] On disclosure, see below at 2-17.
[31] CPR 54.4.
[32] *R v Criminal Injuries Compensation Board, ex parte A* (above n 19). For exceptions to this principle see *R (Lichfield Securities Ltd) v Lichfield DC* (2001) 4 LGLR 35.
[33] Senior Courts Act 1981, s 31(6).
[34] *R v Dairy Produce Quota Tribunal, ex parte Caswell* [1990] 2 AC 738 and *R v Hammersmith and Fulham London Borough Council, ex parte Burkett* [2002] UKHL 23.
[35] *Ex p Caswell* [1990] 2 AC 738.

a range of reasons—most frequently because a final decision has not yet been reached[36] or the defendant has not yet determined the facts.[37] Another common reason is that a claimant has not exhausted the alternative remedies that may be on offer (see for example the complaints procedure in respect of the police at 4-2 or the range of options in a magistrates' court at 6-3). If these are available, but do not provide an effective remedy, it is important for a claimant to explain the reasons for this in the supporting grounds.

The Administrative Court is generally reluctant to consider applications for judicial review that challenge interim decisions of criminal courts and a statutory bar exists in respect of matters relating to trial on indictment in the Crown Court (see discussion above at 1-25 and below at 7-2).[38] However, there are exceptions (see below at 6-21 and 7-7) and the Court has proven itself willing to consider interim decisions particularly in cases where an individual's liberty is at stake.[39]

Where permission is sought to quash any judgment, order or conviction, or other proceeding of a magistrates' court, which is subject to an appeal to the Crown Court and the 28-day time limit for bringing the appeal remains unexpired, the Administrative Court may adjourn the application for permission until the appeal is determined or the time for appealing has expired.[40] Such a claimant must inform the Administrative Court at the outset when they issue their claim that an appeal is pending before the Crown Court.[41]

C. The Rules for Pre-Action Steps

(1) The Letter Before Claim

The parties are expected to comply with the Pre-Action Protocol for Judicial Review (the 'Protocol' contained in Annex 1).[42]   2-9

The Protocol requires claimants to send a letter before claim. The purpose of this letter is to identify the issues in dispute and establish whether litigation can be avoided.[43] The Protocol sets out the central issues which should be addressed in a letter before claim.[44] A sample letter before claim is set out at Annex A of the Protocol. While claimants are advised to 'normally use' this standard form,[45] deviations are unlikely to attract criticism provided all core matters are addressed.

---

[36] *R (Birmingham Care Consortium) v Birmingham City Council* [2011] EWHC 2656 (Admin).
[37] *R (Paul Rackham Ltd) v Swaffham Magistrates Court* [2004] EWHC 1417.
[38] *R (Hoar-Stevens) v Richmond upon Thames Magistrates' Court* [2003] EWHC 2660; *Streames v Copping* [1985] QB 920, 929.
[39] *R (Secretary of State for the Home Department) v Mental Health Review Tribunal* [2004] EWHC 2194 (Admin); *R v Maidstone Crown Court ex parte Clark* [1995] 1 WLR 831.
[40] See also the discussion above on appeals by of case stated and judicial review at 6-12.
[41] *R v Mid-Worcester Justices, ex parte Hart* [1989] COD 397, DC.
[42] Contained in Annex 1. In *Bahta & Ors v Secretary of State for the Home Department* [2011] EWCA Civ 895 [64], the Court of Appeal emphasised the importance of complying with the pre-action protocols, which are intended to facilitate the settlement of proceedings at an early stage, if possible. For circumstances where the Protocol may not apply, see below at 2-11.
[43] Judicial Review Pre-action Protocol, paras 8 and 12.
[44] ibid, paras 10 and 11.
[45] ibid, para 9.

The following information should be included in the letter before claim:

i.   Details of the proposed claimant and proposed defendant/s (including the details of those in the public body who has been handling the dispute, if possible).

ii. A summary of the issues in the claim including:
    a)   the date and details of the decision, act or omission being challenged;
    b)   a clear summary of the facts on which the claim is based; and
    a)   a brief explanation as to why the decision is wrong.

iii. Details of any interested parties known to the claimant.[46]

iv. Details of information or documentation the claimant is seeking and an explanation of why they are considered relevant. This can include a request for more detailed explanation of the reasons for the decision.

v.   Details of the action the defendant is expected to take, including details of the remedy sought.

vi. Address for reply and service of documents.

vii. Proposed reply date (usually 14 days, although a longer or shorter period may be appropriate, depending on the circumstances of the case).

In essence, the letter before claim must clearly set out what is being challenged, and why. It must do so in such a way that the defendant is clear about the basis of the proposed challenge. A failure to do so sufficiently or at all may have cost implications.[47]

The letter before claim should be sent to the proposed defendant(s). Certain public bodies have specific addresses where letters before claim should be sent.[48]

The letter before claim should also be sent to any interested parties known to the claimant. In judicial review claims arising from decisions of courts or tribunals, a copy of the letter before claim must be sent to any other parties of the proceedings. For example, in judicial review claims arising from the decisions of magistrates' courts or the Crown Court, a copy of the letter before claim must be sent to the CPS as an interested party.[49]

2-10   The defendant should normally respond within 14 days or other period specified in the letter before claim.[50] Compliance with the Pre-Action Protocol does not affect the time limit in the CPR: it is therefore crucial that the letter before claim is sent promptly and well within the three-month time limit for judicial review.[51] If this is not possible, the claimant should send a letter before claim to the defendant indicating that it is not possible to give an opportunity to respond before issuing proceedings but explaining that they will consider the defendant's reply in deciding whether to continue with the claim. The claimant should then lodge the Claim Form immediately.

The claimant should normally wait until the proposed reply date given in the letter before claim has passed before proceeding to issue the Claim Form.[52]

---

[46] ibid, para 11. For more, see below at 2-14.

[47] See Chapter 16 below.

[48] Section 2, Annex A of the Protocol. It is advisable to check the online version of the Pre-Action Protocol to ensure addresses remain up to date: www.justice.gov.uk/courts/procedure-rules/civil/protocol/prot_jrv.

[49] CPR PD54A, paras 5.1–5.2.

[50] The Protocol, para 13. Once again, a recommended standard form letter is set out at Annex B of the Protocol.

[51] CPR 54.5.1. See above at 2-4. See also the Protocol, fn 1 which states that compliance with the Protocol alone is unlikely to be sufficient to persuade the Court to allow a late claim.

[52] The Protocol, para 12.

Any response received should be carefully considered to see if the defendant has addressed the complaint or alternatively whether the response reveals additional useful grounds on which to proceed with the claim.

(2) The Limits of the Pre-Action Protocol

Although the Protocol is a 'code of good practice', it is clear that where its use is appropriate, the Court will normally expect all parties to have complied with it.[53] Failure, by either the claimant or the defendant to comply with the Protocol may have cost implications and/or may be taken into account by the Court when making case-management decisions (for example, affording a defendant who was not sent a letter before claim a longer period to file an acknowledgement of service).[54] For analysis of the cost implications of non-compliance with the rules of court, especially in the post-Jackson era, see below at 16-19.   **2-11**

The Protocol recognises two occasions when sending a letter before claim will not be appropriate:[55]

i.   When a defendant does not have the legal power to change the decision being challenged. (This status is called 'functus officio', or 'functus' for short). While there is no need to send a letter before claim in such cases, it can be advisable to do so in strong claims in the hope that the defendant will submit to judgment.

ii. Where the application is urgent. This usually occurs where interim relief is sought because a contested decision is due to be implemented or where the claimant requires the claim to be determined in a particularly short timeframe such that delay would defeat the purpose of the application.[56] In such cases, it is good practice to fax to the defendant the draft Claim Form which the claimant intends to issue.[57]

Any failure by the claimant to comply with the Protocol, whether because the claim is urgent or otherwise, must be explained in the Claim Form.

D. How to Issue a Claim

(1) The Claim Form

An application for permission to apply for judicial review must be made with the Claim   **2-12**
Form (Form N461—contained in Annex 2).[58]

---

[53] ibid, para 7. The Protocol also states that claimants will need to satisfy themselves whether they should follow the Protocol, depending upon the circumstances of his or her case.

[54] ibid, para 7. See also below at 16-19.

[55] ibid, para 6.

[56] See above challenges to adjournments in the magistrates' courts or challenges concerning youths at note 93 in Chapter 6 and at 6-71.

[57] Judicial Review, Pre-Action Protocol for Judicial Review, para 7. Claimants will need to satisfy themselves whether they should follow the Protocol, depending upon the circumstances of their case.

[58] Available from the website of the Ministry of Justice.

Paragraph 5.6 of PD 54A sets out the documents which must be included in or accompany the Claim Form:

i.   a detailed statement of the claimant's grounds for bringing the claim for judicial review;
ii. a statement of the facts relied on;
iii. any application to extend the time limit for filing the Claim Form; and
iv. any application for directions.[59]

Many claimants provide a combined 'Detailed Statement of Facts and Grounds' as a separate document attached to the Claim Form. There is no set approach to drafting this document. However, it should certainly summarise the facts, the law and the grounds of challenge, and deal with any issues of timing or delay. It may also anticipate any defences likely to be raised by the defendant.

In addition to the statement of facts and grounds, the Claim Form requires a claimant to explain reasons for any non-compliance with the Pre-Action Protocol and to specify any relief sought, including interim relief (in section 6 of the Form). For a full analysis of the types of remedies available in judicial review, see Chapter 3. In particular, note that remedies for breaches of human rights should be stated on the Claim Form (see below at 2-12) and that applications for interim relief should generally be made when the claim is lodged—see below at 3-36.

The form also requires a claimant to consider any other applications they may wish to make such as disclosure, protective costs order, reporting restrictions and abridgment or extension of time for the defendant's Acknowledgment of Service (section 7 of the Form).

2-13   Where a claimant raises an issue or seeks a remedy under the Human Rights Act (HRA)1998, the Claim Form must include the following information as required by paragraph 15 of CPR PD 16:

i.   precise details of the Convention right which it is alleged has been infringed and details of the alleged infringement;
ii. the relief sought;
iii. whether the relief sought includes:
   a)   a declaration of incompatibility in accordance with section 4 of that Act; or,
   b)   damages in respect of a judicial act to which section 9(3) of that Act applies;
iv. where the relief sought includes a declaration of incompatibility in accordance with section 4 of that Act, precise details of the legislative provision alleged to be incompatible and details of the alleged incompatibility;
v.   where the claim is founded on a finding of unlawfulness by another court or tribunal, details of the finding; and
vi. where the claim is founded on a judicial act which is alleged to have infringed a Convention right of the party as provided by section 9 of HRA 1998, the judicial act complained of and the court or tribunal which is alleged to have made it.

2-14   The claimant must also set out in the Claim Form the name and address of any person he considers to be an interested party (section 2).[60] An interested party is defined in

---

[59] Para 5.6 of PD 54A.
[60] CPR 54.6(1)(a).

Gráinne Mellon

CPR 54.1.2(f) as 'any person (other than the claimant and defendant) who is directly affected by the claim'. It is clear that a person will only be directly affected for the purposes of CPR 54.1.2(f) if they would be 'affected by the decision without the intervention of any intermediate agency'.[61] In criminal proceedings, the other parties to those proceedings must be named as interested parties.[62] In a claim by a defendant in proceedings before a Crown Court or a magistrates' court, the prosecution must always be named as an interested party.[63] The claimant must serve interested parties with a copy of the Claim Form.[64]

It is not necessary to name a government department or Minister as an interested party simply because a declaration of incompatibility under section 4 of the HRA 1998 is sought. In such cases, it is more appropriate to allow the High Court to order notice to the Crown.[65]

(2) The Bundle

The Claim Form must also be accompanied by a bundle of evidence and authorities, which PD 54A, para 5.6 states should include:

    2-15

i.   any written evidence in support of the claim or application to extend time;
ii.   a copy of any order that you are seeking to have quashed;
iii.   where the claim for judicial review relates to a decision of a court or tribunal, an approved copy of the reasons for reaching that decision;
iv.   copies of any documents upon which you propose to rely;
v.   copies of any relevant statutory material;
vi.   a list of essential documents for advance reading by the court (with page references to the passages relied upon). Where only part of a page needs to be read, that part should be indicated, by sidelining or in some other way, but not by highlighting.[66]

Typically, the bundle contains the letter before claim, the response and other relevant correspondence. The claimant has a duty of candour and should not fail to disclose unhelpful documents that are relevant.[67]

Where it is not possible to file all the above documents, the documents that have not been filed must be listed and reasons given as to why they are not currently available.[68] The claimant must also indicate when the documents are expected to be available. The defendant and/or interested party may seek an extension of time for the lodging of their Acknowledgment of Service pending receipt of missing documents.

---

[61] *R v Liverpool City Council, ex parte Muldoon* [1996] 1 WLR 1103.
[62] PD 54A, para 5.1.
[63] PD 54A, para 5.2.
[64] CPR 54.7(b).
[65] Practice Direction 19A, para 6.1.
[66] See Administrative Court Guidance, Notes for Guidance on applying for Judicial Review, available online at http://www.justice.gov.uk/downloads/courts/administrative-court/applying-for-judicial-review.pdf.
[67] See below at 2-17.
[68] Practice Direction 54A, para 5.8.

The claimant must file two copies of a paginated and indexed bundle containing all the documents referred to above for the Court's use.[69] Although not strictly required, it is advisable to file any authorities upon which the claimant relies at this stage (usually along with statutory material). The claimant must also lodge sufficient copies of the Claim Form so that the court may seal them and return them to the claimant to serve on the defendant and interested parties.

2-16   The Administrative Court may not accept applications that do not comply with the requirements of CPR Part 54 and PD 54A, even when accompanied by an undertaking to comply with the requirements of the CPR within a specified period, save in exceptional circumstances. For these purposes, the Administrative Court has stated that it equates exceptionality with urgency, and considers a matter to be exceptional where a decision is sought from the Court within 14 days of the lodging of the application.[70] Therefore, the fact that the time limit for a claim is due to expire is unlikely to be sufficient. In such circumstances, the Court will return the papers to the claimant to enable him to comply with the relevant requirements. In such circumstances, it is possible (but difficult) to seek an extension of time and provide reasons for the delay in lodging the papers in proper form.

(3) Duty of Disclosure

2-17   Claimants in judicial review proceedings are under a duty to disclose all material facts to the court. This is particularly the case when there are impediments to their claim such as delay,[71] an alternative remedy,[72] a statutory ouster clause[73] or an adverse authority.[74] It is also particularly the case in urgent or interim relief applications when the defendant may not be represented. The duty is a continuing duty: even after the papers have been lodged, claimants have a duty to update the court as to any material change in circumstances. For instance, a claimant must inform the court if the remedy sought by way of judicial review is no longer necessary, even if the claimant wishes to continue the claim as a test claim.[75]

The court has discretion both as to whether or not to take action in respect of nondisclosure, and as to what action to take. The court may refuse the relief sought[76] (or set aside permission or relief previously granted),[77] or may take the non-disclosure into account in making orders as to costs.[78]

---

[69] Practice Direction 54A, para 5.9.

[70] Administrative Court Guidance, 'Notes for guidance on applying for judicial review', para 7.10.

[71] *R v Lloyds of London ex parte Briggs* (1993) 5 Admin LR 698, 707 D.

[72] *R v Law Society, ex parte Bratsky Lespromyshlenny Complex* [1995] COD 216.

[73] *R v Cornwall County Council, ex parte Huntingdon* [1992] 3 All ER 566.

[74] *R v Secretary of State for the Home Department, ex parte Li Bin Shi* [1995] COD 135.

[75] *R (Tshikangu) v Newham London Borough Council* [2001] EWHC Admin 92.

[76] *R v Leeds City Council, ex parte Hendry* (1994) 6 Admin LR 439.

[77] *R (Khan) v Secretary of State for the Home Department* [2008] EWHC 1367 (Admin).

[78] Cost implications can be in the form of wasted costs orders (*R v Secretary of State for the Home Office, ex parte Shahina Begum* [1995] COD 176) but also in the form of inter-partes cost orders (*R v Liverpool City Council, ex parte Filla* [1996] COD 24). See at 16-6 below.

Gráinne Mellon

Defendants also have a duty of disclosure. This duty is a 'very high duty ... to assist the court with full and accurate explanations for all the facts relevant to the issue the court must decide'.[79] Defendants must make full and frank disclosure of all relevant material and cannot be selective in the material they disclose or present.[80] The duty of candour includes disclosure at the permission stage, if permission is resisted.

(4) Where to Issue

Claims are issued in the Administrative Court. The Administrative Court is a special-   **2-18**
ist court within the Queen's Bench Division of the High Court. It sits in London, with District Registries in Birmingham, Manchester, Leeds and Cardiff. If the claimant is not located in London the claim can be issued in one of the District Registries. If the claimant is not based in one of those cities, they may need to contact an agent to issue on their behalf. Agents will charge a fee to issue documents at the Court. Papers can be lodged in person or via the Document Exchange or postal system.

The general expectation is that proceedings will be administered and determined in the region with which the claimant has the closest connection. Practice Direction 54D (*Administrative Court (Venue)*) provides the following considerations as applicable:

i.   any reason expressed by any party for preferring a particular venue;
ii.   the region in which the defendant, or any relevant office or department of the defendant, is based;
iii.   the region in which the claimant's legal representatives are based;
iv.   the ease and cost of travel to a hearing;
v.   the availability and suitability of alternative means of attending a hearing (for example, by video link);
vi.   the extent and nature of media interest in the proceedings in any particular locality;
vii.   the time within which it is appropriate for the proceedings to be determined;
viii.   whether it is desirable to administer or determine the claim in another region in the light of the volume of claims issued at, and the capacity, resources and workload of, the court at which it is issued;
ix.   whether the claim raises issues sufficiently similar to those in another outstanding claim to make it desirable that it should be determined together with, or immediately following, that other claim; and
x.   whether the claim raises devolution issues and for that reason whether it should more appropriately be determined in London or Cardiff.[81]

If the claimant wishes his or her case to be heard in a region other than that in which the claim was issued, that should be addressed in the Claim Form and/or grounds. The court may, on an application by a party or of its own initiative, direct that the claim be determined in a region other than that of the venue in which the claim is currently assigned.[82]

---

[79] *R (Quark Fishing Ltd) v Secretary of State for Foreign and Commonwealth Affairs* [2002] EWCA Civ 1409 [50].
[80] *Lancashire County Council v Taylor* [2005] EWCA Civ 284.
[81] CPR PD 54D para 5.4.
[82] ibid, para 5.3.

'Expected classes of claim' should be issued at the Administrative Court Office in the High Court in London.[83] These include cases involving control orders, terrorist cases, special advocate cases and cases under the Proceeds of Crime Act 2002 and appeals to the Administrative Court under the Extradition Act 2003.

(i) Costs of Issuing

2-19 A fee is payable in order to lodge an application for permission to apply for judicial review. The current fee is £140. A further £700 is payable if permission is granted.[84]

Where the Court refuses permission to proceed, the claimant may not appeal but may request the decision to be reconsidered at a hearing. If such a request is made, the claimant must pay an additional fee of £350. A further £350 is payable if permission is granted. If the Claim Form is lodged in person at the Administrative Court Office, personal cheques must be supported by a cheque guarantee card presented at the time the Claim Form is lodged. A full or partial remission on fees may be available to some applicants. In such circumstances, an EX160 (Application for Fee Remission) should then be filled in and lodged with the Claim Form.

Fees may be paid by credit or debit card in London when presented in person to the Royal Courts of Justice Fees office. The Administrative Court Office in Cardiff will accept payment by debit card only when presented in person at their office. The Birmingham, Manchester and Leeds offices accept payment by both credit and debit cards at their counters and over the telephone. Cheques should be made payable to "HM Courts and Tribunals Service".

(5) Service of the Claim Form

2-20 The Administrative Court will return one sealed copy of the bundle. The claimant must then serve the original sealed copy of the Claim Form (and accompanying documents) on the defendant and (unless the court directs otherwise) any interested party within seven days of the date of issue (ie the date shown on the court seal).[85] Whilst there is no requirement to serve the defendant and any interested party with an Acknowledgment of Service (N462—contained in Annex 4) for completion by them, it is good practice to do so.

A Certificate of Service (Form N215) should be lodged in the relevant Administrative Court Office within seven days of serving the defendant and other interested parties.

The date of deemed service and method of service is calculated in accordance with CPR Parts 6.14 and 7.5.1. Documents may be served by: personal service, first class post, leaving the document at an address for service, document exchange, fax or other means of electronic communication.[86]

---

[83] ibid, para 3.1.
[84] The Civil Proceedings Fees (Amendment) Order 2014, SI 2014/874. This is an increase from £60 to apply for permission and £215 if permission was granted prior to 22 April 2014 under the Civil Proceedings Fees (Amendment) Order 2011 (SI 2011/586).
[85] CPR 54.7.
[86] CPR 6.3.1.

Gráinne Mellon

(6) Urgent Cases

There is no guidance in CPR Part 54 as to urgent applications for permission to apply   **2-21**
for judicial review. Instead the *Practice Statement (Administrative Court: Listing and
Urgent Cases)*[87] introduced a relatively simple system which enables claims to be considered at very short notice and often within hours:

Urgent cases procedure

CPR Pt 54 makes no express provision for urgent applications for permission to apply for
judicial review to be made orally. As the result of user's concerns I now issue guidance on the
procedure to be applied for urgent applications and for interim injunctions. Advocates must
comply with this guidance; and where a manifestly inappropriate application is made, consideration will be given to a wasted costs order. The full terms of the guidance and the form for
use in this procedure are annexed to this statement (Annex B).[88]

1. The Administrative Court currently allocates paper applications for judicial review on a
   daily basis and one judge also act as the 'urgent judge'.
2. Where a claimant makes an application for the permission application to be heard as a
   matter of urgency and/or seeks an interim injunction, he must complete a prescribed form
   which states: (a) the need for urgency; (b) the timescale sought for the consideration of the
   permission application, eg within 72 hours or sooner if necessary; and (c) the date by which
   the substantive hearing should take place.
3. Where an interim injunction is sought, a claimant must, in addition, provide (a) a draft
   order; and (b) the grounds for the injunction.
4. The claimant must serve (by fax and post) the claim form and application for urgency on
   the defendant and interested parties, advising them of the application and that they may
   make representations.
5. Where an interim injunction is sought, the claimant must serve (by fax and post) the draft
   order and grounds for the application on the defendant and interested parties, advising
   them of the application and that they may make representations.
6. A judge will consider the application within the time requested and may make such order
   as he considers appropriate.
7. If the judge directs that an oral hearing take place within a specified time the representatives of the parties and the Administrative Court will liaise to fix a permission hearing
   within the time period directed.

Where a claimant wishes to apply for the permission application to be heard as a matter   **2-22**
of urgency and/or seeks an interim injunction, an application should be made on Form
N463: Application for Urgent Consideration (contained in Annex 3). This form can
also be obtained from the HMCS website or the relevant Administrative Court Office.
For a detailed consideration of the rules on applications for interim relief see below at
section J in Chapter 3 below.

The Urgent Consideration form requires the claimant's advocate to:

i.   set out the reasons for urgency;
ii. disclose the timescale sought for consideration of the permission application,
     eg within 72 hours, or sooner if necessary;

---

[87] *Practice Statement (Administrative Court: Listing and Urgent Cases)* [2002] 1 WLR 810 (QBD).
[88] Annex B has now been superseded by Form N463.

   iii.   state the date by which the substantive hearing should take place;

   iv.   set out the grounds for interim relief (if required);

   v.   provide a separate draft order for interim relief;

   vi.   demonstrate that the form (and draft order and grounds, if required) has been served (by fax and post) on the defendant and interested parties advising them of the application and that they may make representations.

The Urgent Consideration form must be submitted along with a Claim Form and both must be served (by fax and post) on the defendant and interested parties before being lodged with the Court. If it has not been appropriate or possible to comply with the Pre-Action Protocol and send a letter before claim, the reasons must be fully explained in the Claim Form.

The duty judge will consider the Urgent Consideration form and accompanying Claim Form. On the Urgent Consideration form there is a section asking within how many hours or days the application for permission should be considered. The form includes a section on 'Immediate consideration', which must be filled in if consideration is sought within 48 hours, in which case the claimant will need to justify why immediate consideration is required.[89]

2-23   A judge will consider the application within the time requested and may make such order as he/she considers appropriate. The judge may grant interim relief on the papers and/or direct an oral hearing, in which case permission will usually be dealt with at the same time, with time for Acknowledgment of Service abridged. If the judge directs that an oral hearing must take place within a specified time, the Administrative Court will liaise with the representatives of the parties to fix a permission hearing within the time period directed.

The judge may also refuse the application for urgent permission and/or interim relief at this stage. If this occurs, it is possible to seek to renew the application orally to the High Court.[90]

2-24   A CL Application 6 Emergency Legal Aid form may be used in urgent circumstances.[91] The Administrative Court may also take a written undertaking from solicitors in lieu of the issue fee in urgent cases.

Where a manifestly inappropriate urgency application is made, consideration may be given to making a wasted costs order.[92] It is always important to consider whether an application is truly urgent or could in fact be dealt with within a reduced time for response to a letter before claim.

(7) Out of Hours Applications

2-25   In the event that it is necessary to make an out-of-hours urgent application (in which case the procedure set out above is not possible), an application may be made to the

---

[89] The absolute importance of completing the recently introduced Form N463 and the duty of full and frank disclosure in any ex parte hearing has been emphasised on a number of occasions, primarily in the context of immigration removals. See *R (Hamid) v Secretary of State for the Home Department* [2012] EWHC 3070 (Admin); *R (Rehman) v Secretary of State for the Home Department* [2013] EWHC 1351 (Admin) [3]: '[T]his court always deals with applications submitted within court hours through the judge who is dealing with them in court hours ... If the solicitors have not heard, they must wait.' See also below at 3-37.

[90] See below at 2-31.

[91] See below at 15-34.

[92] *Practice Statement (Administrative Court: Listing and Urgent Cases)* (n 87).

duty judge at the Royal Courts of Justice. In such cases, the duty judge's clerk should be contacted by telephone. The clerk will then forward an Out of Hours Application Form ('OHA'), which should be completed and returned to the clerk in advance of the judge considering the papers. The application will then typically be heard in person on the telephone. The defendant is normally unrepresented although there is no reason in principle why they cannot participate.

Extra caution is required when making an out-of-hours application and claimants must bear in mind the warning to legal representatives issued in *R (Hamid) v Secretary of State for the Home Department* by Sir John Thomas P:

> If any firm fails to provide the information required on the form and in particular explain the reasons for urgency, the time at which the need for immediate consideration was first appreciated and the efforts made to notify the defendant, the court will require the attendance in open court of the solicitor from the firm who was responsible, together with his senior partner. It will list not only the name of the case but the firm concerned. Non-compliance cannot be allowed to continue.[93]

If the out-of-hours application is successful, the duty judge frequently directs the claimant to lodge the Claim Form and related documents at the start of business on the next working day.

If the judge makes a determination, whether or not the out-of-hours application is successful, the claimant must file their out-of-hours application with the court the next working day, together with an application fee of £45. The form and the fee should be sent to the Royal Courts of Justice Fees Office.

E. The Defendant's Acknowledgement of Service

(1) The Acknowledgment of Service

Any person who has been served with the Claim Form and who wishes to take part   **2-26**
in the judicial review should file an Acknowledgment of Service (Form N462—also referred to as an 'AoS' and included in Annex 4).[94] The form should be filed in the Administrative Court Office within 21 days of service of the Claim Form.[95]

The Acknowledgment of Service must then be served upon the claimant and the interested parties as soon as practicable and in any event not later than seven days after it is filed with the Court.

The purpose of the Acknowledgment of Service is for the defendant and any interested parties to state whether or not permission is resisted and if so to explain why it should be refused. The Acknowledgment of Service therefore must set out the summary of grounds for contesting the claim (both factual and legal). The level of detail required will depend on the nature of the claim and the extent to which the defendant's case is already clear from the response to the letter before claim. While there is no express provision for submitting documentation to accompany the Acknowledgment of Service, it

---

[93] *R (Hamid) v Secretary of State for the Home Department* [2012] EWHC 3070 (Admin) [7].
[94] CPR 54.8(1).
[95] CPR 54.8(2).

is not prohibited and it is not uncommon for defendants to serve the key documents on which they rely at this stage. The format and presentation of any accompanying bundle should mirror that detailed above.[96]

The Acknowledgment of Service must also set out the name and address of any person considered to be an interested party (who has not previously been identified and served as an interested party).

(2) Extensions of Time

2-27   The parties cannot agree to extend time: permission for any extension must be sought from the Court.[97] However, in practice, if the parties are in agreement to this course of action, the Court is likely to give its permission.

(3) Failure to File

2-28   A party who fails to file an Acknowledgment of Service may not take part in any permission hearing, unless the Court allows him to.[98] Further, the failure may be taken into account in later decisions as to costs.[99] However, such a party is not precluded from taking part in the substantive hearing, subject to complying with the relevant rules for detailed grounds and evidence in CPR 54.9(1)(b).

(4) Claimant's Reply

2-29   There is a growing practice for claimants, in advance of the consideration of permission, to put in a 'Reply' submission which typically responds to the defendant's summary grounds. It is advisable to liaise with the Administrative Court Office in this respect so that a decision on permission is not given before the reply is received. The defendant can also submit a Rejoinder, but this is more unusual.

F. Obtaining Permission for a Claim to Proceed

(1) Consideration on the Papers

2-30   Applications for permission to proceed with the claim for judicial review are considered by a single judge on the papers.[100] The purpose of this procedure is to ensure that applications are dealt with speedily and without unnecessary expense.

---

[96] See above at 2-15.
[97] CPR 54.8.3.
[98] CPR 54.9(1)(a).
[99] CPR 54.9(2).
[100] There may be exceptions in judicial reviews of decisions by the Criminal Cases Review Commission. In such cases the permission decision may be dealt with at an oral hearing (see below for further discussion at section C in Chapter 9).

Gráinne Mellon

The papers will be forwarded to a judge by the Administrative Court Office upon receipt of the Acknowledgement of Service or at the expiry of the time limit for lodging such acknowledgement—whichever is earlier.

The judge's decision and the reasons for it (Form JRJ) will be served upon the claimant, the defendant and any other person served with the Claim Form.

The judge may:

i. grant permission (on some or all grounds);
ii. order the parties to attend an oral hearing and make submissions;
i. refuse permission; or
ii. refuse permission and certify the claim as 'totally without merit'.[101]

The test as to whether or not permission should be granted is a flexible one. The claimant must be able to show that there is 'an arguable ground for judicial review having a realistic prospect of success and not subject to a discretionary bar such as delay or an alternative remedy'.[102] The question is whether 'there is a point fit for further investigation on a full inter partes basis with all such evidence as is necessary on the facts and all such argument as is necessary on the law'.[103]

On occasion, the permission application is conducted as if it is a mini-hearing with detailed evidence and argument. In such cases, permission will be granted where the claimant shows a 'reasonably good chance of success'.[104] The Court of Appeal has stated that cases where the issues are explored in depth at permission stage are 'quite exceptional'.[105]

It is possible for the parties to invite the Court to dispense with the paper sift and invite the Court to hold a hearing on permission.

It is also possible for the permission hearing to be followed immediately by the substantive hearing—known as a 'rolled up' hearing. This may be requested by the parties or by the judge reviewing the papers.

(2) Challenging the Refusal of Permission

(i) Reconsideration at an Oral Hearing

In either criminal or civil cases, if permission is refused, or is granted subject to conditions or on certain grounds only, it is possible to request a reconsideration of that decision at an oral hearing.[106] In criminal cases, the renewed application is usually made to a Divisional Court; in other cases the application is made to a single High Court Judge.

2-31

---

[101] Civil Procedure (Amendment No 4) Rules 2013 (SI 2012/1412). The meaning of the words 'totally without merit' was considered in *R (Grace) v Secretary of State for the Home Department* – judgment handed down after law cut-off date of this edition.

[102] *R v Legal Aid Board, ex parte Hughes* (1992) 5 Admin LR 623.

[103] *R v Secretary of State for the Home Department, ex parte Rukshanda Begum* [1990] COD 107,108 CA. See also *Sharma v Browne-Antoine* [2006] UKPC 57 [14(4)].

[104] *Mass Energy v Birmingham City Council* [1994] Env LR 298.

[105] *Davey v Aylesbury Vale District Council* [2008] 1 WLR 878 [12].

[106] There is no right to request reconsideration at an oral hearing in cases which have been certified as totally without merit. See below at 2-34.

A request for an oral hearing must be made on the Notice of Renewal, Form 86b, and must be filed within seven days after service of the notification of the judge's decision.[107] This form requests a statement of grounds for renewing. In practice, these are typically quite brief.

The claimant must pay a fee of £350 when requesting a renewal hearing.[108] It is likely that an extension to the claimant's funding certificate will need to be sought. The claimant will once again have to meet the merits test in order for an extension to be granted.[109]

An oral hearing is allocated a total of 30 minutes of court time. If it is considered that 30 minutes of court time is insufficient, it is possible to provide a written estimate of the time required for the hearing and request a special fixture.

There is no requirement on any party to provide a skeleton argument in advance of a permission hearing however it is good practice to do so. Any such skeleton should typically rebut the reasons for refusal of permission given by the judge reviewing the matter on the papers.

Although CPR PD 54 indicates that neither the defendant nor any other interested party need attend a hearing on the question of permission unless the court directs otherwise,[110] in practice the defendant and any interested party will normally attend the renewed hearing.

For criminal causes or matters, there is no further remedy in the domestic courts after a refusal of permission by the Administrative Court.

2-32   *(ii) Further Appeals against a Refusal of Permission*

In criminal causes or matters, once permission has been refused after an oral hearing, there are very limited routes for appeal. There is no appeal to the Court of Appeal from a refusal by a Divisional Court to grant permission to apply for judicial review in a criminal case.[111] The Supreme Court has no jurisdiction to hear an appeal against a refusal by a Divisional Court of permission to apply for judicial review in a criminal case.[112] So, if a Divisional Court refuses permission to apply to it for judicial review in a criminal matter, there is no further remedy in the domestic courts. The only circumstances in which an application may be made to the Supreme Court for permission to appeal from a Divisional Court in a criminal cause or matter are when the High Court certifies that a point of law of general public importance arises from its decision.[113]

---

[107] CPR 54.11 and 54.12.
[108] See n 125 in Chapter 3.
[109] See Chapter 15 below at 15-16.
[110] Practice Direction 54A, para 8.5.
[111] Senior Courts Act 1981 s18(1)(a).
[112] Administration of Justice Act 1960 s1(1) & (2) and the decisions of the House of Lords in *Re Poh* [1983] 1 WLR 2, [1983] 1 All ER 287, *R (Burkett) v Hammersmith and Fulham LBC (No 1)* [2002] UKHL 23, [2002] 1 WLR 1593, and *R (Eastaway) v Secretary of State for Trade and Industry* [2001] 1 WLR 2222. See n 158 below.
[113] Supreme Court Practice Direction 12.2.6.

In practice, it is unlikely that the Administrative Court will agree to issue a certificate of general public importance on an application for permission. A possible solution to this quandary is for the Administrative Court to grant permission and also refuse the substantive claim so that a claimant can appeal to the Supreme Court in the usual way (see below at 2-44).

In cases, which are not criminal causes or matters, if permission is refused after an oral hearing, it is possible to renew the permission application to the Court of Appeal.[114] The application must be made within 7 days[115] and the appeal procedure in Part 52 of the CPR is followed. The application is considered first on the papers and an oral hearing can also be ordered if necessary. If the Court of Appeal grants permission to apply for judicial review, it can proceed to determine the substantive claim. It will do this, typically where an oral hearing for permission is ordered as this avoids the need for two hearings. In other cases however, the Court of Appeal will remit the claim back to the Administrative Court for the substantive hearing.

(iii) Totally Without Merit Appeals

2-33

Where a judge certifies an application for permission to bring a judicial review claim as 'totally without merit', the claimant does not have a right to have the permission application reconsidered orally.[116] In such cases, the only appeal is to the Court of Appeal on the papers only, with no right to an oral hearing before the Court of Appeal.[117]

In criminal causes or matters, it appears that CPR 54.12.7 applies and therefore a decision to refuse permission and certify a case as totally without merit is final. As with criminal causes or matter generally (see section above) the Court of Appeal has no jurisdiction to consider an appeal from a judgment of the High Court.[118] Further, the Supreme Court typically only has jurisdiction to consider refusals of permission to apply for judicial review when a certificate of a point of general public importance has been granted.[119] It is likely that the courts will be asked to consider the issue of whether or not CPR 54.12.7 applies to judicial reviews in criminal causes or matters in due course.

G. Preparation for a Substantive Hearing

(1) Grant of Permission

On granting permission the Court may make case management directions for the progression of the case.[120] These directions may include directions as to venue, service of the Claim Form and any evidence on other persons and as to expedition. Where a claim

2-34

---

[114] 52.15 (2) CPR.
[115] 52.15 (2) CPR.
[116] CPR 54.12(7).
[117] CPR 52.15(1A)(b). See *R(RG-Albania) v Secretary of State for the Home Department (C4/13/2419).*
[118] Senior Courts Act 1981, s 18(1)(a).
[119] See also Supreme Court Practice Direction, para 12.2.5 and *Eastaway* (n 112).
[120] CPR 54.10(1).

is made under the HRA 1998, a direction may be made for the giving of notice to the Crown or joining the Crown as a party.[121]

If the judge grants permission and the claim is pursued, a further fee of £700 (or a further Application for Remission of Fee (Form EX160)) must be lodged with the relevant Administrative Court Office within seven days of service of the judge's decision. Failure to lodge this fee can result in the file being closed. If this occurs, it is possible to apply to the Administrative Court to re-open the file. A good explanation for the delay will usually be required.[122]

(2) Defendant's Detailed Grounds of Opposition and Evidence

2-35   If a defendant or interested party wishes to contest the claim (or support it on additional grounds), they must, within 35 days of service of the order granting permission, file and serve on the court and all of the other parties detailed grounds for contesting the claim (or supporting it on additional grounds) and any written evidence relied upon.[123] Where documents are relied on, they must be served in a paginated bundle.[124]

In theory, a defendant who has not complied with these requirements cannot take part in the hearing without seeking an extension of time. In practice, however, it is possible for a defendant to rely on their summary grounds of defence, particularly if they are detailed and accompanied by supporting documentation.

The duty of candour imposed on defendants applies in the drafting of the detailed grounds and the decision as to what documents to disclose.[125]

(3) Reconsideration by the Claimant and/or Amending of Claimant's Case

2-36   The claimant is under a duty to reconsider the claim following service of the defendant's detailed grounds and evidence.[126]

If the claimant wishes to amend his case, or rely on grounds other than those for which permission was granted, they require permission and must give not less than seven clear days' notice before the hearing (or warned) date.[127] The claimant must serve all parties with copies of the proposed amendments and any additional written evidence.

(4) Interim Applications[128]

2-37   Once permission has been granted, the parties should consider whether they wish to make any interim applications, such as for disclosure, further or expert evidence or cross-examination.

---

121 CPR 19.4A and para 6 of PD supplementing s 1 of Pt 19.
122 CPR 3.9 permits a party to apply for relief from any sanction imposed by the Court.
123 CPR 54.14.
124 PD 54A, para 10.1.
125 See above at 2-17.
126 *R v Liverpool City Justices & Crown Prosecution Services v Price* (1998) 162 JP 766; *R (Bateman & Ors) v Legal Services Commission* [2001] EWHC Admin 797.
127 CPR 54.15 and PD 54A, para 11.1.
128 Applications for interim relief are dealt with below at section J in Chapter 3.

The Administrative Court rarely engages in factual disputes, and orders for cross-examination or oral evidence of any kind are unusual. Most commonly, where factual disputes exist, the court will resolve them in favour of the defendant.[129] The court will make orders for cross-examination in some cases, in particular where there is a disputed allegation of a 'hard-edged question of fact' relating to a human rights breach,[130] or where fundamental rights are at stake and the court has to review the merits of the decision.[131] The court has considered oral evidence in cases which do not engage the ECHR. If necessary, the court has the power to transfer a case for trial.[132]

Likewise, although it is unusual for further evidence to be served after the defendant's detailed grounds, permission may be given for further evidence.[133] In practice, most applications to admit further evidence are dealt with by consent. Permission is specifically required for any party to rely on expert evidence.

Where an interim application is required, a specific notice of application (N244) should be lodged in the Administrative Court.[134] A fee of £80 must be paid. The applicant should set out what is being sought and why (a draft order should be attached) and explain whether the matter requires a hearing or not.[135] The court may order that a hearing should take place.[136] The applicant must serve the application notice, and any evidence in support, on the other parties as soon as practicable and in any event at least three days before the court is due to deal with the application.[137]

(5) Listing for the Full Hearing

The Administrative Court Listing Office typically liaises with counsel to fix a date for the hearing.[138] However, if the parties do not contact the court within 48 hours to agree a date, the date will be fixed by the court. If this occurs, an adjournment must be agreed by all parties or obtained following an application on notice to the court. It is possible to request an order for expedition if there is a reason why the matter should be heard quickly.   **2-38**

While the Administrative Court usually gives fixed dates for hearings, some cases are placed in the short warned list, where they can be called on at less than a day's notice from the warned date.[139] The parties must keep the court informed of any matters likely to affect the length of the hearing.

---

[129] *R v Board of Visitors of Hull Prison, ex parte St Germain (No 2)* [1979] 1 WLR 1401.
[130] *R (Al-Sweady) v Secretary of State* [2010] HRLR 2 [19].
[131] *R (Wilkinson) v RMO Broadmoor Hospital* [2002] 1 WLR 419.
[132] CPR 54.20.
[133] CPR 54.16.
[134] CPR 23.3(1).
[135] CPR 23.6 and PD 23A, para 2.1.
[136] PD 23A, para 2.5.
[137] CPR 23.7(1).
[138] *Practice Statement (Administrative Court: Listing and Urgent Cases)* (n 87).
[139] The Administrative Court Listing Policy is available at: www.justice.gov.uk/courts/rcj-rolls-building/administrative-court/listing-policy.

(6) Skeleton Arguments and Bundles

2-39   The claimant must file a skeleton argument not less than 21 working days before the date of the hearing of the judicial review (or the warned date).[140]

At the same time as filing his or her skeleton argument, the claimant must file a paginated and indexed bundle of all relevant documents required for the hearing of the judicial review.[141] This bundle must also include those documents required by the defendant and any other party who is to make representations at the hearing.[142]

The defendant and any other party wishing to make representations at the hearing of the judicial review must file and serve a skeleton argument not less than 14 working days before the date of the hearing of the judicial review (or the warned date).[143]

Paragraph 15.3 of PD 54A requires that skeleton arguments must contain:

i.   a time estimate for the complete hearing (including delivery of judgment);
ii. a list of issues;
iii. a list of the legal points to be taken (together with relevant authorities with page references to the passages relied on);
iv. a chronology of events (with page references to the bundle of documents (see paragraph 16.1);
v.   a list of essential documents for the advance reading of the court (with page references to the passages relied on) (if different from that filed with the Claim Form) and a time estimate for that reading; and
vi. a list of persons referred to.

Skeleton arguments may now be lodged in the Administrative Court London Office and each of the Regional Offices, by email. Each region has its own dedicated email address for skeleton arguments, with London having dedicated addresses for extradition and criminal matters.[144] Note that if skeleton arguments are received after 4.30pm the day before the hearing they may not reach the judge, and, if they are received on the day of the hearing they will not reach the judge. An automated confirmation email is sent when a skeleton argument has been received. It is always advisable to bring copies of skeleton arguments to court.

The claimant should provide a paginated and indexed trial bundle with all the documents relied upon by any party to the proceedings.[145] This is usually prepared in advance of the submission of skeleton arguments, which should refer to pages of the bundle. While there is no requirement to provide a bundle of authorities, it is good practice for the claimant to agree one with the defendant and lodge it two to three days in advance of the hearing, to enable the court to refer to the authorities as part of their preparation.

If the case is being heard by a single judge, only one copy of the skeleton and the bundles needs to be lodged with the Administrative Court. However, if it being heard by a Divisional Court, two or three copies should be supplied as appropriate.

---

[140] PD 15.1.
[141] PD 54A, para 16.1.
[142] PD 54A, para 16.2.
[143] PD 15.2.
[144] See www.justice.gov.uk/courts/rcj-rolls-building/administrative-court. A helpful skeleton argument template is also available on this page.
[145] PD 54A, para 16.1.

Gráinne Mellon

H. The Substantive Hearing

(1) Composition of the Court

When permission has been granted on the papers or subsequent to a permission hear-   **2-40**
ing, a full hearing on the merits of the claim for judicial review will usually take place
some months later. In urgent criminal matters, it is not unusual for the permission
hearing to be followed immediately by the substantive hearing—known as a 'rolled up'
hearing. As indicated above at 2-30, this may be requested by the parties in the application for permission or ordered by the judge reviewing the papers.

While, in principle, criminal causes or matters may be heard by a single judge, in
practice most such cases are heard by a Divisional Court[146] of two or, on rare occasions
in cases of particular importance three judges.[147] Civil matters may also be heard by a
Divisional Court. The composition is almost always a Lord or Lady Justice of Appeal
and a High Court judge.

The Queens' Bench Divisional Court is not a court of first instance or a court of
appeal. It has a unique and multi purpose function that is generally, a court of review.[148]
Where two judges of a Divisional Court disagree, the appeal is dismissed.[149]

Urgent cases may be heard by a single judge, and this is the prescribed practice for
judicial reviews of decisions on bail in the Crown Court (see below at 7-17). The order
granting permission may specify whether the case is suitable for a single judge. If a judge
has refused permission on the papers, the case will not normally be listed before them.[150]

(2) Evidence and Procedure

The claimant usually makes his or her submissions first, followed by the defendant and   **2-41**
any interested party. The claimant makes the final submissions. There is very rarely any
live evidence (see 2-37 above).

(3) Judgment

The time estimate given in the skeleton argument assumes that judgment will be given   **2-42**
at the hearing. If so, it will be transcribed but it is advisable to make a note in case

---

[146] See above at 1-37.
[147] *Wilcock v Muckle* [1951] 2 KB 844 [1951] All ER 367. By virtue of the Senior Courts Act 1981, s 66 a
Divisional Court 'may be held' for any business which 'is required to be heard' by 'or by virtue' of the 'rules of court
or any other statutory provision'. According to the Administrative Court website, judicial reviews in a criminal
cause or matter 'can be' or are 'usually' heard by a Divisional Court. This is a reflection of the old RSC Ord 53(1),
which required any judicial review in a criminal cause or matter to be heard by a Divisional Court. RSC Ord 53
was repealed by Civil Procedure (Amendment No 4) Rules 2000, SI 2000/2092, r 23. Divisional Courts will also
hear any applications to extend time for an application for permission to appeal to the Supreme Court or for the
criminal defendant to be present at such a hearing (RSC Ord 109 as preserved in CPR Sch 1). A Divisional Court
will hear an application for habeas corpus if the Court so directs (RSC Ord 54(1)(1) as preserved in CPR, Sch 1).
[148] *R v Leeds County Court, ex parte Morris* [1990] 1 QB 523, [1990] All ER 550 (DC).
[149] *Cambridgeshire County Council v Associated Lead Mills Ltd* [2005] EWHC 1627 (Admin).
[150] *R (Mohammed) v Special Adjudicator* [2002] EWHC 2496 (Admin) [4].

Gráinne Mellon

of an urgent appeal. If an appeal is sought, a party can ask for leave to appeal after judgment is delivered and if publicly funded, an assessment of costs.

Often, a confidential judgment will be prepared in advance with a direction for the parties to submit typing corrections and notes of other obvious errors. The parties need not attend for handing down of judgment if all consequential orders have been agreed and may not recover costs if they attend unnecessarily.

Counsel will usually be asked to agree a draft minute of Order to be lodged with the court. Once sealed, the Order of the court is final, subject to correction under the slip rule.[151]

I. Appeal[152]

(1) Criminal Cause or Matter: the Supreme Court

2-43 In the case of a criminal cause or matter (discussed above at 1-168 and 2-33) before the Administrative Court, the only route of appeal lies to the Supreme Court by a prosecutor or a defendant.[153] The Court of Appeal has no jurisdiction to consider appeals in criminal judicial reviews, whether an appeal against a refusal of permission or against a decision at a substantive hearing.[154]

In order to appeal to the Supreme Court, permission from the Administrative Court or the Supreme Court is required. Permission may only be granted if the Administrative Court certifies that a point of law of general public importance is involved and it appears that the point is one that ought to be considered by the Supreme Court.[155] If the Administrative Court does not grant a certificate the Supreme Court has no jurisdiction to hear an application for permission.[156] A certificate is not required on a criminal application for habeas corpus or by a minister of the Crown, where they have been joined to criminal proceedings, and they seek to appeal a declaration of incompatibility under section 5(4) of the Human Rights Act 1998.

An application for permission to appeal should be made first to the Administrative Court within 28 days of the date of the decision.[157] An application for a certificate of public importance is usually considered at the same time. An application for leave to appeal to the Supreme Court should be made within 28 days from the date on which

---

151 CPR 40.12.

152 This section considers appealing substantive judicial review decisions. For consideration of appealing decisions to refuse permission, see above at 2-33.

153 Administration of Justice Act 1960, s 1.

154 Senior Courts Act 1981, s 18(1)(a) and Supreme Court Practice Direction para 12.2.6.

155 Administration of Justice Act 1960, s 1(2) and Supreme Court PD paras 12.2.1 and 12.1.4

156 Supreme Court PD 12.1.4 and 12.2.5, which also refers to *Gelberg v Miller* [1961] 1 WLR 459 and *Jones v DPP* [1962] AC 635.

157 The Administration of Justice Act 1960, s 2(1) and Supreme Court PD 12.3.1. This date is the date on which permission is refused, rather than when a point of law was certified (PD 12.3.2). Note under s 2(3) that the Supreme Court or the Administrative Court may extend the time on application by the (criminal) defendant.

the Administrative Court refused permission.[158] Applications for permission to the Supreme Court must follow the provisions of Supreme Court Practice Direction 3. It is unusual for the Administrative Court to grant permission to appeal. In practice, it is likely to be necessary to obtain leave from the Supreme Court.

Time begins to run from the date of the decision of the Administrative Court or, if later, the date on which the Court provided reasons for its decision.[159]

In order to dispose with an appeal, the Supreme Court may exercise any of the powers of the Administrative Court or may remit the case to that Court.[160]

Guidance for preparation of appeals to the Supreme Court can be found in the Supreme Court's Practice Directions 3–7.[161] These apply equally to criminal and civil appeals. Practice Direction 12 deals with criminal proceedings. Applicants should consult Parts 2–4 of the Rules of the Supreme Court 2009 (SI 2009/1603).[162] The forms for appeals to the Supreme Court can be found on the Supreme Court website.[163]

(2) Civil Appeals

In civil cases it is possible to appeal to the Court of Appeal (Civil Division).[164] Permission is required from either the Administrative Court or the Court of Appeal.[165] It is not necessary to seek permission from the Administrative Court, but it is usual to do so. An application for permission to the Administrative Court is usually made when judgment is handed down, but can be made in writing following the circulation of a draft judgment.

2-44

If this is not done (or the application is refused), an application for permission can be made to the Court of Appeal by way of a Notice of Appeal (N161). The notice should be accompanied by grounds of appeal and a skeleton argument[166] lodged within 21 days of the judgment.[167]

Permission will only be granted if there is a real prospect of success or there is some other compelling reason why the appeal should be heard.[168]

At a substantive hearing an appeal will only be allowed if the decision of the lower court was either wrong or it was unjust because of some serious procedural or other irregularity (CPR 52.11(3)). 'Wrong' can mean that the judge erred in law, erred in fact or erred in the exercise of his/her discretion.

In the event the Court of Appeal dismisses the appeal, it is possible to appeal to the Supreme Court for permission to appeal. This must be made within 28 days of the

2-45

---

[158] ibid, s 2(1).
[159] The Administration of Justice Act 1960, s 2(1A). Note the shorter time limits that apply to certain matters under the Extradition Act 2003 and Proceeds of Crime Act 2002 (PD 12.3.3).
[160] The Administration of Justice Act 1960, s 1(4).
[161] These can be accessed online at http://supremecourt.uk/procedures/practice-directions.html.
[162] http://supremecourt.uk/docs/uksc_rules_2009.pdf.
[163] http://supremecourt.uk/procedures/court-forms.html.
[164] Please see the definition of what is a 'criminal cause or matter' above at 1-168.
[165] Practice Direction 52A, para 4.1.
[166] Practice Direction 52, para 5.9 (1).
[167] CPR 52.4(2).
[168] CPR 52.3(6).

decision appealed against.[169] Time runs from the date of the substantive order appealed and not from the date on which the order is sealed or the date of any subsequent procedural order (e.g. an order refusing permission to appeal.)[170]

Permission to appeal is granted for applications that, in the opinion of the Appeal Panel, raise an arguable point of law of general public importance which ought to be considered by the Supreme Court at that time, bearing in mind that the matter will already have been the subject of judicial decision and may have already been reviewed on appeal. [171]

For guidance on the preparation of appeals to the Supreme Court, see 2-43 above.

J. Settlement and Discontinuance

(1) Settlement

2-46   Parties are encouraged to seek settlement at every stage of the process. The receipt of the letter before claim or the grant of permission are often crucial stages for settlement negotiations. If the parties do settle, they must inform the court promptly, to avoid wasting court time.[172]

Paragraph 17 of CPR PD54 requires the consent of the court for all settlements (except those that relate to costs only):

> 17.1: If the parties agree about the final order to be made in a claim for judicial review, the claimant must file at the court a document (with 2 copies) signed by all the parties setting out the terms of the proposed agreed order together with a short statement of the matters relied on as justifying the proposed agreed order and copies of any authorities or statutory provisions relied on.
> 17.2: The court will consider the documents referred to in paragraph 17.1 and will make the order if satisfied that the order should be made.
> 17.3: If the court is not satisfied that the order should be made, a hearing date will be set.
> 17.4: Where the agreement relates to an order for costs only, the parties need only file a document signed by all the parties setting out the terms of the proposed order.

(2) Discontinuance

2-47   If a claimant wishes to discontinue his or her claim before service of the Claim Form on the other parties, he or she may do so simply by notifying the court by way of a letter of withdrawal.

---

[169] Supreme Court Rules 2009 (SI 2009/1603), r. 11 and Supreme Court Practice Direction 1, para 1.2.9
[170] Supreme Court Practice Direction 2, para 2.1.12 (a)
[171] Supreme Court Practice Direction 3, para 3.3.3
[172] *R (Craddock) v PCA* [2005] EWHC 95 Admin.

Gráinne Mellon

At any other stage in the proceedings, a claimant may discontinue their claim at any time by giving notice under CPR Part 38. Discontinuance usually renders the claimant liable for the defendant's costs, unless the court orders otherwise.[173]

Permission is required if an injunction has been granted and may be required, unless all parties agree to the discontinuance, where an undertaking is given, an interim payment has been made, or there is more than one claimant.[174]

A Notice of Discontinuance (N279) must be filed at the Administrative Court Office and served on all other parties. A defendant may apply to set aside the Notice of Discontinuance within 28 days of being served with it.[175]

---

[173] See below at 16-12.
[174] CPR 38.2(2).
[175] CPR 38.4.

3

Remedies

DAVID BALL AND PIERS VON BERG

A. General Principles

(1) Introduction

3-1   An essential quality of remedies in judicial review is that they interfere in the decision-making of public bodies. They can quash a decision—that is, set it aside and remove its effect in law and require a defendant to take the decision again. They can compel a public body to take a decision or prohibit it from taking a particular course. The court can also make declarations to clarify a disputed issue and thereby narrow or eliminate options available to a decision-maker. The remedies available are:

  i.   a quashing order (see below 3-12–3-16);
  ii.   a prohibiting order (see below 3-17);
  iii. a mandatory order (see below 3-18–3-19);
  iv.   a declaration (see below 3-20–3-21);
  v.   an injunction (see below 3-20 and 3-22);
  vi.   monetary remedies including damages (in conjunction with other remedies) (see below 3-23–3-25); and
  vii. damages and/or declarations of incompatibility (see below 3-29–3-30).

These remedies can have powerful effects in the criminal justice system. For example, a conviction can be quashed. A court can be ordered to conduct a trial. A sentence can be varied. A period in police detention can be declared unlawful and damages awarded.

   This chapter gives an account of how the various remedies operate, with particular regard to certain criminal contexts. The case law is the main source of guidance in this respect. Several specific examples from criminal cases can be found in the text and in the footnotes. Practitioners will find that the type of remedy required depends very much on the factual circumstances of their case and what the claimant seeks to achieve. In relation to certain public bodies, there are considerations specific to them, for example, the police (strictly speaking, a chief constable or commissioner—see Chapter 4) and coroners (see Chapter 10).

   However, first it is vital to understand that all of these remedies are discretionary, and are not awarded as of right. The ensuing section considers the grounds on which the court may exercise or refuse to exercise that discretion.

(2) Statutory Basis

3-2   A claimant must state on the Claim Form what remedy they seek (CPR 54(6)(c)).[1] Section 31 of the Senior Courts Act (SCA) 1981 sets these out as follows:

31.—Application for judicial review.

   (1)   An application to the High Court for one or more of the following forms of relief, namely—

---

[1] Note that they have been renamed as follows: mandamus as mandatory order, prohibition as prohibiting order and certiorari as quashing order, as per the Senior Courts Act 1981, s 29(1). It is not unknown for a judge having given judgment to express a view on a more appropriate remedy than the one sought and to invite submissions on the point.

(a) a mandatory, prohibiting or quashing order;

(b) a declaration or injunction under subsection (2); or

(c) an injunction under section 30 restraining a person not entitled to do so from acting in an office to which that section applies,

shall be made in accordance with rules of court by a procedure to be known as an application for judicial review.

Judicial review must be used in order to obtain a mandatory, prohibiting or quashing order (CPR 54.2), known as prerogative orders. Judicial review may also be used to seek a declaration, injunction, damages, restitution or recovery of a sum due (CPR 54.3). A claim may only seek a monetary remedy as part of a claim for one of the injunctive or declaratory orders (CPR 54.3(2)).

(3) Remedies for Breaches of Human Rights

If the claim raises an issue or seeks a remedy under the Human Rights Act (HRA) 1998, the Claim Form must include the information required by paragraph 15 of CPR PD16 (paragraph 5.3 of CPR PD54A):[2]   **3-3**

i. That the claimant seeks to rely on any provision of, right or remedy under the HRA 1998.

ii. The statement of case should give precise details of the right relied on and how it was infringed, specify the remedy and whether it includes a declaration of incompatibility (see below at 3-30)[3] under section 4 HRA 1998 or damages in respect of a judicial act to which section 9(3) of HRA 1998 applies.

iii. If the claimant seeks a declaration of incompatibility, it should state the precise details of the legislative provision alleged to be incompatible and details of the alleged incompatibility.

iv. If the claim alleges unlawfulness of a decision by a court, details of that finding.

v. If the claim alleges that a judicial act infringed a Convention right as provided by section 9 of HRA 1998, details of that act and the court or tribunal.

Any party that seeks to amend their claim and include matters set out above must do so as soon as possible (see CPR 17).

(4) Choice of Remedy

For judicial reviews in the criminal justice system, whether of a public body such as the police, or a prison, or of a court during proceedings, applicants must carefully consider whether any alternative remedies, such as complaint mechanisms, applications to the court or appeal to another court, are more suitable and, if so, have been exhausted (see the relevant chapter on the applicable defendant below). Claimants should also consider   **3-4**

---

[2] Potential claimants should note the different rules on standing for such claims—discussed in Ch 1 above at 1-45–1-49.

[3] Note that applications for a declaration of incompatibility must comply with Practice Direction 19A on providing notice to other parties to be joined.

whether their complaint is really an attempt to secure compensation for alleged loss, and therefore might be better pursued by a private action. This is because claimants cannot seek only damages by way of judicial review. This is particularly apposite for actions against the police (see below at 3-24 and at 4-3). These considerations are equally valid for defendants who may raise this in opposition to a claim that has not exhausted alternative routes or is unsuitable for the Administrative Court because it essentially a claim for damages.

B. Discretionary Nature of Relief

(1) General Principles

3-5   In judicial review, the granting of a remedy at any particular stage is always at the discretion of the court. This means that even if a claimant has succeeded in establishing that a public body has acted unlawfully, the court may refuse to grant a remedy.[4] This is not to say that remedies can be refused out of hand:[5]

> The court will need to identify a good and principled reason to exercise its residual discretion by declining a practical and effective remedy to a claimant who has succeeded in showing a public wrong.[6]

3-6   Before considering those reasons, practitioners should note that it is not the case that the court will simply accede to or refuse the request for a particular remedy. There are a number of other positions:

    i.   The court may refuse to grant the remedy sought, and instead provide one which it considers more appropriate. Often this involves a refusal to grant injunctive relief and the grant of a declaration instead.[7] As with any declaratory relief, the court informs the public authority of the legal position and expects it to consider this guidance in taking any appropriate measures.

    ii.   There are cases where the court may refuse to make an order or a declaration and state that its judgment speaks for itself.[8] Claimants can seek a direction that they

---

[4] At time of writing, the Criminal Justice and Courts Bill 2014 had recently been put before Parliament. Cl 50(1) will amend s 31 of the SCA 1981 so that Court must refuse relief and may not grant an award 'if it appears to the court to be highly likely that the outcome for the applicant would not have been substantially different if the conduct complained of had not occurred'.

[5] Zamir and Woolf, *The Declaratory Judgment*, 3rd edn (London, Sweet & Maxwell, 2002), para 4.005: 'it is vital that the discretion is, and can be seen to be, exercised judicially. Thus reasons should be given which make it clear that the discretion is not being exercised in a selective and discriminatory manner, and neither arbitrarily nor idiosyncratically. Otherwise the rights of the parties could become, or at least appear, dependent upon judicial whim'. Cited in Feldman (ed), *English Public Law*, 2nd edn (Oxford, Oxford University Press, 2009).

[6] Fordham, *Judicial Review Handbook*, 6th edn (Oxford, Hart Publishing, 2012), para 24.3. Relied on in *Woomera Co Ltd v Commissioner for Transport* [2009] UKCFI 377 [37] (see fn 177).

[7] Eg, in *R v Boundary Commission, ex parte Foot* [1983] 1 QB 600, [1983] 2 WLR 458, 634G (Sir John Donaldson MR), obiter. Cited in Zamir and Woolf (n 5) 123, fn 1 and in Feldman (n 5).

[8] Eg, in *R (Zeqiri) v Secretary of State for the Home Department* [2002] UKHL 3 it was said that in cases involving the Secretary of State (for the Home Department) 'the court frequently adopts the view that the Secretary of State will be guided by its opinion without the necessity of a formal order of mandamus or declaration', ibid [12] (Lord Mackay). Cited in Fordham (n 6) and see the authorities listed there.

David Ball and Piers von Berg

have 'liberty to apply' to return the matter to the court if an injunction proves necessary.[9]

iii. The court may grant an order but suspend its implementation (see below with quashing orders at 3-12), or it may adjourn the issue of granting a particular order to give a public body an opportunity to take further actions.[10]

iv. It may make what are called partial quashing orders.[11]

An example of the above was in *R (Mehmet) v Secretary of State for Justice*.[12] This concerned a failure to provide a psychologist's report about a prisoner for the Parole Board in order to assess risk to the public. Bean J granted a declaration but refused an application for a mandatory order to provide the report within 14 days. But he gave liberty to apply where no report was produced within just over 21 days of the judgment.

(2) Reasons for Exercising the Discretion to Refuse or Grant Remedies

The possible reasons that impinge on the court's discretion are wide-ranging: 3-7

> The discretion of the court in deciding whether to grant any remedy is a wide one. It can take into account many considerations, including the needs of good administration, delay, the effect on third parties, the utility of granting the relevant remedy.[13]

(i) Needs of Good Administration

The needs of good public administration are an important overarching principle.[14] It   3-8
can include many factors such as concern with the substance rather than the form of a decision, the speed of decision-making, a requirement for proper consideration of the public interest, the legitimate interests of private citizens and 'decisiveness and finality, unless there are compelling reasons to the contrary'.[15]

Good administration and the interests of others arise under section 31(6)(b) of SCA 1981: 'Undue' delay can be a reason to decline a remedy if the 'granting of the relief sought would be likely to cause substantial hardship to, or substantially prejudice the rights of, any person or would be detrimental to good administration'.[16] This section

---

[9] Eg, *R (Mehmet) v Secretary of State for Justice* [2009] EWHC 1202 (Admin) [31]–[33].

[10] Eg, in *R v St Albans Magistrates' Court, ex parte Read* (1994) 6 Admin LR 201, [1993] Fam Law 518, cited in Fordham (n 6).

[11] *Crédit Suisse v Allerdale Borough Council* [1996] 3 WLR 894, [1997] QB 306, 355C.

[12] [2009] EWHC 1202 (Admin).

[13] *Crédit Suisse* (n 11), 355C. This fundamental principle was restated in *R (Green) v Gloucestershire CC* [2011] EWHC 3216 (Admin).

[14] Eg *Bahamas Hotel Maintenance & Allied Workers v Bahamas Hotel Catering & Allied Workers* [2011] UKPC 4 [40]. Cited in Fordham (n 6), para 24.3.1—this paragraph in Fordham was relied on in *R (Jones) v Mansfield District Council* [2003] EWCA Civ 1408 [59].

[15] This list was set out by Sir John Donaldson MR in *R v Monopolies and Mergers Commission, ex parte Argyll Group PLC* [1986] 1 WLR 763, [1986] 2 All ER 257, 774E–H. This guidance was given in the context of a case concerning the financial industry.

[16] This relates to the requirement of CPR 54.5(1) that the Claim Form must be filed promptly and in any event not later than three months after the grounds first arose (for guidance on this provision, see above at 2-3-2-5).

was considered in *R v Dairy Produce Quota Tribunal, ex parte Caswell*.[17] In that case, Lord Goff considered 'good administration' to involve a 'regular flow of consistent decisions, made and published with reasonable dispatch' allowing citizens to know where they stand; of particular importance 'will be the extent of the effect of the relevant decision, and the impact which would be felt if it were to be reopened'.[18]

An example of where the Divisional Court did not grant the relief sought because of undue delay is *R (DPP) v Swindon Magistrates' Court* [2013] EWHC 4237 (Admin). The CPS issued it's claim a few days before the three month period elapsed. Although the Divisional Court agreed with its case that the justices' decision was unlawful, and granted a declaration to that effect, King J held that the claimant had not acted promptly and refused to quash the decision. For example, there was a period of six to seven weeks after the justices' decision and before the case came before the Crown Court when the CPS appeared not to have progressed its judicial review claim at all. King J held that the defendants, who had been awaiting sentence in the Crown Court for almost seven months, had suffered 'substantial prejudice' and said:

> The delay which has occurred in this case is obviously detrimental to the good administration of the criminal justice system, which requires that criminal process be pursued with due expedition.[19]

(ii) Nature of the Decision and Interests of Justice

3-9   Another key consideration is the 'nature of the illegality of the decision, and its consequences'.[20] The claimant is unlikely to prevail if there are no prejudicial consequences to him of the decision. Linked to this is the necessity or desirability of a remedy 'in the interests of justice'.[21] A strong example is where a claimant has shown unfairness in his trial.[22] Key to this consideration is the nature of the claimant's interest in a remedy as well as consideration of the interests of third parties who may be affected by any remedy.[23]

(iii) Conduct

3-10   The court will consider the claimant's conduct in adhering to the requirements of CPR Part 54 including the Pre-Action Protocol. Of importance for criminal practitioners is

---

[17]   *R v Dairy Produce Quota Tribunal, ex parte Caswell* [1990] 2 AC 738, [1990] 2 WLR 1320.

[18]   ibid 749E–750B.

[19]   *R (DPP) v Swindon Magistrates' Court* [2013] EWHC 4237 (Admin), [45].

[20]   See the authorities cited in Fordham (n 6) para 24.3.1–*R v Secretary of State for the Environment, ex parte Waters* (1998) 30 HLR 328, 381 and *R (Fudge) v South West Strategic Health Authority* [2007] EWCA 803 [67].

[21]   ibid, *R v Inner London south District Coroner, ex parte Douglas-Williams* [1999] 1 All ER 344, 347D–F and *R (Onwumere) v Secretary of State for the Home Department* [2004] EWHC 1281 (Admin) [22].

[22]   *R v Marylebone Magistrates' Court, ex parte Perry* (1992) 156 JP 696. Any discretion to deny relief when an applicant for certiorari had made out his case should not be exercised where there had been an apparent unfairness in the conduct of the trial.

[23]   Eg *R v Felixstowe Justices, ex parte Leigh* [1987] QB 582. A journalist was granted a declaration that a policy was unlawful not to disclose names of magistrates, but was refused a mandamus naming specific magistrates because he was not party to proceedings.

David Ball and Piers von Berg

understanding the rule of full and frank disclosure of all material facts known to them, which is a continuing duty.[24] Examples are where a claimant does not inform the court that their situation has been remedied by the defendant, or where a claimant does not disclose the true extent of their interest, making any application academic.[25]

(iv) Alternative Remedies and Criminal Proceedings

Judicial review is always a remedy of last resort. This is particularly true in criminal pro-   **3-11**
ceedings where the criminal court can provide remedies. Although this factor is usually considered at the permission stage, it frequently arises at the substantive hearing with Divisional Courts repeatedly giving this as a reason not to intervene in ongoing criminal proceedings, especially where it would disrupt or delay those proceedings.[26] This was restated in *R v DPP, ex parte Kebilene*[27] by Lord Bingham LCJ:

> Where the grant of leave to move for judicial review would delay or obstruct the conduct of criminal proceedings which ought, in the public interest, to be resolved with all appropriate expedition, the court will always scrutinise the application with the greatest care, both to satisfy itself that there are sound reasons for making the application and to satisfy itself that there are no discretionary grounds (such as delay or the availability of alternative remedies or vexatious conduct by the applicant) which should lead it to refuse leave. The court will be very slow to intervene where the applicant's complaint is one that can be met by appropriate orders or directions in the criminal proceedings.[28]

It is submitted that claimants should consider carefully the context of their application as regards its impact on ongoing criminal proceedings.[29]

Certainly there are cases where alternative remedies existed but claimants have succeeded by showing them to be ineffective.[30] The chapters on the police, CPS and criminal courts below cover the alternative remedies or types of proceedings that should be considered depending on type of defendant encountered. Special care should be used when dealing with courts or tribunals. By their very nature, courts will be able to provide a range of remedies within the proceedings. For example, the most obvious and drastic is a stay of proceedings. The magistrates' courts have a large range of remedies available (see below at 6-3–6-5) in addition to the statutory rights of appeal to the Crown Court and the option to request that a case is stated for appeal to the High Court. The Crown Court has a wide range of powers to control its proceedings but it is in a

---

[24] *R (Tshikangu) v Newham LBC* [2001] EWHC Admin 92 [23].

[25] See *Tshikangu* and *R (Done Bros (Cash Betting) Ltd) v Cardiff Crown Court* [2003] EWHC 3516 (Admin).

[26] See *R v Oxford City Justices, ex parte Berry* [1988] QB 507, [1987] 3 WLR 643, where the Divisional Court refused to quash committal proceedings due to complaints of inadmissible evidence stating that this could be dealt with at trial. See the decisions referred to at 512H, including *R v Ipswich Justices, ex parte Edwards*, 143 JP 699, 706 (Lane LJ) and *R v Norfolk Quarter Sessions, ex parte Brunson* [1953] 1 QB 503, 505 (Lord Goddard LCJ).

[27] *R v DPP, ex parte Kebilene* [1999] 3 WLR 175.

[28] ibid 183H. Note that the House of Lords reversed the Divisional Court's decision as to whether the courts should intervene in ongoing proceedings in the Crown Court in that case.

[29] See the discussions below on the application of *Ex p Kebilene* to decisions to charge at 5-12 the timing of challenges to decisions of magistrates' courts at 6-16–6-25 and the scope of the jurisdiction over the Crown Court at 1-27–1-31 and at 7-2–7-3.

[30] Eg *R v Deputy Governor of Parkhurst Prison, ex parte Leech* [1988] AC 533, where a prisoner's ability to petition the Home Secretary would not have led to a quashing of a disciplinary decision.

very different position to the magistrates' courts in relation to the High Court. The High Court's jurisdiction to review its decisions is restricted only to matters that do not touch on trial by indictment (see above at 1-27–1-31 and below at 7-2–7-3).

C. Quashing Orders

(1) Quashing Orders

3-12   A quashing order is the most common remedy. It quashes or sets aside the unlawful decision. It can be used for almost any decision by a public body.[31] As a result, the decision ceases to have legal effect.[32] Section 31(5) of SCA 1981 gives the court options of:

i.   quashing a decision and remitting the matter to the decision-maker with a direction to reconsider the case in accordance with the court's judgment; or
ii. substituting the decision for its own.[33] But it can only substitute the decision if the decision was taken by a court or tribunal in error of law, and there is only one decision that could have been reached.[34]

The court can suspend a quashing order if this would allow the defendant time to take remedial action. There is authority to suggest that the claimant can also be directed to undertake certain actions.[35]

In the criminal domain, the High Court can amend verdicts[36] and sentences.[37] As can be seen from the chapters below, it can also quash decisions to arrest, search, charge, caution, detain as well as intervene in a vast range of decisions in the magistrates' courts. The range of decisions of the Crown Court that may be quashed is tightly constrained by section 28(2)(a) of SCA 1981. There are special considerations regarding convictions and acquittals in the magistrates' courts.

(2) Quashing Convictions and Acquittals

3-13   The High Court can quash a conviction obtained in the magistrates' courts but not the Crown Court, unless it is a decision of the Crown Court to dismiss an appeal.[38]

---

[31] The obvious exceptions are Acts of Parliament and acts of the monarch, eg giving Royal Assent.

[32] See *A v HM Treasury* [2010] UKSC 2, [2010] 2 WLR 378 [4]–[8].

[33] See also CPR 54.19(2)(a).

[34] SCA 1981, s 31(5)(b), (5A) and (5B) and CPR r 54.19(2)(b). Examples of cases within the scope of this work include *R (Thames Water Utilities Ltd) v Bromley Magistrates' Court* [2005] EWHC 1231 (Admin); *R (Y) v Aylesbury Crown Court* on reporting restrictions (see below at 11-43); *R (O'Connor) v Avon Coroner* [2009] EWHC 854 (Admin), [2011] QB 106.

[35] Eg, in *R v Bow Street Magistrates' Court, ex parte Mitchell* [2001] FSR 18, the case was remitted to the stipendiary magistrate on the condition that the claimant provide full and exhaustive details of his financial position (this was a claim against a decision on costs).

[36] *R (Longfield Care Homes) v HM Coroner for Blackburn* [2004] EWHC 2467 (Admin).

[37] SCA 1981, s 43(1). Eg, *R (Corner) v Southend Crown Court* [2005] EWHC 2334 (Admin) and *R v St Helen's Justices, ex parte Jones* [1999] 2 All ER 73.

[38] SCA 1981, s 29(3). Note comments by Leveson LJ in *Balogun v DPP* on whether a conviction could be quashed unless it is the decision under challenge (see below at 6-71).

(i) Convictions

A quashing order will be available if a defendant has been denied a fair trial due to   **3-14**
a failure by the court.[39] It is also appropriate if there is an error by the prosecution
that prevents a fair trial subject to specific rules. These rules developed in a series of
road traffic cases where there were errors in the acquisition and presentation of expert
evidence relating to blood alcohol levels. Essentially, defendants had tested positive to
excessive alcohol, entered unequivocal pleas of guilty and then sought to quash their
convictions when they discovered the police had not followed correct procedures.
A three-judge Divisional Court, led by Stuart-Smith LJ, reviewed the authorities in *R v
Dolgellau Justices, ex parte Cartledge*[40] and endorsed the summary of the principles
by Buxton J, with whom Beldam LJ agreed, in *R v Burton upon Trent Justices, ex parte
Woolley*:[41]

1. Where complaint is made of the conduct of judicial proceedings, the court's jurisdiction
    to intervene to quash a decision by way of certiorari is not limited to cases of error by the
    tribunal, but may be also founded on conduct on the part of the prosecutor.
2. The jurisdiction is sui generis, in the sense that it cannot be, or at least does not have to be,
    forced under any of the three heads of judicial review recognised by Lord Diplock in *Council
    of Civil Service Unions v Minister for the Civil Service* [1985] AC 374, 410. In that respect, the
    jurisdiction recognised in *Al-Mehdawi* [1990] 1 AC 876 may represent an extension of the
    categories of judicial review that were identified in *Council of Civil Service Unions v Minister
    for the Civil Service* [1985] AC 374.
3. The jurisdiction is of a limited nature, and there is no authority for recognising it as extend-
    ing beyond conduct on the part of the prosecutor that can be fairly categorised as being
    analogous to fraud.
4. It is however possible for conduct to be so categorised where there is no actual fraud or dis-
    honesty. That is Lord Bridge's analysis of *Reg. v Leyland Justices, Ex parte Hawthorn* [1979]
    RTR 109 and also the view of this court in *Reg. v Bolton Justices, Ex parte Scally* [1991] 1 QB
    537, 556C: see per Watkins LJ and per Hutchison J, at p 557E.
5. Whether the conduct can be so categorised must be a matter of judgment for the court
    seised of the case, looking at all the facts.
6. There is no separate rule or sub-category applying to cases where the applicant's advisers
    are alleged to have been at fault. Whether the result complained of has been contributed to
    by the applicant or his advisers in any significant way is to be taken into account as one of
    the facts involved in deciding whether the result has been caused by conduct on the part of
    the prosecution, and whether in all the circumstances that conduct can be categorised as
    analogous to fraud.[42]

---

[39] See Lord Widgery LCJ in *R v Leyland Justices, ex parte Hawthorn* [1979] QB 283, 286 followed in *R v
Secretary of State for the Home Department, ex parte Al–Mehdawi* [1990] 1 AC 876, 895D–896D (Lord Bridge).
[40] *R v Dolgellau Justices, ex parte Cartledge* [1996] RTR 207.
[41] *R v Burton upon Trent Justices, ex parte Woolley* [1995] RTR 139.
[42] ibid. Note *R v Bolton Magistrates' Court, ex parte Scally* [1991] 1 QB 537, [1991] 2 WLR 239 is relied
on by more recent authorities, which appear not to have been referred to *Ex p Woolley*. Eg see *R (Harrison) v
Birmingham Magistrates' Court* [2011] EWCA Civ 332 and *R (Wilmot) v Taunton Dene and West Somerset
Magistrates' Court* [2013] EWHC 1399 (Admin).

(ii) Examples of Prosecution Misconduct or Failures

3-15 The types of prosecution misconduct evidenced in these authorities can be summarised under the principle that they prevented the defendant from having a fair trial.[43] They included non-disclosure of key witnesses (*Ex p Hawthorn*) or evidence (*Ex p Scally*), perjury or fraud (guidance in *Ex p Hawthorn*), and bringing a case without evidence (*Ex p Khanna*).[44] In *Ex p Scally*, the court held that it had jurisdiction to quash a conviction, notwithstanding a lack of dishonesty by the Crown. In that case, the swabs used for the blood alcohol readings were contaminated with alcohol. Watkins LJ said:

> What happened here was that, there being no dishonesty, the prosecutor (a combination of police and CPS) corrupted the process leading to conviction in a manner which was unfair, for it gave the defendants no proper opportunity to decide whether to plead guilty or not guilty; indeed it wrongly denied them a complete defence to the charge. In my view, that is conduct analogous to fraud, collusion or perjury if ever there was.[45]

It is important to note that the conduct is 'analogous' to fraud and not actual fraud or dishonesty.[46]

(iii) Acquittals

3-16 The higher courts are averse to quashing an acquittal in the magistrates' courts, as it may infringe the rule of double jeopardy.[47] However, if the court acted in excess of its jurisdiction in dismissing the information, then it can be said the proceedings and the acquittal are a nullity. If necessary, the Crown may seek a mandatory order to compel the court to hear the case.[48] These principles derive from *R v Dorking Justices, ex parte Harrington*,[49] where a magistrates' court had dismissed an information after the defendant had objected that the trial was adjourned to a date when he was on holiday. Lord Roskill held that the justices breached their duty under section 9(2) of MCA 1980 to hear the case. He said this:

> The dismissal of these informations was without jurisdiction and was a nullity ... Both on principle and authority I see no reason why, had the prosecution sought to take the matter further, mandamus should not have issued to the justices directing them to hear and determine these informations according to law. Since in my view their orders were a nullity I do not think that it would have been right to order certiorari to issue as well.

---

[43] See Lord Widgery LCJ in *Ex p Hawthorn* (n 38).

[44] For an example in a civil case see *R (Marsh) v Lincoln District Magistrates' Court* [2003] EWHC 956 (Admin) a decision was quashed due to failures by the Child Support Agency to provide relevant evidence concerning enforcement of a liability order in respect of child maintenance.

[45] *Ex p Scally* (n 42) 556B–D.

[46] ibid 556F–557F. Criminal practitioners used to dealing with offences of fraud should be aware of the guidance on pleading fraud in a civil case see *Medcalf v Mardell* [2002] 3 All ER 721.

[47] See *R v Simpson* [1914] 1 KB 66, 75 where Scrutton J said 'there never has been a case in which an acquittal by a court of summary jurisdiction has been quashed by certiorari', cited in *R v Hendon Justices, ex parte Director of Public Prosecutions* [1993] 2 WLR 862, [1994] QB 167, 174H. A number of authorities are reviewed in the judgment which stress the principle of double jeopardy. Note that the reverse is true in an appeal by case stated where the court has the power under ss 111 and 112 of MCA 1980 to order a conviction after an acquittal.

[48] This approach was taken in *R v Horseferry Road Magistrates' Court, ex parte DPP* [1997] COD 172.

[49] *R v Dorking Justices, ex parte Harrington* [1984] AC 743, [1984] 3 WLR 142, 753B.

　　　　　　　　　　　　　David Ball and Piers von Berg

This was considered in *R v Hendon Justices, ex parte Director of Public Prosecutions*[50] where it was said: 'In our judgment, certiorari can go to quash a decision which is a nullity and which by hypothesis is accordingly not an acquittal'. In that case the proceedings were held to be a nullity because the justices had acted irrationally.[51]

D. Prohibiting Orders

(1) Prohibiting Orders

This order prohibits a public body from acting in a way that is unlawful or from imple-   **3-17**
menting an unlawful decision. In criminal proceedings it can generally be used to prevent a court from acting outside its jurisdiction or abusing its powers. For example, it has been used to prevent a magistrates' court from holding a committal hearing for reason of abuse of process.[52] It also includes preventing a public body from taking advantage of an unlawful decision. For example, to prevent admission of evidence after an unlawful adjournment,[53] or to prevent a new trial after parts of the Crown's case were held to be inadmissible.[54]

E. Mandatory Orders

(1) Mandatory Orders

A mandatory order can compel a public body to perform its public duties or act to avoid   **3-18**
a breach of its duties.[55] This may include exercising their discretion lawfully. A well known example in criminal judicial review is to compel a magistrates' court or Crown Court to state a case where it has refused to do so (see below at 6-10).[56]

The High Court is slow to grant mandatory orders to force public authorities to act. The case law tends to show reluctance for such orders, and a preference for declarations.[57] One of the difficulties is that public authorities can advance policy-based arguments such as lack of resources, or that they are simply doing everything possible but the circumstances are beyond their control.[58] Therefore, the normal rules on seeking alternative remedies and abiding by the Pre-Action Protocol will apply with some

---

[50] *Hendon Justices* (n 47) 178F.
[51] This approach was taken in *R (Crown Prosecution Service) v Reading and West Berkshire Magistrates' Court* [2010] EWHC 3260 (Admin), where the Crown's application was refused.
[52] *R v Bow Street Magistrates, ex parte Mackeson* (1982) 75 Cr App R 24, *R v Guildford magistrates' court, ex parte Healy* [1983] 1 WLR 108 and *R v Telford Justices, ex parte Badhan* [1991] 2 QB 78. This practice was approved in *R v Horseferry Road Magistrates' Court, ex parte Bennett* [1993] 3 WLR 90, [1994] 1 AC 42, 78E–80B.
[53] Eg in *R (Watson) v Dartford Magistrates' Court* (see below at 6-21).
[54] *R v Faversham and Sittingbourne Justices, ex parte Stickings* [1996] COD 439.
[55] Note by virtue of the Crown Proceedings Act 1947, s 40 a mandatory order cannot be made against the Crown but it can be directed to an officer of the Crown, eg a minister. See *M v Home Office* [1994] 1 AC 377, 425.
[56] This is provided for under statute in MCA 1980, s 111(6) and SCA 1981, s 29(3) respectively.
[57] Eg, *R v Barnet London Borough Council, ex parte Nilish Shah* [1983] 2 AC 309.
[58] In *R v Bristol Corp, ex parte Hendy* [1974] 1 WLR 498 the court considered the circumstances in which a mandamus (mandatory order) could be granted.

vigour (see above at 2-9–2-11 and Annex 1B). The claimant may be expected to show that they have taken reasonable steps to give the defendant sufficient information, warning and opportunity as part of a request to the defendant to perform its obligations.[59] This would normally be the purpose of the Letter Before Action and subsequent exchanges. If the matter is not resolved and the claimant issues proceedings, they may be expected to address the defendant's Acknowledgement of Service and any evidence setting out any purported compliance with its duty or obstacles preventing such actions.

There may be other difficulties depending on the legal form of the particular statutory duty. For example, the court will wish to see precision. It will refrain from making orders that require a public authority to comply with a vague or ambiguous provision; or it may simply find that the statutory duty in question is not legally enforceable in the manner sought by the claimant. A good example of such issues, albeit in an application for a declaration, can be found in *R (M) v Gateshead Metropolitan Borough Council*[60] (discussed below at 11-20). This concerned the duty of the police to transfer children remanded in custody to local authority accommodation and the corresponding duty of a local authority to provide accommodation to such a child. Key to that case was the scope of the duty under section 21(2)(b) of the Children Act 1989. The court held that section 21(2)(b) provided a discretionary power to provide secure accommodation on request by the police, so far as it was practicable to do so. It did not impose an absolute duty on a local authority to provide secure accommodation for a juvenile in police custody whenever it was requested under section 38(6) of PACE 1984. That case demonstrated the importance of identifying the nature of the duty, which the public authority is alleged to have breached.

Another question the court may ask is whether the outcome sought by the claimant is the only possible result. The courts have indicated that a mandatory order may be the appropriate form of relief when the Administrative Court finds that it will achieve the only and lawful result open to the decision-maker below.[61] It follows that when it is not the only lawful outcome open to a decision-maker, a mandatory order may not be granted.

(i) Examples of Mandatory Orders

3-19   A mandatory order can direct a magistrates' court to rehear a case where the proceedings were a nullity and the defendant acquitted. However, in exercising its discretion the court will consider various factors: the length of time that has elapsed since the alleged offence, the public interest in trying the particular offence, and whether the defendants can reasonably believe they are or are not in jeopardy.[62]

---

[59] See *R v Horsham DC, ex parte Wenman* [1995] 1 WLR 608.

[60] *R (M) v Gateshead Metropolitan Borough Council* [2006] EWCA Civ 221, [2006] QB 650.

[61] *R (Luminar Leisure Ltd) v Crown Court at Norwich* [2004] EWCA Civ 281, [2004] 1 WLR 2512 [20] (Laws LJ). The Court of Appeal dismissed an appeal regarding a quashing order of a Crown Court's decision in a licensing case. Laws LJ agreed with the quashing order granted by the Administrative Court and stated that the 'proper course' was to grant a mandatory order requiring the Crown Court to dismiss the appeal (from the magistrates' court).

[62] *Hendon Justices* (n 47) 178G–179A.

A mandatory order can require a court to accept jurisdiction over a matter where it has declined to do so.[63] However, where Youth Courts unlawfully commit youths to the Crown Court (see below at 6-64), claimants usually apply for quashing orders. On successful applications, the High Court remits the case to the Youth Court.[64]

F. Declarations and Injunctions

(1) General Principles

A declaration and/or an injunction can be sought alongside a mandatory, prohibiting **3-20** or quashing order. On such applications, the court has a power to grant one instead of a prerogative order. Section 31(2) of the SCA 1981 provides:

(1)   A declaration may be made or an injunction granted under this subsection in any case where an application for judicial review, seeking that relief, has been made and the High Court considers that, having regard to—
    (a)   the nature of the matters in respect of which relief may be granted by mandatory, prohibiting or quashing orders;
    (b)   the nature of the persons and bodies against whom relief may be granted by such orders; and
    (c)   all the circumstances of the case,
it would be just and convenient for the declaration to be made or the injunction to be granted, as the case may be.

See also CPR 40.20: 'The court may make binding declarations whether or not any other remedy is claimed.'

(2) Declarations

A declaration states the legal position on a disputed issue. For example, the court may **3-21** state that a particular course of action or ruling was unlawful, that a particular duty has been breached or is owed, or, that a policy is unlawful or contravenes EU law.[65] An example is a declaration concerning the criminality of proposed conduct (see below at 5-41). It can be used against unlawful conduct that has already occurred and from which the claimant no longer suffers prejudice, but wishes the court to declare unlawful for some other purpose, such as recovery of damages. An example of this is unlawful detention where the claimant has been released and seeks compensation.

---

[63] Eg in *R v Oxford Justices, ex parte D* [1987] QB 199, [1986] 3 WLR 447 (although note the scope of Waite J's order to compel a magistrates' court to issue a summons against a local authority was doubted in *Re M and H (Minors) (Local Authority: Parental Rights)* [1987] 3 WLR 759, [1988] 1 FLR 151. See also *R v Reading Crown Court, ex parte Hutchinson* [1988] QB 384.

[64] Eg, *R (H, A, and O) v Southampton Youth Court, R (D) v Manchester City Youth Court* (see below at 6-64) and *R (Crown Prosecution Service) v Redbridge Youth Court* [2005] EWHC 1390 (Admin).

[65] A declaration of incompatibility with the ECHR under s 6 of the HRA 1998 is discussed below at 3-21.

There are limits to the subject matter of a declaration—the issue has to be justiciable, it cannot be an issue for the sole and exclusive jurisdiction of Parliament[66] or relate to questions of international law or those that fall within the jurisdiction of foreign courts.

Although a court will not consider hypothetical and academic points, a case can be made for the clarification of an issue of public importance. This can be addressed through what is known as an advisory declaration. The courts have been inclined to provide declarations where there is a clear public interest in doing so and such a declaration may be of assistance.[67] However, the courts will not engage in an extended discussion or treatise.[68] The courts have refused to entertain such applications where the lawfulness of a particular decision or policy is not in doubt.[69]

It is a flexible and pragmatic but less intrusive remedy. It is available as an interim remedy.[70] The form of words used can be carefully sculpted to identify the reasons why an action is unlawful and what steps should be taken to ensure compliance with any statutory provisions. However, unlike prerogative orders, it cannot compel an authority and carries no consequences such as contempt of court proceedings, if it is ignored. It is useful in situations when a quashing, mandatory or prohibiting order may not be available.[71] As such, providing the claimant has not fallen foul of any other considerations (see the grounds affecting the exercise of the discretion, above), recent authority suggests the court should be inclined to grant a declaration.[72] In practical terms, a claimant should provide the terms of the declaration sought. If granted, this may be subject to some amendment and change flowing from the position taken in the judgment; judges may invite submissions on the terms of the declaration after handing down judgment.

---

[66] For a modern-day application of the principle of parliamentary privilege in the context of criminal proceedings, see *R v Chaytor & Ors* [2010] EWCA Crim 1910. See also *Bradlaugh v Gossett* (1884) 12 QBD 271 and Art 9 of the Bill of Rights: 'That the freedom of speech and debates or proceedings in Parliament ought not to be impeached or questioned in any court or place out of Parliament.'

[67] Eg, *R (Customs and Excise Commissioners) v Canterbury Crown Court* [2002] EWHC 2584 (Admin) [27] (Laws LJ). In contrast, note the refusal of the Supreme Court to provide an advisory declaration in *R (Smith) v Oxfordshire Assistant Deputy Coroner* [2010] UKSC 29, [2011] 1 AC 1 [155].

[68] *R (Howard League for Penal Reform) v Secretary of State for the Home Department (No 2)* [2002] EWHC 2497 (Admin), [2003] 1 FLR 484 [140] (Munby LJ) granting the application but limiting himself to four points.

[69] *R (Ellis) v Chief Constable of Essex* [2003] EWHC 1321 (Admin), [2003] 2 FLR 566 where the court held that there was insufficient evidence to decide whether a proposed scheme to display offenders' names and faces on posters was unlawful. See below at 4-129.

[70] CPR 25.1(1)(b). See also Tomlinson J in *Amalgamated Metal Trading Ltd v City of London Police Financial Investigation Unit* [2003] EWHC 703 (Comm), [2003] 1 WLR 2711 [10], where an interim declaration was refused. It was suggested there was still some uncertainty as to when exactly an interim declaration might have been appropriate.

[71] *R v Secretary of State for Employment, ex parte Equal Opportunities Commission* [1995] 1 AC 1, 34.

[72] See the language used by Singh J in *R (First Stop Wholesale Ltd) v Revenue and Customs Commissioners* [2012] EWHC 106 (Admin) [38]. Note that this decision was reversed in part by the Court of Appeal on the substantive points, but no comment was made on Singh J's statement of principle: 'in principle, if a claimant has succeeded in establishing that there has been an error of public law in the Administrative Court, normally, other things being equal, the court should reflect that in some form of declaratory relief. Justice would tend to suggest no less.'

(3) Injunctions

Injunctions are directed to a party to the proceedings to refrain from or to perform a particular act.[73] In addition to section 31(2) SCA 1981 they are also governed by section 37, the relevant sub-sections of which provide:

3-22

37.—Powers of High Court with respect to injunctions and receivers.

(1)   The High Court may by order (whether interlocutory or final) grant an injunction or appoint a receiver in all cases in which it appears to the court to be just and convenient to do so.

(2)   Any such order may be made either unconditionally or on such terms and conditions as the court thinks just.

...

This repeats the test of 'just and convenient' and adds different characteristics to pre-rogative orders giving the court a more versatile remedy. As per sub-section (1), they can be granted at an interim stage. The language of sub-section (2) reflects the highly flexible character of injunctions. They may be granted for a specific time period or until certain conditions are satisfied. A claimant can apply to extend an injunction.

G. Monetary Remedies

(1) Damages, Restitution and Recovery of Sum Due

Under section 31(4) of SCA 1981 the High Court may award damages, restitution or the recovery of a sum due on an application for judicial review.[74] However, a judicial review claim cannot seek such a remedy alone (CPR 54.3(2)). The award of any monetary remedy is also discretionary. An award of damages can only be made if the claimant would have succeeded in a private law claim or a claim under the HRA 1998.[75] In essence, this creates an additional hurdle for a claimant, who needs to succeed under principles of negligence, for example, in order to recover his loss, as well as demonstrating the public law wrong.[76] Claimants should be mindful of the rules on recovery for breaches of statutory duties. They should ask whether the underlying policy of the statute makes it

3-23

---

[73]   Eg, in *R v North Yorkshire CC, ex parte M* [1989] QB 411 a claimant was granted an injunction to prevent a local authority placing a child for adoption after a decision had been quashed.

[74]   The High Court also has the power to award interest: SCA 1981, s 35A. CPR Pt 16 will apply to claims for damages. This requires statements of case and full particulars of any loss or damage.

[75]   There is no free-standing public law right to damages caused by unlawful acts of public bodies *R (Quark Fishing Ltd) v Secretary of State for Foreign and Commonwealth Affairs* [2005] UKHL 57, [2006] 1 AC 529 [96]. This gap in the law has been the subject of much judicial concern and criticism, eg see *Stovin v Wise* [1996] AC 923, 933F–G (Lord Nicholls). The principle is that: 'The justification for not giving damages for judicial review is that the proceedings are brought for the benefit of the public as a whole': Lord Woolf, 'Has the Human Rights Act made Judicial Review Redundant?' Administrative Law Bar Association, Annual Lecture (23 November 2005).

[76]   See *Anufrijeva v Southwark LBC* [2003] EWCA 1406, [2004] QB 1124.

irrational for a public body not to exercise the power and whether there are exceptional grounds to show that an individual merited compensation in circumstances where the power is not exercised.[77]

This 'mixed' jurisdiction was considered recently in *Robert Tchenguiz, R20 Ltd v Director of the Serious Fraud Office* [2014] EWCA Civ 472, where Pitchford LJ used a helpful discussion in *De Smith's Judicial Review*:

> In such cases [claims for monetary compensation that turn on factual disputes], it may be more convenient for the Administrative Court first to determine the public law issues, and then make an order transferring the issues relating to tortious or other private law liability to proceed as if begun under CPR Part 7. Among other possible ways of determining issues are: the court may award damages at the judicial review hearing but leave quantum to be assessed by a master; where a claim is started in the County Court but it is thought that expertise in public law issues is needed, the case may be transferred to the High Court to be heard by a judge with Administrative Court experience; or a High Court judge with Administrative Court expertise may sit as a judge in the County Court pursuant to section 5(3) of the County Courts Act 1984.[78]

3-24   Claimants bringing a public law action against the police for damages should consider whether such an action should be properly brought in a private law suit (see below at 4-5). Claims for damages against a magistrates' court or a legal adviser (clerk) acting in their professional capacities will face a defence of immunity provided under section 31 of the Courts Act 2003. The only exception to this defence is if it can be proved that the justice of the peace or legal adviser has acted in excess of jurisdiction and that this was done in bad faith (section 32(1)).[79]

3-25   Damages can be sought as part of a judicial review claim based on breaches of rights under the ECHR (see below) or breaches of EU law. The latter includes failures to implement Directives.[80] The following principles will apply:[81]

i.   the provision concerned must be intended to confer rights on individuals;

ii.   the breach must be sufficiently serious; and,

iii. there should be a direct causal connection between the breach and the damage sustained.

---

[77] *Stovin v Wise*, 952F–953B, 953D–E (Lord Hoffmann). In essence, it involves establishing a public duty to act. In *Stovin v Wise*, compensation was refused because the Council had a discretion to decide whether to act (957E).

[78] *Robert Tchenguiz, R20 Ltd v Director of the Serious Fraud Office* [2014] EWCA Civ 472, [8], citing from *De Smith's Judicial Review*, 7th Edition, 19-009.

[79] The Courts Act 2003, s 33 allows a judge to strike out a claim and order costs if it falls outside the conditions of s 32. See *Benham v United Kingdom* (1993) 22 EHRR 293. The court wished to avoid encouraging claims for compensation against courts brought by those who had overturned their convictions or sentences on appeal. There were powerful dissenting judgments in that case. After that case HRA 1998, s 9(3) was enacted which permits recovery of damages against judicial officers for unlawful detention (Art 5(5)). *R v Governor of HMP Brockhill Prison, ex parte Evans (2)* [2001] 2 AC 19, which considered the question of arbitrariness of unlawful detention and bad faith, also postdated that decision.

[80] Case C-6 & 9-90 *Francovich v Italy* [1991] ECR I-5357.

[81] See *R v Secretary of State for Transport, ex parte Factortame (No 5)* [2000] 1 AC 524.

H. Claims under the Human Rights Act (HRA) 1998

(1) Claims under the Human Rights Act 1998

Section 8 of HRA 1998 sets out the court's powers and considerations in granting remedies for breaches of rights under the ECHR: **3-26**

8.—Judicial remedies.

(1) In relation to any act (or proposed act) of a public authority which the court finds is (or would be) unlawful, it may grant such relief or remedy, or make such order, within its powers as it considers just and appropriate.

(2) But damages may be awarded only by a court which has power to award damages, or to order the payment of compensation, in civil proceedings.

(3) No award of damages is to be made unless, taking account of all the circumstances of the case, including—
   (a) any other relief or remedy granted, or order made, in relation to the act in question (by that or any other court), and
   (b) the consequences of any decision (of that or any other court) in respect of that act, the court is satisfied that the award is necessary to afford just satisfaction to the person in whose favour it is made.

(4) In determining—
   (a) whether to award damages, or
   (b) the amount of an award, the court must take into account the principles applied by the European Court of Human Rights in relation to the award of compensation under Article 41 of the Convention.

Therefore, sub-section (1) provides a very wide ambit for the court to provide any of the above remedies (prerogative orders, injunctions, declarations or damages). It follows that a person can apply to a criminal court at first instance for a remedy for a breach of their human rights, for example by seeking to exclude evidence, stay proceedings or simply by way of appeal after conviction or sentence.

Practitioners should be aware that complaints of breaches of ECHR rights in criminal **3-27** investigations or proceedings do not automatically entitle an individual to a remedy (reference should be made to the relevant section in the chapters below, for example, in applications to stay proceedings for abuse of process or delay below at 6-34–6-35). In any event, the criminal courts do not have jurisdiction to award damages. A magistrates' court or Crown Court is more limited than the High Court in the remedies it can provide, for example a stay of proceedings, dismissing an information, or a direction to enter a verdict, as well as using their general powers to control procedure and evidence. The Court of Appeal has more sweeping powers to amend a sentence or quash a conviction. A coroner's court will also be able to provide some relief through the use of similar powers to control its proceedings. It has a discretion to control the scope of the inquiry and, as seen below (at 10-12), this is affected by considerations of Article 2.

Section 9 of HRA 1998 controls awards of damages made against judicial officers, in **3-28** particular:

(3) In proceedings under this Act in respect of a judicial act done in good faith, damages may not be awarded otherwise than to compensate a person to the extent required by Article 5(5) of the Convention.

(4)   An award of damages permitted by subsection (3) is to be made against the Crown; but no award may be made unless the appropriate person, if not a party to the proceedings, is joined.

(2) Damages under the Human Rights Act 1998

3-29   Under sections 8(3) and 9 of the HRA 1998, damages may be awarded, but only as a last resort. A key part of the ECHR is the principle of 'just satisfaction', found in Article 41:

Just satisfaction

If the court finds that there has been a violation of the Convention or the Protocols thereto, and if the internal law of the High Contracting Party concerned allows only partial reparation to be made, the court shall, if necessary, afford just satisfaction to the injured party.

In *R (Greenfield) v Secretary of State*,[82] Lord Bingham interpreted Article 41. Whilst emphasising that awards of damages are of secondary importance in ECHR case law, there was this general guidance:

i.   First, there are three preconditions (Article 41): the court must find a violation, the domestic law should only allow for partial reparation and it should be necessary to afford just satisfaction to provide compensation.[83]

ii.   The court will only award compensation where the loss was caused by the violation of the particular right.[84]

iii.   Where there is no finding of a clear causal connection, the court's finding of a violation of a right will in itself provide 'just satisfaction'.[85]

iv.   However, the approach is fact sensitive and the courts proceed on a case-by-case basis meaning that the above principle may be 'softened' where justice demands it.[86]

v.   With breaches of Article 6, it is not necessary for the claimant to show that any frustration or anxiety would not have occurred but for the breach although awards are 'very sparing' and the 'ordinary practice' is not to make awards.[87]

vi.   As per section 8(4), courts must look to the jurisprudence of the ECtHR for guidance on whether to make an award and on quantum.[88]

vii.   Awards are not precisely calculated, but are judged by the court to be fair and equitable in the particular case; although domestic judges are not 'inflexibly bound' by the ECtHR's awards, 'they should not aim to be significantly more or less generous'.[89]

This restrictive approach is illustrated in *Cullen v Chief Constable of the Royal Ulster Constabulary*.[90] The claimant was held in police custody and denied access to a solicitor. The defendant breached a statutory duty to give the reasons for authorising the delay

---

[82] *R (Greenfield) v Secretary of State* [2005] 1 WLR 673.
[83] ibid [6].
[84] ibid [14].
[85] ibid [15].
[86] ibid [15].
[87] ibid [16].
[88] ibid [19].
[89] ibid [19].
[90] *Cullen v Chief Constable of the Royal Ulster Constabulary* [2003] UKHL 39, [2003] 1 WLR 1763. See also below at 4-4 and 4-82.

of the claimant's right of access to a solicitor. The court held that the claimant was not entitled to recover damages in respect of that breach, as he had suffered no personal injury, injury to property or economic loss.

(3) Declarations of Incompatibility

The High Court may grant a declaration of incompatibility under section 4 of HRA   **3-30**
1998 if it is satisfied that a part of primary legislation is incompatible with a right under the ECHR. This is also a discretionary remedy. It may declare a provision of secondary legislation incompatible if the primary legislation prevents a removal of incompatibility.[91] Where a court is considering granting a declaration of incompatibility, the Crown should be given at least 21 days' notice (CPR 19.4A(1) and PD 19A, para 6.1) and is entitled to become a party to the proceedings (CPR 19.4A(2)). This is not a remedy as such, because where a provision is found to be incompatible with the ECHR it does not affect its applicability in the proceedings.

The declaration is only granted as a last resort because the court is under a strong duty to interpret the legislation in a manner that is compatible with the ECHR.[92] This may involve the court reading in words that are not present, or reading down words to restrict their meaning.[93]

Declarations can be sought in order to challenge a piece of legislation if the purpose of the litigation is to serve the public interest and try to force the Government to reconsider a particular provision. These cases are rare but not unknown in criminal judicial review.[94]

I. Habeas Corpus

(1) Habeas Corpus

Habeas corpus ad subjiciendum, to give it its full title, is a remedy for unlawful deten-   **3-31**
tion. It is not a remedy flowing from an application for judicial review, but simply from an application for habeas corpus. It is included here as it may be a suitable alternative remedy in cases of unlawful detention, for example if a judicial review of a prison is contemplated. If granted, it requires a public authority, which has detained a person, to explain the lawfulness of that person's detention and to produce that person before the court. If the detention cannot be justified, the detainee is entitled to release. In

---

[91] HRA 1998, s 4(3) and (4).

[92] ibid, s 3. See *R v A (No 2)* [2001] UKHL 25, [2002] 1 AC 45 [44] (Lord Steyn) and *Sheldrake v DPP* [2005] 1 AC 264 [28] (Lord Bingham). The duty is to interpret the provision in question 'so far as is possible' unless 'it is plainly impossible' *R v A (No 2)* [45]. This may lead to the court interpreting a provision in a manner that is contrary to its clear meaning: *Ghaidan v Godin-Medoza* [2004] UKHL 30, [2004] 2 AC 557 [29]–[30] (Lord Nicholls).

[93] An example of each is respectively *R v A (No 2)* (n 92), concerning the cross-examination of alleged victims of rape, and *R v Lambert* [2002] UKHL 37, [2002] 2 AC 545, on reading down a legal burden of proof on a defendant to become an evidential burden.

[94] Eg, *R (HC) v Secretary of State for the Home Department* [2013] EWHC 982 (Admin). See below at 11-16–11-17.

contrast to the prerogative orders, the remedy is granted as of right, not by the court's discretion.[95] Its purpose is no more than that—to secure release; it cannot be used to seek redress for any previous illegality.[96] It was described by Lord Birkenhead as 'the most important writ known to the constitutional law of England, affording as it does a swift and imperative remedy in all cases of illegal restraint or confinement'.[97] Article 5(4) of the ECHR specifically protects the writ of habeas corpus.

The proper respondent for an application is the authority which has actual control of the detained person or, at a minimum, a reasonable prospect of being able to exert such control.[98] If it was not clear if the respondent had control, then the writ could be issued to enable a fuller investigation of the facts.[99]

3-32   As stated above, it is not a remedy sought or obtained by way of judicial review; although it may be sought alongside an application for judicial review.[100] It is not correct to think that it is only available when judicial review is available.[101] There is a separate procedure contained in Schedule 1 of the CPR which preserves the old rules for applications for habeas corpus in RSC Order 54 and PD RSC 54. The application is made without notice and with supporting evidence. If the judge is satisfied there is an arguable case, the application is served on the respondent and any interested parties. There then follows a substantive hearing at which, if the applicant is successful, the court must order his release.

Applications for habeas corpus should be approached with great care. In *R v Holmes, ex parte Sherman*,[102] a case which arose in the context of police detention, Donaldson LJ warned that 'habeas corpus is a remedy for an abuse of power and it should rarely be necessary to invoke it'.[103] Although the remedy did remain 'real and available', with such applications being accorded absolute priority by the court, due note should be taken that 'considerable' costs consequences may result from any 'frivolous' applications.[104]

3-33   The writ of habeas corpus cannot be used to subvert or avoid judicial review. The courts have repeatedly expressed a preference for challenges to be brought by way of judicial review as opposed to habeas corpus.[105] In holding that an application for habeas corpus constituted an abuse of process where issues should properly have been raised in the course of earlier (unsuccessful) judicial review proceedings, *Abdul Sheikh v Secretary*

---

[95] *R v Secretary of State for the Home Department, ex parte Khawaja* [1984] AC 74, 111 (Lord Scarman), followed in *R (Rahmatullah) v Secretary of State for Foreign and Commonwealth Affairs* [2012] UKSC 48, [2013] 1 AC 614 [41] (Lord Kerr, with whom the other six justices agreed on the applicable principles).

[96] *R v Secretary of State for Home Affairs, ex parte O'Brien* [1923] 2 KB 361 (CA), [1923] AC 603 (HL(E)), 391 and *Rahmatullah*, ibid [44].

[97] *O'Brien*, ibid 609.

[98] Control is a question of fact, not of law; eg an issue of enforceability of any right to control. This was the central issue and principle established in *Rahmatullah* where the applicant was held by a foreign government in a foreign country (the United States detained him in Afghanistan). Note it was held that habeas corpus can lie against a respondent who has removed a detainee from the jurisdiction: *Rahmatullah* (n 95) [91]–[92].

[99] ibid. The Supreme Court in *Rahmatullah* held that the purpose of the writ was to ascertain whether in fact the UK Government had control of the detainee and to permit it to demonstrate why it could not produce him.

[100] *Ex p Khawaja* (n 95), 99.

[101] *Rahmatullah* (n 95) [72]–[73] (Lord Kerr).

[102] *R v Holmes, ex parte Sherman* (1981) 72 Cr App R 266.

[103] ibid 271.

[104] ibid 271–72.

[105] *B v Barking, Havering & Brentwood Community Health Care NHS Trust* [1999] 1 FLR 106; *Ex p Khawaja* (n 95) [99]; and *R v Leeds Crown Court, ex parte Hunt* [1999] 1 WLR 841 (DC).

of State for the Home Department[106] distinguished between the two mechanisms of redress as follows:

> The principle underlying Habeas Corpus is that each day's detention has to be justified and if someone is wrongfully detained the fact that he does not challenge the legality of his detention for three years does not prevent him from challenging it thereafter, at any rate whilst he is still detained. The principle underlying judicial review is that if someone wishes to challenge the legality of an administrative action he must do so expeditiously; if he does not, the court, although it can grant him extra time, can refuse him relief simply because he failed to act expeditiously.[107]

The courts have been somewhat inconsistent in their approaches to the interaction between judicial review and habeas corpus. Although in *R v Secretary of State for the Home Department, ex parte Rahman*[108] any difference between these mechanisms was seen to be insubstantial, the following distinction was drawn by the Court of Appeal in *R v Secretary of State for the Home Department, ex parte Cheblak*:[109]

> the two forms of relief ... are essentially different. A writ of habeas corpus we will issue where someone is detained without any authority or purported authority or the purported authority is beyond the powers of the person authorising the detention and so is unlawful. The remedy of judicial review is available where the decision or action sought to be impugned is within the powers of the person taking it, but due to a procedural error, a misappreciation of law, a failure to take account of relevant matters, and taking account of all relevant matters or the fundamental and reasonableness of the decision or action, it should never have been taken. In such a case the decision or action is lawful, unless and until it is set aside by a court of competent jurisdiction.[110]

J. Interim Relief

(1) Stay of Proceedings

Where permission is granted, the court may order a stay of the proceedings which are **3-34** subject to the review.[111] Such a remedy may be necessary to preserve the status quo where the application concerns the granting of an adjournment, the decision to prosecute, or an unlawful bad character decision. Indeed, if such a remedy were not available the challenge might not be of practical benefit to the claimant at all.

In most cases where a stay is sought it will be necessary to make an application for urgent consideration (see above at 2-21).

R v Barry Magistrates' Court, ex parte Malpas[112] concerned a refusal by a magistrates' court to stay a charge of rape on the grounds of delay. The court emphasised the very high threshold for interfering with the magistrates' decision. Gage J said:

> The test that this court must apply was conveniently set out in the case of *R v Willesden Justices, ex parte Clemmings* (1988) 87 CrApp R 280 Bingham LJ (as he then was) made it perfectly

---

[106] *Abdul Sheikh v Secretary of State for the Home Department* [2001] INLR 98.
[107] ibid [9].
[108] *R v Secretary of State for the Home Department, ex parte Rahman* [1996] 4 All ER 945.
[109] *R v Secretary of State for the Home Department, ex parte Cheblak* [1991] 2 All ER 319.
[110] See also *R v Secretary of State for the Home Department, ex parte Muboyaye* [1991] 4 All ER 72.
[111] CPR 54.10(2). For the general principles applied when considering a stay see also *R v HM Inspectorate of Pollution, Ministry of Agriculture, Fisheries and Food, ex parte Greenpeace Ltd* [1994] COD 56 (QBD).
[112] *R v Barry Magistrates' Court, ex parte Malpas* [1997] EWHC Admin 874, [1998] COD 90 (QBD).

clear that this court, when dealing with an application of this nature, could only interfere with a decision of the Justices if that decision was a decision which no reasonable Bench of Magistrates, properly directing itself, could have reached.

It should be noted that the power to grant a stay is not limited to judicial reviews involving judicial proceedings. In *R v Secretary of State for Education ex parte Avon County Council*[113] the Court of Appeal held that the Court has the power to grant a stay of any administrative decision-making process by a public body.[114] It would therefore appear potentially open in some circumstances to apply for a stay of a charging decision by the CPS pending production of a report (for example a psychiatric or social work report) which might go to the Public Interest Stage of the Full Code Test. In practice there may well be nothing to choose between applying for a stay or applying for an interim injunction. Using the above example, there is no practical difference between a stay, pausing the CPS's decision-making process, and an injunction restraining the CPS from making a charging decision until a particular piece of evidence has become available.

As the commentary to the White Book sets out, 'The criteria for granting a stay, and in particular the relationship between stays and interim remedies, remains to be worked out'.[115] The commentary goes on to suggest that where a stay just concerns the claimant and defendant, this should be treated as if it were an application for an interim injunction and the same procedure and principles for interim relief should apply (paras 54.3.5–54.3.6). It is suggested that such an approach appears entirely apposite.[116]

(2) Interim Injunctions

3-35   The High Court may grant injunctions under section 37(1) of the Senior Courts Act 1981 where it is 'just and convenient to do so'. Such an order is not dependent upon the grant of permission and may be made at any time, including before the issue of proceedings if the matter is urgent.[117]

The general test for interim injunctions was test set out in *American Cyanamid Co v Ethicon Ltd*.[118] The test in considering whether to grant an interim injunction is as follows:

i.   Does the claim for judicial review raise a serious issue to be tried?
      In considering whether there is a serious issue to be tried the court will consider whether the claimant can show a real prospect of success at the substantive hearing.[119]

ii.   If so, does the balance of convenience justify the court exercising its discretion to grant the injunction?
      In considering the balance of convenience the court will have regard to the wider public interest.[120]

---

[113] *R v Secretary of State for Education ex parte Avon County Council* [1991] 1 QB 558.
[114] Jackson (ed), *Civil Procedure*, vol 1 (London, Thomson Reuters, 2013) (the 'White Book'), 54.10.2.
[115] CPR 54.10.4.
[116] For example, a stay may be ordered but conditional on a cross undertaking for damages (*R v Inspectorate of Pollution, ex parte Greenpeace Ltd* [1994] 1 WLR 570).
[117] CPR r 25.
[118] *American Cyanamid Co v Ethicon Ltd* [1975] AC 396.
[119] *R (Medical Justice) v Secretary of State for the Home Department* [2010] EWHC 1425 (Admin); see also commentary to the White Book at 54.3.6.
[120] *Smith v Inner London Education Authority* [1978] 1 All ER 411; *Sierbein v Westminster City Council* (1987) 86 LGR 431.

In relation to the first test, a serious question to be tried, the House of Lords held as follows:

> the court should not restrain a public authority by interim injunction from enforcing an apparently authentic law unless it is satisfied, having regard to all the circumstances, that the challenge to the validity of the law is, *prima facie*, so firmly based as to justify so exceptional a course being taken.[121]

In relation to the second test, the balance of convenience, the court will consider the inconvenience to the claimant if interim relief is refused if the claim is successful, as against the inconvenience to the respondent if relief if granted and the claim is unsuccessful. Though undertakings in damages are typically required in cases of commercial significance to the parties, they are unlikely to be relevant in claims arising from magistrates' court proceedings.[122]

In deciding whether to grant a mandatory injunction, that is to say an injunction compelling a decision-maker to do something, it will generally be necessary to show a strong prima facie case.[123] However, in some cases the courts have been prepared to apply a lower test. In the context of homelessness cases, it has been held that where permission is granted, an injunction requiring the authority to provide temporary accommodation would generally follow.[124]

(3) Procedure

An interim remedy is generally sought at the time at which the claim is lodged (for the procedure on lodging a claim see above at 2-12). Further to CPR 54.6(1)(c) a claimant must set out on the Claim Form any interim remedy that is being sought. Further to rule 25.3(1), generally notice must be given to the other side for any application for an interim remedy. Good reasons must be given for not giving notice. **3-36**

If a claimant applies for an interim remedy at the same time as applying for judicial review, the claimant will need to complete section 8, 'Other Applications' on the Claim Form (see Annex 2). This sets out, 'I wish to make an application for...'. It is advisable to set out in this box a summary of the interim relief sought and to attach a draft order of the interim injunction sought. The Claim Form must be accompanied by a £140 fee for permission to apply for judicial review.[125] Cheques should be made payable to 'HM Courts & Tribunals Service'.

---

[121] *R v Secretary of State for Transport, ex parte Factortame Limited (No 2)* [1991] AC 603, 674 (Lord Goff).
[122] In *De Falco v Crawley Borough Council* [1980] QB 460, the court considered an application for interim relief in the context of a homelessness case and commented: 'This is not the same sort of case as *American Cyanamid Co v Ethicon Ltd* [1975] AC 396, because the plaintiffs here cannot give any worthwhile undertaking in damages'. *Belize Alliance of Conservation Non Governmental Organisations v Department of the Environment of Belize (Practice Note)* [2003] UKPC 63, [39]: '[T]here may be cases where the risk of serious uncompensated detriment to the defendant cannot be ignored. The rich plaintiff may find, if ultimately unsuccessful, that he has to pay out a very large sum as the price of having obtained an injunction which (with hindsight) ought not to have been granted to him.'
[123] *R v Kensington and Chelsea RLBC ex parte Hammell* [1989] QB 518 (CA).
[124] *R v Cardiff City Council ex parte Barry* [1989] 22 HLR 261 (QBD).
[125] The Civil Proceedings Fees (Amendment) Order 2014/874, Sch 1, para 1.9(a)). Note there is a further £700 fee if permission is granted, payable by the claimant within 7 days of service on the claimant of the order granting permission (para 1.9(c)). In the event of an application for oral renewal of a permission decision the fee for the oral renewal is £350 followed by a further £350 if permission is granted (para 1.9(b)).

For a summary of the procedure for urgent applications and for out-of-hours applications, see above at 2-21–2-22.

3-37   If the application is urgent, which it invariably will be where interim relief is sought, then in addition to a Claim Form, an Application for Urgent Consideration (N463—see Annex 3) should be completed. Section 4 again requires setting out 'what interim relief is sought and why'. It may well be advisable to include this in a separate free-standing document, or as a subheading in any free-standing detailed statement of grounds and facts relied on for the accompanying judicial review. The Urgent Consideration Form requires a draft order of the interim relief sought to be attached. As is clear from the Urgent Consideration Form, considerable thought and justification should be given as to why urgent consideration is required. This includes setting out the date and time when it was first appreciated that an immediate application might be necessary. The application must be served on the defendant and any interested party. The defendant and interested party must be advised that they may make representations on the application.[126]

3-38   The judge who considers an application for interim relief can do any number of things:

i.   they may grant interim relief and permission;[127]
ii.   they may grant interim relief on the papers, pending a decision on permission;
iii.   they may grant interim relief pending an on-notice oral hearing (to consider just the interim relief, or the interim relief and permission);
iv.   they may refuse interim relief and refuse permission; or
v.   they may refuse interim relief and be silent on permission.

3-39   In the event that interim relief and permission are refused, then further to CPR 54.12(3) a claimant can request that the decision granting permission be reconsidered at an oral hearing. The application for interim relief could be re-ventilated at that stage. Further to CPR 54.12(4) the request for reconsideration must be filed in the Administrative Court Office within seven days of service of the reasons for refusal. There is no right to orally renew if the court records the fact that the application is totally without merit in accordance with CPR 23.12 (CPR 54.12(7)). The CPR and Practice Statement are not explicit about whether the out-of-hours telephone procedure can be used to orally renew where permission has been refused on the paper, given the requirement of CPR 54.12(4). Guidance from the Court of Appeal in *R (MD) Afghanistan v Secretary of State for the Home Department*[128] suggests that the out-of-hours procedure would be available in such circumstances:

> If the case is one of sufficient urgency, and there is no time to apply in court, the claimant may renew his application to the out-of-hours duty High Court judge, although if that judge is not provided with the relevant papers he may understandably be reluctant to come to a different decision from the judge who had the advantage of the papers.[129]

In the event that interim relief is refused on the papers and there is no express decision on permission, or permission has already been granted, then the claimant has a

---

[126] Maurice Kay LJ (ed), *Blackstone's Civil Practice* (Oxford, Oxford University Press, 2013) 31.
[127] The court should not normally grant permission without the defendant having an opportunity to file an acknowledgment of service. There could be an abridged timetable for acknowledgment of service. *The White Book* Vol 1 (2013), 54.4.1.
[128] *R (MD) Afghanistan v Secretary of State for the Home Department* [2012] 1 WLR 2422.
[129] ibid [21].

right to orally renew. Again it would appear that this right can be exercised through the out-of-hours telephone procedure where appropriate.[130]

In cases of extreme urgency then it may be necessary to make an out-of-hours appli-   **3-40**
cation by telephone to the duty judge applying for interim relief. It should be noted that it is:

> the advocate's personal responsibility before coming to court to be entirely satisfied that there were good and proper grounds for making a late application and … that there [are] proper grounds for making the application.[131]

Out-of-hours applications should be reserved for only the 'most exceptional circumstances'.[132] It is hard to see how such circumstances are likely to arise in the vast majority of judicial reviews arising in the context of criminal proceedings. As Maurice Kay LJ commented, 'In most cases, the hardship which has been endured for days or hours can be endured until the following day without serious further risk.'[133]

If there are good and proper grounds for making an application out of hours, then an undertaking will need to be given to issue a claim form as soon as possible afterwards if this has not been done. Equally, if the application for an injunction is unsuccessful then it is still incumbent on the claimant and the claimant's advocate the next day to submit the appropriate application, namely an Urgent Consideration Form (N463):

> In respect of the out of hours applications, it is the case that those concerned must, in accordance with the rules, make an appropriate application the following day, even if the court refuses to grant the relief.[134]

In the event that there are grounds to make an out-of-hours injunction, then the advocate should telephone the Royal Courts of Justice. They will be put in contact first with security and then with the clerk to the duty judge in the High Court. They will then be called back by the High Court judge. There is a heavy duty on an advocate at an ex parte hearing to provide full and frank disclosure.[135] The advocate should make as full a note as possible of the hearing, including a detailed note of the reasons given, which should be provided to the other side after the hearing.

(4) Bail

Where a defendant applies for permission to seek an order quashing a conviction or sen-   **3-41**
tence in the magistrates' court, there is a statutory right to apply to the Administrative Court for bail.[136] But some caution is necessary. If a claimant is serving a criminal sentence, applying for bail in the course of an unsuccessful judicial review claim may require a return to prison without any reduction in the time served.[137]

---

[130] ibid. CPR 54.4(1).
[131] *R (Rehman) v Secretary of State for the Home Department* [2013] EWHC 1351 (Admin) [6].
[132] *R (Q, D, KH, OK, JK, H, T, and S) v Secretary of State for the Home Department* [2003] EWHC 2507 (Admin). See also above at 2-25.
[133] ibid [13].
[134] *Rehman* (n 131) [17].
[135] *R (Lawer) v Restormel* [2007] EWHC 2299 (Admin) [64]–[66] (Munby J).
[136] Criminal Justice Act 1948, s 37(1)(d).
[137] Senior Courts Act 1981, s 81(1)(e).

The bail application should be made on the Claim Form and must be served on the prosecutor and the Director of Public Prosecutions. The application should include details of the bail address and any sureties, and be served in time to allow the defendant to properly consider the application. Further procedural rules are set out CPR Schedule 1, RSC Order, rule 9.

There is no rule requiring permission to have been granted before the application for bail has been considered, although in practice a High Court judge is unlikely to grant the application unless satisfied that the judicial review itself is arguable. Therefore, the application should be heard at the permission hearing. In such cases an application for urgent consideration should be made.

On appeals to the Supreme Court from the Administrative Court (see above at 2-41–2-43), any application for bail must be made to the Administrative Court—see Supreme Court Practice Direction 12.13.1–3, which governs bail in appeals to that court.

Part II
Identifying Grounds for Judicial Review

4

The Police

RACHEL TAYLOR AND PIERS VON BERG

A. General Principles

(1) Introduction

The scope for judicial review of the police is substantial, more so than any other defen- **4-1** dant in criminal judicial review. Recent years have seen a marked increase in the number of challenges, especially since the passing of the Human Rights Act 1998. New areas have emerged, including challenges to police handling of personal data, which has seen a high volume of case law. This has been encouraged by the fact that almost of all of these cases are civil rather than criminal causes or matters, and so have been able to reach the Court of Appeal. It is a dynamic area, and at the time of writing several of the cases discussed below are pending appeal or awaiting judgment.

However, despite this fertile ground, it is very important to remember that judicial review is a remedy of last resort. In addition, many complaints against the police may only relate to compensation for alleged loss. Therefore, identifying when and how judicial review is most appropriate, rather than using alternative remedies or bringing a private action, is crucial, as discussed in the first section below.

The subsequent sections identify the circumstances when judicial review will be appropriate in relation to certain police actions and procedures. This chapter cannot however provide an exhaustive list, and readers are reminded to refer to the common grounds for judicial review above at section G of Chapter 1, which can apply in any potential claim.

(2) Alternative Remedies

4-2   It is a first principle of judicial review that a claimant should exhaust any alternative remedies. There is a statutory system for making complaints against police officers, which may constitute such an alternative. A person can make their complaint known to the force which will ordinarily be obliged to record it.[1] The process can provide remedies such as the provision of information, explanations, an apology, a meeting with the person complained about, a change in force policy or procedure, further investigation, and disciplinary measures against officers. More serious complaints are either investigated by the force concerned or referred to the Independent Police Complaints Commission (IPCC). Case law on whether a matter should be investigated by the IPCC or the police has suggested that the IPCC has a wide discretion under section 10 of the Police Reform Act 2002 to decide how to deal with any matter within its remit.[2] However, the way in which the report is framed is restrictive—it cannot express an actual determination, but merely an opinion.[3] Remedies from this procedure can include changes to force procedures, advice to an officer concerned, disciplinary action, or a referral to the CPS (which can also result from a local investigation). If an outcome is unsatisfactory, complainants may appeal.

Importantly, claimants should consider if the procedure as a whole can provide an effective and suitable remedy in light of the above and any delays that would be likely to ensue. Concerning the former, complainants should be mindful that the outcome of the procedure is that a report is submitted for consideration by the appropriate authority. Whether any action will be taken depends on the content of the report and whether the appropriate authority considers that any matters should be referred to the DPP or if there is a disciplinary case to answer.[4] As regards delays, in light of the limitation periods for judicial review (see above at 2-6), claimants may be compelled to issue a claim before the procedure is complete, for example, if the matter is urgent or time-sensitive. In such circumstances, they would be expected to inform the defendant and the court of any outstanding complaints and account for the timing of their actions (see above at 2-4).

There are cases where a claimant can follow the complaint procedure and, if unsuccessful, challenge the decision,[5] or if the complaint is upheld, request a force to act on the outcome of their complaint. If the response is unfavourable, that decision can be targeted by a judicial review.[6]

---

[1] For exceptions, see Police Reform Act 2002, Sch 3, para 2 and Police (Complaints and Misconduct) Regulations 2012, reg 3.

[2] *R (Reynolds) v Chief Constable of Sussex* [2008] EWHC 1240 (Admin), [2008] Po LR 77. This may include investigating whether a person was injured before they had contact with the police in order to identify causation of an injury. IPCC decisions may also be challenged by judicial review—see below section D in Chapter 9.

[3] In *R (Chief Constable of West Yorkshire) v IPCC* [2013] EWHC 2698 (Admin) the Court held that the language of s 10(2) was deliberately restrictive in referring to handling complaints rather than determining them and recording matters that 'may' amount to criminal or disciplinary misconduct.

[4] Police Reform Act 2002, Sch 2, para 24.

[5] Eg as in *R (Driver) v Independent Police Complaints Commission* [2012] EWHC 1271 (Admin).

[6] See *R (Lee) v Chief Constable of Essex* [2012] EWHC 283 (Admin).

Rachel Taylor and Piers von Berg

(3) Judicial Review or Private Action

If a claimant seeks only damages for alleged losses caused by actions of a police officer, **4-3** the proper route is a private claim not a claim for judicial review. For example, the most common civil wrongs by the police against an individual are malicious prosecution, wrongful arrest, assault, false imprisonment and wrongful interference with goods.[7] The matters considered in the course of a judicial review are likely to be strictly limited to issues of lawfulness. As Lord Neuberger MR explained in *R (McClure and Moos) v The Commissioner of Police of the Metropolis*[8] (discussed in detail below at 4-63), which concerned a challenge to police policy:

> it has rightly been accepted that judicial review proceedings in this case are appropriate only to the consideration of the strategic decisions. If there are allegations of excessive force or other tortious behaviour against individual, or groups of, police offices, in the course of the operations consequent on those decisions, those allegations must be made in ordinary Queen's Bench Division actions and their rights or wrongs are not the concern of this case.[9]

Conversely, as there are considerably less obstacles to bringing a private action, the courts take a dim view of claimants who try and bypass these hurdles. For example, the court's permission is not required to bring the claim, the limitation periods are considerably longer and a remedy can be awarded as of right. In *O'Reilly v Mackman*,[10] the court held that it is an abuse of process to attempt to enforce one's public law rights by way of a private law action thereby avoiding the hurdles of the judicial review procedure. This rule was modified by the introduction of the Civil Procedure Rules. In *Clark v University of Lincolnshire and Humberside*,[11] Lord Woolf MR said the court would not strike out such a claim without considering whether there has been unjustified delay in bringing the proceedings, the nature of the claim, and whether the issue affects the general public.[12] It was said that the court did not need to prohibit the use of a private law action, as costs sanctions are available under the CPR. In addition, under the CPR, the court has the power to transfer out claims started in the Administrative Court (CPR 54(20)) and to transfer in proceedings started elsewhere (CPR 30(5)).

A good example of a claim that was correctly brought as a private claim rather than by way of judicial review is the Scottish case of *Ruddy v Chief Constable of Strathclyde*.[13] The case concerned a claim for damages at common law and under the Human Rights Act 1998 for i) an alleged assault by police officers and ii) breach of the claimant's right under Article 3 to an effective investigation into the same allegations. The Supreme

---

[7] See R Clayton, H Tomlinson with E Buckett and A Davies, *Civil Actions Against the Police*, 3rd edn (London, Sweet & Maxwell, 2004). It is also possible for a claim to proceed as a challenge to an investigatory body's findings in respect of a complaint that might normally be brought by way of private action, eg *Driver* (n 5).

[8] *R (McClure and Moos) v The Commissioner of Police of the Metropolis* [2012] EWCA Civ 12.

[9] ibid [2]. Note also that the Court, at [47], identified that concerns regarding the use of shield strikes and lack of communication and training were not suitable for consideration in judicial review proceedings. This approach was also endorsed in *Castle v Commissioner of Police for the Metropolis* [2011] EWHC 2317 (Admin) [71].

[10] *O'Reilly v Mackman* [1983] 2 AC 237, [1982] 3 WLR 1096.

[11] *Clark v University of Lincolnshire and Humberside* [2000] 1 WLR 1988, [2000] 3 All ER 752.

[12] ibid [35]–[37].

[13] *Ruddy v Chief Constable of Strathclyde* [2012] UKSC 57, 2013 SLT 119.

Court disagreed with the Chief Constable's defence that the action should have been brought by judicial review. The appellant was not seeking to control the actions of the Chief Constable or to review and set aside any of his decisions, and as such the court concluded that the 'essence of his claim is simply one of damages'.[14]

That is not to say judicial review claims cannot seek compensation in damages but they can only do so in conjunction with an application for a public law remedy.[15] An example of such a claim against the police would be a declaration of breach of a person's human rights—for example, unlawful detention—together with compensation for losses arising from the breach.[16]

4-4   Moreover, there are some cases that are not amenable to a private law claim. For example, a breach of a statutory duty by the police may not in certain cases found a private action. In *Olotu v Home Office*[17] the CPS failed in their statutory duty to bring the claimant to court before the expiry of the custody time limit. The claimant brought an action for false imprisonment. The court refused the claim on the basis that she did not have a private law right to damages for a breach of a statutory duty. Mummery LJ stated:

> It is a question of available remedies. The plaintiff was undoubtedly entitled to remedies in the criminal proceedings (bail) and in judicial review proceedings. The issue is whether she is entitled to an additional remedy against the CPS by way of a civil law claim for damages ... There are strong indicators against the implied creation of a statutory tort of strict liability in a case such as this: the availability to the plaintiff of other remedies both in the criminal proceedings (bail) and in public law proceedings (habeas corpus and mandamus).[18]

The above authority was considered by the House of Lords in *Cullen v Chief Constable of the Royal Ulster Constabulary*.[19] Lord Hutton said that judicial review would be a suitable remedy for failure by the police to allow a detainee access to a solicitor (see section 58 of PACE 1984, and below at 4-82). The key factor in the majority's decision was that there was no injury, harm or loss to the claimant but it was rather an attempt to overturn a decision.[20] His Lordship was clear this could be an effective remedy in England.[21]

(4) The Overlap Between Public and Private Law Actions against the Police

4-5   There is considerable overlap between police decisions that can be challenged under private and public law. For example, a claimant can challenge a decision to arrest and detain through the tort of false imprisonment or as decisions to arrest and detain reached unlawfully on public law grounds. Some of the factors that the court may consider are illustrated in the cases below.

---

[14] ibid [15].
[15] Eg, *R (Mengesha) v Commissioner of Police of the Metropolis* [2013] EWHC 1695 (Admin). See below at 4-6(
[16] An example is *R (T) v The Secretary of State for Justice and Birmingham Magistrates' Court* [2013] EWHC 1119 (Admin).
[17] *Olotu v Home Office* [1997] 1 WLR 328.
[18] ibid 338–39.
[19] *Cullen v Chief Constable of the Royal Ulster Constabulary* [2003] UKHL 39, [2003] 1 WLR 1763.
[20] ibid [32].
[21] ibid [39].

Rachel Taylor and Piers von Berg

In *Sher v Chief Constable of Greater Manchester*[22] (for the facts see below 4-57) the court refused permission for judicial review on the grounds that the claims could be brought by private action and involved complex disputes of fact for which the judicial review procedure under CPR Part 54 is not designed to address; additionally, the claimants did not seek public law remedies. Notably, the argument that the claimants might lose public funding and would be subject to a different costs regime in private proceedings, for example, orders for security for costs, was dismissed.

Significantly, Coulson J, with whom Laws LJ agreed, emphasised that had the claimants been able to demonstrate that there were other parts of the claim that were arguable in respect of which judicial review offered the only remedy, dealing with all of the matters together in one set of judicial proceedings might constitute a pragmatic and flexible option.[23]

This 'pragmatic' approach was arguably evident in the earlier case of *R (C) v The Chief Constable of 'A' Police, 'A' Magistrates' Court*.[24] The claimant challenged (i) the issuing of a search warrant leading to the claimant's arrest and (ii) the continuation of a criminal investigation. Underhill J, whilst noting that judicial review proceedings in these circumstances were 'very unusual', and that typically actions would be pursued by way of private law remedy 'where the court will have the opportunity to hear all evidence and have the reasons for their actions taken fully explored in cross-examination', emphasised that where judicial review 'may be the only practical available route', the application would not be refused 'in limine' [at the start].[25]

Another example is the exercise of search and seizure powers. Pursuing a judicial review can result in the quashing of search warrants and/or an injunction to deliver up goods, together with damages, where appropriate. A similar injunction can be obtained through a private law action on the basis that the warrant was issued unlawfully, and of course, damages may also be recoverable.

(5) Types of Decision Subject to Challenge

In pursuing a judicial review of a police decision the claimant must consider whether it is the type of decision that can be reviewed. The types of decision that can be challenged are set out below. Generally speaking, where the police purport to exercise a statutory or common law power to the detriment of an individual, the decision will be reviewable. If it falls within that category, there are advantages to the judicial review route. It will in most cases be quicker than the county court, as there are very few interlocutory hearings due to the fact that the procedure is front-loaded (see above in Chapter 2). Judicial review is flexible and can target and influence high-level strategic decisions, or alternatively it can concentrate on the decision of a front-line officer. However, in relation to the former, claimants must be careful of the rules on standing (see above at 1-45). Section 31(3) of the Senior Courts Act 1981 requires a claimant to show that he/she has

4-6

---

22 *Sher v Chief Constable of Greater Manchester* [2010] EWHC 1859 (Admin), [2011] 2 All ER 364.
23 ibid [84].
24 *R (C) v The Chief Constable of 'A' Police, 'A' Magistrates' Court* [2006] EWHC 2352 (Admin).
25 ibid [6].

'sufficient interest in the matter to which the application relates'. For example, alleged victims of crime can seek judicial review of police decisions.[26]

(6) Identifying the Correct Defendant

4-7   Police officers are public officials therefore their decisions are subject to challenges by way of judicial review. The correct defendant in each case is the chief officer who is liable by statute for any unlawful conduct of a constable under his direction and control in the performance or purported performance of his or her functions.[27]

Police staff may be employees of Police and Crime Commissioners (PCCs) or of a chief constable.[28] A chief constable may confer on police staff powers to act as community support officers, investigating officers, detention officers, or escort officers.[29] The police staff of each force is under the direction and control of the chief officer.[30] An employing chief constable or local policing body is liable for unlawful conduct by police staff in the exercise of powers such as those listed above.[31] The correct defendant is likely to be the chief constable, who has direction and control of such persons.

Broadly speaking, the functions and duties of local policing bodies (PCCs) remain the same as the old police authorities concerning the maintenance of a police force.[32] PCCs are also required to hold chief constables to account, and may appoint or dismiss the chief officer. On the latter point, they have been the target of judicial review claims relating to disciplinary matters.[33] On the former point, it remains to be seen whether PCCs will be challenged on how they hold chief constables to account.[34]

In some cases litigants must be careful to distinguish between what is the province of central government, for example, a Secretary of State, and what is a matter for a chief

---

[26] For example in the case of cautions in *R (Omar) v Chief Constable of Bedfordshire* [2002] EWHC 3060 (Admin), [2002] Po LR 413. See below at 4-89.

[27] Police Act 1996, s 88. The same applies for special constables. See also s 24(3) where officers are serving under the direction and control of another force.

[28] Police authorities outside London were abolished and replaced by Police and Crime Commissioners (a 'local policing body') by the Police Reform and Social Responsibility (PRSP) Act 2011, s 1(9). The exceptions in London relate to the London Mayor's office, which acts as 'local policing body' for the Metropolitan Police, and the Common Council for the City of London, which remains the police authority for the City of London Police. The relationship between the PCCs, the Mayor's Office for Policing and Crime, chief constables, Police and Crime Panels and the London Assembly Police and Crime Panel is set out in the Schedule to the Policing Protocol Order 2011, SI 2011/2744. (Police Crime Panels were set up to scrutinise the actions of the PCCs.) The duties and functions of PCCs and the arrangements for London are set out in PRSP 2011, ss 1–4.

[29] Police Reform Act 2002, s 38A.

[30] PRSP 2011, s 2(3).

[31] Police Reform Act 2002, s 42(7). The same applies for contractors—see s 42(9). Note *Woodland v Swimming Teachers Association* [2013] UKSC 66, [2013] 3 WLR 1227, which set out the criteria at [23] for a non-delegable duty of care, which included *inter alia* that the claimant was dependent on the protection of the defendant from risk of injury, (eg such as a prisoner), and where there was an antecedent relationship which put the claimant in the custody of the defendant. Eg *Nyang v G4S Care & Justice Services Ltd* [2013] EWHC 3946 (QB).

[32] PRSP 2011, s 1(6)(a). The general functions of an authority were to 'secure the maintenance of an efficient and effective police force for its area'. Police Act 1996, s 6 (repealed).

[33] For example, *R (Rhodes) v Police and Crime Commissioner for Lincolnshire* [2013] EWHC 1009 (Admin).

[34] See *Police and Crime Commissioners: power to remove Chief Constables* (Cm 8766, 2013), which notes that whilst there is a procedure for PCCs to follow, the circumstances in which they can call for resignation or retirement are not defined.

Rachel Taylor and Piers von Berg

constable (see footnote 28 and the Policing Protocol). This is illustrated by *R v Secretary of State for the Home Department, ex parte Northumbria Police Authority*[35] which highlighted the prerogative power of the minister to keep a central supply of police equipment to provide to chief constables. Any decision to use such stores such as plastic bullets or tear gas, was a decision for the chief constable.

If there is a challenge to a refusal to amend rules or laws on police practices, the proper defendant is likely to be the relevant Secretary of State (perhaps in addition to the chief constable), who may have a statutory power to amend those rules, subject to any approval by Parliament.[36]

(7) Timing of a Challenge

The usual rules on promptness will apply (see above at 2-4). Judicial review of police **4-8** action will very rarely be the appropriate remedy during the course of criminal proceedings. Potential claimants should first consider whether their complaint can and should be dealt with within the trial process. For example, if police conduct has affected the fairness of the proceedings against a defendant in a criminal trial, an application can be made to exclude evidence thereby obtained (under section 78 of PACE) or to stay the proceedings in the event of an abuse of process. Claimants should also be aware of the limited nature of the High Court's jurisdiction over the CPS and the Crown Court (see above at 1-25 and below at 5-8 and at 7-2) and the manner in which judicial review of the magistrates' courts operates (see below at 6-16).

(8) Criminal Cause or Matter

Some judicial review challenges to police decisions will not be a 'criminal cause or **4-9** matter' under section 18(1)(a) of the Senior Courts Act 1981 (see above at 1-168). For example, challenges to policies or procedures will be a civil matter,[37] whereas challenges to police cautions will be a criminal matter. This has important consequences for applying for appeals and legal aid (see below at 2-41 and at 15-9–15-10).

B. General Duties to Prevent and Investigate Crime

(1) Duty to Prevent Crime and Challenges to Police Policy

In principle, a claimant can challenge a decision by a police force not to act against **4-10** certain alleged criminal behaviour. For example, a force may promulgate a policy on

---

[35] *R v Secretary of State for the Home Department, ex parte Northumbria Police Authority* [1989] QB 26.
[36] See Police and Criminal Evidence Codes of Practice in *R (HC) v Secretary of State for the Home Department* [2013] EWHC 982 (Admin).
[37] As with *R v Commissioner of Police of the Metropolis, ex parte Blackburn (No 1)* [1968] 2 QB 118, [1968] 2 WLR 893.

how they will police particular offences. These claims are unusual and very difficult to succeed on as the police are granted a wide margin of discretion in how they devise and implement their policies.

The first consideration is whether a claimant has standing (see above at 1-45). In *R v Oxford, ex parte Levey*[38] the court held that the claimant had sufficient standing to bring a claim challenging police policy not to enter the Toxteth area of Liverpool in circumstances in which he had been robbed near that area. It was irrelevant whether the complainant was from Liverpool or was merely visiting. However, the court refused the substantive application in any event. Although the local police policies could be subject to review, the chief constable was granted the widest possible discretion in how he implemented them.

4-11   This wide remit of discretion is a constant theme in challenges to police policies. In *R v Commissioner of Police of the Metropolis, ex parte Blackburn (No 1)*,[39] a claimant attempted to obtain a mandatory order to compel the police to overturn a decision not to enforce provisions of the Betting, Gaming and Lotteries Act 1963. Lord Denning MR said:

> Although the chief officers of police are answerable to the law, there are many fields in which they have a discretion with which the law will not interfere. For instance, it is for the Commissioner of Police of the Metropolis, or the chief constable, as the case may be, to decide in any particular case whether inquiries should be pursued, or whether an arrest should be made, or a prosecution brought. It must be for him to decide on the disposition of his force and the concentration of his resources on any particular crime or area. No court can or should give him direction on such a matter. He can also make policy decisions and give effect to them, as, for instance, was often done when prosecutions were not brought for attempted suicide. But there are some policy decisions with which, I think, the courts in a case can, if necessary, interfere. Suppose a chief constable were to issue a directive to his men that no person should be prosecuted for stealing any goods less than £100 in value. I should have thought that the court could countermand it. He would be failing in his duty to enforce the law.[40]

The court confirmed this approach in *R v Commissioner for the Police for the Metropolis, ex parte Blackburn (No 3)*[41] and in *R v Metropolitan Police Commissioner, ex parte Blackburn (No 4)*.[42] In the former case, Lord Denning MR said that the discretion was not absolute and the court would intervene in extreme circumstances. Both cases involved attempts by the same claimant to challenge police policies on prosecuting offences of pornography and obscenity.

4-12   In *R v Chief Constable of Devon and Cornwall, ex parte CEGB*,[43] the claimant challenged a decision not to remove protestors from land. Despite a strong case being made out for the claimant the application was refused. Templeman LJ said:

> The court cannot tell the police how and when their powers should be exercised, for the court cannot judge the explosiveness of the situation or deal with the individual problems which will arise as a result of the activities of the obstructers.[44]

---

[38] *R v Oxford, ex parte Levey* (1987) 151 LG Rev 371.
[39] *Ex p Blackburn (No 1)* (n 37).
[40] ibid 136D-F.
[41] *R v Commissioner for the Police for the Metropolis, ex parte Blackburn (No 3)* [1973] QB 241, [1973] 2 WLR 43.
[42] *R v Metropolitan Police Commissioner, ex parte Blackburn (No 4)* The Times, 1 December 1979.
[43] *R v Chief Constable of Devon and Cornwall, ex parte CEGB* [1982] QB 458, [1981] 3 WLR 867.
[44] ibid 481C.

Rachel Taylor and Piers von Berg

Other examples include failed attempts to compel the police to intervene in a custody dispute over a child[45] and, more recently, to declare as unlawful a police initiative to name offenders on public posters (discussed in more detail below at 4-129).[46] The court also refused a prisoner's application to prevent the provision of information by the police to a prison governor concerning potential risk of harm to the claimant on release.[47]

(2) Duty to Investigate

Judicial review of police actions is possible during the course of a police investigation **4-13**
(for example regarding questions of arrest and search, as discussed below at 4-16 and 4-50) but challenges to the investigation itself are extremely rare. More common are actions at private law where a claimant challenges a failure to investigate or investigate promptly as a breach of human rights. This is relevant for judicial review as claims can be brought on the same grounds. Under Article 2(1) the European Court of Human Rights (ECtHR) has held that the State has a duty to investigate where a person has been killed by the use of force.[48] Such an investigation must be effective in that it should be capable of identifying and punishing any found to be responsible.[49]

The scope and nature of the police's duty to investigate serious crimes was considered in substantial detail by Green J in *DSD v Commissioner of Police for the Metropolis*[50]. Various principles were established which will inform potential challenges by victims to alleged failures by police investigators. Practitioners should note that at the outset there is a common law duty to detect crime and bring offenders to justice.[51] Furthermore, Green J rejected the notion that a duty to investigate under Article 3 was inconsistent with domestic authorities such as *R (NM) v Secretary of State for Justice* and *Allen v Chief Constable of Hampshire*.[52] In *NM* the Court rejected the claim that a prison had not adequately investigated a complaint of sexual assault by a prisoner. Rix LJ said that in the absence of State complicity there was a duty to provide a system to investigate and prosecute criminal wrongs. This was cited with approval by Gross LJ in *Allen v Chief Constable of Hampshire*, where the court, including Lord Dyson MR, said Article 3 gave rise to a duty to conduct an effective investigation into the violations of a person's rights. Building on these authorities, *DSD* delineates questions of justiciability and breach under the HRA 1998, particularly Article 3.

The case was a private law claim for damages and declarations for an alleged failure to conduct an effective investigation into the claimants' allegations of sexual assault. The claimants were two of the victims of a prolific rapist, who committed numerous rapes and sexual assaults against women travelling in his taxi. The Commissioner did not

---

[45] *R v Chief Constable of Cheshire ex parte K* [1990] 1 FLR 70, [1990] FCR 201.
[46] *R (Ellis) v Chief Constable of Essex* [2003] EWHC 1321 (Admin); [2003] 2 FLR 566 and *R (Stanley) v Commissioner of Police of the Metropolis* [2004] EWHC 2229 (Admin), (2004) 168 JP 623.
[47] *R (Regan) v Chief Constable of the West Midlands* [2010] EWHC 2297 (Admin).
[48] *McCann v United Kingdom* (A/324) (1996) 21 EHRR 97 and *Kaya v Turkey* (1999) 28 EHRR 1.
[49] *Osmanoglu v Turkey* (2011) 53 EHRR 17 [87]–[88], [92].
[50] *DSD v Commissioner of Police for the Metropolis* [2014] EWHC 436 (QB).
[51] *Rice v Connolly* [1966] 2 QB 414 and *Ex p Blackburn (No 1)*—see above at 4-11.
[52] *R (NM) v Secretary of State for Justice* [2012] EWCA Civ 1182 and *Allen v Chief Constable of Hampshire* [2013] EWCA Civ 967.

accept that the HRA 1998 provided a remedy to victims of crimes committed by private parties where the central allegation was a failure to investigate. The court disagreed. It held that there was a duty on the police to conduct investigations into particularly severe violent acts perpetrated by private parties 'in a timely and efficient manner'.[53] However, it did not follow that damages would flow from every act or omission that may be classed as a failing or that every failure to follow operating standards and procedures leads to liability (see below).[54] After an extensive survey of the ECtHR's authorities on Article 3 Green J identified the following principles:[55]

i. Article 3 imposes a duty upon the police to investigate across the 'entire span' of the case, which may include incidents that came to the police's attention before the alleged offence;

ii. This duty is not conditional on the State being guilty, directly or indirectly of the conduct itself;

iii. It is engaged by a credible or arguable claim by a victim or third party that a person has been subject to treatment that would meet the standard of torture, degrading or inhuman treatment in Article 3—allegations of 'grave' or 'serious' crime will suffice;

iv. The police must investigate such allegations in an 'efficient and reasonable manner which is capable of leading to the identification and punishment of the perpetrator'—'capability' is referred to as the gravamen of the test;

    a. Questions of efficiency and reasonableness shall include promptitude and whether the offender was adequately prosecuted;

    b. Whether an investigation is 'reasonable' or 'capable' is a fact sensitive exercise;

    c. If officers took steps that were 'capable' of leading to identification and arrest, this did not discharge them from liability for omitting to take other steps that they could and should have taken;

    d. However, the police will be accorded a broad margin of appreciation in that: 'A failure to perform an individual act that really could have been performed will not trigger liability if: (a) notwithstanding that omission the investigation viewed in the round did in fact lead to the arrest of the suspect within a reasonable time; or (b) the investigation (even absent a prosecution) may still be said to encompass a series of reasonable and efficient steps';

v. Breaches may occur regardless of the outcome of the investigation;

vi. Not every failing incurs liability and the court will adopt a cautious approach to avoid setting an unacceptable burden on the police—'An operational failing which, had it <u>not</u> occurred, would <u>not</u> have been 'capable' of leading to the apprehension and prosecution of the offender is also not actionable. Police are only liable for failing to meet an operational standard that is capable of leading to the apprehension and prosecution of an offender';

vii. Article 3 requires a criminal investigation and so a civil claim against the offender or disciplinary action against an officer does not discharge the duty;

---

[53] *DSD v Commissioner of Police for the Metropolis* [2014] EWHC 436 (QB), [14].
[54] ibid, [14].
[55] ibid, [212]–[226].

            Rachel Taylor and Piers von Berg

viii. The vulnerability of the victims will at most be a 'contextual factor' in assessing the application of the principles to any case;

ix. The court should not take a sweeping or generalised approach to the facts and must be able to identify the causal connections 'which are innate in capability' before making any findings;

x. Article 8 does not provide a complainant with a broader level of protection than Article 3.[56]

The question of whether an investigation itself could be challenged on the basis that it may **4-14** not result in any eventual prosecution was considered in *R (C) v Chief Constable of A*[57] (see below at 4-86). Although Underhill J stated that there was no precedent for such a challenge he did not rule it out, instead confining it to the 'most exceptional cases'. This was explained by the following factors:

i. The court would need to have all the material that was before the police.

ii. It would require a good understanding of the factors to be taken into account in taking the decision.

iii. The decision itself would be 'highly laborious' and 'would also involve an unwelcome blurring of the separate roles of Court and prosecutor/investigator'.

iv. The type of appropriate relief was unclear, as an investigation is 'a factual rather than a legal state of affairs' with 'no formal status and until proceedings are commenced by a charge there is no public action taken', and investigations continue at various levels of intensity and could be shelved 'without prejudice to the possibility of being later revived in different circumstances: they do not therefore necessarily have a defined conclusion'.[58]

This sets a very high bar for future claims. Although the court did go on to consider the claimant's case, it was ultimately rejected.

A decision not to investigate was upheld in *R (Corner House Research) v Director of the Serious Fraud Office*.[59] This was a very unusual challenge involving threats by a foreign government to withdraw cooperation on counter-terrorism initiatives if a police investigation was continued into allegations that there had been payments to that government's agents or officials. The House of Lords dismissed the challenge to the Director's decision not to terminate the investigation. It recognised that it had been legitimately taken on the basis of a greater concern to protect the public from terrorism that may arise had the cooperation been withdrawn. He had acted within the discretion granted to him and he had not handed over his decision-making powers to the Foreign Office but was right to consult them.[60] This case demonstrated the high hurdle faced by any claimant in challenging the decision-making of an independent investigator as it is reserved to 'highly exceptional cases'. His office alone was entrusted with this decision,

---

[56] ibid, [242] following *Allen v Chief Constable of Hampshire*, [56]–[57].
[57] *R (C) v Chief Constable of A* [2006] EWHC 2352 (Admin), [2008] Po LR 23.
[58] ibid [33].
[59] *R (Corner House Research) v Director of the Serious Fraud Office* [2008] UKHL 60, [2009] 1 AC 756. See also below at 5-8.
[60] See also *R (Bermingham) v Director of Serious Fraud Office* [2006] EWHC 200 (Admin), [2007] QB 727—another challenge to a decision by the Director not to investigate. This involved interpretation of Criminal Justice Act 1987, s 1(3) that contained a power but not an obligation to investigate.

and the power conferred was broad and unprescriptive. But it is not unfettered, and the applicable constraints were described as follows:

> He must seek to exercise his powers so as to promote the statutory purpose for which he is given them. He must direct himself correctly in law. He must act lawfully. He must do his best to exercise an objective judgment on the relevant material available to him. He must exercise his powers in good faith, uninfluenced by any ulterior motive, predilection or prejudice.[61]

4-15   Where the police know or ought to know of the existence of a real and immediate risk to the life of a particular person from the criminal action of another, they have a positive obligation to take steps which might be reasonably expected to avoid that risk. This was established in the European case of *Osman v United Kingdom*.[62] The domestic courts have since held that the same obligation applies to Article 3.[63] More recently, in *Sarjantson v Chief Constable of Humberside*[64] Lord Dyson MR has interpreted the authorities since *Osman* as not to require an identification of the victim in order for the duty to be engaged. It is sufficient for the police to know or ought to know that there is a real and immediate risk to the life of a victim regardless of whether they know or ought to know the identities of such a victim.[65]

In *OOO v Commissioner of Police of the Metropolis*,[66] a private law claim, the claimants were five Nigerian women, who, after being brought into the country illegally, were forced to work for no pay and had been subject to emotional and physical abuse. The claimants argued that breaches of Articles 3 and 4 of the ECHR had been brought to the police's attention but not investigated. The Commissioner submitted that the scope of the investigative duty was equivalent to the preventive duty set out in *Osman* and as provided by the common law. The court rejected that position and applied the approach of the ECtHR in *Rantsev v Cyprus and Russia*.[67] This meant that the police are under a duty:

> to carry out an effective investigation of an allegation of a breach of Article 4 once a credible account of an alleged infringement had been brought to its attention. The trigger for the duty would not depend upon an actual complaint from a victim or near relative of a victim. The investigation, once triggered, would have to be undertaken promptly.[68]

Wyn Williams J also rejected the Commissioner's arguments that (i) the duty was not engaged unless there was a complaint from an identified victim and, (ii) in order for a breach to be found, it had to be particularly egregious.[69]

---

[61] *Corner House Research* (n 59) [32].

[62] *Osman v United Kingdom* [2000] 29 EHRR 245. Applied in *Van Colle v Chief Constable of Hertfordshire* [2008] UKHL 50, [2009] 1 AC 225.

[63] *E (A Child) v Chief Constable of Ulster* [2008] UKHL 66, [2009] 1 AC 536. Note the ECtHR has taken a similar line in relation to cases of domestic violence, which on the correct facts, may engage the operational duty to prevent ill treatment, as opposed to fatal injury, *Opuz v Turkey* (2010) 50 EHRR 28, 27 BHRC 159.

[64] *Sarjantson v Chief Constable of Humberside* [2013] EWCA Civ 1252, [2014] QB 411.

[65] ibid, [25].

[66] *OOO v Commissioner of Police of the Metropolis* [2011] EWHC 1246 (QB), [2011] HRLR 29.

[67] *Rantsev v Cyprus and Russia* [2010] 51 EHRR 1.

[68] *OOO* (n 66) [154].

[69] ibid [163] and [166].

C. Stop and Search

(1) General Principles

There are limited occasions on which a stop and search encounter can or should be   **4-16**
challenged by way of judicial review. A private law action will often present a more
appropriate method of redress due to both the available remedies and applicable procedural restrictions.[70]

The most prominent powers of stop and search are:

i.   section 1 of the Police and Criminal Evidence Act (PACE) 1984;
ii.   section 23(2) of the Misuse of Drugs Act 1971;
iii. section 43 of the Terrorism Act 2000;
iv.   section 163 of the Road Traffic Act (RTA) 1988;[71]
v.   section 60 of the Criminal Justice and Public Order Act (CJPO) 1994;
vi.   section 47A of the Terrorism Act 2000; and
vii. schedule 7 of the Terrorism Act 2000.

These powers can be categorised according to those which carry a condition of reasonable suspicion (i–iii above) and those which do not (iv–vii above). Varying conditions
and safeguards apply to these provisions, as set out in the legislation and accompanying codes of practice.[72] However, in *R (Rutherford) v Independent Police Complaints
Commission*[73] it was held that officers acting under an erroneous belief that they were
exercising a particular power would not be acting unlawfully where an alternative power
could legitimately have been relied on.[74]

(2) Challenges to Statutory Powers (Stop and Search)

Judicial review proceedings can be effectively utilised to challenge a particular statutory   **4-17**
power, or the operation of that power.[75] In *Gillan v United Kingdom*,[76] an important and

---

[70] For example, in *R (CC) v Commissioner of Police of the Metropolis and Another* [2011] EWHC 3316
(Admin), Collins J emphasised the rarity of cross-examination in judicial review proceedings, which would be
permitted only where factual issues required resolution in order for the claim to be considered appropriately.

[71] RTA 1988, s 163 simply imposes an obligation on a driver to stop when requested to do so by an officer and
thereafter to remain at the scene, and does not directly confer a police power to stop. However, there appears to
have been an acceptance of such a power in recent case law: see, for example *R (Smith) v DPP* [2002] EWHC
113 (Admin); and *R (Rutherford) v Independent Police Complaints Commission* [2010] EWHC 2881 (Admin). In
R (Beckett) v Aylesbury Crown Court [2004] EWHC 100 (Admin) the Court held that a police officer in uniform
was entitled under this power (or under common law) to stop any person driving a motor vehicle, and without
grounds to do so, although he was required to act in good faith, absent any malpractice, oppression, caprice or
opprobrious behaviour (ibid [13]). RTA 1988, s 163 does not confer a power to search.

[72] Most notably PACE 1984, ss 2 and 3 which apply to all stop and searches other than those undertaken
under PACE 1984, s 6 and the Aviation Security Act 1982, s 27(2), together with PACE 1984 Code A.

[73] *R (Rutherford) v Independent Police Complaints Commission* [2010] EWHC 2881 (Admin).

[74] Although the Court's reasoning was predicated on the basis that there was no requirement for the power
exercised to be identified absent a statutory provision to that effect. PACE 1984, ss 2(2)(ii) and 2(3) supply
such a statutory requirement.

[75] Whereas the way in which a power was exercised in particular circumstances will often be more suited
to private law proceedings.

[76] *Gillan v United Kingdom* (2010) 50 EHRR 45.

influential judgment in this area on the application of an individual's rights under the ECHR, the ECtHR dismissed an argument that an individual's ability to bring private law proceedings to challenge a specific stop constituted a sufficient safeguard on the exercise of the relevant power, recognising that:

> in the absence of any obligation on the part of the officer to show a reasonable suspicion, it is likely to be difficult if not impossible to prove that the power was properly exercised.[77]

Any theoretical safeguard would inevitably be rendered ineffectual.

What follows is a summary of the statutory powers that have been subject to challenge by way of judicial review, followed by an analysis of the legal arguments presented in those challenges.

(i) Section 44 of the Terrorism Act 2000

4-18   Section 44, an 'exceptional power'[78] purportedly introduced to combat terrorism, enabled an officer of at least the rank of commander to grant an authorisation for a specified area within which any uniformed constable was empowered to stop any vehicle and/or individual, and conduct a search.

This power was ostensibly subject to restrictions, including:

i.   the authorisation could be given only if considered to be expedient for the prevention of acts of terrorism;[79] and

ii.   the purpose of the stops was restricted to searching for articles which could be used in connection with terrorism.[80]

However, the ineffectiveness of these safeguards was exposed by the circumstances which led to the challenge of the power,[81] in which:

i.   the authorisation had been granted on a rolling basis since first made, and extended to the whole Metropolitan Police District; and

ii.   the claimants had been stopped and searched during a protest at an arms fair, absent any association with terrorism.

It was therefore contended that the power was incompatible with Articles 5, 8, 10 and 11 of the ECHR. Although unsuccessful in the domestic courts,[82] the ECtHR found that the powers were not 'in accordance with the law', being insufficiently restricted and not subject to appropriate safeguards. As such, both the process of authorisation and the powers of stop and search themselves constituted breaches of Article 8 of the ECHR.[83]

---

[77] ibid [86].
[78] One that does not require reasonable grounds of suspicion.
[79] Terrorism Act 2000, s 44(3).
[80] ibid, s 45.
[81] Which culminated in *Gillan* (n 76), as discussed below.
[82] See below at 4-24–4-32.
[83] The court did not therefore make any findings in relation to Arts 5, 10 and 11, although it provided guidance on the operation of Art 5, as discussed below at 4-24.

Rachel Taylor and Piers von Berg

The operation of section 44 was consequently suspended. It was repealed in July 2012 and replaced by a more restricted power under section 47A of the Terrorism Act 2000.[84]

(ii) Section 60 of the Criminal Justice and Public Order Act 1994

Section 60 is also an exceptional power, originally introduced to counter football hooliganism. It may only be used where an officer of at least the rank of inspector has granted an authorisation on the basis that he 'reasonably believes' that: **4-19**

i.   incidents involving serious violence may take place in a locality within his police area, and it is expedient to give an authorisation to prevent their occurrence; or

ii.   persons are carrying dangerous instruments or offensive weapons in a locality within his police area without good reason.

Where an authorisation has been granted, uniformed officers are permitted to stop and search any person or vehicle within the specified locality, without requiring any reasonable grounds of suspicion.

The section 60 power was challenged in *R (Roberts) v Commissioner of Police of the Metropolis*,[85] where the claimant sought a declaration of incompatibility with Articles 5 and 8 (discussed in detail below at 4-24–4-32). The Divisional Court rejected the claim and the subsequent appeal was refused by the Court of Appeal.[86] At the time of writing, leave to appeal to the Supreme Court was being sought.

(iii) Schedule 7 of the Terrorism Act 2000

Schedule 7 empowers an 'examining officer' in ports and airports to stop and search **4-20**
any person reasonably believed to be in the area in connection with their entering or leaving Great Britain or Northern Ireland (or travelling by air within Great Britain or within Northern Ireland) for the purpose of determining whether they appear to be a terrorist.[87] That person is then under an obligation to answer questions and cooperate in any search; failure to do so constitutes a criminal offence.[88] A person may be detained for this purpose.[89] Once detained, treatment is governed by Part I of Schedule 8. The Schedule 7 power is not subject to any standard of reasonable suspicion.

---

[84] However, there has been minimal use of this power, and in July 2013 it had only been used once, in Northern Ireland (David Anderson QC, 'The Terrorism Acts in 2012, Report of the Independent Reviewer on the Operation of the Terrorism Act 2000 and Part 1 of the Terrorism Act 2006', July 2013).

[85] *R (Roberts) v Commissioner of Police of the Metropolis* [2012] EWHC 1977 (Admin).

[86] *R (Roberts) v Commissioner of Police of the Metropolis* [2014] EWCA Civ 69.

[87] As defined by Terrorism Act 2000, s 40(1)(b). The very broad definition of terrorism under Terrorism Act s 1 was recognised in *R v Gul* [2013] UKSC 64.

[88] Schedule 7, para 18 (at the time of writing, amendments were pending). Powers of seizure of property also apply.

[89] There are pending legislative amendments under the Anti-Social Behaviour, Crime and Policing Act 2014 which will reduce the time that somebody can be examined from 9 hours to 1 hour. However, if a decision is made to 'detain' the person, the examination can proceed for a maximum of 6 hours (Schedule 7, para 6A Terrorism Act 2000—not yet in force).

The operation of Schedule 7 has proved to be particularly controversial, resulting in a government consultation, the response to which was published on 11 July 2013.[90] This consultation prompted in legislative reform, embodied in section 148 and Schedule 9 of the Anti-Social Behaviour, Crime and Policing Act 2014.[91] However, these proposals largely concern procedural and ancillary issues such as access to legal advice, time limits on detention, training, the issuing of a Code of Practice,[92] and the taking of biometric samples. These matters, while very important, do not impact on the substance of the power itself.[93] This led the Joint Committee on Human Rights to conclude, prior to the enactment of the Bill, that significant ECHR compatibility issues remained, notwithstanding the proposed amendments to the power, and importantly, to recommend that the powers of detention, seizure of property, and DNA and fingerprint sampling be subject to a condition of reasonable suspicion.[94] It is of note that the legislative amendments do introduce a standard of reasonable suspicion in relation to strip-searches.[95]

The lawfulness of Schedule 7 was considered by the High Court in *Beghal v Director of Public Prosecutions*,[96] in which the appellant contended that the statutory powers breached her rights under Articles 5, 6 and 8, and her right to freedom of movement under Articles 20 and 21 of the Treaty on the Functioning of the European Union (TFEU). Although each of these arguments was rejected, the court did express some concern regarding the operation of the power,[97] and approval of the statutory proposals referred to above.[98]

4-21   Schedule 7 remains controversial, and concerns have arisen that the powers are being used perversely, for purposes other than determining whether or not somebody may be a terrorist. This was indeed the case in *R (CC) v Commissioner of Police of the Metropolis and Another*.[99]

Concerns have also arisen regarding the conduct of Schedule 7 examinations. In *R (Elosta) v Commissioner of Police for the Metropolis*[100] the claimant, who had been detained under Schedule 7, challenged the refusal of the examining officer to await the attendance of his solicitor before proceeding with questioning, and the fact that he had only been permitted to speak with his solicitor on the telephone, within the hearing of the officers. The court declared this to be unlawful,[101] and held that the claimant had a right to consult

---

[90] Home Office, 'Review of the Operation of Schedule 7: A Public Consultation', July 2013, available at www.gov.uk/government/uploads/system/uploads/attachment_data/file/212548/WEB_-_2013_07_15_Review_of_the_operation_of_Schedule_7_A_Public_Consulta___.pdf.

[91] Section 148 is to be partially in effect from 13 May 2014, as are parts of Schedule 9.

[92] A draft version of which, at the time of writing, was subject to consultation, https://www.gov.uk/government/uploads/system/uploads/attachment_data/file/304300/DraftCodeOfPracticeSch7.pdf.

[93] This was criticised by David Anderson QC, the Independent Reviewer of Terrorism Powers, in his 2013 report.

[94] Joint Committee On Human Rights, *Legislative Scrutiny: Anti-social Behaviour Crime and Policing Bill* (HC 2013–14, 713).

[95] Schedule 9, para 3 Anti-Social Behaviour, Crime and Policing Act 2014, amending Schedule 7, para 8 Terrorism Act 2000.

[96] *Beghal v Director of Public Prosecutions* [2013] EWHC 2573.

[97] Namely, the absence of a statutory bar to any admissions made being adduced as evidence in criminal proceedings, ibid [146].

[98] ibid [150]. Note that permission to appeal to the Supreme Court was granted to the claimant on 6 February 2014.

[99] *R (CC) v Commissioner of Police of the Metropolis and Another* [2011] EWHC 3316 (Admin), discussed below at 4-24.

[100] *R (Elosta) v Commissioner of Police for the Metropolis* [2013] EWHC 3397.

[101] ibid [34] and [54].

with his solicitor in person.[102] However, notwithstanding this, the claimant had been lawfully detained throughout this period due to the obligation on him to answer questions.[103]

At the time of writing the following cases were also before the courts:

i. *R (Miranda) v Secretary of State for the Home Department*,[104] in which David Miranda, the partner of a former *Guardian* journalist, sought to challenge his detention under Schedule 7 on the basis that:

    (a) the power was exercised unlawfully, for the improper purpose of obtaining material in his possession that may have been sensitive or classified;

    (b) the exercise of the power was a disproportionate interference with his right to freedom of expression, in part because less intrusive measures could have been used to obtain the desired information, but were not pursued;[105] and

    (c) Schedule 7 powers are incompatible with Articles 10 as they are disproportionate and lacking in adequate safeguards (the claimant also relied on Articles 5 and 8, though to a lesser degree).[106]

Particular emphasis was placed on the statutory protections ordinarily afforded to journalistic information, primarily the requirement that seizure be authorised by court order.

However, the claim was refused, with the High Court determining that:

    (a) the purpose of the stop was to ascertain the nature of the material being carried and, if on examination it proved to be as feared, to neutralise the effects of its release or dissemination, and this fell properly within the scope of Schedule 7;[107]

    (b) an application to a circuit judge under Schedule 5 for an Order to seize the material would have been pointless and ineffective, as (i) the material was unknown and could not be particularised; (ii) there would have been no obligation for the claimant to answer questions about the material; and (iii) the only tool of compulsion would have been the threat of contempt proceedings subsequently being pursued;[108]

    (c) the data itself did not constitute 'journalistic material';[109]

    (d) the interference with the claimant's freedom of expression was justified and proportionate, and the balance lay in favour of national security;[110] and

---

[102] ibid [45].

[103] ibid [52]. The case had been subject to appeal by the defendant, but the appeal was withdrawn on 20 February 2014. The right to consult a solicitor when detained under Schedule 7 is now set out in Schedule 8, paras 7A and 16A Terrorism Act 2000, although at the time of writing this was not yet in force. However, subsequent to the judgment in Elosta, this entitlement was also set out in *Circular 015 / 2013: guidance on the rights of persons detained under Schedule 7 to the Terrorism Act 2000*.

[104] *R (Miranda) v Secretary of State for the Home Department* [2014] EWHC 225 (Admin).

[105] Such as a Production Order under Sch 5 of the Terrorism Act 2000.

[106] *Miranda* (n 104), [16].

[107] ibid, [36], [52]. In making this determination, the court aggregated the knowledge of various different individuals, as opposed to considering that of just the examining officer. This constitutes a significant departure from the principle established in *O'Hara v Chief Constable of Royal Ulster Constabulary* [1997] AC 286 that the state of mind of the arresting officer is determinative of the legality of the exercise of police powers of arrest.

[108] ibid, [60]–[61].

[109] ibid, [64].

[110] ibid, [72]–[73].

  (e) there had been no breach of Article 10 (or Articles 5 and 8) as the Schedule 7 powers were sufficiently certain and subject to effective safeguards.[111]

At the time of writing permission to appeal had been sought on behalf of the claimant.

ii. *Sabure Malik v UK*, a case brought by Liberty challenging the compatibility of Schedule 7 with Articles 5(1) and 8 of the ECHR. A declaration of admissibility was granted in May 2013,[112] meaning that the case has proceeded directly to the ECtHR.[113] This is particularly significant due to the outcome of *Miranda*[114] and *Beghal*.[115]

(3) Summary of the Legal Bases of Challenges to Stop and Search

4-23 Challenges in the context of stop and search will most commonly be brought in reliance on Articles 5, 8 and 14 of the ECHR, although Articles 10 and 11 will also often be engaged, particularly in cases concerning political protest.[116]

(4) Article 5 of ECHR (Challenges to Stop and Search)

4-24 A principal issue is whether a stop and search constitutes a deprivation of liberty, contrary to Article 5 of ECHR. Although the House of Lords in *R (Gillan) v Metropolitan Police Commissioner and another*[117] held that a stop lasting 20 minutes could not be termed as such, the ECtHR disagreed:

> during this period the applicants were entirely deprived of any freedom of movement. They were obliged to remain where they were and submit to the search and if they had refused they would have been liable to arrest, detention at a police station and criminal charges. This element of coercion is indicative of a deprivation of liberty within the meaning of art. 5(1).[118]

The Court of Appeal relied on this passage in *Commissioner of Police of the Metropolis v ZH*,[119] rejecting an argument that 30 minutes' detention would not amount to a deprivation of liberty. Although recognising that the ECtHR in *Gillan v United Kingdom* did not make a final determination on this point, the ECtHR was seen to have given a clear indication of its views, and in any event *Gillan v United Kingdom* was not a 'paradigm detention case', concerning detention in a police or prison cell. Conversely, *ZH* was seen to be 'closely analogous to' such a paradigm case, and the court concluded that Article 5

---

[111] ibid, [74]–[89]. Discussed further below at 4-24–4-32.
[112] *Sabure Malik v UK* App no 32968/11 (admissibility decision of 28 May 2013).
[113] On the basis that neither a declaration of incompatibility nor a claim for damages had been shown to provide an alternative effective remedy, ibid [26]–[30].
[114] *Miranda* (n 104).
[115] *Beghal* (n 96).
[116] As in *Gillan v United Kingdom* (n 76).
[117] *R (Gillan) v Metropolitan Police Commissioner and another* [2006] UKHL 12.
[118] ibid [57].
[119] *Commissioner of Police of the Metropolis v ZH* [2013] EWCA Civ 69.

would be engaged where an individual has been deprived of movement throughout the relevant period.[120]

However, in *Roberts* (mentioned above at 4-19) the court held that no deprivation of liberty had occurred in circumstances in which the claimant had not been confined, required to move to a police station, handcuffed or restrained.[121] The court relied upon the formulation of deprivation of liberty provided by the ECtHR in *HL v United Kingdom*:[122]

> in order to determine whether there has been a deprivation of liberty, the starting point must be the specific situation of the individual concerned and account must be taken of a whole range of factors arising in a particular case such as the type, duration, effects and manner of implementation of the measure in question. The distinction between a deprivation of, and restriction upon, liberty is merely one of degree or intensity and not one of nature or substance.

Consequently, challenges to 'stops' would be more appropriately considered within the context of Article 8.[123] This reasoning was upheld by the Court of Appeal, where determination of a stop and search encounter as a deprivation of liberty was said to be decided solely on the basis of its duration.[124]

This approach appears to have been endorsed, albeit implicitly, in the context of Schedule 7 of the Terrorism Act 2000. In *CC*,[125] Collins J relied on evidence indicating that '97% of all examinations last less than one hour' and 'only 0.05% last more than six hours', and concluded that, 'in the vast majority of cases detention is not required and does not occur'.[126] However, the claimant was found to have been detained on the facts as he had been subject to examination for over six hours.[127]

In *Beghal*, the DPP accepted that the two-hour period for which the appellant was examined engaged Article 5, but the court held that that interference was justified in the circumstances.[128]

(5) Article 8 of ECHR (Challenges to Stop and Search)

Arguments predicated on Article 8 of the ECHR have been more successful than Article 5 challenges, and will usually be accorded priority when both are pleaded, as will ordinarily be the case.   **4-25**

The House of Lords in *Gillan v Metropolitan Police Commissioner* accepted that Article 8 was engaged on the facts, but it was not accepted that this would always be the

---

[120] ibid [83].

[121] Other than restraint arising from her resistance to the stop, without which, the Court found, the detention would have been likely to last for no longer than three minutes.

[122] *HL v United Kingdom* (2005) 40 EHRR 32 [89].

[123] Reliance was also placed on *Austin v United Kingdom* [2012] All ER (D) 208 (Mar) and *Gillan v United Kingdom* (n 76).

[124] *Roberts* [2014] (n 86).

[125] *CC* (n 99). Although breach of Art 5 was not pleaded in that case, and the challenge was brought against the particular exercise of the Sch 7 powers on the facts, as opposed to the statutory regime itself

[126] ibid [12].

[127] Notwithstanding the fact that he was engaging in the process voluntarily, and that the available powers of compulsion had not been exercised.

[128] For purposes, it appears, of national security: *Beghal* (n 96) [113]. Permission to appeal to the Supreme Court was granted to the claimant on 6 February 2014.

case. Lord Bingham considered that 'an ordinary superficial search of the person and an opening of bags, of the kind to which passengers uncomplainingly submit at airports, for example, can scarcely be said to reach that level'.[129] The ECtHR disagreed and found that the use of coercive powers requiring an individual to submit to a detailed search amounted to a 'clear interference' with his Article 8 rights: such searches were wholly incomparable to consensual searches carried out at airports.[130]

In *Howarth v Commissioner of Police of the Metropolis*,[131] the court left this issue undecided in view of the contrasting authorities. However, the reasoning of *Gillan v United Kingdom* was applied in *Roberts*, where the court held that the humiliation and embarrassment resulting from the section 60 search was sufficient to engage Article 8(1). The court was able to distinguish *Gillan v Metropolitan Police Commissioner* as it concerned a different statutory power.[132] This approach was also taken in *Beghal*, where the court made a distinction on the basis of (i) the application of a different statutory code; and, (ii) the context of port and border controls in which the powers are exercised (as opposed to a 'normal' stop and search).

Although these cases indicate that stop and search encounters are now likely to be accepted as engaging Article 8, a three-judge Divisional Court in *Beghal*, led by Gross LJ, asserted that this will not be the case where the exercise of powers falls below the threshold of a 'minimum level of seriousness'.[133] Similarly, the Court of Appeal in *Roberts* described Article 8 as only 'marginally' engaged.[134]

(6) Significant Factors in Determining Article 8 Breaches

4-26   Of course, even where Article 8 of the ECHR is engaged, further consideration will need to be given as to whether that engagement is lawful, in compliance with Article 8(2) (ie that it is in accordance with the law and necessary in a democratic society, that is, 'proportionate'). To be 'in accordance with the law', a measure must:

    i.   have a legal basis;
    ii. be accessible and foreseeable; and
    iii. be non-arbitrary.[135]

The following formulation of proportionality was recently set out by Lord Sumption in *Bank Mellat v Her Majesty's Treasury (No 2)*,[136] giving the lead judgment of the Supreme Court:

the question depends on an exacting analysis of the factual case advanced in defence of the measure, in order to determine (i) whether its objective is sufficiently important to justify the limitation of a fundamental right; (ii) whether it is rationally connected to the objective;

---

[129] *Gillan v Metropolitan Police Commissioner* (n 117) [28].
[130] *Gillan v United Kingdom* (n 76) [63]–[64].
[131] *Howarth v Commissioner of Police of the Metropolis* [2011] EWHC 2818 (Admin).
[132] In accordance with *Kay v Lambeth Borough Council* [2006] AC 465.
[133] *Beghal* (n 96) [93].
[134] *Roberts* [2014] (n 86) [15].
[135] *Gillan v United Kingdom* (n 76) [76]–[77].
[136] *Bank Mellat v Her Majesty's Treasury (No 2)* [2013] UKSC 39.

(iii) whether a less intrusive measure could have been used; and (iv) whether, having regard to these matters and to the severity of the consequences, a fair balance has been struck between the rights of the individual and the interests of the community.[137]

In considering Article 8 compatibility in the context of stop and search, the factors listed below have often been considered significant.

(i) Absence of Reasonable Grounds Threshold (Article 8)

As explained above, section 44 of the Terrorism Act 2000,[138] Schedule 7 of the Terrorism Act 2000 and section 60 of CJPO 1994 are 'exceptional powers' as they do not require an officer to have reasonable grounds of suspicion. In *Gillan v Metropolitan Police Commissioner* Lord Bingham asserted that the absence of this threshold could not: **4-27**

> realistically, be interpreted as a warrant to stop and search people who are obviously not terrorist suspects, which would be futile and time-wasting. It is to ensure that a constable is not deterred from stopping and searching a person whom he does suspect as a potential terrorist by the fear that he could not show reasonable grounds for his suspicion.[139]

His Lordship appeared to indicate that there was an operative threshold, unarticulated, but certainly lower than 'reasonable grounds', on the basis of which such searches could be conducted. However, the 'safeguard' of this inferred threshold was not accepted by the ECtHR, which was critical of the breadth of discretion the power conferred on a police officer, seen to give rise to 'a clear risk of arbitrariness'.[140]

Conversely, any concern regarding the absence of the reasonable grounds threshold was dismissed in *Roberts*. Moses LJ, with whom Eady J agreed, commented that the imposition of such a threshold would make it 'all too easy for those who wish to conceal weapons ... to escape detection'.[141] The court reasoned that unless the authorisation could itself be described as arbitrary, random searches carried out pursuant thereto 'cannot and should not be impugned'.[142] It also drew on the margin of appreciation, as endorsed by the Grand Chamber of the ECtHR in *Austin v United Kingdom*,[143] that 'the possibility of being subjected to a random search must seem a justifiable price to pay for greater security and protection from indiscriminate use of weapons.'

---

[137] ibid [20].

[138] Now repealed.

[139] *Gillan v Metropolitan Police Commissioner* (n 117) [35].

[140] *Gillan v United Kingdom* (n 76) [83] and [85].

[141] *Roberts* [2014] (n 86) [40].

[142] ibid [41]. The court relied upon *Colon v Netherlands* (2012) 55 EHRR SE5, noting that a similar power had there been endorsed by the ECtHR (recognising that in that case the relevant power had been subject to greater democratic control, and indeed had been shown to have reduced crime, which was not the case in this instance). At para 20 the court also accorded significance to the particular conduct of the claimant, finding that the power had been exercised by the officer involved due to that conduct. This led the court to conclude that 'it was plainly not a random search, still less arbitrary' as the officer 'had every justification for conducting the search'. However, the court confirmed that the claimant remained a victim for the purposes of the HRA 1998, s 7(1) as the impugned measure had been applied to her detriment, ibid [21]. The approach of the Divisional Court was followed by the Court of Appeal in dismissing the claimant's case, *Roberts* (n 86) [26]. The court drew upon Code A of PACE, indicating that its provisions countered any concerns arising from the absence of a reasonable suspicion standard [27]–[28].

[143] *Austin* (n 123) [45].

This approach was also followed in *CC* in the context of Schedule 7 of the Terrorism Act 2000.[144] The court highlighted the assertion of the Independent Reviewer of Terrorism Powers in his 2004 report that '[I]ntuition ... is not the same as reasonable suspicion: much intuition cannot be rationalised'.[145] It concluded that the absence of reasonable grounds would not, in itself, render a search power unlawful. However, the absence of a requirement of reasonable grounds is in any event less likely to be accorded significance in the context of port and border control.[146]

(ii) Constraints on the Abuse of Power (Article 8)

4-28   The safeguards applied to the operation and exercise of stop and search powers have been accorded particular significance by the courts. However, the approaches taken and conclusions drawn have not been consistent, with the ECtHR generally adopting a far more restrictive view than the domestic courts in relation to the circumstances in which stop and search will be compatible with Article 8.

Whilst in *Gillan v Metropolitan Police Commissioner* the House of Lords confirmed the adequacy of the 11 identified safeguards on the operation of section 44 of the Terrorism Act 2000,[147] the ECtHR determined that those safeguards had not been demonstrated to constitute 'a real curb on the wide powers afforded to the executive so as to offer the individual adequate protection against arbitrary interference'.[148]

The ECtHR emphasised the low threshold applicable for authorisation (where the officer considered it to be 'expedient for the prevention of acts of terrorism', with 'expedient' meaning 'no more than advantageous or helpful'), and the absence of a requirement that the proportionality of the measure be assessed.[149] Emphasis was also placed on the futility of the additional safeguards, in circumstances in which, for example, the 'specified geographical location' had extended to the totality of the Greater London area, and the time-limitation of 48 hours had been circumvented through the practice of a 'rolling renewal'.[150]

The ECtHR concluded that the powers were not in accordance with the law and so breached Article 8.

4-29   However, in *Roberts* the Divisional Court distinguished section 60 of CJPO 1994 from section 44, and found that there were sufficient safeguards on the exercise of that power on the basis that:[151]

    i.   Whilst section 44 authorisations could be issued on grounds of expediency alone, in issuing a section 60 authorisation the officer must 'reasonably believe' that:

        (a)   incidents involving serious violence may take place in a locality in his police area and it is expedient to grant an authorisation to prevent their occurrence;

---

144 See above at 4-21.
145 *CC* (n 99) [11].
146 *Beghal* (n 96) [94] and [97], see also *Miranda* (n 104), [81]–[82].
147 As listed at paragraph 11 of the judgment.
148 *Gillan v United Kingdom* (n 76), [79].
149 ibid, [80].
150 ibid, [80]–[83].
151 *Roberts* (n 85) [31]–[35]. This approach was subsequently endorsed by the Court of Appeal (n 88) [23]–[29].

Rachel Taylor and Piers von Berg

(b)   such an incident has taken place in his police area, a dangerous weapon or
      instrument used in that incident is being carried in his police area and it is
      expedient to grant an authorisation to find that weapon or instrument; or

(c)   persons are carrying dangerous instruments or offensive weapons in the
      area without good reason.

ii.   The authorisation given in section 60 is much more limited than that in section
       44 in terms of its geographical and temporal scope.

iii.   Section 60 powers are exercised for the purpose of carrying out searches for
       dangerous instruments, blades or sharply pointed items or unlawful offensive
       weapons or weapons used in a particular seriously violent incident in that area,
       in contrast with any articles that could be used in connection with terrorism.

iv.   Like section 44, the power to give authorisation is governed by Code A, requiring
       the officer:

(a)   to set the minimum period considered necessary; and

(b)   not to set a geographical area wider than believed necessary.

v.   Officers are warned, as in section 44, not to use the power in a racially discrimi-
       natory way.[152]

(iii) Discriminatory Impact (Article 14)

The absence of a standard of reasonable grounds or any other relevant threshold can   **4-30**
lead to challenges based on the discriminatory impact of a power.

However, in *Gillan v Metropolitan Police Commissioner*[153] this potential risk, and the
difficulty that an individual would face in establishing that a police officer had selected
them on grounds of race in the absence of an operative 'reasonable grounds' threshold,
was dismissed by the House of Lords. To the contrary, Lord Brown stated that ethnic
origin:

> can and properly should be taken into account in deciding whether and whom to stop and
> search provided always that the power is used sensitively and the selection is made for reasons
> connected with the perceived terrorist threat and not on grounds of racial discrimination.[154]

Again, the ECtHR disagreed, stating that the risk of discrimination was 'a very real concern', and one which suggested that the power was not 'in accordance with the law', and
so was contrary to Article 8.[155]

The discriminatory impact of section 60 CJPO 1994 was considered in *Roberts*. The
Divisional Court held that there was no basis to contend that this stop had been motivated by racial discrimination on the facts, and that in any event the challenge was to the

---

[152] The court did not consider that the absence of an independent reviewer was significant in the circumstances, particularly as the ECtHR in *Gillan v United Kingdom* (n 76) did not believe that this safeguarded the
exercise of s 44 in any event (ibid [86]).

[153] In *Gillan v Metropolitan Police Commissioner* (n 117) the claimants submitted that there was a discriminatory impact but there was no suggestion that the power to search had been exercised in a discriminatory
manner on the facts as both of the claimants were Caucasian.

[154] ibid [81] and [92].

[155] *Gillan v United Kingdom* (n 76) [95].

legislative power, which was not itself racially discriminatory.[156] The issue was therefore whether the legislation was being used in a racially discriminatory manner, but the court determined that that could not be resolved in the course of the proceedings.[157] Moses LJ stated that the power of the Commission for Equality and Human Rights to serve 'unlawful act' notices in accordance with section 21 of the Equality Act 2006 would be a more appropriate mechanism for resolving such issues.[158] However, it was accepted that powers of random search give rise to a potential risk of racial discrimination.[159]

(iv) Effectiveness of a Power (Article 8)

4-31   Where a power is shown to be ineffective it is more likely to be considered disproportionate and arbitrary. This was the case in *Gillan v United Kingdom*, where the court drew upon the large number of stops carried out under section 44 of the Terrorism Act 2000 and data evidencing that although many arrests had followed the stops, none had resulted in an arrest for a terrorism offence. This lack of effectiveness was seen to demonstrate the risk of arbitrariness in the exercise of the power.[160]

In contrast, *Roberts* states that section 60 operates as an effective deterrent, and increases the likelihood of discovering prohibited weapons. The court thereby sought to distinguish section 60 from section 44, emphasising that section 60 had resulted in over 2,000 arrests from 2007 to 2008, and 4,273 from 2008 to 2009.[161] Similarly, in *Beghal*, the court drew on the effectiveness of Schedule 7 powers, which had been said by the Independent Commissioner to be 'scarcely in doubt'.[162]

(v) Other Factors

4-32   The extent to which a power is used will also impact on whether it is deemed to be proportionate, in relation to both the frequency of its exercise and the scope of its application.[163]

The conclusions drawn by the courts have also been dependent, to an extent, on context, with counter-terrorism powers generally being afforded a greater degree of latitude.[164] In addition, powers relating to port and border control as opposed to 'normal'

---

[156] *Roberts* (n 85) [47]. The Court of Appeal subsequently agreed with this approach, *Roberts* (n 86) [33]. Permission to appeal to the Supreme Court has been sought on behalf of the claimant.

[157] The court was presented with statistical data to evidence the discriminatory impact of the power but criticised this approach due to the limitations of the court's ability to process and draw conclusions from 'undigested material', *Roberts* (n 85) [50]. The court of Appeal similarly refused to engage with this evidence in its judgment of 4 February 2014, *Roberts* (n 86), [32].

[158] *Roberts* (n 85) [51].

[159] ibid [23].

[160] *Gillan v United Kingdom* (n 76) [84].

[161] Although the court did not specify whether or not those arrests related to the possession of offensive weapons, which was not the case. As above, the Court of Appeal rejected the claimant's appeal in a judgment of 4 February 2014, *Roberts* (n 86).

[162] *Beghal* (n 96) [93] and [151].

[163] ibid [95]–[96], [109].

[164] ibid [98].

stop and searches have been held to decrease the likelihood of a power being considered arbitrary.[165]

(7) Article 6 of ECHR (Challenges to Stop and Search)

One of the arguments pursued in *Beghal* was that the exercise of powers under Schedule 7   **4-33** of the Terrorism Act 2000 breached Article 6 of the ECHR; specifically, the implied protection it affords from self-incrimination.[166] However, the court held that Article 6 was not engaged, as there was no suspicion or intention to commence criminal proceedings sufficient to trigger its application: the appellant was not suspected of the criminal act of terrorism, nor was the purpose of the examination to obtain evidence for use in such proceedings. The possibility that such evidence might be obtained was not sufficient.[167] Further, even if Article 6 had been engaged, there would not have been a violation as it was 'fanciful to suppose' that a court would have allowed any admissions made to be adduced in evidence through the application of section 78 of PACE 1984.[168]

(8) Challenges to Specific Instances of Stop and Search

As indicated above, individual stop and search encounters are unlikely, without more,   **4-34** to give rise to judicial review proceedings, due to both procedural restrictions and the appropriateness of the remedies available. However, the following factors are indicative of an increased suitability of judicial review in this context.

(i) Integrity of Purpose and Proportionality (Challenges to Specific Instances)

In *CC* a challenge was brought against the exercise of powers under the Terrorism Act   **4-35** 2000, Schedule 7. The then applicable Code of Practice[169] echoed the legislation, stipulating that the only lawful purpose of an examination is the determination of whether an individual appears to be a terrorist,[170] although there is no requirement for prior suspicion in order for the questioning to take place.[171]

The court held that there was no power to continue the examination for any other purpose than determining whether or not the individual did or did not appear to be a terrorist, and found on the facts that the examining officers had reached a conclusion in this regard (although the court did assert that the powers should be given a wide

---

[165] ibid [97], [106]–[108].

[166] Although the submissions were largely focused on the facts of the case, as opposed to the application of the powers generally.

[167] *Beghal* (n 96) [125]–[130]. See also *McVeigh v United Kingdom* (1981) 5 EHRR 71 [187].

[168] ibid [134]–[143].

[169] Home Office, 'Examining Officers under the Terrorism Act 2000' (London, TSO, 2009). A new Draft Code of Practice was published by the Home Office in October 2013.

[170] Within the meaning of Terrorism Act 2000, s 40(1)(b). The very broad definition of terrorism under Terrorism Act s 1 was recognised in *R v Gul* [2013] UKSC 64.

[171] 'Examining Officers under the Terrorism Act 2000' (n 169) [9]–[10].

construction).[172] The questions put to the claimant had been unlikely to cast any doubt on that conclusion, and were instead intended to obtain evidence which could be relied upon by the Secretary of State in seeking a control order. As such, the Schedule 7 powers had not been exercised within the specified remit of the legislation.[173]

Although in this instance the examination was largely ineffective, as the claimant denied involvement in any terrorist activity,[174] the case illustrates the potential utility that judicial review proceedings might have in, for example, impacting on evidence adduced in other proceedings.

By contrast, arguments based on improper purpose were unsuccessful in *Miranda*.[175] The court held that the 'proper purpose' of the Schedule 7 power, of assessing whether there is a possibility that an individual might be involved in acts of terrorism, had been fulfilled.[176] The claimant had been detained in order that material in his possession could be examined to determine whether it would be severely damaging to national security if released and, if so, to neutralise the effects of its release or dissemination, and this fell within the 'proper purpose' identified.[177]

In determining whether the exercise of a power is proportionate, the courts should also consider whether any less intrusive measures were available, that should have been adopted. However, in *Miranda*, an argument that a production order should instead have been obtained under Schedule 5 was rejected by the court, on the basis that (i) the requirements of such an application could not have been fulfilled; (ii) a Schedule 5 order would not have conferred any power to ask questions about the material; and (iii) there would have been only a limited sanction should the claimant have failed to comply.[178] Arguments of proportionality were particularly significant in this case as it concerned what was argued to be 'journalistic material',[179] thereby engaging the right to freedom of expression and Article 10 ECHR.

(ii) Component Part of Broader Challenge (Challenges to Specific Instances)

4-36   A claim for judicial review may also be appropriate where the exercise of the power of stop and search forms part of a broader claim or issue that requires or favours resolution by way of judicial review.

This was the position in *Howarth*[180] (see above 4-25), in which the claimant sought to challenge a search to which he was subjected whilst travelling to a demonstration. The claimant contended that the search breached his rights under Articles 8, 10 and 11 of the ECHR. Whilst it was accepted that the search was for the legitimate purpose of preventing crime, it was argued that the measure was disproportionate to this aim and acted

---

[172] *CC* (n 99) [35].
[173] ibid [34].
[174] ibid [33].
[175] *Miranda* (n 103).
[176] ibid, [32].
[177] ibid, [27] and [36].
[178] ibid, [60]–[62].
[179] The court rejected the submission that all of the material could be so termed, and in particular the 'raw data' itself, ibid, [64].
[180] *Howarth* (n 131).

as a deterrent to protest. However, this argument was rejected,[181] and it was held that the measures adopted were intended to enable, rather than prevent, peaceful protest.[182]

Similar arguments were made in *R (Hicks) v Commissioner of Police of the Metropolis and Others*.[183] This was a complex case resulting in a lengthy judgment. It was brought by 20 claimants in relation to the police practices employed at the Royal Wedding in April 2011. The overarching contention was that the first defendant had pursued unlawful policies and practices in pre-emptively exercising police powers against individuals assessed as likely to express anti-monarchist views.

One of the claimants, 'M', a 16-year-old, was stopped and searched under section 1 of PACE 1984[184] purportedly on the basis that the officer reasonably suspected that he was in possession of articles to be used for purposes of criminal damage. The basis for the suspicion was contended to be:

i. the recent student protests, at which disorder and criminality had occurred;
ii. the fact that M was in possession of a bag possibly containing rocks and spray paint; and
iii. M's presentation as nervous and defensive by, for example, immediately justifying his actions.

M contended that the requisite grounds had not been made out, particularly as (i) the officers' witness statements referred only to a suspicion that the bag 'could', as opposed to 'would', contain the relevant articles; and (ii) M had provided a full explanation for his presence. It was submitted that the officers had unlawfully carried out the search in an effort to prevent any expression of protest against the Royal Wedding. The court rejected these arguments and in concluding that the power had been exercised lawfully,[185] emphasised the low threshold constituted by 'reasonable grounds for suspicion'.[186]

It is submitted that although the court's approach was restrictive, it illustrates the difficulties in challenging individual stop and search incidents by way of judicial review. Indeed, at a preliminary hearing[187] it was commented by Elias LJ that M's case, on its own, would not have been suitable for judicial review proceedings, but that the claimants' wider contention that an unlawful policy was being pursued enabled it to proceed as such.[188]

---

[181] The court also rejected the submission that the search was in breach of s 1(3) of PACE 1984, on the basis that there were reasonable grounds to suspect one or more of the protestors to be in possession of the stated articles, which could be used for purposes of criminal damage, and it was not unreasonable for all of the protestors to be searched in the circumstances, *Howarth* (n 131) [24]–[33].

[182] ibid [38].

[183] *R (Hicks) v Commissioner of Police of the Metropolis and Others* [2012] EWHC 1947 (Admin). This is an important and wide-ranging judgment that is referred to below in a range of contexts: 4-42 search warrants, 4-45 the extent of a search, 4-53 arrest without a warrant, 4-56 the necessity requirement, 4-59 protest, 4-64 imminence, 4-65 permitted police action, 4-66 arrest and detention for breach of the peace, 4-69 breaches of Arts 10 and 11 ECHR, 4-70 unlawful policy and 4-71 additional duties. The Court of Appeal's judgment was subsequently handed down on 22 January 2014 in (*R (Hicks) v Commissioner of Police of the Metropolis* [2014] EWCA Civ 3, discussed below at 4-66.

[184] Although a s 60 authorisation was in place, the relevant officer knowingly chose not to use it.

[185] *Hicks* (n 183) [196].

[186] In accordance with *Howarth* (n 131) and *Raissi v Commissioner of the Police of the Metropolis* [2007] EWHC 2842 (QB).

[187] In which an application for limited cross-examination was, unusually, granted, *R (H) v Commissioner of Police of the Metropolis* [2012] EWHC 806 (Admin) [8]–[10] (Elias LJ).

[188] *H*, ibid [7].

(9) Practical and Procedural Considerations (Challenges to Stop and Search)

4-37   A claim for judicial review may also be motivated by practical issues, most significantly of cost and time, both of which will be considerably reduced in a claim for judicial review when compared to a private law action. This will be particularly important where a claimant is publicly funded and the value of their claim is low. However, such factors need to be weighed against the procedural and evidential restrictions applicable in judicial review proceedings, which are likely to disenable claimants from fully contesting evidence presented by the defendant.[189]

(10) Reporting Requirements (Challenges to Stop and Search)

4-38   Powers of stop and search are commonly subject to recording obligations, which are generally seen to provide a safeguard in facilitating the monitoring of those powers.

In March 2011 Code A of PACE 1984 Code was amended,[190] removing a mandatory requirement[191] for all chief constables to monitor the self-defined ethnicity of any persons (i) requested by an officer to account for themselves in a public place; or (ii) detained with a view to a search being carried out, but who were not, in the event, searched. In its place, the amendments conferred a discretion on chief constables to continue such monitoring where concerns existed such as to make it necessary to monitor 'any local disproportionality'.

In *R (Diedrick) v Chief Constable of Hampshire*[192] the claimant challenged these amendments on the basis that the Secretary of State had failed to have due regard to the equality aims set out in section 149(1) of the Equality Act 2010, and had thereby breached the public sector equality duty under the Race Relations Act 1976, section 71 and/or the Equality Act 2010, section 149.

However, the application for permission was refused both on the papers and at a renewal hearing. The Divisional Court found that the amendments were rational, proportionate and lawful:[193]

 i.   The process of recording ethnicity was laborious and could potentially escalate any tension engendered by police intervention and thereafter worsen relations.

 ii.   Individual officers previously had a discretion to dispense with the requirement where it was in place.

 iii.   The amendments allowed chief constables to have discretion in accordance with relevant local factors and there was nothing objectionable in the devolution of this assessment as such decisions could be made more effectively 'on the ground'.

---

[189] As in *Hicks* (n 183), and subsequently emphasised in *R (Pearce and Another) v Commissioner of Police of the Metropolis and another* [2013] EWCA Civ 866 [33], an appeal case arising from *Hicks*.

[190] Police and Criminal Evidence Act 1984 (Codes of Practice) (Revision of Codes A, B and D) Order 2011, SI 2011/412, which came into force on 7 March 2011.

[191] Previously contained in PACE 1984 Code A, paras 4.12–4.20.

[192] *R (Diedrick) v Chief Constable of Hampshire* [2012] ACD 127.

[193] Notwithstanding that no Equality Impact Assessment had been carried out in relation to the proposed amendments and the public consultation had lasted only a month.

Rachel Taylor and Piers von Berg

iv.   The aims of focusing police resources on essential functions of crime prevention and detection, fostering good relations with ethnic minorities and eradicating discrimination required careful exercise of judgment. Reasonable people could differ as to the appropriate measures to be pursued for those purposes, and the Secretary of State had considered the relevant factors and made the amendments accordingly.[194]

This approach may be seen as surprising, and gives cause for concern about the scope for any future challenges to further reductions in reporting requirements.

D. Search Warrants

(1) General Principles

The merits of challenging a search warrant by judicial review will again depend on the facts of each case and the objectives of the potential claimant.[195] Such challenges will be of particular utility, for example, where the claimant is seeking the return of seized property.[196]   **4-39**

As with arrests (see below at 4-51), the lawfulness of a search carried out pursuant to a warrant is determined by the terms of that warrant. Section 6 of the Constables Protection Act 1750 provides that a police officer will not be liable for any act(s) carried out in obedience to a warrant. Therefore, where a warrant has been lawfully procured, issued and executed, a search cannot be successfully challenged. Conversely, acts done outside the remit of the warrant will fall outside section 6 of the 1750 Act even when undertaken in furtherance of the warrant's intended objective.[197]

In *McGrath v Chief Constable of the Royal Ulster Constabulary*[198] it was held that the duty of a police officer executing a warrant was 'to comply with its terms and not to exercise his own discretion as to whether or not he should enforce it'.[199] However, in order for an officer to be protected by section 6 of the 1750 Act the warrant must not be substantially defective. Where 'there is a formal defect on the face of the warrant sufficiently grave to invalidate it', the protection afforded by section 6 of the 1750 Act falls away and officers' actions can be much more readily challenged.[200]

If it appears that the court has issued a search warrant unlawfully, an application for judicial review against the issuing court (and, where appropriate, the police as applicant

---

[194] The court attributed particular weight to the fact that the amendments had been subject to debates in both Houses of Parliament (*Diedrick* (n 192) [43]) and the Secretary of State's assertion that she would keep the matter under review (ibid [44]).

[195] Consideration should also be given to private law remedies such as trespass to land, trespass to goods, malicious process, and breach of Art 8 of ECHR.

[196] Although it is possible that retention will be authorised pursuant to s 59(6) Criminal Justice and Police Act 2001.

[197] *Hoye v Bush* [1840] 1 Man & G 775.

[198] *McGrath v Chief Constable of the Royal Ulster Constabulary* [2001] UKHL 39, [2001] 2 AC 731.

[199] ibid [30].

[200] *Mr Philip Graham Bell v The Chief Constable of Greater Manchester Police* [2005] EWCA Civ 902 [28]–[29].

for the warrant) is often a highly effective way of achieving redress for claimants who may otherwise be prevented from securing a remedy due to the application of section 6.

The courts have consistently applied a high standard in such cases, recognising that the execution of a search warrant is 'a very serious interference with the liberty of the subject'[201] and one that will inevitably engage Article 8 of ECHR. However, even where judicial review proceedings are successful and the relevant warrant quashed, further private law proceedings will often be required to secure damages.[202]

(2) Challenging the Issue of the Search Warrant

4-40   Search warrants will often be issued under PACE 1984, section 8(1).[203] In such cases, a warrant is unlawful unless it has been granted by a magistrate, who is satisfied that there are reasonable grounds to believe that:

    i.   An indictable offence has been committed.

    ii.   There is material on the premises which is likely to be of substantial value to the investigation of the offence and likely to be relevant.

    iii. That material does not consist of or include items subject to legal privilege, excluded material or special procedure material.

    iv. At least one of the following conditions applies:[204]

        (a) It is not practicable to communicate with any person entitled to grant entry to the premises.

        (b) It is practicable to communicate with a person entitled to grant entry to the premises but it is not practicable to communicate with any person entitled to grant access to the evidence.

        (c) Entry to the premises will not be granted unless a warrant is produced.

        (d) The purpose of a search may be frustrated or seriously prejudiced unless a constable arriving at the premises can secure immediate entry to them.

Where these conditions are not fulfilled, the issue of the warrant will be unlawful.

In *R (Global Cash & Carry Ltd) v Birmingham Magistrates' Court*,[205] a search warrant was quashed as the magistrates' court had applied the wrong evidential test: issuing the warrant on the basis that there were reasonable grounds to believe that an indictable offence was being investigated, rather than reasonable grounds to believe an indictable offence had been committed. The court held that it was inappropriate to determine whether

---

[201] *Williams v Somerfield* [1972] 2 QB 512, 518 (Lord Widgery CJ).

[202] *R (Global Cash & Carry Ltd) v Birmingham Magistrates' Court* [2013] EWHC 528 (Admin). This may lead to complications where issues arise which were not dealt with in the public law proceedings as a defendant will not automatically be prevented from raising a defence to a private law claim for trespass simply because the relevant warrants have been quashed, see *Tchenguiz v Director of the Serious Fraud Office; Rawlinson and Hunter Trustees SA v Director of the Serious Fraud Office* [2013] EWHC 1578; *Robert Tchenguiz, R20 Ltd v Director of the Serious Fraud Office* [2014] EWCA Civ 472.

[203] Although not necessarily, as other statutory powers are applicable in certain circumstances, for example, s 9 of PACE 1984 and s 146 Firearms Act 1968.

[204] PACE 1984, s 8(3).

[205] *Global Cash & Carry* (n 202).

the magistrates' court would have issued the warrant had they applied the correct legal test. Where the wrong test is applied, the warrant will be unlawfully issued.[206]

More latitude has been shown in relation to the 'reasonable grounds' standard applied through section 8 of PACE 1984. In *C*,[207] it was held that there were reasonable grounds to believe there might be relevant material at the claimant's premises notwithstanding that:

i.   the putative offence (accessing child pornography) had occurred seven years previously, meaning that the computer sought might not have been retained; and

ii.   the claimant was known to have been the victim of identity theft.

In this case there was no obligation on the police to discount the possibility that somebody else might have committed the offence prior to applying for the warrant, as this would constitute 'an unreasonable and impracticable fetter on the investigation of crime'.[208] However, a challenge based on the absence of reasonable grounds for issuing the warrant in respect of two of the four properties searched was successful in *AC, RC, BK, GST*.[209]

Search warrants, irrespective of the legislative provision under which they are obtained, must also comply with section 15 of PACE 1984, which specifies the requirements applicable to the process of obtaining and executing the warrant, and section 16 of PACE 1984, which governs how warrants must be executed. Section 15(1) provides that an entry on or search of premises under a warrant will be unlawful unless it complies with these sections.

In addition, it has been held that (i) all search warrant application hearings must be recorded as a matter of practice;[210] and (ii) the court must give reasons for either granting or refusing a warrant.[211] When considering the lawfulness of the issue of a warrant, regard should also be had, where applicable, to the Justices' Guidance Booklet on Dealing with Search Warrants, issued on 7 October 2013, and section 7 of Part 6 of the Criminal Procedure Rules.

(i) Breach of Applicable Safeguards in the Procurement and Issuing of the Warrant (Breach of s 15 of PACE 1984)—Challenging the Issue of a Search Warrant

An application for a warrant will be made by an officer setting out the relevant details in an 'information' to be put before the court. The requirements of this document are comprehensively set out in section 15 of PACE 1984. The courts have repeatedly emphasised the need to adhere to these and a failure to do so may result in the warrant being quashed.[212]   **4-41**

---

206 ibid [25] (Kenneth Parker J).
207 *R (C) v Chief Constable of A* (n 57).
208 ibid [15].
209 *AC, RC, BK, GST v Nottingham and Newark Magistrates Court, Her Majesty's Revenue and Customs* [2013] EWHC 3790 (Admin), [66].
210 *R (S, F, L) v Chief Constable of the British Transport Police, The Southwark Crown Court* [2013] EWHC 2189 (Admin) [46].
211 *Van der Pijl v Kingston Crown Court* [2012] EWHC 3745 (Admin), [2013] AC 29 and *R v Lewes Crown Court and another, ex parte Nigel Weller & Co* (CO/28890/98–12 May 1999), 7.
212 See, for example, *S, F, L* (n 210) [43]–[45] and *R (1) F (2) J (3) K v (1) Blackfriars Crown Court (2) Commissioner of Police of the Metropolis* [2014] EWHC 1541 (Admin) [14].

Section 15 of PACE 1984 also requires an applicant to provide full assistance to the court when applying for a warrant,[213] and to draw attention to 'anything which militates against the issue of a warrant'.[214] In *R (Redknapp and others) v Commissioner of the City of London Police*[215] a warrant was invalidated by the failure of the police to disclose material facts when making the application. The court commented that the failures were 'wholly unacceptable', and that the gravity of the search required that 'all the material necessary to justify the grant of a warrant ... be contained in the information provided on the form', with any required additional information requested by the magistrates being appropriately noted.[216]

The application had failed to identify which of the conditions in section 8(3) of PACE 1984 had been relied on, and no evidence appeared to have been supplied to demonstrate that that defect had been remedied with the magistrate. It was not appropriate for an inference to be drawn that the magistrate must have been so informed.[217] Consequently, the court held that the warrant had been issued unlawfully, also rendering the subsequent search unlawful.

However, in *Wood v North Avon Magistrates' Court*[218] Moses LJ held that where non-disclosure was not deliberate, and not due to bad faith, a warrant would only be invalidated if the failure to disclose made a difference to the warrant being issued.[219]

Indeed, in *C*,[220] although the grounds for the application were found to have been poorly expressed in the information, as the magistrate had been made aware of (i) the premises to be searched and (ii) the address of the credit-card holder whose details had been used to access a child pornography website, the applicable conditions were held to have been fulfilled.

Similarly, in *R v (1) Nunaf Ahmad Zinga (2) Mukundin Pilar*,[221] the Court of Appeal, whilst recognising a duty of full disclosure of relevant matters, held that in order for a warrant to be quashed on the basis of non-disclosure a claimant must demonstrate that the warrant would not have been issued had the relevant disclosure been made.[222] *R (Ahmed) v York Magistrates' Court*[223] states that the requirements of PACE 1984 sections 15(2) and 15(2A) do not require the information to include all facts and/or evidence upon which an applicant relies, nor is a magistrate confined, when considering an application, to the content of the information.[224]

4-42   A search warrant will also be subject to challenge where it has been obtained on the basis of misleading information. In *R (G) v Commissioner of Police of the Metropolis*[225]

---

[213] *Gittins v Central Criminal Court* [2011] EWHC 131 (Admin) and *R (Energy Financing Team Ltd) v Bow Street Magistrates Court* [2005] EWHC 1626 (Admin).

[214] See *R (Austen and others) v Chief Constable of Wiltshire Police and others* [2011] EWHC 3385 (Admin) [26] (Ouseley J).

[215] *R (Redknapp and others) v Commissioner of the City of London Police* [2008] EWHC 1177 (Admin).

[216] ibid [13], [27].

[217] ibid [16].

[218] *Wood v North Avon Magistrates' Court* [2009] EWHC 3614 (Admin).

[219] ibid [35].

[220] *R (C) v Chief Constable of A* (n 57).

[221] *R v (1) Nunaf Ahmad Zinga (2) Mukundin Pilar* [2012] EWCA Crim 2257.

[222] In this case, that the prosecutor was a private firm.

[223] *R (Ahmed) v York Magistrates' Court* [2012] EWHC 3636 (Admin).

[224] ibid [53]–[54].

[225] *R (G) v Commissioner of Police of the Metropolis* [2011] EWHC 3331.

the information put before the court falsely indicated that payment had been made for child pornography, and omitted details indicative of the claimant's innocence. The court emphasised the high standard applicable when seeking to obtain a warrant, due to the need for the courts to 'be in a position to trust the police to give full and accurate information when they seek a form of relief that interferes with the liberty of a subject in the cause of fighting crime'.[226]

This standard was also applied in *Global Cash & Carry Ltd*, where a failure to comply with section 15 of PACE 1984 rendered a warrant and the search carried out pursuant thereto unlawful. However, the court commented that in cases where the 'rationale' of section 15 had been respected a court may, as a matter of discretion, not grant any relief beyond declaration of a breach of Article 8 of ECHR. Although not the case in this instance, due to the flagrant breaches of the section 15 requirements, more 'technical' breaches would be unlikely to result in substantive relief for a claimant.[227]

In *Hicks*,[228] an argument that a warrant had been sought on the basis of misleading information, that the magistrates had been informed that individuals suspected of being involved in student demonstrations some months prior to the application were thought to be at the premises to be searched, was found to be 'without foundation' on the facts.[229] Further, the claimants' central contention, that the 'dominant purpose' of the execution of the search warrant had been to prevent any disruption of the Royal Wedding and not to seize stolen goods, or articles intended to be used to commit criminal damage, was also rejected, as discussed below at 4-45.[230]

Finally, the police are required to adopt 'reasonable and available precautions' to verify the apparent connection between the address to be searched and the matter being investigated. Where such steps (such as checking the records of utility companies or local authorities to ensure that the person sought resides at the address) are not taken, the search will be rendered disproportionate and as such constitute a breach of Article 8 of the ECHR.[231]

(ii) Errors on the Face of the Warrant (Breach of s 15 of PACE 1984—Challenge to the Issue of a Search Warrant)

Section 15(6) of PACE 1984 specifies the formality requirements of a search warrant. **4-43** Errors on the face of the document may be sufficient to render both it and any subsequent search unlawful. This is due to the principle that:

> warrants must be sufficiently clear and precise in their terms so that all those interested in their execution may know precisely what are the limits of the power which has been granted.[232]

---

[226] ibid [20] (Laws LJ).
[227] *Global Cash & Carry* (n 202). Although there are indications that a varying standard will be applied, dependant on the context of the case, with complete compliance being necessary in more serious circumstances, G (n 225) [23] (Laws LJ).
[228] *Hicks* (n 183) is referred to in a number of contexts in this chapter—see n 183 above for a full list.
[229] ibid [253].
[230] ibid [235] and [256]. See also *Pearce* (n 189).
[231] *Keegan v United Kingdom* (2007) 44 EHRR 33.
[232] *McGrath* (n 198) [18] (Lord Clyde).

Such errors are constituted where a warrant, for example:

    i.   does not include a schedule of the premises authorised for search;[233]

    ii.   omits to name the person applying for the warrant;[234]

   iii. fails to specify the relevant statutory power under which it was issued;[235]

   iv. does not on its face identify the articles or persons sought (even where a separate document listing the required information was provided);[236]

    v.   fails to specify the material sought with sufficient precision;[237]

   vi. affords discretion to the executing officer(s) as to its terms;[238] or

   vii. has not been certified appropriately as a copy.[239]

However, as above, the impact of any non-compliance on the lawfulness of a search will be dependent on the gravity of the relevant breach. It has been held, for example, that the following errors would not alone be sufficient to render a search unlawful:

    i.   The failure to specify the warrant as either a specific premises warrant or an all premises warrant.[240]

    ii.   The inclusion of a Scottish address on a warrant where the relevant address had also been listed.[241]

(3) Execution of the Search Warrant (Compliance with s 16 of PACE 1984)

4-44   A failure to comply with the procedural safeguards specified by PACE 1984, section 16, may render the execution of the warrant, and the search, unlawful. This will be the case where, for example, officers have failed to supply a copy of the full warrant, including any schedules appended to it.[242]

Although unable to so hold on the facts, in *Redknapp* the court appeared to accept that a search under a warrant will be unlawful where it:

    i.   is carried out at an unreasonable hour;[243] and/or,

    ii.   extends beyond the remit permitted by the warrant.[244]

---

[233] *Global Cash & Carry* (n 202) and *R (Bhatti) v Croydon Magistrates' Court* [2010] EWHC 522 (Admin).

[234] *G* (n 225).

[235] ibid.

[236] *R v Chief Constable of Lancashire Constabulary, ex parte Parker* [1993] QB 577.

[237] *S, F, L* (n 210) and *R (1) F (2) J (3) K* (n 212). In *(1) Robin Lees (2) Anne Lees (3) Karl Morgan (4) Joanne Morgan v (1) Solihull Magistrates' Court (2) Revenue & Customs Commissioners* [2013] EWHC 3779 (Admin) although the entry, search and seizure were declared unlawful due to the imprecision of the warrant [39]–[42], this was not alone sufficient for it to be quashed [57].

[238] *AC, RC, BK, GST* (n 218) [51].

[239] ibid.

[240] *Redknapp* (n 215). However, the fact that an 'all-premises' warrant has erroneously been issued in place of a specified premises warrant was held to be sufficient to invalidate that warrant in *AC, RC, BK, GST* (n 209), [70]–[72].

[241] ibid.

[242] ibid and *Bhatti* (n 233). A search will also be subject to challenge where police fail to make reasonable adjustments in searching the property of a disabled person, as required by the Equality Act 2010 (*Finnigan v Chief Constable of Northumbria Police* [2013] EWCA Civ 1191).

[243] The court did not engage with this matter as to do so would require evidence to be heard in relation to the operational circumstances of the search, which was not appropriate in the context of the application before it, *Redknapp* (n 215) [19].

[244] ibid [20].

                    Rachel Taylor and Piers von Berg

However, failure to return an executed warrant to the court in compliance with section 16(10) of PACE 1984 would be unlikely to render a search unlawful, and even if it technically did, would not in and of itself result in any relief.[245]

(i) Extent of a Search (Execution of a Search Warrant)

PACE 1984 section 16(8) requires that a search extend no further than the purpose for **4-45** which the warrant was issued. In *R (S, F, L) v Chief Constable of the British Transport Police, The Southwark Crown Court*[246] the failure to safeguard legally privileged material was unlawful as it extended beyond the authorised actions.[247]

However, in *Hicks*[248] an argument that a warrant had been executed for a purpose contrary to that for which it had been issued was rejected by the court. Although the execution of the warrant was found to be 'heavily influenced'[249] by concerns regarding the Royal Wedding, there remained a sound legal basis for the search, and in the absence of a challenge to the issue of the warrants the claimants were unable to contend that the 'dominant purpose' of the warrants was to prevent disruption of the Royal Wedding.[250] Instead, '[T]hat the searches had the advantage of furthering the aim of preventing disruption of the Royal Wedding, and were timed to maximise that advantage, did not invalidate the exercise of the powers'.[251] This finding was upheld by the Court of Appeal,[252] where a distinction was drawn between the purpose of the warrant and the operational decision as to the timing of its execution.[253] Actions outside the strict remit of the warrant, such as searching an individual's wallet, are also likely to be considered 'de minimis', and thus will not without more render a search unlawful, nor justify any relief.[254]

(ii) Seizure of Property (Execution of a Search Warrant)

The police powers of seizure pursuant to a search under warrant are generally broad. **4-46** Section 8(2) of PACE 1984, for example, provides that a constable may seize and retain anything for which a search has been authorised.[255] The fact that a warrant has been widely drawn is unlikely to render that warrant or the search carried out pursuant thereto unlawful where the remit of the permitted search is sufficiently clear.[256] However, as above, section 15(6)(b) requires that a warrant specify, insofar

---

[245] *Hicks* (n 183) [247].

[246] *S, F, L* (n 210).

[247] ibid [88].

[248] *Hicks* (n 183) is referred to in a number of contexts in this chapter—see n 183 above for a full list.

[249] ibid [233].

[250] ibid [234]. It was also relevant that on the facts the police had seized quantities of computer equipment falling within the remit of the warrant, ibid [235].

[251] ibid [236].

[252] *Pearce and Another* (n 189).

[253] ibid [29]–[32].

[254] *Hicks* (n 183) [267].

[255] See also PACE 1984, ss 19 and 20.

[256] *Mr Philip Graham Bell v The Chief Constable of Greater Manchester Police* [2005] EWCA Civ 902; *R (Glenn & Co (Essex) Ltd) v HM Commissioners for Revenue and Customs* [2011] EWHC 1998 (Admin) [58]–[66]; *R (Horne) v Central Criminal Court* [2012] EWHC 1350 (Admin); and *Hicks* (n 183) [261]–[263].

as is practicable, any articles sought and the courts have repeatedly emphasised the importance of ensuring precision in the terms of a warrant.[257] In *F J K*[258] the warrant was invalidated, and so quashed, as it had been drawn so widely that the articles sought had not been identified as far as practicable and items were seized that should not have been.

As stated previously, section 16(8) of PACE 1984 requires that a search only extend so far as is required for the purpose stated in the warrant. A search may therefore be challenged on the basis that police sought items falling outside the scope of the warrant.[259] Such challenges will need to consider section 19 of PACE 1984, which permits seizure of items reasonably believed to have been obtained through the commission of an offence, or to be evidence relating to an offence. In addition, it was held by the *Privy Council in PF Sugrue Ltd v Attorney General*[260] that where an officer has mistakenly seized material under one power, his actions will still be lawful if he could (though unknowingly) have acted under another power.[261] It was also held in *R v Chesterfield Justices, ex parte Bramley*[262] that where property has been seized which falls outside the remit of the warrant, the search remains valid for those documents within its scope, although an action for trespass to goods may then arise.[263] Even where property has been seized unlawfully it is possible that its retention will be authorised pursuant to section 59(6) of the Criminal Justice and Police Act 2001.

Potential claimants should also note that the courts have been reluctant to allow use of judicial review in relation to the alleged seizure of excessive material where this requires an extensive fact-finding exercise and hearing of live evidence.[264]

(iii) Special Procedure Material (Execution of a Search Warrant)

4-47   Additional restrictions apply in certain circumstances due to the nature of the articles sought. Most significantly, the police must comply with 'special procedures' when searching for 'excluded material' or 'special procedure material'.[265]

S, F, L concerned the issue and execution of two search warrants obtained by the police for the purpose of seizing items which included a solicitor's notebook and papers relating

---

[257] See, for example, *Piji v The Crown Court at Kingston and others* [2012] EWHC 3745 (Admin) [53], [61] and [65] and *Power-Hynes v Norwich Magistrates' Court* [2009] EWHC 1512 (Admin).

[258] *R(1) F(2) J(3)* (n 212).

[259] See, for example, *S, F, L* (n 210) [71]–[80]. However, such an argument failed in *Hicks* (n 183) despite the fact that material falling outside the scope of the warrant, namely protest literature, was seized, see ibid [239]–[245]. The Court of Appeal upheld this finding in *Pearce* (n 189) [31], reasoning that officers were not required to adopt 'tunnel vision' when conducting searches in accordance with *R v Chesterfield Justices, ex parte Bramley* [2000] QB 576.

[260] *PF Sugrue Ltd v Attorney General* [2005] UKPC 44.

[261] This argument was also raised, though not decided upon, in *R (C) v Chief Constable of A* (n 57).

[262] *R v Chesterfield Justices, ex parte Bramley* [2000] QB 576.

[263] ibid [11].

[264] *R v Chief Constable of the Warwickshire Constabulary and Another, ex parte Fitzpatrick* [1999] 1 WLR 564, [1998] 1 All ER 65, 579D–E. This authority has not been followed on the issue of the interpretation of ss 8 and 15 of PACE 1984. See *Van der Pijl v Kingston Crown Court* [2012] EWHC 3745 (Admin), [2013] ACD 29 and *R (Anand) v HMRC* [2012] EWHC 2989 (Admin).

[265] As set out in PACE 1984, s 9 and Sch 1.

Rachel Taylor and Piers von Berg

to a particular client.[266] In respect of the first warrant, the court held that the 'access conditions' that need to be satisfied for such a warrant to be issued had not been fulfilled, and that the information laid before the court had been wholly inadequate.[267] The second warrant was also quashed as (i) a production order should have been made instead, there being no evidence to suggest that this would have seriously prejudiced the investigation;[268] and (ii) the police had not first established whether the information sought was held by the first claimant before searching the second claimant's property, contrary to the information that had been provided to the court when seeking the warrant.[269]

Where a magistrates' court has no reason to believe that there is any serious possibility that excluded material or special procedure material will be located on the premises, a warrant will not be quashed in the event that such material is so located. A magistrates' court is not under any obligation to request additional information or to obtain assurances regarding this matter: in C,[270] it was held that what was known or should have been known to the police was relevant only to the extent that it was known to the magistrate or should have been established by him on proper enquiry.[271]   **4-48**

No warrant can authorise the seizure of items subject to legal professional privilege and any warrant purporting to do so will be rendered unlawful.[272] It has previously been held that there need not be a specific exclusion to that effect on the warrant, except perhaps where there is 'no doubt' as to which items are privileged.[273] However, in F, J, K[274] the court stated *obiter* that such specific exclusions were necessary in cases where the excluded material fell within the terms of the warrant as drafted (despite the application of section 19(6) of PACE).

If there is uncertainty as to whether property might include legally privileged material, a 'sifting process' may take place to confirm the position. However, any items removed from the property will be 'seized', and such seizure may be unlawful where it falls outside the scope of the warrant.[275] Should there be reason to believe that items are legally privileged subsequent to seizure they should be returned immediately,[276] and any items where this is in dispute stored separately, pending the outcome of that dispute.

(4) Obtaining a Copy of the Information

When considering challenging a warrant, it will ordinarily be important to obtain a copy of the information that was laid before the court. Although it is well established   **4-49**

---

[266] Which, the police contended, were not legally privileged or excluded material, but 'special procedure material'.

[267] *S, F, L* (n 210) [60]–[68].

[268] As required by Sch 1, para 14(d); see also *R (Faisaltex Ltd) v Preston Crown Court* [2009] 1 WLR 1687.

[269] *S, F, L* (n 210) [99]–[101].

[270] *R (C) v Chief Constable of A* (n 57).

[271] ibid [16]–[17].

[272] PACE 1984, s 19(6); *Gittins v Central Criminal Court* [2011] EWHC 131 (Admin) and *S, F, L* (n 210).

[273] *Ex p Bramley* (n 259) [4].

[274] *F, J, K* (n 212) [50].

[275] *Ex p Bramley* (n 259) [9].

[276] ibid. See also *Reynolds v Commissioner of Police of the Metropolis* [1985] QB 881 and *R v Southwark Crown Court, ex parte Sorsky Defries* The Times, 21 July 1995.

that a proper record of the application for, and issuance of, a warrant should be made available to the individual whose property was searched, this has often proved to be problematic in practice.

In making an application for a copy of the information, emphasis should be placed upon the assertion of Lord Woolf LCJ in *Mark Cronin v Sheffield Magistrates' Court*,[277] that, subject to considerations of public interest immunity:

> if a person who is in the position of this claimant asks perfectly sensibly for a copy of the information, then speaking for myself I can see no objection to a copy of that information being provided. The citizen, in my judgment, should be entitled to be able to assess whether an information contains the material which justifies the issue of a warrant.

Similarly, in *Gittins v Central Criminal Court*,[278] the court drew upon the intrusive and grave consequences of searches conducted under warrant, and asserted that a party challenging the grant of such a warrant would ordinarily be entitled to know the basis on which it was obtained. It will not be appropriate for there to be a general policy of non-disclosure while a criminal investigation is continuing,[279] and even where full disclosure is not possible the courts have encouraged a redacted version, or a note backed by affidavit, to be supplied.[280]

Authoritative guidance as to the procedure to be followed in seeking disclosure of the information was provided in *Metropolitan Police Commissioner v B*,[281] an appeal by way of case stated against on order for disclosure of the information in the magistrates' court. Disclosure was successfully opposed by the Commissioner on grounds of public interest immunity. The relevant procedure as applicable in criminal proceedings is set out at rule 5.7 of the Criminal Procedure Rules.

Where it appears clear that a warrant will be amenable to challenge, disclosure can of course be sought by way of pre-action correspondence. It is of note that a party (or potential party) to judicial review proceedings (or proposed judicial review proceedings) cannot unilaterally decide to redact documents for purposes of public interest immunity, and a public interest immunity order will instead be required.[282]

The time taken in obtaining the information where disclosure is contested will often impact on a claimant's ability to issue within the limitation period. However, where reasonable and proper efforts have been made to progress the matter, and the lawfulness of the warrant cannot be ascertained in the absence of the information, it is submitted that a point is unlikely to be taken on this basis, and if it were, little credence should be paid to it by the court.[283]

---

[277] *Mark Cronin v Sheffield Magistrates' Court* (2003) 1 WLR 752 [29].

[278] *Gittins v Central Criminal Court* [2011] EWHC 131 (Admin).

[279] ibid [25], although see also *R (Whiston-Dew) v Revenue and Customs Commissioners* [2009] EWHC 3761 (Admin).

[280] *Gittins* (n 278) [25].

[281] *Metropolitan Police Commissioner v B* [2014] EWHC 546 (Admin). See also *Eastenders Cash & Carry v South Western Magistrates Court* [2011] EWHC 937 (Admin) and *G* (n 225).

[282] *S, F, L* (n 210) [109]–[115]. A party is permitted, however, to withhold documents on this basis, absent a court order.

[283] *G* (n 225) [11].

Rachel Taylor and Piers von Berg

E. Arrest

(1) General Principles

The occasions on which judicial review will be utilised in this context are likely to be limited. Obtaining redress by way of private law action will often be more appropriate, even where a claim involves issues of public importance, as illustrated by *Sher* (see above 4-5 and below 4-57).[284]   **4-50**

(2) Warrants

It is relatively uncommon for arrests to be carried out under warrant.[285] However, where this occurs, an arrest may be amenable to challenge by way of judicial review should the warrant have been procured, issued or executed unlawfully. As in relation to search warrants, the lawfulness of the arrest will be determined by the authority provided by the relevant warrant, in accordance with section 6 of the Constables Protection Act 1750.[286] The remedy sought will ordinarily be a quashing order (together with damages), which cannot result from a private law action.   **4-51**

(3) Lawfulness of an Arrest without Warrant

Practitioners may be familiar with the requisite conditions of a lawful arrest and it is beyond the purposes of this chapter to provide a comprehensive discussion of private law actions for false imprisonment and/or breach of Article 5 of the ECHR arising from an unlawful arrest.[287] However, for ease of reference, the basic requirements of a lawful arrest are set out below, together with examples, where relevant, of occasions on which such matters have been addressed in public law proceedings: **4-52**

(i) Compliance with s 24(1)-(3) of PACE 1984[288]

This states: **4-53**

(1) A constable may arrest without a warrant—
   (a) Anyone who is about to commit an offence;
   (b) Anyone who is in the act of committing an offence;
   (c) Anyone whom he has reasonable grounds for suspecting to be about to commit an offence;
   (d) Anyone whom he has reasonable grounds for suspecting to be committing an offence.

---

[284] *Sher* (n 22).
[285] Issued under Magistrates' Court Act 1980, s 1.
[286] See 4-39–4-49 for a detailed discussion of warrants in the context of searches.
[287] See instead R Clayton, H Tomlinson with E Buckett and A Davies, *Civil Actions Against the Police*, 3rd edn (London, Sweet & Maxwell, 2004).
[288] As amended by the Serious Organised Crime and Police Act 2005.

(2)   If a constable has reasonable grounds for suspecting that an offence has been committed, he may arrest without a warrant anyone whom he has reasonable grounds to suspect of being guilty of it.

(3)   If an offence has been committed, a constable may arrest without a warrant—

(a)   Anyone who is guilty of the offence;

(b)   Anyone whom he has reasonable grounds for suspecting to be guilty of it.

The statute thus imposes both a subjective test (that the arresting officer honestly suspected that the claimant was involved in the commission of a criminal offence) and an objective test (that that suspicion, honestly held, was based on reasonable grounds, with the applicable standard being that of the reasonable person, on the basis of the information known to the arresting officer).[289]

The determination of matters relating to 'reasonable suspicion' for an arrest will ordinarily require the resolution of complex issues of fact, and as such be ill-suited to judicial review. Although unusually in *Hicks*[290] the court was required to make such a determination, it concluded that there was an 'amply sufficient basis' for the arrest.[291]

4-54   In *R (Rawlinson & Hunter Trustees & Others) v Central Criminal Court & another; R (Tchenguiz & another) v Director of the Serious Fraud Office & Others*[292] one of the claimants, Mr Robert Tchenguiz, sought to challenge his arrest on two grounds, one of which was that the arresting officer had been misled into believing that there were reasonable grounds for arrest by an agent responsible for law enforcement, namely the Serious Fraud Office (SFO). It was contended that because the SFO was on notice that the information provided to the arresting officer was incorrect or incomplete, the law should provide a narrow exception to the 'O'Hara principle'[293] and afford Mr Tchenguiz a remedy. However, this argument was rejected by the court on the basis that the police could not be required to duplicate the work of the SFO and independently scrutinise the information provided to it that was thereafter relied upon in executing an arrest.[294]

(ii)   Compliance with s 24(4) of PACE 1984[295]

4-55   Even where an arrest is founded on reasonable grounds of suspicion, it will only be lawful where it is 'necessary', in accordance with section 24(4) of PACE 1984, which provides:

(4)... [T]he power of summary arrest conferred by subsection (1), (2) or (3) is exercisable only if the constable has reasonable grounds for believing that for any of the reasons mentioned in subsection (5) it is necessary to arrest the person in question.

---

[289] *Hussein v Chong Fook Kam* [1970] AC 942 and *O'Hara v Chief Constable of Royal Ulster Constabulary* [1997] AC 286.

[290] *Hicks* (n 183) is referred to in a number of contexts in this chapter—see n 183 above for a full list.

[291] ibid (n 183) [199].

[292] *R (Rawlinson & Hunter Trustees & Others) v Central Criminal Court & another; R (Tchenguiz & another) v Director of the Serious Fraud Office & Others* [2012] EWHC 2254 (Admin). This primarily concerned an application for judicial review regarding the issue and execution of search warrants procured by the Serious Fraud Office working in conjunction with the City of London Police from the Central Criminal Court.

[293] Namely that the question as to whether an officer has reasonable grounds to arrest, in accordance with PACE 1984, s 24, 'is whether a reasonable man would be of that opinion, having regard to the information which was in the mind of the arresting officer', regardless of whether that information was in fact true, *O'Hara v Chief Constable of Royal Ulster Constabulary* [1997] AC 286, 298.

[294] *Rawlinson & Hunter Trustees* (n 292) [222].

[295] As amended by the Serious Organised Crime and Police Act 2005.

(5) The reasons are—

    (a) To enable the name of the person in question to be ascertained (in the case where the constable does not know, and cannot readily ascertain, the person's name, or has reasonable grounds for doubting whether a name given by the person as his name is his real name);

    (b) Correspondingly as regards the person's address;

    (c) To prevent the person in question—

        (i) causing physical injury to himself or any other person;

        (ii) suffering physical injury;

        (iii) causing loss of or damage to property;

        (iv) committing an offence against public decency (subject to subsection (6)); or,

        (v) causing an unlawful obstruction of the highway;

    (a) To protect a child or other vulnerable person from the person in question;

    (b) To allow the prompt and effective investigation of the offence or of the conduct of the person in question;

    (c) To prevent any prosecution for the offence from being hindered by the disappearance of the person in question.

This requirement has been subject to extensive litigation over recent years,[296] with the Court of Appeal most recently formulating the relevant test as follows:

    (i) the constable actually believed that arrest was necessary, and for a subsection (5) reason; and

    (ii) objectively that belief was reasonable on the basis of the information known to the officer.[297]

An arresting officer ought also 'to apply his mind to alternatives short of arrest',[298] paying due regard to the relevant guidance set out in Code G of PACE 1984, paragraphs 2.4–2.9;[299] if he does not do so, the arrest will be vulnerable to challenge.[300] However, the Court of Appeal also emphasised the limitations to this obligation, asserting:

> To require of a policeman that he pass through particular thought processes each time he considers an arrest, and in all circumstances no matter what urgency or danger may attend the decision, and to subject that decision to the test of whether he has considered every material matter and excluded every immaterial matter, is to impose an unrealistic and unattainable burden.[301]

---

[296] *Richardson v Chief Constable of the West Midlands* [2011] EWHC 773; *Hayes v Chief Constable of Merseyside Police* [2011] EWCA Civ 911; *Hicks* (n 183); *Fitzpatrick & Others v The Commissioner of Police for the Metropolis* [2012] EWHC 12 (QB); and *Lord Hanningfield of Chelmsford v Chief Constable of Essex* [2013] EWHC 243 (QB).

[297] *Hayes*, ibid [41]–[42].

[298] Such as attending a voluntary interview, as in *Richardson* (n 296).

[299] Revised in 2012.

[300] *Hayes* (n 296) [39]; see also *Richardson* (n 296).

[301] ibid (n 296) [40].

4-56 Once more, the determination of such matters is likely to require the resolution of complex issues of fact, and as such be unsuitable for judicial review, as in *C*.[302] Although again in *Hicks*[303] the necessity of M's arrest was unusually considered by the Administrative Court, the arguments submitted in furtherance of this claim were rejected[304] on the basis that:

> (i)   the arrest was necessary to ascertain M's name;[305]
>
> (ii) there were reasonable grounds for believing it was necessary to arrest M to prevent damage to property;
>
> (iii) there were reasonable grounds for believing the arrest was necessary to effect an investigation of M's conduct; and
>
> (iv) there was no requirement for the officers to ask M further questions or to consider the possibility of a voluntary interview as an alternative to an arrest.[306]

The court similarly rejected such a challenge in *Rawlinson & Hunter Trustees*,[307] which was distinguished from *Richardson*[308] on the basis that:

> i.   the necessity test had been properly considered;
>
> ii. it was not clear that the claimant had made an unequivocal offer to attend a police interview voluntarily; and
>
> iii. even if such an offer had been made this would not necessarily had obviated the necessity to arrest in view of the risk that relevant documentation would otherwise be destroyed.

Conversely, in *Lord Hanningfield of Chelmsford v Chief Constable of Essex*[309] Eady J concluded, in circumstances in which the claimant had previously been wholly cooperative with police investigations and had prior knowledge of the allegations against him, that the necessity test had not 'on any realistic interpretation of the word, been met'.[310]

(iii) Compliance with the Requirement to Provide Information (s 28 of PACE 1984)

4-57 Officers are additionally required to discharge their duties under section 28 of PACE 1984 when carrying out an arrest, as follows:

> (1) Subject to subsection (5) below, where a person is arrested, otherwise than by being informed that he is under arrest, the arrest is not lawful unless the person arrested is informed that he is under arrest as soon as is practicable after his arrest.

---

[302] *R (C) v Chief Constable of A* (n 56).

[303] *Hicks* is referred to in a number of contexts in this chapter—see n 183 above for a full list.

[304] *Hicks* (n 183) [201]–[220].

[305] Irrespective of the indication in para 2.9 of the May 2012 edition of Code G of PACE 1984 that an individual should be warned that failure to give a name is likely to make his arrest necessary, as this is not incumbent on the police, nor is it required by Code G 2012, nor was that code in force at the material time.

[306] See *Hayes* (n 296) which provides that a failure to consider alternatives does not of itself invalidate an arrest but does expose an officer to the risk of being found to have had no reasonable grounds because believed that arrest was necessary. See also *Richardson* (n 296).

[307] *Rawlinson & Hunter Trustees* (n 292).

[308] *Richardson* (n 296), where such a challenge was successful.

[309] *Lord Hanningfield of Chelmsford v Chief Constable of Essex* [2013] EWHC 243 (QB).

[310] ibid [29].

Rachel Taylor and Piers von Berg

(2) Where a person is arrested by a constable, subsection (1) above applies regardless of whether the fact of the arrest is obvious.

(3) Subject to subsection (5) below, no arrest is lawful unless the person arrested is informed of the ground for the arrest at the time of, or as soon as is practicable after, the arrest.

(4) Where a person is arrested by a constable, subsection (3) above applies regardless of whether the ground for the arrest is obvious.

(5) Nothing in this section is to be taken to require a person to be informed—

    (a) that he is under arrest; or

    (b) of the ground for the arrest,

if it was not reasonably practicable for him to be so informed by reason of his having escaped from arrest before the information could be given.

The entitlement to be informed of the reasons for an arrest is also well established at common law and protected by Article 5(2) of the ECHR.[311]

In *Sher* (discussed above at 4-5), the three claimants, who were of Pakistani nationality, were arrested under section 41 of the Terrorism Act 2000 and detained without charge. The City of Westminster Magistrates' Court granted an application for further detention, which was subsequently extended. The claimants were released without charge some six days later before being served with deportation orders and, five months after their arrest, voluntarily returning to Pakistan.

The claimants argued that they had not been informed of the basis on which they were detained in sufficient detail to allow them to properly challenge its continuation. It was therefore contended that the arrests and detention constituted a breach of Article 5(2) of the ECHR and were contrary to 'the arrest law' as espoused by Lord Carlile QC in his review of this legislative power.[312]

Importantly, it was held that this challenge was not unsuitable for judicial review, but that in any event, there had been no breach of Article 5(2), as:

  i. a 'general statement' was provided to each claimant informing him that he was he was being arrested under section 41 of the Terrorism Act 2000 because the officer arresting him reasonably suspected that he was a terrorist; and

  ii. it appeared that further information as to how and why such suspicions were held was then promptly provided.[313]

(iv) Exercising the Discretionary Power to Arrest in a Manner that is Wednesbury Unreasonable [314]

The introduction of the necessity test[315] means that challenges based on this fourth 'administrative strand' are likely to be rare. However, despite some judicial indication

4-58

---

[311] *Christie v Leachinsky* [1947] AC 573, 593 and *Taylor v Chief Constable of Thames Valley* [2004] 1 WLR 3155. *Fox, Campbell and Hartley v United Kingdom* [1991] 13 EHRR 157.

[312] Lord Carlile of Berriew QC, 'Operation Pathway: Report following review' (October 2009), available at http://tna.europarchive.org/20100419081706/http://security.homeoffice.gov.uk/news-publications/publication-search/legislation/terrorism-act-2000/operation-pathway-report?view=Binary.

[313] *Sher* (n 22) [91].

[314] *Associated Provincial Picture Houses Limited v Wednesbury Corp* [1948] 1 KB 223 explained above at 1-81–1-84; *Castorina v Chief Constable of Surrey* (10 June 1988) and *Cumming and others v Chief Constable of Northumbria Police* [2003] EWCA 1844.

[315] Following the enactment of the Serious Organised Crime and Police Act 2005, ss 110(1), 178; Serious Organised Crime and Police Act 2005 (Commencement No 4 and Transitory Provision) Order SI 2005/3495, art 2(1)(m).

that this strand has consequently been rendered redundant, as in *Fitzpatrick & Others v The Commissioner of Police for the Metropolis*,[316] this has not been fully established.[317] Indeed, in *Redknapp*,[318] Latham LJ asserted:

> as far as a decision to arrest is concerned, I accept that, as this court has said on a number of previous occasions, such a decision is amenable to judicial review in appropriate circumstances. It is the exercise of a discretion which can be challenged on Wednesbury grounds (see *Associated Provincial Picture Houses Limited v Wednesbury Corporation* [1948] 1 KB 223) or other grounds.

Therefore, in appropriate circumstances, it may still be possible for an arrest to be challenged on this basis.

F. Protest

(1) General Principles

4-59   Public law challenges to policies and practices adopted by the police will often arise in this context, where there will be a need, or a perceived need, for an individual's rights to freedom of expression and association to be balanced against the maintenance of order and public security. In addition, the high level of policing at such events increases the likelihood of interactions taking place which then give rise to legal challenges.

Potential claimants should bear in mind the guidance given at the beginning of this chapter on the suitability of judicial review. Although judicial review will not ordinarily present an appropriate remedy where an individual is detained for only a short period, its utility will increase where a claim arises in the context of a protest, particularly where a policy or practice is being challenged. This was the case in *Hicks*[319] where the claimants 'chose deliberately to proceed by way of judicial review because the central theme of the claims was that the defendant had pursued an unlawful policy or practice'.[320]

(2) Breach of the Peace

4-60   The common law power of arrest for breach of the peace, preserved by PACE 1984, is often utilised by the police in the context of protest. The power arises only where 'there has been an act done or threatened to be done which either actually harms a person, or, in his presence, his property, or is likely to cause such harm, or it puts someone in

---

[316] *Fitzpatrick & Others v The Commissioner of Police for the Metropolis* [2012] EWHC 12 (Admin).

[317] With respect, the Divisional Court in *Fitzpatrick* appears to have mistakenly accorded such a finding to Hughes LJ in *Hayes*.

[318] *Redknapp* (n 215) [23].

[319] *Hicks* is referred to in a number of contexts in this chapter—see n 183 above for a full list.

[320] *Hicks* (n 183) [9]. However, this case illustrates the restrictive approach that will be taken to the handling of evidence in the public law sphere, and demonstrates the limitations of these proceedings, which may be critical to a claim. Indeed, at para 148, the court recognised that an individual, Adam Moniz, had succeeded in a private law action brought in relation to the police conduct on the day of the Royal Wedding.

Rachel Taylor and Piers von Berg

fear of such harm being done'.[321] As such, an individual can only be lawfully arrested for breach of the peace:

i.   in circumstances relating to violence; and
ii.   where the arresting officer reasonably believed a breach of the peace to have been occurring or to have been imminent.[322]

The House of Lords engaged in an in-depth analysis of police powers[323] operative in this sphere in *R (Laporte) v Chief Constable of Gloucestershire Constabulary*[324] and the Court of Appeal subsequently endorsed the following to be an accurate summary of the law following *Laporte*:[325]

i.   For a police officer to take steps lawful at common law to prevent an apprehended breach of the peace, the apprehended breach must be imminent.
ii.   Imminence is not an inflexible concept but depends on the circumstances.
iii. If steps are to be justified, they must be necessary, reasonable and proportionate.
iv.   Depending on the circumstances, steps which include keeping two or more different groups apart may be necessary, reasonable and proportionate, if a combination of groups is reasonably apprehended to be likely to lead to an imminent breach of the peace.
v.   Again depending on the circumstances, where it is necessary in order to prevent an imminent breach of the peace, action may lawfully be taken which affects people who are not themselves going to be actively involved in the breach.

This restrictive approach was recently followed in *R (Mengesha) v Commissioner of Police of the Metropolis*,[326] where it was held that containment was not permissible for a purpose alternative to preventing a breach of the peace.[327] Specifically in that case, the purpose of identifying the individuals who had been involved through questioning and filming was not lawful, and release could not be made conditional upon compliance with these police actions.[328]

(i) Conduct Amounting to Breach of the Peace

There is extensive case law illustrating where conduct will be held to amount to a breach   **4-61**
of the peace.[329] Although actions which are wholly peaceful, such as the distribution of leaflets, will not be sufficient, a breach of the peace will be constituted where those

---

[321] *R v Howell* [1982] QB 416, 246G–H.
[322] *Redmond-Bate v DPP* [1999] 163 JP 789.
[323] Including those falling short of arrest.
[324] *R (Laporte) v Chief Constable of Gloucestershire Constabulary* [2006] UKHL 55, [2007] 2 AC 105.
[325] *McClure and Moos* (n 8) [36].
[326] *R (Mengesha) v Commissioner of Police of the Metropolis* [2013] EWHC 1695 (Admin).
[327] ibid [12].
[328] ibid.
[329] See, for example, *Wooding v Oxley* 173 ER 714, where in 1839 'disturbances' of shouting 'hear hear' and posing questions at a public meeting did not amount to a breach of the peace; *Jarrett v Chief Constable of West Midlands Police* [2003] EWCA Civ 397, which held that public agitation or excitement were insufficient for this purpose; and *R (Hawkes) v DPP* [2005] EWHC 3046 (Admin), where demonstrating an 'aggressive manner' did not amount to a breach of the peace.

peaceable actions are reasonably believed to provoke violence by another.[330] However, the refusal of an individual to comply with pre-emptive action taken by the police, such as a request to be voluntarily contained, is unlikely, without more, to be sufficient.[331]

(ii) 'Imminence'

4-62 Lord Mance framed the concept of imminence in the following terms in *Laporte*:

> the requirement of imminence is relatively clear-cut and appropriately identifies the common law power (or duty) of any citizen including the police to take definitive action as a power of last resort catering for situations about to descend into violence [although] [w]hat is imminent has to be judged in the context and the consideration, and the absence of any further opportunity to take preventive action may thus have relevance.[332]

The case concerned protestors travelling by coach to an anti-war demonstration at RAF Fairford. The police stopped the coaches and carried out a search due to a belief that the protestors were members of an anarchist group. Following the search it was concluded that only eight individuals were members of the group and, importantly, that there was no imminent threat of a breach of the peace. However, the chief superintendent directed that the coaches return to London under police escort, purportedly in order to prevent a breach of the peace at RAF Fairford.

It was therefore contended that the respondent chief constable had breached the appellant's rights under Articles 10 and 11 of ECHR, as the action had not been in accordance with the law (on the basis that there had been no imminent threat), and had been disproportionate. In finding for the appellant the Lords emphasised that the requirement of 'imminence' applied equally to all preventative steps taken by the police; even those falling short of arrest.[333] There had been no perception of an 'imminent' risk in the present case, and as 'the focus of any disorder was expected to be in the bell-mouth area outside the base ... police could arrest troublemakers then and there'.[334]

4-63 *Moos and McClure* concerned actions brought by participants in a protest at the Climate Camp in central London on 1 April 2009, who had been subject to 'containment'.[335] This protest had taken place at the same time as an unrelated protest located approximately a quarter of a mile away. Whilst there was evidence of some acts of violence at the second protest these were not, in the main, manifested at the Climate Camp. Despite this, the police contended that there was a concern that the dispersal of the second protest gave rise to a risk of breach of the peace at the Climate Camp, thereby justifying their use of containment.

---

[330] *Austin and another v Commissioner of Police of the Metropolis* [2007] EWCA Civ 989 and *McClure and Moos* (n 8).

[331] *Wright v Commissioner of Police for the Metropolis* [2013] EWHC 2739 [57]–[58].

[332] *Laporte* (n 324) [141].

[333] ibid [66] (Lord Rodger).

[334] ibid [55] (Lord Bingham).

[335] Known also as 'kettling', and discussed below at 4-67. *R (Moos and McClure) v Commissioner of Police of the Metropolis* [2011] EWHC 957 (Admin).

The Divisional Court rejected the police's argument and found that there had been no risk of an imminent breach of the peace as:

i.   The climate camp was largely not hostile.
ii.   Any violence or disorder during the afternoon had been sporadic.
iii. The containment was only precautionary.
iv.   The route between the two protests was lengthy and an appropriate cordon could have been formed at short notice.

However, this decision was overturned by the Court of Appeal,[336] which found that the lower court had applied the wrong test, substituting its own assessment of the imminence of risk for that of the police officers on the ground. The correct test, as stated in *Redmond-Bate v DPP*,[337] was whether the officer(s) had reasonably believed that there was a risk of an imminent breach of the peace.[338] The role of the court is thus to:

> decide not whether the view taken ... fell within the broad band of rational decisions but whether in the light of what he knew and perceived at the time the court is satisfied that it was reasonable to fear an imminent breach of the peace.[339]

The primacy that is thereby accorded to the subjective viewpoint of the officer(s), albeit limited by an objective standard, increases the difficulty of successfully challenging such decisions. This is illustrated by *Wright v Commissioner of Police for the Metropolis*,[340] where the decision of Jay J fell narrowly in favour of the defendant,[341] and also in *Hicks*,[342] where the Divisional Court adopted a more restrictive approach than that observed in previous case law.   **4-64**

Hicks concerned various police practices and policies adopted on the day of the Royal Wedding in April 2011 and included challenges to a number of arrests that were carried out for breach of the peace.[343] One of the grounds relied upon by the claimants in this regard was that the arresting officers did not apprehend an imminent breach of the peace, and/or did not have reasonable grounds for any such apprehension. This formed part of the claimants' overarching argument that the arrests had been carried out pursuant to an unlawful policy or practice of pre-emptive arrest.[344]

However, the court, in applying an unusually low threshold for 'imminence', rejected all of the claims. A close examination of the facts of the individual cases is beyond the scope of this book, but it is of note that varying combinations of the following factors were held to provide the requisite grounds to legitimise the arrests:

i.   proximity to the location of a protest (it is of note that a distance of over a mile was sufficient for these purposes);[345]
ii.   known affiliation with protest or anarchist groups;

---

[336] *McClure and Moos* (n 8).
[337] *Redmond-Bate* (n 322).
[338] ibid [68]–[76].
[339] *Redmond-Bate* (n 322) [5] (Sedley LJ).
[340] *Wright v Commissioner of Police for the Metropolis* [2013] EWHC 2739.
[341] ibid [55].
[342] *Hicks* (n 183) is referred to in a number of contexts in this chapter—see n 183 above for a full list.
[343] As above.
[344] *Hicks* (n 183) [4].
[345] Indeed, somewhat surprisingly when considering *Laporte*, the Court held that a belief that a breach of the peace could result in approximately 20 minutes was sufficiently 'imminent' for purposes of effecting a lawful arrest.

iii.   intelligence that the protest would be countered by opposing groups;

iv.   partial covering of an individual's face (even where the reasons for the concealment were explained and the covering removed);

v.   possession of literature relating to the subject matter of the protest; and

vi.   possession of equipment relevant to protesting, such as placards and a loudspeaker.

In addition, the fact that officers had recorded that the arrests had been made on the authority of senior officers did not mean that the officers themselves lacked the requisite subjective belief for those arrests,[346] it being held that officers are entitled to rely on information provided to them by other officers.[347] It is submitted that this conclusion is questionable in the circumstances, as one might expect that a risk of an imminent breach of the peace would have been apparent to officers present at the scene.

(3) Permitted Police Action

4-65   Police officers are not simply empowered to take action where there is a breach of the peace—they are under a legal duty to do so.[348] Officers are permitted to exercise reasonable force in carrying out this duty.[349]

The fact that alternative statutory powers, such as section 14 of the Public Order Act 1986 cannot be invoked, does not mean that common law powers cannot be lawfully exercised.[350] The powers available to police when faced with circumstances giving rise, or likely to give rise to a breach of the peace include:

i.   arrest;[351]

ii.   diverting individuals to an alternative location;[352] and

iii.   preventing individuals from proceeding to an intended location.[353]

Where a breach of the peace is occurring, the police must not take more intrusive action than is necessary:[354] '[i]t is only when the police reasonably believe that there is no other means whatsoever to prevent an imminent breach of the peace that they can as a matter of necessity curtail the lawful exercise of their rights by third parties'.[355] In addition, the police are required to take all possible steps to ensure that proper and advance preparations have been made to address any foreseen breach of the peace: failure to do so will mean that any resulting interference with the rights of third parties will be unlawful.[356]

---

[346] *Hicks* (n 183) [165]. The restrictions imposed upon the evidence available in relation to this issue demonstrates the limitations of judicial review where there are issues of factual dispute, as the court made repeated reference to the fact that the notebooks were incomplete, but this evidence could not, of course, be tested further through oral examination.

[347] *Hicks* (n 183) [134].

[348] *Laporte* (n 324) [29], see also *Albert v Lavin* [1982] AC 546, 565 (Lord Diplock).

[349] *King v Hodges* [1974] Crim LR 424 and *Piddington v Bates* [1961] 1 WLR 162.

[350] *Wright* (n 340) [68].

[351] See *Foulkes v Chief Constable of Merseyside* [1998] 3 All ER 705.

[352] See *Duncan v Jones* [1936] 1 KB 218.

[353] As in *Moss v McLachlan* [1985] IRLR 76.

[354] *Austin* (n 330).

[355] *Moos and McClure* (n 335) [56] (Sir Anthony May P), approved by the Court of Appeal in *McClure and Moos* (n 8) [95].

[356] *Austin* (n 330), although in *Castle v Commissioner of the Police of the Metropolis* [2011] EWHC 2317 (Admin) [58], it was held that this did not mean that 'if the only action reasonably available is containment,

Again, however, in *Hicks* a more restrictive approach was adopted. Whilst various submissions were made on behalf of the claimants as to alternatives to arrest that could have been pursued, these were dismissed as being 'wholly unrealistic', as 'without constant police supervision it would have been all too easy for the claimants to carry on with their intended actions'.[357] Similarly, in *Wright* it was held that officers are entitled to take police resources into account when determining the likelihood of a breach of the peace.[358]

(4) Arrest and Detention for Breach of the Peace (Article 5 of ECHR)

Steel v United Kingdom[359] confirms that there will be a breach of Article 5(1) of the **4-66** ECHR where an individual has been wrongfully arrested for breach of the peace. In addition, an individual arrested to prevent a breach of the peace may only be detained for such time as that risk remains imminent.[360]

In *Hicks* it was argued that the claimants' detention could not be justified under Article 5(1)(c) as there was no intention to bring them before a court, but merely that they be detained for the duration of the wedding.[361] However, the court, relying on *Nicol and Selvanayagam v United Kingdom*,[362] concluded that the justification for detention on the basis that it is 'reasonably considered necessary to prevent his committing an offence' is not qualified by the words 'for the purpose of bringing them before the competent legal authority'.[363] As such, the detention was justified, and lawful.

This finding was challenged in *R (Hicks) v Commissioner of Police of the Metropolis*.[364] The appellants contended, partly in reliance on *Ostendorf v Germany*,[365] that Art 5(1)(c), (i) does not permit preventative detention of an individual perceived by the authorities to be dangerous or having propensity to commit unlawful acts; and (ii) requires that the purpose of the detention be that a detainee is brought before a competent legal authority. The court dismissed the appeal. Although recognising that Article 5(1)(c) is limited to detention for the prevention of a concrete and specific offence, in the current case the detention was 'reasonably considered to prevent' the claimants from committing a breach of the peace, and thus fell within its remit. Further although (contrary to the finding of the Divisional Court) the detention did have to be for the purpose of bringing the appellant before the competent legal authority, that had been the case in this instance.[366] Somewhat surprisingly, the court held that this requirement was satisfied

---

containment is, by reason of an earlier failure to anticipate events, to be treated as an excessive and therefore unlawful use of power in respect of *all* those contained'.

[357] *Hicks* (n 183) [172]. The court accorded little weight to the fact that the primacy of oral dialogue in the agreed tactical strategy appeared to have been largely disregarded.
[358] *Wright* (n 340) [60].
[359] *Steel v United Kingdom* [1999] 28 EHRR 603.
[360] *Williamson v Chief Constable of the West Midlands Police* [2003] EWCA Civ 337.
[361] In reliance on *Lawless v Ireland (No 3)* (1961) 1 EHRR 15 [13]–[15]. *Hicks* is referred to in a number of contexts in this chapter—see n 183 above for a full list.
[362] *Nicol and Selvanayagam v United Kingdom* App no 32213/96 (admissibility decision, 11 January 2001).
[363] *Hicks* (n 183) [184].
[364] *R (Hicks) v Commissioner of Police of the Metropolis* [2014] EWCA Civ 3.
[365] *Ostendorf v Germany* [2013] Crim LR 601.
[366] *Hicks* [2014] (n 364), [82]–[88].

by a court reviewing the lawfulness of the detention alone, and did not require a trial on the merits, as asserted in *Ostendorf*.[367] This seems to mark a significant departure from established Strasbourg case law, in which Article 5(1) has been held to permit the deprivation of liberty only in connection with criminal proceedings.[368] At the time of writing, leave to appeal to the Supreme Court had been granted.

(5) 'Kettling': Breach of Article 5 of ECHR

4-67   The police will often adopt measures short of arrest in the context of a protest or demonstration in order to exercise 'control', as explained above. One of the most prominent measures used is that of containment or 'kettling'.

This tactic was first considered in *(1) Lois Austin (2) Geoffrey Saxby v The Commissioner of Police of the Metropolis*,[369] a case arising from the use of kettling in the course of a May Day demonstration in 2001. In a private law action for false imprisonment and breach of Article 5 of the ECHR it was contended on behalf of the claimants that they had been unlawfully deprived of their liberty. It was agreed between the parties that whilst the claimants had not themselves been threatening breach of the peace, others in the group of approximately 3,000 had been.[370]

Although it was held at first instance that the detention fell within the remit of Article 5(1)(c),[371] the Court of Appeal concluded that the containment, whilst restricting the claimant's movement, did not amount to an 'arbitrary deprivation of liberty', as required to constitute a breach of Article 5.[372] Instead, where the police had shown that it had been necessary to adopt the policy of containment as a whole, each appellant was required to demonstrate that the individual police officer had acted unreasonably in a *Wednesbury* sense in refusing to release him or her.[373]

The case came before the House of Lords in *Austin v Commissioner of Police of the Metropolis*,[374] where it was similarly concluded[375] that no violation of Article 5 had occurred, although the court emphasised that the determination of this issue was 'a matter of degree and intensity'[376] and highly fact-sensitive. Their Lordships directed that a pragmatic approach should here be adopted, even in relation to absolute rights,

---

[367] ibid, [35]–[38].

[368] *Ciulla v Italy* (1991) 13 EHRR 346 [38], *Al-Jedda v United Kingdom* (2011) 53 EHRR 23, *Schwabe v Germany* 32 BHRC 141. However, the Court of Appeal drew upon *Lawless v Ireland (No 3)* (1961) 1 EHRR 15, *Brogan v United Kingdom* (1989) 11 EHRR 117 and *Steel v United Kingdom* (1998) 28 EHRR 603 in support of its finding. From this, the court held that it was not obliged to follow *Ostendorf*, as it was not indicative of 'clear and constant' Strasbourg jurisprudence, *Hicks* [2014] (n 364), [69]–[81].

[369] *(1) Lois Austin (2) Geoffrey Saxby v The Commissioner of Police of the Metropolis* [2005] EWHC 480 (QB).

[370] It is also of note that the second claimant had not in fact attended the demonstration and had been in the locality for other purposes.

[371] Art 5(1)(c) of ECHR permits 'the lawful arrest or detention of a person effected for the purpose of bringing him before the competent legal authority of reasonable suspicion of having committed and offence or when it is reasonably considered necessary to prevent his committing an offence or fleeing after having done so'.

[372] *Austin* (n 330) [105].

[373] ibid [70]; see also *Al Fayed v Commissioner of Police for the Metropolis* [2004] EWCA Civ 1579.

[374] *Austin v Commissioner of Police of the Metropolis* [2009] UKHL 5.

[375] In reliance on *Saadi v United Kingdom* (2008) 47 EHRR 17.

[376] *Austin* (n 374) [21].

as 'a fair balance is necessary if these competing fundamental rights [of political protest and public order] are to be reconciled with one another'.[377]

In such cases, it was seen to be 'unrealistic' to argue that Article 5(1) was engaged, subject to the actions of the police being, as was found on the facts of the current case:

i.   proportionate and reasonable (for example, being maintained for no longer than was necessary and with measures being in place, or intended to be in place, for those accidentally caught in the protest or requiring medical attention to be released);

ii. restricted to a reasonable minimum as to discomfort and time as is necessary for the relevant purpose; and

iii. carried out in good faith.[378]

This conclusion was subsequently endorsed by the ECtHR,[379] where it was held in a   **4-68** majority judgment that an absolute cordon was 'the least intrusive and most effective means to be applied' in the circumstances.[380]

However, the court emphasised that the present case involved 'specific and exceptional facts', seemingly intending to restrict its influence.[381] It was also subject to a strong dissenting opinion which highlighted how the majority decision appeared to conflict with *Gillan v United Kingdom*. Although that case (see above at 4-17) focused primarily upon Article 8 of the ECHR and as such did not require a final determination in relation to Article 5, the court's observation remains significant:

> although the length of time during which each applicant was stopped and searched did not in either case exceed 30 minutes, during this period the applicants were entirely deprived of any freedom of movement. They were obliged to remain where they were and submit to the search and if they had refused they would have been liable to arrest, detention at a police station and criminal charges. This element of coercion is indicative of a deprivation of liberty within the meaning of Article 5(1).[382]

That reasoning seems directly applicable to the circumstances of *Austin*, particularly in view of the fact that *Gillan v United Kingdom* itself concerned the exercise of police powers at an arms fair protest. However, the majority in *Austin v United Kingdom* did not address this conflict.

(6) Protest and Breaches of Articles 10 and 11 of ECHR

Police actions in the sphere of protest and demonstrations will inevitably engage   **4-69** Articles 10 and 11 of ECHR, which are, respectively, the right to freedom of expression and the right to freedom of peaceful assembly. The state has a positive duty to facilitate

---

[377] ibid [34] (Lord Hope), see also Lord Neuberger at [59].
[378] ibid [60].
[379] *Austin v United Kingdom* (2012) 55 EHRR 14.
[380] ibid [66].
[381] ibid [68].
[382] *Gillan v United Kingdom* (n 76) [57]; see also *Foka v Turkey* App no 28940/09 (24 June, 2008) [74]–[79].

and protect these rights.[383] The ECtHR has consistently emphasised that any infringement on freedom of expression requires careful scrutiny.[384]

Despite this accorded importance, the ECtHR has also held that the protection of these rights may be denied where a demonstration is either unauthorised and unlawful,[385] or where conduct is likely to disturb public order.[386] However, these rights are not forfeited simply in consequence of violent acts being committed by others in attendance at a demonstration, provided that an individual 'remains peaceful in his or her own intentions or behaviour'.[387] This approach was also adopted in *Laporte*, where Lord Bingham asserted that:

> [i]t was wholly disproportionate to restrict [the] exercise of ... rights under Articles 10 and 11 because [the appellant] was in the company of others some of whom might, at some time in the future, breach the peace.[388]

It is well established that preventative measures regarding breach of the peace may be taken against an individual provoking violence as opposed to threatening it.[389] This will inevitably be problematic where two groups of competing political affiliations are in close proximity to one another, giving rise to a question as to whose presence or expression of opinion should be subverted.[390]

This issue was explored in *Hicks*[391] as the claimants submitted that, as the police action was justified by concerns about violent reactions to the protests, the duty of the police was in fact to protect the antimonarchist protesters from that violence.[392] The court rejected that argument on the basis that the protests would have had the 'natural consequence of causing violence'.[393] The facts were seen to be distinct from a scenario in which there were simply two 'rival' demonstrations countering one another, which, it has been recognised, may well lead to an 'invidious choice' on the part of the police as to which demonstration to target.[394]

The problems caused by competing interests is illustrated by *R v Chief Constable of Sussex, ex parte International Trader's Ferry Ltd*[395] which concerned an animal rights protest against the transport of livestock for export. The House of Lords determined that the Chief Constable's decision to (i) restrict police protection to the livestock

---

[383] *Plattform Arzte fur das Leben v Austria* (1991) 13 EHRR 204. However, in *R (Gallastegui) v Westminster City Council* [2013] EWCA Civ 28 [48]–[50], it was held that a positive obligation will only arise where the state prevents any effective exercise of freedom of expression; see also *Abbleby v United Kingdom* (2003) 37 EHRR 38.

[384] *The Sunday Times v United Kingdom (No 2)* [1991] 14 EHRR 229 and *Hashman v United Kingdom* (2000) 30 EHRR 241.

[385] *Ziliberberg v Moldova* App no 61821/00 (4 May 2004).

[386] *Chorherr v Austria* [1993] 17 EHRR 358.

[387] *Ziliberberg* (n 385) [2].

[388] *Laporte* (n 324) [55]; see also *Cumming v Chief Constable of Northumbria Police* [2003] EWCA Civ 1844, which was distinguished as in that case (i) a crime was known to have been committed and (ii) six suspects had been identified.

[389] *Albert v Lavin* [1982] AC 546.

[390] As discussed by Lord Carswell in *Laporte* (n 324) [95]–[99].

[391] *Hicks* is referred to in a number of contexts in this chapter—see n 183 above for a full list.

[392] As in *Öllinger v Austria* (2008) 46 EHRR 38.

[393] *Hicks* (n 183) [135]–[137], applying *Laporte* (n 324) [95]–[99] and [161], and *Steel* (n 368) [55].

[394] *Laporte* (n 324) [98]–[99].

[395] *R v Chief Constable of Sussex, ex parte International Trader's Ferry Ltd* [1999] 2 AC 418, [1998] 3 WLR 1260.

Rachel Taylor and Piers von Berg

vehicles to two days a week; and (ii) turn back vehicles on days when it was believed that a breach of the peace might occur, was lawful. There was no rule that the police could never restrain lawful activity in order to prevent a breach of the peace, and the restrictions applied were seen to be proportionate in view of the resources available to the police.[396]

(7) Unlawful Policy

In *Hicks*[397] actions were brought by 20 claimants, grouped into one class of 15, two **4-70** classes of two and a single youth aged 16. The claims were heard together as they each related to the lawfulness of the policing of events surrounding the Royal Wedding on 29 April 2011.

The claims were brought by way of judicial review, largely because the central issue in contention was:

> whether the defendant operated a policy, or practice on the ground, of equating intention to protest with intention to cause unlawful disruption and adopted an impermissibly low threshold of tolerance for public protest, resulting in the unlawful arrest of persons who were viewed by his officers as being likely to express anti-monarchist views.[398]

Richards LJ concluded that irrespective of its findings that all of the arrests had been justified on their facts, even if some individual arrests had been unlawful this would not support the existence of an unlawful policy or practice. Although '[w]idespread unlawful arrests with common features might evidence a systematic problem ... the fact that a small number of arrests were found to have been unlawful on their own facts would tell one nothing about policy or practice'.[399] The involvement of senior officers also failed to assist the claimants' case in this regard[400] and a submission that the police briefing notes and low-level material exposed a misunderstanding of the proper distinction between lawful protest and unlawful disruption was rejected on the basis of the available evidence.[401]

Finally and significantly, Richards LJ rejected the claimants' arguments, pursued in reliance on *R (Lumba) v Secretary of State for the Home Department*[402] that the existence of an unlawful policy would in itself render the arrests unlawful even if there had otherwise been a lawful basis for them. For such a claim to succeed it 'would have to be shown that the policy had been applied or at least taken into account in reaching the decision to arrest, so as to be material to that decision'.[403]

---

396 ibid 430–36.
397 *Hicks* is referred to in a number of contexts in this chapter—see n 183 above for a full list.
398 *Hicks* (n 183) [1].
399 ibid [149].
400 ibid [150].
401 ibid [146].
402 *R (Lumba) v Secretary of State for the Home Department* [2011] UKSC 12, [2012] 1 AC 245.
403 ibid [157].

(8) Additional Duties Regarding Children and Young Persons

4-71   Additional obligations may impact on the lawfulness of police actions in particular circumstances, most notably when those actions affect children.

In *R (Alan Castle, Rosie Castle, Sam Eton) v Commissioner of Police for the Metropolis*[404] a challenge was brought in relation to the detention of two 16-year-old boys and a 14-year-old girl who had been contained in a police cordon when attending a protest.[405] One of the bases of the challenge was that the decision to contain, and so detain, the claimants constituted a breach of the defendant's duty under section 11 of the Children Act 2004 (for further discussion see below at 11-4), which obliges a chief constable, amongst others:

i.   to make arrangements for ensuring that their functions are discharged having regard to the need to safeguard and promote the welfare of children; and

ii.   in discharging their duties under this section, to have regard to any guidance given to them for the purpose by the Secretary of State.

The Divisional Court rejected this argument and held that the statutory duty had not redefined the duties and functions of the police, but simply meant that the existing functions, such as planning, were required to be carried out in a manner which took into account the need to safeguard and promote the welfare of children.[406] If the defendant had been unable to demonstrate that there were no reasonable steps that could have been taken to avoid the use of containment and reduce its impact on children, the duty would have been breached.[407] However, in the present case, as there was a plan for release of the vulnerable, including school children, the action taken was deemed to be necessary, proportionate and lawful.

Notably, the court was reluctant to apply *Lumba* in this context, reflecting the position adopted in *Hicks*.[408] It was 'unlikely' that a decision made in breach of the statutory duty would in itself render that decision unlawful as 'it is the primary duty of a police officer to detect and prevent crime'.[409]

(9) Method of Protest

4-72   As is perhaps obvious, police intervention in protests will or should ordinarily be prompted by the way in which the protest is being carried out as opposed to the substance of the protest. The method selected will, however, sometimes give rise to particular issues.

---

[404] *R (Alan Castle, Rosie Castle, Sam Eton) v Commissioner of Police for the Metropolis* [2011] EWHC 2317 (Admin).

[405] The claimants accepted that the imposition of the cordon in itself was lawful.

[406] *Castle* (n 404) [51].

[407] ibid [60].

[408] As discussed above at n 183.

[409] *Castle* (n 404) [53].

Sections 143–145 of the Police Reform and Social Responsibility Act 2011 empower the police (and others) to issue directions to prevent protestors from undertaking certain 'prohibited activities', such as the erection of tents, in Parliament Square. Non-compliance with such a direction absent reasonable excuse amounts to a criminal offence.

These powers were introduced in order to address perceived problems arising from 'Democracy Village' (a protest which commenced on 1 May 2010 and evolved to become an encampment occupying approximately 70 per cent of Parliament Square). The occupants of Democracy Village had been evicted, but simply moved their tents to the surrounding pavement, and security had been introduced to prevent any trespass. This process of eviction was seen to be cumbersome and expensive, and so motivated the introduction of these statutory powers.

In *R (Gallastegui) v Westminster City Council*[410] the Court of Appeal considered a claim challenging these powers as being incompatible with Articles 6, 10 and 11 of ECHR. The claimant was not part of the Democracy Village and had commenced her campaign, 'Peacestrike', in 2006. She had desisted from her constant presence in Parliament Square on 3 May 2012 after being issued with a direction to move. However, the court dismissed the appeal, and so the claim, on the basis that:

i.   The statute conferred a discretionary power and not a duty to issue directions, although this discretion would usually be exercised in order to ensure that the intention of Parliament was fulfilled.[411]

ii.   The right to protest remained substantially unimpaired.[412]

iii. Although in some circumstances the mode of protest would be of intrinsic importance,[413] the extent of interference with Articles 10 and 11 in the present case would be limited.[414]

iv.   The law was sufficiently certain, with the boundaries of legality clearly discernible through the issuing of directions.[415]

v.   The measures had been carefully considered by Parliament, and even if they did amount to a blanket ban,[416] were proportionate to the legitimate aim pursued and appropriately balanced the competing interests.[417]

vi.   A removal direction did not constitute a determination of civil rights, and sufficient access to the courts remained as an individual could either seek a restraining order against the issue of a direction, or refuse to comply and raise a defence of 'reasonable excuse' under section 143(8) of the 2011 Act.[418]

---

[410] *R (Gallastegui) v Westminster City Council* [2013] EWCA Civ 28.

[411] ibid [18]–[23].

[412] ibid [24] and [27].

[413] *Tabernacle v Secretary of State for Defence* [2009] EWCA Civ 23.

[414] *Gallastegui* (n 410) [24]–[27]. On the facts of the case it was of note that another protestor had maintained her continual protest without a tent or other equipment; ibid [60].

[415] ibid [28]–[30].

[416] Which was rejected on the facts

[417] *Gallastegui* (n 410) [40]–[47].

[418] ibid [54]–[59].

G. Custody

(1) General Principles

4-73   This is an area more commonly associated with private actions for damages for false imprisonment where the police have failed to abide by their duties under PACE 1984. Claimants need to consider whether they are merely seeking damages as a result of an alleged act or omission or whether they seek to challenge a policy or procedure, or otherwise control the action of an officer or force (see above 4-3 and 4-5).[419] The detention of children and young persons by the police (eg association with adult detainees and attendance of an appropriate adult), the use of local authority accommodation, secure accommodation and secure remand are all dealt with below in Chapter 11.

(i) An Overview of PACE 1984

4-74   In summary, sections 34–52 of Part IV of PACE 1984 set out police powers for detaining suspects. Sections 53–65A of PACE 1984 (Part V) concern the questioning and treatment of suspects. Where relevant, specific sections are set out or described below. In addition to the main body of the Act there are a number of Codes of Practice. Code C concerns detention, treatment and questioning, Codes E and F relate to visual and audio interviewing of suspects and Code H relates to detention, treatment and questioning of terrorism suspects.[420] This is a large and complex area of law and this section will focus solely on those areas and statutory provisions that have been subject to judicial review challenges.

The police must comply with Part IV of PACE 1984 when detaining a person arrested for an offence or a person answering bail.[421] The central provisions are sections 34(1) and (2), which state that a person shall not be kept in police detention as defined by PACE 1984 except under Part IV. A custody officer is under a duty to release immediately a person from police detention if they become aware that grounds for their detention have ceased to apply, no other grounds could be justified under Part IV and the person was not unlawfully at large when arrested. Whether a person is in police detention for the purposes of PACE 1984 is defined by section 118:

> (2)   Subject to subsection (2A) a person is in police detention for the purposes of this Act if—
>   (a)   he has been taken to a police station after being arrested for an offence or after being arrested under section 41 of the Terrorism Act 2000, or
>   (b)   he is arrested at a police station after attending voluntarily at the station or accompanying a constable to it,

---

[419] See in particular the case of *Sher* above at 4-5 and 4-57.

[420] The other Codes are as follows: Code A concerns powers to search a person or a vehicle without first making an arrest and the recording of a stop or encounter; Code B deals with powers to search premises and to seize and retain any property found; Code D concerns methods of identification and keeping of accurate and reliable criminal records; Code G relates to powers of arrest under PACE 1984, s 24; and, Code H contains requirements for detention, treatment and questioning of those suspected of terrorism. Revised versions of Codes A, B, C, E, F and H came into force after midnight on 26 October 2013.

[421] PACE 1984, ss 34(1) and (7). See also *Mercer v Chief Constable of Lancashire* [1991] 1 WLR 367, 373G.

Rachel Taylor and Piers von Berg

and is detained there or is detained elsewhere in the charge of a constable, except that a person who is at a court after being charged is not in police detention for those purposes.

(2A) Where a person is in another's lawful custody by virtue of paragraph 22, 34(1) or 35(3) of Schedule 4 to the Police Reform Act 2002, he shall be treated as in police detention.

There are no justifications outside of this regime for police detention: 'In short, the PACE regime prohibits any extra-statutory justification for police detention after arrest'.[422] This is a strict burden on the police:

> where statutory provisions which provide rights to police constables to interfere with the liberty of the subject are concerned those provisions ought to be construed strictly against those purporting to exercise those rights.[423]

An additional source of guidance for the police can be the Association of Chief Police Officers' publications.[424]

(ii) Areas of Challenge

Judicial review can be used to seek remedies for the following: **4-75**

i.   Decisions to detain a person or extend time for detention under Part IV of PACE 1984. A decision may be challenged on the basis that the police or a magistrates' court[425] has acted outside their powers as interpreted in the Act. Appropriate remedies may be a mandatory order to compel a person's release or a declaration of unlawful detention and a claim for damages.

ii. Ill-treatment in custody, for example, assault or degrading treatment. These incidents have been challenged using Article 3 of ECHR. Claimants have sought declarations of unlawful conduct and damages.

iii. Decisions to prevent or restrict access to legal advice. These have been challenged at common law. The courts have upheld the right of the police to refuse access to certain individuals who are not qualified or who may restrict an investigation.

In some cases, claimants can apply for habeas corpus instead of judicial review. The two remedies are discussed and compared above at 3-31. Habeas corpus is an exceptional remedy for abuse of power, and in most cases judicial review has been used and is preferred by the courts (see above discussion at 3-31). Note that the treatment

---

[422] PACE 1984, s 34(1) and (2). See *R (G) v Chief Constable of West Yorkshire* [2008] EWCA Civ 28, [2008] 1 WLR 550 [11] (Sir Igor Judge P).

[423] See *Hill v Chief Constable of South Yorks* [1990] 1 WLR 946, [1990] 1 All ER 1046, 952G–H.

[424] In particular see NPIA and ACPO, *Guidance on the Safer Detention, and Handling of Persons in Police Custody*, 2nd edn (2012), which contains extensive material on topics such as risk assessments, restraint techniques, detainee care, etc. Available from www.acpo.police.uk/documents/criminaljustice/2012/201203CJBA GoSDHoPPCv2.pdf.

[425] A magistrates' court may issue a warrant of further detention or extend such a warrant under PACE 1984, ss 43–44. See below at 4-78 discussion of *R (Chief Constable of Greater Manchester) v Salford Magistrates Court* [2011] EWHC 1578 (Admin), [2011] 3 All ER 521.

of juveniles (those who appear to be aged under 17)[426] and 17-year-olds is dealt with below at 11-16.

(2) Decisions to Detain a Person or Extend Time for Detention under Part IV of PACE 1984

(i) Police Custody Time Limits

4-76 The applicable time limits for which an individual can be detained in police custody are set out in sections 41–44 of PACE 1984 and covered in paragraph 15 of Code C. The key provision is section 41(1), which states that 'a person shall not be kept in police detention for more than 24 hours without being charged'. The 'relevant time' from when this period starts to run is set out in section 41. This period may be extended to up to 36 hours after the 'relevant time' by authorisation from an officer of rank of superintendent or above, who is responsible for the police station at which the person is detained, if certain grounds are made out as specified in section 42. The period may only be extended beyond 36 hours after the 'relevant time' if the person is charged or a warrant for further detention is issued by a magistrates' court under section 43 (see section 42(10)). A warrant of further detention may be extended by a magistrates' court for another 36 hours, but this is subject to an absolute maximum of 96 hours after the 'relevant time', in accordance with section 44. Where these time limits and the conditions attached thereto are not complied with, public law proceedings may be appropriate, for example, by way of judicial review of an officer's or a court's decision.

R v Holmes, ex parte Sherman[427] was an application for habeas corpus by two individuals detained in a police station for 48 hours without having been charged, or brought before a magistrate, contrary to the old section 38(4) of the Magistrates' Courts Act 1952: 'Where a person is taken into custody for an offence without a warrant and is retained in custody, he shall be brought before a Magistrates' court as soon as practicable.'[428] An application was made for a writ of habeas corpus, and an order issued at the subsequent hearing required the applicants to be produced in court that day.[429]

In seeking to justify the detention in *Ex p Sherman*, the police relied on: (i) the complexity of the investigation; (ii) a number of outstanding burglaries (approximately 100) in relation to which it was intended to question the applicants; and (iii) admissions that had been made by the applicants. The custody sergeant contended that had he charged the applicants, he would have had to comply with his obligations to consider bail, which,

---

[426] Juveniles are defined by PACE 1984, s 37(15) as those who appear to be aged under 17. For a complete description of the various definitions for those aged under 18, see below at 11-13.

[427] *R v Holmes, ex parte Sherman* [1981] 2 All ER 612; also known as *Re Sherman and Apps* [1981] 72 Cr App R 266.

[428] This has since been repealed and replaced by PACE 1984, s 46(2)–(8), which similarly provides for a detained person charged with an offence to be brought before a court 'as soon as is practicable and in any event not later than the first sitting after he is charged with the offence' (s 46(3)).

[429] Although in the event this was not necessary as the custody sergeant undertook to charge the claimants and release them on bail.

Rachel Taylor and Piers von Berg

in the circumstances, was likely to be granted. This would, he submitted, have hindered the police investigations into the outstanding offences.

However, the court determined that the statutory safeguard of 48 hours was unequivocal and imperative in its terms, and had clearly been breached. Therefore, despite the difficulties encountered by the police, the application had been brought appropriately, resulting as it did in expediting the applicants' release. Although the court noted that the words 'as soon as is practicable' meant 48 hours at most, it otherwise denoted some degree of flexibility:

> Practicability is obviously a slightly elastic concept which must take account of the availability of police manpower, transport and Magistrates' courts.[430]

This should be borne in mind by applicants for habeas corpus or judicial review of decisions to detain.

(ii) Pre-charge Detention and the Terrorism Act 2000

There is a separate regime that applies to suspects detained under Schedule 7 (see   **4-77** discussion above at 4-20) or arrested under section 41 of the Terrorism Act 2000. This regime can be found in Schedule 8 of the Terrorism Act 2000. There are several distinct features that affect detention that can be summarised here. A person arrested under section 41 may be detained for 48 hours without charge (section 41(3)). Under both Schedule 7 and section 41, pre-charge detention may be extended by up to 14 days by a judicial authority (a designated district judge).[431] A detainee and his representative may be excluded from a hearing of an application for a warrant to extend the period of detention.[432] This was challenged unsuccessfully in *Sher* (discussed above at 4-5 and 4-57). The Divisional Court applied the House of Lords decision in *Ward v Police Service of Northern Ireland*,[433] in finding that this procedure was compatible with Article 5.[434] *Ward* held that paragraph 33 of Schedule 8 was conceived in the best interests of the detained person and not the police. A judge may exclude them from the hearing where he is satisfied that there are reasonable grounds for believing that further detention is necessary to gather evidence by questioning the suspect, and the judge wishes to satisfy himself that further questioning will cover fresh issues. The detainee and his representative do not have to be informed of the nature of that questioning. In their absence, a judge has to carefully scrutinise the grounds for the application.

---

[430] *Re Sherman* (n 427) 271 (Donaldson LJ) applied in *Huczko v Governor HMP Wandsworth* [2012] EWHC 4134 (Admin) to similar wording in the Extradition Act 2003 s 4(3).

[431] Terrorism Act 2000, Sch 8, para 36(3).

[432] ibid, para 33.

[433] *Ward v Police Service of Northern Ireland* [2007] UKHL 50, [2007] 1 WLR 3013.

[434] See also *Re Duffy Judicial Review (No 2)* [2011] 2 All ER 364 where the Northern Irish High Court rejected a challenge to various parts of Sch 8 as incompatible with Art 5: paras 33(3) and 34 on the requirements of disclosure, there was no requirement under Article 5 that a detainee be charged before the expiry of 28 days in detention, and Art 5(4) did not require a right of appeal or review.

(iii) Police Custody Time Limits and Police Bail

4-78   Section 44 of PACE 1984 was interpreted in *R (Chief Constable of Greater Manchester) v Salford Magistrates' Court* (also known as *Hookway*).[435] The court determined that strictly speaking, the time spent on police bail was included in the calculation of the permissible period a person could spend in police detention before they were charged. Before *Hookway* it was thought that this time period only ran when a person returned to answer bail, and not in the intervening weeks and months when they were on bail and the police investigation was ongoing. When a person answered bail they could only be detained for such hours as remained—including taking into account any extensions that may be granted—for further questioning. Once that time had elapsed, the police had no power to a detain a person any longer and they had to be released without bail. So unless a person voluntarily remained at a police station, the police would be unable to gather further evidence by questioning them. The only way the detention clock could be reset was if fresh evidence came to light and on this basis a person could be re-arrested on a warrant.[436]

The decision in *Hookway* found that the detention clock continued to run whilst a person was on police bail. Therefore, the police could only detain and keep a person on bail for 96 hours before taking a charging decision. This precluded the practice of police investigations taking several months whilst a person was kept on police bail and returned to the police station at regular intervals when they may or may not be subject to further questioning. In effect, after the period had elapsed, the police would have to release suspects without bail if no fresh evidence had come to light. Consequently, the section was quickly re-drafted by Parliament in the Police (Detention and Bail) Act 2011 to exclude the time spent on bail from any calculation of the period of time for which a person on police bail can be detained. The amended section 47(6) of PACE 1984 reads:

> (6) Where a person who has been granted bail under this Part and either has attended at the police station in accordance with the grant of bail or has been arrested under section 46A above is detained at a police station, any time during which he was in police detention prior to being granted bail shall be included as part of any period which falls to be calculated under this Part of this Act and any time during which he was on bail shall not be so included.

(iv) Charging Decisions and Police Custody

4-79   Sections 37(1) and (2) of PACE 1984 allow a custody officer to detain a person for such period as is necessary for the officer to determine whether there is sufficient evidence to charge, secure or preserve evidence connected to the offence for which he was arrested, or to obtain such evidence through a police interview. The officer should make that determination 'as soon as practicable' after an arrested person arrives at a police station or after at an arrest at a police station.[437] Once an officer makes such a determination

---

[435] (n 425).

[436] A person cannot be re-arrested without a warrant for the offence for which he was previously arrested unless fresh evidence has come to light—PACE 1984, ss 41(9), 42(11) and 43(19).

[437] PACE 1984, s 37(10).

in respect of the offence for which he was arrested, he has one of several duties under section 37(7) to the person arrested, who:

  (a) shall be–
      (i)   released without charge and on bail, or
      (ii) kept in police detention,

for the purpose of enabling the Director of Public Prosecutions to make a decision under section 37B below,

  (b) shall be released without charge and on bail but not for that purpose,
  (c) shall be released without charge and without bail, or
  (d) shall be charged.

Before section 37(7)(a)(ii) was inserted,[438] once sufficient evidence was obtained to charge a person there was no power to postpone a charging decision in order to seek advice from the CPS without admitting a suspect to bail. Section 37B(1) and (2) requires a custody officer to send such information as is specified in any guidance to the DPP as soon as practicable to enable the DPP to decide if there was sufficient evidence to charge. A custody officer is required by section 37A(3) to have regard to any guidance issued by the DPP.

This led to difficulties in *R (G) v Chief Constable of West Yorkshire*.[439] In that case, a detainee challenged a decision to delay a charging decision in order to consult the CPS on that decision whilst detaining the suspect for a further three hours. The custody officer felt compelled by section 37A(3) of PACE 1984 to abide by guidance from the DPP that a charging decision must be made by the CPS because the suspect was a persistent young offender. The Court of Appeal, led by Sir Igor Judge P, reversed a decision of the Divisional Court that section 37B does not permit such a course of action. (At the time of the Divisional Court's decision, section 37(7)(a)(ii) had not been inserted.) Furthermore, section 37A does not grant the DPP authority to issue guidance that has the effect of allowing an extension of the time a suspect is kept in detention whilst advice is sought. Once a custody officer has sufficient evidence to charge his alternatives are strictly limited to the options set out in section 37(7)(a)–(d). This case serves as an example of a judicial review of the exercise of police powers under Part IV of PACE 1984 and the fundamental principle that 'each and every detention must be justified by clear, unequivocal, legal authority'.[440]

(3) Ill-Treatment in Custody

Ill-treatment in custody will usually found only a private law claim for compensation   **4-80**
for loss arising from any injury and unlawful detention. Judicial review will be more suitable if the claimant seeks to affect a decision regarding their detention (which can be combined with a claim for damages) and, in rare cases, habeas corpus may be

---

[438] By the Police and Justice Act 2006, s 11. This was not in force when the claimant in *G* (n 422) was detained. It is submitted that it would have been decided differently if it had been. See ibid [29]: 'These alternatives [in s 37(a)–(d)] did not include the power which now exists to keep the suspect in detention for the purpose of consultation with the Director of Public Prosecutions or his representative.'
[439] ibid.
[440] ibid [29] (Sir Igor Judge P).

appropriate if a person seeks their immediate release. Under the first route, damages can be sought under common law torts such as assault, battery and negligence and/or under rights protected by HRA 1998, for example, Article 3, the right not to be subjected to torture or inhuman and degrading treatment or punishment. There is a high threshold for breaches of Article 3 as explained in the next paragraph. Judicial review can be used to challenge decisions regarding complaints or to challenge the detention itself as being unlawful due to the ill-treatment, although habeas corpus can also be used as a remedy for the latter (see the discussion on the two remedies above at 3-31).

4-81   Judicial review was used to challenge the refusal to uphold a complaint about detention in *R (Driver) v Independent Police Complaints Commission*.[441] There are two important lessons from that case:

    i.   The high standard required for a breach of Article 3:

> … ill-treatment must attain a minimum level of severity if it is to fall within the scope of Article 3. The assessment of this minimum is, in the nature of things, relative; it depends on all the circumstances of the case, such as the duration of the treatment, its physical or mental effects and, in some cases, the sex, age and state of health of the victim, etc.[442]

        In *Driver* there was no breach where a detainee with a history of mental health problems was left for 35 minutes with no clothing and no blanket where they had been removed to prevent self-harm.[443]

    ii.   There exists an obligation on the part of the state to investigate breaches of ECHR rights (discussed above at 4-13).

In *Re Gillen's Application*[444] an application for a writ of habeas corpus was issued in circumstances in which there was evidence that an individual arrested on suspicion of terrorist offences and detained for questioning was suffering physical maltreatment in custody.

The Divisional Court held that the applicant's detention had become unlawful at the point at which officers had attempted to extract a confession by assaulting him. A writ of habeas corpus was then issued on the basis that neither (i) the right to recover damages for assault, nor (ii) an injunction restraining the police from further assault would provide the applicant with an adequate remedy or protection.

(4) Access to Legal Advice

4-82   Section 58(1) of PACE 1984 enshrines the right of any person arrested and detained at a police station or other premises 'to consult a solicitor privately at any time' on his request. Paragraph 3.1 of Code C of PACE 1984 states that a custody officer must make sure a detained person is told of the continuing right to consult privately with a solicitor and that free independent advice is available. This right may be exercised face to face, in writing or over the telephone (paragraph 6.1). A person may waive their right to legal

---

[441] *R (Driver) v Independent Police Complaints Commission* [2012] EWHC 1271 (Admin).

[442] *The Republic of Ireland v United Kingdom* (1979-80) 2 EHRR 25 [162], applied in *Driver*, ibid [19], as the 'well-established principle'.

[443] Hickinbottom J considered at [21] the following factors as relevant to his decision—a lack of evidence of suffering during this period, eg from the cold, the period was not arbitrary as the custody officer thought it necessary to allow the risk of self-harm to recede and the claimant did not appear to find it demeaning (although a victim's perception of their suffering may be distorted there was no evidence it was in this case).

[444] *Re Gillen's Application* [1988] NILR 40.

Rachel Taylor and Piers von Berg

advice but the officer must ask them why and record the reason in the custody record (paragraph 6.5). The right of access to legal advice was described as 'one of the most important and fundamental rights of a citizen' in *R v Samuel*.[445] Non-compliance with Code C may affect the admissibility in subsequent criminal proceedings of any statements made by the detainee. Therefore, judicial review is unlikely to be an appropriate remedy as a defendant can apply to exclude such evidence under sections 76 or 78 of PACE 1984. If any such application is unsuccessful, an appeal can be sought by way of case stated from the magistrates' courts or to the Court of Appeal from the Crown Court.[446]

In *R v Chief Constable of South Wales, ex parte Merrick*[447] a claimant challenged a policy that no legal visits at court were permitted after 10am, despite manpower being available. The Divisional Court granted the application and upheld a right at common law of a person detained at court to consult a solicitor as soon as reasonably practicable.

The police are entitled at common law to refuse access to persons in custody to those who are not genuinely qualified and could not properly advise a detainee.[448] The same applies to those whose criminal associations are likely to obstruct an investigation.[449] The Court of Appeal has rejected any notion of a blanket ban on a police station representative and stated that the police's role is confined to assessing if an investigation would be hindered by a representative on a case-by-case basis.[450] If a particular representative was adjudged likely to hold back an investigation, an officer could decide whether their attendance might hinder a particular investigation.[451] The police should not interfere because of poor-quality advice[452] or because of likely conflicts of interest.[453] Those were matters for the solicitor or their regulating body. But the police could intervene if they reasonably believed that the representative was a witness to the alleged offences, if their role was unclear and another solicitor was available.[454] This was held by Beatson J in *Malik,* stating that it was open to police to exclude the advisor in question where it did not preclude access to another solicitor.

There are certain exceptional cases where an urgent application for judicial review in circumstances where a detainee is denied his or her rights to access legal advice may be appropriate. *Cullen v Chief Constable of the Royal Ulster Constabulary*[455] concerned

---

[445] *R v Samuel* [1988] Cr App R 232, 245.
[446] For example, see *Beeres v Crown Prosecution Service West Midlands* [2014] EWHC 283 (Admin), *Charles v DPP* [2009] EWHC 3521 (Admin) and *R v McGovern* (1991) 92 Cr App R 228. See also below in the context of juveniles at 11-15.
[447] *R v Chief Constable of South Wales, ex parte Merrick* [1994] 1 WLR 663, [1994] 2 All ER 560.
[448] *R v Chief Constable of Avon and Somerset, ex parte Robinson* [1989] 1 WLR 793, [1989] 2 All ER 15. Note however different provisions concerning the appropriate adults for those aged under 18 and those with mental health disorders (see below at 11-15 and at 12-23).
[449] ibid.
[450] *R (Thompson) v Chief Constable of Northumbria* [2001] EWCA Civ 321, [2001] 1 WLR 1342 (Lord Woolf LCJ, applying *Ex p Robinson*).
[451] ibid [22]. This is in relation to a specific case. The issue in that case involved a blanket ban, which could not be justified.
[452] ibid [23].
[453] *R (Malik) v Chief Constable of Greater Manchester* [2006] EWHC 2396 (Admin), [2007] ACD 15 applying *Thompson.*
[454] ibid.
[455] *Cullen v Chief Constable of the Royal Ulster Constabulary* [2003] UKHL 39, [2003] 1 WLR 1763.

whether a breach of section 15 Northern Ireland (Emergency Provisions) Act 1987, which provided a qualified right to access to legal advice in custody, could found a claim for damages. Lord Hutton said that a:

> speedy hearing of an application for judicial review … is a much more effective remedy for a claimant to seek than the bringing of an action for nominal damages months or years after the period of detention has ended.[456]

H. Police Bail

(1) The Statutory Framework

4-83 The power to remand on bail arises from an arrest without warrant. There are two types of police bail: pre-charge and post-charge. The relevant provisions are contained in Part IV of PACE 1984 and the Bail Act 1976. What follows is a summary of some of the key provisions, the areas where judicial review may be used and a discussion of some of the obstacles to such claims.

Pre-charge bail can be granted by a constable elsewhere than a police station or when a civilian brings a person to a police station (sections 30A–30D). This is called 'street bail'. It was introduced by the Criminal Justice Act (CJA) 2003. The initial Home Office Circular 061/2003 stated the following criteria should be considered when granting street bail:

    i.   the severity or nature of the offence committed;
    ii. the need to preserve vital evidence;
    iii. the person's fitness to be released back on to the streets;
    iv. the person's ability to understand what is being said or what is happening;
    v. the likelihood that the person may continue to commit the offence or a further offence.[457]

This Circular sits alongside subsequent guidance issued by ACPO and individual police forces, and it is superseded to some extent by amendments to PACE 1984, such as the addition of a power for constables to impose bail conditions (sections 30A(3A)).[458]

Pre-charge bail can also be granted by a custody officer at a police station under sections 30, 37, 37A–37D, 38, 40, 47 of PACE 1984 and sections 3, 3A, 5 and 5A of the Bail Act 1976. If the custody officer finds there is insufficient evidence to charge, he must release a person with or without bail unless he has reasonable grounds for believing that he must detain the person to secure or preserve evidence or obtain evidence by

---

[456] ibid [39]. Lord Hutton was explicit that the same would apply in England. Lord Millett agreed that this failure was 'remediable by judicial review', ibid [73]. Note the dissenting speeches of Lord Bingham and Lord Steyn who pointed out practical obstacles such as providing instructions for a judicial review if there is no access to a lawyer ibid [20]. Lord Hutton said a friend or family member could instruct a solicitor on their behalf ibid [40].

[457] Available at http://205.139.89.196/about-us/corporate-publications-strategy/home-office-circulars/circulars-2003/061-2003/.

[458] See *Guidance on the Safer Detention, and Handling of Persons in Police Custody* (n 443) para 2.1.3, which broadly reflects the Home Office Circular above.

                    Rachel Taylor and Piers von Berg

questioning.[459] If a custody officer finds there is sufficient evidence to charge a person, one of the various options under section 37(7)(a)–(d) must follow, as discussed above.

Street bail and bail by a custody officer are distinct. The key difference is that street bail is governed solely by PACE 1984 and not the Bail Act 1976.[460] Street bail is a discretionary measure intended to allow officers greater flexibility to remain on patrol, as there is otherwise a duty to take arrested persons to a police station.[461] Whereas bail granted at a police station follows from the decisions made by custody officers in light of the sufficiency of evidence before them and whether there are reasonable grounds to detain a person in order to secure, preserve or obtain evidence. It is also part of the range of options post-charge. The scope of the conditions that can be imposed under street bail is narrower than those available to a custody officer or a court.[462] There is no power to take a recognisance, security or surety. A constable must require a person to attend a police station, whilst a person granted bail under the Bail Act 1976 must surrender to custody. There is a separate mechanism for enforcement for each—sections 30D and 46A of PACE 1984 for street bail and section 6 of the Bail Act 1976 for other types of police and court bail.

There are alternative remedies for individuals who wish to challenge decisions on bail. For street bail an individual can apply to a police officer, and failing that apply to a magistrates' court to vary the conditions of bail on different grounds.[463] In respect of bail decisions by custody officers, a person can apply to the magistrates' court to grant bail or vary the conditions.[464] There is right of appeal to the Crown Court from these decisions in the magistrates' court but only in certain cases,[465] and the High Court does not entertain appeals by case stated at an interlocutory stage in criminal proceedings, so judicial review can be an important remedy (see also below at 6-47 for judicial review of magistrates' court decisions on bail). For decisions on street bail, judicial review of a police decision may be a suitable remedy when a person is refused a variation of their bail conditions, and that decision was taken unlawfully due to its failure to consider the grounds put forward (for example, see discussion of ECHR rights below), as any application to the court must rely on different grounds.[466] For persons who have been charged, and who wish to challenge a refusal of bail or imposition of certain conditions, they will have an opportunity to do so when they brought before a magistrates' court pursuant to section 46 of PACE 1984.

---

[459] PACE 1984, s 37(2).

[460] ibid, s 30C(3).

[461] ibid, s 30(1A).

[462] ibid, s 30A(3B).

[463] ibid, s 30CA.

[464] MCA 1980, s 43B. Note that the Joint Committee on Human Rights found this to be one of the important restrictions and safeguards which led it to conclude that there was not a significant risk of breach of Arts 5, 8, 10 or 11 of ECHR. Cited in E Cape and R Edwards, 'Police bail without charge: the human rights implications' [2010] *Cambridge Law Journal* 529.

[465] CJA 2003, s 16 contains a right of appeal where a decision on bail was made after an adjournment of trial (MCA 1980, s 10), adjournment after a intention as to plea (MCA 1980, ss 17C and 24C), initial procedure against an adult for an either-way offence (MCA 1980, s 18), adjournment under Crime and Disorder Act 1951, s 52(5) or remand for medical examination under Powers of Criminal Courts (Sentencing) Act 2000, s 11. A person may also appeal against the following conditions—that they reside away from a particular place or area, that they reside at a particular place other than a bail hostel, the provision of a surety or giving of a security, that they remain indoors between certain hours, electronic tagging, or that they may have no contact with another person.

[466] PACE 1984, s 30CB(2)(b).

(2) Challenges to Police Bail[467]

4-84   It is submitted that there are two principal aspects of the power to grant bail at the pre-charge stage by an officer, which might lead to unlawful interferences with a person's rights under the ECHR as incorporated by the HRA 1998:

    i.   The statutory framework prescribes no time limit on police bail or the number of times it can be renewed.

    ii.   Aside from certain conditions which a constable cannot impose, and the mandatory requirement to surrender to bail on certain date, the precise scope and limits of bail conditions is not defined by statute except that they must 'appear … to be necessary' to secure future attendance, prevent offending, ensure non-interference with witnesses or to safeguard the person's own protection (or best interests or welfare if under 17).[468]

The duration of police bail and conditions imposed can restrict a person's travel, employment, place of residence and interaction with others.[469] For example, curfews can be imposed for as long as 16 hours, amounting in effect to house arrest,[470] and a suspect can be prevented from living at or visiting their home address or prevented from contacting family or other members of a group.[471]

It might be argued that the use of these powers to extend the period of police bail and impose conditions could result in disproportionate interference with Article 5 (right to liberty), Article 6 (right to a trial in a reasonable time and the presumption of innocence), Article 8 (right to privacy and family life), Article 10 (freedom of expression) and Article 11 (freedom of assembly and association).[472] Thus far, reported judicial reviews based on Articles 5 and 6 have failed, whilst there is one decision suggesting that Article 8 may have greater application. It is important for practitioners to understand the obstacles.

4-85   One debate is whether Article 6, specifically the right to a presumption of innocence and a trial within a reasonable time, can apply pre-charge. This could be the basis for a complaint where a person has been on police bail pre-charge for a considerable time on suspicion of a serious offence. The central obstacle, so far as Article 6 and police bail is concerned, is that the domestic courts take the view that it does not apply to bail jurisdiction.[473] This is derived from decisions regarding how magistrates' courts approach

---

[467] This section draws partly on Cape and Edwards [2010] CLJ 529, 7.

[468] PACE 1984, s 30A(3B) in respect of street bail and the Bail Act 1976, s 3(6) in respect of custody officers.

[469] It is not unknown for suspects to be on police bail without charge for as long as three years. During that time they may be suspended from work or unable to run their business, have items of property seized, or required to abide by a nightly curfew. For recent statistics see Gary Slapper, 'It is wrong to impose pain before proving blame' [2013] *Journal of Criminal Law* 355.

[470] Eg by analogy see the case law on control orders and Art 5—*Secretary of State for the Home Department v JJ & Ors* [2007] UKHL 45, [2008] 1 AC 385, which considered an 18-hour curfew and prohibited social contact; and *Secretary of State for the Home Department v MB and AF* [2007] UKHL 46, [2008] 1 AC 440, which included a 14-hour curfew and an electronic tag. The court will need to assess whether such conditions merely restrict a person's liberty or deprive him of it.

[471] See Cape and Richards (n 464) 558.

[472] Eg see *Steel v United Kingdom* (1999) 28 EHRR 603.

[473] Eg see *R (Thomas) v Greenwich Magistrates' Court* [2009] EWHC 1180 (Admin) [12].

Rachel Taylor and Piers von Berg

hearings for breach of bail, principally, *R (DPP) v Havering Magistrates' Court*[474] (see below chapter on magistrates' courts at 6-48 and 6-51). This principle has been applied in cases concerning challenges to magistrates' courts' decisions not to overturn police bail decisions.[475] Despite this, there are principles derived from ECtHR case law that may be worth considering.

The question of at what point Article 6 is engaged in a criminal investigation and prosecution was addressed by the House of Lords in *Attorney-General's Reference (No 2 of 2001)*.[476] It stated that time starts to run from the moment a person is formally charged or served with a summons.[477] Lord Bingham, giving the lead judgment, did not approve this as an inflexible rule but instead said that: 'As a general rule, the relevant period will begin at the earliest time at which a person is officially alerted to the likelihood of criminal proceedings against him', which would ordinarily be when they are formally charged. He conceded that 'An official indication that a person will be reported with a view to prosecution may, depending on all the circumstances' mark that time.[478] This view was reached with reference to authorities of the ECtHR, including *Eckle v Germany*,[479] which stated that time can start from the 'date of arrest, the date when the person concerned was officially notified that he would be prosecuted or the date when preliminary investigations were opened'.[480] But in *R (R) v Durham Constabulary*,[481] Lord Bingham expressed some reservations about a concession by the Secretary of State that Article 6 was engaged when a youth had been formally notified by the police that allegations against him were being investigated.[482] Nevertheless, His Lordship expressed the view that Article 6 covers 'the preparatory and preliminary processes preceding trial'.

It is submitted that the basis for Article 6 applying at a pre-charge stage can be found in the ECtHR's definition of the meaning of being 'charged'.[483] In *Serves v France* (1999) 28 EHRR 265,[484] a French soldier was considered to be charged for the purposes of Article 6(1), as he was subject to a preliminary enquiry in which he was implicated, and was described as 'wholly responsible' in another report. An application to have him formally charged had been declared void. The soldier had refused to take the oath at a hearing and argued that the consequent fine was a breach of his right not to incriminate himself. Although the claim ultimately failed the ECtHR held Article 6 to be engaged. It defined 'charged' as having an 'autonomous' meaning to include when 'the official notification [is] given to an individual by the competent authority of an allegation that he has

---

[474] *R (DPP) v Havering Magistrates' Court* [2001] 1 WLR 805.

[475] *R (Ajaib) v Birmingham Magistrates' Court* [2009] EWHC 2127 (Admin) [35].

[476] *Attorney-General's Reference (No 2 of 2001)* [2004] 2 AC 72, [2004] 2 WLR 1.

[477] ibid [27]–[28]. A decision by a panel of nine judges of the House of Lords. See also *R (R) v Durham Constabulary* [2005] UKHL 21, [2005] 1 WLR 1184 [11].

[478] *Attorney-General's Reference (No 2 of 2001)* (n 476) [27]–[28]. Lords Nicholls, Steyn, Hoffmann, Hobhouse, Millett and Scott agreed with Lord Bingham.

[479] *Eckle v Germany* (1982) 5 EHRR 1.

[480] ibid [73].

[481] *R (R) v Durham Constabulary* (n 477).

[482] ibid [11].

[483] See authorities cited in Cape and Edwards (n 464) 550–51 and fnn 124–133. Note that the relevant date from which various rights under Art 6 are engaged may be different. For example, the right to access to legal advice has been held to be a separate guarantee in this context—see *Allen v United Kingdom* App no 25424/09, The Times, 30 July 2013.

[484] *Serves v France* (1999) 28 EHRR 265.

committed a criminal offence'.[485] The court stated this was a definition that also corresponds to the test whether 'the situation of the [suspect] has been substantially affected'.[486]

In *Fatullayev v Azerbaijan*,[487] the applicant complained that a public statement by a prosecutor that he was guilty of the offence contemplated, made before he was charged, was a breach of Article 6(2) and the presumption of innocence. The court found Article 6(2) to be engaged as the applicant had been detained and an investigation was underway although he had not been formally charged.[488] In *Howarth v United Kingdom*,[489] the applicant submitted that the two-year delay between his non-custodial sentence and custodial sentence following a reference to the Court of Appeal breached his right to a trial within a reasonable time. The ECtHR stated a person's right to trial within a reasonable time was engaged from the point of the police interview.[490]

4-86   As far as the domestic courts are concerned, claimants have encountered considerable difficulties. In *R (C) v Chief Constable of A*, a challenge based on Article 6 (above at 4-13) was given short shrift.[491] This case demonstrated the key difficulty in challenging a decision to continue to bail a suspect and postpone a charging decision. It might appear that the claimant is effectively asking the police to complete their investigation within a specified time frame. It is highly unlikely that a court would wish to circumscribe police discretion in such a way especially in long and complex investigations.[492] In *Ajaib v Birmingham Magistrates' Court* the claimant challenged the refusal of a court to vary his bail conditions. He relied on Lord Bingham's statements in *Attorney-General's Reference (No 2 of 2001)*. Dobbs J held that Article 6 did not apply as the imposition of conditions did not amount to a charge. The submissions on Article 5 were not relevant because there was no risk of loss of liberty and Article 8—although it may be engaged in such cases—was found on the facts not to be engaged.

A different approach can be found in *R (HC) v Secretary of State for the Home Department*[493] (discussed in detail below at 11-16), which concerned access to appropriate adults for youths in police custody. Moses LJ suggested that Article 6 should be considered in light of the emphasis on prevention, diversion and welfare with youths, and referring to Lord Bingham's statement above: 'The early exchanges between police and detainee are an important part of the preparatory and preliminary process.'[494]

A successful claim was brought in *R (Carson) v Ealing Magistrates' Court*[495] where it was accepted that it was disproportionate for bail conditions to require a person to leave their home in a domestic dispute between neighbours. Although the claim was

---

[485] ibid [42]. In adopting this approach it relied on *Deweer v Belgium* (1980) 2 EHRR 30 [42], and *Eckle v Germany* (n 479) [73].

[486] See also *Deweer v Belgium* (n 485).

[487] *Fatullayev v Azerbaijan* (2011) 52 EHRR 2.

[488] ibid [155].

[489] *Howarth v United Kingdom* (2001) 31 EHRR 37.

[490] ibid [20].

[491] *R (C) v Chief Constable of A* (n 57) [30]. The period was just over six months. The claimant argued that this placed enormous stress on his family and caused significant difficulties at work ibid [4].

[492] For example, see a failed challenge on the basis of Art 8 in a private action in *Fitzpatrick & Ors v Commissioner of the Police for the Metropolis* [2012] EWHC 12 (QB) in which the suspects, who were solicitors, were on bail for 21 months.

[493] *R (HC) v Secretary of State for the Home Department* [2013] EWHC 982 (Admin).

[494] ibid [91].

[495] *R (Carson) v Ealing Magistrates' Court* [2012] EWHC 1456 (Admin).

Rachel Taylor and Piers von Berg

not brought or decided explicitly on the basis of Article 8, it is submitted that given the facts, it was engaged in effect.

I. Out of Court Disposals

(1) General Principles

Out-of-court disposals include police cautions and conditional cautions. A caution is **4-87** not a sentence or a criminal conviction. It is an admission of guilt by the person who receives it. It forms part of a person's criminal record and may in certain circumstances be disclosed to others in the future (see below at 4-99). A separate system exists for children and young persons of youth cautions and youth conditional cautions. This is described below at 11-26.

A decision by the police to issue or refuse to review[496] a simple caution or conditional caution can be challenged if there is a significant breach of the established policy and guidelines, even if that breach was unintentional.[497] The policy and guidelines change over time.[498] In previous years they were contained in Home Office circulars. This has now been replaced, following the introduction of the Legal Aid, Sentencing and Punishment of Offenders Act (LASPO) 2012, with a Ministry of Justice document 'Simple Caution for Adult Offender guidance'.[499] The new guidance, applicable to decisions taken after 14 November 2013 replaces the 'Guidance on Simple Cautions' introduced on 8 April 2013.[500] The former sets out a complex series of guidelines to which practitioners should refer as necessary in advising on cases of this sort. A decision-maker should also refer to the Director's Guidance on Charging. Simple cautions, youth cautions and adult and youth conditional cautions will require a decision on whether there is a realistic prospect of conviction and whether it is in the public interest for an offender

---

[496] Eg in *R v Commissioner of Police of the Metropolis, ex parte Thompson* [1997] 1 WLR 1519, [1997] 2 Cr App R 49 and *R (Cordell) v Chief Constable of Nottinghamshire* [2010] EWHC 3326 (Admin), [2011] ACD 36.

[497] This has been the position since *R v Commissioner of Police of the Metropolis, ex parte P* (1996) 8 Admin LR 6, Times, 24 May 1995. The word 'significant' was used by the Divisional Court in *R (Lee) v Chief Constable of Essex* [2012] EWHC 283 (Admin). At the time of writing there was an ongoing review by the Ministry of Justice on the use of police cautions and mention of proposals for magistrates to have oversight of them. The Criminal Justice and Courts Bill 2014 was laid before Parliament on 5 February 2014. It contains measures to restrict the use of cautions for those aged over 18 (cl 14) (note it does not apply to conditional cautions). Indictable-only offences may only be cautioned in 'exceptional circumstances relating to the person and the offence' and with the consent of the DPP. Either-way offences specified by the Secretary of State may not receive a caution except in 'exceptional circumstances relating to the person and the offence'. Other either-way offences and summary offences, where the person concerned has been convicted or cautioned for a similar offence in the preceding two years, may not attract a caution except in exceptional circumstances relating to the person, the offence admitted or the previous offence.

[498] For an example of where there is an absence of settled policy or guidance see *R (Mondelly) v Commissioner of Police of the Metropolis* [2006] EWHC 2370 (Admin), (2007) 171 JP 121.

[499] www.justice.gov.uk/downloads/oocd/adult-simple-caution-guidance-oocd.pdf.

[500] There is a national framework for out of court disposals, a Code of Practice for Adult Conditional Cautions, Director's Guidance on adult and youth conditional cautions as well as guidance on cautions and conditional cautions for youths. See http://www.justice.gov.uk/out-of-court-disposals.

to be prosecuted. This will require reference to the Code for Crown Prosecutors (see below at 5-10).

Breaches that are vulnerable to a claim involve a lack of a clear and reliable admission of guilt[501] and the police inducing a confession.[502] It can also include a failure to assess the facts of the case and apply the Code for Crown Prosecutors.[503] With the introduction of a system for allowing employers to request checks of a person's criminal record including cautions, there are added consequences to accepting a caution which will often be very significant to the individual concerned. The Administrative Court has recently held that the police should make a person aware of those implications when confirming whether a person consents to a caution (see paragraphs 65-74 in the updated November 2013 guidance).[504] Cases will be fact-specific and may turn on evidence of what was said and done in the police station, including the interpretation of interviews.

(2) Margin of Appreciation Granted to Police

4-88   The court will not exercise its discretion to grant a remedy merely because of a breach of the guidelines:

> So far as the jurisdiction of this court is concerned, it is common ground that judicial review is available as a remedy in respect of a caution; that this court will not invariably interfere, even in the case of a clear breach of the guidelines relating to the administration of cautions, as the availability of a remedy is a matter for the discretion of the court; that police officers responsible for applying the Home Office Circular which sets out the guidelines 'must enjoy a wide margin of appreciation as to the nature of the case and whether the preconditions for a caution are satisfied'; and that it will be a rare case where a person who has been cautioned will succeed in showing that the decision was fatally flawed by a clear breach of the Guidelines. That much is clear from a decision of this court, *R v Commissioner of Police for the Metropolis, Ex parte P* (1995) 160 JP 367.[505]

An example of this approach is in *Lee*[506] where a claimant sought a declaration that the police erred in law in refusing to quash a caution, an order quashing that decision and an order quashing the caution. The officer was not aware that the Home Office Circular which he applied had been replaced by an updated version. The updated Circular, in summary, required the officer to explain the consequences of accepting a caution and thus to obtain the claimant's informed consent, especially where the offence was listed in Schedule 3 of the Sexual Offences Act 2003. The officer was also required to request that the claimant sign a form to that effect. However, the court found that the claimant was not induced into accepting a caution. He was made aware of or had access to legal

---

[501] *Ex p P* (n 497).

[502] *Ex p Thompson* (n 496).

[503] Eg in *R (Caetano) v Commissioner of the Police for the Metropolis* [2013] EWHC 375 (Admin) which is a good example of a failure to properly assess the seriousness of a domestic violence incident and difficulties the police can face with the increase in sources of guidance and policy.

[504] *R (Stratton) v Chief Constable of Thames Valley Police* [2013] EWHC 1561, a decision of Sir John Thomas P, which refers to the April 2013 guidance. See also below at 4-99.

[505] *Ex p Thompson* (n 496) 1521B–D. This decision, along with *Ex p P* (n 497), was followed in *R (W) v The Chief Constable of Hampshire Constabulary* [2006] EWHC 1904 (Admin) and in *Lee* (n 497).

[506] *Lee* (n 497).

Rachel Taylor and Piers von Berg

advice on the consequences of accepting a caution for a sexual offence and so was seen to have given informed consent. Consequently, the application was dismissed.

In *R (A) v South Yorkshire Police*[507] the claimants argued that had the officer followed the Final Warning Scheme and Home Office Circular in force at the time, they would have received final warnings as opposed to being charged. They sought orders that their cases be reconsidered. It is of note that the case concerned a joint enterprise offence on public transport, which involved knives and resulted in serious damage to a bus. The defendant's decision that this 'was so serious that it was in the public interest for all the youths to be prosecuted' was therefore accepted; this was an exercise of discretion that could not be challenged.[508]

An example of a caution that was successfully overturned was in *Caetano*,[509] which applied *Ex p Thompson*. The claimant challenged a caution for common assault of her partner. Goldring LJ summarised the facts as:

> two impulsive slaps by a vulnerable and unwell woman of excellent character which caused no injury. The context was the return home in the early hours of the morning of a drunken partner who would not leave.[510]

The claim succeeded primarily because the police officer concerned incorrectly assessed the facts of the offence as more serious than they actually were. The officer considered that it involved domestic violence and this was an aggravating factor when the facts did not support this. As Goldring LJ found, this incident did not come near to the definition provided in the CPS Policy.[511] This case is a good example of the difficulties in applying several sources of guidance (Home Office Circular 016/2008, the Code for Crown Prosecutors, the ACPO Gravity Matrix and the CPS 'Policy for Prosecuting Cases of Domestic Violence'). There is also a reminder of the severe consequences a person might face in their employment, in this case a medical professional who wished to travel overseas for work.

(3) Challenges by Victims

Victims can challenge the use of cautions by the police. In *R (Omar) v Chief Constable of Bedfordshire*[512] the victim was not consulted prior to a decision to caution for actual bodily harm. This in itself was a breach of the guidance in force at the time. Significantly, the case involved a mistake of fact in that the police officers admitted that had they known of the full extent of the claimant's injuries, they would have taken a different decision. Another example is *R (Guest) v DPP*[513] where a victim challenged a decision

4-89

---

[507] *R (A) v South Yorkshire Police* [2007] EWHC 1261 (Admin).

[508] ibid [100] (May LJ).

[509] *Caetano* (n 503).

[510] ibid [44]. The claimant also alleged an assault by her partner, ibid [4].

[511] '"Domestic violence" is a general term that describes a range of controlling and coercive behaviours, which are used by one person to maintain control over another with whom they have, or have had, an intimate family relationship. It is the cumulative and interlinked physical, psychological, sexual, emotional or financial abuse that has a particularly damaging effect on the victim.' CPS, 'Policy for Prosecuting Cases of Domestic Violence', March 2009, para 2.1.

[512] *R (Omar) v Chief Constable of Bedfordshire* [2002] EWHC 3060 (Admin), [2002] Po LR 413.

[513] *R (Guest) v DPP* [2009] EWHC 594 (Admin), [2009] 2 Cr App R 26.

not to prosecute where it was contended that a conditional caution should not have been administered (this is discussed below at 4-91).

(4) Expunging of Records

4-90   Claimants can seek an order that not only quashes the caution but also expunges all record of it.[514] This may be necessary in respect of any future disclosure of their criminal record to prospective employers or in criminal proceedings. In certain circumstances where the record of interview is agreed, this may not be destroyed, as some prosecuting agencies may wish to prosecute the claimant in light of the quashing of the caution.[515]

(5) Conditional Cautions (Adults)

4-91   Adult conditional cautions may also be challenged. There is a different set of criteria the police must follow when administering such cautions, which are set down by statute. The five requirements set out in section 23 of the CJA 2003 must be met, and there is a revised Code of Practice and guidance from the DPP from April 2013 which should be accorded with.[516] The latter sets out exceptional conditions where serious offences likely to attract a custodial sentence or community order can be dealt with using a conditional caution.

The case of *Guest* involved an assault at a person's home at night incurring injuries to which the suspect had made admissions and given an apology to the victim. The CPS had conceded that the decision not to prosecute was flawed, as was the decision to issue a conditional caution, albeit it submitted that the latter was not unlawful. The Divisional Court found the use of a conditional caution unjustified. It was contrary to the DPP's guidance in several respects: i) the assault occasioning actual bodily harm passed both the evidential and public interest tests, ii) serious violence was threatened, used and pre-meditated, and iii), in all the circumstances it was a serious assault. (This case is also considered in the next paragraph on the issue of abuse of process and subsequent prosecutions).

(6) Can a Person be Prosecuted after a Caution is Quashed?

4-92   The guidance on simple cautions requires that if a caution is quashed the case must be reviewed to decide the appropriate disposal (para 88). It also states that a person may be prosecuted if there is a substantial change in the material circumstances or if new evidence comes to light that suggests that the offence was more serious that originally thought. It is submitted that the law on abuse of process will apply to the above

---

[514] For example in *Ex p P* (n 497) and *R (Game) v Chief Constable of Avon & Somerset* [2011] EWHC 3567 Admin.
[515] For example in *R (W) v The Chief Constable of Hampshire Constabulary* [2006] EWHC 1904 (Admin). There is a useful example of an Order in the conclusion of the judgment.
[516] These were revised from 8 April 2013 under LASPO 2012. There is also a revised Code of Practice and revised Directors Guidance (7th edn, April 2013). These can be found on the CPS website www.cps.gov.uk.

Rachel Taylor and Piers von Berg

situations. In *R v Abu Hamza*[517] (discussed below at 6-38), Lord Phillips LCJ stated that where there is an unequivocal representation by the police or the CPS that the defendant will not be prosecuted and the defendant acted on that representation to his detriment, there may be an abuse (it is not a binding rule). The court added that if facts came to light that were not known at the time of the representation 'these may justify proceeding with the prosecution despite the representation'. Similarly, in the context of a judicial review of a caution the Administrative Court has said that:

> in the absence of an express undertaking that there will be no future prosecution even if circumstances materially changed, the legitimate expectation argument does not prevent a later and exceptional decision to charge for good reasons, particularly if this Court had quashed the caution.[518]

This issue arose in *Guest* (discussed above at 4-91). On the facts set out above, the court quashed a decision to administer a conditional caution and a decision not to prosecute. The CPS has raised a defence that it would be academic to quash the decisions because any subsequent attempt to prosecute the offender would be an abuse of process. Sweeney J was of the view that, if anything, the reverse appeared true—it was an affront to justice that the CPS had decided not to prosecute the offender. The court considered *Abu Hamza* and *Jones v Whalley*.[519] In the latter case the House of Lords held that a private prosecution would be an abuse of process where an offender had agreed to accept a caution with the assurance that he would not be prosecuted. Lord Bingham said the correct approach was for a victim to obtain an order quashing the caution first, before seeking to institute a private prosecution:

> If Mr Jones had legal grounds for attacking the police decision to caution Mr Whalley, he could apply for judicial review to quash that decision. If successful, the slate would be clean. There would be no citable caution on Mr Whalley's record and Mr Jones would be free to prosecute. But so long as that formal caution stood, induced by a representation that he would not be prosecuted, the private prosecution of Mr Whalley did in my opinion amount to an abuse, as the justices held.[520]

The court observed in *Guest* that the issue of abuse of process is always considered in light of the facts of a case. If the conditional caution was quashed and compensation that was paid by the offender was repaid, it was hard to see how the offender in that case was in any worse position than before.[521]

(7) Human Rights and Cautions

Challenges to cautions brought under Article 6 have not succeeded because the decision to issue a caution 'rules out the possibility of any trial, or condemnation, or punishment'.[522]   **4-93**

---

[517] *R v Abu Hamza* [2007] 1 Cr App R 27.
[518] *Omar* (n 512). On the question of a legitimate expectation, the Court was applying the case of *R v DPP, ex parte Burke* (1997) COD 169.
[519] *Jones v Whalley* [2006] UKHL 41, [2007] 1 AC 63.
[520] ibid.
[521] *R (Guest) v DPP* [2009] EWHC 594 (Admin), [2009] 2 Cr App R 26 [51]–[52].
[522] *R (R) v Durham Constabulary* (n 477) [12], discussed below at 11-30. See also *Commission in X v United Kingdom* (1979) 17 DR 122 and *S v Miller* 2001 SC 977.

In *R (R) v Durham Constabulary*, the House of Lords held that a warning given under the old system was not a determination of a criminal charge. The House of Lords rejected the submission that the entry on the Police National Computer and the sex offenders register were 'public declarations of guilt', because only a limited number of persons had access to them. Whilst no point was taken on Article 8, Lord Bingham asserted that although it was engaged any interference was justified in the terms set out in Article 8(2).[523]

In *R (Mohammed) v Chief Constable of West Midlands*,[524] Wyn Williams J awarded £500 for breach of Article 8 arising from an unlawful caution on the grounds that it would have been apparent to the police that the claimant's Article 8 rights would be interfered with.

Judicial reviews of cautions or adult or youth conditional cautions will be treated as a criminal cause or matter.[525] However, other such disposals, e.g. penalty notices for disorder (PNDs), would, it is submitted, not constitute a criminal cause or matter. It is not an admission of an offence and does not create a criminal record, although it is recorded on the Police National Computer.[526]

(8) Decisions to Charge

4-94 A claimant can challenge a decision to charge and, in appropriate cases, not to grant an out-of-court disposal.[527] Again, a claimant will have to show that the decision was completely outwith the guidance provided to the police or the CPS.[528] For the approach to decisions to charge by the CPS see Chapter 5.

J. Data Retention and Disclosure

(1) Introduction

4-95 Issues relating to the retention and disclosure of data have become increasingly prominent in recent years. As methodologies employed by the police have grown in sophistication, the impact on individuals' private lives has increased accordingly, which in turn has been reflected in a vast amount of litigation.

Challenges in this area have predominantly been based on Article 8 of ECHR, although the 'data protection principles' as set out in the Data Protection Act 1998,

---

[523] *R v Durham Constabulary* (n 477) [20]. His Lordship agreed for 'similar' reasons with *R (M) v Inner London Crown Court* [2003] 1 FLR 994 and *R (S) v Chief Constable of the South Yorkshire Police* [2004] 1 WLR 2196.

[524] *R (Mohammed) v Chief Constable of West Midlands* [2010] EWHC 1228 (Admin), [2010] ACD 90.

[525] *R (Aru) v Chief Constable of Merseyside* [2004] EWCA Civ 199, [2004] 1 WLR 1697 [9]–[11].

[526] See the new guidance published on 1 July 2013, Ministry of Justice, 'Penalty Notices for Disorder (PND's)', www.justice.gov.uk/downloads/oocd/pnd-guidance-oocd.pdf. *R v Gore* [2009] 1 WLR 2454, a decision of Judge LCJ, was followed in *R v Hamer* [2010] EWCA Crim 2053, [2011] 1 WLR 528, where the Court held that a recipient of a PND was entitled to a good character direction.

[527] See *A* (n 507).

[528] *D v Commissioner of Police of the Metropolis* [2008] EWHC 442 (Admin), [2008] Po LR 41. On decisions of the CPS, see *R (O) v DPP* [2010] EWHC 804 (Admin).

Rachel Taylor and Piers von Berg

Schedule 1, will also often be relevant.[529] This area continues to develop rapidly through legislation, policy and case law.

(2) Data Retention

By way of background, the Police National Computer (PNC) became operational in **4-96** 1974. It is a database of 'nominal records', which detail recordable offences for which an individual has been convicted, as well as any cautions, reprimands, warnings or arrests for recordable offences. This record will be retained until a person's 100th birthday and conviction data will ordinarily be disclosed as part of a criminal records check.[530]

Previously, under the ACPO 'Retention Guidelines for Nominal Records in the Police National Computer' (March 2006), information recorded on the PNC would be 'stepped down' after a period of time, which was dependant on factors such as the event history and the individual's age. However, in *Chief Constable of Humberside Police and others v Information Commission and another*[531] it was held that retention of the record until an individual's 100th birthday did not infringe data protection principles.[532] Consequently, all records held on the PNC, whether or not stepped down, would be retained as above, subject to the 'exceptional case procedure' provided for in the ACPO guidelines, 'Exceptional Case Procedures for the Removal of DNA, Fingerprints and PNC records'.[533]

The Police National Database (PND) is used instead to record 'soft' police intelligence, that is, non-arrest data. The disposal of material held on the PND is governed by the Home Office (2005) Code on the Management of Police Information (MOPI), which is supplemented by other policies, notably the College of Policing's Guidance 'Authorised Professional Practice' on 'Information management, retention, review and disposal'.[534] This guidance consolidates those documents previously applicable, some of which have now been decommissioned.[535] Each force must also have an 'Information Management Strategy', owned by the Chief Officer, and this must be compliant with national policies. These policies require that all records retained are in accordance with the 'National Retention Assessment Criteria'; that they are necessary for a policing purpose, accurate, adequate and up to date. Information must also be reviewed regularly

---

[529] A Chief Constable is the 'data controller' for the relevant police force and 'owns' the data that force has entered onto the PNC.

[530] Although this general position was subject to change following the case of *R (T) v Chief Constable of Greater Manchester Police and others* [2013] 1 Cr App R 27, as discussed below at 4-112.

[531] *Chief Constable of Humberside Police and others v Information Commission and another* [2009] EWCA Civ 1079.

[532] As set out in Sch 1 of the Data Protection Act 1998.

[533] Available at Appendix 2 of the 'Retention Guidelines for Nominal Records in the Police National Computer' (March 2006), http://www.acpo.police.uk/documents/PoliceCertificates/SubjectAccess/Retention%20of%20Records06.pdf.

[534] http://www.app.college.police.uk/app-content/information-management/retention-review-and-disposal-of-police-information/.

[535] The decommissioned documents appear to include the Management of Police Information (MOPI) Code of Practice and Guidance on the Management of Police Information (Second Edition), though it continues to be frequently referred to (http://library.college.police.uk/docs/APPREF/decommissioned-documents.pdf). Other 'local' policies may also be in place, as in *R (TD) v (1) The Commissioner of Police for the Metropolis; (2) Secretary of State for the Home Department* [2013] EWHC 2231 (Admin). See, for example, the Metropolitan Police's 'Information Management in the MPS', January 2014.

where retention is in excess of six years, although the exact requirements are dependent on the nature of the information held.

(i) General Principles

4-97 As stated above, challenges in this sphere will most often be founded on Article 8. The case law discussed below reveals certain issues to which the courts are likely to accord particular weight when considering whether Article 8 is engaged. These include the nature and subject matter of the information/data held, the circumstances in which the data was obtained (ie, whether in a public forum, and whether consensual), the purpose, or purported purpose, of the retention, and the way in which the data is stored (for example, whether this allows the identification of the claimant).

Should Article 8 be engaged, the following factors will be indicative of whether that right has been breached:

i.   length of retention;
ii.   frequency of review;
iii. level of transparency in the applicable policy/practice;
iv.   existence of a 'blanket' or inflexible policy/practice;
v.   circumstances in which the data was obtained;
vi.   nature of the data held;
vii. purpose and utility of retention; and
i.   likely or actual impact on individual concerned.

(ii) Convictions

4-98 As mentioned above, in *Chief Constable of Humberside v Information Commissioner* the Court of Appeal found that the data protection principles as set out in Schedule 1 of the Data Protection Act 1998 did not compel the police to delete even minor and old convictions from the PNC. The retention was lawful and justified for policing purposes such as 'vetting and licensing'.[536]

(iii) Cautions

4-99 One of the claimants in *Chief Constable of Humberside v Information Commissioner* sought to challenge the retention of the record of a reprimand received when she was a minor. In so doing she relied, in part, on the fact that she had been informed at the time the reprimand was administered that the record would be removed under the policy of 'weeding' then in force.

However, the Court of Appeal held that the retention was lawful, notwithstanding the information that she had been given, as the relevant policy had changed. The court reasoned that the deletion of the reprimand would lead to the deletion of many others and that this would 'be likely to prejudice the prevention and detection of crime and

---

[536] In its reasoning the court also drew upon Art 8(5) of Directive 95/46/EC (the Data Protection Directive), which specifically refers to the maintenance of a complete record of criminal convictions.

the apprehension or prosecution of offenders'.[537] It emphasised the potential relevance of such information to the courts and CPS should an individual be subject to criminal proceedings in the future, and in so doing dismissed the claim.[538]

A contrary view was then taken in *MM*,[539] in which the Grand Chamber found that the indefinite retention of a caution under Northern Ireland's equivalent of MOPI breached Article 8 of ECHR. In drawing this conclusion, the ECtHR attached considerable weight to the absence of a clear legislative framework, the lack of transparency regarding the relevant police powers, and the absence of any independent review mechanism. Although the case concerned Northern Ireland, it remains very relevant to this jurisdiction, particularly when considering the similarities between the applicable policies.

Indeed, in *R (Stratton) v Chief Constable of Thames Valley*, the claimant successfully challenged a caution for assault, administered in January 2008. The Divisional Court, in a judgment by Sir John Thomas P, held that as the claimant had not been informed that the caution would be disclosed in a criminal records check, she could not have given the 'informed consent' required for the caution to have been lawfully administered.[540] It is of note, however, that the circumstances of this case differ to those in *Humberside v Information Commissioner* as the caution was administered after the current criminal records system was introduced through Part V of the Police Act 1997. As such, the issue was not simply that the policy had changed, but that the claimant had been misinformed of the applicable policy.

(iv) Challenging Data Retention: PNC Records and Arrest

There has been some considerable dispute as to whether the retention of arrest records **4-100** on the PNC engages Article 8(1) of the ECHR. The position appeared to be clear following *S & Marper v United Kingdom*,[541] in which the storage and retention of data alone was held to amount to an interference with Article 8(1), thereby requiring justification in accordance with Article 8(2).[542]

Similarly, in *R (GC) v Metropolitan Police Commissioner*,[543] the Supreme Court held by a majority that the Commissioner's practice of retaining data on the PNC database in accordance with the ACPO guidelines[544] was incompatible with Article 8 of ECHR. Although the primary issue in that case was the retention of biometric data (namely fingerprints and DNA), it appeared implicit in the judgment that the policy regarding retention of the PNC record was, and is, also unlawful.

However, it was held in *R (RMC and FJ) v Commissioner of Police of the Metropolis*[545] that the retention of the second claimant's arrest record on the PNC could not with certainty be said to engage Article 8, and that in any event such an infringement would

---

[537] *Chief Constable of Humberside Police v Information Commissioner* [2009] EWCA Civ 1079; 2010 1 WLR 1136 [105] (Hughes LJ).
[538] ibid [48].
[539] *MM v the United Kingdom* App no 24029/07 (The Times, 16 January 2013).
[540] *Stratton* (n 504), [54].
[541] *S & Marper v United Kingdom* [2009] 48 EHRR 50.
[542] ibid [67].
[543] *R (GC) v Metropolitan Police Commissioner* [2011] 1 WLR 1230.
[544] See above at 4-96.
[545] *R (RMC and FJ) v Commissioner of Police of the Metropolis* [2012] EWHC 1681.

be proportionate.[546] Richards LJ emphasised that if the incident was deleted the record would be incomplete and potentially misleading, and in consequence any subsequent allegation of a similar nature would not be considered in its appropriate context.[547]

This reasoning was employed in *R (V) v Commissioner of Police for the City of London*,[548] with the court asserting that 'the contention that the retention of the record or arrest on the PNC is unlawful is … untenable'.[549] The findings of the Supreme Court in *GC* were found to relate to specific issues, and not to amount to a general assertion regarding the lawfulness of the retention of data: 'the Supreme Court cannot have meant … that the conclusions reached about DNA and fingerprints were equally applicable to an entirely different feature of the PNC, namely the arrest record'.[550] This was held to be the case notwithstanding Lord Dyson's clear assertion that 'it is common ground that the retention of [such] information raises no separate issues from those raised by the retention of seized DNA material and his fingerprints'.[551]

4-101   Significantly, however, in *R (Catt) v Association of Chief of Police Officers of England, Wales and Northern Ireland*[552] the Court of Appeal, including Lord Dyson MR, countered this approach and asserted that:

> the systematic collection, processing and retention on a searchable database of personal information, even of a relatively routine kind, involves a significant interference with the right to respect for family and life.[553]

It would therefore fall on the defendant to prove the justification for any such interference.[554] The implications of this for the retention of PNC records was recognised in *R (TD) v (1) The Commissioner of Police for the Metropolis; (2) Secretary of State for the Home Department*,[555] a case concerning the retention of information regarding the claimant's arrest for sexual assault some nine years previously.[556]

In seeking to contend that any interference with TD's Article 8 rights was only small, the defendant relied upon Richard LJ's reasoning in *RMC and FJ*, discussed above at 4-100. However, the court in *TD* appeared to reject this approach, instead emphasising the significance of *Catt* and *S & Marper*. Although on the facts it was held that the retention was justified due to the potential utility of the data in circumstances in which only nine years had

---

[546] Reflecting the approach of the Supreme Court in *Kinloch (James) v HM Advocate* [2012] UKSC 62.

[547] *RMC and FJ* (n 545) [61].

[548] *R (V) v Commissioner of Police for the City of London* [2012] EWHC 3430 (Admin).

[549] ibid [25].

[550] ibid [27].

[551] *GC* (n 543) [51]. An alternative argument that there should be a requirement for a PNC record to include fuller information regarding the particular circumstances of the arrest in order to facilitate greater understanding of the context, and importantly, any limitations to the credibility of the allegation, was also rejected by the court on the basis that this additional detail could be readily ascertained from the relevant local records, *V* (n 570) [30]. However, in practice, police forces appear to be more willing to insert additional information in agreeing terms of settlement.

[552] *R (Catt) v Association of Chief of Police Officers of England, Wales and Northern Ireland* [2013] EWCA Civ 192, [2013] 1 WLR 3305.

[553] ibid [44].

[554] However, at the time of writing an appeal before the Supreme Court was being sought.

[555] *TD* (n 535).

[556] On both the PNC and Criminal Reporting Information System (CRIS) reports.

elapsed since the allegation,[557] the court delivered a very strong indication that arrest data stored on the PNC does indeed engage Article 8, and as such can be subject to challenge.

However, the case was subject to appeal in *R (TD) v (1) The Commissioner of Police for the Metropolis; (2) Secretary of State for the Home Department.*[558] Here, the Court of Appeal distinguished *Catt* from *RMC and FJ*, with Laws LJ stating that the later decision 'by no means overrules or calls into question the conclusion of the Divisional Court in the case of C'.[559] Although the retention of the information[560] was recognised to impact on the claimant's private life, this was said to be 'extremely modest'[561] and the information was seen to have an 'objective utility',[562] The court did heavily criticise the absence of a policy for any systematic review, particularly where the information would otherwise be retained for a period of one hundred years, but ultimately refused to make a declaration regarding the need for periodic reviews of retention,[563] as this was a matter of an ongoing policy review.

This approach was also taken in *R (AR) v (1) Chief Constable of the Greater Manchester Police; (2) Secretary of State for the Home Department (Defendants); and (3) Disclosure and Barring Service (Interested Party)*[564] in which the claimant sought to challenge the retention of acquittal information. In this, he relied on *MM v the United Kingdom*[565] and submitted that the absence of clear and detailed statutory guidelines as to the applicable safeguards to the retention of the data rendered that retention unlawful.[566] HHJ Raynor QC rejected the claim. He distinguished *MM* on the basis that the information was over 12 years old and related to a caution given in private, whereas in the present case there had been a public trial only two and a half years previously. As such, the time had not yet come when the retention of the records constituted a disproportionate interference with the claimant's right to private life. Notably, HHJ Raynor QC also expressed some scepticism as to whether Article 8 was engaged in any event.[567]

(v) Harassment Warnings and Criminal Reporting Information System (CRIS) Reports

As intelligence systems have become more complex, the police recording systems have been extended accordingly, and there are now a number of different databases and mechanisms upon and by which personal data may be stored. This has led to a proliferation of case law in this area.   **4-102**

---

[557] *TD* (n 535) [16].
[558] *R (TD) v (1) The Commissioner of Police for the Metropolis; (2) Secretary of State for the Home Department* [2014] EWCA Civ 585.
[559] ibid, [9].
[560] Which was comprised of a PNC record and a CRIS report.
[561] *TD* (n 535),[10].
[562] ibid, [12].
[563] ibid [16]–[23].
[564] *R (AR) v (1) Chief Constable of the Greater Manchester Police; (2) Secretary of State for the Home Department (Defendants); and (3) Disclosure and Barring Service (Interested Party)* [2013] EWHC 2721 (Admin).
[565] *MM* (n 539).
[566] *AR* (n 564) [45].
[567] ibid [48]–[49].

In *R (T & R) v Commissioner of Police of the Metropolis*[568] conjoined challenges were brought against the policy of retaining harassment warnings for periods of at least seven years. 'T' was reported by a neighbour to have made homophobic comments but had never been interviewed by the police in relation to this, whilst 'R' had been the subject of a complaint by an ex-girlfriend, and although arrested and interviewed, it had subsequently been determined that no crime had been committed.

Although the claim was unsuccessful at first instance, this was overturned by the Court of Appeal in *Catt*.[569] The court noted that the retention of the reports was a blanket policy which allowed no differentiation, even in relation to the gravity of the offence, and indeed, did not take into account whether a matter was or should be classified as an offence at all.

Although it was understandable, particularly in the context of allegations of harassment, that the police would seek to (i) inform an individual of the risk of an offence being committed should behaviour(s) continue or be repeated; and (ii) retain a record in case further allegations were made,[570] the length of retention was excessive and disproportionate to those purposes. The court observed that it was difficult to see how retention for any longer than three years could be of any assistance to a prosecution for the offence of harassment.[571] The initial recording of the matter was however held to be proportionate and in accordance with Article 8(2) of the ECHR.

The retention of CRIS records was also considered in *TD*.[572] Although on the facts, retention for nine years of the information relating to the claimant's arrest for sexual assault could be justified,[573] the court was clear that retention of data of this sort could amount to a breach of Article 8 of ECHR. Indeed, the policy in question[574] was strongly criticised for its failure to include any provision for review throughout the envisaged 100-year period of retention.[575] Although, as above, the Court of Appeal was less attracted by the claimant's factual case, and sceptical as to the extent to which Article 8 was infringed, it was also extremely critical of the absence of a system of review, particularly where the data would otherwise be retained for one hundred years.[576]

(vi) 'Extremist' Databases

4-103   As noted above, the evolution of intelligence systems has resulted in the introduction of new databases to be utilised by the police. One of these, the 'National and Domestic Extremist Database', was challenged in *Catt v Association of Chief Police Officers*.[577] The

---

[568] *R (T & R) v Commissioner of Police of the Metropolis* [2012] EWHC 1115.

[569] *Catt* (n 552). It is of note that upon T being granted permission to appeal the police agreed to expunge the record of her letter but, irrespective of the academic nature of the claim, the court agreed to determine the appeal due to the importance of the issue.

[570] ibid [57].

[571] ibid [61].

[572] Discussed above at 4-101.

[573] *TD* (n 535) [12]–[17].

[574] The Metropolitan Police's Corporate Review Retention and Disposal Schedule, available at www.met. police.uk/foi/pdfs/policies/rmb_review_retention_disposal2012.pdf.

[575] *TD* (n 535) [17].

[576] *TD* [2014] (n 535), [16]–[23].

[577] *Catt v Association of Chief Police Officers* [2012] EWHC 1471 (Admin).

Rachel Taylor and Piers von Berg

data that had been retained, and which was in issue in the case, related to a non-violent protester and, amongst other things, his attendance at demonstrations. There was no suggestion that the claimant had, or would, engage in criminal or violent conduct.

At first instance, the Divisional Court accepted the defendant's submissions that the retention complied with Article 8(2) of ECHR as:

i.   there was a value in knowing identities of attendees at protests organised by extremist groups even if they had not themselves been convicted of any offence; and,

ii. the suggestion that individual reports should be analysed in order to determine whether information continued to be of value was unworkable.

Significantly, the court also held that in any event, as the claimant's activities and his association with extremist groups took place in a public forum, it would be 'unreal and unreasonable' to assert that the police response engaged Article 8. On the contrary, the claimant 'did not enjoy a reasonable expectation and privacy', and no such expectation was triggered by the 'wholly understandable' compilation and retention of intelligence reports by the defendant.[578]

This approach was, however, wholly rejected by the Court of Appeal, which held that the inclusion of the claimant's personal information on the database did constitute an interference with his Article 8 rights and thus required justification. Although the demands of modern policing were recognised, the court emphasised that the police needed to exercise caution in identifying the information likely to provide them with assistance in carrying out their role. In the circumstances of the present case the assistance afforded by virtue of the recording and retention of the data could not be identified, and so the public interest could not be seen to have been served in a sufficiently important way. The interference was therefore disproportionate and unjustified, in breach of Article 8.[579]

Importantly, the court also asserted more generally that 'the systematic collection, processing and retention on a searchable database of personal information, even of a relatively routine kind, involves a significant interference with the right to respect for family and life', emphasising that the burden to prove the justification of any such interference lay firmly on the defendant.[580] This means that the retention of personal information by the police on any police database will potentially be subject to challenge, subject of course, to the conditions applied through Article 8(2) of ECHR.[581]

(vii) Biometric Data

Biometric data refers to data that is used to identify individuals, such as fingerprints or DNA. The indefinite retention of such data by the police[582] was challenged in *R (S) v Chief*   **4-104**

---

[578] ibid [40]–[46].

[579] *Catt* [2013] (n 552) [44].

[580] ibid.

[581] Although as noted above at 4-101, the Court of Appeal in *TD* (n 535) took steps to restrict the wide application of this assertion.

[582] Save 'exceptional circumstances', as provided for by the ACPO guidelines, 'Exceptional Case Procedures for the Removal of DNA, Fingerprints and PNC records'.

Constable of the South Yorkshire Police[583] on the basis that it constituted an unjustifiable breach of Articles 8 and 14 of the ECHR. Surprisingly, the House of Lords held that:

i.   there had been no interference contrary to Article 8;[584]

ii.   but in any event, any such interference would have been justified and proportionate; and

iii. the retention of the data was not in consequence of the claimant's 'status', and so could not be discriminatory, in accordance with Article 14.[585]

The Grand Chamber found to the contrary in *S & Marper;*[586] holding that the indefinite retention of such data constituted a breach of Article 8 of ECHR. The Supreme Court then accepted this approach in *GC*.[587] Although it was submitted by the defendants that the empowering provision for the policy, section 64(1A) of PACE 1984, should be declared incompatible with Article 8, the majority held that Parliament had conferred a discretion on the police to retain the data and that there was no reason to conclude that it must have intended the discretion to be exercised in a non-Convention-compliant manner. A declaration of incompatibility was therefore inappropriate.

This conclusion was drawn notwithstanding the fact that Parliament was seized of the issue at the time, yet it was seen to be inappropriate for the Supreme Court to order either a change in the legislative scheme within a specific period or the destruction of the data in issue. Instead, it was open to ACPO to reconsider and amend the guidelines in the intervening period prior to any legislative reform.

The relevant legislative provisions have now been embodied in the Protection of Freedoms Act 2012 (PFA 2012), which amends PACE 1984 accordingly. The relevant provisions for material obtained subsequent to this enactment are set out at sections 63D to 63U PACE.

In brief, the legislation provides that section 63D material[588] can be retained:

1.   until the conclusion of the investigation, or the consequential proceedings, where arrested and/or charged for an offence which is not a qualifying offence.[589]

2.   for three years where the individual is arrested for a qualifying offence and not charged, provided that a successful application has been made to the Biometrics Commissioner[590] (however, where the person has a previous conviction for a recordable offence,[591] or is subsequently convicted of such an offence before the destruction of the s.63D material is required, the retention may be indefinite).[592]

---

[583] *R (S) v Chief Constable of the South Yorkshire Police* [2004] UKHL 39.

[584] Lady Hale dissented on this point.

[585] As the rules applied to all arrested individuals.

[586] *S & Marper* (n 541).

[587] By the time the case came before the Supreme Court this had also been accepted by the defendants, with the sole issue being that of redress.

[588] Fingerprints and DNA profiles obtained under a PACE power or taken by consent in the course of a police investigation.

[589] PACE 1984, s 63E.

[590] ibid, s 63F(5). This application can only be made, pursuant to s 63G in certain circumstances, as set out in s 63G(2) and (3). An individual whose data is subject to such an application has the right to make representations against further retention.

[591] Where this is not an excluded offence, as defined in PACE, s 63F(11).

[592] PACE 1984, s 63F(2).

Rachel Taylor and Piers von Berg

3. for three years where the individual is charged with a qualifying offence but not convicted, subject to a possible extension of two further years upon application to a District Judge (magistrates' court).[593]
4. indefinitely where the individual has been convicted of a recordable offence.[594]

Although there is also a procedure by which applications can be made for early deletion of section 63D material, this will only be relevant in very limited circumstances. The applicable grounds are also extremely restricted and applications are likely to prove difficult.[595]

Even where destruction of biometric data is required, the Act allows for a speculative search to be carried out in order to ascertain whether there is any match to a crime recorded on the database.[596]

Notably, section 63R of PACE 1984[597] requires the destruction of all DNA samples taken under any power conferred by the Act or given voluntarily in the course of an investigation, regardless of whether an individual has been convicted. Samples must be destroyed as soon as a profile has been derived, and in any event within six months,[598] although this may be extended in certain circumstances.[599]

The retention of DNA profiles and fingerprints taken before the commencement of **4-105** the relevant provisions (31 October 2013) is governed by section 25(3) of the PFA 2012, and the Protection of Freedoms Act 2012 (Destruction, Retention and Use of Biometric Data) (Transitional, Transitory and Saving Provisions) Order 2013/1813 ('the Order') made pursuant thereto.

Essentially, this stipulates:

i. Where the data was taken or derived three or more years before 31 October 2013, and a person was arrested and/or charged but not convicted[600] of a qualifying offence,[601] the maerial had to have been destroyed prior to the coming into force of the Order.
ii. Where the data was taken or derived less than three years before 31 October 2013, and a person was arrested and/or charged but not convicted of a qualifying offence, the material would have to be destroyed three years from the date on which it was taken or derived.
iii. Where the data was taken or derived before 31 October 2013, and a person was arrested and/or charged but not convicted of an offence other than a qualifying offence, the material had to have been destroyed prior to the Order coming into force.

---

[593] ibid, s 63F(7). Such an application can also be made in relation to s 63F(5) material. Again, where the person has a previous conviction for a recordable offence, or is subsequently convicted of such an offence before the destruction of the s 63D material is required, the retention may be indefinite.
[594] PACE, s 63I.
[595] See further 'Early Deletion Process: Guidance to Chief Officers on the Destruction of DNA Samples, DNA Profiles and fingerprints under section 63AB(2) of the Police and Criminal Evidence Act 1984' and PACE s 63D(2).
[596] PACE 1984, s 63D(5).
[597] Inserted by PFA 2012, s 14.
[598] PACE 1984, s 63R(4).
[599] As set out at ibid ss 63R(4)–(9). Samples must also be destroyed where PACE 1984, s 63R(2) applies.
[600] It should be noted that 'conviction' includes cautions, reprimands and final warnings, in accordance with ibid, s 65B.
[601] As listed at ibid, s 65A.

However, section 25(4) specifically allows for exceptions to the foregoing by way of Order made pursuant to the Act, and due reference should be paid to the Order referenced above.[602] Importantly, all profiles and fingerprints not compliant with the PFA 2012 provisions were destroyed by September 2013.[603]

(viii) Collection of DNA Samples: Operation Nutmeg

4-106 'Operation Nutmeg' is a national police scheme[604] that has as its objective the collection of DNA samples from convicted offenders not already on the DNA database.[605]

The relevant provisions are contained in section 63(3B) of PACE 1984, which came into force on 7 March 2011, and authorises an officer to take a non-intimate sample where a person has a conviction, caution, warning or reprimand for a recordable offence, provided that no sample has previously been taken. A sample may only be taken without consent where an inspector is satisfied that this is 'necessary to assist in the prevention and protection of crime'.[606]

An individual may be compelled to attend a police station in order that a non-intimate sample can be taken where an officer of at least the rank of inspector has authorised the taking of the sample,[607] although since 7 March 2013 this power has been applicable only to qualifying offences.[608] Refusal to attend a police station for this purpose can lead to arrest.[609]

These legislative provisions were challenged in *R (R) v A Chief Constable*[610] on the basis that the operation constituted a breach of the claimant's Article 8(1) rights.

Although the claimant succeeded in establishing that there was no power for an individual to be compelled to attend the police station to provide a sample without consent in the absence of authority being granted by an officer of at least the rank of inspector (as had happened in this case), the claim largely failed. Whilst the requirement to provide a non-intimate sample interfered with the claimant's Article 8(1) rights, this was (i) in accordance with the law[611] and (ii) proportionate.

In considering proportionality, Pitchford LJ held that the statistical probability that a sample would result in a positive match was not determinative,[612] and that the defendant was justified in relying on propensity to commit offences on the basis of previous offending as a measure of probability in the proof of further offences.[613] The absence of specific grounds of suspicion did not render the exercise of the power disproportionate

---

[602] See the Protection of Freedoms Act 2012 (Destruction, Retention and Use of Biometric Data) (Transitional, Transitory and Saving Provisions) Order 2013, (SI 2013/1813).
[603] National DNA Database Strategy Board Annual Report 2012–13, Home Office.
[604] Extending throughout England and Wales.
[605] Which will usually be due to the age of their conviction, as DNA sampling dates back only to 1994.
[606] PACE 1984, s 63(3BC).
[607] ibid, Sch 2A, paras 11 and 15.
[608] As defined by ibid, s 65A.
[609] ibid, Sch 2A, para 17.
[610] *R (R) v A Chief Constable* [2013] EWHC 2864.
[611] As indeed had been accepted by the claimant.
[612] *R* (n 610) [40] (Pitchford LJ).
[613] ibid.

Rachel Taylor and Piers von Berg

and significant weight should be attached to the legitimate interest being pursued of detecting crime.[614]

The claimant further contended that his Article 8 rights had been breached, as he had not been provided with an opportunity to make representations against the sample being taken. Whilst the court seemed to accept that such an opportunity should be afforded, there had been no breach in the present case as the claimant had submitted a witness statement as to why the requirement to provide a sample was unlawful, and this had been taken into account by the inspector when deciding to grant the authorisation.[615]

(ix) Custody Photographs

Whilst section 64A of PACE 1984 allows for custody photographs to be taken on arrest,   **4-107**
there exists no power relating to their retention. This has caused uncertainty as to the length of time for which photographs will be stored.

The retention of custody photographs was subject to challenge in *RMC and FJ*. Neither of the two claimants had been charged: one was a minor who had been arrested for a sexual offence, and the other an adult arrested for assault. The defendant submitted that the MOPI Code of Practice and Guidance governed the retention of this data. This stipulated that information held by the police (other than that listed on the PNC) would ordinarily be retained for six years, subject to extension on the basis of the gravity of the offence.

The claimants argued that this policy breached Article 8 of ECHR and the court agreed both that Article 8(1) was engaged and that the policy of retention was disproportionate. In so holding, it was emphasised that:

i.   The policy included no distinction on the basis of:
    a)   whether an individual had been charged, or charged and then acquitted; or
    b)   the age of the claimant at the time of arrest;
ii.   the length of retention was in reality likely to be greater than six years, and could be significantly longer; and
iii. reviews of the retention were likely to be infrequent, and entirely absent in certain circumstances.

The MOPI Code and accompanying guidance were therefore declared unlawful, although the defendant was afforded time to revise the existing policy.[616] As discussed above, the PFA 2012 makes no reference to the retention of custody photographs.[617]

(x) Images Obtained Through Police Surveillance

In *R (Wood) v Commissioner of Police of the Metropolis*[618] the claimant sought to appeal   **4-108**
against a decision that there had been no breach of his Article 8 rights caused by the

---

[614] ibid [41] (Pitchford LJ).
[615] ibid [43] (Pitchford LJ).
[616] *RMC and FJ* (n 545) [58].
[617] At the time of writing ACPO, the College of Policing and the Home Office were carrying out a review into information management arrangements within the police service, scheduled to report in April 2014. In the interim, each police force should have in place a local policy regarding the retention of custody photographs.
[618] *R (Wood) v Commissioner of Police of the Metropolis* [2009] EWCA Civ 414.

police photographing him and retaining the images. The photographs had been taken outside the annual general meeting of a company associated with the arms industry. The defendant stated that its intention had been to use the photographs for purposes of identifying potential offenders, should offences have been committed at the meeting, and that the claimant's image had not therefore been added to any police databases.

The Court of Appeal, by a majority, found for the appellant. Although the taking of a photograph in a public place[619] would not itself engage Article 8, it did so in the present context due to the implication that the images would be used and retained, which constituted an intrusion by the state. Although initially pursuing a legitimate aim,[620] the practice could not be justified pursuant to Article 8(2) of ECHR. It was clear after no more than a few days that the appellant had not been involved in the commission of any criminal offences and at this point the identified legitimate aim was no longer applicable.[621]

Similarly, in *R (Mengesha) v Commissioner of Police of the Metropolis*,[622] where police had filmed individuals being released from containment at a trade union march, the taking and retention of the images was held to be contrary to Article 8 of ECHR. This was principally due to the absence of any police power to require individuals to be filmed in the circumstances.[623] However, the court held that the retention would have been contrary to Article 8[624] in any event due to the lack of a clear and published policy regarding retention, which could not therefore be said to be 'in accordance with the law'.[625]

(xi) Alternative Mode Of Redress: Enforcement Notices

4-109   In *V*,[626] the defendant sought to contend that judicial review proceedings were inappropriate due to the existence of an alternative remedy by virtue of section 40(1) of the Data Protection Act 1998. This provision empowers the Information Commissioner to serve an enforcement notice requiring deletion of data wrongly obtained or wrongly held.[627]

The argument was dismissed as the matter had already proceeded to a substantive hearing. However, the court indicated that this process would be ineffective as a means of alternative redress in any event as the defendant would be likely to resist such an order on the same basis as the defence that had been put forward in the present proceedings. In *TD* the defendant submitted the same argument, but the court again paid little credence to it due to (i) previous case law and (ii) the limited 'vigour' with which it had

---

[619] Permitted at common law.

[620] Namely (i) the prevention of disorder or crime; (ii) the interests of public safety; and (iii) the protection of the rights and freedoms of others.

[621] The court also indicated that a far stricter view would be taken in cases concerning photographs taken of individuals who are not suspected of having committed any criminal offence: *Wood* (n 618) [100].

[622] *R (Mengesha) v Commissioner of Police of the Metropolis* [2013] EWHC 1695 (Admin).

[623] Which clearly fell outside the remit of s 64A of PACE 1984.

[624] Which was engaged due to the involvement of the state, even absent a reasonable expectation of privacy, *Mengesha* (n 622) [19].

[625] ibid [20].

[626] *V* (n 548).

[627] As in *Chief Constable of Humberside Police* (n 531).

been pursued.[628] It therefore appears unlikely that the section 40(1) provision will be accepted as a bar to proceedings brought in the future.

(3) Disclosure of Data

Although the retention of data will be a matter of concern to many clients, the disclosure of that data will often be considered more important, due to the direct impact it is likely to have on their lives. Challenges to disclosure will ordinarily be by way of judicial review on the basis that the disclosure is in breach of Article 8 of ECHR.[629]   **4-110**

(i) 'Conviction' Data

The Rehabilitation of Offenders Act 1974 provides that convictions or cautions become   **4-111**
spent after a specified period of time (the rehabilitation period), although prison sentences over 48 months are excluded from the scope of the Act. [630] The intention of this statute is to ensure that once rehabilitated (that is, once a conviction is spent), an offender will generally be treated as if the offence had never been committed.[631]

The length of a rehabilitation period[632] will depend upon:

i.   the gravity of the offence;
ii.   whether any additional offences have been committed during the relevant period; and,
iii. whether the individual was a minor at the time of commission.

However, the Rehabilitation of Offenders Act 1974 (Exceptions) Order 1995 (SI 1975/1023) provides that for 'excepted positions' (namely those relating to children and vulnerable individuals, or those in which an individual would be employed in a position of trust), a person can be required to disclose full details of their criminal record, including any spent convictions or cautions.[633] These details will also be revealed on a

---

[628] *TD* (n 535) [18].

[629] Private law actions for negligence, breach of confidence, breach of s 7 of HRA 1998 and breach of the Data Protection Act 1998 may also be relevant in this sphere, and an action for libel may also be available in appropriate circumstances, see *Wood v Chief Constable of the West Midlands* [2004] EWCA Civ 1638.

[630] Increased to 48 months upon the coming into force of s 139 of LASPO 2012 on 10 March 2014.

[631] As protected by s 12 of the Rehabilitation of Offenders Act 1974.

[632] On 10 March 2014 ss 139 and 141 and Sch 25 of LASPO 2012 came into force, substantially altering the time in which a conviction or a caution is spent. For adult offenders, the period for custodial sentences of 0–6 months has been reduced from seven to two years (18 months for those under 18 at the date of conviction), for sentences of 6–30 months from 10 to four years (24 months for those under 18 at the date of conviction), and sentences of 30 months to four years shall be spent after seven years (42 months for those under 18 at the date of conviction). As above, sentences over four years will never be spent. For non-custodial sentences community orders and youth rehabilitation orders there is a buffer period of one year from the end of the sentence instead of five years (six months for those under 18 at the date of conviction). The period for fines will be reduced from five years to one year (six months for those under 18 at the date of conviction). Absolute discharges will be automatically spent and all other non-custodial orders shall be spent after the life of the order.

[633] A full list of the 'excepted positions' for which a criminal records check can be obtained has been published by the DBS, available at https://www.gov.uk/government/uploads/system/uploads/attachment_data/file/315179/DBS_guide_to_eligibility_v4.pdf.

criminal records certificate, obtained through the Disclosure and Barring Service (DBS), in accordance with sections 113A and 113B of the Police Act 1997.

(ii) R (T) v Chief Constable of Greater Manchester Police and others

4-112   The statutory scheme laid out above[634] was successfully challenged in *R (T) v Chief Constable of Greater Manchester Police and others*,[635] where the Court of Appeal, including Lord Dyson MR, considered conjoined appeals brought by three appellants:

i.   'T', aged 21, sought to challenge the disclosure of information to his university which related to two warnings that had been administered when he was 11 years old. The disclosure was made as T's course involved contact with children.

ii.   'JB' contested the disclosure of a caution administered in 2001 for theft of a packet of false nails. This disclosure had been made in the context of JB's application for the position of a care worker.

iii. 'W' sought to challenge the disclosure of her conviction as an accessory to manslaughter and robbery that had been committed by her boyfriend. She had pleaded guilty to this offence, which took place in 2003, when she had been 16.

Lord Dyson MR held that records of criminal convictions engaged Article 8.[636] First, although it was recognised that conviction data is in a way public due to the forum in which criminal proceedings are conducted, 'as the conviction recedes into the past, it becomes part of the individual's private life'.[637] His Lordship also noted that cautions are in any event administered in private and therefore are always part of an individual's private life. Secondly, and irrespective of the above, the court highlighted that disclosure of information of this nature can lead to exclusion from employment; potentially adversely impacting on an individual's earning potential and the development of their personal relationships. Consequently, such disclosure clearly amounts to an interference with the right to respect for private life.[638]

Whilst accepting that this interference was in accordance with the law, the court held that the requirement that all conviction and caution data relating to recordable offences be disclosed was disproportionate to the relevant legislative aim. This was principally due to the absence of any assessment of the relevance of the information to the particular circumstances and purposes of disclosure.[639] Lord Dyson MR further reflected that whilst 'bright-line' rules can be legitimate in some circumstances, if those rules fail to achieve their stated purposes in a 'significant way', or are disproportionate, they are unlikely to be saved simply by virtue of the simplicity and administrative ease that they afford.[640]

---

[634] Albeit that in force prior to the amendments in force from 10 March 2014.

[635] *T* (n 530).

[636] In contrast to the approach that had been taken in the count below.

[637] *T* (n 530) [31].

[638] In accordance with *Sidabras v Lithuania* (2006) 42 EHRR 6 [48].

[639] However, whilst this resulted in the appeals of T and JB being upheld, the Court rejected that of AW on the basis that parliament was entitled to take the view that some offences were so serious that they should never be regarded as 'spent', and that this was not a blanket policy but instead one that drew distinctions based upon the gravity of offences.

[640] *T* (n 530) [40], see also *R (F) v Secretary of State for the Home Department [2010] UKSC 17.*

The court therefore issued a declaration of incompatibility in relation to the disclosure provisions of the Police Act 1997, and a declaration that the 1975 Rehabilitation of Offenders Act Order was *ultra vires* the 1974 Act. In making these declarations the court commented that '[t]his is not a case where we can be confident that Parliament will move quickly to find a solution'.[641] However, notwithstanding this, the court did direct that the decision not take effect pending the determination of an application for permission to appeal by the Supreme Court.[642]

Subsequent to *T* the DBS announced that as of 29 May 2013 certain old and minor convictions and cautions would be filtered and so not disclosed in a DBS criminal record certificate.[643] This filtering policy is, however, restricted, and its adequacy following the Court of Appeal's decision is likely to be determined by the Supreme Court in due course.

(iii) Non-Conviction Data: Enhanced Criminal Records Certificate

Non-conviction data can be disclosed on an 'enhanced criminal records certificate' (ECRC), which is required for certain positions of employment or voluntary work.[644] The relevant disclosure regime is now contained in section 113B(4) of the Police Act 1997,[645] which provides that:

4-113

> Before issuing an enhanced criminal record certificate the DBS must request any relevant chief officer to provide any information which—
>
> (a) The chief officer reasonably believes to be relevant for the purpose described in the statement in the sub-section (2) (matters, relevant to the position for which you are applying); and,
>
> (b) In the chief officer's opinion, ought to be included in the certificate.

The disclosure of non-conviction data has been the subject of extensive litigation over recent years, signalling both the importance of this issue to individuals and the conflict to which it gives rise between the rights of the individual and issues of public protection.

---

[641] *T* (n 530) [69]. This can be contrasted to the approach that has been taken following *GC* (n 565) and *RMC and FJ* (n 567), as discussed above at 4-100.

[642] Permission was granted and judgment was handed down, subsequent to the completion of this chapter, in *R (T and another) v Secretary of State for the Home Department and another* [2014] UKSC 35.

[643] Disclosure and Barring Service, *Filtering Rules for Criminal Record Check Certificates*, 28 May 2013, issued pursuant to the Rehabilitation of Offenders Act 1974 (Exceptions) Order 1975 (Amendment) (England and Wales) Order 2013/1198 and the Police Act 1997 (Criminal Record Certificates: Relevant Matters) (Amendment) (England and Wales) Order 2013/1200. The document was updated on 11 and 13 June 2013, and on 13 December 2013.

[644] Most commonly those in which the individual will be working with children or vulnerable people.

[645] In effect from 10 September 2012, following the enactment of the PFA 2012. This legislative change was prompted by the Mason Review (Sunita Mason, *A Common Sense Approach—Report on Phase 1*, February 2011), which also recommended, amongst others, (i) the development of an open and transparent representations process for individuals to challenge inaccurate or inappropriate disclosures to be overseen by an independent expert; and (ii) the introduction of a statutory code of practice for the police to follow in deciding whether or not make disclosure (recommendation 7), both of which were introduced through s 82 of the PFA 2012.

(iv) Framework and Principles

4-114   The best starting point is *R (L) v Commissioner of Police of the Metropolis*,[646] in which the Supreme Court held that the collection and retention of information in central records could engage Article 8(1) of ECHR. The fact that a matter has been in the public arena, for example through a criminal trial, does not mean that Article 8 will not be engaged.[647]

The court held that although section 115(7) of the Police Act 1997[648] would not be unlawful as long as the test 'ought to be included'[649] was applied in a manner compatible with Article 8, the protection of vulnerable people needed to be balanced against the rights of individuals in respect of their private life, and that disclosure of information would often constitute a 'killer blow' to an individual seeking employment in an excepted position.[650] On this basis it was held that:[651]

   i.   there was no presumption of disclosure absent a good reason; and

   ii.   if any doubt existed as to whether sensitive information ought to be disclosed, the chief officer should give the individual concerned an opportunity to make representations prior to making that disclosure.

This framework has now largely been embodied into statutory guidance to which a chief officer is required to have regard when making disclosure decisions, in accordance with section 113B(4A) of the Police Act 1997.[652] Failure to pay due regard to all factors applicable under the statutory guidance can itself provide a basis of challenge.[653]

(v) 'Reasonably be Thought to be Relevant'

4-115   The 2012 statutory guidance provides that the following should be taken into account in determining relevance:

   i.   relevance to prescribed purpose for which the ECRC is sought;[654]

   ii.   gravity and number of allegations;[655]

   iii.   age of information;[656]

---

[646] *R (L) v Commissioner of Police of the Metropolis* [2010] 1 AC 410.

[647] *R (AR) v (1) Chief Constable of the Greater Manchester Police; (2) Secretary of State for the Home Department (Defendants); and (3) Disclosure and Barring Service (Interested Party)* [2013] EWHC 2721 (Admin) [28].

[648] The relevant statutory provision at that time.

[649] The amended statutory test reflects that in existence previously, other than the insertion of the standard of 'reasonable belief' in s 113B(4)(a).

[650] *R (L)* (n 646) [75].

[651] Contrary to the previous position of *R (X) v Chief Constable of West Midlands* [2005] 1 WLR 65.

[652] See www.gov.uk/government/uploads/system/uploads/attachment_data/file/118017/statutory-disclosure-guidance.pdf. This Guidance should be read together with the Quality Assurance Framework jointly published by ACPO and the DBS, CRB/ACPO, Quality Assurance Framework (Version 9), 2013.

[653] *R (A) v Chief Constable of Kent Constabulary* [2013] EWHC 424 [60].

[654] *R (C) v Secretary of State for the Home Department* [2011] EWCA Civ 175; *R (L) v Chief Constable Cumbria Constabulary* [2013] EWHC 869 (Admin) [88].

[655] *R (J) v Chief Constable of Devon and Cornwall* [2012] EWHC 2996 (Admin); *R (W) v Chief Constable for Warwickshire* [2012] EWHC 406 (Admin); *R (L)* (n 646) [88]; *R (RK) v (1) Chief Constable of South Yorkshire; (2) Disclosure and Barring Service* [2013] EWHC 1555 (Admin).

[656] *C* (n 654); *RK*, ibid.

       Rachel Taylor and Piers von Berg

iv.   age of applicant at the time of the alleged incident; and,

v.   credibility of information.[657]

In determining credibility, chief officers are required to directly assess the available evidence and take reasonable steps to 'ascertain the truth'. A defence based on lack of resources to carry out this task is unlikely to be accepted.[658] In considering this matter, the court will take into account (i) the standard of investigation initially carried out and (ii) whether the matter has been before a court forum.[659]

Findings made by other bodies should also ordinarily be taken into account. For example, in *R (A) v Chief Constable of Kent Constabulary*,[660] the High Court held that the fact that other bodies, such as the CPS, NMC and ISA, had not upheld the allegations was 'highly relevant'.[661] However, in *R (W) v Chief Constable for Warwickshire*[662] the High Court held that the Chief Constable had been entitled to pay limited weight to the claimant's successful claim for unfair dismissal, and to reach a different decision to the Employment Tribunal, which:

i.   had limited evidence presented to it;

ii.   was considering a different issue involving different factors; and,

iii.   was in any event concerned with a different legal test.[663]

(vi) 'Ought to be Disclosed'

Even where information is deemed to be relevant, an issue remains as to whether the   **4-116**
interference is proportionate;[664] balancing an individual's private life against the 'pressing social need' to protect vulnerable people.[665] In determining whether information 'ought to be disclosed', the statutory guidance requires that the following be taken into account:

i.   The impact of disclosure on the private life on the applicant or a third party, which will require that the disclosure:

(a)   has a legitimate aim;[666]

(b)   is necessary to pursue that aim; and

(c)   is proportionate.[667]

ii.   Any adverse impact of disclosure on the prevention or detection of crime.

---

[657]   *C* (n 654); *J* [2012] (655); *L* (n 654) [74].

[658]   *A* (n 653) [58].

[659]   *L* (n 654).

[660]   *A* (n 653).

[661]   ibid [66]. See also *L* (n 654).

[662]   *R (W) v Chief Constable for Warwickshire* [2012] EWHC 406 (Admin).

[663]   ibid (n 655) [43]–[55].

[664]   *AR* (n 564) [6]–[8], see also *Huang v Home Secretary* [2007] 2 AC 167 [13], *R (SB) v Governors of Denbigh High School* [2007] 1 AC 100 [30] (Lord Bingham).

[665]   *L* (n 654) [42] (Lord Hope).

[666]   Which will not normally be in dispute.

[667]   *RK* (n 655).

(vii) Standard of Review

4-117 There has been some dispute over the appropriate role of the court in considering these cases, and the extent to which deference should be paid to the primary decision-maker. The courts have largely resisted any restriction to their role in this respect, instead engaging in a direct and comprehensive examination of the issues in dispute and the available evidence.[668] Indeed, a failure to apply such an approach has been said to itself constitute a breach of section 6(1) of the HRA 1998.[669] As Stuart-Smith J stated in *L*:[670]

> my primary concern is to look at the substance of the arguments and evidence that should go into the balance on one side or another with a view to determining whether the defendant's decisions were sustainable or were wrong.

However, in *R (B) v Chief Constable of Derbyshire Constabulary*,[671] Munby LJ, giving judgment, cautioned against 'narrow textual analysis' which could technically enable a claim that a decision-maker had misdirected themselves, and instead endorsed a 'broad and common sense' approach to these matters.[672] Through this, Munby LJ warned against the over-extension of the court's role, and expressed disapproval of any judicial attempt to reformulate or revise an ECRC.[673]

Yet in *A*,[674] Lang J appeared not to heed Munby LJ's warning, and carried out an intensive review of the evidence, and the process by which the decision was made to disclose, even considering material that had not been known to the Chief Constable at that time. The court was highly critical of the decision maker, and concluded that the disclosure was disproportionate, quashing the decision to disclose, declaring it as unlawful and ordering that damages be awarded (to be assessed).

However, the case was then appealed in *R (A) v Chief Constable of Kent Constabulary*[675] principally on the grounds that (i) the standard of review employed had gone beyond the 'higher intensity review' appropriate in a judicial review where Convention rights are at issue; substituting the court for the primary decision maker; and (ii) the court had improperly taken into account material unavailable to the Chief Constable at the time the original decision had been made.[676] Importantly, the appellate court held that the court was required to make an objective assessment of proportionality. However, the standard of scrutiny employed should not be that of a full merits review, nor should it require the determination of issues of fact.[677] It was further held that information post-dating the decision should not be taken into account when there was no continuing duty imposed on the decision maker.[678]

---

[668] See, for example, *L* (n 654) [69] and *A* (n 653) [68]–[95].

[669] *L* (n 654) [69] and *A* (n 653) [43]. See also *Belfast City Council v Miss Behavin* [2007] 1 WLR 1420 [31], *Huang* (n 664) and *Manchester City Council v Pinnock* [2011] 2 AC 104.

[670] *L* (n 654) [68].

[671] *R (B) v Chief Constable of Derbyshire Constabulary* [2011] EWHC 2362 (Admin).

[672] ibid [66]; see also *Piglowska v Piglowski* [1999] 1 WLR 1360, 1372.

[673] ibid [88].

[674] *A* (n 653).

[675] *R (A) v Chief Constable of Kent Constabulary* [2013] EWCA Civ 1706.

[676] ibid, [6], [35].

[677] ibid, [43], [56].

[678] ibid, [67]–[92], contrary to the approach of Stuart-Smith J in *L* (n 654), [24]–[27].

Rachel Taylor and Piers von Berg

The Court of Appeal then itself considered the proportionality of the disclosure and concluded that it had been unlawful, largely due to concerns about the reliability of the allegations.[679] In doing so, the court stated that a prosecutor's decision that a prosecution should not proceed as the evidence was not such to provide a 'realistic prospect of conviction' would be a 'significant factor' in considering whether to make disclosure. A decision by a safeguarding body not to take any action would also be highly relevant.[680]

(viii) Representations

As above, the requirement that an individual be afforded an opportunity to make rep- **4-118** resentations against disclosure in 'cases of doubt' was fully established in *L* [2010]. This position is protected by the statutory guidance,[681] which stipulates that only 'in cases where there is no room for doubt that the information should be disclosed should a decision to disclose be taken without first giving the applicant an opportunity to make representations'.[682]

In *R (C) v Secretary of State for the Home Department*[683] the Court of Appeal affirmed the decision of the Divisional Court that the disclosure had been unlawful, in part, because of the failure of the chief officer to provide an opportunity for the claimant to make representations.[684] Although the court refused to set out in detail when representations would be required, emphasising that each case would be fact specific, helpful direction was provided by Toulson LJ in the formulation of the rhetorical question 'was it obvious that nothing [the applicant] could have said could rationally or sensibly have influenced the mind of the chief constable?'[685]

In *B*, Munby LJ emphasised that:

typically where a chief officer is considering the issue of an ECRC, it is likely to be appropriate for him to afford the applicant an opportunity to make representations, unless, for example, the facts are clear and not in dispute, and that typically this will appropriately be done by sending the applicant a draft of the proposed certificate and inviting his comments.[686]

A chief officer will thus be required to provide an opportunity to make representations prior to disclosure in the majority of cases, as was confirmed by Foskett J in *R (J) v Chief Constable of Devon and Cornwall*,[687] stating, 'it must be in very few such cases that such an opportunity should not be given'.[688]

---

[679] ibid, [93]–[99]
[680] ibid, [96].
[681] Home Office, Statutory Disclosure Guidance, July 2012, available at www.gov.uk/government/uploads/system/uploads/attachment_data/file/118017/statutory-disclosure-guidance.pdf.
[682] *L* (n 646) [27]. Para 26 lists the factors that should be taken into account in making these representations.
[683] *C* (n 654).
[684] Although the Court of Appeal held that the wide injunctive relief granted by the Divisional Court had been too broad. The court also held that there was no requirement for an oral hearing.
[685] *C* (n 654) [12].
[686] *B* (n 671) [60].
[687] *R (J) v Chief Constable of Devon and Cornwall* [2012] EWHC 2996 (Admin).
[688] ibid [46].

(ix) Disclosure of Documents

4-119   In order to make appropriate representations it will be advantageous to obtain disclosure of documents relating to the allegation. However, in *B* Munby LJ directed that full disclosure of documents would not ordinarily be required unless the gist of the information was insufficient to meet the requirements of Article 8 of ECHR. Even where additional disclosure is required, it should be limited and focused.[689]

Similarly, his Lordship was clear that an applicant will not be entitled to an oral hearing, or to be provided with an opportunity to cross-examine witnesses, prior to disclosure being made.[690]

(x) Article 6 of ECHR (Disclosure of Data)

4-120   As is clear from the above, challenges to disclosure will ordinarily be based on Article 8 of ECHR. However, an additional ground was put forward in *AR*, namely that disclosure was counter to the principle that 'everyone charged with a criminal offence shall be presumed innocent until proved guilty according to law', as protected by Article 6(2) of the ECHR. This argument was wholly rejected by Judge Raynor QC, on the basis that:

   i.   The purpose of Article 6(2) is to protect an individual from being treated in subsequent proceedings or by public officials as if he or she is guilty of the offence.
   ii.   Disclosure does not imply that an individual should have been convicted or is in fact guilty, but that he or she may have committed the offences.
   iii. The implication that, notwithstanding the acquittal, an individual might in fact have committed the relevant act does not constitute a breach of Article 6(2).[691]

In *B* the claimant submitted that Article 6 applies to the process by which disclosure is considered. This submission was rejected by the court, in reliance on the decision of the Supreme Court in *R (G) v Governors of X School (Secretary of State for the Home Department and another intervening)*.[692] In that case it was held, unanimously, that the 'civil right' in question in such cases is the right to practice one's profession and that the decision as to whether to disclose must therefore have 'a substantial influence or effect' on a subsequent determination of one's right to practise in order for Article 6 to be engaged.[693] In the present case this necessary causal connection was seen to be 'manifestly absent', rendering Article 6 inapplicable.[694] The claimant's alternative submission that Article 6 was engaged because there had been breaches of Article 8 was equally dismissed as a 'non sequitur'.[695]

4-121   Since 17 June 2013, ECRCs have only been sent to the individual applicant, whereas previously a copy was also supplied to the body requiring it.[696] This is of course likely to reduce

---

[689] *B* (n 671) [61].
[690] ibid [68]–[70].
[691] *AR* (n 564) [50]–[56].
[692] *R (G) v Governors of X School (Secretary of State for the Home Department and another intervening)* [2011] UKSC 30, [2011] 3 WLR 237.
[693] *G* (n 225) [69] (Lord Dyson), [90] (Lord Hope), [96] (Lord Brown) and [103] (Lord Kerr).
[694] *B* (n 671) [39]–[40] (Munby LJ).
[695] ibid [41].
[696] PFA 2012 (Commencement No 6) Order 2013.

the impact of any disclosure on the individual, who will her/himself be responsible for forwarding the ECRC to the registered body. Consequently, should an individual succeed in challenging the disclosure there is a reduced risk that a potential employer will have learnt of it, although problems may arise due to any consequential delay in delivering the ECRC.

An appeal mechanism has also been introduced, through which applicants can raise disputes with the DBS. The DBS will then pursue this with the police in order to ascertain whether the matter can be resolved. Where resolution is not possible, an Independent Monitor will consider the matter, and can direct the DBS to issue a new, amended certificate if appropriate. In accordance with the general principles, it will only be when this alternative remedy has been exhausted that judicial review proceedings should ordinarily be commenced.

(xi) Alternative Forms of Disclosure to Third Parties: Common Law

The disclosure of information is not solely effected through the system of criminal **4-122** records checks. The courts have consistently held in a variety of contexts that disclosure can be made notwithstanding the absence of any specific legislative power where it is in the public interest provided, of course, that an individual's rights under Article 8 of ECHR are appropriately balanced and the disclosure is in accordance with the data protection principles as listed in Schedule 1 of the Data Protection Act 1998.[697]

In *R v Chief Constable of North Wales Police, ex parte Thorpe*[698] the Court of Appeal upheld the finding of Lord Bingham LCJ in the Divisional Court that the police could inform the owner of a caravan site that certain residents were convicted paedophiles, due to the gravity of the risk posed.

In making this determination, Lord Woolf MR listed the following principles in relation to disclosure:[699]

i.   There is a general presumption against disclosure due to the impact this would have and the consequential risk to the public of individuals being driven underground.
ii. In certain circumstances there is a strong public interest in ensuring the police are able to disclose certain information should it be necessary for the prevention or detection of crime or protection of vulnerable people, put simply, where there is a 'pressing social need'.
iii. There should be no blanket policy regarding disclosure.
iv. The police should ordinarily consult with other relevant agencies prior to making disclosure.

These principles have been applied in a variety of contexts, as illustrated below.

---

[697] Although in *R (Regan) v Chief Constable of the West Midlands* [2010] EWHC 2297 (Admin) disclosure of information to a prison governor regarding threat to a prisoner's life was held not to constitute 'decision-making' in a way that would give rise to judicial review, ibid [14].

[698] *R v Chief Constable of North Wales Police, ex parte Thorpe* [1999] QB 396.

[699] Although this case was heard prior to the HRA 1998 coming into force, regard was had to the influence of Art 8 of ECHR.

(xii) Disclosure to a regulator

4-123   The appellant in *Woolgar v Chief Constable of Sussex*[700] sought to contest the refusal of the court to grant an injunction restraining a chief constable from disclosing the contents of a police interview to the relevant regulator. It was contended that comments made in interview should be treated as confidential unless later used in bringing a criminal prosecution. The Court of Appeal held that although comments made in police interviews were indeed confidential if not used in criminal proceedings,[701] disclosure to a regulatory body could be justified by the public interest served through that body's proper functioning.

The court stated that where the police were in possession of confidential information which in their reasonable view should be considered by a professional regulatory body in the interests of public health or safety, that information could be disclosed. However, it was accepted that there was a need for a balance to be struck between the competing interests and that therefore the reasonableness of such disclosure could be subject to challenge. The court directed that due regard had to be paid to the requirements of Article 8 and that accordingly the police should inform an individual where disclosure was likely to occur in order that they could, if appropriate, seek the assistance of a court to obtain an injunction.

(xiii) Disclosure to Employer/Contracting Body

4-124   *R v Local Authority in the Midlands, ex parte LM*[702] concerned the disclosure of alleged sexual offences against children committed by the owner of a bus company providing transport to local schools, which had resulted in the termination of the company's contract.[703] In holding that the disclosure was unlawful in the circumstances, the court emphasised that in cases of alleged child or sex abuse, the police must balance the need to protect children against the individual's right to private life.[704] Although it would be neither possible nor desirable to set out an exhaustive list of factors to be taken into account, the following would ordinarily require consideration when contemplating such disclosure:

i.   the extent of the defendants' belief as to whether the events as said occurred, ie the credibility of the information;

ii.   the legitimacy of the interest of the third party in obtaining the proposed information; and

iii. the degree of risk posed if disclosure was not made.

---

[700] *Woolgar v Chief Constable of Sussex* [2000] 1 WLR 25.

[701] In accordance with *Taylor v Director of Serious Fraud Office* [1999] 2 AC 177.

[702] *R v Local Authority in the Midlands, ex parte LM* [2000] 1 FLR 612.

[703] The allegations made were that the claimant had (i) sexually abused his daughter; and (ii) sexually abused a child in his care during his employment as an officer in a hostel for vulnerable children. No further action had been taken pursuant to either the subsequent police investigations into the abuse of his daughter or internal investigations regarding the abuse in the hostel, although the family name had been placed on the Central Register of Child Protection as a multiagency conference had been of the view that LM's daughter had been sexually abused. The allegations dated back a number of years, and no subsequent allegations had been made, during which time he had been employed as a bus driver and teaching young individuals.

[704] Although this case was decided before the HRA 1998 came into effect due regard was paid to the relevant case law from the ECtHR.

In the present case the disclosure had been irrational, as it had not been required by any 'pressing social need'.[705] This conclusion was only strengthened by the fact that the defendant had erroneously adopted a blanket approach in making the disclosure.

(xiv) Schemes Relating to Specific Categories of Offender

As above, the common law permits disclosure to be made where it is deemed to be in the **4-125** public interest. However, increased concerns regarding sex offenders' access to children resulted in the Home Office Review of the Protection of Children from Sex Offenders in July 2007. This in turn led to the introduction of several measures aimed at protecting children from sexual abuse, two of which relate to disclosure.

The first was implemented through section 327A of the CJA 2003 and imposes a duty on each Multi-Agency Public Protection Arrangements ('MAPPA') authority to consider whether to disclose 'information in its possession about relevant previous convictions of any child sex offender managed by it' to any particular member of the public. There is a presumption in favour of disclosure where the authority has reasonable cause to believe that:

i.   a child sex offender managed by it poses a risk in that or any other area of caus-ing serious harm to any particular child or children or to children of any par-ticular description; and

ii. the disclosure of information about the relevant previous convictions of the offender to the particular member of the public is necessary for the purpose of protecting the particular child or children, or the children of that description, from serious harm caused by the offender.[706]

Comprehensive guidance has been issued in relation to the exercise of this disclosure duty.[707]

Secondly, in March 2010 the Home Secretary introduced 'The Child Sex Offender **4-126** (CSO) Disclosure Scheme Guidance Document' (CSOD), and Chief Constables have been able to adopt the (non-statutory) scheme since 1 August 2010. This enables mem-bers of the public to request the police to provide details to enable them to ascertain whether an individual that has contact with children has any convictions for sexual offences against children, or whether any other relevant information is held about them. CSOD provides that there will be a presumption of disclosure:

[i]n the event that the subject has convictions for sexual offences against children, poses a risk of causing harm to the child concerned and disclosure is necessary to protect the child.[708]

The scheme is broader than the MAPPA measures, principally because it:

i.   requires only risk of harm and not serious harm;
ii. is intended to give the public a right of disclosure; and
iii. is not confined to the disclosure of conviction data alone.

---

[705] See also *R (A) v B* [2010] EWHC 2361 (Admin).
[706] CJA 2003, ss 327A(2) and 327A(3).
[707] 'MAPPA Guidance 2012, version 4', available at www.gov.uk/government/uploads/system/uploads/attachment_data/file/281225/mappa-guidance-2012-part1.pdf.
[708] Home Office, 'The Child Sex Offender (CSO) Disclosure Scheme Guidance Document', para 2.2.

4-127 In *X (South Yorkshire) v Secretary of State for the Home Department*,[709] in which the Chief Constable of South Yorkshire was an interested party, the claimant sought to quash the CSOD Guidance on the basis that (i) it failed to provide an opportunity to make representations and (ii) the presumption of disclosure was not in accordance with the balancing exercise required by Article 8 of ECHR. The claim was upheld. Although the defendant sought to argue that *L* [2009] established that the disclosure of convictions did not give rise to a right to make representations, Sir John Thomas P distinguished the present case as:

    i.   The CSOD scheme applied to everyone who might come into contact with children.

    ii. The ECRC scheme considered in *L* had been approved by Parliament and was more limited in scope.

    iii. And, in any event, the CSOD scheme was not confined to disclosure of previous convictions.

The President also held that the Guidance required further revision to make it clear that the presumption of disclosure in paragraph 2.2 was subject to the procedural guidance laid out at section 5, thereby constituting the 'balancing exercise' required. The presumption of confidentiality is therefore retained, and disclosure should only be made where:

    i.   it is necessary to protect the child from being the victim of a crime by that offender;

    ii. there is a pressing need for such disclosure;

    iii. interfering with the rights of the offender under Article 8 is necessary and proportionate (with consideration being accorded to the impact on the offender); and

    iv. the disclosure is in accordance with the eight principles set out in the Data Protection Act 1998.[710]

The court also agreed that there should be a requirement that an individual be afforded an opportunity to make representations. However, it was seen to be disproportionate to quash the scheme, particularly as this would itself put children at risk of harm. Indeed, the court held that this step would not be necessary provided the defendant supplied a timetable for amendment of the Guidance.[711]

4-128 A similar system, the 'Domestic Violence Disclosure Scheme' was rolled out on 8 March 2014. This scheme, which has already been piloted, provides members of the public with a 'right to ask' whether an individual with whom they are associated has a history of domestic violence and a 'right to know', whereby the police may choose to disclose certain information to individuals seen to be at risk of such violence. The scheme does not have any statutory basis, and so disclosure will be made within the framework provided by existing legislation and case law.[712]

---

[709] *X (South Yorkshire) v Secretary of State for the Home Department* [2012] EWHC 2954.

[710] ibid [46].

[711] ibid [37]–[43].

[712] The applicable guidance can be found at www.gov.uk/government/uploads/system/uploads/attachment_data/file/224877/DV_Disclosure_Scheme_Guidance_-_REVISED_W.pdf.

     Rachel Taylor and Piers von Berg

(xv) Publication of Information Relating to Offenders

Less common are decisions that have been made to publicise information relating to   **4-129**
offenders or alleged offenders, ordinarily for the purpose or, purported purpose, of
protecting the public and/or deterring crime.

In *R (Ellis) v Chief Constable of Essex Police*[713] a police practice of displaying posters
featuring the names and photographs of offenders, their offence and their sentence was
held to engage Article 8(1) of ECHR. However, Lord Woolf LCJ was unable to determine
whether or not this practice was proportionate, as this would be dependent on the specific circumstances of each individual case. Relevant factors would include whether the
individual remained in custody and whether they had children who could potentially
be impacted by the disclosure.

Similarly, in *R (Stanley) v Commissioner of Police of the Metropolis*[714] the claimants
sought to challenge decisions made by the police force and local authority to distribute
leaflets containing their photographs, names and ages and the details of Anti-Social
Behaviour Orders (ASBOs) said to have been made against them.[715] The Divisional
Court refused the application on the basis that ASBOs were orders requiring publicity
to ensure their effective operation, and the objective of providing information, reassur-
ance, enforcement and deterrence would be ineffective without the inclusion of an individual's photograph, names and partial addresses. In addition, there was no requirement
that the distribution of information be confined to the area from which the claimants
had been excluded.

Despite the severity of this approach, the court emphasised the need for the relevant
body, whether it be the local authority or the police, to have due regard to an individual's rights under Article 8 of ECHR; a blanket policy prioritising 'the rights of the
community' would not be sufficient for this purpose.[716] Yet it appears from the above
that objectives of crime prevention are likely to be accorded considerable weight by the
courts when balancing any infringement of an individual's Article 8 rights caused by
such policing methods.

(4) Undercover Policing

Concerns regarding covert policing have increased significantly over recent years, par-   **4-130**
ticularly as technological advancements have been reflected in more sophisticated police
practices. Surveillance activity is largely governed by the Regulation of Investigatory
Powers Act 2000 (RIPA), the Police Act 1997 Part III and the Protection of Freedoms
Act 2012, together with accompanying codes of practice.[717]

---

[713] *R (Ellis) v Chief Constable of Essex Police* [2003] EWHC 1321 (Admin).
[714] *Stanley* (n 46).
[715] Information was also published on the local authority's website and in a newsletter.
[716] *Stanley* (n 46) [42].
[717] See, for example, Home Office, 'Surveillance Camera Code of Practice', June 2013.

The level of public concern in this arena has been further heightened by revelations of practices of phone hacking, Project Tempora,[718] and disclosures by undercover police operatives.

(i) AKJ and others v Commissioner of Police of the Metropolis and others

4-131 *AKJ and others v Commissioner of Police of the Metropolis and others*[719] concerns claims relating to undercover police officers who, whilst operative, had engaged in intimate and sexual relationships with individuals who were unaware of their true identities. The claims being brought by the claimants are, variously, that the activities:

i. constituted a breach of Articles 3 and 8 of ECHR;
ii. constituted the torts of deceit, misfeasance in public office, assault and negligence; and
iii. breached the Data Protection Act 1998.

At the time of writing, the substantive cases had yet to be heard, but preliminary issues had arisen, primarily relating to the appropriate tribunal before which the cases should proceed.

The claimants contended that the cases should not be put before the IPT, which was created by RIPA in order to hear claims under HRA 1998 relating to conduct falling within the statute's remit. Extensive restrictions apply to these proceedings, which will ordinarily be heard in secret due to the sensitivity of the subject matter. Such procedural restrictions are likely to impact upon decisions regarding how a relevant claim can most appropriately be pleaded.

In determining this issue the High Court held that:

i. The IPT has exclusive jurisdiction to hear HRA claims regarding conduct falling within the remit of RIPA.[720]
ii. RIPA cannot authorise conduct amounting to an interference with a fundamental common law right or an unqualified ECHR right, and so such conduct cannot fall within its remit.[721]
iii. The IPT does not have jurisdiction to hear common law claims.[722]
iv. The fact that a common law claim arises from the same facts as a HRA claim does not render that claim an abuse of process, notwithstanding the existence of a 'neither confirm or deny' policy maintained by the defendant.[723]
v. In the interests of justice, IPT proceedings should precede those in the High Court.[724]

---

[718] Project Tempora was a secret programme run by GCHQ to intercept and store vast amounts of phone and internet data. At the time of writing, a challenge to practices of mass surveillance employed by the security services was pending before the Investigatory Powers Tribunal (IPT), to be heard in July 2014.
[719] *AKJ and others v Commissioner of Police of the Metropolis and others* [2013] EWHC 32.
[720] ibid [155]–[163].
[721] ibid [156].
[722] ibid [195]–[197].
[723] ibid [216]–[218].
[724] ibid [222].

Rachel Taylor and Piers von Berg

The Court of Appeal subsequently confirmed the IPT as the appropriate body to hear the HRA claims.[725] In so doing, the court held that the statutory authority[726] permitted officers to engage in sexual relationships (with such conduct falling within the definition of 'personal or other relationships'),[727] and thus that this had been intended by Parliament, despite that fact that this had never been contemplated by Parliament when the legislation was enacted.[728] However, the appellate court also determined that the High Court proceedings should not be stayed behind the IPT proceedings. It had not been shown that there was 'a real risk of injustice' if the High Court proceedings were to continue, and certainly not a risk outweighing the appellants' right to have the claims heard in open court.[729]

(5) Third Party Practices

The collection and retention of personal data by private persons has also caused a high level of concern over recent years and journalistic practices of 'phone hacking', for example, prompted a full public inquiry.[730] Although actions taken by private individuals or bodies will not ordinarily give rise to judicial review proceedings, it may be arguable in some circumstances that the state has a positive obligation to address such practices and ensure the protection of an individual's rights under the ECHR.[731]

4-132

In *R (Bryant) v Commissioner of Police of the Metropolis*,[732] the claimants sought to challenge the failure of the police to inform them of material which indicated that they might or had been victims of phone hacking. At an oral renewal hearing it was held to be at least arguable that the police were subject to such a positive obligation, in accordance with Article 8 of ECHR. Settlement was subsequently reached in the case, with the Metropolitan Police apologising for its failure to inform victims of the criminal acts that had been committed against them.

---

[725] *AJA and others v Commissioner of Police of the Metropolis and others* [2013] EWCA Civ 1342 [43] (Maurice Kay LJ).

[726] RIPA, s 27.

[727] Ibid, s 26(8)(a).

[728] *AJA and others* (n 725), [32].

[729] ibid [65].

[730] 'An inquiry into the culture, practices and ethics of the press: report [Leveson]', The Stationery Office, 29 November 2012, available at www.gov.uk/government/uploads/system/uploads/attachment_data/file/270939/0780_i.pdf.

[731] See *Osman* (n 62).

[732] *R (Bryant) v Commissioner of Police of the Metropolis* [2011] EWHC 1314 (Admin), [2011] HRLR 27.

5

The Crown Prosecution Service

(Including Other Prosecuting Authorities and Agencies)

PIERS VON BERG[1]

---

[1] The author is grateful to Sian Cutter for help with the initial drafts of this chapter.

A. General Principles

(1) Introduction

5-1 Judicial reviews of decisions by the Crown Prosecution Service (CPS) are relatively rare. They can provide some of the most interesting cases. The decisions that are usually subject to challenge are:

    i.   decisions to charge or to prosecute;

    ii. decisions not to charge or to discontinue a prosecution; and

    iii. refusals to give undertakings not to prosecute.

Claimants have also challenged the CPS's policy, for example the policy on prosecuting those who assist others to take their lives. This chapter will also consider applications to obtain declarations concerning the lawfulness—in the criminal sense—of future conduct.

Generally, judicial reviews of the first category are very difficult to bring. The courts consider the CPS to have a wide margin of discretion in deciding whether to charge a person.

The courts also are very reluctant to allow judicial review to delay ongoing proceedings, especially where the criminal court can provide alternative remedies. These decisions are considered in section B.

Claimants in the second category have a lesser hurdle to surmount. They cannot apply to the criminal court to stay proceedings and, as proceedings have not been instituted, they cannot be criticised of delaying any. They are expected to first make use of the CPS's own review mechanisms, and in any event, they still have to show that the decision fell outside a very wide ambit of discretion. These decisions are considered in section C.

(2) The Role of the CPS

5-2 The Director of Public Prosecutions (DPP) as head of the Crown Prosecution Service (CPS) is primarily responsible for taking over the conduct of criminal proceedings instituted on behalf of a police force.[2] The police commence proceedings when they have made the arrest, conducted the investigation and brought the defendant into custody.[3] The DPP has a discretion to take over prosecutions in any other case.[4]

The CPS advises the police on possible prosecutions and reviews cases sent to it for prosecutorial decisions. The division of labour is set out in the 'Director's Guidance on

---

[2] The Prosecution of Offences Act 1985, s 3(2)(a). There is a wide range of prosecutions which the DPP is under a duty to undertake or may take over (see ss 3(2)(b)–(g)). The DPP's position under s 1(1)(a) of the 1985 Act is 'head of the Service'.

[3] See *R v Stafford Justices, ex parte Customs and Excise Commissioners* (1991) 2 All ER 201 and *R (Hunt) v Criminal Cases Review Commission* [2001] QB 1108, [2001] 2 WLR 319. See below at 5-43–5-44 on the relationship with other prosecuting bodies.

[4] The Prosecution of Offences Act 1985, s 6(2).

Charging'.[5] This states that the CPS will take the charging decision in all cases except those set out at paragraph 15, which include:

(i)   any Summary Only offence (including criminal damage where the value of the loss or damage is less than £5000) irrespective of plea;

(ii) any offence of retail theft (shoplifting) or attempted retail theft irrespective of plea provided it is suitable for sentence in the magistrates' court; and

(iii) any either way offence anticipated as a guilty plea and suitable for sentence in a magistrates' court;

provided that this is not:

— a case requiring the consent to prosecute of the DPP or Law Officer;
— a case involving a death;
— connected with terrorist activity or official secrets;
— classified as Hate Crime or Domestic Violence under CPS Policies;
— an offence of Violent Disorder or Affray;
— causing Grievous Bodily Harm or Wounding, or Actual Bodily Harm;
— a Sexual Offences Act offence committed by or upon a person under 18;
— an offence under the Licensing Act 2003.

Note that the CPS may take charging decisions in the above cases (i)–(iii) if those offences are related to an offence which has been referred to them. It follows that judicial reviews of CPS decisions to charge will inevitably involve more serious offences.

The CPS prepares and presents cases at court. It can be involved in judicial reviews of criminal courts as an interested party by virtue of being party to the proceedings.[6] It also brings judicial reviews against the criminal courts.[7]

The vast majority of judicial review challenges to prosecutions concern prosecutions instituted by the CPS, as it is the principal prosecuting authority for England and Wales and so these are the main focus of this chapter.[8]

(3) Identifying the Defendant, the Decision and Timing of the Challenge

It is submitted that the correct practice in challenging decisions by CPS prosecutors is to name the CPS as the defendant, unless the decision involves the DPP himself or is taken under his direction. The DPP is the respondent to appeals by way of case stated, although it is not unknown for the CPS to be named as the respondent in such appeals.[9] There are a range of different stages the CPS may be involved in, and it is important to distinguish whether it is a decision by the CPS or the police. If the decision is taken by another prosecuting agency, for example the Environment Agency, then that decision-maker should be named as the defendant. These bodies may have their own separate procedures for decision-making as concerns enforcing sanctions and undertaking

5-3

---

[5] Crown Prosecution Service, *Director's Guidance on Charging*, 5th edn, May 2013, paras 15-16. Available on the CPS website at www.cps.gov.uk/publications/directors_guidance/dpp_guidance_5.html#a02. This was issued under PACE 1984, s 37A.
[6] CPR PD 54A paras 5.1–5.2.
[7] Eg *R (Crown Prosecution Service) v Norwich Magistrates' Court* [2011] EWHC 82 (Admin) or *R (Crown Prosecution Service) v Ipswich Crown Court* [2010] EWHC 1515 (Admin).
[8] For judicial reviews concerning other prosecuting bodies, see below at 5-43–5-44.
[9] Eg *H v Crown Prosecution Service* [2010] EWHC 1374 (Admin), [2012] QB 257.

prosecutions that are distinct from the CPS, and they may take those decisions within the context of and with reference to a regulatory framework.[10]

Challenges to decisions to prosecute will arise when a criminal defendant invites the prosecuting body to discontinue a prosecution or offer no further evidence and it refuses. Conversely, challenges to CPS decisions not to prosecute will arise when the CPS elects to follow either of these routes. In addition, in certain cases, set out above, the CPS may also take a charging decision. A claimant may challenge a decision of the CPS to charge, a decision to charge a particular offence or not charge a certain offence, or, a decision not to charge any offence(s) at all. A claimant may also challenge a decision to administer an out-of-court disposal, such as a caution, or refuse to consider such an option. All these decisions are described below. The latter two types of decision are far more common as the others fall within scope of the proceedings, which for reasons explained below, are unlikely to be susceptible to challenge.

To be clear, a prosecutor has various options to seek a termination of the proceedings. He can i) apply to discontinue the proceedings under section 23 (magistrates' court) or section 23A (Crown Court) of the Prosecution of Offences Act 1985, ii) apply to withdraw the case, or iii) offer no evidence. In Crown Court the Attorney General can enter a *nolle prosequi* and the court has a power to quash the indictment on application by either of the parties. It is important to distinguish between these, as they apply at different stages in the proceedings and have different effects. Under discontinuance and withdrawal, proceedings can be reinstituted, but this is rare in the absence of fresh evidence. In the case of discontinuance, they cannot be taken without leave of the court and after the trial has begun; whereas an application to withdraw cannot be made after a plea has been taken. A decision to offer no further evidence is available to a prosecutor at any time before the completion of the prosecution case. It is ultimately a matter for the prosecutor and results in the acquittal of the defendant.[11]

If a prosecutor accedes to a request not to prosecute and there is no acquittal, parties should be aware of the rules on abuse of process in respect of breaches of representations not to prosecute (see below at 6-38), if any proceedings are re-instituted or are contemplated at a later date.

The timing of a judicial review challenge is of vital importance. First, if the matter is already before the Crown Court, the High Court has very limited jurisdiction. The exact rules on this are set out in Chapter 7 at 7-2–7-3 and see also above at 1-25 Therefore, if a claimant is of the view that judicial review is an appropriate challenge to a prosecutorial decision relating to an indictable offence or an offence for which the magistrates' court is unlikely, or would not accept jurisdiction, that challenge should be made before the Crown Court is seized of the matter.[12] Secondly, if the matter is before a magistrates' court, a claimant should exhaust any suitable remedies in the ongoing proceedings before resorting to judicial review. For example, if the complaint is that it is

---

[10] For example, see Environment Agency, *Enforcement and Sanctions—Guidance*, Operational Instruction 1356-10, Version 2, 2011, pp 11–15.

[11] See *R v Grafton* [1993] QB 101, [1992] 3 WLR 532, 107B: 'It cannot in our judgment be right that a judge can refuse to allow the prosecution to discontinue before their case is concluded if he believes the evidence already called raises a prima facie case'.

[12] See discussion below at 7-5 of the decision in *R (Securiplan Plc, Phillip Ullmann,Sabrewatch Ltd, Luke Lucas) v Security Industry Authority* [2008] EWHC 1762 (Admin), [2009] 2 All ER 211.

unfair to try the defendant because of some alleged fault on the part of the CPS, then an application can be made to stay the proceedings on grounds of abuse of process. Judicial review can be sought of any adverse decision resulting from such an application (see below at 6-34–6-37) Therefore, potential claimants should be mindful of limited utility of judicial review in proceedings in the Crown Court and careful to identify what faults in the prosecutorial decision-making that can be, or not, as the case may be, adequately remedied within summary proceedings.

In any case, at whatever stage, once the CPS has the matter before it, a prosecutor is under a continuing duty to review a case and 'must take account of any change in circumstances that occurs as the case develops'.[13] The CPS will also review charging decisions made by the police prior to the first hearing.[14]

Before proceedings are instituted there are various stages at which the CPS may be involved.

(i) Criminal Investigations

The CPS may be involved in the very early stages of the criminal process in advising   **5-4** on the conduct of criminal investigations. However challenges to decisions made in criminal investigations should properly be made against the police and, in any event, are extremely rare due to the wide scope of discretion granted to the police (see above at 4-13–4-15). As can be seen from the preceding chapter, decisions made to arrest, search or detain a person are those of the police, and the relevant chief constable is the correct defendant.

(ii) Out-of-Court Disposals

The same principle applies to decisions by the police to grant or refuse out-of-court   **5-5** disposals also known as 'diversion from prosecution'. A decision to grant an out-of-court disposal is most commonly take by a police officer but it may be taken by the CPS under section 37B of PACE 1984 if the case is sent to it for a charging decision.[15] For example, indictable only offences that are considered by an officer suitable for a caution or conditional caution must be referred to the CPS.[16] A common challenge is to decisions to prosecute rather than offer an out-of-court disposal. An account of these types of judicial reviews is given at 4-87 and at 11-26.

(iii) Decisions to Charge

Potential claimants should be careful to distinguish whether this is a decision made by   **5-6** the police, for example, by a custody officer under section 37(7)(b) of PACE 1984, or by

---

[13] Crown Prosecution Service, *Code for Crown Prosecutors*, January 2013, para 3.6.
[14] See the *Director's Guidance* (n 5), para 21.
[15] *Code for Crown Prosecutors* (n 13), para 3.6.
[16] *Director's Guidance* (n 5), para 19.

the CPS under section 37B of PACE 1984.[17] Offences that can and cannot be charged by the police are set out above.

(iv) Decisions to Charge Particular Offences

5-7   Claimants can in principle challenge a decision to choose a particular offence to charge. An example of an area of controversy is the charging of section 5 (rape of a child under 13) or section 13 (sexual activity with a child) under the Sexual Offences Act 2003. Broadly speaking, criminal defendants have argued that in cases where a victim has consented, section 13 should be preferred (this is discussed in detail below at 11-35).[18]

(4)   The Decision-Making Process

5-8   A decision to prosecute by the CPS is based on the criteria set out in the *Code for Crown Prosecutors* (the 'Code'),[19] Director's Guidance on Charging[20] and the CPS's legal guidance for particular offences. There may also be policies on particular areas, for example, on domestic violence or religious or racist crime.[21] There is a two-stage process, called the 'Full Code Test':

    i.   The 'evidential stage': 'Prosecutors must be satisfied that there is sufficient evidence to provide a realistic prospect of conviction against each suspect on each charge.'[22] A realistic prospect of conviction is understood as a balance of probabilities test. Only if this stage is satisfied should a prosecutor go on to consider the second stage.

    ii. The 'public interest stage': 'A prosecution will usually take place unless the prosecutor is satisfied that there are public interest factors tending against prosecution which outweigh those tending in favour.'[23] It is at this stage that out-of-court disposals are considered. If a prosecutor considers that the case merits court proceedings, then there is a range of factors listed in the Code that should be considered.

Judicial reviews of decisions to prosecute or not to prosecute can target failures or errors by a decision-maker at either or both stages. For example, a claimant can argue that a prosecutor has make mistakes of fact in assessing the evidence, or has omitted to consider a material piece of evidence or given weight to irrelevant evidence (see below at 5-36). A claimant can contend that the CPS has not considered factors pertaining to the public interest, for example, in the case of youths, the age, background and criminal record of a suspect (see below at 5-22). Overall, a decision that has substantially departed from the CPS's applicable policies can be challenged for that reason as well (see below at 5-20).

---

[17]   Note that there is a range of offences for which the consent of the DPP is required in order to commence a prosecution.

[18]   See *R (S) v DPP* [2006] EWHC 2231 (Admin). This is covered below at 11-35.

[19]   *Code for Crown Prosecutors* (n 13).

[20]   *Director's Guidance* (n 5).

[21]   See the 'Other Guidance' on the CPS website—www.cps.gov.uk/publications/prosecution/index.html.

[22]   *Code for Crown Prosecutors* (n 13), para 4.4.

[23]   ibid, para 4.8.

(5) The Constitutional Position of the DPP

The first issue in any judicial review involving the CPS is that the scope for review is very **5-9**
narrow. The courts recognise that the DPP and other independent prosecuting bodies[24]
have an important constitutional position, as bodies independent of the executive, solely
entrusted with powers to make difficult judgments and assessments in the public interest. This will apply to decisions to prosecute and decisions not to prosecute.[25] Therefore,
judicial review of their actions is 'highly exceptional'. In *R (Corner House Research) v
Director of the Serious Fraud Office*,[26] Lord Bingham said:

> The reasons why the courts are very slow to interfere are well understood. They are, first that the
> powers in question are entrusted to the officers identified, and to no one else. No other author-
> ity may exercise these powers or make the judgments on which such exercise must depend.
> Secondly, the courts have recognised (as it was described in the cited passage of *Matalulu v
> Director of Public Prosecutions* [2003] 4 L.R.C. 712 at 735–736]) 'the polycentric character of
> official decision-making in such matters including policy and public interest considerations
> which are not susceptible of judicial review because it is within neither the constitutional func-
> tion nor the practical competence of the courts to assess their merits.'

> Thirdly, the powers are conferred in very broad and unprescriptive terms.[27]

(6) Grounds for Review

This is not to say that the CPS is immune from judicial review. In the above-cited case, **5-10**
Lord Bingham went on to set out the various bases on which a challenge can be brought:

> the discretions conferred on the Director are not unfettered. He must seek to exercise his pow-
> ers so as to promote the statutory purpose for which he is given them. He must direct himself
> correctly in law. He must act lawfully. He must do his best to exercise an objective judgment on
> the relevant material available to him. He must exercise his powers in good faith, uninfluenced
> by any ulterior motive, predilection or prejudice.[28]

This holds as a general statement of principle but as shall be seen below there are differing considerations applicable to decisions to prosecute as opposed to decisions not
to prosecute.

---

[24] Note that not all prosecuting bodies will be independent of the state—see below for how this might affect
the level of deference granted by the court at 5-44.

[25] See *L v DPP and Commissioner of the Police for the Metropolis* [2013] EWHC 1752 (Admin) [5]–[6] (Sir
John Thomas P).

[26] *R (Corner House Research) v Director of the Serious Fraud Office* [2008] UKHL 60, [2009] 1 AC 756. See
also above at 4-14.

[27] ibid [31] (Lord Bingham), with whom Lord Hoffmann, Lord Rodger and Lord Brown agreed. Although
this case involved the Director of the Serious Fraud Office, its principles have been applied in challenges to
decisions by the DPP (eg *R (Gujra) v Crown Prosecution Service* [2011] EWHC 472 (Admin), [2012] 1 WLR
254 [40], a decision upheld on appeal to the Supreme Court—see below at 5-42). For a statement of the
three interests a prosecutor must take into account—the state, the defendant and the victim—see *R v B* [2003]
2 Cr App R 197 [27] (Lord Woolf LCJ). See above at 1-14.

[28] ibid [32].

5-11   There may be cases where there is insufficient evidence to charge a suspect, but there is a substantial risk of bail offences if the suspect is released. Prosecutors must then apply the 'Threshold Test':

    i.   There is insufficient evidence currently available to apply the evidential stage of the Full Code Test; and

    ii.   There are reasonable grounds for believing that further evidence will become available within a reasonable period; and

    iii.   The seriousness or the circumstances of the case justifies the making of an immediate charging decision; and

    iv.   There are continuing substantial grounds to object to bail in accordance with the Bail Act 1976 and in all the circumstances of the case it is proper to do so.[29]

If these criteria are met, two further questions must be addressed: i) is there reasonable suspicion (explained at paragraph 5.6 of the Code), and ii) can further evidence be gathered to provide a realistic prospect of conviction (explained at paragraphs 5.8–5.10 of the Code)? If both these criteria are met, a prosecutor should apply the public interest test.

B. Decisions to Prosecute

(1) The General Rule: *Ex p Kebilene*

5-12   *R v DPP, ex parte Kebilene and Ors*[30] is an important authority in this area. In short, the House of Lords sharply curtailed the scope for review of a decision to prosecute by the CPS. The claimants challenged a decision of the DPP to consent to continue with a retrial of an offence. They argued this was contrary to Article 6(2) of the European Convention on Human Rights (ECHR). The principal ground of review was that section 16A of the Prevention of Terrorism (Temporary Provisions) Act 1989 created a reverse burden on the defendant, thus undermining the principle of the presumption of innocence.[31] This was an issue on which the original trial judge had ruled in the claimants' favour. The DPP had subsequently taken independent legal advice which concluded that the trial judge had ruled incorrectly and, as a consequence, the decision was made to continue with the prosecution. The claimants argued this was an error of law and the Divisional Court, led by Lord Bingham LCJ, agreed.

---

[29] *Code for Crown Prosecutors* (n 13), para 5.2.

[30] *R v DPP, ex parte Kebilene and Ors* [2000] 2 AC 326, [1999] 3 WLR 972.

[31] See Lord Hope's speech in particular (ibid 377B–378E, 383E–386D) and his important remarks on the question of deference to an elected body or person on issues of 'high constitutional importance' (381B–D). The issue of reverse burdens and the presumption of innocence is a complex area that has developed subsequently in appeals to the Court of Appeal and by way of case stated, but not by way of judicial review. The lead case is *Sheldrake v Director of Public Prosecutions* [2004] UKHL 43, [2005] 1 AC 264. There have been a number of successful and failed challenges to 'read down' a legal burden to an evidential burden under HRA 1998, s 3(1). See *Sheldrake* for an example of both and a review of the ECHR and domestic case law.

The House of Lords reversed this decision on appeal. Lord Steyn, giving the lead judgment, with whom Lord Slynn and Lord Cooke agreed, accepted that the defendants could apply to the trial judge for a ruling on the interpretation of section 16A and, if convicted, they could raise the issue on appeal.[32] The matter could also be addressed by submitting that the prosecution was an abuse of process.[33] Quite simply, they were not without an alternative remedy.

More importantly, as a matter of principle, section 29(3) of the Senior Courts Act 1981 excluded the High Court's jurisdiction over the Crown Court from any matters relating to trial on indictment. Section 29(3) provides:

> In relation to the jurisdiction of the Crown Court, other than its jurisdiction in matters relating to trial on indictment, the High Court shall have all such jurisdiction to make orders of mandatory, prohibiting or quashing orders as the High Court possesses in relation to the jurisdiction of an inferior court.[34]

Although Lord Steyn accepted the Divisional Court's interpretation that this only affected 'orders directed to and affecting the Crown Court's exercise of its jurisdiction in matters relating to trial on indictment',[35] the effect of the Divisional Court's judgment, in allowing a judicial review during ongoing proceedings, was highly disruptive: 'The potential for undermining the proper and fair management of our criminal justice system may be considerable.'[36] By allowing the claim, the Divisional Court had introduced unnecessary delay to the criminal process with satellite litigation on matters which should have been dealt with within the trial process itself.[37] As counsel for the criminal defendants accepted, there was in fact a common law principle, independent of section 29(3), that 'provides a strong presumption against the Divisional Court entertaining a judicial review application where the complaint can be raised within the criminal trial and appeal process'.[38]

Essentially, the court held that decisions to prosecute were not amenable to judicial review unless there was dishonesty, bad faith or other exceptional circumstances (these are explored in more depth below).[39] The rationale is that the trial process itself allows

---

[32] *Ex p Kebilene* (n 30) 370H–371A. Lord Hope observed that even if judicial review was available, a mandatory order could only require the DPP to reconsider, not change, his decision. However, the trial judge or the Court of Appeal could provide a more favourable interpretation of s 16A and therefore a more effective remedy (ibid 376C).

[33] ibid 371B.

[34] The Senior Courts Act 1981, s 29(3). For more detailed analysis on how this affects challenges to decisions of the Crown Court, see above at 1-25 and below at 7-2-7-3.

[35] ibid 369C. Lord Bingham's view was that the words of s 29(3) 'relate and relate only to orders directed to and affecting the exercise of its jurisdiction by the Crown Court. There is nothing to suggest that the words are intended to limit in any way the power of the High Court to make orders against any party other than the Crown Court'. Ibid 337A. See Laws LJ, 350C.

[36] ibid 370D.

[37] ibid 371G-H. That is not to say the three-judge Divisional Court, comprised of Bingham LCJ, Laws LJ and Sullivan J, did not properly entertain such considerations. In fact the judgment expresses acute awareness of them, but there were special circumstances in the case which merited intervention. Lord Bingham said that such applications must be scrutinised with the greatest care to avoid unnecessary delay in criminal proceedings, but if 'strongly arguable grounds for making application are shown … and if there are no discretionary grounds for refusing relief, leave to move may properly be granted; and if on full argument grounds for granting relief are established and no discretionary grounds shown for refusing it, such relief may properly be granted even though the consequence is a delay in the resolution of criminal proceedings'. Ibid 337E–F. See also 350D–E (Laws LJ).

[38] ibid 370D.

[39] ibid 371F.

for arguments by the defence concerning the appropriateness of the prosecution. It is, in effect, an extension of the policy behind section 29(3):

> If the substance of what is sought to review is the answer to some issue between the prosecution and defence arising during a trial on indictment, that issue may not be made the subject of review proceedings.[40]

It is vital to note that this ratio in *Ex p Kebilene* does not apply to decisions not to prosecute. As Lord Steyn said: 'That is, however, a wholly different situation because in such a case there is no other remedy.'[41] It is also notable that subsequent to *Ex p Kebilene* the courts have entertained challenges on grounds of breaches of human rights.[42]

5-13   An example of 'exceptional circumstances' is *R (D) v Central Criminal Court*[43] where Scott Baker LJ considered the claim by a defendant in proceedings in the Crown Court that his defence statement should not be disclosed to his co-defendants because it would endanger his safety and that of his family. The court accepted that there was a duty on the prosecutor under Articles 2 and 3 of ECHR to consider such risks, but in the instant case the prosecutor had satisfied himself that those risks could be minimised and the defendant adequately protected. The 'exceptional circumstances' test was reiterated in *R (Pepushi) v CPS*[44] by Thomas LJ:

> In view of the frequency of applications seeking to challenge decisions to prosecute, we wish to make it clear … that, save in wholly exceptional circumstances, applications in respect of pending prosecutions that seek to challenge the decision to prosecute should not be made in this court. The proper course to follow, as should have been followed in this case, is to take the point in accordance with the procedures of the Criminal Courts. In the Crown Court, that would ordinarily be by way of defence in the Crown Court and, if necessary, on appeal to the Court of Appeal Criminal Division. The circumstances in which a challenge is made to the bringing of a prosecution should be very rare indeed, as the speeches in *Kebilene* make clear.[45]

The claimant in *Pepushi* was being prosecuted by the CPS for using a false instrument, after entering the country with a false passport. Had he chosen to continue with his application, it would therefore have been dismissed as the issues raised could properly be dealt with as part of his trial.

(2) Challenges to Decisions to Prosecute in the Magistrates' Courts

5-14   The emphasis above on section 29(3) of the Senior Courts Act 1981 raises the question as to whether *Ex p Kebilene* applies to cases before the magistrates' courts. Lord Steyn

---

[40] ibid 394B. Note that this case was decided before the Human Rights Act (HRA) 1998 came into force. Lord Hope said that even if the HRA 1998 had been in force the defendants would still have a remedy within the trial process (ibid 375D). For challenges to advice based on Art 6 see *R (Barclay) v Secretary of State for Justice* [2013] EWHC 1183 (Admin).

[41] ibid 369F. Reliance was placed on *R v DPP, ex parte Chaudhary* [1995] 1 Cr App R 136, mentioned further below at 5-28.

[42] For example, see *SXH v Crown Prosecution Service* [2014] EWCA Civ 90 [68]–[71], discussed below at 5-34.

[43] *R (D) v Central Criminal Court* [2003] EWHC 1212.

[44] *R (Pepushi) v CPS* [2004] EWHC 798 (Admin).

[45] ibid [49] (Thomas LJ).

expressly distinguished such considerations and related authority.[46] In *Pepushi* the magistrates' court had committed the case to the Crown Court. Thomas LJ considered the general principle in *Ex p Kebilene* and said that if the challenge was to the decision of the magistrates' court on the issues in that case, or a decision not to prosecute, then the High Court 'would of course be the correct forum'.[47] Thomas LJ otherwise maintained the 'exceptional circumstances' test in *Ex p Kebilene* 'whether in the Magistrates Court or the Crown Court, [decisions to prosecute] cannot be challenged in this Court, save in exceptional circumstances of the kind described in *Kebilene*'.[48]

His Lordship subsequently elaborated on this as President of the Queen's Bench **5-15** Division in *R (Barons Pub Company) v Staines Magistrates' Court*[49] where the claimant argued that the prosecution was an abuse of process. The district judge refused the application, and the claimant applied for judicial review of that decision. The single judge invited the claimant to pose the question whether magistrates are permitted to conduct a 'mini judicial review' of a decision to prosecute. The Divisional Court rejected that notion: 'the Magistrates' Courts have no power of review of a prosecutorial decision other than through an abuse of process application'.[50] The magistrates' courts' jurisdiction is defined by statute in the Magistrates' Courts Act (MCA) 1980, the Courts Act 2003 and the Criminal Procedure Rules. Sir John Thomas P observed:

> if there is a challenge to the decision to prosecute, it must always be made in the criminal proceedings, unless there is some reason why it cannot be so made. The only way in which it can be made in Magistrates' Court proceedings is by an abuse of process application. That in itself is an exceptional remedy. It is only if that cannot be done, that there can be an application of this court.[51]

The court strongly discouraged applications for judicial review that may delay criminal proceedings, especially summary proceedings.[52] In light of this decision, it is submitted that defendants may not be criticised for challenging a decision of the CPS in the magistrates' court by way of abuse of process and, if unsuccessful, seeking judicial review.[53] Reference should be made to Chapter 6 below on when judicial reviews of magistrates' courts are appropriate (see below at 6-16–6-25).

---

[46] ibid 369F–G. Note however the similar concerns expressed in *R v Rochford Justices, ex parte Buck* (1979) 68 Cr App R114 regarding the potential disruption caused by judicial review applications during trials in the magistrates' courts, discussed below at 6-16–6-25.

[47] *Pepushi* (n 44) [46].

[48] ibid [47]. With respect, it may be queried to what extent this takes into account the differences between the Crown Court and magistrates' court—the former being a superior court of record afforded the protection of s 29(3) and the latter being an inferior court over which the High Court has a more express duty of supervision. See *R v Hereford Magistrates' Court, ex parte Rowlands* [1998] QB 110, [1997] 2 WLR 854 and *Haggarty's (Gary) Application* [2012] NIQB 14.

[49] *R (Barons Pub Company) v Staines Magistrates' Court* [2013] EWHC 898 (Admin).

[50] ibid [36].

[51] ibid [36].

[52] Although an example of its application could not be found, the Divisional Court (Kennedy LJ and Mance J) said in *R v Inland Revenue Commissioners, ex parte Allen* [1997] STC 1141 that if a judicial review of a decision to prosecute was used to deliberately obstruct criminal proceedings, the claimant would be subject to costs sanctions.

[53] For a recent example see *R (Kinsella) v DPP and Wrexham Magistrates' Court* [2013] EWHC (Admin).

(3) Where the Prosecution has Shown Bad Faith

5-16 'Bad faith' on the part of a prosecutor is a form of abuse of process namely that, if shown, it would be unfair for the defendant to be tried. It is defined in the criminal context as where:

> a court is not prepared to allow a prosecution to proceed because it is not pursued in good faith, or because prosecutors have been guilty of such serious misbehaviour that they should not be allowed to benefit from it to the defendant's detriment.[54]

Accordingly, there is a high hurdle to cross before a court will be satisfied that the prosecution has shown bad faith. In *R v DPP, ex parte Burke*,[55] proceedings were discontinued by the Crown, which agreed not to reinstate them in the absence of fresh evidence. The Crown reneged on that promise and recommenced proceedings against the claimant in the absence of fresh evidence. The DPP had formed the view that the original decision to discontinue was wrong. The application for judicial review was refused, on the grounds that the DPP retains a discretion to reinstate a prosecution without being required to demonstrate special circumstances in support of that decision (note the CPS's policy in the next paragraph). However, the Divisional Court appeared to accept that a complaint could be brought on grounds that the CPS had raised a legitimate expectation on the part of the defendant that he would not be prosecuted.[56] Such considerations may go to issues of abuse of process (see below at 6-34).

In subsequent cases the Divisional Court has stated that challenges to prosecutions alleging improper motive must show that the conduct was truly oppressive. The court would be slow to halt prosecutions brought for mixed motives.[57]

5-17 It is part of the CPS's policy to reconsider decisions to prosecute in certain circumstances. The Code identifies four specific scenarios:

  i.   cases where a new look at the original decision shows that it was wrong and, in order to maintain confidence in the criminal justice system, a prosecution should be brought despite the earlier decision;
  ii. cases which are stopped so that more evidence which is likely to become available in the fairly near future can be collected and prepared. In these cases, the prosecutor will tell the defendant that the prosecution may well start again;

---

[54] *R (Ebrahim) v Feltham Magistrates' Court* [2001] EWHC 130 (Admin), [2001] 1 WLR 1296 [19]. See also *Warren v Attorney General for Jersey* [2011] UKPC 10, [2012] AC 12: 'where the court's sense of justice and propriety is offended if it is asked to try the accused in the particular circumstances of the case'. Note the Privy Council accepted a category of abuse of process to include improper motives such as political pressure or influence, in *Sharma v Brown-Antoine* [2006] UKPC 57, [2007] 1 WLR 780. If what is alleged amounts only to incompetence, a claimant will not succeed *R (Samir) v Crown Prosecution Service* [2013] EWHC 2660 (Admin).
[55] *R v DPP, ex parte Burke* [1997] COD 169.
[56] Philips LJ said: 'I consider that if a letter is written which creates an expectation that there will be no further prosecution, this can be a material factor in deciding what the public interest requires'. This was relied on and considered in *R (SA) v DPP* [2002] EWHC 2983 (Admin) [34]. Another example is *R (O) v DPP* [2010] EWHC 804 (Admin).
[57] See *R v Bow Street Metropolitan Stipendiary Magistrate, ex parte South Coast Shipping* [1993] QB 645 followed in *R (Dacre) v Westminster Magistrates' Court* [2008] EWHC 1667 (Admin), [2009] 1 WLR 2241. Discussed in context of challenges to decisions of the magistrates' courts below at 6-32.

iii. cases which are stopped because of a lack of evidence but where more significant evidence is discovered later; and

iv. cases involving a death in which a review following the findings of an inquest concludes that a prosecution should be brought, notwithstanding any earlier decision not to prosecute.[58]

There is also a new scheme called the Victim's Right of Review, discussed in detail below at 5-36.

The claimants in *R (Gavigan) v Enfield Magistrates' Court*[59] applied for judicial review **5-18** of a decision made by the magistrates' court to refuse a stay of their prosecution for public order offences. The defendants chose to contest alleged offences under section 5 of the Public Order Act 1986, rather than pay fines under fixed penalty notices, which the police had issued to them. The police reviewed the case and charged them with more serious offences. Their case was that the prosecution had taken an unfair course by charging them with an offence more serious than that within the penalty notices. The High Court refused the application and stated that there was no established principle that a person who refuses a penalty notice should not be charged with a more serious offence based on the same set of circumstances.

Conversely, the CPS cannot substitute a lesser charge for a more serious offence unless it is proper and appropriate to do so on the facts of the case. In *DPP v Hammerton*,[60] Davis J rejected the argument that the CPS had an unfettered discretion to amend and proceed on any appropriate charge absent bad faith.

An example of a successful challenge is *R (Smith) v Crown Prosecution Service*.[61] **5-19** The defendant was charged with harassment. The parties agreed before the court that the matter could be disposed of with a restraining order without a trial. The case was adjourned, as the defendant was not present. At a later hearing, the prosecution reneged on this position, stating that the complainant or supporting agencies should be consulted. Ouseley J held that whilst a prosecutor is entitled to change his mind and was right to consider consultation, especially in this type of case, there had been an agreement before the court with no reservation that the matter would be reconsidered later.

(4) Where the CPS has not Followed its Own Policies

This was not a ground of review mentioned in *Ex p Kebilene,* but it is more akin to **5-20** Lord Bingham's test in *Corner House.* It is where the decision to prosecute has unjustifiably departed from usual prosecution practices, such as those in the Code and other CPS written policies (these are extensive, and specific policies may exist for particular

---

[58] *Code for Crown Prosecutors* (n 13),para 10.2.
[59] *R (Gavigan) v Enfield Magistrates' Court* [2013] EWHC 2805 (Admin).
[60] *DPP v Hammerton* [2009] EWHC 921 (Admin), [2010] QB 79.
[61] *R (Smith) v Crown Prosecution Service* [2010] EWHC 3593 (Admin).

offences, classes of offences or victims).[62] Lord Judge LCJ gave the following guidance in *R v A*,[63] which echoes the concerns of Lord Bingham in *Corner House*:

> In summary, when it is sought to advance an argument for a stay by reference to policy or guidance issued by the Director of Public Prosecutions, by way of emphasis it is worth repeating, first, that the decision whether to prosecute or not must always be made by the Crown Prosecution Service and not the court. The court does not make prosecutorial decisions.

> Second, provided there is evidence from which the jury may properly convict, it can only be in the rarest circumstances that the prosecution may be required to justify the decision to prosecute.

> Third, the decision whether or not to prosecute in most cases requires a judgment to be made about a multiplicity of interlocking circumstances. Therefore even if it can be shown that in one respect or another, part or parts of the relevant guidance or policy have not been adhered to, it does not follow that there was an abuse of process. Indeed, it remains open to the prosecution in an individual case, for good reason, to disapply its own policy or guidance.

5-21   Only CPS policies in force at the time of the decision are relevant, and CPS policies cannot be applied retrospectively. In *R v A* the Court of Appeal expressed a view which would apply to judicial reviews of decisions to prosecute. It was argued on behalf of the appellant that the decision to prosecute her for making a false retraction of rape against her husband would not have been taken in light of later CPS policy on victims of domestic abuse. That, however, was a policy which had not been in place at the time she was convicted of perverting the course of justice. The court stressed that, if the CPS has conscientiously applied its guidance and policy, it should not 'substitute its own view for that of the Crown about whether there should be a prosecution'.[64] The judgment also gives a reminder of the powers the criminal court has at its disposal, as opposed to remedies by way of judicial review, including an order for absolute or conditional discharge, and a grant of a stay in cases of oppression and misconduct.[65]

(5) Challenges to Prosecutions Involving Youths

5-22   A good example of a challenge to a CPS decision to prosecute on grounds of a failure to follow its policy concerns cases involving youths (understood as those aged under 18 for the purposes of this section). This area is expanded upon in the context of youths accused of sexual offences against other youths and vulnerable youths in Chapter 11 on children, young persons and juveniles below at 11-32. Review on these grounds will only succeed if it can be clearly shown that the CPS has i) completely failed to follow its own policies or ii) breached its policies by failing to properly enquire into the particular circumstances of the defendant.

---

[62] For details of the CPS's policies on prosecuting various offences and on dealing with issues such as violence against women and girls, see www.cps.gov.uk. See also the ACPO website for joint agreements between the CPS, ACPO and other public bodies on how to charge certain offences, offenders and seek other disposals (such as ASBOs)—eg CPS, NPIA and ACPO, *Guidance on Investigating and Prosecuting Rape*, abridged edn (2010), and ACPO, CPS and NHS Protect, 'Tackling violence and antisocial behaviour in the NHS, Joint Working Agreement between the Association of Chief Police Officers, the Crown Prosecution Service and NHS Protect', October 2011.
[63] *R v A* [2012] EWCA Crim 434 [84].
[64] ibid [83].
[65] ibid [83]–[84].

In *R v Chief Constable of Kent, ex parte L; R v DPP, ex parte B*,[66] applications for judicial review were refused.[67] In both cases it was argued that the CPS had failed to follow its own guidance on the prosecution of youths. As far as L was concerned, the argument was that a caution could, and therefore should have been administered. In B's case, it was submitted that although she could not receive a caution, the CPS, in deciding to prosecute her, had failed to examine all the circumstances of the case. With regards to L, it was held that the CPS had not failed to follow procedure on the cautioning of youths. The seriousness of the offence justified proceeding with prosecution against the defendant. As for B, there was nothing noted in the decision-making process of the CPS which demonstrated it had failed to enquire into the circumstances of B or to consider the effects of a conviction on her future prospects and welfare (a consideration required by the 1983 Attorney General's guidelines on prosecuting youths). The CPS had not therefore failed to properly consider whether it was in the public interest to prosecute her. The court commented that judicial review on such grounds would be unlikely to succeed:

> unless it could be demonstrated, in the case of a juvenile, that there had been either a total disregard of the policy or, contrary to it, a lack of enquiry into the circumstances and background of that person, previous offences and general character and so on, by the prosecutor and later by the CPS. But here too I envisage the possibility of showing that such disregard had happened as unlikely.[68]

In *R v Chief Constable of Kent, ex parte L (a minor)*,[69] Watkins LJ re-stated the position from *Ex p L, Ex p B*:

> in respect of juveniles, the discretion of the CPS to continue or to discontinue criminal proceedings is reviewable by this court but only where it can be demonstrated that the decision was made regardless of or clearly contrary to a settled policy of the Director of Public Prosecutions evolved in the public interest, for example the policy of cautioning juveniles, a policy which the CPS are bound to apply, where appropriate, to the exercise of their discretion to continue or discontinue criminal proceedings. But I envisage that it will be only rarely that a defendant could succeed in showing that a decision was fatally flawed in such a manner as that.[70]

An interesting example of a successful judicial review in this area is *R (E, S and R) v DPP*.[71] This highly unusual case was described by Lord Judge LCJ in *R v A*[72] as 'wholly exceptional'. The claimants were the defendant and the two complainants. They challenged the DPP's decision to prosecute a child, (E) aged 12, for the alleged sexual abuse of her two younger sisters (S, aged three and, R, aged two). A local authority multi-agency group produced a report for the CPS in which it was made clear that the police were alone in thinking the prosecution of E was in the best interests of the children concerned. The group had emphasised that whilst there was an ongoing prosecution, neither E nor her sisters would receive the vital support of which they were urgently in need, and that any further delay would severely impair their future recovery. There was a risk that if a prosecution went ahead, the parents might fail to cooperate with the

5-23

---

[66] *R v Chief Constable of Kent, ex parte L; R v DPP, ex parte B* [1991] 93 Cr App R 416.
[67] Applied in *R (F) v Crown Prosecution Service* [2003] EWHC 3266 (Admin), (2004) 168 JP 93.
[68] *Ex p L, Ex p B* (n 66) 428.
[69] *R v Chief Constable of Kent, ex parte L (a minor)* [1993] 1 All ER 756.
[70] ibid, 770.
[71] *R (E, S and R) v DPP* [2011] EWHC 1465 (Admin), [2012] 1 Cr App R 6.
[72] *R v A* (n 63) [82].

various agencies working to rehabilitate E and her sisters. Despite these factors, the CPS went on to conclude that there was both a reasonable prospect of conviction and that prosecution was in the public interest.

The claimants submitted that the CPS, in deciding to institute proceedings regardless of advice from outside agencies, had failed to follow its own policy on the prosecution of youths, a policy which emphasises the 'welfare' of the child. Of relevance was guidance laid down both in the Code and in the policy on the Sexual Offences Act 2003: 'Prosecutors must consider the interests of the youth when deciding whether it is in the public interest to prosecute'.[73] The High Court agreed and found that the CPS had failed to adhere to key elements of its own policies. It was emphasised that the welfare and interests of both the complainants, their families and the defendant are to be taken into consideration. For example, the decision letter from the CPS, which outlined its grounds for prosecution, made no reference to the need of all three girls for therapy and the risk to their rehabilitation posed by any delay. As Munby LJ stated, 'there is simply no explanation of how the report has been considered or as to why, given what had been said in the report, the decision was nonetheless to prosecute'.[74] In His Lordship's view, this was a wholly unsatisfactory way in which to proceed.

(6) Where the Decision to Prosecute is Perverse or Irrational[75]

5-24   A challenge on these grounds failed in *R (F) v CPS and Chief Constable of Merseyside Police*.[76] It is a good illustration of how the court approaches such a case, and it affirmed a high threshold for such challenges. Again, it was a case involving youths. The facts in this case deserve some description, as they demonstrate a common predicament. The claimant, aged 14, was stopped with four others in a stolen car. He refused to admit his part and so was not eligible for a reprimand or final warning under section 65 of the Crime and Disorder Act 1988. At the first court hearing his solicitor said he would be willing to accept a reprimand or final warning. A memorandum from the CPS to the police came to light advising that a final warning would be appropriate if the youth admitted the offence. However, the police decided not to re-interview the defendant, as proceedings were already underway. In response to representations from the defendant, the CPS elected not to discontinue.

The claimant submitted that both Merseyside Police, in refusing to re-interview him and administer a final warning, and the CPS, in refusing to discontinue proceedings against him, had failed to comply with sections 65–66 of the Crime and Disorder Act, or to follow the 2002 Home Office Guidance on the issue of reprimands and final warnings. The claimant stated that in light of the memorandum, and the refusal of the police to administer such warning, it was not in the public interest to pursue the prosecution, and therefore the CPS decision to continue was irrational and perverse.

The Divisional Court disagreed. Once the police made a decision not to administer a reprimand or final warning, the matter was taken out of their hands and it was for

---

[73] *Code for Crown Prosecutors* (n 13), para 8.2.
[74] *E, S and R* (n 71) [60].
[75] See discussion above of irrationality at 1-81–1-97.
[76] *R (F) v CPS and Chief Constable of Merseyside Police* [2003] EWHC 3266 (Admin).

the CPS to decide whether a prosecution should be pursued. The Crown Prosecutor in this case had considered all the evidence, come to the rational conclusion that there was a reasonable prospect of conviction and had given sound reasons for why it was in the public interest to continue with prosecution, given the prevalence of this sort of offending. The court stated it was unwilling to interfere with that discretion. Jackson J, with whom Rose LJ agreed, stated that:

> save in exceptional circumstances, it is quite inappropriate for this court to step into the shoes of the crown prosecutor and to retake decisions which Parliament has entrusted to the crown prosecutor under the Prosecution of Offences Act 1985.[77]

(7) Delay

Article 6(1) provides a right to a trial within a reasonable time: 5-25

> In the determination of his civil rights and obligations or of any criminal charge against him, everyone is entitled to a fair and public hearing within a reasonable time by an independent and impartial tribunal established by law.

An application to stay proceedings for abuse of process, rather than a claim for judicial review, will be the first step for a defendant who believes he has had to wait an unreasonable period of time to be tried (this form of abuse of process is also considered in above at 4-85 and below at 6-39). If proceedings have not been initiated, for example if a person has not been charged, and they allege that there has been an excessive delay by the CPS in reaching its charging decision, a question might arise as to whether judicial review would be appropriate. This section provides cautionary guidance for those contemplating judicial review of the CPS in such circumstances.

Article 6 may not be engaged and the time period for a delay may not start to run if the person has not been charged (see domestic case law above at 4-85). In contrast, the ECtHR understands time to run from the moment an individual is officially notified or substantially affected.[78] In the case law considered above at 4-85 this may be where a person is implicated in a police investigation, is interviewed, or the police or prosecutors have publicly declared an intent to prosecute a person. If a person has not been charged, claimants should be mindful of the Court's significant reluctance to intervene during an ongoing police investigation (see above at 4-14).

For periods of delay, the case law demonstrates that a reasonable period of time, as far as Article 6 is concerned, can be quite long. In *Dyer v Watson*[79] the Privy Council found that 20 months was not an unreasonable period of time between the charging decision and trial of two police officers for perverting the course of justice; although, in the case of a child, three and a half years between the date of charge and trial was considered unreasonable (see below at 11-6 and 11-41). If the period gives rise to real concern, a court should go on to consider the detailed facts and circumstances and the explanations provided by the state for the delay. This will include consideration of the complexity of the case, the conduct of the defendant and of the prosecuting authorities.

---

[77] ibid [77].
[78] See *Eckle v Germany* and *Dewer v Belgium* above at 4-85.
[79] *Dyer v Watson* [2004] 1 AC 379, [2002] 3 WLR 1488.

In *Dyer v Watson* the court was especially critical on the latter point (see further discussion below at 11-6 and 11-41 in the context of children).

Even if a person can make out an unjustified breach to their Article 6 rights, it does not necessarily follow that they will not be prosecuted. In *Attorney-General's Reference (No 2 of 2001)* (discussed below at 6-40) the House of Lords held that a court may only stay a prosecution where it would be unfair to try the defendant at all, or where there was some other compelling reason not to try the defendant.[80] The category of such cases included where there had been bad faith, unlawfulness or executive manipulation. The remedy must be fair, just and proportionate in the circumstances, including consideration of the stage of the proceedings, pursuant to section 8(1) of HRA 1998. A lesser remedy could be provided, if it would vindicate the defendant's Article 6 right, before the proceedings should be stayed. For example, such a measure might include compensation or mitigation of sentence.

5-26   Having considered these factors, it remains the case that the CPS is a public body that is obliged to act within the bounds of the law and pay proper consideration to its policies. Guidance issued under PACE 1984 to the CPS states that:

> Where Crown Prosecutors receive a 'Report to Crown Prosecutor for a Charging Decision' (MG3) accompanied by the information specified in Paragraph 7.2 below, it is the duty of the Crown Prosecutor to review the evidence as soon as is practicable, having regard to any bail return dates, and decide whether it is appropriate or not, at that stage, to charge the person with an offence or divert them from the criminal justice system.[81]

If a decision cannot be taken immediately, a person may be released on bail 'to permit the required information to be provided as soon as is practicable' (also note the threshold test above at 5-11).

Furthermore, the Code also states that the CPS should swiftly stop cases which do not meet the evidential stage of the Full Code Test and which cannot be strengthened by further investigation, or where the public interest clearly does not require a prosecution.[82]

C. Decisions Not to Prosecute

(1) General Principles

5-27   The scope for review for decisions not to prosecute is wider, because victims have no recourse to the trial process. Any such decision is final and, until the CPS introduced its Victim's Right to Review (VRR) policy, there was no effective remedy other than judicial review. The introduction of the VRR followed the case of *R v Killick (Christopher)* (discussed below at 5-37).[83] The Court of Appeal recognised that victims now have a

---

[80] *Attorney-General's Reference (No 2 of 2001)* [2003] UKHL 68; [2004] 2 AC 72, [29]. See also *Spiers v Ruddy* [2007] UKPC D2, [2008] 1 AC 873.

[81] Director of Public Prosecutions, *Guidance to Police Officers and Crown Prosecutors Issued by the Director of Public Prosecutions under S37A of the Police and Criminal Evidence Act 1984*, 3rd edn, February 2007, para 5.4

[82] *Code for Crown Prosecutors* (n 13), para 3.3.

[83] *R v Killick (Christopher)* [2011] EWCA Crim 1608, [2012] 1 Cr App R 10. The import of this decision and the case law in this area is helpfully described by the DPP at the time in Keir Starmer QC, 'Finality in criminal justice: when should the CPS reopen a case?' [2012] *Criminal Law Review* 526.

'right' to seek a review of a decision not to prosecute. This right is now given effect in the VRR scheme, which allows victims to seek a review of a prosecutorial decision. It is essential that practitioners are aware of it, as a failure to use it prior to issuing a claim for judicial review may incur costs (see below at 5-39). Also, as a note of caution, these types of decision are very difficult to challenge because due to their very nature they are speculative on how a case may fare before a court or jury:

> In most cases the decision will not turn on an analysis of the relevant legal principles but on the exercise of an informed judgment of how a case against a particular defendant, if brought, would be likely to fare in the context of a criminal trial before (in a serious case such as this) a jury. This exercise of judgment involves an assessment of the strength, by the end of the trial, of the evidence against the defendant and of the likely defences. It will often be impossible to stigmatise a judgment on such matters as wrong even if one disagrees with it. So the courts will not easily find that a decision not to prosecute is bad in law, on which basis alone the court is entitled to interfere.[84]

In *R (F) v Director of Public Prosecutions*[85] Lord Judge LCJ summarised the position today as follows:

> the decision not to prosecute may be shown to follow a perverse decision to disregard compelling evidence or inexplicably to ignore the relevant prosecutorial policy or policies, or a combination of both. It may, although as far as we know there have never been any such examples, follow some impropriety or abuse of power by those entrusted by the Director with the relevant responsibility. It may also be based on an error of law.[86]

Furthermore, victims must be aware that due to the constitutional position of the DPP and the attitude of the courts to prosecutorial decision-making (see above at 5-9), the High Court will not compel a prosecution to go ahead but merely quash the decision and remit to the CPS for reconsideration. This in itself does not guarantee a different outcome although any decision-maker would of course have to have regard to any relevant matters in the judgment.

(2) Categories of Review

In *R v DPP, ex parte Chaudhary*,[87] Kennedy LJ provided guidance on when a court may set aside a decision not to prosecute. First, the power to set aside such decisions would be used sparingly. The circumstances in which this may happen are: **5-28**

  i.   where the DPP has failed to act in accordance with his own settled policy;
  ii. where the policy is found to be unlawful; or
  iii. where the decision not to prosecute is perverse as one which no reasonable prosecutor could have made.[88]

These categories were confirmed by Sir John Thomas P in *L v DPP and Commissioner of the Police for the Metropolis*.[89]

---

[84] *R v DPP, ex parte Manning* [2001] QB 330 [23] (Lord Bingham LCJ).
[85] *R (F) v Director of Public Prosecutions* [2013] EWHC 945 (Admin) [2014] 2 WLR 190.
[86] ibid [6].
[87] *R v DPP, ex parte Chaudhary* [1995] 1 Cr App R 136, 140–41.
[88] This follows the test set out in *Ex p Chaudhary*.
[89] *L v DPP and Commissioner of the Police for the Metropolis* [2013] EWHC 1752 (Admin).

The claimant in *Ex p Chaudhary* sought a review of the CPS decision not to prosecute her husband, who was a police officer, for the offence of buggery against her. Medical evidence demonstrated damage consistent with repeated acts over a prolonged period of time, and her husband made no comment when questioned about the allegation. The High Court found that the DPP's decision not to prosecute was flawed. First, with the exception of consensual buggery between adult males over the age of 21, under the Sexual Offences Act of 1956 both consensual and non-consensual buggery were offences. The lawyer who made the decision not to prosecute had questioned in his affidavit whether it was appropriate to prosecute two consenting adults of different genders, when two males would not be guilty of any offence. This part of his decision-making process revealed that he was unduly influenced by consideration of the evidence supporting the consensual offence, when in fact what was alleged by the claimant was the more serious non-consensual offence. As such, the decision failed to have regard to a material consideration and was thus unreasonable.

In view of this the court maintained that the CPS had failed to adhere to its own policy. The lawyer failed to consider all possible lines of defence, as required by paragraph 4 of the Code. The court quashed the decision not to prosecute and remitted the matter to the DPP for reconsideration.

5-29   In *R v DPP, ex parte Manning*,[90] Lord Bingham LCJ developed the position further. The claimants' brother died in custody and they sought a review of a CPS decision not to prosecute any of the prison officers. A key feature of the case was that the deceased died in the custody of the state, and an inquest verdict was reached of unlawful killing. The court held that whilst there was no absolute duty of the CPS to give reasons not to prosecute, in cases that engaged the right to life in the context of detention by the state, there must be compelling grounds not to give reasons for the decision. The court found that the CPS had applied too high a standard to the evidence vis-à-vis that found in the Code.

In coming to this decision, the court again stressed that this power should be used sparingly and should respect the independence and expertise of the CPS, particularly where their task involved an exercise of judgment and an assessment of the strengths of the case at the end of a criminal trial. In contrast to the stringency of *Ex p Kebilene* (see above at 5-12), the court said this:

> the standard of review should not be set too high, since judicial review is the only means by which the citizen can seek redress against a decision not to prosecute and if the test were too exacting an effective remedy would be denied.[91]

5-30   This decision was challenged in *R (Da Silva) v DPP*.[92] The claimant's cousin (Jean Charles de Menezes), an innocent member of the public, was accidentally shot dead by police. The claimant sought judicial review of the DPP's decision not to charge any of the officers with murder or gross negligence manslaughter. It was argued that a more intensive standard of review should apply where Article 2 of ECHR, the right to life was potentially breached by the state.[93] A three-judge Divisional Court rejected this. It held that *Ex p Manning* applied and the CPS should be expected to abide by the Code in

---

[90]   *R v DPP, ex parte Manning* (2001) QB 330, [2000] 3 WLR 463. See above at 1-87.
[91]   ibid [23].
[92]   *R (Da Silva) v DPP* [2006] EWHC 3204 (Admin), [2006] Inquest LR 224.
[93]   The claimant relied on *Oneryildiz v Turkey* (2005) 41 EHRR 20 and *Bekos and Koutropoulos v Greece*, 13 December 2005, unreported.

coming to its decisions. It found that the evidential test in the Code did not contravene Article 2. Providing the decision was reasonably open to the prosecutor on the material before him, the decision could not be impugned.

(3) Human Rights Based Challenges[94]

R (B) v DPP[95] is an important decision because it is a clear application of the *Ex p Manning* categories and it involved a breach of Article 3 of the ECHR, for which damages were awarded. The claimant was a victim of an assault where his ear was bitten off. He identified his assailant, whom he knew. The CPS discontinued the case on the grounds that in the absence of other evidence the claimant would be an unreliable witness. The claimant had a history of psychotic illness during which he had suffered paranoid beliefs and auditory and visual hallucinations. A psychiatric report indicated that this might affect his memory and perception of events.

5-31

The Divisional Court held that the decision was irrational. The prosecutor had not properly informed himself of the facts or asked himself the right questions. On the basis of the psychiatric report, the prosecutor could not say that it was more likely than not that the claimant's evidence was caused by a hallucination. There was no reasonable basis to conclude that the claimant would not be a credible witness on any matter. The court also held that the termination of the proceedings, the claimant's sense of vulnerability and being outside the effective protection of the law was a breach of Article 3 and merited compensation (£8,000).

In *R (Waxman) v Crown Prosecution Service*[96] the claimant successfully challenged a decision not to prosecute as contrary to Article 8 of ECHR. The issue was whether service of civil proceedings on the claimant constituted a breach of a restraining order. The court found it to be conduct that might cause anxiety, alarm and distress; this was aggravated by the fact that the civil claims were entirely devoid of merit. On Article 8, Moore-Bick LJ said it gave rise to a duty on the state 'to maintain and operate an adequate system for affording protection against acts of violence by private individuals'.[97] An award of £3,500 was made.

5-32

Re MacMahon's Application for Judicial Review[98] is an example from Northern Ireland of a successful challenge to a prosecutor's decision based on the ECHR. The court found that the Public Prosecution Service (PPS) breached its Victims and Witnesses Policy in not explaining to the family of a murder victim its decision to accept guilty pleas to lesser offences. This was the outcome of an earlier decision.[99] The court then invited submissions on whether this constituted a breach of Article 8 of ECHR. It found that:

5-33

the right of the partner of a person whose life is unlawfully taken to be appropriately involved in and informed about prosecutorial decisions concerning that death do properly come within that broad range of interests protected by Article 8.[100]

---

[94] Readers should refer to the general rules on these types of challenges set out above at 1-64.
[95] *R (B) v DPP* [2009] EWHC 106 (Admin), [2009] 1 WLR 2072. See above at 1-103.
[96] *R (Waxman) v Crown Prosecution Service* [2012] EWHC 133 (Admin), (2012) 176 JP 121.
[97] ibid [21].
[98] *Re MacMahon's Application for Judicial Review* [2012] NIQB 93. See above at 1-88.
[99] ibid.
[100] ibid [22].

The PPS's decision not to adhere to its Code of Practice constituted a breach of those rights.

5-34   The authorities in this area[101] were recently considered by the Court of Appeal in *SXH v Crown Prosecution Service*[102] a private law claim for damages arising out of a decision to prosecute. Pitchford LJ identified two circumstances in which Article 8 may be engaged, the first on an assessment of the evidence and the second as regards the public interest:

i)   A decision to prosecute may engage Article 8 even if the offence charged does not constitute an interference with that person's private life, for example, if the prosecutor is aware of facts that constitute an unanswerable statutory defence;

ii) A decision to prosecute a dying woman may constitute a disproportionate interference in her private life.

(4) Where the Law has not been Properly Applied

5-35   In *R v DPP, ex parte Jones (Timothy)*,[103] the brother of a deceased man successfully overturned the CPS's decision not to prosecute his brother's employer for gross negligence manslaughter. The court found the CPS had misapplied the test for recklessness when concluding there was insufficient evidence to proceed. Buxton LJ held that there were three considerations potentially relevant:

(1) has the decision-maker properly understood and applied the law?
(2) has he explained the reasons for his conclusions in terms that the court can understand and act upon? And
(3) has he taken into an irrelevant matter or is there a danger that he may have done so?[104]

The court found that the prosecutor has failed to apply the law and to take in to account relevant matters. As Buxton LJ explained, the latter 'was not a point about weight or rationality, but rather a factor that stands out from the basic facts as requiring to be addressed'.[105] Decisions not to prosecute gross negligence manslaughter have been subject of several judicial reviews on grounds of an incorrect application of the law, for example in *R (Rowley) v DPP*.[106] The latter criterion of failing to properly assess the evidence is considered next.

(5) Errors in Assessing Evidence

5-36   *R (Lewin) v Crown Prosecution Service*[107] was also a case of gross negligence manslaughter. The claimant failed to establish that the decision not to prosecute was outwith the

---

[101] For further discussion of how a decision to prosecute may engage Article 8 in the context of child defendants see below at 11-35.
[102] *SXH v Crown Prosecution Service* [2014] EWCA Civ 90.
[103] *R v DPP, ex parte Jones (Timothy)* [2000] IRLR 373, [2000] Crim LR 858.
[104] ibid [26].
[105] ibid [48].
[106] *R (Rowley) v DPP* [2003] EWHC 693 (Admin). See the leading authorities of *R v Adomako* [1995] 1 AC 171 and *R v Misra* [2004] EWCA Crim 2375, [2005] 1 Cr App R 21.
[107] *R (Lewin) v Crown Prosecution Service* [2002] EWHC 1049 (Admin).

Piers von Berg

available medical evidence. However, the claimant succeeded in *R (Dennis) v DPP*,[108] where it was found that a different decision might have been reached if proper account had been given to the employer's failure to give adequate instructions. This involved an application of the evidential stage of the Code. Of importance in *Dennis* was an inquest's verdict of unlawful killing, in light of which any decision not to proceed would have to be a legally and evidentially robust. Waller LJ considered *Ex p Chaudhary, R v DPP, ex parte Treadaway*,[109] *Ex p Jones* and *Ex p Manning* and said this:

> My approach to the arguments in the instant case, guided by the above authorities, is as follows. If it can be demonstrated on an objective appraisal of the case that a serious point or serious points supporting a prosecution have not been considered, that will give a ground for ordering reconsideration of the decision. Second, if it can be demonstrated that in a significant area a conclusion as to what the evidence is to support a prosecution is irrational, that will provide a ground. Third, the points have to be such as to make it seriously arguable that the decision would otherwise be different, but the decision is one for the prosecutor and not for this court. Fourth, where an inquest jury has found unlawful killing the reasons why a prosecution should not follow need to be clearly expressed.[110]

A similar decision was reached in *R (Joseph) v DPP*,[111] where the court found the CPS had not given proper consideration to evidence relating to self-defence in a case of assault.

(6) The Victim's Right to Review (VRR) Policy

On 4 June 2013, the DPP announced a new policy called the Victim's Right to Review (VRR). The introduction of the VRR followed the Court of Appeal's decision in *R v Killick*.   **5-37**

R v Killick was an appeal against conviction for sexual offences. One of the issues raised by the appeal was whether the proceedings had been an abuse of process due to the CPS reneging on unequivocal representations to the criminal defendant that he would not be prosecuted. The appellant had indeed been told he would not be prosecuted but, consequently, as a result of representations and a Letter Before Action from the complainants, the decision was reversed.[112] The court found that, in assessing whether there had been an abuse of process, it should take into account that in reviewing the decision the CPS was responding to the rights of the complainants. This should be distinct from any notion of a complaint about a level of service. Thomas LJ observed that:

> As a decision not to prosecute is in reality a final decision for a victim, there must be a right to seek a review of such a decision, particularly as the police have such a right under the charging guidance.[113]

---

[108] *R (Dennis) v DPP* [2006] EWHC 3211 (Admin).
[109] *R v DPP, ex parte Treadaway* The Times, 31 October 1997 (QB).
[110] *Dennis* (n 108) [30].
[111] *R (Joseph) v DPP* [2001] Crim LR 489.
[112] Interestingly, one of the points taken in the Letter was that the decision was unlawful under the provisions of the Disability Discrimination Act 1995. As was seen in *B* (n 95) the CPS, as a public authority, is caught by statutory obligations, not just the common law grounds of review.
[113] *R v Killick (Christopher)* [2011] EWCA Crim 1608, [2012] 1 Cr App R 10 [48].

The court observed that such a right is in accordance with that expressed in Article 10 of the EU Directive on the rights of victims of crime 2012/29/EU (see below at 14-8), which obliges all Member States to ensure that victims of crime have the right to request review of any decision not to prosecute. It had to be taken into account when considering whether there had been an abuse of process. The court said it was for the DPP to consider whether the right to review, as distinct from a complaint, required a clearer procedure.

5-38   In response to the judgment, the DPP introduced the VRR Scheme.[114] The intention is to give effect to the principles in *R v Killick* and Article 10 of the Directive. The relevance for judicial review is obvious—there is a clear alternative remedy that claimants should exhaust. It applies to all cases from 5 June 2013. It excludes decisions on selection of charges and where cases are disposed of by way of an out-of-court disposal.[115]

(i) Guidance on the VRR

5-39   In *L v DPP and Commissioner of the Police for the Metropolis*, Sir John Thomas P provided guidance on the High Court's approach to judicial reviews of decisions not to prosecute in light of the VRR:

    i.   No judicial review will be entertained by the High Court unless the CPS has already conducted a review under its new procedure.

    ii.   Where such internal review has already been taken place and the decision to prosecute deemed correct, the prospects of success at the High Court would be slim indeed, unless one of the three conditions in *Ex p Chaudhary* were met.

    iii.   If the claimant has not used the VRR, the CPS should state their position in their acknowledgement of service on whether it is appropriate or not in the case.

    iv.   There is no reason why the CPS should not be entitled to seek costs from a claimant who is not successful.[116]

This authority reinforces the point above that practitioners should be conversant with the VRR in advising on claims against the CPS brought by victims.

D. Challenges to the DPP's Policy and Declarations on Future Conduct

(1) Assisted Suicide Litigation

5-40   These cases have involved terminally ill individuals who wished to know if family members would be prosecuted for assisting them to die. The issues were profound but for the

---

[114] It can be found at http://www.cps.gov.uk/victims_witnesses/victims_right_to_ review/ index.html.

[115] The former would exclude challenges to charging of section 5 rather than section 13 of the Sexual Offences Act 2003 eg see below at 11-35.

[116] *L v DPP and Commissioner of the Police for the Metropolis*, [11]-[17].

Piers von Berg

purposes of this chapter they centre on when it is in the public interest to prosecute.[117] The cases are extremely rare and they serve as examples of attempts to influence or change CPS policy, including the Code, rather than a prosecutor's decision. The finer detail is of greater relevance for the assisted dying litigation.[118]

In *R (Pretty) v DPP*[119] the claimant suffered from a terminal illness and wished to end her life, but was unable to do this herself. The claimant judicially reviewed the DPP's refusal to give an undertaking that her husband would not be prosecuted for assisting her. She submitted that criminalisation of her husband's role was an unlawful interference with her Article 2, 3, 8, 9 and 14 rights under the ECHR. The House of Lords dismissed the appeal. It held that Article 2 did not confer a right to self-determination as regards to life and death and a right to assistance in suicide. Article 8 also did not provide a right to decide when and how to die. The DPP had no power to dispense with or suspend laws without Parliament's consent. Any suffering alleged under Article 3 was a consequence of the illness, not the DPP's decision.

The ECtHR also dismissed the case in *Pretty v United Kingdom*.[120] It agreed that Article 2 did not confer a right to die. It also found that Article 3 applied to positive acts by the state. But importantly it differed on Article 8. It held that it was engaged, albeit the interference was justified in that the law served to protect those who were terminally ill and who could be susceptible to abuse.

In *R (Purdy) v DPP*[121] a claimant also suffered from a debilitating condition and wished to end her life. She sought clarification from the DPP on whether her husband would be prosecuted if he assisted her to end her life in another country where it was lawful. The DPP refused to provide guidance beyond what was contained in the Code. The claimant's case was that the lack of an offence-specific policy was an unlawful breach of her Article 8 rights. The House of Lords agreed and followed the ECtHR rather than its own decision in *Pretty*, in holding that the right to decide when and how to die was part of how a person lived her life.[122] Crucially, in assessing the interference with Article 8, it applied the ECHR's principle of legality.[123] The court asked itself whether the Code was:

> sufficiently accessible to the individual who is affected by the restriction, and sufficiently precise to enable him to understand its scope and foresee the consequences of his actions so that he can regulate his conduct without breaking the law.[124]

It found that the Code did not provide sufficient accessibility and foreseeability for offences of assisted suicide of a terminally ill person. The factors it listed did not apply

---

[117] For the classic statement of principle, see *Smedleys Ltd v Breed* [1974] AC 839, 856 (Viscount Dilhorne). For a concise outline of the issues of euthanasia and assisted dying see *R (Pretty) v DPP* [2001] UKHL 61, [2002] 1 AC 800 [54] (Lord Steyn).

[118] *Pretty v United Kingdom* App no 2346/02 [2002] 2 FLR 45, (2002) 35 EHRR 1 also established principles in the area of Art 3, which have been applied in judicial reviews in immigration and asylum, and mental health law.

[119] *Pretty* (n 117).

[120] *Pretty v United Kingdom* (n 118).

[121] *R (Purdy) v DPP* [2009] UKHL 45, [2010] 1 AC 345.

[122] This approach to Art 8 has been followed in other assisted suicide cases. See also *Haas v Switzerland* App no 31322/07 (2011) 53 EHRR 33.

[123] See *Sunday Times v UK* (1979) 2 EHRR 245 [49].

[124] *Purdy* (n 121) [40]. See also *Hasan and Chaush v Bulgaria* (2000) 34 EHRR 1339 [84], cited at [43].

to such cases and many relevant considerations were not included. It simply offered 'almost no guidance at all'.[125] It was vital to have such guidance in order to achieve predictability and consistency. Accordingly, the DPP issued guidance in February 2010 to clarify his position.[126]

Since these seminal cases, there has been one further reported attempt to influence policy. *R (Nicklinson) v Ministry of Justice*[127] was a challenge to the DPP's policy created after *Purdy*. The court, including Lord Judge LCJ and Lord Dyson MR, refused to create a defence of necessity, but held that the DPP's policy was insufficiently clear on the position of healthcare professionals. The policy contained a list of factors that did not enable a person to foresee the consequences of their actions, and left several questions unanswered.[128] It followed the ECtHR in *Pretty* that the blanket ban on assisted suicide was not incompatible with Article 8(2).[129]

(2) Declarations of Lawfulness of Future Conduct

5-41   Claimants have attempted to use judicial review as part of efforts to obtain declarations on whether proposed conduct is lawful. These types of proceedings will normally not be entertained by a court as it entails consideration of a hypothetical question. This was the decision in *R (Rusbridger) v Attorney General*[130] where journalists sought a declaration that it was no longer an offence to publish articles seeking the peaceful overthrow of the monarchy, or that such an offence was incompatible with Article 10 of ECHR. The court stated that such proceedings could only be brought in 'exceptional circumstances' and as the state of the law was clear, the litigation was unnecessary. The guidance was as follows: the appropriate defendant is the Attorney General. There were three criteria: i) there must be an absence of a genuine dispute, ii) the claim must not be fact-sensitive, and iii) there is a cogent public or individual interest that can be advanced by a declaration.[131] Lord Rodger accepted that the interests of justice must allow a litigant to obtain a ruling of a court before continuing with a course of conduct that may result in prosecution.

The criteria and principles in *Rusbridger* were applied in *Blackland Park Exploration Ltd v Environment Agency*,[132] a case concerning landfill waste. This was followed by *R (OSS Group Ltd) v Environment Agency Ltd*,[133] which again concerned dealing with waste (oil). These were successful bids to obtain a declaration. A failed effort can be found in *R (Zoolife International Ltd) v Secretary of State for Environment, Food and*

---

[125] ibid [53].

[126] www.cps.gov.uk/publications/prosecution/assisted_suicide_policy.html.

[127] *R (Nicklinson) v Ministry of Justice* [2013] EWCA Civ 961. At time of writing, judgment is awaited from the Supreme Court in an appeal from the Court of Appeal.

[128] See *R (Nicklinson) v Ministry of Justice* [2013] EWCA Civ 961 [138]–[140]. Note that Lord Judge LCJ dissented on this point.

[129] This principle was also applied by the Irish High Court in *Fleming v Ireland* [2013] IEHC 2, (2013) 131 BMLR 30. The decision was upheld by the Supreme Court ([2013] IESC 19, (2013) 132 BMLR 1).

[130] *R (Rusbridger) v Attorney General* [2003] UKHL 38, [2004] 1 AC 357.

[131] ibid [22]–[24] (Lord Steyn).

[132] *Blackland Park Exploration Ltd v Environment Agency* [2003] EWCA Civ 1795, [2004] Env LR 33.

[133] *R (OSS Group Ltd) v Environment Agency Ltd* [2006] EWHC 2390 (Admin).

Rural Affairs,[134] where the claim was considered to be academic and there were no exceptional circumstances. It was notable that nevertheless the court did give its views on the issues in the case.

E. Private Prosecutions

(1) Private Prosecutions[135]

As stated in the introduction, private citizens have a common law right to instigate pros-   **5-42**
ecutions under section 6(1) of the Prosecution of Offences Act 1985. Under section 6(2) the DPP has a discretion to take over such prosecutions, and once doing so, may discontinue it.

The CPS has a policy on when it will exercise that discretion.[136] It will take over and continue a prosecution where the requirements of the Code are met and there is a particular need for the CPS to take over. The policy states that the latter includes a non-exhaustive list of where the private prosecution involves i) serious offences, ii) detailed disclosure issues, iii) disclosure of sensitive material, or iv) it requires applications for special measures or witness anonymity.

The CPS will take over private prosecutions for the purpose of stopping them if the requirements of the Code are not met.[137] It may also take over to halt a prosecution where i) the case interferes with the investigation or prosecution of another offence, ii) is vexatious or malicious, iii) where the CPS or police have promised the defendant he will not be prosecuted, or iv) where the defendant has already received an out-of-court disposal.[138] Claimants have attempted to argue that when the DPP takes over a case he should incline towards discontinuance. This was rejected in *R v DPP, ex parte Duckenfield*.[139]

The policy was challenged in *R (Gujra) v DPP*[140] as unlawful, in that it frustrated the right in section 6(1) of the 1985 Act. The CPS took over and discontinued on grounds of insufficient evidence the claimant's private prosecutions for common assault and threatening, abusive or insulting words and behaviour. The case failed because the Supreme Court found that section 6(2) does not expressly limit the DPP's discretion, a prosecution that lacks reasonable prospects of success is an inappropriate drain on court

---

[134] *R (Zoolife International Ltd) v Secretary of State for Environment, Food and Rural Affairs* [2007] EWHC 2995 (Admin).

[135] See discussion below at 6-32 relating to decisions of Magistrates' Courts concerning private prosecutions.

[136] www.cps.gov.uk/legal/p_to_r/private_prosecutions/.

[137] This decision as well as a decision not to intervene can both subject to judicial review. See *R v DPP, ex parte Duckenfield* [2000] 1 WLR 55, [1999] 2 All ER 873. Note that authority involved a different earlier policy of the DPP.

[138] For an example of the last point see *Jones v Whalley* [2007] 1 AC 63 (discussed above at 4-92). Note that the Attorney General may be requested to exercise his power to enter a *nolle prosequi*. This is a common law power to stay criminal proceedings. See *R v Dunn* (1843) 1 C & K 730.

[139] *R v DPP, ex parte Duckenfield* [2000] 1 WLR 55, [1999] 2 All ER 873. The claimants relied on obiter dicta in *Gouriet v Union of Post Office Workers* [1978] AC 435, [1977] 3 WLR 300. Note that Laws LJ's own obiter dicta in *Ex p Duckenfield* on the lawfulness of the DPP's policy were not followed in *R (Gujra) v DPP* [2012] UKSC 52, [2013] 1 AC 484 [72].

[140] *Gujra*, ibid.

resources and a defendant could legitimately complain that he was subject to prosecution at private hands for allegations that a public prosecutor would not pursue.[141]

It is submitted that the other categories of review of decisions to prosecute and refusals of applications for abuse of process will apply, for example, see the allegation of improper motive in *R (Dacre) v Westminster Magistrates' Court*.[142]

F. Judicial Reviews Concerning other Prosecuting Bodies

(1) Other Prosecuting Bodies

5-43 Section 6(1) of the 1985 Act preserves a common law power to instigate private prosecutions. In addition there are statutory powers to commence proceedings.[143] As a result there are a large number of bodies that bring prosecutions. The CPS has a working agreement, called the Prosecutor's Convention, with the Attorney General's Office, Civil Aviation Authority, Department for Business, Innovation and Skills, Department of Work and Pensions, Environment Agency, Financial Services Agency, Food Standards Agency, Gambling Commission, Health and Safety Executive, Maritime and Coastguard Agency, Office of Fair Trading, Office of Rail Regulation, Serious Fraud Office and the Service Prosecuting Authority.[144] The Convention governs situations such as where bodies have a common interest in pursuing the same prosecution.

There are other prosecuting bodies including, for example, local authorities, the Gangmasters Licensing Authority, the Driver and Vehicle Licencing Agency and the Royal Society for the Prevention of Cruelty to Animals (RSPCA). The CPS considers that the Convention should be followed where practicable with non-signatory agencies.[145]

The CPS's approach to whether a prosecution should be conducted by another body is set out in its Legal Guidance, which states that if any of the following factors apply, it should be conducted by another body:

i.   the police did not conduct the majority of the investigation;
ii. the police were only involved in overseeing a search, effecting an arrest or assisting other investigators in the conduct of an interview;
iii. the other authority is in possession of all the main exhibits; or
iv. someone other than a police officer is named on the charge sheet as the person accepting the charge or as the officer in the case.[146]

---

[141] ibid [36] (Lord Wilson), with whom Lord Neuberger agreed, ibid [52]–[58] and Lord Kerr agreed.
[142] *R (Dacre) v Westminster Magistrates' Court* [2008] EWHC 1667 (Admin), [2009] 1 WLR 2241. See below at 6-32.
[143] For an example of a challenge to a prosecution by the Security Industry Authority on the basis of a lack of statutory power to institute the proceedings see *R (Securiplan) v Security Industry Authority* [2008] EWHC 1762 (Admin), [2009] 2 All ER 211.
[144] The Revenue and Customs Prosecutions Office (RCPO) was merged with the CPS on 1 January 2010. The DPP became the Director for Revenue and Customs Prosecutions. There is a detailed statutory regime concerning the commencement of prosecutions for customs and revenue offences. The DPP has been assigned the power to prosecute all United Kingdom Border Agency investigated offences. There are also protocols in place relating to prosecutions concerning work-related deaths, offences under service law and contempt of court in Employment Tribunals.
[145] www.cps.gov.uk/legal/p_to_r/prosecuting_agencies_relations_with_other _agencies/.
[146] ibid.

(2) Judicial Review of Prosecutors other than the CPS

It is submitted that unless there is an issue of the independence of the body concerned,   **5-44**
the principles remain the same (see above at 5-9). A key issue is whether the independent body conducting the prosecution is truly independent of the state. If it is not, it is
possible that the wider standard of discretion than that granted to the CPS will apply.
Moss & Son Ltd v Crown Prosecution Service[147] was an appeal by way of case stated
against the dismissal of an application to stay for abuse of process. The Gangmaster's
Licensing Authority (GLA) brought the prosecution. The appellant argued that the case
was brought in breach of the GLA's own policy. An executive body rather than an independent body such as the CPS drafted the policy. Sir John Thomas P said that whilst
it would be 'highly undesirable' for a different standard of review to apply to abuse of
process applications concerning decisions made by part of the executive:

> There must nonetheless be a powerful argument that a court should apply a more stringent
> standard to prosecution policy devised and implemented by the Executive Government.[148]

The standard to be applied would be 'little different' to that applied to the executive. His
Lordship added that prosecutorial decisions should be in the hands of those who were
independent of the executive.[149]

In *Moss & Son*, the court noted the approach taken in cases involving prosecutions by
local authorities in *R v Adaway*[150] and *Wandsworth LBC v Rashid*,[151] which presumed
that decisions were made independent of the executive. Therefore, the 'wide test', which
is applied to the CPS, was also applied to these decisions.

---

[147] *Moss & Son Ltd v Crown Prosecution Service* [2012] EWHC 3658 (Admin), (2013) 177 JP 221.
[148] ibid [29].
[149] See above at 5-9. The 'highly exceptional' test that applies to 'the decisions of an independent prosecutor
and investigator', *Corner House Research* (n 21) [30] (Lord Bingham).
[150] *R v Adaway* [2004] EWCA Crim 2831.
[151] *Wandsworth LBC v Rashid* [2009] EWHC 1844 (Admin).

6

Magistrates' Courts

SARAH PARKES AND PIERS VON BERG[1]

---

[1] The authors are grateful to David Ball and Pranjal Shrotri for their help with the initial drafts of this Chapter.

A. General Principles

(1) Introduction

6-1 There is significant scope for judicial review of magistrates' courts decisions. A leading case states that the High Court provides a supervisory jurisdiction to guarantee the integrity and fairness of summary proceedings.[2]

---

[2] *R v Hereford Magistrates' Court, ex parte Rowlands* [1998] QB 110, [1997] 2 WLR 854, 125 (Lord Bingham LCJ).

Sarah Parkes and Piers von Berg

This does not mean that criminal defendants can challenge every instance of alleged unfairness by bringing a claim for judicial review. Potential claimants should consider first the guidance in this Part A. It sets out the wide range of alternative remedies that may be available depending on the nature of the complaint and the stage at which proceedings have reached. Among these remedies, there is appeal by way of case stated, which is also an application to the High Court. A complete analysis of appeal by way of case stated is outside the scope of this work as it is not a form of judicial review. But there is significant overlap between the two areas, particularly regarding challenging errors of law in the magistrates' courts, and readers will find several appeals by way of case stated mentioned below. (See below from 6-12 for the factors to be considered when deciding between this route and judicial review). Following this at 6-16 the specific instances and occasions when judicial review is appropriate are identified. Potential claimants, and defendants who think that a claim has been brought inappropriately or prematurely, should consult these sections first.

In the remainder of the chapter, sections B–D are devoted to a range of issues that have been brought by way of judicial review and where possible, indications of where new avenues may be explored. When considering the authorities in sections B–D, practitioners should be aware that some may be merely examples of how a decision may be reached on a particular set of facts concerning a specific point of law. It is common in this area to find that a judgment does not describe the grounds on which a claim was made, or the grounds pleaded are not immediately recognisable as public law arguments. It is also not uncommon to find that authorities do not refer to prior authority, or only refer to the relevant statutory provisions or cases from criminal law. This is not to say that precedents are not important, but simply that they should be deployed with care, as they may be confined to particular facts or the working of a specific provision. Despite this, the grounds of review can be found in Chapter 1 and there are several areas where the practitioner can rely on settled case law applied in a series of cases.

Generally speaking, the most common grounds of review are *Wednesbury* unreasonableness, errors of law, and procedural unfairness or breaches of the common law right to a fair trial and Article 6 of ECHR (see Chapter 1). There are some common areas of dispute, such as adjournments, where general precedents are established, and a failure by a magistrates' court to follow the principles of those cases can be grounds for judicial review. There are also topics such as abuse of process and breach of human rights, which have been dealt with in substantial detail by the appellate courts and the ECtHR. Practitioners should be aware that some decisions have been made by senior judges sitting in the Divisional Court, such as the Lord Chief Justice or President of the Queen's Bench Division, which will inevitably carry more weight.

Magistrates' courts usually take a neutral position on judicial review applications against them, and may not respond to a claim or be represented at a hearing of an application. In many cases they do not have a power to reverse or amend an impugned decision so the Pre-Action Protocol will not apply to them.[3] Therefore, in claims by a criminal defendant, the prosecution will often take the role of the defendant, even though they are an interested party. The magistrates' court may occasionally provide evidence or a note to assist the High Court as to what transpired in the proceedings

---

[3] Pre-Action Protocol para 6.

below. There are special provisions governing costs against magistrates' courts in judicial review, see below at 16-13.

There is some degree of overlap with other chapters—challenges to search warrants issued by a magistrates' court can be found above at 4-39 and decisions in respect of those with mental health disorders (to issue a warrant to remove to place of safety or orders on disposal) are addressed below at 12-18. Chapter 11 covers judicial reviews of Youth Courts relating to trial, young victims and witnesses, special measures, reporting restrictions, sentencing and Anti-Social Behaviour Orders. This chapter includes challenges to decisions of Youth Courts on sending of youths to the Crown Court and preliminary issues around trial, such as adjournments and remittals due to age.

(2) Statutory Framework

6-2   This chapter does not provide comprehensive guidance to the criminal law and procedure in the magistrates' courts. Instead, it aims to describe the most common areas for judicial review, and where necessary the statutory framework, for example, where there have been recent and significant changes. Magistrates' courts deal with a wide range of criminal, civil and family proceedings. This chapter covers only judicial reviews arising from criminal cases or related proceedings such as under the Proceeds of Crime Act 2002. Part 1 of the Magistrates' Court Act (MCA) 1980 describes the criminal jurisdiction and procedure of the magistrates' courts. Proceedings in a magistrates' court are also governed by the Criminal Procedure Rules, the Practice Directions issued by the Lord Chief Justice and the Magistrates' Courts Rules 1981 (as amended).[4] There are numerous other statutes that contain provisions relating to procedure and proceedings before the magistrates' courts.[5] Among the most commonly referred to for present purposes are the Bail Act 1976, the Police and Criminal Evidence Act (PACE) 1984, the Crime and Disorder Act (CDA) 1998 and the Criminal Justice Act (CJA) 2003.

(3) Alternative Remedies

6-3   It has been said that where an adequate alternative remedy exists, the court should only exercise its discretion to grant judicial review in exceptional circumstances.[6] The potential alternative remedies that ought to be considered, and ordinarily exhausted, prior to judicial review are listed below.

(i) *The Power to Reopen a Case (The 'Slip Rule')*

6-4   Section 142 of the MCA 1980 provides for the reopening of any order, determination, conviction or sentence where it would be in the interests of justice to do so. The magistrates'

---

[4] See also the *Adult Criminal Case Management Framework*, 3rd edn, 2007. The purpose of the Framework is to give 'useful, practical guidance to participants, enabling them to comply with the Rules', Sir Igor Judge P, in Foreword. 'It is not a substitute for the Criminal Procedure Rules or any part of them', Introduction to Framework. It can be viewed online at http://webarchive.nationalarchives.gov.uk/20100512160448/http://ccmf.cjsonline.gov.uk/.

[5] See *Stone's Justices' Manual*, Vol 1 (London, Butterworths, 2013), 1.4620 et seq.

[6] *R v High Peak Magistrates Court, ex parte B* [1995] 1 FLR 568.

court has a wide discretion, providing it does not go further than to simply rectify a mistake.[7] Where a person has been convicted it permits a magistrates' court to direct that they be retried by a different bench, if it is in the interests of justice (section 142(2)). It gives a power to reopen and vary sentence to any that could have been imposed on the date of the original sentence. It is not exercisable in respect of any sentence or conviction where the Crown Court has determined the matter by way of appeal or the High Court has determined an appeal by way of case stated.

It is clear that the concept of the 'interests of justice' includes considerations of certainty and finality.[8] This provision is unlikely to be an effective remedy for many defendants, due to its limited scope. For example, where a criminal defendant believes he has been wrongly convicted, it cannot be used to remit the matter for a retrial.[9] It would be 'wholly wrong' to use it as a substitute for an appeal to the Crown Court where a defendant has unequivocally pleaded guilty.[10] In cases of unfairness, it is unlikely to provide the wholesale procedural scrutiny that necessarily follows a judicial review application.

Unlawful use of the section may provide grounds for judicial review, in that a magistrates' court has exercised its discretion unlawfully, or for an appeal by way of case stated, if it can be said that the court has acted outside its jurisdiction by using the section for an unlawful purpose. In particular, the Divisional Court has quashed decisions where the magistrates' court has gone beyond its jurisdiction to rectify a mistake. In *Roman Zykin v Crown Prosecution Service*[11] it was held that section 142(2) does not confer a wide and general power to reopen decisions on the grounds of the interests of justice. The Divisional Court upheld a magistrates' court's decision not to reopen a committal hearing, on grounds that it was being asked to review or effectively consider an appeal of the decision of a previous court.

Whether the court had been misled on the earlier occasion will be a relevant consideration as to whether the power should be exercised.[12] For example, a sentence may be said to have been imposed by mistake if the magistrates' court failed to appreciate a relevant fact, according to Collins J in *R (Holme) v Liverpool City Justices & Crown Prosecution Service*[13] (see below at 6-4). Although, His Lordship added that this may well give the magistrates' court jurisdiction to use the section but it does not follow that it should necessarily be used. The interests of justice will be a key factor. In *Trigger v Northampton Magistrates' Court*,[14] Ramsey J cautioned that 'it would not usually be in the interests of justice to increase a sentence imposed earlier unless the power is exercised speedily after the date of the original sentence'.[15] This is particularly the case when the intention is to use the power to impose a custodial sentence.

---

[7] *R v Croydon Youth Court, ex parte DPP* [1997] 2 Cr App R 411, DC. In that case a magistrates' court wrongly allowed a defendant to be retried after he applied to change his plea of guilty. There was no mistake that needed to be corrected.

[8] ibid.

[9] *R (Williamson) v City of Westminster Magistrates' Court* [2012] EWHC 1444 (Admin), [2012] 2 Cr App R 24.

[10] *Ex p DPP* [1997] (n 7), 417 and followed in *DPP v Chajed* [2013] EWHC 188 (Admin).

[11] *Roman Zykin v Crown Prosecution Service* [2009] EWHC 1469 (Admin).

[12] *R (Holme) v Liverpool City Justices & Crown Prosecution Service* [2004] EWHC 3131 (Admin).

[13] ibid [30].

[14] *Trigger v Northampton Magistrates' Court* [2011] EWHC 149 (Admin) [33].

[15] This case provides a useful discussion and overview of the law on MCA 1980, s 142.

(ii) Statutory Declarations

6-5   Section 14 of MCA 1980 allows for a person to make a declaration that they did not
know of the summons or the proceedings until after the court had begun to try the
offence. A declaration that contains valid information voids the summons and all subsequent proceedings.[16] Such a declaration must be made within 21 days but a magistrates'
court has a discretion to extend that time. Clearly, if a person has recourse to such a
remedy, judicial review will not be appropriate.[17]

(iii) Appeal to the Crown Court

6-6   If the complaint is one of error of fact by the magistrates' court, then the correct route is
appeal to the Crown Court. Appeals to the Crown Court are governed by section 108(1)
of the MCA 1980 and Part 63 of the Criminal Procedure Rules, which permit appeals as
of right against sentence and/or against conviction:

> (1)   A person convicted by a magistrates' court may appeal to the Crown Court—
>   (a)   if he pleaded guilty, against his sentence;
>   (b)   if he did not, against the conviction or sentence.

The powers of the Crown Court under section 48 of the Senior Courts Act 1981 include
quashing the conviction, remitting the case, or varying the sentence. There is no right of
appeal against conviction where a guilty plea is entered unless it can be shown the plea
was improperly taken.[18] The Crown Court can remit a case where there is an equivocal
plea or it was entered under duress.[19] For judicial reviews of the Crown Court in its
appellate capacity, see below at 7-25.

6-7   The vexed issue of whether a judicial review application can be made without previously exercising an appeal to the Crown Court was addressed in *R v Hereford Magistrates'
Court, ex parte Rowlands*[20] [1998] QB 110, [1997] 2 WLR 854 by Lord Bingham LCJ,
who held that the right to seek for judicial review existed even if the defendant also had
a right of appeal to the Crown Court and that to hold otherwise 'would be to emasculate
the long-established supervisory jurisdiction of this court over magistrates' courts'.[21]

---

[16] Note the Lord Chief Justice introduced a new form in February 2014. It can be found at http://www.
justice.gov.uk/courts/procedure-rules/criminal/formspage.

[17] See *R v Brighton Justices, ex parte Robinson* [1973] 1 WLR 69, [1973] Crim LR 53, a decision of Lord
Widgery LCJ that refers to the now repealed s 24 of the Criminal Justice Act 1967, which governed statutory
declarations. It has been replaced by s 14 of the MCA 1980. It is submitted that the case remains authority
for statutory declarations.

[18] In *R v Rochdale Justices, ex parte Allwork* [1981] 3 All ER 434, Lord Lane LCJ held that unless there was
prima facie evidence as to the equivocal nature of the plea, the Crown Court should simply proceed to hear
any appeal against sentence. If there was such evidence it should request affidavit evidence from the clerk and
the justices, if necessary.

[19] *R v Plymouth Justices, ex parte Hart* [1986] QB 950, [1986] 2 WLR 976 and *R v Huntingdon Justices,
ex parte Jordan* [1981] QB 857. Where there is nothing to suggest that the plea was equivocal, it cannot be
quashed by way of judicial review *R (Golrokhi) v Chelmsford Crown Court*, 10 October 2013.

[20] *R v Hereford Magistrates' Court, ex parte Rowlands* [1998] QB 110, [1997] 2 WLR 854.

[21] ibid 125. Note *R v Huyton Justices, ex parte Roberts* [1988] COD 43, where it was more appropriate to
appeal to the Crown Court where facts emerged post-conviction.

The following principles concerning appeals to the Crown Court can be distilled from the judgment:

i.   A defendant should exhaust any alternative remedies if they are available otherwise the court may exercise its discretion and refuse relief. But for defendants seeking relief from unfairness or procedural irregularity it was not argued that they should exhaust their right of appeal first.

ii. The High Court should refuse relief where an application is made for judicial review with the purpose of delaying or frustrating an appeal before the Crown Court.[22]

iii. It was not the case that relief should be refused simply because the defendant could appeal to the Crown Court or had an appeal underway—it was a matter for the High Court's discretion.[23]

iv. Examples of issues that could not be remedied on appeal to the Crown Court included the magistrates' exercise of discretion to amend a charge.[24]

As for the procedure on appeals to the Crown Court where a judicial review is sought, see above at 2-8. It is open for a defendant to issue a claim in the High Court and file a notice of appeal with the Crown Court. In such cases the defendant must inform the Administrative Court at the outset whether any appeal is pending.[25]

(iv) Appeal Against Sentence to the Crown Court

On an application for a quashing order in respect of a sentencing decision made by a **6-8** magistrates' court or the Crown Court (on appeal or a committal for sentence) the High Court may substitute for the sentence any sentence which the court below could have passed, if that court had had 'no power to pass the sentence'.[26] However, the High Court has strongly discouraged applications for judicial review of sentencing decisions in the magistrates' courts (although note below at 6-83 judicial reviews concerning reopening of sentencing decisions in light of fresh evidence).

In *Allen v West Yorkshire Probation Service*[27] and *Tucker v DPP*[28] it was said that the defendant should appeal against a sentence to the Crown Court unless there were clear and substantial grounds for proceeding with judicial review. It is submitted that if there is a complaint of unfairness, procedural impropriety or bias that cannot be dealt with by the Crown Court on appeal, then a defendant is entitled to invite the High Court to consider the matter as per *Ex p Rowlands*. However, the interests of a defendant in

---

[22] *R v Peterborough Magistrates' Court, ex parte Dowler* [1997] QB 911, [1997] 2 WLR 843, approved in *Ex p Rowlands* (n 20) on this narrow ground. Note the comments in *Ex p Rowlands* at 124F–125A disapproving of other parts of the judgment.

[23] *Ex p Rowlands* (n 20) 124F–G, 125E–G.

[24] ibid 125B. It is submitted that another example could be a grant of an adjournment in circumstances where the Crown would have had to have offered no evidence if it was refused. Such unfairness, if shown, cannot be remedied on an appeal in the Crown Court, which is a re-hearing of the facts.

[25] *R v Mid-Worcester Justices, ex parte Hart* [1989] COD 397, DC.

[26] See *R (Corner) v Southend Crown Court* [2005] EWHC 2334 (Admin) and *R v St Helen's Justices, ex parte Jones* [1999] 2 All ER 73.

[27] *Allen v West Yorkshire Probation Service* [2001] EWHC Admin 2, (2001) 165 JP 613.

[28] *Tucker v DPP* [1992] 4 All ER 901.

custody must be borne in mind, especially where there may be significant delay in bringing proceedings in the High Court. Lord Woolf LCJ gave the following warning in *Allen*:

> Even if there were not the delays which had occurred in this case, the procedure of coming to this court by way either of judicial review or of case stated is one which created difficulties and problems ... The delays today are nothing like as great as they have been in the past, but inevitably some months must go by before the matter can come before the court. Even if the appeal or application for judicial review is successful, the best that a defendant can hope to achieve is that he will have to be sentenced again. He is therefore either in a position where he remains in custody if a sentence of imprisonment has been imposed (as it was here), pending the matter coming before this court, or (as did the appellant) he applies for and obtains bail, and then is faced with the danger months later of having to return to prison to complete a sentence, a sentence which may be of short duration... Appeals by case stated, or applications for judicial review, in the generality of cases are not appropriate procedures for appeals against sentence. If the sentence imposed by a magistrates' court is wrong, the right place to go to is the Crown Court.[29]

(v) Appeal by Way of Case Stated

6-9   Any party to proceedings before the magistrates' court or who is aggrieved[30] by the conviction, order, determination or ruling of the court may apply to the High Court on the grounds that the decision was wrong in law or in excess of jurisdiction.[31] The procedure is set out in Part 64 of the Criminal Procedure Rules and in section II of CPR Part 52E. The party concerned should apply to the magistrates to state a case for the opinion of the High Court within 21 days of the decision.[32] The magistrates' court may refuse to state a case if the court considers it to be frivolous.[33] This means 'futile, misconceived, hopeless or academic'.[34] The applicant may seek judicial review of that decision and apply for a mandatory order for the court to state a case (for mandatory orders see above at 3-18).[35]

In order for the magistrates' court to state a case it needs to complete the proceedings before it and make a final determination. Hence the authorities state that the High Court does not have jurisdiction to entertain interlocutory appeals.[36] It has been held

---

[29] *Allen* (n 27) [20]–[22] (Lord Woolf LCJ).

[30] In *Cook v Southend-on-Sea Borough Council* [1990] 2 WLR 61, [1990] 2 QB 1 this was defined as any party to the proceedings for whom the decision was adverse, except in the case of an acquittal of another in criminal proceedings. It can also include a person who is simply 'aggrieved' by the decision and is not a party, including a local authority. See also *Drapers' Co v Hadder* (1892) 57 JP 200 and *R v Newport (Salop) Justices, ex parte Wright* [1929] 2 KB 416. This is a different test to one of sufficient interest for judicial review applications. It is a formula used for statutory appeals to the High Court, eg under the Road Traffic Act 1988, ss 100 and 119.

[31] MCA 1980, s 111(1). A separate provision applies to family proceedings to allow appeals to be sent to the county court (s 111A).

[32] The procedure is set out in CPR Pt 52 and the accompanying Practice Direction. In relation to the magistrates' courts see also the Magistrates' Courts Rules 1981. A defendant may seek bail under MCA 1980, s 113.

[33] MCA 1980, s 111(5).

[34] *R v Mildenhall Magistrates' Court, ex parte Forest Heath District Council* (1997) 161 JP 401.

[35] MCA 1980, s 111(7). In such cases the applicant is entitled to withdraw his appeal without the High Court's leave *Collen v Bromsgrove District Council* (1996) 160 JP 593, [1997] Crim LR 206.

[36] *Streames v Copping* [1985] QB 920, [1985] All ER 122. See the discussion below at 6-21 as there is some controversy on this point.

that the court has a discretion to state a case at an interlocutory stage in civil proceedings but it should be used sparingly and in exceptional circumstances.[37]

A person may also apply to the Crown Court to state a case for the High Court on the grounds that an order, judgment or decision of the court was wrong in law or made in excess of jurisdiction.[38]

The High Court may reverse, affirm or amend the decision, or remit[39] the matter back to the magistrates' or Crown Court with its opinion to be considered, or to make such an order as the court sees fit, including on costs.

(vi) A Court's Refusal to State a Case

A refusal to state a case can be challenged on the usual judicial review grounds (see **6-10** section G in Chapter 1 above) However, a court is only obliged to state a case where there is some evidence that there has been an error of law. It was reiterated in *R v North West Suffolk (Mildenhall) Magistrates Court, ex parte Forest Heath District Council*[40] that errors of fact cannot form the basis of an appeal by way of case stated unless it can be said that there is no evidential foundation for the decision. Where a point of law or procedure is settled, justices are entitled to refuse to state a case.[41]

The magistrates' court cannot refuse to state a case on the grounds that a defendant has a pending appeal to the Crown Court: asking for a case to be stated automatically extinguishes the Crown Court appeal.[42] Magistrates can refuse to state a case unless the defendant pays a surety contingent on the expeditious prosecution of the appeal, provided that in setting the level of the surety, they take into account the defendant's means.[43]

For example, in *R (Coxon) v Manchester City Magistrates Court*,[44] a refusal to state a case was held to be reasonable as any suggestion of error was wholly frivolous. The claimant, during his trial for drink driving, argued that the breath analysis machine used to measure the alcohol in his breath had been altered, so that it was no longer approved. The judge rejected this argument and refused to state the case. It was held that the claimant had failed to discharge the evidential burden on him to show that the device was not approved. The challenge was therefore unsuccessful.

Examples of successful challenges to refusals to state cases can be found in *R v Thames Metropolitan Stipendiary Magistrate, ex parte Hackney London Borough Council*,[45]

---

[37] *R v Chesterfield Justices, ex parte Kovacs* [1992] 2 All ER 325.

[38] The procedure is set out in the Crown Court Rules 1982, SI 1982/1109, r 26 and CPR 64.7.

[39] This may include an order to conduct a rehearing before the same or different bench *Griffiths v Jenkins* [1992] 2 AC 76, [1992] 1 All ER 65. There is old authority that if the High Court states that the lower court should have convicted, the court should reinstate the case and proceed to conviction, or the lower court risks judicial review proceedings with consequences in costs *R v Haden Corser* (1892) 8 TLR 563. This unusual decision is cited in *Stone's Justices' Manual*, Vol 1 (London, Butterworths, 2013), para 1.832, fn 13.

[40] *R v North West Suffolk (Mildenhall) Magistrates Court, ex parte Forest Heath District Council* [1998] Env LR 9 CA.

[41] *R v Uxbridge Justices, ex parte Webb* [1994] 2 CMLR 288 DC.

[42] *R v Fylde and Wyre Justices, ex parte Gornall* [1996] COD 434 decided on the old law. The current law is MCA 1980, s 111(4).

[43] *R v Croydon Justices, ex parte Morgan* [1997] COD 176 DC decided on the old law. The current law is MCA 1980, s 114.

[44] *R (Coxon) v Manchester City Magistrates Court* [2010] EWHC 712 (Admin).

[45] *R v Thames Metropolitan Stipendiary Magistrate, ex parte Hackney London Borough Council* [1994] 92 LGR 392 DC.

R v Lowestoft Magistrates, ex parte Adamson[46] and *R v Aldershot Justices, ex parte Rushmoor Borough Council*.[47] Costs were awarded in the latter case against the justices, who refused to state the case even after permission for judicial review had been granted. In refusing to state a case, a court must not take into account irrelevant considerations such as the lack of seriousness of an offence, the leniency of the sentence passed or the defendant's previous convictions.[48]

If a claimant is successful, the court may grant a mandatory order compelling the magistrates' court to state a case, or it may go on to hear the appeal by way of case stated using the evidence before it. This flexible approach can also apply where a case is brought by way of appeal case stated that should have been brought by way of judicial review.[49]

(vii) The High Court's Approach to Appeals by Case Stated

6-11 As stated above, appeal by way of case stated will not be appropriate where there is an alleged error of fact; for example where the court prefers the evidence of one person over another.[50] Such complaints should be addressed to the Crown Court in the form of an appeal. The court will not consider issues that depend on further findings of fact, and is bound by the findings of the court below.[51] It will not disturb any inferences from the facts, providing they have been validly made. The parties should be aware that they cannot take points on the facts that were not taken before the lower court. It will also not be appropriate if the impugned decision is a discretionary one. For example, this includes decisions to exclude evidence under section 78 of PACE 1984.[52]

(viii) Appeal by Case Stated or Judicial Review?

6-12 The overall position was addressed by Lord Bingham LCJ in *Ex p Rowlands*:

i.   If a magistrates' court convicts a defendant and in doing so radically departs from 'well known principles of justice and procedure', the decision can be challenged by case stated.[53]

ii. Judicial review is the usual 'if not invariable' means of challenging unfairness, bias or procedural irregularity and the cases that demonstrate this 'are legion'.

---

[46] *R v Lowestoft Magistrates, ex parte Adamson* [1996] COD 276.

[47] *R v Aldershot Justices, ex parte Rushmoor Borough Council* [1996] COD 2.

[48] *R v Crown Court at Portsmouth, ex parte Thomas* [1994] COD 373 DC.

[49] An example is *Balogun v Director of Public Prosecutions Practice Note* [2010] EWHC 799 (Admin), [2010] 1 WLR 1915, discussed in more detail below at 6-25 and at 6-71.

[50] *Oladimeji v DPP* [2006] EWHC 1199 (Admin).

[51] *Ross v Moss* [1965] 2 QB 396, [1965] 3 All ER 145; *Skipaway Ltd v Environment Agency* [2006] EWHC 983 (Admin) and *M v DPP* [2009] EWHC 752 (Admin). Costs may be awarded against the court if the case is not stated fairly—see *Edge v Edwards* (1932) 48 TLR 449 cited in *Stone's Justices' Manual*, Vol 1 (London, Butterworths, 2013), para 1.831, fn 13.

[52] Eg *Braham v DPP* (1994) 159 JP 527.

[53] *Ex p Rowlands* (n 20) 118F. There are extreme examples of decisions which were so patently wrong it would have been absurd to have appealed by case stated and posed a question in law—Lord Bingham cites *Rigby v Woodward* [1957] 1 WLR 250, where a defendant was denied an opportunity to cross-examine a co-defendant and *R v Wandsworth Justices, ex parte Read* [1942] 1 KB 281 where a defendant was convicted without an opportunity to give evidence.

Judicial review is not suited for determining factual disputes or for lengthy investigations **6-13** of complex factual issues.[54] This theme was repeated by Lord Woolf LCJ in *R v North Essex Justices, ex parte Lloyd*[55] (court was not referred to *Ex p Rowlands*). The claimant challenged a decision to commit him for sentence to the Crown Court and His Lordship said this:

> A case stated for appeal is very useful and valuable when the magistrates have determined facts. It is a useful vehicle for them to record their findings of fact. But in a case where the issue is of the sort that exists here as to the extent of their jurisdiction to commit for sentence, an application for judicial review is the most convenient procedure and it is the procedure which should ordinarily be used. It has the advantage, first of all, that it saves the cumbersome procedure of appealing by way of case stated; and secondly, it has the advantage that the matter comes before a judge of the High Court who decides whether or not to give permission to apply for judicial review. That avoids this Court being troubled with cases that lack merit. It also provides assistance to the applicant because at a relatively modest cost he knows whether or not he has an arguable case.

There are a number of competing considerations; these were considered by Collins J in **6-14** *R (P) v Liverpool City Magistrates*[56] (the court was not referred to the above authorities). This was a challenge to a conviction of a parent where a child had not attended school regularly without reasonable justification, under section 444 of the Education Act 1996. It was brought on the grounds that the court had made an error of law by imposing a burden of proof on the defendant under section 444(1A). The claimant also contended that the justices had misinterpreted the phrase 'reasonable justification'. Collins J said these matters could have been raised by way of appeal by case stated and went on to explore the relationship between the two remedies:

   i.   The time limit for appeal by case stated is much shorter than for judicial review (three months), although three months is a long stop position, and any application should be brought promptly. However, the court may decline relief if judicial review has been used to bypass the short time limits in a case where appeal by case stated is more appropriate.[57]

   ii.   The authorities are conflicting, and it is not clear which may be the appropriate route in the circumstances of any given case. Judicial review would be more appropriate where there is an issue of fact that must be raised and determined that the court below has not resolved.[58] This relates to cases of unfairness in the way in which the magistrates' court conducts the case including i) bias, ii) problems preventing the defendant in putting his case, or iii) improper interference from the clerk.

---

[54] *R v Felixstowe Justices, ex parte Baldwin* [1981] 1 All ER 596, (1981) 72 Cr App R 131 followed in *R v Morpeth Ward Justices, ex parte Ward* (1992) 95 Cr App R 215, [1992] Crim LR 497.

[55] *R v North Essex Justices, ex parte Lloyd* [2001] 2 Cr App R (S) 15.

[56] *R (P) v Liverpool City Magistrates* [2006] EWHC 887 (Admin), [5]–[8].

[57] Eg in *Pall Mall Investments Ltd v Leeds City Council* [2013] EWHC 3307 (Admin). See also *R (Brighton and Hove City Council) v Brighton and Hove Justices* [2004] EWHC 1800 (Admin). Both these cases concerned a magistrates' court's decision to set aside a liability order for non-domestic rates. In the latter case Stanley Burnton J stated that the appropriate procedure was to appeal by way of case stated.

[58] See contrary authority in *R v Morpeth Ward Justices, ex parte Ward* (1992) 95 Cr App R 215.

iii. Case stated is more appropriate where the lower court has misdirected itself in law or simply got the law wrong.

iv. 'Generally speaking a failure to go by way of case stated in such a situation is likely to result in a refusal of permission for judicial review on the basis that it is the wrong way of dealing with it'.[59]

Notably, in that case, the application was not dismissed for taking the wrong route. Aside from the claimant obtaining permission (for which the reasons are not given), Collins J found that the court was in possession of a statement of the facts found by the justices, which put him in 'as good a position in the circumstances of this case as I would have been had it been brought by way of case stated'.[60] This was held to be a reason not to refuse relief.

6-15   There are other considerations:

i. First, a defendant forfeits his right to appeal to the Crown Court on making an application to appeal by case stated under section 111(4) of MCA 1980. As stated above, one can in principle apply for judicial review if one has already appealed to the Crown Court. Although the High Court may not consider the matter until such an appeal is determined, or at all (see above on the procedure 2-8 and on the relationship with appeals to the Crown Court at 6-7).

ii. The time limit for appeal by case stated (21 days) may be much shorter than for judicial review (note that the latter requires claimants to act promptly, and not simply within three months—see above at 2-3–2-4). If there is any doubt, claimants preferring judicial review where appeal by way of case stated is possibly appropriate, and who issue their claim after the shorter time limit for an appeal has expired, may assist their case by explaining their choice of remedy in their grounds. This may pre-empt any criticism that they have chosen judicial review in order to bypass the shorter time limit for appeal.

iii. There is no permission stage for appeals by way of case stated. Instead, applicants have to persuade the justices to state a case. Potential applicants can weigh up their chances of persuading the magistrates' court which has heard the matter to state a case, or with a High Court judge, who will only consider the case on the papers or failing a grant of permission, at a short oral hearing.[61]

iv. An applicant cannot challenge an interlocutory decision by way of appeal by case stated. Equally, there are barriers to challenging such decisions by judicial review (see discussion below at 6-21), but much less so.

v. Judicial review remedies are discretionary (see above at 3-5).

vi. A magistrates' court may ask a defendant who requests them to state a case to provide recognisances that they will proceed with the appeal as expeditiously as possible as a condition for stating a case (section 114 of MCA 1980). This is likely to be more applicable to privately funded criminal defendants.

---

[59] *P* (n 56) [8].

[60] ibid [10].

[61] Judicial review applicants in criminal causes or matters must be aware that if the judge at the permission stage certifies the application as 'totally without merit', they have no further remedy in the domestic courts (see above at 2-31).

Sarah Parkes and Piers von Berg

vii.   Judicial review has a procedure for urgent cases where appeal by way of case stated does not (see above 2-21). In cases where speed is important, judicial review may be more appropriate; for example, if the defendant is vulnerable, or there is a risk to a person's safety or health or to the public at large.[62]

viii.   There are different tests for standing—see above at 6-9 for appeals by way of case stated and above at 1-45 for the 'sufficient interest' test in judicial review.

On the other hand, the remedies available by either route are broadly comparable. The court can quash a conviction in either case. The matter can be remitted for a rehearing by either route. Although damages can be sought by way of judicial review, magistrates and their clerks have immunity for acts conducted in a judicial capacity, unless they acted in excess of their jurisdiction and in bad faith.[63]

(4) When to Challenge by Way of Judicial Review

(i) General Principles

The High Court's supervisory jurisdiction over the magistrates' courts provides 'an   **6-16** invaluable guarantee of the integrity of proceedings in those courts', according to Lord Bingham LCJ in *Ex p Rowlands*.[64] Certiorari (a quashing order) provides 'the usual if not invariable means of pursuing challenges based on unfairness, bias or procedural irregularity in the magistrates' courts'.[65] His Lordship gave this guidance:

> First, leave to move should not be granted unless the applicant advances an apparently plausible complaint which, if made good, might arguably be held to vitiate the proceedings in the magistrates' court. Immaterial and minor deviations from best practice would not have that effect, and the court should be respectful of discretionary decisions of magistrates' courts as of all other courts.[66]

Another important reason for the High Court accepting jurisdiction to intervene in proceedings before the magistrates' courts is where a judicial review raises wider questions of policy beyond any issues of unfairness in the instant proceedings. This derives from the decision in *R v Horseferry Road Magistrates' Court, ex parte Bennett (No 1)*,[67] where the House of Lords said that where confronted with an alleged abuse of process that raised questions about the rule of law, the magistrates should decline jurisdiction and adjourn to allow the High Court to consider the matter (discussed in more detail under abuse of process claims below at 6-34).

An application of this principle can be seen in *R (A) v South Yorkshire Police*[68] concerning the administering of out-of-court disposals. That was a case where six young

---

[62] As can be seen below at n 93 expedition and urgency are encouraged in judicial reviews concerning youths and adjournments.

[63] The Courts Act 2003, s 31.

[64] *Ex p Rowlands* (n 20) 125D. See also discussion above at 1-20.

[65] ibid 120B. Note this decision pre-dated the Human Rights Act (HRA) 1998.

[66] ibid 125E.

[67] *R v Horseferry Road Magistrates' Court, ex parte Bennett (No 1)* [1994] 1 AC 42, [1993] 3 WLR 90, 64. See above at 1-9 and below at 6-35 and 6-43.

[68] *R (A) v South Yorkshire Police* [2007] EWHC 1261 (Admin).

defendants challenged decisions by the police to charge them rather than issue final warnings, and of the CPS to continue to prosecute them. It was alleged that both defendants failed to follow the applicable guidance at the time to such decisions issued by the Home Office. The Youth Court agreed to adjourn the proceedings whilst the High Court heard the case. There was no application to the Youth Court to stay the proceedings for abuse of process. Gray J, with whom May LJ agreed, accepted that there were wider issues of policy in the case that went beyond the complaint of unfairness in the proceedings.[69]

(ii) Waiting for the Outcome of the Case

6-17   Many of the issues outlined in this chapter are ones that may occur at a pre-trial stage or during a trial. Judicial review challenges should not be brought simply as and when a criminal defendant or prosecutor considers it the appropriate remedy. *R v Rochford Justices ex parte Buck* is an important early authority.[70] The prosecution brought a judicial review claim against the justices' ruling on admissibility of evidence at the start of a trial. Lord Widgery LCJ said it was highly unsatisfactory for the High Court to be invited to intervene in proceedings which had not run their course. It was not only a question of practical convenience, but also one of the jurisdiction of the High Court: 'The obligation of this Court to keep out of the way until the magistrate has finished his determination seems to me to be a principle properly to be applied both to summary trial and to committal proceedings'; consequently, 'there was no jurisdiction in this Court to interfere with the justices' decision, that not having been reached by termination of the proceedings below'.[71]

6-18   In an appeal by way of case stated, *Streames v Copping*[72] held that the magistrates do not have a power under section 111(1) of the MCA 1980 to state a case at an interlocutory stage.[73]

6-19   *Ex p Buck* was followed in *R (Hoar-Stevens) v Richmond upon Thames Magistrates' Court*,[74] which was also a case where a challenge was brought mid-trial:

> It was of the utmost importance that the course of a criminal trial in the magistrates' court should not be punctuated by applications for an adjournment to test a ruling in the High Court, especially when in reality if the case proceeded the ruling may turn out to be of little or no importance. Even where, as in the instant case, there was an important substantive point arising during a trial [of inadequate disclosure by the prosecution], the High Court should not and indeed could not intervene, Buck followed. The proper course was to proceed to the end of the trial in the lower court and then to test the matter, almost certainly by way of case stated.[75]

6-20   The above authorities may be interpreted as applying to challenges brought to a decision made during the course of a trial or an interlocutory hearing with the effect of staying

---

[69] ibid [31].

[70] *R v Rochford Justices ex parte Buck* (1979) 68 Cr App R 114.

[71] ibid 118. The court relied on *R v Carden (Robert)* (1879) 5 QBD 1, where Cockburn CJ said 'we have no authority, as it seems to me, to control the magistrate in the conduct of the case, or to prescribe to him the evidence which he shall receive or reject, as the case may be'.

[72] *Streames v Copping* [1985] QB 920, [1985] All ER 122.

[73] This was applied in *R (Paul Rackham Ltd) v Swaffham Magistrates' Court* [2004] EWHC 1417 (Admin)— see below at 6-23. However, note the concerns of Sedley LJ in *Essen v Director of Public Prosecutions* [2005] EWHC 1077 (Admin) discussed below at 6-21.

[74] *R (Hoar-Stevens) v Richmond upon Thames Magistrates' Court* [2003] EWHC 2660 (Admin) (Kennedy).

[75] ibid [18].

Sarah Parkes and Piers von Berg

that hearing whilst the High Court determines the issue.[76] In *R (Singh) v Stratford Magistrates' Court*[77] the claimant challenged a decision to adjourn a trial in order to obtain a psychiatric report. Although The court did not hear argument on the point, Hughes LJ saw it necessary to draw attention to the rule in *Ex p Buck*:

> In general terms the Divisional Court would not entertain, whether by application for judicial review or by way of appeal by case stated, a purely interlocutory challenge to proceedings in the magistrates' court ... It is necessary, in nearly every case, to wait until the end result of the proceedings is known before anyone can tell whether there is a source for complaint or not, and also before the facts of the case can reliably be known for the purposes of decision here.[78]

Despite this statement, there are exceptions where the court accepted jurisdiction. For example, the following reasons were mentioned in *Singh*:

   i.   there had been a delay of one year and any further delay was undesirable;
   ii.   the parties were prepared to argue the issues and were anxious to resolve them;
   iii.   the case did not turn on any factual dispute; and,
   iv.   the claimant sought a mandatory order for the judge to conduct a trial, which the judge had refused to do.[79]

On that day the same Divisional Court also decided *R (Crown Prosecution Service) v Sedgemoor Justices*[80a] which restated the above principles. Again, the court dealt with the case for similar reasons: i) a remittal to the magistrates' court would cause further delay, ii) the magistrates' ruling would have been a terminating one that led to an acquittal, and iii) there was no need to find facts.

(iii) Problems with and Exceptions to the Rule in Ex p Buck

In *Singh* the court recognised that there can be good reasons for accepting jurisdiction   **6-21**
and referred to *R (Watson) v Dartford Magistrates' Court*[80] and *Essen v Director of Public Prosecutions*.[81] With respect, it is submitted that this underplays the objections in those authorities to the rule in *Ex p Buck*.

   Watson concerned a challenge to a grant of an adjournment on the morning of trial. The prosecution, attending as an interested party, contended that following *Ex p Buck* the application was premature. Mitting J, with whom Sedley LJ agreed, rejected that submission: 'In a case such as this, where the issue is straightforward and the principle clear, I do not see that there is any fetter on this court intervening'.[82]

   Essen v Director of Public Prosecutions, an appeal by way of case stated, concerned   **6-22**
complicated challenges to the adjournment of a trial. Beatson J pointed out that *Ex p Buck*

---

[76] Eg *R (K) v Bow Street Magistrates' Court* [2005] EWHC 2271 (Admin), a decision relating to preliminary rulings by a district judge at the beginning of a hearing.
[77] *R (Singh) v Stratford Magistrates' Court* [2007] EWHC 1582 (Admin).
[78] ibid [7]–[8].
[79] This might be seen an example of the application of the overriding objective of the CPR to the particular facts of that case rather than a statement of any guiding principles as Hughes LJ then goes on to discourage applications of this type.
[80] *R (Watson) v Dartford Magistrates' Court* [2005] EWHC 905 Admin.
[80a] *R (Crown Prosecution Service) v Sedgemoor Justices* [2007] EWHC 1803 (Admin).
[81] *Essen* (n 73).
[82] *Watson* (n 80) [7].

applies not only to rulings during a trial but also to other rulings.[83] Sedley LJ observed that the appellant was prevented by *Ex p Buck* from judicially reviewing the initial decision of the magistrates and had to wait two years before he sought relief because of the long delays in the case. As a result, Sedley LJ said this:

> It may be in the light of the present case that this group of decisions could usefully be revisited. If neither judicial review nor appeal by a case stated is available against an interlocutory decision which would arguably have been dispositive of a case at an early and much less costly stage, a fixed rule that any challenge must abide a final outcome is capable of working injustice.[84]

There then followed *Lauderdale & Ors v Mid Sussex Magistrates' Court*,[85] which concerned a grant of an adjournment apparently not on the day of trial but in advance of a fixed date. The court considered the conflicting authorities of *Ex p Buck*, *Hoar-Stevens*, *Watson* and *Essen v DPP*. Gage LJ preferred the view of Mitting J in *Watson* but did not elaborate on his reasons. In *Gillan v DPP*[86], an appeal by way of case stated, the Court refused to entertain an appeal against an interlocutory decision (a decision to hold a fresh *Newton* hearing). Forbes J, with whom Latham LJ agreed, said 'the correct procedure for challenging the lawfulness of an interlocutory decision in criminal proceedings such as the present one is by way of an appropriate claim for judicial review' although the circumstances in which it would be necessary were 'relatively rare and exceptional'.[87]

6-23   In contrast to these authorities there is *R (M) v Bow Street Magistrates Court*,[88] which also considered *Ex p Buck*, *Hoar-Stevens*, *Watson* and *Essen v DPP* but elected to follow *Ex p Buck* and *Hoar-Stevens*. This involved forfeiture of money and arguments over the criminal standard of proof. The Divisional Court found itself unable to address the point, as no evidence had been served and there was no determination of the factual issues. Therefore, it could not identify the legal issues. This authority followed *R (Paul Rackham Ltd) v Swaffham Magistrates Court*,[89] which reached similar conclusions that a claim for judicial review could not be decided because the facts were not available.

6-24   This area has been more recently considered in *Balogun v Director of Public Prosecutions*.[90] This was an appeal by way of case stated challenging the grant of an adjournment. The court permitted judicial review proceedings to be issued out of time as the more appropriate course. Leveson LJ considered *Ex p Buck*, *Hoar-Stevens*, *Sedgemoor Justices*, *Watson* and *Essen v DPP*. He distinguished cases where there was an issue over an adjournment:

> In my judgment, where the issue of an adjournment is raised, different considerations may apply: that is so not only because of the unsatisfactory nature of quashing a conviction which

---

[83] *Essen* (n 71) [20]. See also *Loade v DPP* [1990] 1 QB 1052, [1989] 3 WLR 1281.

[84] ibid [34].

[85] *Lauderdale & Ors v Mid Sussex Magistrates' Court* [2005] EWHC 2854 (Admin).

[86] [2007] EWHC 380 (Admin), [2007] 1 WLR 2214.

[87] ibid, [13]. The Court followed *Loade v DPP* and *Ex p Buck*, *Hoar-Stevens*, *Watson* and *Essen v DPP* were cited in argument.

[88] *R (M) v Bow Street Magistrates Court* [2005] EWHC 2271 (Admin).

[89] *R (Paul Rackham Ltd) v Swaffham Magistrates Court* [2004] EWHC 1417 (Admin).

[90] *Balogun* (n 49).

Sarah Parkes and Piers von Berg

is not itself before the court but also because, in the interim, considerable expense has been incurred, not merely by the parties but also by the court in conducting a hearing which in the event has proved entirely nugatory and thereafter setting aside the original decision.[91]

Leveson LJ advised any seeking to challenge an adjournment to do so as 'a matter of extreme urgency—within days rather than weeks—so as not to affect the continued progress of the case'.

(iv) A Proposed Approach to Challenging Interlocutory Decisions

It is submitted that there are threads which can be drawn out of the various lines of authorities. *Balogun v DPP* identifies the different approach to adjournments evident in *Watson* and *Essen v DPP* that distinguishes *Ex p Buck*. The ratio of these judgments may be extended to other decisions, which if left unchallenged, may incur expense and injustice. It is in line with Lord Bingham's guidance in *Ex p Rowlands* of a claimant advancing a complaint which 'might arguably be held to vitiate the proceedings in the magistrates' court' (see above at 6-16).   **6-25**

On the other hand, none of these decisions alters other principles in *Ex p Buck* that are common to all judicial review matters—claims may be premature if the issues may be resolved within the ongoing proceedings (in other words, an alternative remedy exists). Secondly, judicial review proceedings are unsuited to matters which depend on disputes of fact. Thirdly, there is an understandable unwillingness to disrupt and delay summary proceedings with time-consuming applications to the High Court.

Despite these observations, a comprehensive review of the authorities is clearly needed, not least because the Administrative Court has entertained many challenges to interlocutory decisions, as can be seen from below.[92] There are commonplace interlocutory challenges, such as to decisions on bail, the committal of youths to the Crown Court[93] and the amendment of an information; less common, but also with no mention of *Ex p Buck,* are challenges to the admission of bad character evidence, decisions on special measures and re-opening of the Crown's case. It is submitted that several of these examples are similar to adjournments in the sense of *Ex p Rowlands* and *Balogun* that if the decision was found to be unlawful any subsequent proceedings would be vitiated or nugatory. For example, a conviction or acquittal could be quashed following a trial that is conducted on the basis of unlawfully admitted or rejected bad character evidence or, where the Crown were wrongly permitted to or prevented from reopening their case.   **6-26**

---

[91] ibid [31].

[92] An exception is *R (O) v Batley and Dewsbury Youth Court* [2003] EWHC 2931 (Admin) see below at 6-68).

[93] The High Court has given guidance on such interlocutory challenges in the Youth Court in *Crown Prosecution Service v Newcastle upon Tyne Youth Court* [2010] EWHC 2773 (Admin). It echoes the stress on urgency in *Balogun* (n 49) particularly in cases involving young defendants (the CPS, which was the claimant, was criticised for taking five weeks to consider the matter before making an application).

B. Pre-Trial Matters

(1) Refusal of Legal Aid[94]

6-27   The decision by a magistrates' court to refuse legal aid may be subject to judicial review, as illustrated by the following cases (challenges to decisions by the Legal Aid Agency are dealt with below in section B of Chapter 9). Claimants have succeeded on grounds that i) the court has not provided adequate reasons for its decision, ii) the court has misapplied the guidance and law on granting legal aid to those at risk of custody, or iii) a refusal of legal aid has jeopardised a person's right to a fair trial.

(i) Irrationality

6-28   In *R v Calderdale Magistrates' Court, ex parte Foulger*,[95] Rose LJ quashed a decision to refuse a representation order when the conduct of a defence required legal argument on the failure to conduct an identification parade and the admissibility of evidence under section 78 of PACE 1984. The trial might also have involved a dock identification. The Divisional Court said that it was in the interests of justice for legal aid to be granted, and the magistrates' court decision was irrational.

(ii) Misapplication of Relevant Guidance or Regulations

6-29   In *R (Sonn and Co) v West London Magistrates' Court*,[96] the court endorsed the guidance given by the then Lord Chancellor's Department that legal aid should normally be granted 'where there is a real and practical (as opposed to a theoretical) risk of imprisonment or other form of deprivation of liberty'. This was applied in *R (Sonn MacMillan) v Grays Magistrates' Court*,[97] a decision of Keith J relating to bail and absconding.[98] The court dismissed an application on the basis that the risk of a person being deprived of their liberty was remote, given the facts of the case.

In *R (Punatar) v Horseferry Road Magistrates' Court*[99] the defendant had originally been charged with an imprisonable offence. Due to his previous record of offending there was a strong possibility that the defendant would be given a sentence of imprisonment. At the door of the court the charge was changed to a lesser, non-imprisonable offence. In such circumstances, the court was wrong to not grant a representation order applied for after the charge had been changed. The risk of imprisonment was not to be viewed from the perspective of those passing sentence, but retrospectively from that of solicitor who is considering taking the case.[100]

---

[94] See R Young and A Wilcox, 'The merits of legal aid in the magistrates' courts revisited', [2007],*Criminal Law Review* 109-128.

[95] *R v Calderdale Magistrates' Court, ex parte Foulger*, 14 December 1999.

[96] *R (Sonn and Co) v West London Magistrates' Court*, 30 October 2000.

[97] *R (Sonn MacMillan) v Grays Magistrates' Court* [2006] EWHC 1103 (Admin).

[98] See also authorities on custodial penalties for breaches of bail cited in *Evans v Chester Magistrates' Court* [2004] EWHC 536 (Admin).

[99] *R (Punatar) v Horseferry Road Magistrates' Court* [2002] EWHC 1196 (Admin).

[100] ibid [18] (Sedley LJ).

Regulation 17 of the Criminal Defence Service (General) (No 2) Regulations 2001 (SI 2001/1437) as amended requires the trial court to consider whether to withdraw a right of representation where the charge has been varied and to consider for this purpose whether the interests of justice continue to require representation. In *Punatar*, Sedley LJ considered whether representation could or would have been withdrawn on the day of trial under the provision if representation had been granted in advance of the trial date, and on the day of trial the charge faced by the defendant was reduced from an imprisonable to a non-imprisonable offence. His Lordship could see little point in doing so, on the grounds that practically all the costs would already have been incurred and the only effect would be to deprive the defendant and the court of assistance which had already been paid for.

In *R (Clive Rees Associates) v Swansea Magistrates' Court*[101] a solicitor's firm challenged a transfer of legal aid from one solicitor's firm to another due to a loss of confidence under regulation 16 of the Criminal Defence Service (General) (No 2) Regulations 2001 (SI 2001/1437). The transfer was made by the court and then confirmed by a legal advisor in respect of three defendants jointly charged. First, the Divisional Court agreed with the claimant that the legal advisor had had no jurisdiction to confirm such an order, as regulation 16(1) conferred the power on the justices (section 148(1) of MCA 1980). It was accepted that the duration of the relationship and the quantity of work done were relevant considerations, and the fact that the application was made at an early stage of the proceedings did not of itself justify a transfer. Lloyd Jones J, with whom Beatson J agreed, said this:

> The court must consider in each case whether a substantial compelling reason exists in the sense explained in these authorities. In exercising its discretion within that context, the fact that only limited work has been done by the original representatives may be a factor tending in favour of transfer.[102]

The claimant was hindered in its response to the application in respect of the first two defendants, as no reasons were given for their loss of confidence:

> Simply to assert there has been a breakdown in the relationship will not be sufficient. The court needs to be fully informed in order that it may investigate whether there has been a genuine breakdown for a reason which would justify a transfer of the of the representation order, as opposed, for example, to the mere giving of proper but unpalatable advice.[103]

The claimant did not succeed in obtaining a quashing order, as Lloyd Jones J said this would have disrupted the representation of the first two defendants, who had been committed to the Crown Court, and would have led to additional cost. But the principle above can be relied upon.[104] Regarding the third defendant, the court found that conflicting advice on his fitness to plead had led to his loss of confidence. This entitled the magistrates' court to find that the claimant could no longer represent him.

---

[101] *R (Clive Rees Associates) v Swansea Magistrates' Court* [2011] EWHC 3155 (Admin).

[102] ibid [29]. See the lead authorities of *R v Ashgar Khan*, 10 July 2001, approved in *R v Ulcay (Erdogan)* [2007] EWCA Crim 2379, [2008] 1 WLR 1209, a decision of Sir Igor Judge P, cited at [15]–[16].

[103] ibid [28].

[104] ibid, [41]–[42].

(iii) Breach of Right to Fair Trial

6-30 In *R (Matara) v Brent Magistrates' Court*[105] it was unreasonable to deny legal aid to a defendant with limited knowledge of English, even though an interpreter was provided. This case succeeded on grounds of breach of the defendant's right under Article 6 to participate effectively in his trial. A key issue was that his defence to a charge of failing to provide a breath specimen (section 7 of the Road Traffic Act 1988) was that he could not understand what was being said at the time of his arrest.

In *R (GRK Solicitors) v Liverpool Magistrates' Court*[106] the court should have granted a representation order for a defendant's special reasons hearing. The defendant wished to call her 11-year-old son as a witness, and special measures would have to have been taken to assist a young child in giving evidence to the court.

(2) Commencement of Proceedings

6-31 Decisions to commence proceedings can be challenged as an abuse of process. Abuse of process is considered in more detail below at 6-34. This form of abuse of process relates to misconduct on part of the prosecutor. In *R v Derby Crown Court, ex parte Brooks*[107] a Divisional Court of Lord Lane LCJ and Sir Roger Ormrod confirmed that a magistrates' court has a discretion to stay a case where there is an abuse of process on account of misconduct by the prosecutor:

> It may be an abuse of process if either (a) the prosecution have manipulated or misused the process of the court so as to deprive the defendant of a protection provided by the law or to take unfair advantage of a technicality, or (b) on the balance of probability the defendant has been, or will be, prejudiced in the preparation or conduct of his defence by delay on the part of the prosecution which is unjustifiable: for example, not due to the complexity of the inquiry and preparation of the prosecution case, or to the action of the defendant or his co-accused, or to genuine difficulty in effecting service.[108]

An example of such conduct in commencing proceedings is in *R v Brentford Justices, ex parte Wong*.[109] The prosecutor laid information shortly before expiry of the six-month time limit purely in order to gain time and without having finally decided whether or not to prosecute. The case was remitted for the magistrates to investigate the matter. The court stated that the justices could stay the matter where an abuse of process was found.

(3) Bringing a Private Prosecution

6-32 Private prosecutions can occur i) in the wake of a decision by the CPS not to prosecute, ii) where a jury has failed to reach a verdict, or iii) where a defendant has received a

---

[105] *R (Matara) v Brent Magistrates' Court* [2005] EWHC 1829 (Admin).
[106] *R (GRK Solicitors) v Liverpool Magistrates' Court* [2008] EWHC 2974 (Admin).
[107] *R v Derby Crown Court, ex parte Brooks* (1985) 80 Cr App R 164, 169A.
[108] This was approved in *R v Telford Justices, ex parte Badhan* [1991] 2 WLR 866, [1991] 2 QB 78, 86G by a three-judge Divisional Court of Watkins, Mann LJJ and Otton J. For further discussion of this case, see below at 6-37.
[109] *R v Brentford Justices, ex parte Wong* [1981] QB 445.

Sarah Parkes and Piers von Berg

caution. Note that the CPS's decisions in respect of private prosecutions can be challenged by judicial review (see above at 5-42).

In *R (Charlson) v Guildford Magistrates' Court*[110] Silber J explained that when considering an application to issue a summons for a private prosecution, where the CPS had discontinued a prosecution on the same facts, a magistrates' court should ascertain the following:

i. Whether the allegation was an offence known to the law and, if so, whether the ingredients of the offence were prima facie present;
ii. Whether the summons was time barred;
iii. Whether the court had jurisdiction;
iv. Whether the informant had the necessary authority to prosecute;
v. Any other relevant facts.

Challenges to private prosecutions have been brought by way of an application for a stay of the proceedings on grounds of abuse of process. Claimants have judicially reviewed a magistrates' court's decision to accede to or refuse such applications. Abuse of process is discussed in detail below at 6-34. For example, a challenge may relate to the role of the DPP in not intervening in such cases. In *R v Bow Street Metropolitan Stipendiary Magistrate, ex parte South Coast Shipping*,[111] a private prosecution was brought by families of the victims of the *Marchioness* riverboat disaster after a jury in a public prosecution had twice failed to reach a verdict in a trial of the master of the *Bowbelle*. The defendant applied for judicial review of the judge's refusal to stay the case for abuse of process. The application was refused on the basis that although a private prosecutor was precluded from bringing cases covered by sections 3(2)(a), (c) and (d) of the Prosecution of Offences Act 1980, where a DPP had a duty to bring prosecutions, this did not apply to section 3(2)(b). In these cases the DPP might take over the conduct of the case, but he was not under a duty to do so. The court stated that an indirect or improper motive behind a private prosecution could be a ground for staying a prosecution, although mixed motives could often be present in such prosecutions, but a judge should be slow to accede to such an application unless the conduct complained of was truly oppressive.[112]

This principle was applied in *R (Dacre) v Westminster Magistrates' Court*.[113] The claimant submitted that the case was brought partly to publicise the message of a campaign body. The prosecution was brought against the defendant for the offence of publicising information that was likely to identify a child (section 97 of the Children Act 1989). The Divisional Court applied the principle relating to mixed motives in *Ex p South Coast Shipping* and cited the following principle from *Re Serif Systems Ltd*:[114] 'It is for consideration whether there is a primary motive and one which is so unrelated to the proceedings that it renders it a misuse or an abuse of the process'.[115]

Latham LJ, giving judgment, went further and found that:

there is, however, no reason in principle why, by analogy, a private prosecution should not be considered an abuse of process if the crime which is the subject of the prosecution is one that

---

[110] *R (Charlson) v Guildford Magistrates' Court* [2006] EWHC 2318 (Admin), [2006] 1 WLR 3494.
[111] *R v Bow Street Metropolitan Stipendiary Magistrate, ex parte South Coast Shipping* [1993] 2 WLR 621.
[112] See also on this point *R v Belmarsh Magistrates' Court, ex parte Watts* [1999] 2 Cr App R 188.
[113] *R (Dacre) v Westminster Magistrates' Court* [2008] EWHC 1667 (Admin), [2009] 1 WLR 2241.
[114] *Re Serif Systems Ltd* [1997] CLY 1373 (QBD).
[115] *Dacre* (n 113) [28].

has been encouraged by the private prosecutor or when in some other way the private prosecutor has essentially created the same mischief as that about which he or she complains.[116]

Consequently, the court overturned the district judge's refusal of a stay, as there was evidence that the private individual that brought the prosecution had provided material willingly and deliberately that was likely, if not certain to, identify the child as subject of the proceedings.

In *Jones v Whalley*,[117] a private prosecution was held to be an abuse of process because the defendant had already been cautioned for the matter. The case is similar to the species of abuse of process where a defendant has been given an assurance that he would not be prosecuted (discussed below at 6-38). In essence, the court said that the correct route would be to apply to quash the caution.

(4) Amending an Information

6-33   An information can be amended after six months has elapsed under section 127 of MCA 1980 if it arises from the same or substantially the same facts as the original information—specifically the 'same misdoing'—and the amendment is in the interests of justice.[118] Whether the amendment arises from the same facts is obviously a fact-specific exercise.[119] These decisions are discretionary, and accordingly any judicial review challenge will need to show how the court's decision fell outside the ambit of that discretion. Examples of where an amendment was not in the interests of justice are as follows (note these were brought either by way of appeal by case stated or judicial review):

i.   Where the prosecution has not sought the amendment in a timely fashion, for example, by not raising it at the first hearing devoted to case management or when it first became apparent, but instead waiting to amend the information on the eve of trial (and thereby not adhering to the principles of case management in the Criminal Procedure Rules).[120]

ii.   A decision to refuse a prosecution application to amend on the grounds that it was not in the interests of justice was upheld in *R (DPP) v Everest*,[121] where the magistrates' court considered the following factors:
(a)   a failure to follow the Code of Crown Prosecutors;
(b)   a failure to review the file promptly;
(c)   the new offence had a greater penalty and placed a burden on defendant;[122]
(d)   the defendant was not represented.

---

[116] *Dacre* (n 113) [31]. See also *R v Looseley* [2001] UKHL 53, [2001] 1 WLR 2060.

[117] *Jones v Whalley* [2006] UKHL 41, [2007] 1 AC 63. See above at 4-92.

[118] *Simpson v Roberts*, Times, 21 December 1984, [1985] CLY 2095 (DC). Followed in *R v Scunthorpe Justices, ex parte M* (1998) 162 JP 635.

[119] *Ex p M*, as applied in *Williams v DPP* [2009] EWHC 2354 (Admin).

[120] *Williams* (Thomas LJ) (n 119).

[121] *R (DPP) v Everest* [2005] EWHC 1124 (Admin).

[122] Another example of an amendment being against the interests of justice on the basis that the new offence carried a heavier penalty than the previous one is *Shaw v DPP* [2007] EWHC 207 (Admin).

Sarah Parkes and Piers von Berg

(5) Abuse of Process

(i) General Principles

It has long been held that a court has the power to ensure that the process of justice is not abused.[123] In *R v Beckford*,[124] Neill LJ identified the jurisdiction to stay proceedings for abuse of process in two main areas or limbs: i) where the defendant cannot receive a fair trial or ii) where it would be unfair to try the defendant.[125] These cases will often engage a criminal defendant's rights under Article 6, and practitioners should be mindful of its various provisions as applicable to a magistrates' court under section 6(1) of the HRA 1998 (see discussion above at 1-68).

A magistrates' court has a power to stay the proceedings if they amount to an abuse of process.[126] This is subject to the exception of the types of abuse of power identified in *Ex p Bennett (No 1)* discussed above at 6-16. Where it should decline jurisdiction and refer the matter to the High Court.

Commentators have identified several types of abuse of process from the case law (note also the discussions above on commencement of proceedings and private prosecutions):[127]

i.   reneging on a representation or undertaking not to prosecute;
ii. inordinate or unreasonable delay in trying the defendant;
iii. manipulation of procedure by the prosecution or abuse of power/breach of human rights by the state;
iv. adverse publicity;
v.   loss of evidence by the police or prosecution; and
vi. issue of a summons by the magistrates' court.

These headings are explored in more detail below. Abuse of process can also be encountered in proceedings under the Proceeds of Crime Act 2002 and in extradition proceedings, and the latter is addressed separately below at in Chapter 13. Note that this work

---

[123] *Metropolitan Bank Ltd v Pooley* (1885) 10 App Cas 210, 214 (Earl of Selborne LC): 'The power seemed to be inherent in the jurisdiction of every court of justice to protect itself from the abuse of its own procedure'. *DPP v Connelly* [1964] AC 1254, [1964] 2 WLR 1145, 1354 (Lord Devlin): 'The courts cannot contemplate for a moment the transference to the Executive of the responsibility for seeing that the process of law is not abused'. In *DPP v Humphrys* [1977] AC 1, [1976] 2 WLR 857, 46, Lord Salmon said this: 'It is only if the prosecution amounts to an abuse of the process of the court and is oppressive and vexatious that the judge has the power to intervene', although note dicta of Lord Morris, Lord Pearce and Lord Hodson in *Connelly* was not applied.

[124] *R v Beckford* [1996] 1 Cr App R 94, 100.

[125] The same division was set out by Lord Lowry in *Ex p Bennett (No 1)* 72G, (n 67). It has been said more recently that these are two separate distinct categories, in *Warren v Attorney General for Jersey* [2012] 1 AC 22, PC.

[126] *Dacre* (n 113) [26], discussed above at 6-32. The improper motive in that case was said to be under the second limb of abuse of process.

[127] See D Young, M Summers and D Corker, *Abuse of Process in Criminal Proceedings*, 3rd edn (Haywards Heath, Tottel Publishing, 2009) and C Wells, *Abuse of Process*, 2nd edn (Bristol, Jordans, 2011). There are arguably several more, including entrapment. Where the question of entrapment has arisen in the magistrates' courts, it has been in the context of arguments over the admissibility of evidence of police officers, allegedly acting as agents provocateurs. These challenges have been brought by way of appeal by case stated, eg *Nottingham City Council v Amin* [2000] 1 WLR 1071, [2000] 2 All ER 946 and *Williams (Gary John) v DPP* [1993] 3 All ER 365, (1994) 98 Cr App R 209.

deals elsewhere with challenges to decisions to charge (above at 5-12), commence proceedings (above at 6-31) and decisions relating to private prosecutions (above at 5-42 and 6-32).

6-35   The appellate courts have repeatedly stated that the power to stay proceedings must be used very sparingly.[128] A criminal defendant can challenge a refusal to stay the proceedings by way of judicial review, or he can invite the magistrates' court to decline jurisdiction and seek a stay of proceedings in the High Court. The latter category of cases (per *Ex p Bennett (No 1)*) concerns complex or novel points or those relating to the wider application of the rule of law, which should be dealt with in the High Court or in the Crown Court, if the case is sent there.[129] If there is any doubt, the magistrates' court should decline jurisdiction.[130] This does not prevent a magistrates' court from enquiring into a complaint prior to sending a case to the Crown Court. It may stay the proceedings, including those for indictable offences, before they reach the Crown Court.[131] The higher courts have stressed the lower courts' jurisdiction should be used to entertain points directed to matters affecting the fairness and propriety of the trial before it, rather than wider points touching on the rule of law.[132]

6-36   Claimants should exhaust alternative and effective remedies first. For example, relevant points to consider are rulings on the admissibility or exclusion of certain evidence that has been obtained unfairly.[133] The defence may be able to exploit gaps in the prosecution case and they may invite the court to dismiss the case for lack of sufficient evidence after hearing the prosecution's evidence.[134]

Potential claimants must also bear in mind that judicial review is unsuited for prolonged investigation into disputed facts. Permission may well be refused on this point alone if the application involves a lengthy examination of the factual background, which may not be agreed by the Crown.[135]

Practitioners should also be aware that the High Court does not consider itself a readily available appellate court for failed abuse of process applications in the magistrates' courts. As with any application for judicial review, a claim should show grounds why the action of a public body is unlawful, for example, that it was 'plainly irrational and untenable that no reasonable bench of justices, properly directed, could have reached it'.[136] As the power to stay proceedings should be used sparingly, it is understandable that a refusal to exercise it will only be quashed in 'a very exceptional case'.[137]

---

[128] *Ex p Bennett (No 1)* (n 125) 63H. See above at 1-9, 6-16 and below at 6-43.

[129] ibid 64D (Lord Griffiths); *Ex p Watts* (n 112); and, on sending to the Crown Court, *R v Horseferry Magistrates' Court, ex parte DPP* [1999] COD 441, DC.

[130] *Ex p Watts* (n 112).

[131] *R (Salubi) v Bow Street Magistrates' Court* [2002] 1 WLR 3073.

[132] *Ex p Watts* (n 112) 195A (applying *Ex p Bennett (No 1)*).

[133] See in particular *R (Ebrahim) v Feltham Magistrates' Court* [2001] 2 Cr App R 23, DC discussed below at 6-45.

[134] On the former point, see *DPP v S* [2002] EWHC 2982 and on the latter see the principles in *R v Galbraith* [1981] 1 WLR 1039.

[135] See Young, Summers and Corker (n 127) pp 369–370. The authors also point out that a voir dire procedure is available in the Crown Court that permits the calling of live evidence on a disputed point. They remind potential applicants that an adverse decision in the High Court may also weigh substantially with any trial judge asked to reconsider the matter.

[136] *R v Liverpool City Justices and Crown Prosecution Service, ex parte Price* [1998] COD 453, 455.

[137] ibid, 455 (Brooke LJ).

(ii) Procedure (Abuse of Process)

The burden of proof rests on the party claiming there is abuse and it must be met to   **6-37**
a balance of probabilities.[138] In *R (Salubi) v Bow Street Magistrates' Court*[139] the court
made it clear that when a case is committed to the Crown Court, an abuse of process
application can be made at committal stage.

On hearing an application, if a magistrates' court hears evidence from the prosecution,
it may well infringe the principles of natural justice to refuse a request of the defendant
to give evidence; the court should hear the full facts before it comes to its decision.[140]
However, the court does not have power to order disclosure and summon witnesses, as
the Criminal Procedure (Attendance of Witnesses) Act 1965 only applies to trial.

If a magistrates' court's decision is challenged in the High Court, advocates should
provide an agreed note of the decision and of any evidence heard. The application can
be made for a conviction to be quashed on the basis that the proceedings below were
unfair and cannot be addressed on appeal.[141]

(iii) Representations not to Prosecute

In *R v Abu Hamza*,[142] Lord Phillips LCJ stated that it may constitute an abuse of process   **6-38**
where:

   i.   there is an unequivocal representation by the police or the CPS that the defen-
        dant will not be prosecuted; and
   ii. the defendant acted on that representation to his detriment.

The court added that if facts came to light that were not known at the time of the representation, 'these may justify proceeding with the prosecution despite the representation'.
In coming to the above statement of principle, Lord Phillips LCJ considered the following cases. In *R v Croydon Justices, ex parte Dean*[143] a defendant, who had assisted
to destroy evidence after a murder, was assured he would not be prosecuted if he gave
evidence for the Crown. He then gave evidence and admitted his role. It was held
to be an abuse to prosecute in such exceptional circumstances. In *R v Townsend*,[144]
Rose LJ said that an abuse will be more likely if there is a significant period of time
during which a defendant believed he would not be prosecuted. In *R v Bloomfield*[145]
there was an abuse of process where prosecuting counsel had unequivocally informed
the court that no further evidence would be offered and there were no changes
in circumstances.

---

[138] *Ex p Badhan* (n 108) 91D.
[139] (n 131).
[140] *R v Clerkenwell Stipendiary Magistrate, ex parte Bell* (1991) 159 JP 669 and *R v Crawley Justices, ex parte DPP* (1991) 155 JP 841.
[141] On both points in this paragraph see *Ebrahim* (n 133).
[142] *R v Abu Hamza* [2006] EWCA Crim 2918, [2007] QB 659 [51].
[143] *R v Croydon Justices, ex parte Dean* [1993] QB 769.
[144] *R v Townsend* [1997] 2 Cr App R 540.
[145] *R v Bloomfield* [1997] 1 Cr App R 135.

The Court of Appeal emphasised in *R v Gripton*[146] that since *R v Abu Hamza* the above principles are not a binding rule. The court is concerned with considerations of fairness, and must be free to respond to the circumstances of the case. In *R v Gripton*, prosecution counsel had made an unequivocal representation in open court. Although there had been no detrimental reliance on it by the defendant, the court was prepared to consider whether there was an abuse. The court expressed the view that it would undesirable to go back on a statement in open court.

Other examples include *R (H) v Guildford Youth Court*,[147] where a defendant was prosecuted for grievous bodily harm. The prosecution was an abuse of process where the representation had been made by the police in an interview that they would deal with the matter by way of a final warning. The seriousness of the charge was not a relevant factor in deciding whether there had been an abuse. For a different outcome in a case where it could not be said that there was any prejudice to the defendant, see *R (Tunbridge Wells BC) v Sevenoaks Magistrates' Court*.[148]

(iv) Delay[149]

6-39 In the leading case of *Attorney General's Reference (No 1 of 1990)*[150] it was held that a stay on grounds of delay was to be imposed only i) in exceptional circumstances where the delay was unjustifiable, ii) even more rarely in the absence of fault on the part of complainant or prosecution, and, iii) never when the delay was due to the complexity of the case or the actions of the defendant.

Further, a stay would not be imposed unless a criminal defendant established that he would suffer serious prejudice because of the delay to the extent that no fair trial could be held. When deciding whether a fair trial could be held, a court should bear in mind the powers of the judge and the trial process itself to provide protection from prejudice.[151]

In *R v S (SP)*,[152] Rose LJ, giving the judgment of the Court, restated that:

i.   where there has been no fault on part of either party it would be very rare to grant a stay;

ii. a stay should not be granted where there is no serious prejudice to the defendant; and

iii. when assessing the level of prejudice, the court must consider its power to regulate the admissibility of evidence.

---

[146] *R v Gripton* [2010] EWCA Crim 2260.

[147] *R (H) v Guildford Youth Court* [2008] EWHC 506 (Admin). Note *R v Abu Hamza* was not cited.

[148] *R (Tunbridge Wells BC) v Sevenoaks Magistrates' Court* [2001] EWHC Admin 897. See also *Jones v Whalley* [2007] 1 AC 63 above at 6-32.

[149] Note this is discussed in context of challenges to decisions by the CPS at 5-25 above and trial of young defendants below at 11-37.

[150] *Attorney General's Reference (No 1 of 1990)* [1992] QB 630, [1992] 3 WLR 9.

[151] These principles were approved as the general test in *R v F* [2011] EWCA Crim 1844, [2012] QB 703 by a five-judge Court of Appeal led by Lord Judge LCJ. The court also approved *R v S (SP)* [2006] 2 Cr App R 23, see above.

[152] *R v S (SP)* [2006] 2 Cr App R 23.

In *Attorney General's Reference (No 2 of 2001)*,[153] a judgment of a nine-member panel of   **6-40**
the House of Lords, the court considered the requirement under Article 6(1) of ECHR
to hold a trial within a reasonable time. It was held that a failure by a public authority to hold a hearing within a reasonable time constituted a breach of the defendant's
rights under Article 6(1), and a remedy should be afforded which was effective, just and
proportionate. This did not necessarily mean a defendant was entitled to a stay to the
proceedings.

The appropriate remedy would depend on the nature of the breach and all the circumstances, including the stage of the proceedings at which the breach was established.
The public interest in the final determination of criminal charges required that a charge
should not be stayed or dismissed if any lesser remedy would be just and proportionate
in all the circumstances. Consequently, a stay or dismissal of proceedings would not be
appropriate unless there could no longer be a fair trial or it would otherwise be unfair
to try the defendant.

In the past the courts have been reluctant to set any time limit. For example, the court   **6-41**
in *R v Grays Justices, ex parte Graham*[154] refused to set any specific limitation period after
which delay would constitute an abuse of process. The ECtHR dismissed a complaint
under Article 6 of a delay of 56 years in the somewhat exceptional case of *Sawoniuk v
United Kingdom*.[155]

One important consideration is the defendant's age. In cases concerning youths   **6-42**
the wording of Article 6 must be read in light of international law on the rights of
children.[156] At common law it is accepted that criminal proceedings involving youths
should be brought with all due expedition.[157] For a discussion of these points see
above at note 93. There are cases where the court has approved of differential treatment on the basis of age, allowing longer delays for adults and prohibiting similar
periods for youths. For in example, in *R (Knight) v West Dorset Magistrates' Court*[158]
it was held that the court was correct not to stay proceedings in respect of two adults
on grounds of undue delay, where it had been stayed for their co-defendant who was
a youth (aged 17).

(v) *Abuse of Power or Manipulation of Procedures (Including Conduct of Legal Advisors)*

In *Ex p Bennett (No 1)* Lord Griffiths said: **6-43**

If the court is to have the power to interfere with the prosecution in the present circumstances
it must be because the judiciary accept a responsibility for the maintenance of the rule of law
that embraces a willingness to oversee executive action and to refuse to countenance behaviour
that threatens either basic human rights or the rule of law.[159]

---

[153] *Attorney General's Reference (No 2 of 2001)* [2003] UKHL 68, [2004] 2 AC 72.
[154] *R v Grays Justices, ex parte Graham* [1982] QB 1239.
[155] *Sawoniuk v United Kingdom* [2001] Crim LR 918.
[156] See *Dyer v Watson* [2002] UKPC D1, [2004] 1 AC 379 and discussion below at 11-6 and at 11-41.
[157] See above *Crown Prosecution Service v Newcastle upon Tyne Youth Court* (n 93).
[158] *R (Knight) v West Dorset Magistrates' Court* [2002] EWHC 2152 (Admin).
[159] *Ex p Bennett (No 1)* (n 125) 63A. See above at 1-9, 6-16 and 6-35.

The first application of this principle is to the manner in which the defendant is brought before the courts. Regardless of whether a fair trial could be had, if pre-trial conduct of the state was found to 'compromise the integrity of the judicial process, dishonour the administration of justice', the proceedings could be stayed.[160] The examples in the case law include where evidence is obtained by torture or where the defendant is forcibly brought from overseas outside of the lawful extradition procedure.[161] The court will have to balance the competing interests of trying offences and not undermining public confidence in the criminal justice system.[162]

Cases involving alleged misconduct or manipulation of procedures by the prosecution are considered above at 5-16 and the applicant will usually need to show bad faith or serious misconduct that prevents him receiving a fair trial, or that it is unfair to try him.[163] An example in the context of the magistrates' courts is the conduct and interaction with legal advisors. In *R v Faversham and Sittingbourne Justices, ex parte Stickings*[164] justices had ruled certain evidence inadmissible on the advice of their clerk. The prosecution then complained to a senior clerk. This clerk, who was not present at the hearing, intervened and advised the justices, who then reversed the ruling. This was only disclosed to the defence when they arrived for the trial. Pill LJ held it was wrong for the prosecution to discuss with the clerk rulings that were adverse to them after the fact, where there was to be a further hearing.

The Divisional Court interpreted *Ex p Stickings* in *R (Hussain) v Peterborough Magistrates' Court*.[165] It cautioned applicants for judicial review that even where this type of unfairness exists, it does not necessarily follow that the court will grant an application, as it will depend on the facts and circumstances of the case.[166] In *Hussain*, the prosecution complained about the conduct of a clerk after he advised on a decision that was adverse to the prosecution. This advice turned out to be incorrect and the case was adjourned. The clerk did not then appear at a subsequent hearing. The defence based an abuse of process application on the fact that the prosecution had complained about the clerk and the clerk did not attend the subsequent hearing. The district judge made findings that there was no intentional manipulation of the court process. Furthermore, the advice of the clerk had no impact on the subsequent hearing. Notably, the claimant conceded that he would receive a fair trial, and confined his submissions to the second limb that it was unfair to try him. The court distinguished *Ex p Stickings* and ruled that where the prosecution correspond with a clerk without informing the defence, and that has an effect on a case (intentional or not), that will not of itself justify a stay of proceedings. These cases demonstrate how fact-sensitive these applications can be.

---

[160] *A & Ors v Secretary of State for the Home Department* [2005] UKHL 71, [2006] 2 AC 221 [87] (Lord Hoffmann).

[161] Eg in *A & Ors* and *Ex p Bennett (No 1)* (n 125).

[162] *Warren* (n 125) [26] (Lord Dyson). This was said to apply to both abduction and entrapment cases.

[163] See *Ex p Wong* (n 109) (above at 6-31) and *R v Rotherham Justices, ex parte Brough* [1991] COD 89, DC.

[164] *R v Faversham and Sittingbourne Justices, ex parte Stickings* (1996) 160 JP 801.

[165] *Ex p Stickings* in *R (Hussain) v Peterborough Magistrates' Court* [2007] EWHC 667 (Admin).

[166] *Hussain* (n 165) [21].

Sarah Parkes and Piers von Berg

(vi) Adverse Publicity

This issue may rarely arise in the magistrates' courts either because there is a profes-   **6-44**
sional judge sitting or because lay justices are experienced in dealing with cases. On
the latter point note the principle in *R v Central Criminal Court, ex parte The Telegraph
Plc*[167] that 'a court should credit the jury with the will and ability to abide by the judge's
direction to decide the case only on the evidence before them', and Sir Igor Judge P's
comments in *R v B*[168] on the integrity of juries.[169]

(vii) Loss of Evidence

In *R (Ebrahim) v Feltham Magistrates' Court*,[170] the defendant sought a stay for abuse of   **6-45**
process where videotape evidence relevant to the defence had been destroyed. A defendant in the magistrates' court may seek judicial review of a court's refusal to accede to
such an application. Brooke LJ set out the following guidance:

i.   What was the nature and extent of the police and/or prosecutor's duty to obtain
      or retain the evidence?
ii.   If the duty was not engaged before the defence sought the evidence in question,
      then there can be no unfairness.
iii. If the evidence is not obtained and/or retained in breach of the code of practice
      issued under section 25 of the Crime and Procedure and Investigations Act 1996
      and the Attorney General's guidelines on disclosure, it is necessary to ascertain if
      the defence have proved that as a result of this failure, the defendant will suffer
      serious prejudice such that a fair trial could not happen.
iv.   A stay can also be granted if the prosecution's behaviour shows bad faith or seri-
      ous misconduct.[171]

This guidance has been applied in many subsequent reported cases. It is submitted that a key issue was whether the defendant could have still received a fair trial
despite the loss or destruction of evidence (as per *Attorney General's Reference (No 2
of 2001)*[172]):

i.   In *R v Dobson*[173] an alleged failure by the police to obtain and investigate CCTV
      footage did not constitute an abuse of process. There was no certainty the evi-
      dence would have assisted the defence. The defendant had also had ample time
      to procure additional supporting evidence, so the preparation of his case had not
      been prejudiced.

---

[167] *R v Central Criminal Court, ex parte The Telegraph Plc* (1994) 98 CR App R 91, 98.
[168] *R v B* [2006] EWCA 2692, [31].
[169] For an example of how such an issue may arise where a case is sent to the Crown Court see *R v Bow
Street Stipendiary Magistrate, ex parte DPP* [1992] 95 Cr App R 9, DC.
[170] (n 133).
[171] Applied in *DPP v S* [2002] EWHC 2982 (Admin).
[172] *Attorney General's Reference (No 2 of 2001)* (n 153).
[173] *R v Dobson* [2001] EWCA Crim 1606.

ii.   *Dobson* was applied in *Leatherland v Powys CC*,[174] where Owen J ruled that the destruction of evidence was an abuse of process. In that case sheep carcasses had been destroyed where the sole issue was the condition of the sheep on arrival at market.

iii. In *DPP v Cooper*,[175] a case of drugs possession, the issue was whether the defendant was able to challenge evidence of a forensic scientist who had found traces of the drugs. The court overturned a stay of proceedings despite a loss of a video record of the scientist's tests due to police negligence and the inability of the defence to have their own tests done. Silber J held that the expert witness could be cross-examined on the issue and allowance could have been made for the lack of defence evidence.

iv.   For a case in which delay led to a loss of material documents by which a victim's credibility could be assessed and thereby caused prejudice resulting in an unfair trial, see *Ali v CPS West Midlands*.[176]

(viii) Issue of Summonses

6-46 In *R v Redbridge Justices, ex parte Whitehouse*[177] the prosecution issued an additional summons to ensure trial on indictment. It was held that there was enough evidence to justify committal for trial. It was held that:

> the fact that the prosecution wish to add or substitute new charges either to ensure that the case is tried summarily or to ensure that it is tried in the Crown Court is not a ground for refusing the issue of a summons or other process provided that on the facts disclosed the justices are satisfied that the course proposed by the prosecution is proper and appropriate in the light of the facts put before them.[178]

Clearly, the justices should not agree to the addition of a charge which is triable only on indictment, if the facts are incapable of supporting such a charge and the fresh charge can be seen to be a device to deprive the justices of their jurisdiction to try the case themselves. In this case, it was held that there was enough evidence to justify committal for trial and thus no abuse.

In *R v Rotherham Justices, ex parte Brough*,[179] the prosecution did not seek a summons until the defendant reached 17 years of age. At that point the Youth Court had to exercise a discretion not to send the case to the Crown Court. This example of calculated delay was held to be deliberate manipulation of the process.

(6) Bail

6-47 Under section 4 of the Bail Act 1976 a person who is brought before a magistrates' court has a right to bail unless one of the conditions in Schedule 1 is made out. The test is that

---

[174] *Leatherland v Powys CC* [2007] EWHC 148 (Admin).
[175] *DPP v Cooper* [2008] EWHC 507.
[176] *Ali v CPS West Midlands* [2007] EWCA Crim 691.
[177] *R v Redbridge Justices, ex parte Whitehouse* [1992] 94 Cr App R 332.
[178] ibid 339.
[179] *R v Rotherham Justices, ex parte Brough* (n 163).

Sarah Parkes and Piers von Berg

the court must be satisfied that there are substantial grounds for belief that one of these conditions may occur.[180] When a magistrates' court grants or refuses bail or imposes or varies conditions, it must give reasons.[181]

There are exceptions to the general right to bail under section 25(1) of the Criminal Justice and Public Order Act (CJPO) 1994. The absolute prohibition on pre-trial bail for defendants charged with murder, attempted murder, manslaughter, rape or attempted rape with a previous conviction for such an offence under section 25(1) of CJPO has been removed as a consequence of the decision in *Caballero v United Kingdom*,[182] which found this section to breach Article 5(3).[183] However, it is notable that such a prohibition has survived in respect of extradition proceedings where a defendant charged with an offence that would be triable as an either-way or indictable offence, committed at a time when he was on bail for another offence, cannot apply for bail.[184]

There are a range of different challenges that may arise either on grounds of error of law, procedural impropriety or breach of rights under the ECHR, especially Article 5 (see a discussion on Article 5 above at 1-67). What follows below is a summary of the main areas (statutory references are to the Bail Act 1976). Challenges to police bail are dealt with above at 4-83. Practitioners should bear in mind that there is an alternative remedy in the form of an appeal to the Crown Court against a grant or refusal of bail and a decision on bail conditions.[185]

(i) Bail Procedure

Section 7 provides an enforcement mechanism of arrest without warrant of persons for anticipated and actual breaches bail (section 7(3)), who are then brought before a magistrate (section 7(4)). There have several judicial review challenges to the procedure adopted at such hearings. Section 7(5) states: **6-48**

> (5)—A justice of the peace before whom a person is brought under subsection (4) or (4B) above may, subject to subsection (6) below [children and young persons and remands to local authority care], if of the opinion that that person—
>
> (a)   is not likely to surrender to custody, or
> (b)   has broken or is likely to break any condition of his bail,

---

[180] See *R v Nottingham Justices, ex parte Davies* [1981] 1 QB 38. A judge should also have regard, in respect to Sch 1, para 2 to the factors set out in para 9.

[181] Bail Act 1976, ss 5(2A)–(2B) and 5(3). The Law Commission stated that these must be 'clear and adequate and deal with the substantial issues in the case', and 'any refusal of bail which is recorded in the standard form [that is by repeating the statutory wording on a standard form] is in danger of being held to violate Article 5', Consultation Paper No 157, *Bail and the Human Rights Act 1998*, paras 4.20–4.21, cited in B Emmerson QC, A Ashworth QC and A MacDonald with A L-T Choo and M Summers (gen eds), *Human Rights and Criminal Justice*, 3rd edn (London, Sweet & Maxwell, 2012), 8-121.

[182] *Caballero v United Kingdom* (2000) 30 EHRR 643.

[183] See also *SBC v United Kingdom* (2002) 34 EHRR 21. Note also *R (O) v Crown Court at Harrow and Governor of HMP Wormwood Scrubs* [2006] UKHL 42, [2007] 1 AC 249, a judicial review of a Crown Court's decision on bail. It was held that a refusal of bail beyond the applicable custody time limits was not a breach of Art 5(3). The application was dismissed in *O'Dowd v United Kingdom* (2012) 54 EHRR 8.

[184] See Bail Act 1976, Sch 1, para 2B. This is argued to be a provision 'highly unlikely to withstand challenge' in Emmerson et al (gen eds) (n 181), 8-59.

[185] See Criminal Procedure Rules, rr 19.8–19.9 and CJA 2003, s 16 for the limited class of bail conditions that can be appealed. These are set out in the above section on police bail at 4-83.

remand him in custody or commit him to custody, as the case may require, or alternatively, grant him bail subject to the same or to different conditions, but if not of that opinion shall grant him bail subject to the same conditions (if any) as were originally imposed.

In *R v Liverpool Justices, ex parte DPP*[186] the defendant was brought before the court pursuant to section 7(4). The single justice adjourned the case on being told that formal evidence would have to be called, and that the hearing would require at least two justices as it would in effect be a trial. A three-judge Divisional Court held that the single justice was wrong to adjourn. Proceedings under section 7(5) can be conducted by a single justice and can take place as an information inquiry without the giving of evidence on oath or cross-examination.[187]

In contrast, an adjournment was permitted in *R (Hussain) v Derby Magistrates' Court*.[188] Here, the defendant was brought before the justices under section 7(4)(a). They began to hear the application in the morning and adjourned it to be heard by the district judge in the afternoon. This was acceptable on the basis that the procedure was one where speed was critical, and, not involving say a trial, section 7(5) was not to be construed as subject to procedural rigidities which might lead to delay.

Importantly, the Divisional Court in *R (DPP) v Havering Magistrates' Court*[189] held that Article 6 has no application to proceedings under section 7(5) as they are not a determination of a criminal charge. However, Article 5(4) does apply:[190]

> (4) Everyone who is deprived of his liberty by arrest or detention shall be entitled to take proceedings by which the lawfulness of his detention shall be decided speedily by a court and his release ordered if the detention is not lawful.

In that case, it was said that a person was entitled to natural justice, including a truly adversarial hearing with equality of arms between the parties. The following points from the case law of the ECtHR were agreed:[191]

i.   It was a breach of Article 5 where a detained person did not have an opportunity to see and respond to the submissions of the prosecution.

ii. It was a breach of the principle of the equality of arms where defence counsel did not have an opportunity to view documents relied upon for justification to detain the defendant.

iii. It was held to be a breach where the hearing was conducted without notifying the defendant or offering him an opportunity to be present.

---

[186] *R v Liverpool Justices, ex parte DPP* [1993] QB 233 D, [1992] 3 WLR 20.

[187] This has been followed in *R (Culley) v Dorchester Crown Court* [2007] EWHC 109 (Admin) (although this is later doubted on a different point see below at 6-52), *R (Vickers) v West London Magistrates' Court* [2003] EWHC 1809 (Admin) and *R (DPP) v Havering Magistrates' Court* [2001] 1 WLR 805, [2001] 3 All ER 997—see below at 6-51.

[188] *R (Hussain) v Derby Magistrates' Court* [2001] EWHC Admin 507.

[189] *R (DPP) v Havering Magistrates' Court* (n 183).

[190] This is considered in more detail below at 6-51.

[191] These were respectively: *Sanchez-Reisse v Switzerland* (1986) 9 EHRR 71, *Lamy v Belgium* (1989) 11 EHRR 529 and *Toth v Austria* (1991) 14 EHRR 551. Note that commentators have argued that there was a misinterpretation of *Sanchez-Reisse v Switzerland*—see n 205 below.

Sarah Parkes and Piers von Berg

(ii) Fresh Applications for Bail (Change of Circumstances)

In *R v Nottingham Justices, ex parte Davies*,[192] the defendant made two consecutive **6-49** bail applications, both of which were refused. The justices, on being informed that the defendant's circumstances had not changed since the previous applications, refused bail on the third application without considering the facts. It was held that on renewed applications the court's duty is to consider new circumstances and not to review findings of fact made on previous applications.[193]

It was decided in *R v Dover and East Kent Justices, ex parte Dean*[194] that where a defendant does not make an application for bail, does not appear[195] and consents to further remand in custody, these hearings do not constitute occasions when an application for bail is considered. Therefore, the justices are bound to hear his application at a subsequent hearing.

In *R (B) v Brent Youth Court*,[196] in respect of youths it was held that even if no new grounds are advanced, the court is compelled by section 44 of the Children and Young Persons Act 1933 to consider the welfare of the defendant, and had erred in declining to consider his application. The case is also an interesting example of the application of *Ex p Davies*, as Wilkie J accepted that the proposal by the defendant of new bail conditions that had not been canvased before, which appeared to address the prosecution's concerns, constituted an argument of fact not previously considered. Furthermore, an assessment of the prosecution's evidence suggested its case was not as strong as previously thought. The Youth Court erred in law in refusing to entertain these new arguments of fact and law.

(iii) Bail Conditions

In *R v Bournemouth Magistrates' Court, ex parte Cross (Barry)*[197] it was held that as there **6-50** is no power to withhold bail except on the grounds set out in the Bail Act 1976, a refusal to grant bail because a defendant would not consent to a condition of bail was wrong. The Divisional Court pointed out that if consent to the requirement had been a condition to be complied with before release, the case would have been different.

In *R v Mansfield Justices, ex parte Sharkey*[198] the court decided that the tests for refusing bail and imposing conditions must not be confused. A bail condition was imposed on the ground that the defendant was likely to commit further offences whilst on bail. The claimant argued that there were no substantial grounds for believing this. It was held that the justices did not have to be satisfied that there were substantial grounds for believing that the defendant would commit further offences. That requirement applied

---

[192] *R v Nottingham Justices, ex parte Davies* [1981] QB 38.
[193] See also *R v Slough Justices, ex parte Duncan* (1982) 75 Cr App R 384.
[194] *R v Dover and East Kent Justices, ex parte Dean* [1992] Crim LR 33.
[195] Although MCA 1980, s 122 allows the court to proceed in his absence if the defendant is represented, a decision by a court to proceed in his absence against his wishes is liable to challenge by judicial review. See Consultation Paper No 157, *Bail and the Human Rights Act 1998*, para 11.14, fn 18, cited in Emmerson et al (gen eds) (n 181), 8-108.
[196] *R (B) v Brent Youth Court* [2010] EWHC 1893 (Admin).
[197] *R v Bournemouth Magistrates' Court, ex parte Cross (Barry)* (1989) 89 Cr App R 90.
[198] *R v Mansfield Justices, ex parte Sharkey* [1985] QB 613, [1984] 3 WLR 1328.

where it was proposed to refuse bail rather than grant it with conditions. The test for imposing conditions was whether the justices perceived a real rather than fanciful risk of a further offence being committed.[199]

In *R (Crown Prosecution Service) v Chorley Justices*,[200] Latham LJ found that the justices have a power to impose a doorstep condition in addition to a curfew under section 3(6) and added that whether it was necessary to impose such a condition is a question of fact to be determined in each case.[201]

(iv) Human Rights (Bail)

6-51   Under section 6(1) and 6(3)(a) of the HRA 1998, it is unlawful for a magistrates' court as a public body to act in a way that is incompatible with a Convention right (see above comments on Article 5 and procedure at 6-48). There are several examples of how ECHR rights have been relied upon (see also general discussion of these rights above at 1-64):

i.   Inhuman and degrading treatment (Article 3): in *R (Smith) v Uxbridge Magistrates' Court*[202] the claimant sought judicial review of a decision of the magistrates' court to remand him into custody under section 152 of the Criminal Justice Act 1988. The claimant had been subjected to an X-ray that was inconclusive about the presence of a package of drugs inside him. He had refused to eat for 23 days. On the facts, the claimant had not reached a point where his remand had become unlawful by reference to his Article 3 rights, but in such a case the judge should keep the matter under a regular review and ensure she was fully informed of the medical evidence (for the test on Article 3 see above at 4-81 and below at 8-22).

ii.   Unlawful detention (Article 5) and fair trial (Article 6): in *R (DPP) v Havering Magistrates' Court*[203] (discussed above at 6-48) the justices had decided that proceedings brought against the defendant under section 7(5)[204] for breach of the conditions of his bail should be withdrawn, on the grounds that oral evidence was needed to show that the defendant had acted in breach of the conditions. The Divisional Court disagreed. Liability for detention under section 7 did not equate to the facing of a criminal charge, and therefore Article 6 did not have any direct relevance.[205] It was held that Article 5 did not limit the court to only

---

[199]   ibid, 625 (Lord Lane LCJ).
[200]   *R (Crown Prosecution Service) v Chorley Justices* [2002] EWHC 2162 (Admin).
[201]   ibid [24].
[202]   *R (Smith) v Uxbridge Magistrates' Court* [2010] EWHC 996 (Admin).
[203]   *R (DPP) v Havering Magistrates' Court* (n 183).
[204]   Note the guidance in *R v Liverpool Justices, ex parte DPP* [1993] QB 233, [1992] 3 WLR 20, cited in *R (DPP) v Havering Magistrates' Court* (n 183) [11] and approved as compliant with Art 5.
[205]   This decision was followed in *R (Thomas) v Greenwich Magistrates' Court* [2009] EWHC 1180 (Admin). For further comment on Art 5 see *R (Ajaib) v Birmingham Magistrates' Court* [2009] EWHC 2127 (Admin) above at 4-86. Commentators have queried this approach to ECHR case law: see Emmerson et al (gen eds) (n 181), 8-129 and fn 329, which cites a wealth of case law in support of the contention that 'an adversarial oral hearing is required' in cases under Art 5(1)(c). The authors there contend that the English courts in *R (DPP) v Havering Magistrates' Court* (n 187) and *Wildman v DPP* [2001] EWHC 14 (Admin) misunderstood *Sanchez-Reisse v Switzerland* (n 191) as holding that written proceedings were sufficient for Art 5(1)(c) when in fact the ECtHR was referring to Art 5(1)(f).

considering evidence that was admissible in the strict sense. The court gave guidance on such hearings stating that the criminal standard of proof did not apply. Instead the magistrates must allow the defendant a 'full and fair opportunity' comment on and challenge the evidence, including an opportunity to give evidence himself, and if the prosecution calls oral evidence, to cross-examine witnesses. A key issue for the court is how weight is attached to such material when a witness is not available for cross-examination:[206] 'What undoubtedly is necessary is that the justice, when forming his opinion, takes proper account of the quality of the material upon which he is asked to adjudicate.'[207]

iii.   Family and private life (Article 8): in *R (Ajaib) v Birmingham Magistrates' Court*[208] the magistrates' court refused to vary bail conditions imposed by the police, who were concerned that the claimant was a flight risk (discussed above at 4-86). In reaching this decision, and in the absence of a prosecution file, it had considered the opinion of an officer involved in the investigation. It was held that whilst Article 8 might be relevant to such a case, on the facts there was little material to suggest that it was engaged, as the claimant had visited Pakistan twice in the preceding months to see his sick mother. The claimant also argued his case on Article 5, in that the police refused to disclose to him evidence on which they relied in opposing his application on the grounds that this might reveal an informant.[209] The court rejected this submission because the claimant knew the essence of the case against him and because this information was not disclosed to the magistrates.[210]

(v) Time Limits (Bail)

In *McElkerney v Highbury Corner Magistrates' Court*,[211] an application for habeas corpus, Richards LJ stated that, although a decision was not required on the point, section 7(4) did not necessarily require a person to be brought before a magistrates' court within 24 hours of arrest, as it included the words 'as soon as practicable';[212] although the submission that the judge lacked jurisdiction to deal with the case was rejected on different grounds.   **6-52**

---

[206] See *R (DPP) v Havering Magistrates' Court* (n 187) [48].

[207] ibid [41].

[208] *R (Ajaib) v Birmingham Magistrates' Court* (n 205).

[209] Note the court's decision that a special advocate need not be appointed was not a view taken in *R (KS) v Northampton Crown Court* [2010] 2 Cr App R 23 (DC). In control order cases the House of Lords has held that the involvement of a special advocate was essential where closed material would be determinative of the issue.

[210] However, see the case of *R v DPP, ex parte Lee* [1999] 1 WLR 1950, where it was held that there should be a residual duty of disclosure in a complex case. See further the Attorney General's Guidelines on Disclosure 2005, paras 55–56, which state that 'disclosure ought to be made of significant information that might affect a bail decision'. This means that the defence should have access to documents to enable an effective application to be made.

[211] *McElkerney v Highbury Corner Magistrates' Court* [2009] EWHC 2621 (Admin).

[212] The decision in *R (Culley) v Dorchester Crown Court* [2007] EWHC 109 (Admin) was doubted. This held that there is a 'strict time limit' of 24 hours and a decision by a magistrates' court outside that limit was *ultra vires*. See above at 4-76 for discussion of the meaning of the words 'as soon as practicable'.

In *R (Chief Constable of Greater Manchester) v Salford Magistrates' Court*[213] an extension of time granted under a warrant for further detention of a suspect was not suspended during the suspect's release on bail. This was primarily a question of the interpretation of section 44 of PACE 1984 in relation to police bail. (The magistrates' court was the defendant, as it had refused the Chief Constable's application for an extension of the warrant.) In *R v Sheffield Justices Court, ex parte Turner*[214] it was held that once a custody time limit had expired and the prosecution had failed to obtain an extension of time, the magistrates had no power to extend time and were required to grant bail. For a case on whether good and sufficient cause to extend a time limit had been established, see *R v Folkestone Magistrates' Court, ex parte Bradley*.[215]

(vi) Bail and the Relationship with the Crown Court

6-53   In *R (Ellison) v Teesside Magistrates' Court*,[216] Lord Woolf LCJ held that magistrates must deal with a defendant who is brought before them for a breach of bail under section 7(5) even though the Crown Court had granted him bail. The justices had committed the defendant to custody to await his next hearing before the Crown Court. Lord Woolf LCJ stated that the justices must exercise their jurisdiction to either grant bail or remand in custody under section 7(5). In *R v Lincoln Magistrates' Court, ex parte Mawer*[217] it was held that the magistrates had no power to vary bail conditions under section 3(8) once the defendant had surrendered to bail in the Crown Court.

(vii) Securities and Sureties (Bail)

6-54   In *R (Stevens) v Truro Magistrates' Court*[218] an order for security made pursuant to sections 3(5) and 5(7) was quashed by a three-judge Divisional Court where i) it failed to make clear the nature of the defendant's interest in the property, and ii) where the owner of the property was not a surety, had not entered into a recognisance, and had not been given notice of the possibility of forfeiture.

(7) Disclosure

6-55   In *R v Bromley Magistrates Court, ex parte Smith*[219] the magistrates refused to adjudicate on an application to disclose unused material, falsely believing that they held no jurisdiction to do so. Simon Brown LJ said that magistrates have jurisdiction to rule on disputed issues of disclosure, as distinct from disclosure of unused material at the committal stage. Any dispute as to whether any document—for example items from

---

[213] *R (Chief Constable of Greater Manchester) v Salford Magistrates' Court* [2011] EWHC 1578 (Admin) (also know as *Hookway*). See above at 4-78.
[214] *R v Sheffield Justices Court, ex parte Turner* [1991] 2 QB 472.
[215] *R v Folkestone Magistrates' Court, ex parte Bradley* [1994] COD 138.
[216] *R (Ellison) v Teesside Magistrates' Court* [2001] EWHC Admin 11.
[217] *R v Lincoln Magistrates' Court, ex parte Mawer* (1996) 160 JP 219.
[218] *R (Stevens) v Truro Magistrates' Court* [2001] EWHC Admin 558.
[219] *R v Bromley Magistrates Court, ex parte Smith* [1995] 1 WLR 944.

Sarah Parkes and Piers von Berg

the schedule of unused materials—should be disclosed or not was to be determined by the magistrates after looking at the document in question.

In *R v Leyland Justices, ex parte Hawthorn*,[220] a prosecution failure to disclose witnesses' statements favourable to the defence was a denial of natural justice and the conviction was quashed, even though the blame lay with the prosecution and not the tribunal. In *R v Peterborough Magistrates' Court, ex parte Dowler*[221] it was held that the procedural unfairness caused by a failure to disclose witness statements could be rectified by a fair hearing before the Crown Court.[222]

In *R v Knightsbridge Crown Court, ex parte Goonatilleke*[223] the defendant was convicted of shoplifting on the evidence of a store detective who failed to disclose at trial that he had resigned from the police for misconduct and had subsequently been convicted of an offence. It was held that the detective's failure to disclose his true character, where credibility was vital, amounted to denying natural justice, and the conviction was quashed.

In *R v South Worcestershire Magistrates, ex parte Lilley*[224] it was stated that if a bench has accepted a submission not to disclose information to the defence on grounds of public interest immunity (PII), it has a discretion whether to direct that a new bench hear the trial in the interests of justice, depending on the circumstances of the case.

Another issue that can arise on applications for disclosure is questions of bias (for further discussion see below 6-77) as to whether a bench should refuse to hear a trial after considering an ex parte application for non-disclosure. In *R v Stipendiary Magistrate for Norfolk, ex parte Taylor*,[225] the test was whether there was a real danger of bias occurring such as to prevent there being a fair trial following the principle in *R v Gough (Robert)*.[226] On the facts, at no time was material presented to the magistrate that would have resulted in a real danger of bias.[227] **6-56**

(8) Reversing Previous Decisions[228]

In *R v Newham Juvenile Court, ex parte F*[229] it was held that: **6-57**

> such a review is permissible if a change of circumstances has occurred since the original decision was taken and also if circumstances are brought to the attention of the court which, although existing when the original decision was taken, were not then drawn to the attention of the court.

This was approved in *R v Acton Youth Court, ex parte DPP*,[230] which was applied in the context of adjournments in *Watson* (see above at 6-75) and *R (Jones) v South East Surrey*

---

[220] *R v Leyland Justices, ex parte Hawthorn* [1979] QB 283.
[221] *R v Peterborough Magistrates' Court, ex parte Dowler* [1997] QB 911.
[222] Note *Ex p Rowlands* (n 20) considered *Ex p Dowler* and decided that this should not be a reason to refuse a claim for judicial review on account of the defendant not seeking an alternative remedy in the Crown Court. See above at 6-7.
[223] *R v Knightsbridge Crown Court, ex parte Goonatilleke* [1986] QB 1.
[224] *R v South Worcestershire Magistrates, ex parte Lilley* [1995] 1 WLR 1595.
[225] *R v Stipendiary Magistrate for Norfolk, ex parte Taylor* (1997) 161 JP 773.
[226] *R v Gough (Robert)* [1993] AC 646, [1993] 2 WLR 883.
[227] This was applied in *R (DPP) v Acton Youth Court* [2001] EWHC Admin 402.
[228] See discussion above at 6-4.
[229] *R v Newham Juvenile Court, ex parte F* [1986] 1 WLR 939, 947F.
[230] *R v Acton Youth Court, ex parte DPP* [2002] Crim LR 75.

Local Justice Area.[231] A similar approach was taken in *R (Crown Prosecution Service) v Gloucester Justices*.[232] A deputy district judge set aside a previous bench's ruling to amend a charge as contrary to the interests of justice, and stayed the prosecution of the defendant as an abuse of process. It was held that for one bench to set aside a previous bench's ruling in this way was contrary to the interests of justice, unless there was compelling reason, such as a change of circumstances or fresh evidence.

(9) Allocation, Sending for Trial and Committal for Sentence

6-58   Committal proceedings were substantially reformed and removed as of 28 May 2013 in all parts of England and Wales (they were abolished progressively in specified areas before that date).[233] This affects both adult and youth courts. Note that the Sentencing Guidelines Council's guidelines on allocation still apply.[234]

Prior to the reforms, judicial review of committal proceedings was not common, but equally not unheard of, with at least one case reaching the House of Lords. The reforms leave the process of transferring cases to the Crown Court a complex one, and so mistakes can easily be made. If there are no alternative remedies open to the magistrates' court, or the Crown Court, and grounds can be made out, it is submitted that these can be remedied by judicial review, especially as appeal by way of case stated will not be available at an interlocutory stage (see above at 6-21).

First, the key changes can be summarised as:[235]

i.   There are no committal proceedings for indictable-only offences, which are sent forthwith.[236]

ii.   Either-way offences will be subject to amended plea before venue and allocation procedures, which may be presided over by a single justice.[237]

Certain either-way offences shall be sent forthwith:

(a)   serious and complex fraud cases where the Crown has served a notice, under rule 9.6 of the Criminal Procedure Rules;

(b)   certain cases involving children where they may be called as a witness and to avoid any prejudice to their welfare the case should be heard in the Crown Court (notice also required under rule 9.6);

(c)   either-way offences related to an indictable-only offence or either of the above two offences or related summary offences punishable with a sentence

---

[231]   *R (Jones) v South East Surrey Local Justice Area* [2010] EWHC 916 (Admin).

[232]   *R (Crown Prosecution Service) v Gloucester Justices* [2008] EWHC 1488 (Admin).

[233]   This is effected by CJA 2003, s 41 and Sch 3, paras 15 and 17.

[234]   These are contained within the Magistrates' Courts Sentencing Guidelines and can be found separately at http://sentencingcouncil.judiciary.gov.uk/docs/Allocation_guideline2.pdf. The Sentencing Guidelines should be referred to when determining whether the court's sentencing powers are sufficient. At time of writing these have yet to be changed to reflect the amended MCA 1980, s 19. See also Part 9 of the *Practice Direction (Criminal Proceedings)*, [2013] EWCA Crim 1631, [2013] 1 WLR 3164.

[235]   For a very useful description of the effects of the changes and flow-charts for both adult and young offenders, see the training materials developed by the Judicial College for Legal Advisors, 'Allocation, Sending for Trial and Committal for Sentence—CJA 2003', Judicial College, May 2013, at www.crimeline.info/uploads/docs/committalabolitionv2.pdf.

[236]   Crime and Disorder Act (CDA) 1998, s 51(2)(a) or (c) and s 51(3).

[237]   See MCA 1980, ss 17A–17D and ss 19–23 as amended by CJA 2003, Sch 3.

Sarah Parkes and Piers von Berg

of imprisonment or discretionary or obligatory disqualification from driving;[238]

(d) defendants jointly charged with either-way offences in the above three categories or summary offences as described above;

(e) the courts have a discretion to send a defendant who appears on a subsequent occasion on a related either-way offence or jointly charged on a related either-way offence.[239]

If a defendant does not fall into any of the above categories the plea before venue procedure under section 17 of MCA 1980 shall be followed.

The prosecution may disclose the defendant's previous convictions for the purposes of allocation.

iii. The courts may still commit for sentence after summary trial or plea of guilty.

iv. Two justices are required to hear a trial or sentence.

v. In cases that are suitable for summary trial the magistrates' courts have a new discretionary power to indicate if a custodial or non-custodial sentence would be more likely if a plea of guilty is entered—note the following apply after such an indication:[240]

(a) the court may not impose a custodial offence unless such an indication was given, the defendant is committed to the Crown Court as they meet the criteria for an extended sentence or they are committed for sentence for a related offence;[241]

(b) a defendant may reconsider their plea after an indication;

(c) if there is no change of plea after an indication, the indication is not binding on any other court and there is a bar to any appeals on such a basis;[242] and

(d) the court may grant a non-custodial sentence after an indication of a custodial one.

vi. The prosecution may apply to send an either-way offence that was allocated for summary trial to the Crown Court, but only before trial and before any pre-trial rulings have been made.[243]

vii. The court may adjourn if either party seeks it of their own initiative.[244]

(i) Application of Old Case Law

It is submitted that aspects of the previous approach to judicial reviews of committal proceedings will still apply. In *Neill v North Antrim Magistrates' Court*[245] the court held that committal proceedings should be judicially reviewed only in cases of 'really substantial error leading to demonstrable injustice' requiring the Divisional Court to

6-59

---

238 CDA 1998, ss 52(A) or 51(11).
239 ibid, s 51(4).
240 MCA 1980, ss 20(3)–(7) and 20A.
241 The latter two refer to PCC(S)A 2000, ss 3A and 4.
242 MCA 1980, s 20A(3).
243 CJA 2033, Sch 3, para 11.
244 CDA 1998, s 52(5).
245 *Neill v North Antrim Magistrates' Court* [1992] 1 WLR 1220.

consider a remedy. In *Ex p Dean* (see above at 6-38) it was stated that an application to quash a committal to the High Court by way of judicial review may be appropriate in exceptional cases, such as if the point could be decided on the undisputed facts without hearing oral evidence.

In *R v Bedwellty Justices, ex parte Williams*[246] the defendant was committed for trial without any admissible evidence of her guilt before the justices. The prosecution argued that admissible evidence to this effect had subsequently been served on the defence. The court held that where a committal was influenced by inadmissible evidence, it should be quashed, even if there was admissible evidence upon which the magistrates could have relied.[247]

R v Warley Magistrates' Court, ex parte DPP[248] concerned the old section 17A of MCA 1980 and challenges to committal for sentence. These decisions are fact-dependent, in that the reviewing court revisits the sentencing exercise. For example, that case involved consideration of the discount available on a plea of guilty, the aggravating and mitigating factors of each offence, and consideration of a defendant's character and record in assessing the lawfulness of the magistrates' court's decision.

It will be interesting to see if the following authorities on legitimate expectation on the issue of committal will remain good law (as distinct from any expectation on indication of sentence, which is now expressly excluded). In *R (Harrington) v Bromley Magistrates' Court*[249] it was held that subsequent benches are bound by any previous unequivocal indications not to commit for sentence (although it was found that the first bench had been entitled to reach the decision it had). In *R (Merritt) v Peterborough Magistrates' Court*[250] the defendant was given an unequivocal assertion that the magistrates' court would retain jurisdiction and the matter was then adjourned for pre-sentence reports. The decision of the bench at the next hearing to commit to the Crown Court for sentencing was contrary to the defendant's legitimate expectation and thus unlawful.

(ii) Transfer of Cases involving Youths[251]

6-60 Any person between the ages of 10 and 17 inclusive will usually be tried before the Youth Court unless an exception applies. As with the rules above on transferring cases involving adults, there have been some recent significant changes and the law remains complex. The volume of case law illustrates that judicial review is an important, and sometimes the only effective remedy where there are errors of law in committing youths to the Crown Court for trial or sentence. It is not the function of the Crown Court on appeal to consider such matters, and appeal by way case stated is best suited to issues arising at the conclusion of proceedings. The High Court has encouraged expedition in respect of such judicial review applications.[252]

---

[246] *R v Bedwellty Justices, ex parte Williams* [1997] AC 225, [1996] 3 WLR 361.
[247] Note though that a committal will not be quashed merely because inadmissible evidence had been received: *R v Highbury Magistrates' Courts, ex parte Boyce* (1984) 79 Cr App R 132.
[248] *R v Warley Magistrates' Court, ex parte DPP* [1998] 2 Cr App R 307.
[249] *R (Harrington) v Bromley Magistrates' Court* [2007] EWHC 2896 (Admin).
[250] *R (Merritt) v Peterborough Magistrates' Court* [2009] EWHC 467 (Admin).
[251] See Sentencing Guidelines Council Definitive Guideline: Overarching Principles, Sentencing Youths.
[252] See above at n 93.

Sarah Parkes and Piers von Berg

A defendant who attains the age of 18 during the criminal proceedings for an either-way offence may elect trial on indictment. This is providing he attains that age by the date by which the court makes its decision as to mode of trial.[253]

(iii) Transfer of Youths to the Crown Court—the New Rules

A child or young person (hereafter 'youths') shall be sent to the Crown Court for trial forthwith if:[254] **6-61**

i.   they are charged with homicide;[255]

ii.   they are charged with a firearms offence and the conditions under section 51A(1) of the Firearms Act 1968 or section 29(3) of Violent Crime Reduction Act 2006 apply;

iii. they are charged with an offence (a 'grave crime') mentioned in section 91(1) of the Powers of the Criminal Courts (Sentencing) Act (PCC(S)A) 2000 and the court considers that the sentencing court should have available to it the possibility of sentencing the offender to be detained at Her Majesty's pleasure (section 91(3))—note that the Youth Court's sentencing powers are limited to two years' detention;

iv.   the court has received notice that the offence is one of serious or complex fraud or is a case that involves children (see above);

v.   they are charged with a 'specified offence' under section 224 of CJA 2003, and if convicted, the criteria for imposing a sentence of detention for life under section 226 or extended sentence under section 226B are met.[256]

In the following specified cases the Youth Court shall follow the new plea before venue procedure in section 24A of MCA 1980:[257] **6-62**

i.   if it is an offence which is related to one that is being transferred that day or that has already been transferred;

ii.   if it is an offence that is a grave crime;

iii. if the youth is jointly charged with an adult who has been transferred.[258]

Note that the new section 24B of MCA 1980 allows for the plea before venue to occur without the defendant being present, providing he has legal representation, if it is not practicable to conduct it because of their disorderly conduct.

---

[253] *Re Daley* [1982] 2 All ER 974. See also *R v Lewes Juvenile Court, ex parte Turner* (1985) 149 JP 186 and *R v Nottingham Justices, ex parte Taylor* [1992] QB 557, [1991] 4 All ER 860 on youths who turned 18 after the decision was taken. *R v West London Justices, ex parte Siley-Winditt* (2000) 165 JP 112, [2000] Crim LR 926 (DC) concerned a youth charged with an offence for which detention under PCC(S)A 2000, s 91, was available.

[254] See CDA 1998, s 51A. These proceedings can be presided over by a single justice (s 51A(11)).

[255] Note that the term 'murder' is not used (CDA 1998, s 51A(3)(a) and (12)(a)). It is unclear how this may or may not apply to offences that cause death, particularly driving offences.

[256] CDA 1998, s 51A(2) and (3)(d).

[257] See the guidance in Judicial College, 'Allocation, Sending for Trial and Committal for Sentence—CJA 2003', May 2013, www.crimeline.info/uploads/docs/committalabolitionv2.pdf.

[258] Note that if a youth is jointly charged with an adult and is transferred to the Crown Court, and the adult pleads guilty and the youth pleads not guilty in the Crown Court, the court does not have the power to send the youth back to the Youth Court for trial. See *R (W) v Leeds Crown Court* [2011] EWHC 2326 (Admin), [2012] 1 WLR 2786 and below at 11-36.

6-63   In the above cases, if a plea of guilty is indicated the Youth Court:

    i.   must commit for sentence where the defendant will receive an extended sentence under the dangerousness provisions (section 3C of PCC(S)A 2000);

    ii.   may commit for sentence if the defendant will receive long-term detention for an offence under section 91(1) of PCC(S)A 2000 (section 3B of PCC(S)A 2000) or pleads guilty to an offence under section 91(1) and has been sent for related offences (section 4A of PCCA(S)A 2000)—note, a defendant cannot be committed under both sections 3B and 3C; or

    iii.   can otherwise sentence the defendant or direct pre-sentence reports and adjourn the matter.

Note that if a defendant is committed for sentence under the above three criteria, they can be committed for sentence for any other offences that are indictable, summary, or carry a sentence of imprisonment or disqualification from driving.[259]

Where a not guilty plea is indicated, a Youth Court must send the case to the Crown Court forthwith if either i) the offence is a grave crime that will receive a sentence of long-term detention, or ii) the youth is jointly charged with an adult, who has been transferred to the Crown Court and it is necessary to transfer the case in the interests of justice. The Youth Court has a discretion to send a youth charged with an offence which is related to an offence that is sent the same day or has already been sent.

(iv) Case Law on Committing Youths

6-64   The lead authority is *R (H, A, and O) v Southampton Youth Court*[260] which set out the follow the factors to be taken into consideration:

    i.   The general policy of the legislature was that offenders under 18 years old, and in particular those under the age of 15, should wherever possible be tried in a youth court. A Crown Court trial with greater formality should be reserved for the most serious cases.

    ii.   Generally, first offenders aged 12-14 and younger should not be detained in custody and should only be tried in the Crown Court exceptionally where grave offences had occurred, which would be rare.

    iii.   In each case a court should ask itself whether there was a real prospect, having regard to the offender's age, that a two year detention would be ordered or whether the offence had other unusual features.

This has been reinforced by the amendment of section 24(1) of MCA 1980 which contains the general presumption that youths charged with indictable offences shall be

---

[259] PCC(S)A 2000, s 6.

[260] *R (H, A, and O) v Southampton Youth Court* [2004] EWHC 2912 (Admin). For a recent application see *R (B) v Norfolk Youth Court* [2013] EWHC 1459 (Admin). See also on the trial of young persons the *Practice Direction (Crown Court: Trial of Children and Young Persons)* [2000] 1 WLR 659, in response to *T v United Kingdom* App no 24724/94 (2000) 30 EHRR 121 (see below 11-38). See also below at 11-36.

tried in the Youth Court subject to the rules set out above at 6-61–6-63 (as derived from sections 51 and 51A of CDA 1998 and sections 24A and 24B of MCA 1980).

It is submitted that the following case law holds good in light of the reforms to the **6-65** MCA 1980 and CDA 1998 by section 41 and Schedule 3 of CJA 2003.

In *R (DPP) v South East Surrey Youth Court*[261] a three-judge Divisional Court, led by Rose LJ, gave general guidance:[262]

i.   Courts should consider the principles in *R v Lang*[263] when assessing non-serious specified offences, and in most cases of such offences, dangerousness should not be assessed until after conviction.

ii.   It will not be appropriate to conclude that there is a significant risk of serious harm from a person under 18 without the assistance of a pre-sentence report, and any such analysis should be 'rigorous'.

iii. Where a youth is jointly charged with an adult, before committing the defendants to the Crown Court to be tried together, the court should consider their age and maturity, comparative culpability, previous convictions, and the feasibility of separate trials.

The Court must consider any question of venue for trial or sentence before the defendant enters any pleas. If pleas are entered and a decision is then taken on transfer, the prosecution cannot then apply to the Court to reopen its decision.[264] The Court does not need to give expansive reasons for the transfer, but the decision must show that the bench had properly directed itself and had regard to the relevant authorities.[265] Each defendant must be considered separately.[266] The test to be applied in deciding whether the Court's sentencing powers are sufficient is whether there is a 'real possibility', 'real prospect' or 'reasonable prospect' that the defendant could be sentenced to a greater custodial term than was available.[267] The court should consider the prosecution's case at the highest, aggravating and mitigating factors with reference to the applicable sentencing guidelines or case law, and the possibility of a plea of guilty.[268] The duty to consider a youth's welfare under section 44 of the Children and Young Person's Act 1933 should not deflect a court from abiding by the requirements under the MCA 1980.[269]

---

[261] *R (DPP) v South East Surrey Youth Court* [2005] EWHC 2929 (Admin), [2006] 1 WLR 2543.

[262] Followed in *W v Warrington Magistrates' Court* [2009] EWHC 1538 (Admin) and *R (G) v Llanelli Magistrates' Court* [2006] EWHC 1413 (Admin).

[263] *R v Lang* [2005] EWCA Crim 2864, [2006] 1 WLR 2509.

[264] *R (D) v Sheffield Youth Court* [2008] EWHC 601 (Admin).

[265] *R (C) v Leeds Youth Court* [2005] EWHC 1216 (QB).

[266] *R (W) v The Brent Youth Court* [2006] EWHC 95 (Admin) followed in *R (W) v Oldham Youth Court* [2010] EWHC 661 (Admin).

[267] *R (Crown Prosecution Service) v Redbridge Youth Court* [2005] EWHC 1390 (Admin), *R (R) v Manchester City Youth Court* [2006] EWHC 564 (Admin) and *W v Oldham Youth Court* (n 261).

[268] *W v Oldham Youth Court* (n 266).

[269] *R v Devizes Youth Court, ex parte A* (2000) 164 JP 330. A decision of Brooke LJ followed in *D v Sheffield Youth Court* and *Crown Prosecution Service v Newcastle upon Tyne Youth Court* (n 93).

6-66   These authorities are fact-dependent, but give an overview of some of the decisions and offences in reverse chronological order:[270]

  i.   *R (W) v Warrington Magistrates' Court:*[271] a 13-year-old charged with attempted rape of an eight-year-old and sexual assault of 13-year-old and five-year-old—a decision not to commit was upheld, as the full facts only emerged during trial;

  i.   *R (G) v Burnley Magistrates' Court:*[272] defendants aged 13 and 14 of good character, charged with a sexual assault on a 13-year girl of a short duration, should not have been committed;

  ii. *R (C) v Croydon Youth Court:*[273] two defendants aged 15 and 16 assaulted a 14-year-old with intent to rob, and a third defendant was also charged with assault with intent to rob of a 14-year-old—a decision to commit for sentence was upheld and there was real prospect of sentence in excess of two years;

  iii. *R (G) v Llanelli Magistrates' Court:*[274] a 14-year-old defendant charged with robbery of a 78-year-old complainant should not have been committed;

  iv. *R (W) v Brent Youth Court:*[275] 12-year-old defendant charged with rape of a 13-year-old complainant should have been committed but (obiter) there may be circumstances where it is appropriate to try 12-year-old for rape in Youth Court;[276]

  v.   *R (C) v Balham Youth Court* [2003] EWHC 1332 (Admin): a 14-year-old accused of robbery did not warrant a sentence of two years.

(10) Bad Character

6-67   Bad character means 'evidence of or a disposition towards misconduct', which is taken to mean commission of an offence or other reprehensible conduct.[277] The magistrates' court is bound by the substantive and procedural law on the admission of evidence of bad character, a full account of which is beyond the scope of this section. The key provisions can be found in sections 98–112 of the CJA 2003, the Criminal Procedure Rules Part 35 and extensive case law. The case law demonstrates that judicial review challenges are brought on i) the proper exercise of the court's discretion and application of the Criminal Procedure Rules, and ii) issues of fairness.

Examples of challenges include attacks on the magistrates' exercise of discretion to extend time under rule 35(8) of the Criminal Procedure Rules to allow an application by the prosecution. Such a claim failed in *R (Robinson) v Sutton Coldfield Magistrates' Court.*[278] The Divisional Court found that the discretion was not limited to exceptional

---

[270] See also the recent decision of *R (BH) v Llandudno Youth Court*, [2014] EWHC 1833 (Admin), where Andrews J reviews the lead authorities and several comparable authorities.

[271] *R (W) v Warrington Magistrates' Court* [2009] EWHC 1538 (Admin).

[272] *R (G) v Burnley Magistrates' Court* [2007] EWHC 1033 (Admin).

[273] *R (C) v Croydon Youth Court* [2006] EWHC 2627 (Admin).

[274] *R (G) v Llanelli Magistrates' Court* [2006] EWHC 1413 (Admin).

[275] *R (W) v Brent Youth Court* [2006] EWHC 95 (Admin).

[276] See *R v Millberry* [2002] EWCA Crim 2891, [2003] 1 WLR 546. See also *W v Brent Youth Court* (n 275) [44].

[277] Criminal Justice Act 2003, ss 99 and 112.

[278] *R (Robinson) v Sutton Coldfield Magistrates' Court* [2006] 2 Cr App R 13.

Sarah Parkes and Piers von Berg

circumstances. The two key considerations were whether there was a good reason for the delay and whether the opposing party would suffer prejudice.[279]

A successful challenge was brought in *R (Kelly) v Warley Magistrates' Court*[280] to a deputy district judge's decision to compel a defendant to disclose names, addresses and dates of birth of his witnesses. Litigation privilege attached to the information entitling the defendant not to disclose the information until he wished to present it.

As regards fairness, a successful judicial review was brought in *R v Knightsbridge Crown Court and Another, ex parte Goonatilleke*[281] in circumstances where a prosecution witness had deliberately concealed his bad character. Another challenge to the Crown Court on appeal was in *R (Jefferies) v St Albans Crown Court*[282] where a defendant unsuccessfully challenged a decision not to admit evidence of a complainant's bad character.

The issue of disclosure of a person's bad character arose in *R (Gleadall) v Huddersfield Magistrates' Court*.[283] The prosecution had disclosed that none of its witnesses had any previous convictions. The defence sent a questionnaire designed to discover if any of them were of bad character, but the prosecution had refused to respond to it. The Divisional Court held that there was nothing inappropriate in this refusal. The prosecutor's code of practice placed the prosecution under a duty to consider the credibility and reliability of prosecution witnesses and to make enquiries appropriate to the facts and circumstances of individual cases. In the absence of evidence to show that those duties were not being performed, it had to be assumed that they were. The interests of justice did not demand that, in every case, comprehensive enquiries be made about the character of every prosecution witness whose evidence was to be challenged. The interests of justice demanded an investigation that was reasonable in the circumstances of the individual case. The gravity of the offence and the centrality of the evidence of the particular witness would be important factors.

(11) Special Measures

The special measures regime is governed by the Youth Justice and Criminal Evidence Act (YJCEA) 1999.   **6-68**

It has been held that there is no strict requirement for a party making a special measures application to adduce specific evidence as to a witness's state of mind. Where the witness is very young, or the incident to be described very distressing, the court may infer that their evidence would be diminished if special measures were refused (see below at 11-43 for further discussion on youths and special measures).[284]

In *R (D) v Camberwell Green Youth Court*[285] the defendants were aged under 16 and were charged with robbery. They sought judicial review of the magistrates' decision to give a special measures direction enabling the child witnesses for the prosecution to give their

---

[279] See also *R v Hassett (Kevin)* [2008] EWCA Crim 1634.
[280] *R (Kelly) v Warley Magistrates' Court* [2008] 1 WLR 2001.
[281] *R v Knightsbridge Crown Court and Another, ex parte Goonatilleke* (n 223).
[282] *R (Jefferies) v St Albans Crown Court* [2012] EWHC 338 (Admin).
[283] *R (Gleadall) v Huddersfield Magistrates' Court* [2005] EWHC 2283 (Admin).
[284] See *R (H) v Thames Youth Court* [2002] EWHC 2046 (Admin) and *R (DPP) v Redbridge Youth Court* [2001] EWHC Admin 209, [2001] 1 WLR 2403.
[285] *R (D) v Camberwell Green Youth Court* [2005] UKHL 4, [2005] 1 WLR 393.

evidence via a live video link. This was a challenge to the compatibility of YJCEA 1999 with Article 6. In one of the cases the district judge had refused the application for special measures, as it would have led to a significant inequality of arms in that the defendant was not entitled to the same measures. The claim failed because the court found that the defendant's Article 6 rights could be safeguarded by the criminal court in allowing him to know and challenge the evidence against him. Importantly, it held that Article 6 did not guarantee face-to-face confrontation and so the special measures regime did not breach Article 6.

R (O) v Batley and Dewsbury Youth Court[286] saw an application of the rule in *Ex p Buck* (see above at 6-17) to judicial review challenges in the Youth Court. The issue was one of delay and the court expressed its favour with *Hoar-Stevens*. Maurice Kay J said that 'discouragement must apply all the more in relation to a Youth Court where there is such a strong policy reason to see the case through to an early stage'.[287] Whilst it is difficult to argue with the need for expedition where children and young persons are concerned, this authority must be set in context of the other decisions above that take a different view. For example, if a decision to grant or refuse special measures was found to be unlawful and a conviction or acquittal quashed as a result, the case could be remitted for a retrial.

C. Trial

(1) Adjournments

(i) General Principles

6-69   The magistrates' court has a discretionary power to adjourn proceedings before trying the defendant or during the trial, or before the case is committed to the Crown Court under sections 5, 10 and 18 of MCA 1980.[288] This is probably one of the areas of greatest activity for judicial review of magistrates' courts' decisions. Practitioners should be mindful of the case law on challenges to interlocutory decisions above at 6-17.

In *R v Aberdare Justices, Ex p DPP*[289] Bingham LJ emphasised that due to the discretionary nature of the decision it is only open to challenge in exceptional circumstances:

> First, a decision as to whether or not proceedings should be adjourned is, as counsel for the defendant rightly urged, a decision within the discretion of the trial court. It is pre-eminently a discretionary decision. It follows, as a matter of undoubted law, that it is a decision with which any appellate court will be very slow to interfere. It will accordingly interfere only if very clear grounds are shown for doing so.[290]

---

[286] *R (O) v Batley and Dewsbury Youth Court* [2003] EWHC 2931 (Admin)
[287] ibid [8].
[288] This discretion is not open-ended in MCA 1980. A Youth Court cannot be required to adjourn only on the basis that it has committed the defendant for another offence or the defendant is charged with another offence (MCA 1980, s 10(3A). There are time limits after conviction (four weeks) and after conviction with remands in custody (three weeks) (MCA 1980, s 10(3)). Note there is no power to adjourn hearings for breach of bail under the Bail Act 1976, s 7. See *DPP v Havering Magistrates' Court* (n 187) [44].
[289] *R v Aberdare Justices, Ex p DPP* [1991] 155 JP 324.
[290] ibid, 330–31.

In *Ex p Rowlands* Lord Bingham LCJ restated the principle that a trial should not be adjourned unless there are good and compelling reasons for doing so. This has been reiterated as part of the Stop Delaying Justice Initiative, which urges justices to restrict proceedings wherever possible to two hearings: one for plea and one for trial. Accordingly, applications to adjourn should be subject to 'rigorous scrutiny' in terms of reasons for the application, with the delay, the consequences to either party, especially fairness, as a key factor:

> It is not possible or desirable to identify hard and fast rules as to when adjournments should or should not be granted. The guiding principle must be that justices should fully examine the circumstances leading to applications for delay, the reasons for those applications and the consequences both to the prosecution and the defence. Ultimately, they must decide what is fair in the light of all those circumstances.

> This court will only interfere with the exercise of the justices' discretion whether to grant an adjournment in cases where it is plain that a refusal will cause substantial unfairness to one of the parties. Such unfairness may arise when a defendant is denied a full opportunity to present his case. But neither defendants nor their legal advisers should be permitted to frustrate the objective of a speedy trial without substantial grounds. Applications for adjournments must be subjected to rigorous scrutiny.[291]

These two authorities are often taken as the starting point of the law in this area, for example, see Leveson LJ's analysis in *Balogun v DPP* (see above at 6-24 and below at 6-71). See also the discussion on use of irrationality as a ground of review above at 1-87.

(ii) Development of the Case Law

In *R (Walden and Stern) v Highbury Corner Magistrates' Court*,[292] Mitchell J stressed **6-70** the court's intolerance for delay, especially where the party seeking the adjournment is responsible for its own lack of readiness (witnessing not warned to attend):

> The longer the courts tolerate the sort of inefficiency which seems, in each of these cases, to be the explanation for the failure of the witnesses to attend court on the date fixed for the hearing, the longer it will continue. To tolerate it is to encourage it … delays in the administration of justice are a scandal. They are the more scandalous when it is criminal proceedings with which the court is concerned.[293]

Sedley LJ made a similar point in *Essen v DPP* (discussed above at 6-22) where 'the purpose and effect of [the adjournment] which would be simply to rescue it [the CPS] from the consequences of its own neglect'.[294]

---

[291] *Ex p Rowlands* (n 20) 127G–128A. See a list of possible factors, again with a stress on prejudice to the parties, in *R v Kingston-upon-Thames Justices, ex parte Martin* [1994] Imm AR 172.

[292] *R (Walden and Stern) v Highbury Corner Magistrates' Court* [2002] EWCA 708 (Admin).

[293] ibid [17]. These comments were approved by Leveson LJ in *Balogun* (n 49). One example of the importance of delay is whether the magistrates consider the length of any delay caused by the adjournment, eg see *Nadour v Chester Magistrates' Court* [2009] EWHC 1505 (Admin), [2010] Crim LR 955.

[294] *Essen* (n 73) [39].

In *Crown Prosecution Service v Picton*,[295] another case where the prosecution failed to bring its witnesses to court, the court helpfully summarised the law from *Aberdare Justices, Ex p Rowlands* and *Essen v DPP*:

i.   A decision whether to adjourn is a decision within the discretion of the trial court. An appellate court will interfere only if very clear grounds for doing so are shown.

ii.   Magistrates should pay great attention to the need for expedition in the prosecution of criminal proceedings; delays are scandalous; they bring the law into disrepute; summary justice should be speedy justice; an application for an adjournment should be rigorously scrutinised.

iii.   Where an adjournment is sought by the prosecution, magistrates must consider both the interest of the defendant in getting the matter dealt with, and the interest of the public that criminal charges should be adjudicated upon, and the guilty convicted as well as the innocent acquitted. With a more serious charge the public interest that there be a trial will carry greater weight.

iv.   Where an adjournment is sought by the accused, the magistrates must consider whether, if it is not granted, he will be able fully to present his defence and, if he will not be able to do so, the degree to which his ability to do so is compromised.

v.   In considering the competing interests of the parties the magistrates should examine the likely consequences of the proposed adjournment, in particular its likely length, and the need to decide the facts while recollections are fresh.

vi.   The reason that the adjournment is required should be examined and, if it arises through the fault of the party asking for the adjournment, that is a factor against granting the adjournment, carrying weight in accordance with the gravity of the fault. If that party was not at fault, that may favour an adjournment. Likewise if the party opposing the adjournment has been at fault, that will favour an adjournment.

vii.   The magistrates should take appropriate account of the history of the case, and whether there have been earlier adjournments and at whose request and why.

viii.   Lastly, of course the factors to be considered cannot be comprehensively stated but depend upon the particular circumstances of each case, and they will often overlap. The court's duty is to do justice between the parties in the circumstances as they have arisen.[296]

The above principles have been applied in several subsequent authorities.[297] For example, Toulson LJ considered them to be the relevant factors in assessing the exercise of the discretion to adjourn in *R (Taylor) v Southampton Magistrates' Court*.[298]

The 'good and compelling' reasons test, the avoidance of delay and the prohibition on parties using their own failures as a reason for adjournment can be seen in *Visvaratnam v Brent Magistrates' Court*:[299]

I have no doubt that there is a high public interest in trials taking place on the date set for trial, and that trials should not be adjourned unless there is a good and compelling reason to do

---

[295] *Crown Prosecution Service v Picton* [2006] EWHC 1108 (Admin), (2006) 170 JP 567.

[296] ibid [9].

[297] In *R (Drinkwater) v Solihull Magistrates' Court* [2012] EWHC 765 (Admin), Beatson J, with whom Sir John Thomas P agreed, observed these factors to be 'widely followed', ibid [31].

[298] *R (Taylor) v Southampton Magistrates' Court* [2008] EWHC 3006 (Admin).

[299] *Visvaratnam v Brent Magistrates' Court* [2009] EWHC 3017 (Admin), (2010) 174 JP 61.

so. The sooner the prosecution understand this—that they cannot rely on their own serious failures properly to warn witnesses—the sooner the efficiency in the magistrates' court system improves.[300]

(iii) Recent Cases—the Importance of Procedure and Case Management

Balogun v DPP is an important decision (entitled 'Practice Note') that reviews and restates much of the case law in the above section. Leveson LJ, with whom Cranston J agreed, stressed the test of 'rigorous scrutiny' in *Ex p Rowlands*. His Lordship applied the test in *R v Aberdare Justices, ex parte DPP* that a decision to adjourn is a discretionary decision that should only be interfered with in exceptional circumstances. Such challenges should be brought extremely urgently, in a matter of days not weeks, by way of judicial review and not by appeal by way of case stated. If permission is granted, then interim relief may be ordered in the form of a stay of proceedings whilst the High Court considers the matter. Unlike earlier authorities it reminds parties of their obligations under the Criminal Procedure Rules to actively assist the court in its case management duties under rule 3.2(2) and in the context of the overriding objective under rule 1.1(2). This approach has continued in newer cases where a failure by a party to adhere to its obligations under the Rules has influenced the court's decision to dismiss a claim.[301] Close attention to the Criminal Procedure Rules and active case management was emphasised by Sir John Thomas P in *R (Drinkwater) v Solihull Magistrates' Court*, in particular, maintaining a timetable for the case (see below at 6-76).[302]

6-71

Below are various authorities, which it is submitted, provide illustrations of the above principles.

(iv) Failure to Grant an Adjournment to Allow the Attendance of a Complainant or Witness

This situation was in issue in some of the above lead authorities. The above principles would apply particularly to avoid disadvantaging one side in the presentation of its case. An important example is where the complainant fails to attend. This occurred in *R v Neath and Port Talbot Magistrates' Court, ex parte DPP*[303] where the complainant was unaware of the trial date. The magistrates refused an application to adjourn and the prosecution offered no evidence. The decision was quashed and remitted to the magistrates to be heard. In *R (DPP) v Birmingham Justices*[304] the court quashed an acquittal where magistrates refused an adjournment when the complainant did not attend where she was a victim of serious crime the night before.

6-72

---

[300] ibid [19], approved in *Balogun* (n 49) [26].
[301] *R (O'Brien) v City of London Magistrates' Court* [2013] EWHC 3831 (Admin).
[302] *Drinkwater* (n 297) [47]. Note in *R (Chinaka) v Southwark Crown Court* [2013] EWHC 3221 (Admin) the Divisional Court stated that a judge had a discretion under the Criminal Procedure Rules, r 63 to proceed if he considered that the appeal would be unreasonably delayed if adjourned. This was without one lay justice, contrary to SCA 1981, s 74(1)(a).
[303] *R v Neath and Port Talbot Magistrates' Court, ex parte DPP* [2000] 1 WLR 1376.
[304] *R (DPP) v Birmingham Justices* [2003] EWHC 177 (Admin).

Specific factual examples can be found in *R v Swansea Justices, ex parte DPP*[305] where magistrates were criticised for being over-hasty (less than half an hour) in refusing an adjournment for prosecution witnesses to attend. In a similar situation to *R (DPP) v Birmingham Justices,* the court in *R (Price) v Southern Derbyshire Magistrates' Court*[306] said that stress brought on by having to attend court could be a ground for adjournment. It is submitted that these authorities are fact-specific.

As regards defence witnesses, in *R (Costello) v North East Essex Magistrates,*[307] Collins J held that if, through no fault of the accused, witnesses do not attend who should have attended, magistrates ought generally to grant an adjournment. In that case, the defendant's son had attempted suicide 36 hours before the trial and his wife was not able to attend.[308] Concerning applications to adjourn where a witness is not present, the Divisional Court has held that magistrates' courts ought to exercise their discretion under section 97 of MCA 1980 to summons a witness whose evidence is critical to an issue in the case.[309]

(v) Failure to Grant Adjournment when the Defendant is Absent

6-73 Section 11(1) of MCA 1980 states that the court must proceed in the absence of the defendant, unless it is contrary to the interests of justice. This does not apply if the defendant is under 18. Rule 37.11 of the Criminal Procedure Rules will apply. The court should consider whether the defendant was notified of the hearing in reasonable time. The overriding concern is that the trial is fair. The court should have 'due regard' to the factors set out in *R v Jones,*[310] and failure to do so may lead to the court quashing a decision to adjourn, as in *Drinkwater* where defendants were unable to attend due to illness and injury where they wished to give evidence in their defence:[311]

    i.   A defendant had a right to be present at his trial and a right to be legally represented which could be waived, separately or together, wholly or in part, by the defendant himself;

    ii.   The trial judge had a discretion whether a trial should take place or continue in the absence of the defendant or his legal representatives, and only in exceptional cases should the discretion be exercised to permit a trial in the absence of the defendant, particularly if he was unrepresented;

---

[305] *R v Swansea Justices, ex parte DPP* (1990) 154 JP 709.

[306] *R (Price) v Southern Derbyshire Magistrates' Court* [2005] EWHC 2842 (Admin).

[307] *R (Costello) v North East Essex Magistrates* (2007) 171 JP 153, [11].

[308] See also *R v Bradford Justices, ex parte Wilkinson* [1990] 1 WLR 692 and *R v Bristol Magistrates' Court, ex parte Rowles* [1994] RTR 40. Note authority exists for judicial reviews by witnesses of witness summons—see *R (Cunliffe) v Hastings Magistrates' Court* [2006] EWHC 2081 (Admin), which concerned expert witnesses.

[309] *Ex p Wilkinson,* 695 (Mann LJ). In that case defence witnesses, for whom summonses had been granted, failed to attend a trial. Their evidence was critical to the defence case. The justices' decision to refuse an application for a warrant under MCA 1980, s 97 was quashed as it prevented the defendant from receiving a fair trial.

[310] *R v Jones* [2002] UKHL 5, [2003] 1 AC 1.

[311] As derived from the judgment of the Court of Appeal and endorsed by Lord Bingham, with whom Lord Hoffmann, Lord Nolan and Lord Rodger agreed. Lord Bingham disagreed with the Court of Appeal that the seriousness of the offence was a relevant factor. See the *Practice Direction (CA (Crim Div): Criminal Proceedings: General Matters)* [2013] EWCA Crim 1631, [2013] 1 WLR 3164, 19E.3.

        Sarah Parkes and Piers von Berg

iii. In exercising the discretion fairness to the defendant was of prime importance, but account also had to be taken of fairness to the prosecution, and the judge had to have regard to all the circumstances of the case, including:

    (a) the nature of the defendant's behaviour;

    (b) the length and effect of an adjournment;

    (c) the possibility of the defendant being able to instruct his legal representatives;

    (d) the extent of the disadvantage to the defendant in not being able to give his account of events;

    (e) the risk of an improper conclusion by the jury about the defendant's absence;

    (f) the public interest; and,

    (g) the effect of delay on the recollection of witnesses and, where there was more than one defendant, the effect on the trial of the other defendants.

iv. If a trial did take place or continue in the absence of an unrepresented defendant the judge had to take reasonable steps to expose weaknesses in the prosecution case, to make such points on behalf of the defendant as the evidence permitted and to warn the jury that absence was not an admission of guilt.

In *R (M) v Burnley Pendle and Rossendale Magistrates' Court*,[312] it was held that only in rare and exceptional cases should a discretion be exercised in favour of a trial taking place or continuing in the defendant's absence.[313] As a result, it was incumbent on the defendant court to make clear what factors make the case exceptional. To this extent if an adjournment allows the defendant to have a fair trial, this takes precedence over any inconvenience to prosecution witnesses.[314] Clearly, a defendant's rights under Article 6 of ECHR will be engaged, as Munby LJ said in *R (Evans) v East Lancashire Magistrates' Court*:[315]

> it is in the final analysis the interests of the defendant (and, indeed of the public at large) in having a fair trial which must take priority over the interests of the prosecution witnesses in not being inconvenienced.

In cases where the defendant has a medical complaint that prevents attendance, the court can express doubts and call for better evidence.[316] If the court is not satisfied by evidence of the defendant's conduct that suggests he is able to attend, the decision is likely to be upheld.[317]

---

[312] *R (M) v Burnley Pendle and Rossendale Magistrates' Court* [2009] EWHC 2874 (Admin).

[313] The court applied the authorities of *R v Jones (Anthony William)* (n 310) and *R v O'Hare (Leigh James)* [2006] EWCA Crim 471, [2006] Crim LR 950.

[314] *R (Evans) v East Lancashire Magistrates' Court* [2010] EWHC 2108 (Admin). See also the stress on fairness in *Price* (n 306).

[315] ibid [48].

[316] *R v Bolton Justices, ex parte Merna* (1991) 155 JP 612. See also *R (Iqbal) v Liverpool Magistrates' Court*, 13 October 2000, QBD (Admin) on difficulties with medical evidence. Note also the decision in *Drinkwater* (n 297).

[317] Eg see *R v Ealing Magistrate's Court, ex parte Burgess* (2001) 165 JP 82 where it was said the defendant did not have an unlimited right to be present.

(vi) Failure to Grant Adjournment to Allow Time to Prepare Defence Case

6-74   This was the issue in *R v Thames Magistrates' Courts, ex parte Polemis*[318] and *R (Halpin) v Northwich Magistrates' Court*,[319] where refusals to grant adjournments were overturned because they did not permit the defence sufficient time to gather witnesses and evidence or consider material disclosed late that was of importance in the trial. In the more recent case of *Halpin* the prosecution failed to comply with its duty under the Criminal Procedure and Investigations Act 1996 to disclose the schedule of unused material within the specified time limit (it was provided eight days before trial). The schedule contained details of the complainant's bad character. The defence wished to obtain details of a relevant matter (cautions for violent offences) in order to make an application to adduce the evidence.

(vii) Repeated Adjournments

6-75   Often there may be a series of adjournments leading to an extended period of delay. Conceivably, one party could argue that because of the number of adjournments and the cumulative delay, a further adjournment should not be granted. This argument was made in *Ex p Rowles*,[320] where there had been five separate adjournments and it was rejected. However, in *R (Chinaka) v Southwark Crown Court*[321] a decision to proceed without the requisite two lay justices was upheld because of the cumulative delays caused by two adjournments.

   If an application has been made and refused, the court should not accede to any subsequent application unless there has been a material change in circumstances. This principle was applied in *Watson* (see above at 6-21) and in *R (F) v Knowsley Youth Court*.[322]

(viii) Adjourning Part-Heard Trials for Substantial Periods

6-76   In *Drinkwater*, Sir John Thomas P gave this guidance:

> where a case does not conclude within the estimate, every effort must be made to see if the trial can continue the following day, there are obvious practical difficulties, particularly given the commitments of the Magistrates and other business that has been scheduled for succeeding days. The practice has thus developed of adjourning a case that has not concluded for a period of two to three weeks, as we are told that that is the sort of time which is needed to find a time at which the availability of a courtroom, staff and, more importantly, the Magistrates, can be secured. A delay in the middle of a case for a period of two to three weeks is plainly inimical to the principles of speedy and summary justice. It is for these reasons and those given in *Jisl*[323]

---

[318] *R v Thames Magistrates' Courts, ex parte Polemis* [1974] 1 WLR 1371.
[319] *R (Halpin) v Northwich Magistrates' Court* [2011] EWHC 1349 (Admin).
[320] *Ex p Rowles* (n 308).
[321] *R (Chinaka) v Southwark Crown Court* [2013] EWHC 3221 (Admin).
[322] *R (F) v Knowsley Youth Court* [2006] EWHC 695 (Admin).
[323] See *R v Jisl* [2004] EWCA Crim 696 [114]–[115], per Judge LJ's comments on the efficient running of trials.

Sarah Parkes and Piers von Berg

essential that the closest attention is paid to timetabling, that the case is actively managed and concluded within the estimate.[324]

Following this decision, an adjournment was not considered unreasonable in *R (O'Brien) v City of London Magistrates' Court*[325] where the magistrates' court considered that it could not complete the case in a day due to late witnesses.

(2) Magistrates Dealing with Interlocutory Applications Later Hearing the Trial (Allegations of Bias)

Applications for judicial review are extremely difficult to succeed with on this issue. **6-77**
For example, magistrates are not barred from hearing a trial where they have heard bad character disclosed during a bail hearing.[326] There are very few examples in recent times of a claimant successfully demonstrating bias. In *KL v DPP*,[327] Richards J gave a firm judgment dismissing a claim that magistrates who had heard an application for special measures could not hear the trial:

> In my judgment, there can be no objection in principle to justices continuing to hear a case after listening to and ruling on an application for the witness to be screened from a defendant. The fact that evidence or submissions adverse to the defendant are advanced in support of such an application does not necessarily prevent fair-minded consideration of the case after the application has been determined, whether it has been allowed or refused.

His Lordship went on to say that it was 'necessary to look at whether there was anything in the particular circumstances that made it unfair for the justices to proceed' in the circumstances of the case.

For authorities on how this issue applies to magistrates who have heard previous applications for disclosure see above at 6-56.

(3) Trial in the Youth Court: Preliminaries

The procedure for conduct of a trial in an adult magistrates' court applies to the Youth **6-78**
Court unless specifically excluded.[328] It is a mandatory requirement for a man and a woman to sit. If it is not so constituted, the bench may only decide that it is inexpedient in the interests of justice to adjourn after hearing submissions from the parties in open court.[329]

The important issue of how a youth should be tried as a person who almost always has significantly less awareness, understanding and maturity than an adult is dealt with below at 11-37. A key issue for potential judicial review claims will be effective participation, as safeguarded at common law and by Article 6 of ECHR.

---

[324] *Drinkwater* (n 297) [48].
[325] *R (O'Brien) v City of London Magistrates' Court* [2013] EWHC 3831 (Admin).
[326] This restriction in MCA 1980, s 42 was abolished by CJA 2003, Sch 3, para 14.
[327] *KL v DPP* [2001] EWHC Admin 1112, (2002) 166 JP 369 [13] and [15].
[328] CYPA 1933, s 101 and MCA 1980, s 152.
[329] *R v Birmingham Justices, ex parte F* (1999) 164 JP 523, [2000] Crim LR 588, DC.

(i) Age and Remittals

6-79 There have been a number of judicial reviews on this topic. They have led to the following principles being decided, which indicate the scope for possible challenges. If a youth turns 18 years during the proceedings, whether he or she has a right to elect trial in the Crown Court depends on their age on the date on which the mode of trial is decided.[330] If a youth commits an offence when aged under 18 but turns 18 before their first appearance, or does not appear on the return date and subsequently turns 18, the Youth Court shall not have jurisdiction to deal with him or her and should remit the case to the adult court.[331] A youth who turns 18 during the course of proceedings and can be tried in the Youth Court is still liable to the orders on conviction for youths.[332]

In certain circumstances a youth can be remitted to the Youth Court from the adult magistrates' court and vice versa for either trial or sentence (see section 29 of MCA 1980 and section 8(1) and (2) of PCC(S)A 2000). Many of these situations are outlined above and concern the rules on dealing with young defendants. In addition, the Youth Court may remit a youth, who has turned 18, at any time prior to hearing the prosecution's evidence at the start of trial, after conviction or before sentence except where they are charged with an indictable only offence.[333] The Divisional Court has held that the power under section 142 of MCA 1980 (the 'slip rule') may be used where a youth has been incorrectly remitted to the adult court.[334]

(ii) Absence of the Defendant in the Youth Court

6-80 As above, this issue has also led to a number of challenges. The court has a discretion to proceed where the defendant is aged under 18 and not present.[335] The court may try a youth in his absence only on rare occasions. A young defendant's common law and Article 6 rights are not contravened where a hospital or guardianship order is made because it does not involve a conviction or punishment.[336] Any challenges under Article 6 place the burden of proof on the defendant.[337] Such a decision cannot be justified on grounds of convenience where the defendant has no criminal record or record of absconding on bail.[338] It has also been held that a defendant did not have a fair trial where he was absent whilst the complainant gave evidence.[339]

---

[330] See *R v Islington North Juvenile Court, ex parte Daley* [1983] 1 AC 347, [1982] 2 All ER 974, HL. See also *R v Nottingham Justices, ex parte Taylor* [1992] QB 557, [1991] 4 All ER 860, and *R v West London Justices* (n 253).

[331] *R v Uxbridge Youth Court, ex parte Howard* (1998) 162 JP 327, DC.

[332] CYPA 1969, s 29. Eg *Aldis v DPP* [2002] EWHC 403 (Admin), [2002] 2 Cr App Rep (S) 400.

[333] CDA 1998, s 47(1) and PCC(S)A 2000, s 9(1).

[334] *R (Denny) v Acton Youth Justices* [2004] EWHC 948 (Admin), [2004] 2 All ER 961.

[335] MCA 1980, s 11(1). See above on adjournments in absence of the defendant 6-73.

[336] *R v M* [2010] EWCA Crim 2024, [2002] 1 Cr App R 283; *Re H (Tyrone)* [2002] EWCA Crim 2988; *R (Singh) v Stratford Magistrates Court* [2007] EWHC 1582 (Admin), [2007] 4 All ER 407. For further discussion of challenges relating to such orders in the magistrates' courts see below at 12-52–12-53.

[337] *R (P) v West London Youth Court* [2005] EWHC 2583 (Admin), [2006] 1 All ER 477.

[338] *R v Dewsbury Magistrates' Court, ex parte K* The Times, 16 March 1994.

[339] *R (R) v Thames Youth Court* [2002] EWHC 1670 (Admin), 166 JP 613.

(4) Admissibility of Evidence and Calling Witnesses

In *R (Crown Prosecution Service) v Sedgemoor Justices* (see above at 6-20) Hughes LJ gave **6-81** general guidance on the admission of expert evidence especially in drink driving cases:

> In every case the court must be satisfied that the evidence being tendered is (a) expert and (b) reliable. Providing that it is, I have no doubt that it is admissible whether it is tendered by certificate of authorised analyst or by evidence of a demonstrated expert.[340]

This area has seen judicial review challenges of decisions on the admission of such evidence. For example, in *R (Gonzales) v Folkestone Magistrates' Court*[341] the claimant (G) applied for judicial review of a decision of the defendant court to refuse to admit into evidence the defendant's interview containing an exculpatory mixed statement raising an issue of self-defence. The court rejected an application to adduce the evidence and refused to allow G to do so on the basis that it was a mixed statement and, to an extent, self-serving. G was convicted of assault and a two-year restraining order was imposed. The application in relation to G's conviction was successful, but it was held that his restraining order had been properly imposed on the civil standard given his criminal record and admissions.

In *R v Haringey Justices, ex parte DPP*,[342] it was held that the justices had a power to call a prosecution witness themselves where the Crown had refused to do so. This was on the basis that the interests of justice required that witness to give evidence and it was unfair to the defence for him not to do so.

(5) Refusal to Allow the Prosecution to Reopen their Case

General principles in relation to the reopening of cases were set out by MacKay J, with **6-82** whom Kennedy LJ agreed, in *Tuck v Vehicle Inspectorate*.[343] These have been relied on in several judicial reviews of magistrates' courts' decisions. The guidance, cited with approval in *R (Malcolm) v the Director of Public Prosecutions*[344] and in *R (Payne) v South Lakeland Magistrates' Court*[345], is as follows:

(1) The discretion to allow the case to be re-opened is not limited to matters arising ex improviso or mere technicalities, but is a more 'general discretion' (see Kennedy LJ *Jolly v DPP* 31st March 2000, unreported).

(2) The exercise of this discretion should not be interfered with by a higher court unless its exercise was wrong in principle or perverse (*R v Tate* [1997] RTR 17 at 22C).

(3) The general rule remains that the prosecution must finish its case once and for all (*R v Pilcher* 60 Cr App R 1 at 5) and the test to be applied is narrower than consideration of whether the additional evidence would be of value to the tribunal (loc cit). The discretion will only be exercised 'on the rarest of occasions' (*R v Francis* 91 Cr App R 271 at 175).

---

[340] *R (Crown Prosecution Service) v Sedgemoor Justices*, [31].
[341] *R (Gonzales) v Folkestone Magistrates' Court* [2010] EWHC 3428 (Admin).
[342] *R v Haringey Justices, ex parte DPP* [1996] 2 WLR 114, [1996] QB 351.
[343] *Tuck v Vehicle Inspectorate* [2004] EWHC 728 (Admin), [15].
[344] *R (Malcolm) v the Director of Public Prosecutions* [2007] EWHC 363 (Admin).
[345] *R (Payne) v South Lakeland Magistrates' Court* [2011] EWHC 1802 (Admin).

(4) The discretion must be exercised carefully having regard to the need to be fair to the defendant (*Matthews v Morris* [1981] JP 262), and giving consideration to the question of whether any prejudice to the defendant will be caused (*Tate* at 23C).

(5) The courts have in the past differed as to whether the mere loss of a tactical advantage can constitute such prejudice. The defendant, having spotted and drawn attention to a gap in the case by way of submission, as to which he could have remained silent, and taken advantage of that gap at the close of the evidence, was thought in *R v Munnery* [1992] 94 Cr App R 164 at 172 to be an important consideration. However, later cases take a discernibly different approach. A different view was expressed in *Khatibi v DPP* [2004] EWHC 83 Admin at 25 to 26 and in *Leeson* [2000] RTR 385 and 391F–G.

(6) Criminal procedure while adversarial is not a game (see *Leeson* (loc cit), *Hughes v DPP* [2003] EWHC Admin 2470, and the overall interests of justice include giving effect to the requirement that a prosecution should not fail through inefficiency, carelessness or oversight (*Leeson*).

(7) Of particular significance is the consideration of whether there is any risk of prejudice to the defendant (see *Jolly* and *Tate*).

An example of point (5) above is *R (CPS) v Norwich Magistrates' Court*.[346] The defence made a submission of no case to answer after a witness, who had been due to attend court, had not been warned. The witness identified the defendant and the defendant submitted that he had not been properly identified. The prosecutor claimed to have been ambushed and was granted a short adjournment to secure the witness's attendance and then reopen his case. The magistrates retired to consider their verdict without hearing from him, and held that there was no case to answer. The Divisional Court held that it was established law that the justices had a discretion to allow the prosecution to adduce further evidence to plug a gap identified in the submission of no case, provided that such a course would cause no injustice. It was contrary to the overriding objective of the Criminal Procedure Rules to prohibit the prosecutor from calling the witness. The defendant was caused no injustice and was at fault for 'sitting tight' in order to ambush the prosecutor. The issues in dispute should have been made clear at the outset.[347]

D. Post-Trial Matters

(1) Fresh Evidence (Reopening of Sentencing Decisions)

6-83   In *R v Northamptonshire Justices, ex parte Nicholson*,[348] the Divisional Court dismissed the prosecution's application for a mandatory order requiring justices to reopen a case after the emergence of new evidence. The defendant had previous convictions for road traffic offences which meant that she should have been disqualified. However, these previous convictions were not known when the magistrates passed sentence. The

---

[346] *R (CPS) v Norwich Magistrates' Court* [2011] EWHC 82 (Admin).
[347] Another example of an adjournment to permit the prosecution to deal with a point raised is *R (Taylor) v Southampton Magistrates' Court* [2008] EWHC 3006 (Admin).
[348] *R v Northamptonshire Justices, ex parte Nicholson* [1974] RTR 97.

Sarah Parkes and Piers von Berg

prosecutor's application to have her disqualified was refused on the basis that there was no residual power to reopen a case where magistrates had made a proper decision on all the evidence before them.

A different approach was taken in the more recent authority in *R (Holme) v Liverpool Magistrates' Court*.[349] The applicant (H) sought judicial review of the decision of the magistrates' court's decision to reopen his sentence following a conviction for dangerous driving. The prosecutor had explained that the pedestrian had suffered serious injuries as a result of the driving, but was not more specific. H was sentenced to 50 hours' community service and was disqualified from driving. A relation of the pedestrian complained about the leniency of this sentence and the Crown applied to reopen the case so that more evidence could be provided concerning the extent of the pedestrian's injuries. The court acquiesced to this application on the basis that there had been a breach of natural justice for them to sentence without full knowledge of the injuries. The Divisional Court granted H's application: this was not one of the exceptional circumstances where it would be appropriate to resort to section 142 of MCA 1980.

(2) Costs

(i) Defendants' Costs Orders

Where an accused is successful, the magistrates' court may order that the defence costs are paid out of central funds. A court's decisions on such applications can be challenged by judicial review. The circumstances in which such an order will be made are set out in section 16(1) of the Prosecution of Offences Act 1985, as follows: i) where an information is not proceeded with, or ii) the magistrates decide not to commit for trial, or iii) the accused is acquitted after a summary trial. Where an information is laid out of time[350] or proceedings are stayed as an abuse of process,[351] orders can still be made. It will also apply where proceedings are discontinued, either wholly or because the matter has been disposed of by a police caution.[352] A Defendants' Costs Order cannot be refused on the sole ground that the applicant has brought proceedings on himself. For such a refusal to be legitimate, more would be required, such as the defendant having misled the prosecution as to the strength of the case against him.[353]

6-84

Under section 16(3), costs can also be awarded upon successful appeal to the Crown Court in respect of either conviction or sentence. In *R (Cunningham) v Exeter Crown Court*[354] the Divisional Court held that the Crown Court should have given reasons for refusing costs from central funds where a magistrates' fine had been reduced on appeal. The refusal to award costs was held to be irrational and the Crown Court was ordered to award costs.

---

[349] *Holme* (n 12).
[350] *Patel v Blakey* [1988] RTR 65.
[351] *R (R E Williams and Sons) v Hereford Magistrates' Court* [2008] EWHC 2585 (Admin).
[352] *R (Stoddard) v Oxford Magistrates' Court* (2005) 169 JP 683.
[353] *R (Spiteri) v Basildon Crown Court* [2009] EWHC 665 (Admin).
[354] *R (Cunningham) v Exeter Crown Court* [2003] EWHC 184 (Admin).

Schedule 7 of the Legal Aid, Sentencing and Punishment of Offenders Act (LASPO) 2012 amended the 1985 Act. The new regime applies to all proceedings commenced on or after 1 October 2012. Although the ability of defendants to recover costs has been significantly restricted by LASPO 2012, individuals may still recover their costs after proceedings in the magistrates' court. However, Schedule 7 of LASPO 2012 empowers the Lord Chancellor to cap the amount the court can award by means of rates and scales or other provision. This power is contained in the Costs in Criminal Cases (General) Regulations 1986 (SI 1986/1335, as amended). Defendants are therefore only able to recover legal costs at legal aid rates. There is therefore likely to be a significant shortfall for those defendants who are ineligible for legal aid and pay for their representation privately.

The costs of a publicly funded defendant acting as a claimant in judicial review proceedings have been subject to recent reform. These provisions are examined below at 16-15.

6-85   Guidance on how and when to make defendants' costs order is provided in *Practice Direction (Criminal Proceedings: Costs)*.[355] No fault is required on the part of the prosecution in order to make a costs order.[356] Costs are deemed as having been incurred by the defendant when he is contractually obliged to pay them; the fact that he has no means and there is therefore no likelihood of him paying them is irrelevant.[357]

In *R v Liverpool Magistrates' Court, ex parte Abiaka*,[358] the Divisional Court held that section 16(1) gave a power to any constitution of the magistrates' court to make a Defendant's Costs Order, and was not confined to the same constitution of justices who had dismissed the case. Moreover, the order stood unless and until referred back to the court, or revoked by a superior court: the clerk was not entitled to ignore it or treat it as a nullity.

(ii) Prosecution Costs

6-86   Section 18 of the Prosecution of Offences Act 1985 authorises the making of orders that a convicted accused or unsuccessful appellant shall pay costs to the prosecutor of an amount that the court considers 'just and reasonable'. When seeking an order for costs against a defendant, the prosecution must give notice to the defendant of its intention to apply for such an order.[359] The magistrates must adjudicate on any such application.[360] The court must satisfy itself that the offender has the means and ability to pay any costs awarded.[361]

The Divisional Court provided detailed guidance in *R v Northallerton Magistrates' Court, ex parte Dove*,[362] where it was held that costs of £4,642 were grossly disproportionate to a fine of £1,000:

i.   The order to pay costs should never exceed the sum which the offender is able to pay, and which it is reasonable to expect him to pay, having regard to his means and any other financial order imposed on him.

---

[355] *Practice Direction (Criminal Proceedings: Costs)* [2010] 1 WLR 2351. See *Hussain v United Kingdom* (2006) 43 EHRR 437 on the interaction between Art 6(2) and cases where the prosecution offers no evidence.
[356] *R v Birmingham Juvenile Court, ex parte H* (1992) 156 JP 445.
[357] *R (McCormick) v Liverpool City Magistrates' Court* [2001] 2 All ER 705.
[358] *R v Liverpool Magistrates' Court, ex parte Abiaka* [1999] 163 JP 497.
[359] *R v Emmett* The Times, 15 October 1999.
[360] *R v Coventry Justices, ex parte Director of Public Prosecutions* [1991] 1 WLR 1153 DC.
[361] *Practice Direction (Criminal Proceedings: Costs)* [2010] 1 WLR 2351, para 3.4.
[362] *R v Northallerton Magistrates' Court, ex parte Dove* [1999] 163 JP 657, (Lord Bingham LCJ and Ognall J).

ii.   Nor should it exceed the sum which the prosecutor has actually and reasonably incurred.

iii. The purpose of such an order is to compensate the prosecutor and not to punish the offender, for example, for exercising his constitutional right to defend himself.

iv.   Any costs ordered should not in the ordinary way be grossly disproportionate to any fine imposed. Where the fine and the costs exceeded the sum which the offender could reasonably be ordered to pay, the costs should be reduced, rather than the fine.

v.   An offender facing a fine or an order as to costs should disclose to the magistrates the data relevant to his financial position, so that they can assess what he can reasonably afford to pay. Failure to make such disclosure could lead the court to draw reasonable inferences as to his means.

vi.   The court should give the offender a fair opportunity to adduce any relevant financial information and make submissions prior to the determination of any financial order.

(iii) Examples of Disproportionate Cost Orders

Further examples of costs orders that were set aside on the basis that they were disproportionate are as follows: **6-87**

i.   *R v Bow Street Magistrates' Court, ex parte Mitchell:*[363] the magistrates' decision that the claimant pay £8,000 towards the prosecution costs was so far outwith the limits of any reasonable discretion as to be grossly excessive.

ii.   *R v Walsall Magistrates, ex parte Garrison:*[364] a costs order was quashed because the justices had omitted to give any consideration to either the defendant's means or how such extensive costs had been incurred.

iii. *R v Old Street Magistrates' Court, ex parte Spencer:*[365] the defendant was fined £250 and ordered to pay £930 costs. The Divisional Court held that the proper bracket was £150 to £250, but it was not within their power to quash part of the order to lower the amount. The order was therefore quashed in its entirety and remitted to the magistrates.

iv.   *R v Newham Justices ex parte Samuels:*[366] the defendant was unemployed and had savings of £50 and debts of £690. The court imposed a fine of £250 on each of the two offences and ordered costs of £2,145.

v.   *R v Nottingham Justices, ex parte Fohmann:*[367] an order for costs of £600 was quashed. The defendant was on benefits and it would have taken him two years to pay off the combined fine and costs. Glidewell LJ said that the offender should be able to pay any order within a year.

---

[363] *R v Bow Street Magistrates' Court, ex parte Mitchell* [2000] COD 282 (DC).
[364] *R v Walsall Magistrates, ex parte Garrison* [1997] COD 14 (DC).
[365] *R v Old Street Magistrates' Court, ex parte Spencer* The Times, 8 November 1994 (DC).
[366] *R v Newham Justices ex parte Samuels* [1991] COD 412.
[367] *R v Nottingham Justices, ex parte Fohmann* (1986) 84 Cr App R 316.

(iv) Costs for a Breach of the Rules

6-88   Rule 3.5(6) of the Criminal Procedure Rules provides for sanctions in respect to breach of the rules:

> If a party fails to comply with a rule or a direction, the court may—
>
> (a) fix, postpone, bring forward, extend, cancel or adjourn a hearing;
> (b) exercise its powers to make a costs order; and
> (c) impose such other sanction as may be appropriate.

The court can also make a costs orders under:

i. section 19 of the Prosecution of Offences Act 1985 where it finds that one party incurred costs as a result of an unnecessary or improper act or omission by, or on behalf of, another party;

ii. section 19A of the 1985 Act if a party has incurred costs as a result of the same actions in section 19 on the part of a legal representative; or

iii. section 19B of the 1985 Act where there has been serious misconduct by a person who is not a party.

In *DPP v Bury Magistrates' Court*[368] the Divisional Court held that, when assessing the quantum of any loss, a court would consider taking into account the failings of the party seeking to claim a loss. A relevant factor was the failure of the party seeking costs to report a breach of the rules by the opposing party, thereby failing in their duty under Part 3 of the Criminal Procedure Rules.

(3) Proceeds of Crime Act (POCA) 2002 Matters

6-89   The magistrates' courts have a number of roles under POCA 2002 in relation to i) authorising searches, ii) extending time for the detention of property and iii) enforcing warrants of arrest and commitment that have been subject to judicial reviews. Their decisions have been challenged by way of judicial review on the basis of incorrect interpretation of the various sections of POCA 2002 or a magistrates' court otherwise misdirecting itself on the law.

(i) Search under POCA 2002

6-90   Although there are no reported cases of judicial review of magistrates' courts' decisions on this topic, the legislation is far from straightforward and errors may occur. Section 289 of POCA 2002 provides powers of search and detention for constables, officers of Revenue and Customs, accredited financial investigators and immigration officers. Section 304(1) of POCA 2002 defines 'recoverable property' as property obtained though unlawful conduct. Section 305(1) states that where original property has been disposed of, property representing that property is recoverable, for example, money from the sale of stolen goods. Approval for searches must be obtained from a magistrate or from a police officer

---

[368] *DPP v Bury Magistrates' Court* [2006] EWHC 3256 (Admin).

Sarah Parkes and Piers von Berg

of at least the rank of inspector or a designated customs officer or accredited financial investigator. Applications to a magistrates' court are governed by the Magistrates' Courts (Detention and Forfeiture of Cash) Rules 2002 (SI 2002/2998).

If a search is conducted without prior approval from a magistrate, and no cash is recovered or any cash is released within 48 hours, a written report must be completed specifying the reasons for the search and why it was not practicable to seek prior authority (section 290(6) and (7)).

Sub-sections 289(1) and (2) stipulate that the powers of search within the section are only exercisable where there are reasonable grounds for suspecting that recoverable property will be found on a person or premises. The minimum amount referred to in the section is defined in the Proceeds of Crime Act 2002 (Recovery of Cash in Summary Proceedings: Minimum Amount) Order 2006 (SI 2006/1699) as not less than £1,000. Where premises are to be searched, the officer must be on the premises lawfully. The powers are exercisable 'only so far as reasonably required for the purpose of finding cash' and must comply with the Proceeds of Crime (Cash Searches: Code of Practice) Order 2008 (SI 2008/947).

(ii) Seizure of Cash under POCA 2002

Seizure of cash is permitted under section 294(1) of POCA 2002 where the relevant person **6-91** has reasonable grounds for suspecting that it is recoverable property or is intended by any person for use in unlawful conduct. Where it is not reasonably practicable to sever recoverable property from a suspected amount, section 294(2) permits seizure of the full amount.

In *R (Iqbal) v Luton and South Bedfordshire Magistrates' Court*,[369] the Divisional Court considered the time after which police were permitted to seize cash under section 294 of POCA 2002 where it had previously been seized and retained under sections 19 and 22 of PACE 1984. The claimant maintained that the application by the police for an extension of time to detain seized cash had not been brought within 48 hours of seizure as required by section 295 of the 2002 Act. The magistrates' court rejected that argument, agreeing with the police that they were entitled to a grace period having made the decision not to institute proceedings for another offence.

The Divisional Court agreed.[370] The police were entitled to retain the cash for a short grace period once the section 22 power had expired. That period had to be reasonable. Where alleged not to be reasonable, the appropriate remedy was an application to stay proceedings (following *Chief Constable of Merseyside v Hickman*[371]). The delay in this case was held to be permissible.

In *R (Chief Constable of Greater Manchester) v City of Salford Magistrates' Court*,[372] the **6-92** Divisional Court considered the use of section 295 of POCA 2002 at an interim stage in proceedings when there was uncertainty as to whether money obtained derived from criminal conduct.

---

[369] *R (Iqbal) v Luton and South Bedfordshire Magistrates' Court* [2011] EWHC 705 (Admin).
[370] The facts of the case were distinguished from *R (Cook) v Serious Organised Crime Agency* [2010] EWHC 2119 (Admin), [2011] 1 WLR 144. In that case, there had been an obligation to restore the property, but only because the original seizure had been unlawful.
[371] *Chief Constable of Merseyside v Hickman* [2006] EWHC 451 (Admin).
[372] *R (Chief Constable of Greater Manchester) v City of Salford Magistrates' Court* [2008] EWHC 1651 (Admin), [2009] 1 WLR 1023.

Under section 294 of POCA 2002, police officers seized cash from S's commercial premises. S applied for the return of the money but the chief constable (C) sought continued detention of the money, on the grounds that it was to be used to pay wages of illegal workers. The judge granted S's application on the basis that even if the workers were illegal, that did not render the entire business unlawful.

C sought a quashing order on the grounds that the judge had misdirected himself in law. He did not need to be satisfied that the business as a whole was unlawful, but rather that there were reasonable grounds for suspecting that the money derived to a material degree from the labour of people whom it was a criminal offence to employ. C argued that his application under section 295 should have been granted, as the illegal workers had made a material contribution to the acquisition of S's money.

C's application was granted; the judge had misdirected himself in law. By virtue of section 297(3), the burden of proof was on S to show that the money could not reasonably be suspected of having been obtained through criminal conduct. It was only at the forfeiture stage that section 298 placed the burden of proof on C to satisfy the court that the criteria in section 242 were made out. Section 295, however, was intended for use at a time when the provenance of money would be uncertain. That question could not be resolved at an interim stage and the judge's decision was therefore quashed.

(iii) Enforcement: Warrants of Commitment and Arrest

6-93 In *R (Johnson) v Birmingham Magistrates' Court*[373] the claimant sought judicial review of a decision of a district judge to issue a warrant of commitment under section 76 of the MCA 1980 specifying 3,211 days' imprisonment in relation to an outstanding confiscation order. J's benefit was certified to be £168 million, but his realisable assets were just over £26 million. J submitted that the judge had acted unlawfully in issuing the warrant: he could not be sure that, as he had to be, that the failure to pay was the result of J's wilful refusal or culpable neglect within section 82(4)(b)(i) of MCA 1980 and that all other methods of enforcement were impractical within section 82(4)(b)(ii). He further submitted that the enforcement officer had been allowed insufficient time to pursue the foreign assets and that the £8 million worth of assets recovered in the UK demonstrated cooperation on his part.

The Divisional Court rejected these arguments on the grounds that J's cooperation had been fruitless. The onus had been on him to realise those assets within the time set by the judge in the confiscation order. If he was seeking to contend that assets identified in the confiscation order were not his, he should have disputed it at the confiscation hearing. Custody must be available as a sanction where such a small proportion of assets had been recovered, otherwise the notion of 'realisable assets' became meaningless. Section 82(4) required the court to have regard to other methods of enforcement, rather than to exhaust those methods.

6-94 The magistrates' court has a power under section 83 of MCA 1980 to compel the attendance at court of a person, who in this context is usually in default of payment of a confiscation order. The purpose is to conduct a means enquiry as provided in section

---

[373] *R (Johnson) v Birmingham Magistrates' Court* [2012] EWHC 596 (Admin).

Sarah Parkes and Piers von Berg

82.[374] In *R (Necip) v City of London Magistrates' Court*,[375] such an order was quashed on the grounds that it had been issued solely to compel his attendance at an enforcement hearing. However, in *R (Lawson) v City of Westminster Magistrates' Court*,[376] a similar application was refused as the defaulter had refused to attend court in response to a summons. The Divisional Court held that section 83(2) which dealt with such circumstances permitted a warrant to be issued separate to any consideration of a means enquiry.

(iv) Delay in POCA 2002 Enforcement (Abuse of Process)

In *R (Lloyd) v Bow Street Magistrates' Court*[377] a delay of two years nine months between a CPS decision to enforce a confiscation order and the confiscation proceedings was unjustifiable. The defendant relied on his Article 6 right to have a criminal charge determined within a reasonable time. *R (Joyce) v Dover Magistrates' Court* made clear that Article 6 submissions would not succeed where part of the delay was attributable to the defendant being unlawfully at large.[378] In *R (Syed) v City of Westminster Magistrates' Court*[379] a delay of over six years in enforcing a confiscation order was unreasonable and infringed both defendants' right to have the confiscation orders enforced within a reasonable time. Note though the case of *Crown Prosecution Service v Derby and South Derbyshire Magistrates' Court*,[380] in which it was held that although there had been an unreasonable delay in pursuing enforcement proceedings, this did not necessarily mean that it was appropriate to bar all methods of enforcement by virtue of Article 6. In particular, in some circumstances it would be inappropriate to invoke a criminal sanction but inappropriate and disproportionate to prevent enforcement by civil law remedies.

6-95

In *R (Chief Constable of Lancashire) v Burnley Magistrates' Court*[381] the Divisional Court considered whether it would be an abuse of process to seize cash under section 298 of POCA 2002 when an application to extend the time limit under section 295 had been refused. Officers had seized cash from the interested party (A). They believed they had reasonable grounds for believing that A was involved in drug crime, and exercised their power under section 294(1). The chief constable (C) then made an application under section 295(2) to extend the initial 48-hour time limit for the detention of the cash. The court refused the application on the ground that the application did not meet the criteria set out in sections 295(5) or 295(6).

6-96

C then made an application for forfeiture under section 298, but the court held that this amounted to an abuse of process: C's sole purpose was to avoid returning the money to A so that more evidence could be gathered against him. C successfully sought judicial review of the court's decision. There was nothing in the statutory provision that

---

[374] For a challenge to a court's approach to applying s 82 see *R (Jestin) v Dover Magistrates' Court* [2013] EWHC 1040 (Admin).

[375] *R (Necip) v City of London Magistrates' Court* [2009] EWHC 755 (Admin), [2010] 1 WLR 1827

[376] *R (Lawson) v City of Westminster Magistrates' Court* [2013] EWHC 2434 (Admin).

[377] *R (Lloyd) v Bow Street Magistrates' Court* [2003] EWHC 2294 (Admin).

[378] *R (Joyce) v Dover Magistrates' Court* [2008] EWHC 1448 (Admin). See also *R (Marsden and McIntosh) v Leicester Magistrates' Court* [2013] EWHC 919 (Admin).

[379] *R (Syed) v City of Westminster Magistrates' Court* [2010] EWHC 1617 (Admin).

[380] *Crown Prosecution Service v Derby and South Derbyshire Magistrates' Court* [2010] EWHC 370 (Admin).

[381] *R (Chief Constable of Lancashire) v Burnley Magistrates' Court* [2003] EWHC 3308.

prohibited an application under section 298 following a refusal under section 295. The judge had failed to have regard to C's duty to the public, and there was no evidence on which C's section 298 application could be characterised as manipulative or abusive. The power to order release of the cash under section 297(1) had not been exercised and the application was therefore within the 48-hour time limit.

7

The Crown Court

LIAM LOUGHLIN AND JAMES McLERNON

A. General Principles

(1) Introduction

The scope for judicial review of Crown Court decisions is limited. It excludes all matters **7-1** relating to trial on indictment by virtue of section 29(3) of the Senior Courts Act 1981. Practitioners need to understand how the courts have delineated the scope of this exclusion, as it affects almost all challenges to the Crown Court. There are several areas that fall outside this exclusion, including decisions on bail, custody time limits, production orders, on appeal from the magistrates' courts and on rare occasions, decisions concerning wasted costs.

(2) The High Court's Jurisdiction over the Crown Court[1]

7-2   The nature of the application of judicial review to decisions of the Crown Court can be considered in light of the exclusionary provisions of section 29(3) of the Senior Courts Act 1981:

> (3) In relation to the jurisdiction of the Crown Court, other than its jurisdiction in matters relating to trial on indictment, the High Court shall have all such jurisdiction to make mandatory, prohibiting or quashing orders as the High Court possesses in relation to the jurisdiction of an inferior court.

It appears at first instance that there is a broad-based jurisdiction to judicially review the Crown Court. The difficulty arises however when it comes to assessing what matters are properly excluded under section 29(3) as relating to 'matters relating to trial on indictment'.

The courts have been reluctant to draw any clear-cut definitions as to what 'matters relating to trial on indictment' encompasses, and it is notable that the enacting legislation does not define the term further. What seems clear from the case law, as Lord Browne-Wilkinson explained in *R v Manchester Crown Court, ex parte DPP*, is that the courts feel that judicial review should be used sparingly, as:

> If it were possible to challenge decisions taken in the course of a criminal prosecution, not only the prosecution but also the accused would be able to put off the conclusion of the trial by taking technical points and then seeking to have the judge's decision reviewed in the Divisional Court. Experience in other jurisdictions shows that those on trial are only too willing to put off the evil day by taking 'interlocutory' points to appeal. English law has set its face against this.[2]

In considering whether the matter was properly reviewable, the House of Lords in *R v Manchester Crown Court, ex parte DPP* expanded on the test set out in *Re Smalley*,[3] asking whether the decision was one affecting the conduct of a trial on indictment given in the course of the trial or in pre-trial directions. The court stated:

> It might be a helpful further pointer to the true construction of section 29 of the 1981 Act to ask the question whether the decision sought to be reviewed was one arising in the issue between the Crown and the defendant formulated in the indictment (including the costs of such issue). If the answer is in the affirmative, then to permit the decision to be challenged by judicial review may lead to delay in the trial: the matter is therefore probably excluded from review by the section. If the answer is in the negative then the decision of the Crown Court is truly collateral to the indictment of the defendant and judicial review of that decision will not delay his trial: therefore, it may well not be excluded by the section.[4]

---

[1] See also discussion above at 1-27.

[2] *R v Manchester Crown Court, ex parte DPP* [1993] 1 WLR 1524, [1993] 4 All ER 928 (HL), 7.

[3] *Re Smalley* [1985] AC 622, [1985] 2 WLR 538 (HL).

[4] *R v Manchester Crown Court, ex parte DPP* (n 2) 2. See also discussion above at 1-25 and *R (Lipinski) v Wolverhampton Crown Court* [2005] EWHC 1950 (Admin).

(i) Examples of Matters Relating to Trial on Indictment

The following decisions have been held to be 'matters relating to trial on indictment' **7-3**
(see also above at 7-2):

i.   an order to discharge the jury;[5]
ii.   the empanelling of a jury;[6]
iii. the issue of a witness summons under section 2(1) of the Criminal Procedure
      (Attendance of Witness) Act 1965;[7]
iv.   the arraignment of a defendant and the way in which a plea and directions
      hearing was conducted;[8]
v.   the refusal to fix a trial date until a certain event has occurred, such as the
      conclusion of a summary trial. The court stated that there is no difference in
      principle between such a decision and the decision to adjourn a trial or a deci-
      sion ordering that a trial should not proceed without leave of the court;[9]
vi.   an order by the judge that an indictment lie on the file marked 'not to be pro-
      ceeded with without leave';[10]
vii. the refusal to grant a further extension of time in which to prefer a bill of
      indictment;[11]
viii. the remand of witness to custody in a trial on indictment until such time as the
      court appointed for the giving of evidence under section 4(3) of the Criminal
      Procedure (Attendance of Witnesses) Act 1965 to remand a witness;[12]
ix.   an order made following an application to stay a criminal trial as an abuse of
      process;[13]
x.   a Crown Court judge's refusal of an application made pursuant to section 18(1)(b)
      of the Extradition Act 1989 for a stay of proceedings on indictment;[14]
xi.   a decision on a dismissal application of a charge sent for trial under section 51
      of the Crime and Disorder Act 1998;[15]
xii. a warrant of imprisonment ordering that a defendant serve their sentence con-
      secutively to a term that he was already serving, where the judge had not stated
      that the sentence was to be consecutive, is not reviewable;[16]
xiii. where a Crown Court judge had mistakenly sentenced a convicted rapist under
      section 227 of the Criminal Justice Act 2003 instead of under the serious

---

[5] *Ex p Marlowe* [1973] Crim LR 294.
[6] *R v Sheffield Crown Court, ex parte Brownlow* [1980] QB 530, [1980] 2 WLR 892.
[7] *R (TB) v Stafford Crown Court* [2006] EWHC 1645 (Admin), [2007] 1 WLR 1524.
[8] *R v Leeds Crown Court, ex parte Hussain* [1995] 1 WLR 1329 (DC), [1995] 3 All ER 527.
[9] *R v Liverpool Crown Court, ex parte Mende* [1991] COD 483.
[10] *R v Central Criminal Court, ex parte Raymond* [1986] 1 WLR 710, [1986] 2 All ER 379.
[11] *R v Isleworth Crown Court, ex parte King* [1992] COD 298 (DC).
[12] *R (H) v Wood Green Crown Court* [2006] EWHC 2683 (Admin), [2007] 1 WLR 1670.
[13] *Re Ashton* [1994] 1 AC 9, [1993] 2 WLR 846.
[14] *R (Rogerson) v Stafford Crown Court* [2001] EWHC Admin 961, [2002] Crim LR 318.
[15] *R (Snelgrove) v Woolwich Crown Court* [2004] EWHC 2172 (Admin), [2005] 1 WLR 3223.
[16] *R v Lewes Crown Court, ex parte Sinclair* (1993) 5 Admin. LR 1, [1992] Crim LR 886 (DC).

offences provisions of the Act, and had refused to correct the decision under the slip rule;[17]

xiv.   a decision by a judge at the end of a trial not to make a compensation order;[18]

xv.   the making of an order under section 51(5) of the Mental Health Act 1983 (making a hospital order in the absence of the defendant);[19]

xvi.   in relation to the making or discharge of an order under section 39 of the Children and Young Persons Act 1933 to protect the anonymity of a child defendant;[20] and

xvii. an order made by the trial judge in relation to the disclosure of documents held by a third party that potentially affected the credibility of a witness to proceedings.[21]

Another example is the case of *R (TB) v Stafford Combined Court*.[22] The court considered an application for the disclosure of psychiatric medical records by witness summons in relation to the medical records of TB, a complainant then aged 15, who was the chief prosecution witness in a case concerning allegations of sexual offences against children. The defence sought to argue that the allegations were the result of a 'schoolgirl fantasy', and sought medical records to support this. With regard to the failure to provide adequate notice and representation for TB in relation to the matter, the court held that:

> procedural fairness in the light of Article 8 undoubtedly required in the present case that TB should have been given notice of the application for the witness summons, and given the opportunity to make representations before the order was made. Since the rules did not require this of the person applying for the summons, the requirement was on the court as a public authority, not on W, the defendant. TB was not given due notice of that opportunity, so the interference with her rights was not capable of being necessary within Article 8(2). Her rights were infringed and the court acted unlawfully in a way which was incompatible with her Convention Rights. This in substance is what the requested declarations seek and I would grant them.[23]

It would seem therefore that the distinction is quite fine and will depend on the nature of the disclosure sought, the potential right infringed, and how the matter is approached.

---

[17] *R (CPS) v Guildford Crown Court* [2007] EWHC 1798 (Admin), [2007] 1 WLR 2886. The court stated that it was not possible to derive a general principle from *R v Maidstone Crown Court, ex parte Harrow LBC* [2000] QB 179 and *R (Kenneally) v Snaresbrook Crown Court* [2001] EWHC Admin 968, [2002] QB 1169. The court had a power in judicial review proceedings to quash any sentence that exceeded the jurisdiction of the sentencing court. *Ex p Harrow* and *Kenneally* were distinguished, on the basis that in those cases there had been no trial on indictment.

[18] *R (Faithfull) v Crown Court at Ipswich* [2007] EWHC 2763 (Admin), [2008] 1 WLR 1636 (DC).

[19] See however *Kenneally* (n 16), where it was held that the High Court retained the power to quash an order if the Crown Court made an error of jurisdiction of the type of which took the case outside the scope of the Crown Court's jurisdiction in matters relating to trial on indictment. See discussion below at 12-4.

[20] See *R v Manchester Crown Court, ex parte H (A Juvenile)* [2000] 1 WLR 760, [2000] 2 All ER 166 that held that such an order would normally fall within the exclusionary ambit of s 29(3) of the Senior Courts Act 1981, although the issue becomes collateral to trial after verdict and sentence.

[21] *R v Chester Crown Court, ex parte Cheshire County Council* [1996] 1 FLR 651, [1996] Crim LR 336.

[22] *R (TB) v Stafford Combined Court* [2006] EWHC 1645 (Admin), [2007] 1 WLR 1524.

[23] ibid [25].

(3) Statutory Rights of Appeal to the Court of Appeal

There are a number of statutory rights of appeal to the Court of Appeal from the Crown   7-4
Court that are prescribed by statute and will therefore take precedence over any judicial
review. They include rights of appeal:

i.   by the Crown in relation to the refusal to make a Football Banning Order;[24]
ii.   against a finding of and sentence for contempt of court;[25]
iii.   against an order restricting or preventing reports of proceedings or limiting
        access to the public to such proceedings;[26]
iv.   in relation to a restraining order following acquittal or conviction;[27]
v.   against the making, variation or non-variation of a Serious Crime Prevention
        Order;[28]
vi.   by a third party against a third party wasted costs order;[29]
vii.   against a wasted costs order;[30]
viii.   where a defendant is found unfit to plead and there is a finding that he com-
        mitted the actus reus;[31] and,
ix.   where as a result of item (viii) the court imposes a hospital order, interim order
        or a supervision order.[32]

(4) Judicial Review of Matters that have not Reached Trial

The decision therefore to challenge the power of a prosecuting authority may well be   7-5
affected by the stage at which any such challenge is brought (for challenges to decisions by prosecuting authorities, see Chapter 5 above). For example, in *R (Securiplan
Plc, Phillip Ullmann, Sabrewatch Ltd, Luke Lucas) v Security Industry Authority*[33] the
claimant challenged the legal authority of the Security Industry Authority to institute a
prosecution for the use of 'unlicensed security operatives', contrary to section 5 of the
Private Security Industry Act 2001. By the time the challenge was brought, the matter
had already been before the Crown Court and a determination of the legal authority of
the agency to bring prosecutions determined by HHJ Rivlin. In deciding that the present
matter now constituted a matter related to trial on indictment, Maurice Kay LJ stated:

> I am prepared to assume that a challenge to the decision to prosecute, in the form of a chal-
> lenge to the *vires* of the prosecutor, if made at a much earlier stage, may not be caught by the
> exclusionary provision of section 29(3). However, when (as here) the case has proceeded to the

---

[24] See the Football and Spectators Act 1989, s 14A(5A) anzd *R v Boggild (Phillip)* [2011] EWCA Crim 1928,
[2012] 1 WLR 1298 for a case on this point.
[25] The Administration of Justice Act 1960, s 13.
[26] Criminal Justice Act 1960, s 159.
[27] Protection from Harassment Act 1997, ss 5 and 5A.
[28] Serious Crime Act 2007, s 24.
[29] Costs in Criminal Cases (General) Regulations 1986 SI 1986/1335, Pt IIB, r 3H.
[30] ibid, r 3C.
[31] Criminal Appeal Act 1968, s 15.
[32] ibid, s 16A. Note that the defendant needs to seek leave from the Court of Appeal, or a certificate from
the trial judge.
[33] *R (Securiplan Plc, Phillip Ullmann, Sabrewatch Ltd, Luke Lucas) v Security Industry Authority* [2008]
EWHC 1762 (Admin), [2009] 2 All ER 211.

Crown Court and has been the subject of a ruling by a judge in the Crown Court, it seems to me that the exclusionary provision bites. If a defendant is then prosecuted to conviction in the Crown Court, he can take the point in the Court of Appeal Criminal Division (CACD) in an appeal against conviction.[34]

In any event, the court made a finding that if they had been able to make an assessment of the lawfulness of the prosecution, the court would have concluded that they did have such authority. What the case demonstrates, however, is that, if a party to proceedings wishes to challenge the lawfulness of any such decision, that decision must be challenged at the earliest possible date, and before the Crown Court is seized of the matter.

(5) Third Parties[35]

7-6   It would appear that judicial review will be available to a third party where a decision is made, although appearing to relate to a matter involving trial on indictment. For example in the leading case of *Re Smalley* (see above at 7-2), it was held that the forfeiture of a surety's recognizance for bail where the surety's brother as defendant had failed to attend his Crown Court trial was judicially reviewable.

Similarly, the court held in the case of *Maidstone Crown Court, ex parte Gill*[36] that a forfeiture order under section 27 of the Misuse of Drugs Act 1971 was again not one 'affecting the conduct of the trial', and that consequently the Divisional Court had jurisdiction to entertain an application for a quashing order in respect of that forfeiture order. The Divisional Court held that it had power to hear the matter otherwise the applicant would have no right of appeal against the decision of the original trial judge. The Divisional Court held that a forfeiture order would be quashed where a person had no knowledge of the purpose to which his goods were being used (in this case, two cars belonging to the applicant that his son had used to facilitate the supply of heroin).

The court did hold that a forfeiture order would have been proper if the lender of the motor car should have been put on notice that the car was going to be used for illegal purposes.

B. Bail

(1) Jurisdiction

7-7   Crown Court decisions on bail can in principle be challenged in the Administrative Court. Claimants must first overcome the hurdle of satisfying the court that their application is not 'a matter relating to trial on indictment' within section 29(3).

---

[34] ibid [22].

[35] Applications under s 23(1) of the Criminal Appeal Act to the Court of Appeal to order the disclosure of relevant records post conviction fall outside of the scope of this book, although an example of one can be found in *Niwar Doski v The Crown* [2011] EWCA Crim 987.

[36] *Maidstone Crown Court, ex parte Gill* (1986) 84 Cr App R 96, [1986] 1 WLR 1405.

Through section 17 of the Criminal Justice Act (CJA) 2003, Parliament chose to abolish the right to apply directly to the High Court for bail, and so the court is careful to guard against this being circumvented by applications seeking review of Crown Court decisions on bail.

The leading case on the High Court's jurisdiction is *R (M) v Isleworth Crown Court*[37] where Maurice Kay LJ sought to deal with these 'two jurisdictional issues requiring comment'. First, His Lordship considered the effect of section 29(3) on the Administrative Court's jurisdiction in respect of Crown Court decisions concerning bail. The court applied the 'helpful pointer' for the proper interpretation of section 29(3), set out by Lord Browne-Wilkinson in *Ex p DPP*[38] [1993] (which is essentially an almost exact restatement of the passage cited above at 7-2) and Maurice Kay LJ held that this test excluded bail decisions 'at an early stage of criminal proceedings' from the scope of section 29(3).

The second jurisdictional question was whether a refusal of bail was susceptible to judicial review in any event. In *R v Croydon Crown Court, ex parte Cox*[39] it was held that there was no jurisdiction to review bail decisions. Maurice Kay LJ distinguished that case because this pre-CJA 2003 judgment had specifically cited the availability of an alternative remedy, namely an application to a High Court judge for bail, which had since been abolished.

Section 17(6)(b) of the CJA 2003 provides that: 'Nothing in this section affects … any right of a person to apply for a writ of habeas corpus or any other prerogative remedy.' Maurice Kay LJ said that he had no doubt that 'prerogative remedies' in that context embraced those set out in section 29(1) of the Senior Courts Act 1981, namely mandatory orders, prohibiting orders and quashing orders

(i) Extent of the Jurisdiction Beyond 'An Early Stage'

The judgment in *M*[40] puts beyond doubt the question of jurisdiction at 'an early stage' **7-8** in criminal proceedings, but gives no further clarification. In the years following this judgment the Administrative Court struggled with this poorly defined phrase. In a series of subsequent decisions the court, without challenge, assumed jurisdiction at stages immediately before and after the trial phase itself.

i. In *Burns v Woolwich Crown Court*[41] the court reviewed a bail decision made after a preliminary hearing and before a Plea and Case Management Hearing (PCMH).

ii. In *R (Fergus) v Crown Court at Southampton*[42] the court assumed jurisdiction over an application in respect of a refusal to continue bail following a guilty plea at arraignment and pending sentence. Fergus was considered in the subsequent case of *R (Uddin) v Leeds Crown Court*.[43]

---

[37] *R (M) v Isleworth Crown Court* [2005] EWHC 363 (Admin).
[38] *Ex p DPP* [1993] see 7-2 and n 3 above.
[39] *R v Croydon Crown Court, ex parte Cox* [1997] 1 Cr App R 20.
[40] *M* (n 36).
[41] *Burns v Woolwich Crown Court* [2010] EWHC 29 (Admin).
[42] *R (Fergus) v Crown Court at Southampton* [2008] EWHC 3273.
[43] *R (Uddin) v Leeds Crown Court* [2013] EWHC 2752 (Admin).

iii. In *R (Shergill) v Harrow Crown Court*,[44] Collins J said: 'I am persuaded that any application that arises, certainly before the trial itself actually starts, is one which can be dealt with by this court'. *Shergill* was also cited in *Uddin*.

iv. In *R (KS) v Northampton Crown Court*[45] the court expressed the view that jurisdiction extended to reviewing a decision on bail pending retrial following discharge of a jury, but not to the actual trial itself. The court noted that following the discharge of the jury the retrial could not be heard for at least another five months. In *KS* the court considered the previous cases of *Burns, Fergus* and *Shergill*.

Counsel instructed by the CPS in *KS* conceded that the Administrative Court had jurisdiction to review the decision of a Crown Court judge in respect of bail at least where no trial was currently in progress. Langstaff J said this concession was rightly made, as the applicant was no longer 'in the middle of a trial' when there would have been no jurisdiction.

7-9 Whilst the jurisdictional question was dealt with tangentially in many of the above decisions it was confronted head on in the recent case of *Uddin*.[46] The applicant's bail was revoked by the trial judge in the midst of a lengthy Crown Court trial. No High Court judge was available in Leeds to hear the matter at short notice, and so it was dealt with by HHJ Jeremy Richardson QC sitting as a Deputy of the High Court, to prevent delay in the ongoing trial.

HHJ Richardson QC reviewed the relevant cases including those set out above. He held that the wording of section 29(3) was clear, and highlighted the use of the phrase 'matters relating to the trial on indictment', which was deliberately broader in scope in his view than simply 'relating to the indictment'. This was felt to be specifically intended to 'prohibit this court trespassing upon the trial process itself'.[47]

The purpose of bail is to ensure the defendant's attendance at the trial so outside the time of the trial, either before or after it, this is a collateral matter.

> Bail decisions before the trial and after the trial, if there to be a retrial or another trial (perhaps in a series of trials) are not decisions relating to the trial itself and are open to challenge by way of judicial review.[48]

The position changes once the trial starts. During the trial, any decision on bail must sensibly be a matter relating to the trial on indictment. HHJ Richardson QC acknowledged the lacuna this created in judicial oversight and the right to challenge judicial decisions, but held that the alternative would interfere with the jurisdiction of the Crown Court entrusted to it by Parliament in the clearest of terms and inevitably mire the trial process in satellite litigation:

> I confess I have a feeling of unease, whereby I may be approving a scenario where an aggrieved individual has potentially no means of challenging by appeal or review a first instance, indeed, only instance decision, during a criminal trial. With that said, subject to very limited statutory exceptions (as an example a terminating ruling) there is no concept of interlocutory appeals

---

[44] *R (Shergill) v Harrow Crown Court* [2005] EWHC 648 (Admin).
[45] *R (KS) v Northampton Crown Court* [2010] 2 Cr App R 23 (QBD).
[46] *Uddin* (n 42).
[47] ibid [31].
[48] ibid [35].

Liam Loughlin and James McLernon

in a Crown Court trial on indictment. That is the choice Parliament has made. It must be respected.[49]

(ii) The Test to Apply where the High Court has Jurisdiction

In M,[50] Maurice Kay LJ said:

> Although we have jurisdiction by reason of s 17(6)(b), I am in no doubt that it is a jurisdiction which we should exercise very sparingly indeed … The test must be on *Wednesbury* principles, but robustly applied and with this court always keeping in mind that Parliament has understandably vested the decision in judges in the Crown Court who have everyday experience of, and feel for, bail applications. Of course if bail were to be refused on a basis such as 'I always refuse in this type of case', or some other unjudicial basis, then this court would and should interfere.[51]

His Lordship felt that he would not have refused bail had he heard the application sitting in the Crown Court at first instance, but that was not the test and the application must fail as the decision was not 'perverse'. Subsequent decisions have reaffirmed a straightforward *Wednesbury* test without the 'robust' gloss attached by Maurice Kay LJ.[52] In *R (I) v Wood Green Crown Court* Collins J disavowed a 'super' Wednesbury test stating that:

> The test is whether this was a decision which was one which was reasonable within that test, and going with rationality is the question whether matters which influence the decision ought to have been taken into account.[53]

In KS[54] [2010], the court held that:

> A decision as to bail by a Crown Court Judge is in principle reviewable, although the parties agree (as, emphatically, do I) that Parliament having decided to remove the right of application to the High Court in respect of any bail decision it will only be in exceptional cases that this court will consider it right to review the decision of a crown court judge in whom is vested the relevant powers.[55]

In *R (Galliano) v Crown Court at Manchester*,[56] Collins J stated that:

> He can only succeed on this claim if he persuades me that the decision made by the learned judge was one which fell outside the bounds of what could be regarded as reasonable. So one is in the realm of irrationality and it is clear that nothing short of that will entitle me to interfere.[57]

7-10

7-11

7-12

---

[49] ibid [29].

[50] *M* (n 36).

[51] ibid [11]–[12].

[52] *Associated Provincial Picture Houses Ltd v Wednesbury Corp* [1948] 1 KB 223, [1947] 2 All ER 680, 230 (Lord Greene MR). Explained above at 1-82.

[53] *R (I) v Wood Green Crown Court* [2014] EWHC 1595 (Admin), [10], was a case where the Crown Court judge refused bail on the basis of what Collins J described as 'entirely speculative' and 'highly improbable' objections, which were not advanced by the Prosecution.

[54] *KS* (n 44).

[55] ibid [6].

[56] *R (Galliano) v Crown Court at Manchester* [2005] EWHC 1125 (Admin).

[57] ibid [11] See also 'Failure to grant bail not irrational' (2005) 169 *Justice of the Peace & Local Government Law* 426.

7-13   An important case on the test to be applied is the recent decision in *R (Charles) v Central Criminal Court*,[58] which dealt with an application for bail on a charge of murder, can be seen as an expansion of the reviewability of Crown Court bail decisions.

Singh J cited and approved of the *Wednesbury* test set out by Maurice Kay LJ in *M*,[59] but stated that this had never been intended to be interpreted (as it had been in many subsequent decisions) in what he termed 'the narrow sense' of *Wednesbury* unreasonableness, which focuses solely on whether the ultimate decision made was irrational or perverse. Singh J stated that the *Wednesbury* principles at the heart of the test set by Maurice Kay LJ also allow the Administrative Court to scrutinise the decision-making process which led to the decision. The court must look not just at the decision that was reached, but how that decision was reached

As Singh J makes clear the application of the *Wednesbury* test is now not to be applied in its most limited sense, in what is sometimes termed *Wednesbury* irrationality, as had previously been suggested in the previous authorities:[60]

> But the Wednesbury principles, as Maurice Kay LJ clearly had in mind ... are not confined to that narrow ground. More broadly, they include, for example, a failure to take a relevant consideration into account, or the taking into account of a consideration which is legally irrelevant.[61]

Singh J stated that the court could intervene and quash a decision where the Crown Court failed to consider a factor that was relevant, took into account a factor that was irrelevant, or failed to apply the correct legal test to the application before it. Throughout, Singh J emphasised the importance of giving a defendant good and sufficient reasons for refusing bail. Even though the judge at first instance was extremely experienced, such that Singh J doubted that he had an incorrect test in mind, the reasons given did not make this sufficiently clear.

The reasoning had to be made clear, first so that any reviewing court could assess its validity, secondly so that the losing party could understand why it is they have lost, and thirdly so that the decision-maker themselves can ensure they are having regard to all relevant considerations and that they are asking themselves the right questions as directed by law.[62]

In applying this test Singh J found that the Crown Court judge had not made it sufficiently clear that he had the right statutory test from the bail act in mind (some of the phrases used in the reasons gave rise to the possibility that the test in section 25 of the Crime Justice and Public Order Act 1994 (CJPO) had been incorrectly used). Furthermore, he did not explain why he had dispensed with strong arguments put forth by the defendant in respect of sureties and bail conditions.

Singh J accepted the submissions that:

> Most fundamentally, what the claimant submits is that when the ruling is read as a whole, the learned judge failed to ask himself the right questions. The claimant submits that although if one took one or two passages in isolation, it would not necessarily be right or fair to criticise the decision when one takes the reasoning as a whole and cumulatively, there are too many

---

[58] *R (Charles) v Central Criminal Court* [2012] EWHC 2581 (Admin), [2013] Crim LR 229.
[59] *M* (n 36).
[60] See for example Collins J in *Galliano* (n 54) [11] and *Shergill* (n 44).
[61] *Charles* (n 56) [20].
[62] ibid [30].

problems and defects in the reasoning adopted by the learned judge for the decision to be able to stand.[63]

The above demonstrates that the Administrative Court will be ready to take a global approach to the reasoning to assess whether the decision falls foul of the *Wednesbury* test in its broadest sense.

The reasoning above reflects the cautious and constructive approach that the courts have taken to the giving of reasons for the refusal of bail, as illustrated in the case of *R (F) v Southampton Crown Court* where the judge's statements that he was 'not sure' that the defendant would 'turn up or stay out of trouble' were held to be insufficient: **7-14**

> it is not a question of him not being sure that the defendant would turn up or stay out of trouble ... he was only entitled to refuse bail if there were substantial grounds for believing that he would breach, he would fail to turn up or would commit further offences.[64]

For a similar approach to the strict application of the correct test for bail, see the decision in *R (Rojas) v Snaresbrook Crown Court*, where Holman J stated:

> Of itself the fact that a person has been convicted and a custodial sentence is inevitable, is not sufficient to trigger the exception to bail. It is still necessary that the court is satisfied that there are substantial grounds for believing that one of the statutory exceptions [to the presumption in favour of bail] applies.[65]

(2) Successful Applications

Despite the jurisdictional hurdles and extremely narrow remit to intervene, the court does continue to exercise its discretion to quash Crown Court decisions on bail in exceptional circumstances. A number of the decisions such as *Rojas* and *Fergus* reflect The court's willingness to scrutinise the way in which decisions are made rather than simply the outcome as highlighted in the formulation of the test to be applied set out in *Charles.*   **7-15**

i.   In *R (Malik) v Central Criminal Court*,[66] the court quashed the decision of the Central Criminal Court to refuse the defendant's request for his bail application to be heard in public with him present.[67] This case was mention in *KS.*

ii.   In *R (Mongan) v Isleworth Crown Court*,[68] the court stated that the reduction in charges, from two counts of robbery to one offence committed on one occasion, constituted a material change in circumstances for the purposes of deciding whether the risk of reoffending remained. The Crown Court judge's refusal to hear a renewed bail application was wrong in law. Although that did not necessarily mean that bail would be granted, it did justify a reconsideration and acceptance of a new application for bail, and the Crown Court was ordered to entertain the defendant's application.

---

[63] ibid [24].
[64] *R (F) v Southampton Crown Court* [2009] EWHC 2206 [8].
[65] *R (Rojas) v Snaresbrook Crown Court* [2011] EWHC 3569 (Admin) [24].
[66] *R (Malik) v Central Criminal Court* [2006] 4 All ER 1141 (DC).
[67] *Malik* was mentioned in *KS* (n 44) [7].
[68] *R (Mongan) v Isleworth Crown Court* [2007] EWHC 1087 (Admin).

iii.   In *R (Allwin) v Snaresbrook Crown Court*[69] a homeless defendant was remanded for psychiatric report, as he had indicated he might harm himself. After consideration of the report and the offer from his parents of a stable address, he was released on conditional bail. The defendant was committed to the Crown Court and although there were no breaches or opposition to renewed bail, the circuit judge stated that he was concerned about self-harm and refused bail. Collins J held that he would not have refused to continue bail at first instance as there was no material change in circumstances, but went further and quashed the decision as being *Wednesbury* unreasonable.[70]

iv.   In *R (Brooks) v Croydon Crown Court*,[71] Forbes J held that where a defendant has been observing his conditions of bail scrupulously and has not acted in breach in any way at all, a reasoned explanation should be given to explain why bail is being withdrawn and this should only occur after a full and proper examination of all the relevant considerations.

> By indicating at the outset of the proceedings that he was minded not to grant bail, the judge clearly exhibited a mind that was very nearly, if not entirely, made up. That gave the appearance of a predetermined approach to a matter which he had to consider and decide.[72]

> I have come to the conclusion that the decision-making by the learned judge on 10th February was so perfunctory and so lacking in any proper analysis of the relevant facts, and so lacking in the proper exploration of such fundamental considerations such as appropriate conditions, as to place it firmly outside the bounds of what was reasonable for the purposes of the decision-making in a bail application.[73]

> Not giving B's counsel the opportunity to explore the possibility of bail conditions also gave the appearance of a closed mind and predetermined approach.[74]

v.   In *Rojas*, a 17-year-old claimant (R) applied for judicial review of the Crown Court's decision to withdraw his bail. R had been arrested for affray, and was released on conditional bail for six months until his trial. The jury unanimously found R guilty, and the judge said that a custodial sentence was inevitable and that R was to be remanded into custody. R indicated that he would seek to persuade the judge otherwise, to which the judge simply answered 'no'.

The Divisional Court quashed the refusal of bail. The trial judge had been under a statutory obligation under section 5(3) of the Bail Act 1976 to give reasons for the withdrawal of bail. At a minimum, this required citing the statutory grounds for refusal of bail and identification of the case-specific factors that this was based on. Furthermore, the court was obliged to give any defendant's advocate the opportunity to make submissions before such a decision was made.

Such a serious procedural flaw would require remittal to the Crown Court for a fresh decision but in the instant case it was held that no reasonable judge,

---

[69]   *R (Allwin) v Snaresbrook Crown Court* [2005] EWHC 742 (Admin).

[70]   *Allwin* was applied in *R (Brooks) v Croydon Crown Court* [2006] EWHC 461 (Admin) and *R (Thompson) v Central Criminal Court* [2005] EWHC 2345 (Admin) and cited in *Mongan*.

[71]   *Brooks* (n 68).

[72]   ibid [16].

[73]   ibid [20].

[74]   ibid [19].

properly directed, could withdraw bail, and so R was granted bail immediately with more stringent conditions.

vi.   In *Fergus* the refusal of bail was quashed not because the result was irrational but because the judge had used an improper formulation of the statutory test to be applied. The matter was remitted to the same judge to make a fresh decision based on the proper test.

vii.   A similar decision was given in the case of *R (Ukaegbu) v Northampton Crown Court*.[75] The court held that in appropriate circumstances that the Crown Court had the power to revoke bail without a material change of circumstances. However the judge in *Ukaegbu* had been wrong to take account of the defendant's recall to prison, as this was an administrative act. The revocation of the claimant's licence was not therefore a decision of a court based on consideration of the relevant features to the grant or withdrawal of bail.

(3) Actions the Court will take on Quashing a Decision to Refuse Bail

In *Rojas*, Holman J set out the options open to the Divisional Court. If the court considers that there has been significant procedural error, it should remit the substantive issue of bail for reconsideration by the judge, who is currently conducting the case in the Crown Court   **7-16**

If however the court can properly conclude that no reasonable judge, properly directing himself, could have withdrawn or could now withdraw bail (subject to any appropriate conditions or varied conditions), then it is a waste of time and expense to remit the matter to the Crown Court.

If there is still room for a discretionary decision to withdraw bail, then that is a decision which should be made by the Crown Court judge, but after hearing submissions on behalf of the claimant and possibly the prosecution.[76]

(4) Practical Procedure for Judicial Review of Decisions on Bail

In two cases heard on the same day, Collins J set out guidance for these types of applications. The principles in the first case of *Allwin* (discussed above at 7-15), are summarised below: **7-17**

i.   Such applications will normally be presented to the court on the basis of a matter of urgency. It would be surprising if it was appropriate in any case that bail be granted on an interim application on the papers.

ii.   Of course, one never should rule out the possibility of a truly exceptional set of circumstances but, in general, that cannot be expected to occur.

iii.   The matter should be put before the court with a view to an oral hearing on notice being sought within as short a time as reasonably possible.

---

[75] *R (Ukaegbu) v Northampton Crown Court* 4 September 2013 (QBD) (Admin).
[76] 64 *Rojas* (n 63) [29].

iv.   Applications should always be made within hours to the Administrative Court and over the weekend.

v.   Unless a judge considers the claim to be unarguable and dismisses it, the normal order would be to direct an oral hearing within a day or two.

vi.   The CPS should have sufficient time to be able to make representations, if they wish to.

vii.   The court will determine the issue at the oral hearing. If it grants bail, it will give permission and abridge all other procedural requirements. In other cases it can decide to grant permission and dismiss the application, or it can view the application as unarguable and refuse permission.

viii.   A single judge will normally deal with the applications. It would not be right to convene a Divisional Court, unless an important point of principle was raised.[77]

In *Shergill* (see above at 7-8), Collins J revisited the topic and added this:

i.   The case should be heard as soon as possible, at the most within 48 hours on notice to the Crown Court and to the prosecution.

ii.   A judge may find there is no possibility that the refusal of bail could conceivably be overturned and could, in those circumstances, reject the matter out of hand. Otherwise it would have to be heard as soon as possible.

iii.   In many cases the court would want to deal with the matter as quickly as possible on the basis of oral submissions. This may help to avoid any problems that may emerge if there are any renewed applications.

iv.   It is essential that the reasons given by the judge at first instance are recorded so that on any application for judicial review the court will have a record of them.[78]

C. Custody Time Limits

7-18   The Administrative Court has been willing to interfere with decisions of the Crown Court in two situations:

i.   where there has been a jurisdictional error; and

ii.   where decisions of the Crown Court that would ordinarily be deemed to be matters that relate to trial on indictment have been made improperly.

In the case of *R v Maidstone Crown Court, ex parte Clarke*[79] the court was prepared to quash an arraignment that was used only to defeat the custody time limits due to the service of a large amount of additional evidence in the case by the Crown the day prior to the expiry of the relevant custody time limits; it had also prevented the defendant from entering informed pleas.

The judge directed that a 'holding plea' be entered that would not be held against the defendant if he later pleaded. The matter proceeded to arraignment, the defendant pleaded not guilty and was subsequently remanded in custody; defence counsel was

---

[77] *Allwin* (n 67) [17]–[18].
[78] (n 44) [2]. This case was considered in *Uddin*.
[79] *R v Maidstone Crown Court, ex parte Clarke* [1995] 1 WLR 831, [1995] 3 All ER 513.

therefore no longer able to challenge the extension of the custody time limits. The court quashed the arraignment following the reasoning of McCowan LJ in *R v Maidstone Crown Court, ex parte Hollstein*:[80]

> I do not consider it permissible for a Crown Court, whether of its own motion or at the request of the prosecution, artificially to create an arraignment situation with the deliberate intention of denying a defendant the fruit of the failure by the prosecution to obey the custody time limits. That is not a real arraignment

Glidewell LJ, in a qualified acceptance of the above case, stated that whilst he found that *Ex p Hollstein* was a just result, he was not so satisfied that the court was correct to conclude that it had jurisdiction. However, he did not go so far as to say the decision was wrong, and indeed held that he was bound by it.[81]

In any event Glidewell LJ felt that the matter was amenable to a free-standing writ of habeas corpus (for a discussion of this remedy, see above at 3-31). It should be noted that Curtis J did not have any such reservations as to the correctness of *Ex p Hollstein*.

Similarly in the case of *R (Raeside) v Luton Crown Court*[82] the court was called upon to assess whether the court had properly applied the test for the extension of custody time limits under section 22(3) of the Prosecution of Offences Act 1985:

> (3) The appropriate court may, at any time before the expiry of a time limit imposed by the regulations, extend, or further extend, that limit; but the court shall not do so unless it is satisfied—
> (a) that the need for the extension is due to—
>   i.   the illness or absence of the accused, a necessary witness, a judge or a magistrate;
>   ii. a postponement which is occasioned by the ordering by the court of separate trials in the case of two or more accused or two or more offences; or some other good and sufficient cause; and,
> (b) that the prosecution has acted with all due diligence and expedition.

In reaching their decision the court found that the original trial judge had approached the issue on the wrong basis and misdirected himself. The matter was therefore susceptible to judicial review. Importantly, Sir John Thomas P reinforced that the assessment was to a stringent standard, a stricter standard of review than as suggested in some previous cases[83] when he stated:

> We must emphasise again the necessity in every case that the court in an application to extend a CTL gives detailed scrutiny to the evidence to see if the Crown has proved that there is good and sufficient cause. As the court said in *McAuley*, such evidence must be served in advance of the hearing so that the defendant has the opportunity of examining it and then testing it in cross-examination, if necessary.[84]

7-19

7-20

The Administrative Court found that the case was not remotely within the category of cases of real complexity such as to justify the extension of the custody time limits without

---

[80] *R v Maidstone Crown Court, ex parte Hollstein* [1995] 3 All ER 503.
[81] *Ex p Clarke* (n 77), 842.
[82] *R (Raeside) v Luton Crown Court* [2012] EWHC 1064 (Admin), [2012] 1 WLR 2777.
[83] See for example the comments of Jowitt J in *Norwich Crown Court, ex parte Parker* [1992] 96 Cr App R 68, [70] and *Wildman v DPP* [2001] EWHC Admin 14 (Lord Woolf LCJ), that seemingly suggest a lower test and a greater discretion for the first instance judge.
[84] *Raeside* (n 80) [16]. See also *R (Clark McAuley) v Coventry Crown Court* [2012] EWHC 680 (Admin), [2012] 1 WLR 2766, a Divisional Court led by Sir John Thomas P.

further efforts being made to establish if another court in the area could have tried the matter within the time limits.[85] The following further observations are worthy of mention:

> We must emphasise again the necessity in every case that the court in an application to extend a CTL gives detailed scrutiny to the evidence to see if the Crown has proved that there is good and sufficient cause.

> … the purpose of the statutory provision and the long tradition of the common law in ensuring that cases are tried speedily would be undermined if the unavailability of a judge or court room was simply treated as amounting to good and sufficient cause, absent other circumstances.[86]

In relation to where the duty to address any issues concerning the listing of trial in accordance with trial dates lies, the court supported the view of Smith J in *R (Norman) v Worcester Crown Court*:

> In my judgment, there is a joint duty upon the prosecution and the court to recognise that fact of life, and to make early arrangements for the fixing of a trial date within the custody time limits.[87]

It is important to note that the court in *Raeside* specifically said that the obligation to resolve the issue is not the responsibility of the defence.[88]

7-21   As a final note, challenges to arraignments on the basis that they have been conducted solely for the purpose of avoiding an expiry of custody time limits, will inevitably fail, as arraignments are a matter relating to trial on indictment.[89]

D. Production Orders

7-22   Following what might be called an alarming increase in the number of production orders made against the media, including in relation to the student protests in 2011 and the 2011 riots, the Divisional Court quashed a production order of Chelmsford Crown Court in relation to the Dale Farm evictions of 2012, in *R (British Sky Broadcasting Ltd) v Chelmsford Crown Court*.[90] The claimants sought to challenge production orders in relation to all footage of a 17-hour period that the police wished to have disclosed to them as potential evidence of substantial value to the police investigations under the Police and Criminal Evidence Act 1984 Schedule 1, paragraph 2(a)(iii), in relation to a number of indictable offences arising from the opposed eviction.

In quashing such a wide-ranging production order, the court held that there was a balance to be struck between the public interest in bringing to justice those involved in public

---

[85] Enquiries were only made of St Albans and Cambridge Crown Courts, with no reference to the regional listing office. Further, no enquiries were made of Wood Green or Harrow Crown Courts where the court found that the matter could have been tried within the custody time limits or extra effort being made to list the case at Luton Crown Court. See *Raeside* [6] and [10].

[86] ibid [15]–[16].

[87] *R (Norman) v Worcester Crown Court* [2000] 3 All ER 267, [2000] 2 Cr App R 33, 40.

[88] *Raeside* (n 80) [28].

[89] *R v Leeds Crown Court, ex parte Hussain* [1995] 1 WLR 1329. In that case what the defendants were asking the court to do, in effect, was to quash the arraignment, and because the custody time limits had expired, release them on bail.

[90] *R (British Sky Broadcasting Ltd) v Chelmsford Crown Court* [2012] EWHC 1295 (Admin).

disorder or violence, and the granting of a production order and the need to protect freedom of expression under Article 10 of ECHR. Eady J, with whom Moses LJ agreed, said:

> It is clear that full account must be taken of Article 10 considerations when determining an application under Schedule 1. It is helpful to have in mind the words of Dyson LJ (as he then was) in *Malik v Manchester Crown Court* [2008] EMLR 19, at [47]-[48], albeit immediately concerned with (comparable) wording from another statute:

> '47. There is no disagreement between the parties as to the relevant legal principles. Courts are public authorities under s.6(3) of the Human Rights Act 1998 (the HRA). Accordingly, a production order cannot be made if and to the extent that it would violate a person's Convention rights. The discretion conferred by para 6 must be exercised compatibly with an affected person's Convention rights even if the two access conditions are satisfied.

> 48. The correct approach to the Art 10 issues as articulated in both the Strasbourg jurisprudence and our domestic law emphasises that: (i) the court should attach considerable weight to the nature of the right interfered with when an application is made against a journalist; (ii) the proportionality of any proposed order should be measured and justified against that weight; and (iii) a person who apples for an order should provide a clear and compelling case in justification of it'.[91]

His Lordship added that:

> In our view, it is relevant to the balancing exercise to have in mind the gravity of the activities that are the subject of the investigation, the benefit likely to accrue to the investigation and the weight to be accorded to the need to protect the sources.[92]

It is clear from the above, and the careful consideration of the relevant case law in *British Sky Broadcasting*, that the imposition of a production order will be the subject of careful review, and that the court will be willing to review any such order and quash it accordingly if the relevant test is not applied appropriately.

Another consideration is the procedure adopted by the Crown Court, in particular, the disclosure of evidence by the police to respondents to an application. In *R (British Sky Broadcasting Ltd) v Central Criminal Court*,[93] the Commissioner of Police for the Metropolis had applied for a production order under section 9 of and Schedule 1 to the Police and Criminal Act 1984 (PACE), requiring the claimant broadcaster to produce copies of e-mails which had passed between one of its journalists and two named persons. The notice of application stated that access to the e-mails was sought for the purposes of an investigation into offences under the Official Secrets Act 1911, and that some of the evidence that was to be provided to the judge in support of the application would not be provided to the claimant. After the hearing of the application had opened *inter partes,* the judge heard counsel for the Commissioner *ex parte* with a view to deciding whether the secret evidence should be disclosed to the claimant. In the course of that secret hearing the judge heard evidence from a police officer in addition to the evidence he had previously read. He concluded that none of the evidence should be disclosed. Having heard further argument *inter partes*, the judge then granted the production order sought by the Commissioner. The claimant brought a claim for judicial review of the production order, on the ground that the procedure by which it had been obtained was fundamentally unfair and unlawful.

---

[91] *R (British Sky Broadcasting Ltd) v Chelmsford Crown Court* [2012] EWHC 1295 (Admin) [14].
[92] ibid [56].
[93] *R (British Sky Broadcasting Ltd) v Central Criminal Court* [2014] UKSC 17, [2014] 2 WLR 558.

The Commissioner appealed to the Supreme Court. The Supreme Court stated that as a general proposition, the court should not apply the *Al Rawi* principle (see above at 1-111) to an application made by a party to litigation (or prospective litigation) to use the procedural powers of the court to obtain evidence for the purposes of litigation from a person who was not a party or intended party to that litigation:

> This is because such an application will not ordinarily involve the court deciding any question of substantive legal rights as between the applicant and the respondent. Rather it is an ancillary procedure designed to facilitate the attempt of one or other party to see that relevant evidence is made available to the court in determining the substantive dispute. Applications of this kind, such as an application for a witness summons in civil or criminal proceedings, are typically made ex parte.[94]

However, applications for productions orders under section 9 of, and Schedule 1 to PACE 1984 presented a different situation. Such proceedings were not a trial in the ordinary sense, but were a special form of statutory procedure:

> Compulsory disclosure of journalistic material is a highly sensitive and potentially difficult area. It is likely to involve questions of the journalist's substantive rights. Parliament has recognised this by establishing the special, indeed unique procedure under section 9 and Schedule 1 [of the Police and Evidence Act 1984] for resolving such questions....

> Parliament recognised the tension between the conflicting public interests in requiring that an application for a production order shall be made 'inter partes'.[95]

When an application for a production order is made, there is a *lis* [law suit] between the person making the application and the person against whom it is made, which may later arise between the police and the suspected person through a criminal charge. Equal treatment of the parties required that each should know what material the other is asking the court to take into account in making its decision and should have a fair opportunity to respond to it. That is inherent in the concept of an 'inter partes' hearing.[96]

Accordingly, the Supreme Court dismissed the Commissioner of Police's appeal and upheld the Divisional Court's decision that it was not permissible for the Crown Court judge to have allowed the Commissioner's application to hear part of the police officer's evidence *ex parte*.[97]

E. Costs

(1) Costs

7-23   The granting of the award of costs in criminal proceedings has been held to be a matter relating to trial on indictment. The refusal to award costs following an acquittal,[98] as

---

[94] ibid [28].

[95] ibid [29]–[30]. See also *R v Lewes Crown Court, ex parte Hill* (1991) 93 Cr App R 60, 65-66 where Bingham LJ set out the proper approach to the statutory scheme; affirmed by the Supreme Court in *British Sky Broadcasting* at [24].

[96] ibid [30].

[97] ibid [31]. For the avoidance of doubt, the Supreme Court made it clear that its ruling did not prevent a court from hearing a public interest immunity ("PII") application ex parte, but that was a different matter (at [32]).

[98] *Re Meredith* [1973] 1 WLR 435, [1973] 2 All ER 234.

well as the refusal of a Crown Court judge to grant legal aid,[99] to revoke legal aid,[100] and refusing to amend an order to allow for representation by Queen's Counsel,[101] have all been held to be matters relating to trial on indictment.

Prior to the case of *Hunter v Newcastle Crown Court*[102] there was some uncertainty in relation to the award of a defendant's costs in relation to matters that had not proceeded to trial, excluding in relation to guilty pleas.[103]

The matter was however revisited in *Hunter,* where Leveson LJ endorsed the judgment in *R v Harrow Crown Court, ex parte Perkins,*[104] [1998] 162 JP 527 where Rose LJ said:

> I can see no difference in principle between a Crown Court judge's refusal to make a costs order in favour of the defendant, when ordering a stay for an abuse of process or when entering a verdict of not guilty under s.17 of the Criminal Justice Act 1967 or at any stage of the proceedings. In each case, it seems to me that such an order, like an order made at the end of the trial as in *ex parte Meredith* [1973] 1 WLR 435, 57 Cr App R 451 relates to trial on indictment.

Leveson LJ went further by stating:

> It is worth noting that in *Reg v Bolton Crown Court ex parte CPS* [2012] EWHC 3570 (Admin), Richards LJ (with whom Ouseley J agreed) observed that, in the light of the decision in Ashton, the Wood Green case should 'be treated with considerable caution'… In my judgment, it goes further than Richards LJ observed: both the decision and its reasoning are entirely undermined and the law has been as expressed in Harrow Crown Court for over 14 years.

It is therefore clear that following the decision in *Hunter* that matters that relate to the award of a defendants costs' will not be amenable to judicial review. The Administrative Court will not be prevented from examining the issue when it is clear that the lower Court has imposed an order for cost that it does not have the power to impose.[105]

(2) Wasted Costs

Whilst it follows from the above that the award or not of costs to a party to proceedings is not amenable to judicial review,[106] it is evident from the case of *R (B) v X Crown Court* that the imposition or award of wasted costs for either the defence or the prosecution is potentially amenable to judicial review in certain limited situations, such as where a potentially determinative interlocutory order is sought to be challenged. Hickinbottom J said that: **7-24**

> The wasted costs jurisdiction under Section 19A is a separate collateral jurisdiction from the Crown Court's primary jurisdiction to try indictments: it is a discrete jurisdiction arising in the Crown Court 'irrespective of whether that which is before the Crown Court judge is a trial on

---

[99] *R v Chichester Crown Court, ex parte Abodunrin* (1984) 79 Cr App R 293, DC.
[100] *R v Isleworth Crown Court, ex parte Willington* [1993] 1 WLR 713, DC, [1993] 2 All ER 390.
[101] *R (Shields) v Crown Court at Liverpool* [2001] EWHC Admin 90, [2001] UKHRR 610.
[102] *Hunter v Newcastle Crown Court* [2013] EWHC 191 (Admin), [2013] 2 Costs LR.
[103] *R v Wood Green Crown Court, ex parte Director of Public Prosecutions* [1993] 1 WLR 723, [1993] 2 All ER 656.
[104] *R v Harrow Crown Court, ex parte Perkins* [1998] 162 JP 527.
[105] See *R (DPP) v Sheffield Crown Court* [2014] EWHC 2014 (Admin): An award of the defendant's costs following acquittal against the Director of Public Prosecutions was amenable to judicial review as the Crown Court had no powers to impose any such order in the circumstances.
[106] See *R v Smith* [1975] QB 531, [1974] 2 WLR 495 where the decision of a judge to order a defence solicitor to pay the costs occasioned by the granting of a defence application for an adjournment was held not to be susceptible to judicial review.

indictment, committal for sentence, an appeal from the magistrates or any other proceedings' (*[R v Snaresbrook Crown Court] ex p Field* [23 March 1994] at page 8, per Rose LJ).[107]

The Administrative Court further held that the trial judge's decision not to consider whether to recuse himself in considering a matter of wasted costs for the appearance of bias in a case considering the conduct of the trial over which he had presided was also amenable to judicial review. Accordingly the trial judge should have considered whether the test for recusal for bias was met, namely whether a fair-minded and informed observer would conclude that there was a real possibility of bias, or have left such an assessment to another judge. A failure to properly consider the question was an interlocutory matter that was susceptible to review.

It is worth noting however that in reaching their decision the court stated that successful challenges under judicial review would be very rare, but that in some cases, such as the present one that sought to challenge an interlocutory order, such cases may succeed.

It is submitted however that cases such as those found *B v X Crown Court* will be rare, and that the proper route of challenge would be through to appeal to the Court of Appeal.[108] In the case of *B v X Crown Court* the court found that whilst there was a right of appeal for wasted costs decisions to the Court of Appeal, there was no such appeal from an interlocutory order (such as judge's refusal to recuse himself). Successful judicial reviews in the wasted costs jurisdiction will be very rare, and *B*'s case had exceptional features.

F. Appeals and Variations of Sentence

(1) Appeals by Way of Case Stated

7-25 Decisions by the Crown Court sitting in an appellate capacity can be challenged by way of judicial review or by an appeal by way of case stated. For example it can be challenged on the basis of a failure to give reasons (see above at 1-120). The differences between the two routes and the factors to be borne in mind when choosing between them is described above at 6-12. Section 28 of the Supreme Court Act 1981 reads:

28.— Appeals from Crown Court and inferior courts.

(1) Subject to subsection any order, judgment or other decision of the Crown Court may be questioned by any party to the proceedings, on the ground that it is wrong in law or is in excess of jurisdiction, by applying to the Crown Court to have a case stated by that court for the opinion of the High Court.

(2) Subsection (1) shall not apply to—
   (a) a judgment or other decision of the Crown Court relating to trial on indictment; or
   (b) any decision of that court under the Local Government (Miscellaneous Provisions) Act 1982 which, by any provision of any of those Acts, is to be final.

(3) Subject to the provisions of this Act and to rules of court, the High Court shall, in accordance with section 19(2), have jurisdiction to hear and determine—
   (a) any application, or any appeal (whether by way of case stated or otherwise), which it has power to hear and determine under or by virtue of this or any other Act; and

---

[107] *R (B) v X Crown Court* [2009] EWHC 1149 (Admin), [2009] PNLR 30 [30i].
[108] See *Smith* [1975] QB 531 and the Solicitors Act 1974, s 50(3).

Liam Loughlin and James McLernon

(b) all such other appeals as it had jurisdiction to hear and determine immediately before the commencement of this Act.

In subsection (2)(a) the reference to a decision of the Crown Court relating to trial on indictment does not include a decision relating to [a requirement to make a payment under regulations under section 23 or 24 of the Legal Aid, Sentencing and Punishment of Offenders Act 2012.

As can be seen from the above, section 28(1) grants any party to proceedings in the Crown Court the right to have a case stated on the grounds that it is 'wrong in law or in excess of jurisdiction'. It is an appeal to the Queen's Bench Division of the High Court to state its opinion on a question of law that has been framed by the magistrates' court or Crown Court in its appellate capacity. The decision in question should be framed as containing the relevant background and facts in a document called the case. It was held in *Loade and others v Director of Public Prosecutions*[109] that an appeal by way of case stated could not be made as an interlocutory application, and could only be made after the final determination of the criminal matter in question. If there is a challenge to an interim decision, it should be made by way of judicial review.[110] However, there are limits to the High Court's jurisdiction in intervening at a interlocutory stage in proceedings (see above at 6-17). The right of appeals by way of case stated is restricted to parties to proceedings.[111]

Where the Crown Court hears appeals from the magistrates' court, this plainly falls outside section 29(3) of the Senior Courts Act 1981, so there is no issue as to the High Court's jurisdiction in considering claims for judicial review. However, there is authority that the appropriate route for a challenge to conviction on appeal in the Crown Court is by case stated.[112] To be clear, the Crown Court's decision on appeal cannot be challenged as wrong on the facts, for example, that it misinterpreted the evidence or placed undue weight on a particular piece of evidence. It can only be challenged in the High Court on the grounds that apply to appeal by case stated (eg wrong in law or excess jurisdiction) or by judicial review (eg unfairness, procedural impropriety, bias, *Wednesbury* unreasonableness or error of law[113]—see section G of Chapter 1).   **7-26**

It is submitted that the correct route depends on the timing of the application, the type of the decision under challenge and the nature of the complaint (see comparison of the two routes in detail above at 6-12).

Under section 81(1)(d) of the Senior Courts Act 1981, bail pending appeal by way of case stated from the Crown Court may be granted by a judge in chambers.

(2) Variation of Sentence

Where the Crown Court passes sentence following: **7-27**

i.   committal for sentence; or
ii. appeal against conviction and /or sentence,

---

[109] *Loade and others v Director of Public Prosecutions* [1990] 1 QB 1052, [1989] 3 WLR 1281.
[110] See *Gillan v DPP* [2007] EWHC 380 (Admin), [2007] 1 WLR 2214.
[111] For a discussion of the expanded group of appellants of 'those aggrieved by the conviction, order, determination or other proceedings of the court under section 111(1) of the Magistrates Court Act 1980', see above at 6-9.
[112] *R v Gloucester Crown Court, ex parte Chester* [1998] COD 365 (DC), Lord Bingham LCJ presiding.
[113] See for example *R (Taffs) v Chelmsford Crown Court* [2014] EWHC 899 (Admin).

and the defendant applies to the Administrative Court for a quashing order under section 31 of the Senior Courts Act 1981, the court may, instead of quashing the conviction, amend the sentence to any one that the Crown Court had the power to impose.

7-28   The High Court has clear jurisdiction to intervene where the sentence is wrong in law, or is in excess of jurisdiction. The line of case law seeking to give guidance on these principles begins with *R v St Albans Crown Court, ex parte Cinnamond*:[114]

> it is not sufficient to decide that the sentence is severe, perhaps even unduly severe or surprisingly severe. It is necessary to decide that it is either harsh and oppressive or, if those adjectives are thought to be unfortunate or in any way offensive, that it is so far outside the normal discretionary limits as to enable this court to say that its imposition must involve an error of law of some description, even if it may not be apparent at once what is the precise nature of that error.[115]

In that case, an 18-month disqualification for careless driving was quashed, and replaced with a six-month sentence. Although the Crown Court sentence was not in excess of any statutory maximum sentence, it was so far beyond the standard disqualification handed down for the same offence across the country as to constitute an error in law

7-29   This case was qualified by a series of cases such as *R v Acton Crown Court, ex parte Bewley*[116] and *Tucker v DPP*.[117] This is best exemplified by the cautious treatment given to *Ex p Cinnamond* by Watkins LJ in *R v Crown Court at Croydon, ex parte Miller* where he stated that *Ex p Cinnamond* 'has to be regarded with circumspection', as its ratio will only apply to unusual and rare circumstances:

> I would utter a warning to anyone who comes here seeking to have a sentence of justices or the Crown Court reviewed upon the basis that the sentence is too severe because it is out of scale, so to speak, that for *St Albans Crown Court, ex parte Cinnamond* to be applied the sentence will in all the circumstances need to appear to be, by any acceptable standard, truly astonishing.[118]

In *R v Swansea Crown Court, ex parte Davies*,[119] the Divisional Court found that the sentence imposed by the Crown Court was untoward, harsh and oppressive. It was held that it so far departed from the norm as to call for intervention by the Administrative Court. In *R (Turner) v Sheffield Crown Court*, Moses J cited *Ex p Miller* and held that the test to be applied was even more restrictive than 'manifestly excessive':

> As a Divisional Court it is not open to this court to interfere with sentence merely because we believe that the sentence of one month's imprisonment which the judge passed was manifestly excessive ... This court can only interfere if the decision was either in excess of jurisdiction or was wrong in law.[120]

---

[114] *R v St Albans Crown Court, ex parte Cinnamond* [1981] QB 480, [1981] 2 WLR 681.
[115] ibid, 484.
[116] *R v Acton Crown Court, ex parte Bewley* 10 Cr App R(S) 105 (DC).
[117] *Tucker v DPP* 13 Cr App R (S) 495 (DC).
[118] *R v Crown Court at Croydon, ex parte Miller* (1987) 85 Cr App R 152, 155.
[119] *R v Swansea Crown Court, ex parte Davies* The Times. 2 May 1989.
[120] *R (Turner) v Sheffield Crown Court* [2003] EWHC 1717 (Admin) [2].

8

Prisons

FLORENCE IVESON

A. General Principles

(1) Introduction

8-1 Prison law is a complex and idiosyncratic area, governed by its own set of rules and guidance. It is beyond the scope of this chapter to consider all areas of prison life which might involve reviewable decisions or to chart the history of judicial review in prisons. This chapter is intended to be used as a reference, to help practitioners get to grips with the way judicial review is currently being approached by UK courts in the field of prison law.

(2) The Scope and Role of Judicial Review

8-2 Judicial review has become more and more prevalent in prison life over the past few decades. Following the case of *R v Board of Visitors of Hull Prison, ex parte St Germain*[1] through to *R v Home Secretary, ex parte McAvoy,*[2] *R v Secretary of State for the Home Department, Ex p Anderson,*[3] *R v Deputy Governor of Parkhurst Prison, ex parte Leech*[4] and *R v Deputy Governor of Parkhurst Prison, ex parte Hague,*[5] judicial intervention in prison life has gradually increased, to the point at which almost all areas of prison life are open to judicial review. Essentially, all of the important decisions affecting prisoners, such as categorisation, release on licence and transfer to open conditions, will be classed as public law exercises and the remedy of judicial review will be available, provided there are grounds.

The importance of judicial review in prisons is now obvious. Regardless of their detention, convicted prisoners retain all civil rights which are not expressly removed or which are not necessarily limited by the very fact of their detention.[6] Prisoners are in a uniquely vulnerable position from a public law perspective, because they are necessarily unable to exercise control over their daily existence. Almost everything affecting their day-to-day lives, sometimes even beyond prison, is decided by people occupying positions of authority, who must apply a variety of rules and exercise a range of discretions. Prisoners must have access to courts to ensure that such decisions are made fairly and justly.

Grounds for review in a prison law context are no different from those in any other area of law, thus decisions can be challenged on the basis of irrationality, illegality and procedural impropriety. In practice, the main areas in which grounds for review arise have been where a law, rule or policy has not been followed by a decision-maker, or decisions have been taken without the required level of procedural fairness.

---

[1] *R v Board of Visitors of Hull Prison, ex parte St Germain* [1979] QB 425.
[2] *R v Home Secretary, ex parte McAvoy* [1984] 1 WLR 1408.
[3] *R v Secretary of State for the Home Department, ex parte Anderson* [1984] QB 778.
[4] *R v Deputy Governor of Parkhurst Prison, ex parte Leech* [1988] 1 AC 533, [1988] 2 WLR 290.
[5] *R v Deputy Governor of Parkhurst Prison, ex parte Hague* [1992] 1 AC.
[6] *Raymond v Honey* [1983] 1 AC 1 [10].

Florence Iveson

Thus it is very important for practitioners to be aware of the plethora of policies and rules relevant to a given situation and to work out what was in force at the time a decision was made. This is especially the case since the outcomes of judicial review will often quickly be incorporated into the guidance or rules affecting a specific area. With regard to what fairness requires, this will often be fact-sensitive, but as a general rule, the closer a decision comes to being judicial in nature, the higher the level of procedural fairness required.

The limits of this remedy must be acknowledged. Prisoners will often want a review of a decision which they think is unfair or simply do not agree with, but where judicial review is of little help. Equally, a decision quashed for procedural reasons may well be re-made, following the appropriate procedure but with the same conclusion. Further, the courts have often shown a willingness to defer to the expertise of prison governors or parole boards in areas such as the management of risk within and outside of prisons, unless there is a clear breach of a public law policy, or blatant unfairness.

However, public law litigation in the prison law field has led to improvements in fairness and procedural safeguards in general, particularly in areas such as disciplinary and parole board hearings. Additionally, the Human Rights Act (HRA) 1998 has allowed for further areas of challenge to decisions made in the prison law context, since acts and omissions which interfere with any protected rights must be demonstrably proportionate, even where limits on those rights are necessarily imposed as a consequence of imprisonment. See for example the case of *R v Secretary of State For The Home Department, ex parte Daly*,[7] where the importance of the common law and the Article 8 right to legal privilege required the court to go further than the traditional irrationality grounds and consider whether a search policy which infringed those rights was proportionate. This case has been influential beyond the prison law field.

Finally, in terms of judicial review procedure, prison cases have been largely treated as civil matters not criminal causes or matters. For a discussion on how this affects rights of appeal, see above at 2-43.

(3) Alternative Remedies

Remedies other than judicial review are available in a prison law context; the main ones are civil claims for assault and battery, claims for negligence, and claims misfeasance in public office. Thought should be given to what is the most suitable remedy, as courts will not be willing to entertain actions in negligence, for instance, if they are being used to circumvent the time limit imposed for judicial review. **8-3**

Since judicial review is intended to be a remedy of last resort, there are also internal appeal and complaints procedures which will often be appropriate to pursue before bringing a claim. Complaints are governed by section 11 of the Prison Rules 1999 (SI 1999/728), and PSI 02/2012. Complaints can also be made to the Prison and Probation Ombudsman (PPO), which may well be best suited to dealing with complaints on narrow issues where a point of policy is not being challenged. In practice, the strict judicial review time limit may mean pursuing a claim in tandem with a complaints procedure. An impending legal claim may well focus the minds of those adjudicating on an internal complaint or appeal such that the need for review falls away.

---

[7] *R v Secretary of State For The Home Department, ex parte Daly* [2001] 1 WLR 2099.

(4) Identifying the Defendant

8-4   Identifying the defendant will in most cases be straightforward. Since judicial review in a prison context usually involves challenging a decision made about an individual, the maker or makers of that decision, whether it is the parole board or prison governor, will be the defendant. If a refusal to amend a policy affecting all prisoners is the impugned decision, then the relevant Secretary of State would be the appropriate defendant.

Complications arise in the case of private prisons and in relation to services provided by outside suppliers. For instance, should an action, omission or policy relating to healthcare be challenged, it will be necessary to determine who is responsible for providing health care to the particular prison in question. At the time of writing, this will usually be the local NHS Primary Care Trust, although note the Secretary of State can also be responsible. However, this may change in respect of private prisons or where healthcare provision is contracted out to private companies.

(5) Sources of Law

8-5   Prison law is a multifaceted area that changes relatively frequently, with a further layer of complication being added by the guidance issued on various topics from differing sources, which affects the way in which prison life and questions of release and recall are administered.

Prison law is derived mainly from the following sources:

   i.   the Prison Act 1952 (PA 1952);
   ii.   the Prison Rules (PR) 1999 (made by the Secretary of State using powers conferred by section 47 of the PA 1952);
   iii. Prison Service Orders (PSOs);
   iv.   Prison Service Instructions (PSIs), Probation Instructions (PIs) and Agency Instructions (AIs); and
   v.   the HRA 1998.

PSOs are long-term mandatory instructions to prison staff on particular topics, which were issued up until August 2009. They were intended to last for an indefinite period, until replaced by new instructions on that topic. Up until that time PSIs were issued as temporary documents containing mandatory actions with a set expiration date, usually 12 months. Many PSOs and PSIs issued before August 2009 are still in force.

After August 2009 a new regime was put in place whereby PSOs would no longer be used and Probation Instructions (PIs) and Agency Instructions (AIs) came into use alongside PSIs. PSIs, PIs and AIs now all convey mandatory instructions to prison staff, probation staff and National Offender Management Service staff, respectively. These instructions all have a set expiry, which can be up to four years from the date of issue, but they can also be i) reissued to extend their validity, or ii) cancelled or iii) amended before the expiry date if required. Regardless of expiry dates, however, they remain in force until expressly cancelled.

Old PSOs still in force can be wide-ranging and cover broad topics like segregation (PSO 1700) and maintaining order in prisons (PSO 1810), or smaller details such as production of prisoners at the request of police (PSO 1801) or video links from court (PSO 1030). It is not always clear which PSOs and PSIs are in force just by searching for a particular topic. Helpfully, new PSIs set out which old PSOs/PSIs they replace or supersede, and the Ministry of Justice website has a list of PSOs still in force (www. justice.gov.uk/offenders/psos) and PSIs in force (www.justice.gov.uk/offenders/psis).

In addition, practitioners need to be aware of the Parole Board Rules 2011 (SI 2011/2947), which came into force in January 2012, revoking the Parole Board Rules 2004 and Parole Board (Amendment) Rules 2009 (SI 2009/408). These were made by the Secretary of State in exercise of powers conferred by section 32(5) of the Criminal Justice Act 1991 and govern the review process employed by the Parole Board.

The Parole Board issues its own guidance, which can be found at www.justice.gov.uk/about/parole-board. Additionally, the Secretary of State is empowered to issue guidance to the Parole Board, which can be found at www.justice.gov.uk/offenders/parole-board/sos-directions, although not all of it is currently in force.

Finally, with regard to case law, this will of course always be important in a judicial review context. However, practitioners will find that new decisions made by the courts, even just the High Court, often become quickly incorporated into new PSIs or into directions issued by the Parole Board to its members, and directions issued by the Secretary of State. PSIs sometimes even refer to case law that has influenced a particular area of policy-making, for example, as to how disciplinary matters should be heard.

B. Prison Life

(1) The System of Categorisation

This section will first explain the system of categorisation and then consider the avenues for judicial review. The policy on categorisation is dealt with in detail in i) PSI 39/2011 for female prisoners, ii) PSI 40/2011 for adult male prisoners, and iii) PSI 41/2011 for young adult male prisoners. The general approach and policy is largely the same for each prisoner group, but with the categories being slightly different.   **8-6**

Male prisoners are categorised as either Category A, B, C or D, with category A being reserved for those who would present the most risk to the public and/or highest risk of escape.[8] Female and young adult male prisoners are categorised into Category A, Restricted Status, Closed Conditions and Open Conditions, Category A again being the highest security.[9]

On reception into prison, all prisoners will be categorised according to the following considerations:

i. risk posed in terms of likelihood of escape;
ii. risk to the public should the prisoner escape; and
iii. any threat posed to the security of the prison, good order and/or the safety of others in the prison.[10]

---

[8] PSI 39/2011.
[9] PSI 39/2011 and 41/2011.
[10] PSI 39/2011, PSI 40/2011, PSI 41/2011. Note, unless otherwise stated, all information in this section relating to general categorisation is derived from these three PSIs. Information relating to Category A is derived from PSIs 05/2013 and 08/2013 unless otherwise stated.

The following principles of security categorisation are the same for all prisoners, and failure to apply these principles would be grounds for review. First, prisoners must be assigned to the lowest category that is consistent with managing the risk they present, and they must meet all the criteria for the category they are assigned.[11] In the relevant PSIs, it is expressly stated that the security category assigned to prisoners must not be adjusted in line with places available within the prison estate. However, the PSIs also state that prisoners may be accommodated in a higher security setting than their categorisation, where there are population pressures or where particular rehabilitation programmes are only available in that security setting, which it is in the interests of the prisoner to complete.

An example of a judicial review challenge regarding categorisation and pressure on resources is *R (Spicer) v Secretary of State for Justice*.[12] A decision to keep a prisoner in closed conditions where previously he was moved to open conditions was judicially reviewed on grounds of irrationality, inconsistency and procedural unfairness. The court held that the decision was not irrational, because it allowed him to participate in a programme for serious violent offenders. This was held to be the case even where it entailed a delay until a space became available on the course. However, the application was upheld in part, because the applicant had not had the opportunity to comment on a report which formed the basis for the decision and as such the decision was self-evidently unfair[13].

The PSIs state that the process for deciding categorisation must be fair, consistent, objective and open. An example of a judicial review on this point is *R (Lowe) v Governor of Liverpool Prison*.[14] In that case a prisoner successfully obtained an order to quash a decision to recategorise him as a Category B prisoner on grounds of irrationality in not following the Secretary of State's policy and considering erroneous material or taking into account material that should not have been considered. The court stated that categorisation involves the application of the principles of consistency and legitimate expectation, particularly the expectation that policy contained in policy documents such as PSOs will be applied and found that the decision to recategorise had been 'in some parts perverse and irrational'.[15] The court was particularly critical of the 'Kafkaesque' attitude displayed by the governor in this case who interpreted the claimant's several successful legal challenges to his categorisation, leading to it being reduced, as 'evincing a will to make a determined escape attempt'.[16]

Prisoners must be provided with a copy of the relevant form (which is annexed to the respective PSIs), setting out the reasons for the categorisation, if it is requested. There are some exceptions to this where the reasons are not disclosable because, for instance, matters of national security are involved.

All convicted and sentenced prisoners, including indeterminate sentenced prisoners (aside from those likely to be assigned to category A) must be assigned a categorisation within four working days of all the core documents being received by prison staff. These will include matters such as i) a record of any previous convictions, ii) details

---

[11] Criteria for security categorisation are set out in the respective PSIs relating to males, females and young adult males, per above.

[12] *R (Spicer) v Secretary of State for Justice* [2009] EWHC 2142 (Admin).

[13] Applying *R (Banfield) v Secretary of State of Justice* [2007] EWHC 2605.

[14] *R (Lowe) v Governor of Liverpool Prison* [2008] EWHC 2167 (Admin).

[15] ibid, [40].

[16] ibid, [51].

Florence Iveson

of the current conviction, and iii) custody record to date. Any prisoner sentenced to a determinate sentence of less than 12 months must be considered for allocation to open conditions/category D, unless they are convicted under terrorism legislation.

With regard to Category A prisoners, there are currently two PSIs in place which set out the relevant policy—PSI 05/2013 and PSI 08/2013. These state that governors must have in place a system for identifying prisoners who might meet Category A or Restricted Status criteria on their first reception into prison, whether pre- or post-conviction. Prisoners will meet this criterion if convicted of or charged with a serious, violent or sexual offence such as murder, rape, armed robbery or drug importation and the facts of such offences demonstrate a high level of dangerousness, for example where the victim of a violent offence is unknown, or the violence is frenzied or sadistic.

Where any such prisoner is identified locally, this should be reported immediately to the Category A Team over the telephone and the relevant documents sent to them. The Category A Team will then inform the prison whether the prisoner should be placed in Category A within three days, and if they are considered to be Category A, they should be moved to a High Security Prison within three days.

(i) Category A Internal Reviews

Those prisoners allocated to Category A, who are on remand, are entitled to an internal review every 12 months, or sooner if new information indicating against Category A becomes available. There will be a further review immediately following conviction and sentence, and a first formal review after three months. If the individual remains in Category A, they will then be reviewed again after two years, following which their status will be reviewed annually. **8-7**

Annual reviews, including the review held after two years, involve consideration by the local advisory panel (LAP), which will then submit a recommendation to the Category A Review Team (CART). If the recommendation is that the prisoner remains Category A, and CART agrees, the matter ends there. If there is a recommendation for a downgrade in status from Category A, the issue will be considered by the Director or Deputy Director of Custody, High Security (DHS, DDHS) or a suitably qualified individual to whom authority has been delegated. The DHS may grant an oral hearing to determine the issue of categorisation, but at present these are relatively rare.

(ii) Challenges to Internal Reviews

The question of whether fairness requires an oral hearing has been the most common ground of review in this area recently. In the case of *R (McLuckie) v Secretary of State for Justice* some general principles are set out.[17] The Court of Appeal first of all acknowledged the significance of being a Category A prisoner, not only in terms of the very restrictive regime, but also with regard to the practical impossibility of obtaining parole **8-8**

---

[17] *R (McLuckie) v Secretary of State for Justice* [2011] EWCA Civ 522. This case also appears to be known as *R (Mackay) v Secretary of State for Justice* [2011] EWCA Civ 522.

while being considered Category A.[18] Thus, the court held the prisoner's liberty is at stake and a high level of procedural fairness is required.

Secondly, the court acknowledged that there will be situations where a prisoner who denies his own guilt will not be allowed to participate in certain rehabilitative courses as a consequence, and this will make it very difficult for him to be recategorised. It was held that this impasse may lead to a possibility of injustice, but that this was unavoidable in the context of the need to protect the public from risk and the fact that a great many prisoners will maintain a denial of guilt. The court did not find that an oral hearing would necessarily be needed to address an apparent impasse of this nature.

The court went on to state that there was a common law duty of procedural fairness that would sometimes require CART to hold an oral hearing. In a review of a decision by CART not to hold an oral hearing, the test is whether the decision not to hold the hearing was wrong, since it is a matter for the court as to what fairness requires. The test is not based on the *Wednesbury* principles.

Importantly, the court held that what fairness requires will be dependent on the facts of each case, and that there was no requirement for 'exceptional circumstances', although the court expressed the view that the need for an oral hearing would be rare. On the facts of the case, the court did not find that a disagreement between LAP and CART on suitability for recategorisation meant that there should have been an oral hearing.

8-9   In *R (Shaffi) v Secretary of State for Justice*[19] the High Court came to a different conclusion when there was a disagreement between LAP and a psychologist, on one hand, who were advocating recategorisation, and the DDHS on the other hand. The court distinguished the cases on the basis that in *McLuckie* there was a tentative suggestion from LAP that the prisoner 'may' benefit from recategorisation rather than, as in this case, a wholesale disagreement.

The court in *Shaffi* referred to *R (Smith and West) v Parole Board*,[20] which concerned oral hearings before the Parole Board on the question of release on licence. From that case the court derived the principle that an oral hearing may be required when there is a dispute of fact.

Further, there was an impasse in *Shaffi* because the Director of High Security (DHS) required evidence that the claimant was sufficiently rehabilitated; meanwhile the prisoner was prepared to undertake any rehabilitative course available to him, but none were ever made available. There was no way to move forward and the court suggested that an oral hearing was necessary to i) help the DHS resolve the discrepancy between the experts, ii) test the reliability of the evidence given by the claimant himself, and iii) also to help the claimant understand better how he might demonstrate sufficient change if he was unsuccessful on that occasion.

8-10   A dispute between professionals will not always give rise to the need for an oral hearing, as was the case in *R (Downs) v Secretary of State for Justice*.[21] In *Downs* there was conflicting evidence between an independent psychologist and a prison psychologist as to whether the claimant needed to attend a sexual offender treatment programme. The

---

[18] This was recognised in the earlier case of *R v Secretary of State for the Home Department, ex parte Duggan* [1994] 3 All ER 277 [280] and [288].

[19] *R (Shaffi) v Secretary of State for Justice* [2011] EWHC 3113 (Admin).

[20] *R (Smith and West) v Parole Board* [2005] UKHL 1, [2005] 1 WLR 350.

[21] *R (Downs) v Secretary of State for Justice* [2011] EWCA Civ 1422 (Admin).

decision not to hold an oral hearing, based in part on the fact that CART had copies of both reports before them and did not believe the dispute could be resolved, was upheld at first instance and by the Court of Appeal.

The fact that a prisoner disagrees with an expert's report does not necessarily give rise to the need for an oral hearing, either. In *R (Willoughby) v Category A Review Team*,[22] the claimant's rejection of the expert's report was not enough for the interests of fairness to require an oral hearing in the absence of other factors. The court stated that the starting point should be that an oral hearing is not normally required.

The court in *Willoughby* did state obiter that there might come a time in respect of the claimant (and presumably other prisoners) when the sheer length of detention would be a compelling reason to hold an oral hearing and that the prisoner might well find a decision given after an oral hearing easier to accept.[23] In the instant case, the claimant having served 14 years where the tariff had been seven, was not seen as sufficient to merit an oral hearing for that reason alone.

In *R (Bourke) v Secretary of State for Justice*[24] the claimant was also unsuccessful in arguing that he should have been given an oral hearing, and one of the factors taken into account was his pre-tariff status. It was held that although not a point of principle, where an individual has reached or passed their tariff they would in most cases be granted an oral hearing. Fairness has to be approached in a different way where an individual was post-tariff and as a result of his or her security status, had no chance of release on parole. This does not seem to accord with the approach in *Willoughby*, where the claimant was several years past his tariff date and was still not granted an oral hearing. *Bourke* was applied in *R (Hussain) v Secretary of State for Justice*[25] as authority for the proposition that fairness did not require a prisoner to have an oral hearing where his or her denial of guilt meant they were unable to show a reduction of risk.

In the cases of *R (Roberts) v Secretary of State for Justice*[26] and *R (Cain) v Secretary of State for Justice*[27] the continued reluctance of the courts to expand the criteria for holding an oral hearing was evident, despite the relative frequency with which the issue is litigated. Both decisions exclude themselves from the class of rare cases referred to in *McLuckie* where an oral hearing is needed, indicating perhaps the height of the bar set by *McLuckie* (despite it having been expressly stated that the test is not one of exceptionality).

In *Roberts* the court held that its role was to consider in detail the circumstances in which the decision was made not to hold an oral hearing in order to assess whether the decision-making could have been improved by an oral hearing.

The case of *Cain* involved a prisoner who had been imprisoned for over 24 years and was post-tariff. This alone was not considered to be a sufficient reason to justify an oral hearing, and neither was an apparent disagreement between the Director of High Security and LAP, with LAP's approach considered to lack clarity on future risk. Using

8-11

---

[22] *R (Willoughby) v Category A Review Team* [2011] EWHC 3483 (Admin).
[23] This view was also expressed by Judge LJ in *R (Williams) v Home Secretary* [2002] 1 WLR 264 and Cranston J in *R (H) v Secretary of State for Justice* [2008] EWHC 2590 (Admin).
[24] *R (Bourke) v Secretary of State for Justice* [2012] EWHC 4041 (Admin).
[25] *R (Hussain) v Secretary of State for Justice* [2013] EWHC 1452 (Admin).
[26] *R (Roberts) v Secretary of State for Justice* [2013] EWHC 697 (Admin).
[27] *R (Cain) v Secretary of State for Justice* [2013] EWHC 900 (Admin).

the approach of *Roberts*, it could be said that holding an oral hearing was likely to have improved decision-making if only to clarify where LAP stood on risk. This was not the finding of the court.[28]

Where a court finds that fairness required that there should have been an oral hearing, a decision not to reclassify from Category A to a lower category may be quashed. An example is *R (H) v Secretary of State for Justice*.[29]

(2) Prisoners' Correspondence and Communications

8-12   The policy regarding prisoner correspondence is set out in PSI 49/2011, set to expire in September 2015, and the relevant PRs are 34 to 39. Prisoners are entitled to send one statutory letter a week under PR 35, the postage for which is paid for by the state. Prisoners are also allowed to send additional letters, paid for out of their own money, as a privilege, subject to restrictions that may be imposed by governors. Statutory letters may not be restricted or withdrawn as a punishment, but privilege letters may be. Prisoners also have access to telephones, but again governors may impose limitations to this, in accordance with the category of the inmate and regime of the particular prison.

Prison governors are entitled to monitor communications within the prison, even legally privileged letters sent or received by prisoners. Rule 39 limits the circumstances in which this can be done, reflecting the approach of the courts to legally privileged communications in *Campbell v United Kingdom* and *R v Secretary of State for the Home Department, ex parte Leech*.[30]

In *Campbell*, originally a Scottish case, the ECtHR found that a blanket policy allowing a governor to read all letters sent or received by prisoners violated prisoners' Article 8 rights. This was followed in *Ex p Leech*, a case regarding a similar English rule which allowed correspondence to be censored. In that case the importance of unimpeded access to the courts for every citizen was emphasised, including access to legal advice. In essence, the rule now provides that legally privileged letters may only be opened if the governor has reasonable cause to believe it contains illicit material, and may be opened, read and stopped if the governor believes its contents represents a danger to prison staff or to others. Prisoners are also entitled to be present when legally privileged letters are opened.

The approach to legally privileged letters already in the prisoner's possession was litigated in the well-known case of *Ex p Daly* (see above at 8-2). In that case a policy of excluding prisoners from their cells during routine searches by staff, to prevent intimidation or disruption, was successfully challenged on the basis that any inspection of legally privileged material should take place in front of the prisoner affected. In *Ex p Daly* the House of Lords advocated a proportionality approach. Legal privilege was described as

---

[28] The judgment in this case contains a very useful survey of the case law in relation to this area.

[29] *H* (n 21).

[30] *Campbell v United Kingdom* (1992) 15 EHRR 137 and *R v Secretary of State for the Home Department, Ex p Leech* [1994] QB 19. Note also the case of *R v Secretary of State for the Home Department, ex parte Simms* [2000] 2 AC 115 in which the House of Lords ruled that a policy preventing journalists from publishing material obtained from visiting convicted murderers seeking to prove their innocence was *ultra vires*. The policy was found to interfere disproportionately with freedom of expression, particularly important in the context of prisoners trying to prove their innocence.

a basic common law right and Article 8 right, and any interference with it therefore had to be justified. A blanket policy whereby all prisoners were excluded from their calls regardless of whether they had ever intimidated staff or disrupted searches was found to be *ultra vires*.

The issue of interference with correspondence was raised again in the more recent case of *R (Thakrar) v The Secretary of State for Justice*.[31] In that case the claimant challenged the policy on legally privileged letters and on telephone calls, as set out in PSI 49/2011. The claimant felt his letters were being deliberately targeted and intercepted by prison staff, and asserted that the policy did not prevent malicious interception of mail or provide a system for dealing with excessive interference with letters. There were further challenges to the policy on legal visits and telephone calls.

The court rejected all of the 14 grounds put forward by the claimant, and held that the policies in place to deal with interference with mail, with telephone calls and regarding legal visits, were systematically adequate. The court also held that the policy was at times necessarily vague to avoid being inflexible, but that the policy should be read as a whole and in the context of the Prison Rules. The case provides a useful review of the law in this area, which the court appeared to view as relatively settled. This is an example of where judicial review as a remedy is unlikely to be helpful to the claimant's particular concerns, since the complaint is essentially one against prison staff interfering with an individual's post.

(i) Communication with the Media

Access to the media for prisoners is relatively limited and in most cases will be restricted to telephone calls. The House of Lords considered visits by the media to serving prisoners in *R v Secretary of State for the Home Department, ex parte Simms*.[32] In that case the House of Lords emphasised the crucial importance of Article 10 (freedom of expression) where a prisoner is attempting to prove their own innocence. The court held that a blanket policy introduced by the Home Secretary requiring all journalists visiting serving prisoners to sign an undertaking not to publish any of the material obtained during the visit was *ultra vires*. Prior to the policy a number of miscarriages of justice had been uncovered following interviews between journalists and prisoners, and the policy was effectively stifling this possibility.

In the subsequent case of *R (Hirst) v Secretary of State for the Home Department*,[33] the policy that permission to contact the media by telephone would only be granted in wholly exceptional circumstances (which in practice meant permission was very unlikely to be granted) was found to be insufficiently flexible. Concerns regarding how to monitor and control what material was published following telephone calls with the media were not held to justify the inflexible approach which resulted from the Home Secretary's policy.

Communication with the press is now governed by PSI 37/2010, due to expire on 1 July 2014. This sets out that most prisoners will be able to contact the media through

8-13

---

[31] *R (Thakrar) v The Secretary of State for Justice* [2012] EWHC 3538 (Admin).
[32] *R v Secretary of State for the Home Department, ex parte Simms* [2000] 2 AC 115.
[33] *R (Hirst) v Secretary of State for the Home Department* [2002] EWHC 602 (Admin).

letters only, and do not need to seek permission for this, although unsurprisingly the letters are subject to certain restrictions with regards to their content. The policy allows for contact with the media through telephone, although only with permission from the governor and where the reason for the telephone call meets certain criteria. Prisoners may also receive visits from members of the media if they have written to the governor for permission and the governor accepts there is a need for a face-to-face interview because the prisoner claims there has been i) a miscarriage of justice or ii) they seek to raise another issue of strong public interest with the journalist. Therefore, relatively tight restrictions remain.

However, the BBC were successful in their application not only to obtain but also to film and broadcast a face-to-face interview with Babar Ahmad in the case of *R (BBC) v Secretary of State for Justice*.[34] Mr Ahmad, a British citizen, was detained pending extradition to the United States in relation to alleged terrorism offences, and had been detained since 2004. The court in that case considered whether the interview should have been allowed under the existing policy set out in PSI 37/2010 on the basis of Article 10, rather than whether the policy itself was lawful.

It was held that although the policy only envisaged one-to-one meetings with journalists in exceptional circumstances, this was one such exceptional case, since the claimant had been detained for seven years without facing any criminal charge in the UK jurisdiction. The reasoning that a televised interview could cause offence to viewers who had been victims of terrorism, was held to be disproportionate since mere offence was not held to be a sufficient basis on which to interfere with Article 10. The court also rejected the contention that such an interview would undermine public faith in the criminal justice system. The case provides a useful survey of the law in this area, but is unlikely to expand the circumstances in which a face-to-face media interview will be allowed.

(3) The Right to Vote

8-14 The struggle to win the right to vote for prisoners has received a huge amount of press coverage but is not currently a particularly fertile ground for judicial review following the decision of the Supreme Court in *R (Chester) v Secretary of State for Justice*.[35] The background to that decision is worth some consideration.

At present all convicted prisoners are unable to vote. Section 3 of the Representation of the People Act 1983 disenfranchises convicts from voting in local government, Scottish Parliament and UK Parliament elections, and the European Parliamentary Elections Act 2002 disenfranchised them from European Parliament Elections.

The compatibility of the blanket disenfranchisement of all convicted prisoners from voting in parliamentary elections with human rights was considered by the Grand Chamber of the ECtHR in the case of *Hirst v United Kingdom*.[36] The challenge, brought by an individual serving a discretionary life sentence for manslaughter, complained that

---

[34] *R (BBC) v Secretary of State for Justice* [2012] EWHC 13 (Admin).
[35] *R (Chester) v Secretary of State for Justice* [2013] UKSC 63.
[36] *Hirst v United Kingdom* [2006] 42 EHRR 41.

Florence Iveson

UK law infringed the right to vote enshrined in Protocol 1, Article 3 of the European Convention of Human Rights (ECHR). In response, it was argued that the right was not an absolute one and determination of this right fell within a wide margin of appreciation that should be accorded to Member States.

The court ruled that although States held a wide margin of appreciation in this sphere, the enshrined right to vote was well established and the fact of imprisonment does not in itself mean that all Convention rights are forfeited. It held that the United Kingdom pursued a legitimate aim in the sanctioning of crime and encouraging civic responsibility, but that a blanket ban on voting amongst all prisoners was not a proportionate means of pursuing that aim.

Subsequently and in light of this decision, a declaration of incompatibility under section 4(5) of HRA 1998 was made by the Registration Appeal Court of Scotland after the repeated refusal to add a prisoner to the electoral register reached the court in *Scott v Smith*.[37] The court considered it impossible to read down the legislation so as to remove in the incompatibility with European law.

Since Parliament took no action to execute the court's judgment in *Hirst*, a pilot judgment was issued in *Greens v UK*[38] giving the United Kingdom six months to act on it. The ECtHR referred in that case to a large number of pending cases, which it was found appropriate to suspend until the time for the United Kingdom to act on the judgment had expired.

Following a number of domestic applications for judicial review, the issue was finally considered by the Supreme Court in *R (Chester) v Secretary of State for Justice*.[39] In that case the court found there was no point in making a declaration of incompatibility as one had already been made in *Smith v Scott*. The Supreme Court agreed with the Scottish Court that section 3 of the Representation of the People Act 1983 could not be read down to comply with EU law, and found the same with regard to section 8 of the European Parliamentary Elections Act 2002. The court also held that EU law did not incorporate any express right to vote on which convicted prisoners could rely. The court did not consider this to be a case where a reference to the ECtHR could usefully be made.

Thus the United Kingdom is in something of a stalemate with the ECtHR and unless Parliament passes a bill to incorporate some form of proportionality in the ban on prisoners voting, convicted prisoners' rights to vote will remain unchanged and legal challenges fruitless. This is borne out by the outcome of the recent case of *Teshome v Lord President of the Council*.[40]

(4) The Right to Family Life

It is a well-established principle that a prisoner's Convention rights, including the right to a private and family life under Article 8, remain intact despite imprisonment.[41]   8-15

---

[37] *Smith v Scott* [2007] CSIH 9.
[38] *Greens v United Kingdom* [2011] 53 EHRR 21.
[39] (n 35).
[40] *Teshome v Lord President of the Council* [2014] EWHC 1468 (Admin).
[41] See *Dickson v United Kingdom* [2008] 46 EHRR 41 below.

The right to a private and family life has been invoked in prison judicial review cases in a number of different contexts—from prison conditions, to parole decisions, to reporting restrictions. This section deals with the interaction between prison life and family relationships in prison.

The maintenance of family relationships is referred to in PR 4:

> (1) Special attention shall be paid to the maintenance of such relationships between a prisoner and his family as are desirable in the best interests of both.
>
> (2) A prisoner shall be encouraged and assisted to establish and maintain such relations with persons and agencies outside prison as may, in the opinion of the governor, best promote the interests of his family and his own social rehabilitation.

Imprisonment and the attendant separation from family necessarily involves interference with Article 8 rights. Subsequent decisions which affect the maintenance of family relationships will often also engage Article 8. These must be justified under Article 8(2) and shown to be proportionate. Usually the grounds of public safety and the prevention of disorder and crime will be relied upon.

8-16   The Court of Appeal in 2001 considered the position of two mothers serving prison sentences whose children were to be removed from them at 18 months, in accordance with prison service policy, in *R (P) v Secretary of State for the Home Department*.[42] The 18 month cut-off date was challenged as being insufficiently flexible. Lord Phillips MR said of the ECtHR jurisprudence:

> It is possible to draw some general conclusions from these authorities: (i) the right to respect for family life is not a right which the prisoner necessarily loses by reason of his or her incarceration; (ii), on the other hand, when a court considers whether the state's reasons for interfering with that right are relevant and sufficient, it is entitled to take into account (a) the reasonable requirements of prison organisation and security and (b) the desirability of maintaining a uniform regime in prison which avoids any appearance of arbitrariness or discrimination; (iii) whatever the justification for a general rule, Convention law requires the court to consider the application of that rule to the particular case, and to determine whether in that case the interference is proportionate to the particular legitimate aim being pursued; (iv) the more serious the intervention in any given case … the more compelling must be the justification.[43]

The court also acknowledged the approach required under the HRA 1998 (as set out in *Ex P Daly*) was to consider the proportionality of the decisions against the legitimate aims of the prison service, rather than simple rationality or *Wednesbury* unreasonableness, when Article 8 rights are in engaged. In such cases, it was held by the court that prison policy must be formulated to allow a reasonable degree of flexibility to enable a proportionate application. In the instant case one appellant succeeded where there was no suitable alternative accommodation for the child and the mother's prison sentence was due to end shortly, and one appellant failed where she had a considerable sentence left to serve and the child would be 5 by the time she was first eligible for parole.

The court indicated that cases of this nature were likely to be aimed at the application of rather than the legality of prison service policy and would only succeed where

---

[42] *R (P) v Secretary of State for the Home Department* [2001] EWCA Civ 1151.
[43] ibid, [78].

Florence Iveson

a significant threat to the best interests of a child could be demonstrated. As such the court indicated they had been greatly assisted by having a family judge on the panel (Baroness Hale) and indeed practitioners involved in these types of cases will be assisted by an understanding of family law in general.

The principles in *P* were applied in *R (CD) v Secretary of State for the Home Department*.[44] In that case, a mother was removed from a mother and baby unit, separating her from her still breastfeeding baby, because she had been behaving erratically. The decision was quashed and remitted back to be made again applying the correct principles as no proper consideration had been given to the best interests of the child, there had been no assessment of risk and no thought given of the proportionality of the decision.   **8-17**

In the case of *R (X) v Secretary of State for the Home Department*[45] the High Court found that Article 8 was engaged when a female prisoner was refused temporary release on license to visit her children, after she was recategorised to a semi-open prison. Bean LJ considered however that the interference with Article 8 was much lower in this case than it had been in *P* or *CD* and that the decision of the governor, based on the safety of the applicant, of other prisoners and staff and of members of the public, was not disproportionate. A relevant factor in this case was that bonds with the applicant's children could have been maintained through them visiting her in prison but she had decided she did not want them to do that as she did not wish for them to know she was incarcerated.

More recently in *R (MP) v Secretary of State for Justice*[46] the High Court considered the application of a prison service policy on childcare resettlement leave (CRL). The policy, contained at the time in PSO 6300, was interpreted as putting a blanket limit on the availability of CRL to prisoners two years away from their release dates. In determining the application of Article 8, the court considered the case of *P* but was also referred to the extradition cases *Norris v Government of United States of America*[47] and *R (HH) v Westminster City Magistrates Court*,[48] as well as the immigration case *ZH (Tanzania) v Secretary of State for the Home Department*.[49] It is clear therefore that an understanding of the development of Article 8 rights across different areas of law, not just family law, is of importance in a prison law context.   **8-18**

The Court in *MP* found that those taking decisions on CRL on behalf of the Secretary of State had misinterpreted PSO 6300 and the CRL policy by limiting its applicability to those two years from the end of their sentences when it could in principle be available at any time during a prison sentence when other eligibility criteria were met. The court was critical of a review of the policy by the Home Secretary which had been carried out in 2009/2010 and found that Article 8 should have been taken into account when the policy was reviewed as well as when the decision was made on CRL

---

[44] *R (CD) v Secretary of State for the Home Department* [2004] EWHC 111 (Admin).
[45] *R (X) v Secretary of State for the Home Department* [2005] EWHC 1616 (Admin).
[46] *R (MP) v Secretary of State for Justice* [2012] EWHC 214 (Admin).
[47] *Norris v Government of United States of America* [2010] 2 AC 487.
[48] *R (HH) v Westminster City Magistrates Court* [2011] EWHC 1145 (Admin), subsequently appealed to the Supreme Court in *R (HH) v Westminster City Magistrates Court* [2012] UKSC 25.
[49] *ZH (Tanzania)v Secretary of State for the Home Department* [2011] 2 AC 166. Mentioned below at 11-5.

in the case of the applicants in the instant case. Lang J made the following ruling at paragraph 188:

> In my judgment, the Secretary of State acted unlawfully when reviewing and applying his policy on CRL because he:
>
> a) misinterpreted PSO 6300, and the policy on the grant of CRL, by taking the view that CRL was only ever intended to be available to prisoners who were in the final stages of their custodial term, and thus close to release;
> b) failed to have regard to Art. 8 ECHR and Article 3(1) UNCRC;
> c) acted in a way which was incompatible with Art. 8 ECHR, contrary to s.6(1) HRA 1998;
> d) fettered his discretion by applying a blanket policy without considering the individual circumstances of prisoners.

8-19   As to policies affecting potential parents, the Court of Appeal in *Dickson v Premier Prison Service Ltd*[50] refused an appeal against the Secretary of State's decision not to grant the applicants access to facilities for artificial insemination. The applicants met via a prison pen pal programme and married while both were still in prison. After Mrs Dickson's release, they applied to have access to artificial insemination facilities in light of the fact that by the time Mr Dickson was released, Mrs Dickson would most likely be too old to conceive.

The decision was challenged on the basis that not allowing the Dicksons access to these facilities effectively extinguished a fundamental right (Article 8) as in all likelihood it prevented them from having children. This argument was dismissed by the court which found that the exercise of the Secretary of State's discretion was proportionate in all the circumstances. Relevant factors were the long-term absence of one of the parents if a child was successfully conceived, the undermining of public confidence in the prison system should access be granted and the fact that losing the opportunity to have children was an inevitable consequence of imprisonment.

The matter was appealed to the ECtHR[51] which found that Article 8 was engaged, ruling that there could be positive obligations attendant to the State's duty to protect the right to private and family life which could extend even to the relationship between two individuals. It was found that the inability to have children was not an inevitable consequence of imprisonment, precisely because of the availability of artificial insemination. The court considered that although punishment was part of the aims of imprisonment, rehabilitative aims were also very important and a prisoner's rights should not be automatically forfeited based on what might offend public opinion. The policy applied in the instant cases, requiring the applicant to show exceptional circumstances, placed an inordinately high burden on the applicant and did not allow for an assessment of whether its application was proportionate. A breach of Article 8 was found.

8-20   With regards to relationships between prisoners, the two pairs of applicants in *R (Bright) v Secretary of State for Justice*[52] were in homosexual relationships and sought to challenge the decision to separate them, and specifically the lack of policy governing how homosexual relationships should be treated within the prison estate.

---

[50] *Dickson v Premier Prison Service Ltd* [2004] EWCA Civ 1477.
[51] *Dickson v United Kingdom* [2008] 46 EHRR 41; this case is authority for the broader proposition that a prisoner's Convention Rights remain intact despite incarceration.
[52] *R (Bright) v Secretary of State for Justice* [2013] EWHC 3514 (Admin).

The defendant conceded that it was arguable a restriction on contact between part-ners in this context that could amount to an interference with Article 8. It was found by the Court however that the reasons for the separation were justifiable in each case and were implicitly therefore proportionate (for instance in the case of one applicant, he was on a particular wing in order to undertake a particular programme recommended for him). It was argued more generally that in the absence of a clearly defined policy, an unlawful risk of inconsistent decision making arose and Article 8 was breached. These submissions failed on the basis that the absence of a clearly defined policy did not, in the Court's view, effect the decisions made in each of the applicants' circumstances. An appeal is currently outstanding in the matter. It seems inevitable this issue will arise again.

(5) Prison Conditions

Claims brought for judicial review on the basis of prison conditions alone have been rel-atively infrequent in the UK. Claims brought to the ECtHR on the basis of Article 3 have been less rare; however, not many of these have been cases brought by UK prisoners.   **8-21**

A notable case involving a UK citizen is that of *Keenan v United Kingdom*[53] which was brought by the mother of a young man who had committed suicide after being given 28 extra days on top of his sentence for a disciplinary offence, including time in segregation, shortly before his release. Mr Keenan suffered from serious mental health problems and it was found that, taking into account his particular vulnerability, the imposition of a further sentence may have affected his mental and physical wellbeing so adversely that it amounted to inhuman and degrading treatment in breach of Article 3 of ECHR.[54]

In the subsequent case of *McGlinchey v United Kingdom*[55] the ECtHR found that the medical treatment given to a prisoner of HMP Newhall in Wakefield had been so inad-equate, her Article 3 rights had been breached. The claim was brought by the family of a woman who had died while withdrawing from heroin. The Court was critical of the prison for having no doctor available over the weekend leading up to her death, other than a locum, as well as having broken weighing scales which prevented medical staff from realising that the woman had lost a dangerous amount of weight over a few days. The severity of the woman's suffering was such as to bring her treatment into the scope of Article 3.

In *P v United Kingdom*[56] the ECtHR considered the case of a young man, detained in Feltham Young Offender's Institute, who suffered from mental health difficulties and engaged in such extreme self-harm that he became at risk of urethral failure, sepsis and ultimately death. The applicant claimed that his treatment in custody, including failure to provide him with adequate medical care for his condition, breached Article 3 and the

---

[53] *Keenan v United Kingdom* [2001] 33 EHRR 38.
[54] The 28 days was imposed as a punishment by the governor for a disciplinary offence. The matter would now have been referred to an independent adjudicator, which might have provided better safeguards against an incident like this.
[55] *McGlinchey v United Kingdom* [2003] 37 EHRR 41.
[56] *P v United Kingdom* [2014] 58 EHRR SE9.

failure to investigate his treatment in prison breached Article 2. The court found that the severity of the applicant's suffering was sufficiently grave as to engage Article 3 but held that his failure to exhaust domestic remedies meant his claim could not succeed. The Article 2 claim was said to be manifestly ill-founded.

8-22   The case of *Grant and Gleaves v Ministry of Justice*,[57] heard by the High Court, was founded on much less extreme circumstances. In that case, Hickinbottom J dismissed the claim brought by two prisoners who argued that the sanitary arrangements in HMP Albany infringed their Article 3 and Article 8 rights.

The claimants brought their claim on the basis that the lack of toilets in their cells was 'degrading' and therefore in breach of their Article 3 rights. They further alleged that their right to private life under Article 8 was infringed by these sanitary arrangements, because it interfered with their dignity. They sought to rely on the case of *Kalashnikov v Russia*,[58] in particular the principle they inferred from that case that although the nature of incarceration may inevitably cause some degrading treatment, prison conditions must be 'compatible with respect for human dignity' and ensure that a prisoner's 'health and well-being are adequately secured'.[59]

Hickinbottom J did not accept the suggestion that *Kalashnikov* effectively 'lowered the threshold' of Article 3 and that anything that is not inherent in serving a prison sentence that might cause prisoners distress was in breach of Article 3. Rather, he found that the court would require there to be a high level of suffering before finding that Article 3 had been infringed, giving the following examples:

'… intense suffering …' *Iovchev v Bulgaria* (2006) Application No 41211/98 , at paragraph 133, '… serious suffering …' R (Limbuela) v Secretary of State for the Home Department [2005] UKHL 66 at [8] per Lord Bingham, and '… intense physical or mental suffering' (*Pretty*, at paragraph 52). In other cases, the court has asked whether the treatment 'adversely affected his or her personality in a manner compatible with Article 3' (*Kalashnikov* at paragraph 95).[60]

Hickinbottom J went on to state that there was an objective 'minimum suffering' test, which depended on the circumstances of each case and that there would normally need to be direct evidence of suffering. The judge found that there was no such evidence in the instant case, and that neither was it a case in which suffering could be assumed because of the inherently degrading or inhuman nature of the treatment itself.[61] This case provides a useful survey of the relevant ECtHR case law. Permission to appeal was refused by the Court of Appeal.

8-23   In the rather unusual case of *R (F) v Secretary of State for Justice*[62] the claimant applied for another prisoner, who he believed represented a threat to him, and who had in the past been involved indirectly on a serious attack on the claimant, to be moved out of the prison they were both serving in. The claimant himself did not wish to move, as the prison he was in was near to his family and provided him access to particular rehabilitative resources. The other prisoner had similar reasons for wishing to remain in

---

57 *Grant and Gleaves v Ministry of Justice* [2011] EWHC 3379 (QB).
58 *Kalashnikov v Russia* [2003] 36 EHRR 34.
59 ibid [85].
60 *Grant and Gleaves* (n 57) [48].
61 ibid [78.1]–[78.2]. For example *Filiz Uyen v Turkey* App no 7496/03 (2009).
62 *R (F) v Secretary of State for Justice* [2012] EWHC 2689 (Admin).

the prison. The claim was founded on Article 3 rights and that it was irrational to place both prisoners in the same prison.

The judge found that, on the facts, the prison had taken reasonable steps to protect the claimant, and there was no 'real and immediate risk'. Haddon Cave J further stated that the decision to place them both in the same prison could not be said to be irrational, and added that courts will defer to the expertise of prison officials, unless decisions of this nature could be shown to be *Wednesbury* unreasonable.

In the case of *R (Hall) v University College London Hospitals NHS Foundation Trust*[63] **8-24** the claimant, who had been sentenced to three years in prison for a drug smuggling offence, suffered from a debilitating brain disease for which he used a wheelchair and needed constant care. In tandem to an appeal against sentence, the claimant issued a claim on the basis that the prison regime to which he was subject breached his Article 3 and 8 rights.

The court found that the Article 3 claim, brought on the basis that the prison was not able to accommodate his disability adequately, came nowhere near to establishing that Article 3 was engaged, let alone breached. The court did not make findings as to the level of care provided, but stated that even if medical care fell below what the claimant should have properly received, this would not have necessarily amounted to a breach of Article 3. The Article 8 claim was similarly dismissed and the claimant also failed to win a claim founded on the Equality Act 2010, namely that the prison had failed to make reasonable adjustments. With regard to the latter, it seems such a claim may have succeeded in other circumstances but on the facts of this case, there was inadequate evidence to support the claim.

It was acknowledged by the Court of Appeal in *R (Smith) v Secretary of State for Justice*[64] that Article 8 was potentially engaged by unwanted exposure to second-hand smoke in a prison. The Court held, however, that the issue could not be looked at in a vacuum and that the facts and circumstances of each case had to be considered. In the instant case, the appellant had shared a cell with a smoker for a week, contrary to policy set out in PSI 09/2007. The necessary minimum level of interference had not been reached on the facts, when the operational needs of the prison were also taken in to account. This case contains a useful survey on European case law on the issue of environmental factors in prisons, and smoking in prisons in particular, breaching Article 8.

C. Discipline

(1) General Principles

An exhaustive list of offences against discipline is set out in PR 51. The disciplinary pro- **8-25** cess is set out in detail in PSI 47-2011, due to expire in September 2015, and the relevant PRs are PR 53, 53A, 54, 55, 55A, 59 (YOI 58, 58A, 59, 60, 60A, 63, 65). These must be consulted initially when considering whether a decision is reviewable. The procedure

---

[63] *R (Hall) v University College London Hospitals NHS Foundation Trust* [2013] EWHC 198 (Admin).
[64] *R (Smith) v Secretary of State for Justice* [2014] EWCA 380.

followed at any adjudication will need to be scrutinised in detail to check whether all rules and guidance was followed. If rules or guidance has not been followed, this is likely to be grounds for review and in some cases will make the outcome invalid. Specific examples of where this has occurred are discussed below.

(2) Laying a Charge

8-26   Where a prisoner is charged with a disciplinary offence, the charge 'shall be laid as soon as possible and, save in exceptional circumstances, within 48 hours of the discovery of the offence'.[65] An offence is discovered when an incident is witnessed by a member of staff, or when evidence regarding the incident first comes to the attention of staff.[66]

In the case of *R (Kamara) v Secretary of State for Justice*[67] it was held that when a prisoner wrote and signed a statement to be used in evidence for another prisoner's disciplinary process, admitting to an offence, that was sufficient evidence to bring a charge against him. Thus the offence was 'discovered' when the reporting officer taking part in the other prisoner's disciplinary process became aware of the written statement, and the 48-hour time limit for laying a charge ran from that time. The charge was not laid in that case until the prisoner concerned gave live evidence, effectively incriminating himself. The charge was quashed as being laid out of time, as there were no exceptional circumstances.

A charge is laid when a notice of report is issued to a prisoner which sets out the details of the accused prisoner, the charge, relevant PR and the arrangements for the hearing.[68] The prison will keep a copy of this on file and should have a record of the time and date of issue.

8-27   The rule regarding the time limit for laying a charge was considered by the Court of Appeal in *R (Garland) v Justice Secretary*,[69] where the claimant sought to have an adjudication struck out on the basis that the Secretary of State could not show the charge was laid within 48 hours (as times recorded were approximate).

The court found that the meaning of the rule was that 'the authorities have 48 hours in any event, and longer if there are exceptional circumstances making it impossible to lay the charge within that time'.[70] The court went on to say that Parliament could not have intended to render invalid any charge laid slightly after the 48-hour period, but that where a charge was laid outside the 48 hours it could and should be struck down if it led to the prisoner being prejudiced, or there was no good reason for the delay.

Therefore where a charge is laid outside of the 48 hours, this should be challenged at the first opportunity and an explanation sought. The Court of Appeal in *Garland* indicated that where a reasonable explanation can be given, prisons will be given some

---

[65] Prison Rules (PR), r 53(1).
[66] Prison Service Instructions (PSI) 47-2011, para 1.12.
[67] *R (Kamara) v Secretary of State for Justice* [2009] EWHC 1403 (Admin).
[68] PSI 47-2011 (n 66), para 2.11.
[69] *R (Garland) v Justice Secretary* [2011] EWCA Civ 1335, [2012] 1 WLR 1879.
[70] ibid [13].

Florence Iveson

latitude. For instance, the need to investigate a charge or to take legal advice where this has caused a delay may amount to good reasons—the question is fact-sensitive.[71]

The claimant in *Garland* did not succeed, and it appears that the courts will not apply a strict approach here, so claimants will need to show a delay of more than an hour or so, and demonstrate that either i) there was no good reason for delay, or ii) some genuine prejudice was suffered.

(3) Time Limits

Once a charge has been laid, the prison governor must determine whether or not an outside adjudicator is required. An outside adjudicator is required when the charge is so serious that it may lead to extra days being added on to a prisoner's sentence, or when 'it is necessary and expedient for some other reason for the charge to be inquired into by the adjudicator'.[72]

8-28

As to the meaning of 'necessary and expedient for some other reason', this reflects the recommendation of Collins J in *R (Smith) v Governor of Belmarsh Prison*,[73] that in exceptional circumstances those serving indeterminate sentences (so not at risk of extra days) may still face charges serious enough to warrant an independent adjudication and its attendant Article 6 rights, and that this should be reflected in the Rules.

The Court of Appeal in *Tangney v Governor of HMP Elmley and Secretary of State for the Home Department*[74] anticipated that there may be a rare case that would normally fall to be adjudicated by a governor but which may still attract Article 6 protection. The test or factors that should be taken into consideration to determine this were identified as the criteria set out in *Engel v The Netherlands*,[75] namely:

8-29

i.   the classification of the offence in domestic law;
ii. the nature of the offence; and
iii. the severity and nature of the punishment.

If the governor is satisfied he can hear the charge, it must be inquired into no later than the day after it is laid, save where that would be a Sunday or public holiday.[76] If at any time during or after the inquiry (but before punishment has been imposed) the governor feels the charge is serious enough to merit a punishment of extra days, he must refer the charge to an adjudicator.[77]

If the charge is to be heard by an independent adjudicator, this must be 'inquired into'—in other words, the case must be opened—within 28 days of the charge being

---

[71] ibid [23], which refers to *R v Board of Visitors of Dartmoor Prison, ex parte Smith* [1987] QB 106, [1986] 3 WLR 61.

[72] PR 53A(1).

[73] *R (Smith) v Governor of Belmarsh Prison* [2009] EWHC 109 (Admin), [2010] 1 Prison LR 126.

[74] *Tangney v Governor of HMP Elmley and Secretary of State for the Home Department* [2005] EWCA Civ 1009.

[75] *Engel v The Netherlands* (1979–80) 1 EHRR 647.

[76] PR 53A(1). Note PSI 47-2011, para 2.2 states that: 'At the discretion of the Governor hearings can be opened on Sundays, however, Prison and Young Offender Institution Rules are unclear about this practice and the legal position remains untested.'

[77] PR 53A(3).

referred.[78] The adjudicator will be a district judge or deputy district judge and the prisoner is currently entitled to legal representation in those circumstances.[79]

8-30   Failure to inquire into a charge within 28 days of referral, or the next day in the case of an inquiry by a governor, would be grounds for review. In practice, especially in the case of an independent adjudication, the case may be opened and then immediately adjourned if there is a need to gather more evidence, or where the prisoner himself makes a reasonable request for an adjournment, for example to seek legal advice.

However, if the case is adjourned and reopened, there may still be grounds for review if the delay in hearing the case prejudices the fairness of the hearing. If an adjournment extends to six weeks or more, adjudicators must consider whether natural justice has been compromised by the delay.[80]

Where a charge may amount to a criminal offence, it should be reported to the police for investigation and possibly to the CPS for prosecution. In those circumstances a charge should be laid as normal within 48 hours and opened the following day. The adjudicator must then take the decision as to whether the case should be referred and if it is, the adjudication will be adjourned pending the outcome of the police investigation. If the CPS initiates a prosecution, the internal adjudication will not proceed. If the CPS does not, the internal adjudication can go ahead. However there could still be grounds for challenging the decision to pursue the charge where the CPS have opted not prosecute since this will raise questions as to whether there is adequate proof to meet the charge.[81]

(4) Adjudication Hearings

8-31   At a disciplinary adjudication a prisoner must be given an adequate opportunity to hear what is alleged against him, and to present his own case in response.[82] This has been held to import the principles of natural justice into disciplinary hearings, although what is required by natural justice will depend on the seriousness of both the charges and the possible consequences. An example is where a Young Offenders Institution failed to provide to the claimants' solicitor any necessary documents including the charge sheet and witness statements. The evidence 'highlighted the wholly inadequate system which existed at Ashfield for disclosure of material information to legal representatives in advance of an Independent Adjudicator hearing'.[83]

Adjudications are intended to be inquisitorial rather than adversarial, but the standard of proof in disciplinary hearings is the criminal standard: beyond reasonable doubt. Adjudications are held within the prison. Prisoners are entitled to legal representation at independent adjudications. They may in some circumstances be granted the right to legal representation for an internal adjudication, but this is not the norm. Independent adjudicators are bound by prison and YOI rules but are not bound by PSI 47-2011 or any other relevant PSIs/PSOs.

---

[78] PR 53(3).
[79] PR 54(3).
[80] PSI 47-2011, para 2.16.
[81] ibid, para 2.17.
[82] PR 54(2).
[83] *R (MA & Ors) v Independent Adjudicator HMYOI Ashfield* [2013] EWHC 438 (Admin).

During an adjudication, a prison officer will normally present the charges against the prisoner and can then be questioned by the prisoner themselves (or their legal representative, in the case of an independent adjudication). The prisoner can give evidence and request the attendance of others to give evidence, although witnesses cannot be compelled to attend.[84] Hearsay evidence is admissible, but it is recognised in the context of governor adjudications that findings of guilt based solely on disputed hearsay evidence will be unsafe.[85]

After the evidence is heard, if the charge is found to be proved, the prisoner or representative is entitled to mitigate and then the adjudicator will decide on an appropriate punishment.

Both governor and independent adjudications can be challenged by way of judicial review. However, it may be appropriate in the case of governor adjudications to seek a review of the decision under PR 61 before applying for review (subject to time limits). This internal review is not available in the case of independent adjudications.

(5) Governor Adjudications

Governor adjudications for less serious disciplinary offences will be held within the prison by the prison governor, although this task can be delegated by the governor to another member of staff at managerial level with the requisite training.[86] In private prisons adjudications can either be carried out by the prison director or suitably trained and experienced staff who would be senior enough to run the prison in the director's absence.   **8-32**

At the start of an adjudication, the adjudicator must satisfy themselves that the accused prisoner is physically and mentally fit enough to participate in the hearing.[87] If the prisoner requests legal representation, this must be considered properly by the adjudicator, taking into account the seriousness of the charge and the potential penalty, whether any points of law are likely to arise, the capacity of particular prisoners to present their own case, procedural difficulties, the need for reasonable speed and the need for fairness.[88]

For a challenge based on the failure to grant legal representation at a governor's adjudication, it seems likely it would have to be demonstrated that the prisoner was unable to cope with the adjudication themselves, for intellectual reasons.[89]

Although adjudications are carried out by prison staff, there must be no actual or apparent bias. The test is whether 'a reasonable and fair-minded bystander, knowing all the facts, would have a reasonable suspicion that a fair trial for the applicant was not possible'.[90]

---

[84] PSI 47-2011, para 2.31.
[85] ibid, para 2.34.
[86] PR 81/YOI 85, see also PSI 47, 2011, para 1.3.
[87] PSI 47-2011, para 1.101.
[88] ibid, para 2.10. These principles are known as the *Tarrant* criteria and are derived from *R v Home Secretary, ex parte Tarrant* [1985] QB 251.
[89] No reported case where any such complaint succeeded has been found, however this was suggested by the judge in *Re Reynolds' Application* [1987] 8 NIJB 82.
[90] *R v Board of Visitors, Frankland Prison, ex parte Lewis* [1986] 1 WLR 130, 134F (Woolf J), which is based on Ackner LJ's formulation in *R v Liverpool City Justices, ex parte Topping* [1983] 1 All ER 490. Affirmed in *Porter v Magill* [2001] UKHL 67, [2002] 2 AC 357.

Challenges of this nature have been relatively rare. One example where a challenge might be successful is where the adjudicator was present during or in some way involved in incidents leading up to the charge. The House of Lords in *R (Carroll) v Secretary of State for the Home Department*[91] stated that there would be an appearance of bias where a deputy governor was present when a search order was confirmed, and was subsequently asked to adjudicate on the lawfulness of the order. His presence when the search order was confirmed implied a tacit acceptance that the search order was lawful.

Other examples were given by Judge J in the case of *R v Governor, Pentonville Prison, ex parte Watkins* [1992] COD 329.[92] Where the prison officer preferring the charges (ie presenting the evidence for the prison) is admitted into the adjudication room before the prisoner, or remained behind after the prisoner left, this could give the appearance of bias.

(6) Independent Adjudications

8-33   Independent adjudicators were introduced following the decision of the Grand Chamber of the ECtHR in the case of *Ezeh v United Kingdom*.[93] In that case the ECtHR held that sufficiently serious disciplinary offences which could result in additional days being added to existing sentences should attract Article 6 protection.

As set out above, all disciplinary procedures must be carried out according to the principles of natural justice, the requirements of which vary according to the seriousness of the offence. As such, hearings where the prisoner is at risk of being allocated extra days require a higher level of procedural safeguards and are held before an independent adjudicator, in practice a district judge or deputy district judge. Prisoners in such circumstances are also entitled to legal representation. The relevant disciplinary rules must be adhered to in the preparation and conduct of the hearing.

The Court of Appeal found in *R (Haase) v Independent Adjudicator*[94] that the requirement demanded by Article 6 for an independent tribunal did not extend to an independent and impartial prosecutor, and that there was no other basis for arguing that this was required in a prison disciplinary hearing. It was therefore found to be acceptable for a prison officer to conduct a prosecution despite the fact that that he was a potential witness. The test is whether the apparent lack of independence or impartiality leads to unfairness to the prisoner.[95]

8-34   As with criminal proceedings, there is a requirement for equality of arms within disciplinary adjudications. HHJ Purle QC, sitting as a Deputy High Court Judge in *R (Smith) v Independent Adjudicator, Secretary of State for Justice*,[96] said that there is a general requirement for a 'level playing field', and this will include the accused being given an opportunity

---

[91] *R (Carroll) v Secretary of State for the Home Department* [2005] UKHL 13, [2005] 1 WLR 688.
[92] *R v Governor, Pentonville Prison, ex parte Watkins* [1992] COD 329.
[93] *Ezeh v United Kingdom* [2002] 35 EHRR 28.
[94] *R (Haase) v Independent Adjudicator* [2008] EWCA Civ 1089, [2009] QB 550.
[95] The difference between *R (Haase) v Independent Adjudicator* [2007] EWHC 3079 (Admin), [2008] 1 WLR 1401 and the case of *R (Carroll) v Secretary of State for the Home Department* [2005] UKHL 13, [2005] 1 WLR 688 is that in the latter case the deputy governor, who was also a potential witness, was the adjudicator, not the prosecutor.
[96] *R (Smith) v Independent Adjudicator, Secretary of State for Justice* [2011] EWHC 3981 (Admin).

to obtain the evidence of other witnesses to the alleged offence, even where not called by the prison. The court held this was implicit in the requirement of Article 6 for individuals to have 'adequate time and facilities for the preparation of his defence'.[97] Failure to provide a prisoner with the opportunity to obtain the evidence of other witnesses and then to call them if required, was held to be fatal to the integrity of the convictions in *Smith*.

In fact, in the case of *Smith*, much of what was required to satisfy Article 6 and general principles of fairness was also set out in the *Prison Discipline Manual* (now replaced by PSI 47-2011). Decisions by independent adjudicators where procedure leading up to or during a hearing is flawed, can often be challenged on the basis that certain specific mandatory instructions set out in PSI 47-2011 have not been followed, as well as on Article 6 grounds.

The right of a prisoner to obtain the evidence of other witnesses however will not, it seems, make an adjudication unfair where a prisoner has failed to request the attendance of a witness they were aware of. In *R (Bates) v Independent Adjudicator, Secretary of State*[98] the claimant and another were both accused of possession of a mobile phone.[99] The other individual was released prior to the adjudication, but not before he submitted a written confession to the governor.

The confession was considered by the adjudicator but not considered credible and the claimant was convicted. The claimant failed to show that the release of the other prisoner, preventing the claimant from relying on his evidence and preventing the judge from assessing the respective credibility of each of them, made his conviction unfair. The claim was dismissed for a number of reasons, the main one being that the claimant, who was legally represented, did not ask for the other witness to attend, and said witness's evidence was heard through the apparent confession in any event. It is clear from this case that confessions written once a prisoner believes they are free from possible sanction are unlikely to be given much weight.

Where an independent adjudicator hears conflicting evidence, the case of *R (Anderson) v Independent Adjudicator*[100] suggests that there is a duty to give reasons for accepting one version of events over another. This is because a finding of guilt by an independent adjudicator can be challenged through the courts, which can only be effective if there are adequate reasons given for the original decision. The claimant in *Anderson* was successful in his application for judicial review where it was clear the adjudicator had preferred the account of a prison officer over prisoners giving evidence but was unclear why the evidence was preferred.

8-35

(7) Challenging Adjudications Generally

Adjudications can be challenged where all elements of the disciplinary charge were not present on the evidence or where an individual's involvement was not proven.[101]

8-36

---

[97] ibid [21].

[98] *R (Bates) v Independent Adjudicator, Secretary of State* [2011] EWHC 3236 (Admin).

[99] Note that possession on a mobile phone in prison is now a criminal offence under s 40D of the Prison Act 1952.

[100] *R (Anderson) v Independent Adjudicator* [2010] EWHC 2260 (Admin).

[101] For a useful breakdown of the elements of all disciplinary offences as seen by the prison service, see PSI 47-2011, paras 2.45–2.106.

In *R (Shreeve) v Secretary of State for the Home Department*[102] a prison service area manager refused to overturn a deputy prison governor's finding after the decision was referred to him for review.

In *Shreeve*, the claimant challenged the outcome of the adjudication on the basis that he was charged with having an unauthorised article, namely a sharpened stabbing instrument, in the absence of any evidence that the article had been actively sharpened. The claimant had been found guilty on the basis of his acceptance of possession, and his submissions that it had not been deliberately sharpened were considered by the adjudicator as merely mitigation. This was upheld by the service area manager, who added that the object was also unauthorised because the prisoner had been given it by another inmate without permission.

The Administrative Court held that because the claimant had been charged with possession of an article which was unauthorised because it had been sharpened, that was an element that must be proved, and the area manager had erred in finding that because the object was unauthorised for another reason, the charge could be upheld. The court quashed the area manager's decision.

8-37   The courts have also been willing to quash findings of guilt where the prisoner's presence at the time of an offence has been proven but his participation in the offence has not. Prisoners may well find themselves in a situation where they are present when other prisoners breach rules and are unable to remove themselves or object for reasons of safety or because for instance, they are sharing a cell with the individual.

The court in *R v Board of Visitors of Highpoint Prison, ex parte McConkey*[103] quashed a finding of guilt against a prisoner for an offence against good order where he was convicted solely on the basis of his presence in a room when others were smoking cannabis.

In *R v Deputy Governor of Camphill Prison, ex parte King*,[104] paraphernalia for drug-taking were found in a cell occupied by the applicant and three other prisoners. The Court of Appeal commented that it would be grossly unfair for knowledge of illicit items in a prisoner's cell to amount to an offence when they were not his and he might be frightened of their owner.[105]

In more recent times the Divisional Court was willing to quash a finding of guilt in *R (Barnsley) v The Secretary of State for the Home Department*[106] for the charge of denying officers access to a prison cell, where the claimant had been in a room with nine others and there was no evidence to establish that he had played any part in actually blocking the door.

As to when the outcome of a disciplinary matter should be challenged by way of judicial review, as opposed to via the PPO, this is considered in detail in the case of *Gifford v Governor of Bure Prison*.[107] Coulson LJ stated that claimants wishing to challenge the

---

[102] *R (Shreeve) v Secretary of State for the Home Department* [2007] EWHC 2431 (Admin), [2008] Prison LR 229.

[103] *R v Board of Visitors of Highpoint Prison, ex parte McConkey* The Times, 23 September 1982.

[104] *R v Deputy Governor of Camphill Prison, ex parte King* [1985] QB 735.

[105] The substantive finding in this case, that the courts could not review disciplinary decisions, has long since been overturned by the House of Lords, in *Ex p Leech* (n 4). Therefore it seems that if the Court of Appeal had considered itself able to review this decision, the claimant would have succeeded in having the disciplinary finding overturned.

[106] *R (Barnsley) v The Secretary of State for the Home Department* [2002] EWHC 1283 (Admin).

[107] *Gifford v Governor of Bure Prison* [2014] EWHC 911 (Admin).

outcome of a disciplinary procedure should do so through the PPO unless they sought to raise an issue outside the experience or jurisdiction of the PPO. The three main circumstances in which judicial review were said to be appropriate are where an injunction is sought (or the claim has some other urgent or emergency element), where underlying the complaint is a challenge to conviction or sentence (and as such is outside the jurisdiction of the PPO) or where policy is being directly challenged. The learned judge indicated that in future all claimants challenging disciplinary hearings should set out on their claim form how and why the claim is not suitable for adjudication.

(8) Punishments

The punishments available to governors following disciplinary hearings are set out at **8-38** PR 1999, rule 55. These range from a caution to loss of privileges, to up to 21 days' confinement in a cell. The punishments available to independent adjudicators are set out in rule 55A. The essential difference is that in addition to the punishments available to governors, independent adjudicators may make an award of up 42 extra days to be added to the prisoner's sentence.

There is a specific duty for governors to be aware of any guidance on suitable punishments for prison disciplinary offences published by the Secretary of State. Governors are required to take the following factors into consideration when deciding on a suitable punishment:

i. The circumstances and seriousness of the offence, and its effect on the victim (if any).
ii. The likely impact on the prisoner (including any health or welfare impact), the prisoner's age, behaviour in custody, and remaining time to release.
iii. The type of establishment and the effect of the offence on local discipline and good order, and the need to deter further similar offences by the prisoner and others.
iv. Any guilty plea, ensuring that the prisoner was not pressured into this plea, and that the decision is based on evidence, not just the plea.[108]

Punishments have been successfully challenged where a governor has devised a punishment themselves. In *R v Governor of Frankland Prison, ex parte Russell*,[109] a governor's policy of preventing prisoners in the segregation unit who refused to wear prison clothes from collecting their three meals a day from the servery, and providing them with one meal a day in their cells, was successfully challenged. It was held that the rights of a prisoner to adequate food must not be withdrawn or limited as a punishment, and that although the governor might lay down conditions for accessing food in the normal way, there is an overriding obligation that adequate food should still be provided.

More recently, the High Court in *R (Coleman) v Governor of Wayland Prison*[110] held that prison governors do not have the right to order the destruction of confiscated property, in this case a contraband mobile phone. The court held that there was no power to permanently deprive a prisoner of their property rights as a disciplinary sanction or at

---

[108] PSI 47-2011, para 2.110.
[109] *R v Governor of Frankland Prison, ex parte Russell* [2000] 1 WLR 2027, [2000] HRLR 512.
[110] *R (Coleman) v Governor of Wayland Prison* [2009] EWHC 1005 (Admin).

all, save for the specific circumstances set down in Prison Rule 43(4), which states that where property belonging to a prisoner remains unclaimed for a year, it can be sold or otherwise disposed of.

(9) Segregation

8-39   As set out above, one of the punishments available to governors and independent adjudicators, in PR 55 and 55a respectively, is cellular confinement, which can be imposed for up to 21 days.

Governors are also entitled to segregate prisoners in between laying the charge and when they first open disciplinary hearings.[111] They should only do so if there is significant risk of collusion or intimidation.[112] An initial health screen should be carried out for all potential segregations, and taken into account before segregation is ordered.[113]

Where a disciplinary hearing is adjourned, governors may continue to segregate prisoners pursuant to PR 45. This is a general provision which allows for the segregation of prisoners where it is 'for the maintenance of good order or discipline or in his own interests'.

Prisoners segregated under this provision can only remain so for a maximum period of up to 72 hours, without the permission of the Secretary of State. The Secretary of State may after the first 72 hours give permission for segregation under PR 45 for a further period of up to 14 days, and this 'may be renewed from time to time for a like period'.[114] Prisoners may also be released from segregation early at the discretion of the governor.[115]

The Secretary of State's powers in this regard are vested in a 'Segregation Review Board' (SRB), the make-up of which is provided for in PSO 1700. In practice the SRB contains an array of professionals, including a healthcare representative, wing or segregation unit personnel officer and the prison chaplain. Although the presence of a member of the Independent Monitoring Board is not mandatory, PSO 1700 recommends their attendance as well, and the prisoner must be present for at least some of the review.

8-40   In the case of *Secretary of State for the Home Department v SP*[116] the Court of Appeal ruled that a young woman in a YOI should have been given the chance to make representations before the decision was taken to segregate her. In this case, the claimant asserted that she should have had the opportunity to explain statements she had made to a member of staff about wanting to hurt other inmates, as she was being bullied and she said her statement was mere bravado.

The court took the view that the decision to segregate was an important one, which the claimant should have had the chance to make representations about and that although the decision would be reviewed after 72 hours or sooner, the court accepted

---

[111] PR 53(4), YOI r 58(3).
[112] PSI 47-2011, para 1.98.
[113] PSO 1700—this very detailed PSO deals with segregation and should be considered in full before a challenge in relation to segregation is brought.
[114] PR 45.
[115] ibid.
[116] *Secretary of State for the Home Department v SP* [2004] EWCA Civ 1750, [2005] 1 Prison LR 84.

that once a decision has been made, it is harder to change it. The court found that the principles of fairness required this, as did the 'principles and spirit of the Children's Act 1989' which the relevant PSO (PSO 4950) acknowledged should underpin the approach to segregation.[117]

The impact of this finding is limited to inmates in a YOI under the age of 18, and exceptions were envisaged by the Court of Appeal where, for instance, urgency required that the decision be taken quickly. However the Court of Appeal repeated the following statement of the judge in the court below, which presumably would apply to all prisoners:

> Although segregation is not a punishment imposed for a disciplinary offence, in cases where the order is made 'for the maintenance of good order or discipline' the difference may often seem slight, particularly to the subject of the order.[118]

As to the rights affected by segregation, the claimant in *Hassan v Secretary of State for Justice*[119] sought to argue that his continued segregation after a disciplinary charge was not pursued breached his rights under Articles 3 and 8 of ECHR. The court did not accept this contention. **8-41**

The main arguments put forward by the claimant were that the reason he was given for his segregation was in relation to an assault on another prisoner. As such he should have been taken out of segregation when the police and internal charges were dropped, and continued segregation was unreasonable. The claimant also argued his mental health should have been given greater weight.

This was given short shrift by the High Court, which considered the segregation regime in detail and stated simply that it could not be said to breach either his Article 3 or 8 rights. The court also found that the documented reasons for continued segregation were not 'unreasonable, let alone unlawful', essentially applying a *Wednesbury* test and showing a reluctance to impose the court's view in a situation where the prison professionals had greater knowledge and expertise.[120]

The court was somewhat scathing of the medical grounds and medical evidence relied on. The claimant had been monitored daily and had shown no signs of worsening mental illness, and relied on medical evidence which referred to the general undesirability of segregation for his condition. It is clear from this judgment that in order to succeed on mental health grounds, a medical report which engages with the precise regime actually imposed on the prisoner would be needed, and very likely some degree of harm would have to be shown.

The Court of Appeal considered Article 8 in the context of segregation in the earlier case of *Malcolm v Secretary of State for Justice*.[121] In that case, the claimant had been on the segregation wing for 157 days, as a consequence of his refusal to move to another wing. While on that wing he had been routinely denied the 60 minutes in open air which was his entitlement, according to the policy set out in PSO 4275 at the time.[122] **8-42**

---

[117] See the case of *R (Howard League for Penal Reform) v Secretary of State for the Home Department* [2002] EWHC 2497 Admin, [2003] 1 FLR 484.

[118] *Secretary of State for the Home Department v SP* [2004] EWCA Civ 1750, [2005] 1 Prison LR 84 [22] ([55] of High Court judgment).

[119] *Hassan v Secretary of State for Justice* [2011] EWHC 1359 (Admin).

[120] ibid [57].

[121] *Malcolm v Secretary of State for Justice* [2011] EWCA 1538.

[122] PSO 4275 has been replaced with PSI 10/2011.

In that case the breadth and potential elasticity of Article 8 was acknowledged and the court accepted that the enjoyment of exercise in the open air was capable of being an interest protected by Article 8, particularly in the context of incarceration. However it was found on the facts of this case that Article 8 was not engaged by the regime on the segregation wing experienced by the claimant, since he regularly received at least 30 minutes' exercise, and often more, and could not show any adverse effect on his health and wellbeing. The case also failed because the claimant had elected to remain on the wing.

The failure of the claim in this case does not preclude future claims of this nature. The court did find that if the restriction of exercise had infringed Article 8, the restriction could not have been justified, as a consequence of the precept that a decision-maker must follow their own published policy unless there are good reasons not to.[123] Success in a case like this would be likely to depend on the claimant being able to show actual distress or detriment as a result of being denied exercise.[124] Detrimental impact on health would then inevitably be weighed against the level of risk imposed by individuals.

In a case reported the year before of *R (Bary) v Secretary of State for Justice,*[125] immigration detainees awaiting extradition or deportation were all prevented from having unmonitored contact with the rest of the prison or the outside world, because of the fear that one of the detainees would use them to plan a terrorist attack. Even where some deterioration in health could be shown, there was found to be no infringement of Article 3, because the measures were not put in place to punish or humiliate, and no breach of Article 8 was found—even though Article 8 was engaged—because of the serious nature of the threat posed.

8-43   In the case of *R (King) v Secretary of State for Justice*[126] the Court of Appeal considered whether Article 6 was engaged when the decision was taken to segregate prisoners. In that case, the appeals of three prisoners against the finding of the High Court about the lawfulness of keeping each of them in segregation were heard, and in conjunction with Article 6, Articles 3 and 8 were also raised.

The appellants submitted that serving prisoners had a right to association with other prisoners and that this constituted a civil right within the meaning of Article 6. On this basis, they argued, the decisions of the governor and subsequently the SRB made to order or maintain their segregation were not Article 6 compliant, as the decision-makers were not sufficiently impartial. They further argued that their segregation interfered with their Article 3 and 8 rights, and as such the decision to segregate them engaged Article 6 in that way, because it was the determination of a civil right.

Maurice Kay LJ, giving the lead judgment, reversed the Divisional Court's decision and found that association with other prisoners was a privilege rather than a civil right, and could be denied by governors using their discretionary powers. He noted that the Prison Rules did not confer any right to association, and found that on the facts of all three cases it could not be said that Article 3 had been engaged.

---

[123] *R (Lumba) v Secretary of State for the Home Department* [2011] UKSC 12, [2012] 1 AC 245.
[124] An unfortunate consequence of this decision appears to be that the entitlement to 60 minutes in the open air on a daily basis has been reduced to 30 minutes.
[125] *R (Bary) v Secretary of State for Justice* [2010] EWHC 587 (Admin).
[126] *R (King) v Secretary of State for Justice* [2012] EWCA Civ 376, [2012] 1 WLR 3602.

It was accepted that in the case of claimants Bourgass and Hassan, Article 8 had been engaged in light of the long periods for which they had been confined (both for around six months), and that misuse of the discretion to segregate prisoners could clearly engage Article 8.[127] However, it was not accepted that seclusion was an infringement of that right in this case, where it was used as a means of protecting others from potential violence from the claimants.

Maurice Kay LJ did not find that the fact that Article 8 may have been engaged meant that Article 6 was automatically engaged. He considered the process of deciding on segregation to be 'administrative decision-making', and for this reason Article 6 would not be engaged.[128] He went on to state that the availability of judicial review was an appropriate safeguard to decisions on segregation.

The question of whether segregation should have been used as an alternative to disciplinary transfer was considered in the case of *R (Odigie) v Serco Limited*.[129] The claimant, who was serving an indeterminate sentence for manslaughter, had his cell searched based on intelligence that he had been bullying other prisoners and was implicated in a serious assault. A homemade weapon was found and the disciplinary process commenced. The claimant was segregated under Rule 45 for a number of weeks but before the evidence was adjudicated upon, a decision was made to transfer him to another prison. The challenge in the High Court was framed in classic judicial review terms, based on the procedural unfairness of the decision to transfer without awaiting the outcome of the disciplinary proceedings or considering other options, such as segregation. The rationality of the decision itself was not challenged. The court found that the correct procedure had been followed in making the decision to transfer (as set out in paragraphs 4.2.6–4.2.13 of PSO 4700) and that the governor was entitled to conclude that transfer was the only way he could discharge his duty to staff and other prisoners to maintain order.

It appears from these cases that there is a judicial reluctance to interfere with decisions made by governors about potentially dangerous or vulnerable prisoners and the containment of risk on prison wings. This is especially the case where other professionals are involved in monitoring the health and progress of prisoners. It is likely that actual harm would need to be shown or some kind of failure in the procedure, either through malice or mistake, in order to succeed in a case of this nature.

D. Parole Board Hearings

(1) General Principles

The Parole Board is an independent body whose role is to assess whether certain prisoners can safely be released back into the community or can be moved to open prisons.   **8-44**

---

[127] See ibid [50], where the case of *R (Munjaz) v Mersey Care NHS Trust* [2005] UKHL 58, [2006] 2 AC 148 is referred to in this regard.

[128] ibid [56].

[129] *R (Odigie) v Serco Limited* [2014] EWHC 3795 (Admin).

The Board is constituted under section 239 of the Criminal Justice Act (CJA) 2003, pursuant to which it can make its own rules of procedure (section 239(5)). The Secretary of State may also give it directions as to the matters to be taken into account by it when discharging its functions (section 239(6))

The Parole Board has changed since its inception, from having an advisory function to assist the Secretary of State, with very little in the way of checks and balances, to having an essentially judicial function in weighing up risk of release against continued deprivations of liberty. There are now a host of procedural safeguards in place, brought about in no small part by numerous successful common law and human rights challenges from prisoners.

(i) Functions

8-45   The Parole Board has the following functions:

  i.   For prisoners serving indeterminate sentences (including life sentences), the Board makes a binding decision on whether they should be released on license and whether they should be re-released after being recalled, as well as making a recommendation as to whether they should be transferred to open conditions;
  ii. For some prisoners serving determinate sentences the Board makes a binding decision on whether to release on license and decides on release following recall;[130]
  iii. For prisoners serving an extended sentence for public protection (EPP) for sentences imposed after but before 14 July 2008, the Parole Board will decide on parole when the individual has served the minimum term.[131]

(ii) Procedure

8-46   The Secretary of State refers all cases to the Parole Board. When cases are referred, the Secretary of State must provide a dossier of documents, as set out in Schedule 1, Parts A and B of the Parole Board Rules (PBR) 2011 (SI 2011/2947) when the Board is considering the release of a prisoner on licence for the first time, or those set out in Schedule 2, Parts A and B of the PBR 2011 when the Board is considering the release of a prisoner recalled for breach of licence conditions.

Where a prisoner is serving a determinate or extended sentence and is eligible for parole, a panel of three members will consider the suitability of the individual for release based on the Secretary of State's dossier, ie without an oral hearing. The prisoner must then be informed of the outcome no later than two weeks before their potential early release date.[132]

---

[130] Most prisoners serving determinate sentences have an automatic release date, apart from those serving sentences of four or more years for sexual or violent offences set out the Criminal Justice Act 2003, Sch 15 for offences committed before 4 April 2005. In the case of the latter category of prisoner, the Board makes a binding decision for those sentenced to between four and 15 years, and a recommendation for those serving more than 15 years.

[131] The release date is now automatic for those serving extended sentences imposed after 14 July 2008.

[132] PSO 6000, para 5.1.1

Florence Iveson

Where a prisoner serving an indeterminate sentence is to be considered for initial release on licence, the case is assessed initially by a single member of the Parole Board without a hearing, within 14 weeks of the case being referred. The single member will then either refer the case to an oral panel, or make a provisional decision that the individual is unsuitable for release. The decision must then be provided in writing within a week. If the case is to be referred for an oral hearing, the single Board member may not sit on the oral panel. The oral panel must consist of, or be chaired by, a judge or retired judge.

For recall of prisoners with indeterminate or life sentences there is now a presumption that an oral hearing will be given unless the prisoner waives their right.[133] For recall of prisoners on determinate and extended sentences, the dossier is considered by a single panel member, who will then decide whether an oral hearing is necessary.

(2) Oral Hearings Before the Parole Board

Decisions by the Board not to hold oral hearing have generated a great deal of case law.   **8-47**
Many cases have been argued on grounds of breach of Article 5, and it has been confirmed by the ECtHR that failure by the Parole Board to hold an oral hearing may in some circumstances breach Article 5(4):

> In matters of such crucial importance as the deprivation of liberty and where questions arise involving, for example, an assessment of the applicant's character or mental state, the Court's case law indicates that it may be essential to the fairness of the proceedings that the applicant be present at an oral hearing. In such a case as the present, where characteristics pertaining to the applicant's personality and level of maturity and reliability are of importance in deciding on his dangerousness, Art. 5(4) requires an oral hearing in the context of an adversarial procedure involving legal representation and the possibility of calling and questioning witnesses.[134]

The test for whether there has been any procedural unfairness on the part of the Board, including the fairness of any decision not to hold an oral hearing, is not *Wednesbury* unreasonableness—the court must make its own assessment of what fairness requires in the given situation.[135]

With regard to the consideration of fairness, *R (West) and R (Smith) v Parole Board*[136]   **8-48**
sets out that the importance of what was at stake for the individual concerned is a factor that should be taken into account when considering whether the decision not to hold an oral hearing is fair:

> The prisoner should have the benefit of a procedure which fairly reflects, on the facts of his particular case, the importance of what is at stake for him, as for society.[137]

In the case of *Roose v Parole Board*[138] the court quashed a decision not to hold an oral hearing where the Board may not have appreciated from the material before it the effect that its decision would have on Mr Roose's future management and

---

[133] See *Re Reilly's Application for Judicial Review* [2013] UKSC 61, [2013] 3 WLR 1020.
[134] *Waite v United Kingdom* (2003) 36 EHRR 54 [59].
[135] *Gillies v Secretary of State for Work and Pensions* [2006] UKHL 2, 2006 SC (HL) 71, [2006] 1 WLR 781 [6].
[136] *R (West) and R (Smith) v Parole Board* [2005] UKHL 1, [2005] 1 WLR 350.
[137] ibid [35].
[138] *Roose v Parole Board* [2010] EWHC 1780 (Admin).

psychological treatment. In that case the Board apparently accepted the suggestion by one psychologist that Mr Roose was suitable for a certain treatment programme, without understanding the practicalities of undergoing the programme or how it would affect his later opportunities for release. This is a clear case where an oral hearing was needed, as it could have prevented this confusion.

Roose also demonstrates the above principle that the importance of what was at stake for individual concerned is a factor that should be taken into account when considering whether the decision not to hold an oral hearing is fair. In *Roose*, the individual had been given a life sentence with a seven-year minimum term, but had already served 25 years.

8-49 Following the subsequent case of *R (Osborn and Booth) v the Parole Board*[139] in which the appellants were unsuccessful in showing they should have been given an oral hearing and the court set out guidance on when one should be held, the Parole Board issued guidance to its members on the topic.

However, the case of *Osborn and Booth* has since been appealed to the Supreme Court (the decision is discussed in detail below at 8-52), and therefore the guidance needs to be looked at in conjunction with the new decision because the Supreme Court allowed the appeals and goes further than the Court of Appeal in suggesting circumstances when an oral hearing is required.

At the time of writing, the Parole Board's website still has available a copy of the guidance issued in 2011 following the Court of Appeal's decision *Osborn and Booth*. It also states that it is being reviewed and will be updated shortly.

The 2011 guidance states that there is no requirement for the Parole Board to hold an oral hearing except in the cases of prisoners serving indeterminate sentences who are not assessed on the papers as unsuitable for release, or for prisoners serving indeterminate sentences, at the first review following recall.

8-50 According to the Parole Board's guidance, an oral hearing should be held for those on indeterminate or life sentences in the following circumstances:

i.   where there is a realistic prospect of release or a move to open conditions; or
ii. in any case where the assessment of risk requires live evidence from the prisoner and/or witnesses.

The guidance was intended to reflect the general principles enunciated by the Court of Appeal in *Osborn and Booth*, that if there is no realistic prospect of an application for parole succeeding, it would be a waste of time and resources to hold an oral hearing, but also that any Board must take into account the power of oral persuasion, and there may be some cases that look hopeless but nevertheless require oral hearings. This should now be read in light of the Supreme Court's decision in that case (see below at 8-52).

8-51 In the case of *R (Newsham) v the Parole Board*[140] the Court of Appeal's decision in *Osborn and Booth* and the Board's own guidelines were applied. The claimant challenged a decision not to hold an oral hearing on the basis that first, he should have been given the opportunity to discuss with the board his attendance on a thinking skills course, to demonstrate its effects on him. This submission failed on the basis that

---

[139] *R (Osborn and Booth) v the Parole Board* [2010] EWCA Civ 1409.
[140] *R (Newsham) v the Parole Board* [2013] EWHC 2750 (Admin).

an oral hearing would not have made a difference as there was no real prospect of the application for parole succeeding.

The claimant also contended that the characterisation by the Board of his offending as being 'instrumental violence' represented a shift in approach to what risk factors he presented. The court did not accept this but made clear that had it been shown the Board had departed substantially from the material provided to it in their findings, or asserted that there was a particular risk factor which had not previously been suggested, an oral hearing would have been necessary.

This case may well have been decided differently now, following the successful **8-52** appeal of *Osborn and Booth* to the Supreme Court. The appeal was conjoined with the Northern Irish case of an individual called Reilly, and the case is also known as *Re Reilly's Application for Judicial Review*.[141]

Lord Reed, giving the lead judgment, stated categorically that prospects of success at an oral hearing should not determine whether fairness requires that an oral hearing should be held:

> In so far as the board's practice is to require that a realistic prospect of success be demonstrated, as a precondition of the grant of an oral hearing, that practice should therefore cease.[142]

His Lordship identified three elements of procedural fairness:

i. The first was the avoidance of a sense of injustice in those subject to legal or administrative proceedings, warning of the danger of a sense of injustice arising where prisoners are denied the opportunity to participate in an oral hearing.[143]

ii. The second element, founded on the rule of law, was that decision-makers should listen to anyone who has something relevant to say.[144]

iii. The third was that the cost of oral hearings should not be determinative of whether they are held.[145] The court stated that the duty to afford an oral hearing where facts are in dispute, does not mean that oral hearings should be reserved for that situation.[146]

His Lordship went on to state that prisoners have a legitimate interest in being involved in proceedings which ultimately have serious implications for them, especially in the case of recalled prisoners whose freedom (albeit conditional) is being curtailed. The judgment also touched on the fact that the Board may well be asked to comment on particular risk factors which need to be addressed by the prisoner, which makes an oral hearing necessary in cases even where release is unlikely.

This represents a sea change in the approach to oral hearings in a Parole Board context, and it is likely that decisions made by the Board relying on the 2011 guidance may well be reviewable. This case would appear to recommend a presumption in favour of an oral hearing. The court was also clear that in the case of prisoners serving indeterminate sentences who have served their minimum term, fairness will require in

---

141 *Re Reilly's Application for Judicial Review* (n 133).
142 ibid [89].
143 ibid [68].
144 ibid [71].
145 ibid [72].
146 ibid [74].

most cases that they be given an oral hearing, which again is not the position in the 2011 guidance.

(i) Procedural Fairness

8-53   There is a common law duty of procedural fairness which applies to the Parole Board (see also above at 1-110). As set out above, the test is not *Wednesbury* unreasonableness—the court must make its own assessment of what fairness requires in the given situation. The Board's role is judicial, but the process is one of risk assessment, it is not a criminal court within the meaning of Article 6; discussions of the burden of proof are inappropriate.

When referring cases to the Parole Board, the Secretary of State must present them with certain proscribed documentation, but may also serve any evidence which s/he 'considers is relevant to the case'.

(ii) Evidence at Parole Board Hearings

8-54   Strict rules of evidence do not apply in Parole Board hearings. The Board is entitled to act on hearsay, but should bear in mind when according weight to evidence that it is hearsay, as well as considering whether procedural fairness requires that the evidence is tested through cross-examination. The Board can consider evidence that would not be admissible in court, but again subject to a general requirement of fairness.

The admissibility of evidence before the Parole Board was considered in detail in *R (Weszka) v Parole Board*.[147] The court accepted the ability of the Board to consider hearsay evidence and found it was entitled to consider the witness statement of a complainant in a criminal case even after an acquittal. It was found that the appellant had had the opportunity to request that the complainant be called to give evidence under the relevant provision in the PBR 2011 and challenge her evidence in that way. His failure to do so did not mean the evidence should be excluded.

The appellant in *Weszka* did succeed on the issues surrounding the late introduction of police intelligence on the day of the hearing. This consisted of police notes on serious crimes of which the appellant was suspected, and which gave no indication of the sources of the information. The court held there should have been an adjournment to allow the appellant's representatives to consider whether to seek to exclude it. It went on to say that the failure of the appellant's representative to ask for an adjournment on the day of the hearing did not make an unfair procedure fair.

The claimant succeeded to the extent that the nature, quality and unknown provenance of the evidence, combined with the fact that it was shown to the claimant for the first time on the morning of the hearing, meant the hearing was unfair. The court also found that the Board in its decision had failed to analyse the reliability or veracity of the police evidence.

8-55   The later case of *R (McGetrick) v Parole Board and Another*[148] also considered the admissibility of hearsay and addresses the conflict between the requirement under

---

[147] *R (Weszka) v Parole Board* [2012] EWHC 827 (Admin).
[148] *R (McGetrick) v Parole Board and Another* [2013] EWCA Civ 182, [2013] 1 WLR 2064.

section 239 of the CJA 2003 for the Board to consider any documents referred to it by the Secretary of State, and its duty to act as an independent, judicial panel, free from the influence of the executive.[149]

The case of *McGetrick* acknowledges however that there are circumstances where evidence provided to the Parole Board by the Secretary of State should be excluded from consideration altogether. The Court of Appeal held that section 239 of CJA 2003 should, if possible, be read so as not to infringe the principle that the Parole Board has an independent judicial function, which could not be interfered with by the Secretary of State, and should have the power to exclude evidence from the Secretary of State of its own volition.

A member of the Board is thus permitted, in what the court predicted to be rare circumstances, to exclude certain evidence from the panel conducting the hearing, while still meeting its obligations under section 239 of CJA 2003 when the dossier of all documents from the Secretary of State is considered by a single panel member. In reality, commentators have indicated the need for this function to be exercised will not in fact be exceptional and practitioners should consider seeking an order from the Board themselves for evidence to be excluded at an early stage in the proceedings.

The Board may also proceed on the basis of evidence which the prisoner never sees. **8-56** The Secretary of State has a power under the Probation Rules 2011 to withhold any information or report from a prisoner and their representative where s/he considers that its disclosure would adversely affect national security, the prevention of disorder or crime or the health or welfare of the prisoner or any other person.

It was held in the case of *R (Roberts) v Parole Board*[150] that the Parole Board has a corresponding ability to control its own procedure in such a way as to deal with a prisoner from whom evidence is withheld fairly, including the use of special advocates where necessary.

Where evidence is withheld from a prisoner and potentially his legal adviser as well, there is certainly a duty to mitigate the effects of any unfairness, and such evidence cannot be relied on where it abrogates the prisoner's right to a fair hearing. Proceedings must be looked at as a whole and where a panel, having heard withheld evidence, comes to a decision adverse to the prisoner, they must consider whether the procedure employed is consistent with Article 5(4) and the minimum standards of fairness.

The case of *R (Rowe) v Parole Board*[151] involved a victim impact statement from the **8-57** former partner of the claimant detailing allegations which went well beyond those for which he was convicted and pleaded guilty to. The statement was given to the chair of the Board on the morning of the hearing labelled 'not to be disclosed' and she disclosed it to the prisoner's representative, directing that it should not be revealed to the prisoner himself. The representative did not ask for further time but stated in submissions that little weight should be accorded to it in the absence of cross-examination.

As in *Weszka*, the court held that the failure of the appellant's legal advisor to request an adjournment did not mean the appellant waived the right to question a defect in the

---

[149] Note the earlier case of *R (Brooke) v Parole Board* [2008] EWCA Civ 29, [2008] 1 WLR 1950 [96], where the Court of Appeal held that the job of the Board is to analyse the evidence placed before it by the Secretary of State and then to reach its own objective conclusions.
[150] *R (Roberts) v Parole Board* [2005] UKHL 45, [2005] 2 AC 738.
[151] *R (Rowe) v Parole Board* [2012] EWHC 1272 (Admin).

procedure. The correct procedure would have been for the Chair to consider whether non-disclosure could have been mitigated, by giving a summary or disclosing limited parts of the statement, or whether the hearing could have been dealt with justly without considering the statement at all.

The judge commented that the real reason for the defect in procedure was: i) the very late service by the Secretary of State of the victim impact statement, ii) this was not an isolated incident, and iii) the proper procedure for service of such documents should be followed.

(3) Transfer to Open Conditions

(i) Introduction

8-58   The Parole Board regularly advises on transfer of a given prisoner to open conditions, even though this is not a role expressly provided for by statute. However it has been held that the Board in so advising is carrying out its duties pursuant to section 239(2) of the CJA 2003, to 'advise the Secretary of State with respect to any matter referred to it by him which is to do with the early release or recall of prisoners'. The Secretary of State is not obliged to follow its recommendation.

(ii) Parole Board Recommendations[152]

8-59   There have been a number of challenges to responses to recommendations. In the case of *R (Wilmot) v Secretary of State for Justice*[153] it was found that in the absence of a published statement of policy that the Secretary of State would always follow the Parole Board's recommendation, there could be no legitimate expectation that he or she would. Failure to follow their recommendation can, it seems, only be challenged on the basis of *Wednesbury* principles (see also above at 1-82). However the Secretary of State in this case did make clear that it would only depart from the board's recommendations on rare occasions.

In a preceding case, *R (Adetoro) v Secretary of State for Justice & The Parole Board*,[154] a claim was brought by a Category A prisoner after the Secretary of State first accepted but then rejected the recommendation of the Parole Board that the claimant be moved to open conditions. It was found that it was not lawful for the Secretary of State to first accept the recommendation and then change the decision without seeking input from the claimant prisoner. The judgment further stated that the new decision was neither properly reasoned nor rational.

In *R (Hill) v Secretary of State for Home Department*[155] a similar finding was made, where a claimant successfully showed that the approach of the Home Secretary in deciding not to accept the advice of the Parole Board on transfer to open conditions was

---

[152] See also in Ch 1 at 1-105.
[153] *R (Wilmot) v Secretary of State for Justice* [2012] EWHC 3139 (Admin).
[154] *R (Adetoro) v Secretary of State for Justice & The Parole Board* [2012] EWHC 2576 (Admin).
[155] *R (Hill) v Secretary of State for Home Department* [2007] EWHC 2164 (Admin).

Florence Iveson

neither rational nor even-handed. The court found that where the percentage of cases in which the Home Secretary did not accept the advice of the Parole Board in this regard suddenly increased significantly from one year to the next, this indicated that there must have been an unpublished change of policy toward scrutinising positive advice more closely. The policy was not even-handed as there was no change in approach by the Home Secretary towards advice where transfer to open conditions was not recommended—in that case the advice continued to be accepted by the Home Secretary as normal.

(iii) The Test for Transfer to Open Conditions

The Secretary of State may invite the Parole Board to consider transfer to open condi- **8-60**
tions either as a stand-alone issue or to be looked at in the alternative where the Board does not consider release appropriate. In the latter case, the Board must first apply the test for release and if the prisoner does not succeed on that test, go on to apply the test for transfer to open conditions. Clearly, these are different tests.

Guidance on the approach to be followed by the Parole Board when considering transfer to open conditions is set out in the Secretary of State's Directions to the Parole Board: August 2004 ('the Directions'). The test for transfer should be 'a balanced assessment of risk and benefits [but] the Parole Board emphasis should be on the risk reduction aspect'.[156] In *R (Gordon) v Parole Board*,[157] Smith J said:

> in my judgement the balancing exercise they are required to carry out is so fundamental to the decision making process that they should make it plain that this has been done and to state broadly which factors they have taken into account.

In the same case, Smith J gave this general guidance, which subsequently has been followed in several cases:

> I remind myself that I must not in any way interfere with the discretion or judgement of the Parole Board, who, as Turner J. observed in *ex parte Hart* (unreported 24th May 2000) are 'uniquely qualified' to make the decisions it is called upon to make. I must ask myself whether they have carried out their task in accordance with the law, as set out in the statutory directions. I must consider whether the decision falls within the range of decisions which a reasonable panel might make. I must ask whether the reasons for the decision are proper, sufficient and intelligible.[158]

The guidance goes on to say that this is a balancing exercise, which should include consideration of the following four factors:

i.   The extent to which the lifer has made sufficient progress during sentence in addressing and reducing risk to a level consistent with protecting the public from harm, in circumstances where the lifer in open conditions would be in the community, unsupervised, under licensed temporary release.

ii. The extent to which the lifer is likely to comply with the conditions of any such form of temporary release.

---

[156] The Secretary of State's Directions to the Parole Board: August 2004 ('the Directions'), para 3.
[157] *R (Gordon) v Parole Board* [2000] Prison LR 275 [38].
[158] ibid [31]. Applied in *R (D'Cunha) v Parole Board* [2011] EWHC 128 (Admin), *Hill* (n 155) and *Rowe* (n 151).

   iii.   The extent to which the lifer is considered trustworthy enough not to abscond.

   iv.   The extent to which the lifer is likely to derive benefit from being able to address areas of concern and to be tested in a more realistic environment, such as to suggest that a transfer to open conditions is worthwhile at that stage.

The guidance also acknowledges that transfer to open conditions is considered to be related to the release of prisoners, because a prisoner serving a life sentence is very unlikely to be released without having spent some time in open conditions.

The Court of Appeal has found that while the Directions should not be considered mandatory on questions of recall or release on licence (and indeed some of these have now been withdrawn by the Secretary of State), they are mandatory on questions of transfer to open conditions.[159] Failure to carry out the correct balancing exercise will be a reviewable error of law, as was the case in *R (D'Cunha) v Parole Board* [2011] EWHC 128 (Admin) where the Board failed to consider the question of transfer separately from the question of release and the decision was remitted back to be considered within the terms of the Directions.[160]

8-61   Nevertheless, the courts have shown themselves reluctant to interfere in cases where the Board has carried out a detailed analysis of the evidence and given lengthy reasons which broadly take in the factors set out in the Directions. In the cases of *R (Austin) v Parole Board*[161] and *R (Leach) v Parole Board*[162] the claimants argued that the Board had failed to give sufficient weight to the benefits of transfer to open conditions and focused too heavily on the risk. This argument was rejected in both cases, the respective judges taking a holistic approach to the reasons given and not requiring explicit reference to every element of the guidance. In both cases it was highlighted that the Directions placed the emphasis on reducing risk in any event.

In the case of *H v Parole Board*[163] a claimant prisoner was successful in having a decision of the Parole Board not to move him to open conditions quashed on the grounds that they had made a material error of fact. The individual had been tried for three counts of rape and convicted of two, with the jury unable to agree on the third count. The Board took into consideration what they considered to be vagueness regarding facts surrounding the count of which he had not been convicted, which they were not entitled to do, leading to their decision being quashed.

8-62   Another area of litigation relating to the transfer to open conditions has been around delay. Following the coming into force of the dangerousness provisions in the Criminal Justice Act 2003, there was a wholesale failure to provide the resources, including places in open prisons, necessary for the prisoners serving indeterminate sentences to prove their rehabilitation to the Parole Board.

In *R (James, Lee and Wells) v Secretary of State for Justice*[164] the House of Lords held that there was a public law duty to give prisoners 'a fair opportunity … to demonstrate

---

[159] *D'Cunha* [59], and applied in *Rowe* [12].

[160] It is also clarified in that case that although the relevant section in the Secretary of State's Directions is entitled 'Transfer of Life Sentence Prisoners to Open Conditions', the test and guidance also applies to IPP sentences.

[161] *R (Austin) v Parole Board* [2011] EWHC 2384 (Admin).

[162] *R (Leach) v Parole Board* [2011] EWHC 2470 (Admin).

[163] *H v Parole Board* [2011] EWHC 2081 (Admin).

[164] *R (James, Lee and Wells) v Secretary of State for Justice* [2009] UKHL 22, [2010] 1 AC 553.

that the risk they presented at the date of sentence has diminished to levels consistent with release into the community'.[165] The Secretary of State for Justice was found to have entirely failed to uphold this public law duty with regard to the claimant prisoners who were serving indeterminate sentences, and whose release had been delayed as a result. Despite this, the House of Lords did not find that the claimants' Article 5 rights had been infringed and did not award damages.

The prisoners appealed to the ECtHR in *James, Wells and Lee v United Kingdom*.[166] The ECtHR disagreed with the House of Lords in finding that Article 5(1) had been infringed in each case. The court found that where a government requires prisoners to demonstrate they fall below a certain level of risk, failure to provide adequate opportunities for them to do so must be reasonable in all the circumstances. The ECtHR found that the detention of the prisoners was arbitrary from the point at which the prisoners' tariffs expired up to the point at which the prisoners were enabled to access the relevant rehabilitative resources.

Two significant factors identified by the ECtHR were that i) the prisoners were unable to move into open prisons and ii) lacked access to the courses they needed to take for the purposes of rehabilitation. This was a consequence of a failure to plan for the inevitable outcome of the new sentences the government had itself introduced, which had resulted in the significant increase of indeterminately sentenced prisoners. The delay the appellants faced, spending two and half years in local prisons with no possibility of furthering their rehabilitation, was also a significant factor. The appellants were awarded damages pursuant to section 7 of HRA 1998, but at the time of writing an appeal is pending to the Grand Chamber.

The House of Lords and ECtHR judgments were considered in detail in the case **8-63** of *R (Haney and Jarvis) v Secretary of State for Justice*.[167] In that case the claimants were serving prisoners with indeterminate sentences, who had been told by the Parole Board that they needed to undertake further rehabilitation in open conditions. They were both pre-tariff and became aware of an unpublished policy of prioritising post-tariff prisoners, implemented to deal with the backlog of indeterminate sentenced prisoners.

The claimants argued, first, that the defendant was in breach of its public law duties in failing to provide adequate access to rehabilitation and open conditions, and secondly, that the policy was unlawful, contrary to the published policy and irrational. They asserted that their Article 5 and Article 8 rights had been breached and also argued that they had been discriminated against as compared to post-tariff prisoners, thereby breaching their Article 14 rights as well.

The court found that the defendant had breached its public duties in regard to the provision of access to rehabilitation, and that the failure to publish its policy in regard to the prioritisation of post-tariff prisoners was also in breach of a public law duty to publish new arrangements, particularly because if the prisoners had known of the policy, they could have asserted that their cases were exceptional and should have been considered outside the policy.

---

[165] ibid [105] (Lord Judge LCJ).
[166] *James, Wells and Lee v United Kingdom* (2013) 56 EHRR 12.
[167] *R (Haney and Jarvis) v Secretary of State for Justice* [2013] EWHC 803 (Admin).

The court did not find that the policy was irrational, unlawful or contrary to pub-lished policy, as there was a need to clear the backlog of post-tariff prisoners serving indeterminate sentences and no published policy suggesting that they would take the opposite approach. For this reason, the policy was not quashed and the court noted that in any event the backlog had been cleared. The court also did not find that there was a breach of Articles 8 or 14 and considered itself bound by *James* with regards to Article 5. The appellants were given immediate permission to appeal on the Article 5 point.

8-64   The appeal was joined with an appeal in the case of *R (Kaiyam) v Secretary of State for Justice*[168] and they were heard together in the Court of Appeal.[169] At first instance in *Kaiyam* the court considered whether the failure of a particular prison to allow a particular prisoner serving an indeterminate sentence to undertake a course thought to be appropriate for him was a breach of Article 5(1), as well as of public law duties. The court considered the facts of the instant case distinguishable from those of *Haney* on the basis that there was not a systemic failure to allow access to particular courses, but rather a failure in one individual case. The argument of the defendant, that in the absence of systemic failure, the only grounds for review in this case would be that the Secretary of State had acted irrationally in denying access to the course, was accepted. On the question of whether there had been a breach of Article 5(1) the court considered itself bound by the decision of the House of Lords in *James* (n 164).

Hearing the conjoined appeals, the Court of Appeal was also bound in terms of Article 5 by the case of *Wells* (see n 164 above) but granted permission to appeal to the Supreme Court to resolve the 'unsatisfactory' conflict between domestic and European jurisprudence. The Court declined to give a view on the correct determination of the issue. At the time of writing that appeal was pending.

The court went on to consider the public law dimension to the claim in Kaiyam's case, which had failed at first instance. The Court was critical of the way the case had been put, in that it was a claim for breach of a public law duty which in the court's view did not identify said duty or the nature of the breach. It upheld the ruling of the lower court, finding that a *James* type claim was bound to fail in the absence of evidence of a systemic failure in the provision of relevant courses for prisoners serving indeterminate sentences.

E. Release on Licence

(1) The Test for Release

8-65   The Secretary of State announced on July 2013 that she was withdrawing her Directions to the Parole Board, issued pursuant to section 32(6) of the Criminal Justice Act 1991, where they apply to early release.

---

[168] *R (Kaiyam) v Secretary of State for Justice* [2013] EWHC 1340 (Admin).
[169] *R (Kaiyam) v Secretary of State for Justice* [2013] EWCA Civ 1587.

In December 2012, with the coming into force of the Legal Aid, Sentencing and Punishment of Offenders Act (LASPO) 2012, a new statutory test for the release of prisoners serving determinate sentences was introduced, and has been inserted into the CJA 2003. It is expressed in the negative, stating that the Parole Board 'must not [direct the release of a prisoner] unless the Board is satisfied that it is no longer necessary for the protection of the public for them to be confined'.

This brings the test for determinate sentenced prisoners into line with those serving indeterminate or life sentences, set out in section 28(6)(b) of the Crime (Sentences) Act 1997.

The change reflects the judgment in *R (Foley) v Parole Board*,[170] which stated that the difference in test for release between those serving determinate and indeterminate sentences (the former being incongruously harder to meet) was not justified. It was found that in *Foley* this was not a breach of Article 14, since the court considered itself bound by a previous decision of the House of Lords to find that Ms Foley could not rely on the difference between herself and those serving indeterminate sentences to bring her under Article 14.[171]

An unsuccessful challenge to the rule applied to the release of prisoners with an IPP **8-66** sentence was made in the case of *R (Sturnham) v Parole Board*.[172] It was argued that the test for release for IPP prisoners should reflect the test for imposition of such a sentence, and therefore focus only on the risk that 'further specified offences' may be committed. The Court of Appeal in *Sturnham* found that Parliament had not provided for differential treatment of prisoners serving IPPs as compared to others serving life sentences, and there was no reason for the test for their release to mirror the test applied when sentencing. This was affirmed by the Supreme Court in *R (Faulkner) v Secretary of State for Justice, R (Sturnham) v Parole Board*.[173]

> The Parole Board issued guidance to its members on the new test for release on license for determinate sentenced prisoners in December 2013, which stated that:

> In order to direct release, the Board should be satisfied that it is no longer necessary for the prisoner to be detained in order to protect the public from serious harm (to life and limb). It is not a requirement to balance the risk against the benefits to the public or the prisoner of release.

> The lawfulness of this guidance was considered by the Divisional Court in *R (King) v Parole Board*.[174]

The challenge to the guidance in *King* was principally to the contention that the Parole Board's members were no longer required to carry out a balancing exercise, taking into account the benefits to the prisoner of release as against any risk they might pose, as part of the test for release. It was argued for the claimant that the balancing test was in fact consistent with both the statutory history of the test and the new framework introduced

---

[170] *R (Foley) v Parole Board* [2012] EWHC 2184 (Admin).
[171] The House of Lords found in *R (Clift) v Secretary of State for Home Department* [2006] UKHL 54, [2007] 1 AC 484 that being a determinate as opposed to indeterminate sentenced prisoner does not constitute 'other' status. This is contrary to the subsequent decision of the ECtHR in *Clift v UK* [2010] ECHR 1106. The conflict between domestic and European law will be considered by the Supreme Court in the appeal following *R v Kaiyam* [2013] EWCA Civ 1587.
[172] *R (Sturnham) v Parole Board* [2012] EWCA Civ 452, [2012] 3 WLR 476.
[173] *R (Faulkner) v Secretary of State for Justice, R (Sturnham) v Parole Board* [2013] UKSC 47, [2013] 3 WLR 281.
[174] *R (King) v Parole Board* [2014] EWHC 264 (Admin).

by LASPO 2012 and the guidance issued indicating that this was no longer a relevant consideration was therefore unlawful.

The Divisional Court considered the statutory history of the test in great detail and looked at the findings of the Supreme Court in *Faulkner*. The Court held that the Parole Board was required to simply apply a 'public protection' test, not the previously applied balancing test which had been contained in the now revoked Secretary of State's Guidance to the Parole Board, as this would put a gloss on the words of the statute which was not permitted by their formulation. For this reason the Parole Board guidance was found to be lawful and the claim dismissed.

(2) Delay

8-67 The Court of Appeal in *Sturnham* held that in a case where there has been a delay in the Parole Board hearing a case, engaging Article 5(4) of ECHR,[175] just satisfaction will normally be achieved by a declaration unless the claimant's detention is extended by reason of the delay or the delay causes a diagnosable illness in the claimant. The court also held that cases where delay merely causes stress and anxiety will not generally attract compensation. The Secretary of State's cross-appeal therefore succeeded in the Court of Appeal, but this was overturned by the Supreme Court in *Faulkner and Sturnham*.

The Supreme Court held that UK courts should be guided by the approach taken by the ECtHR to the award of damages for breach of Article 5(4) in cases brought by UK citizens or citizens from countries with similar living costs.[176] It was held, contrary to the findings of the Court of Appeal, that where there was a delay in breach of Article 5(4), but it is not established that an earlier hearing would have resulted in earlier release, there is still an overriding presumption that the prisoner suffered anxiety and frustration and should be compensated.

In the case of *Sturnham,* there had been a delay of six months but the court had found that there would have been no prospect of release had the claimant been heard by the Parole Board earlier. Referring to the award made in *Betteridge v UK*[177] of 750 for an unjustified delay of 13 months, the Supreme Court awarded Sturnham £300.

With regards to the other appellant, Faulkner, his award of £10,000 for a 10-month delay was reduced to £6,500, the Supreme Court taking into account the fact that the liberty at stake was 'conditional and precarious'.[178] Therefore it would appear that this case does not on the whole set down conditions likely to increase awards of damages to prisoners subject to delayed Parole Board hearings.

---

[175] Art 5(4) reads: 'Everyone who is deprived of his liberty by arrest or detention shall be entitled to take proceedings by which the lawfulness of his detention shall be decided speedily by a court and his release ordered if the detention is not lawful.'

[176] A useful, but ultimately inconclusive survey of such cases is undertaken by Lord Reed in *Faulkner and Sturnham* (n 173) [41]–[74].

[177] *Betteridge v UK* (2013) 57 EHRR 7.

[178] *Faulkner and Sturnham* (n 173) [87].

(3) Recall

Prisoners released on licence may be recalled to prison by the Secretary of State if   **8-68**
they breach their licence conditions. This process is currently governed by sections
254–256A (Recall after release) in Chapter 6 of CJA 2003[179] and guidance is provided
in PSI 30/2014. A prisoner will be recalled to prison if, following a recommendation by
the relevant probation service, the Secretary of State considers that the individual has
breached a licence condition or is exhibiting other behaviour which means that they are
likely to start offending again and should therefore be recalled to prison.

It has been held that the fact that a prisoner is facing a criminal charge cannot alone
be justification for concluding that there is a risk of reoffending—there must be something more to suggest the individual represents a risk to the public.[180] As the House of
Lords set out in *Smith and West* (n 18), recall should not be approached as a punishment, but as a measure to protect the public from further offending.[181] Where a breach
of a licence condition is alleged, the threshold for recall is not high[182]—there must be
some evidence which reasonably leads the Secretary of State to conclude that there has
been a breach.[183]

In the case of *R (Jorgensen) v Secretary of State for Justice*[184] it was held that not every   **8-69**
case where a licence condition has been breached should lead to recall. The judge in
Jorgensen considered that where there has been a breach, the Secretary of State must
then go on to consider what steps (which may include recall) should be taken to deal
with the breach.[185] Relevant considerations in *Jorgensen* were whether the prisoner acted
intentionally to breach their licence conditions, and whether the conduct is very similar
to the index offence for which the prisoner was originally imprisoned—the Secretary of
State must then decide whether recall is a proportionate means of achieving the legitimate aim of protecting the public from risk.

Ultimately, challenging a decision to recall will be difficult because the threshold for
deciding that recall is necessary is low, and so long as the Secretary of State has taken
into account the relevant considerations and is not acting unlawfully or on incorrect
information, the test (according to *Jorgensen*) is one of *Wednesbury* unreasonableness.[186]
In *Jorgensen,* the court also held that a margin of appreciation should be allowed in matters of recall, in light of the expertise required to assess the risk posed by a particular
prisoner.

---

[179] Note the changes introduced by LASPO 2012.
[180] *R (Broadbent) v The Parole Board* [2005] EWHC 1207, [2006] 1 Prison LR 137 [26] and *R (J) v Parole
Board* [2010] EWHC 919 (Admin) [48].
[181] *Smith and West* (n 20) [56].
[182] *R (Howden) v Secretary of State for Justice* [2010] EWHC 2521 (Admin) [14].
[183] *R (Gulliver) v Parole Board* [2007] EWCA Civ 1386 [5] and *R (McDonagh) v Secretary of State for Justice*
[2010] EWHC 396 (Admin) [28].
[184] *R (Jorgensen) v Secretary of State for Justice* [2011] EWHC 977.
[185] The judge is implying there is essentially a balancing exercise, referring to the following quote from
Saadi v United Kingdom (2008) 47 EHRR 17: '70 ... the detention of an individual is such a serious measure
that it is only justified as a last resort where other, less severe measures have been considered and found to
be insufficient to safeguard the individual or public interest which might require the person concerned to be
detained'.
[186] *Jorgensen* (n 184) [22] and [49].

(4) Release Following Recall

8-70   Where the decision is made to recall any person to prison, the Secretary of State is required by section 255A(2) of CJA 2003 to consider whether the person is suitable for automatic release, unless they had been serving an extended sentence. Automatic release means release after 28 days of having been returned to custody.[187] The test for whether someone is suitable for automatic release is whether the person presents a risk of serious harm to the public (section 255A(4) of CJA 2003). If the person is deemed suitable for automatic release they must be informed of this and given a release date.[188]

    If a recalled prisoner is suitable for automatic release they may still make representations in writing under section 254(2) before the 28-day period expires. Indeed all prisoners must be told when they are recalled to prison the reasons for their recall and their right to make representations in writing in respect of them.[189] The Secretary of State must refer the prisoner's representations to the Parole Board under section 255B(4) of CJA 2003, although he may also elect to simply release the prisoner if satisfied that they did in fact comply with all the conditions of their licence.[190] If the Board directs the release of that individual, the Secretary of State must release them.[191]

    Where a prisoner is serving an extended or indeterminate sentence, or is not deemed suitable for automatic release by the Secretary of State, they must be informed of this. Any such prisoners must be referred to the Parole Board, if they make representations under section 254(2) of CJA 2003, at the time such representations are made. If they do not make representations under section 254(2), they must be referred to the Parole Board in any event at the end of 28 days. The Secretary of State must then release any such prisoner if so directed by the Parole Board. In practice, the Secretary of State's powers in regard to recall are deferred to the Public Protection Casework Section (PPCS).

8-71   Chapter 7 of PSO 6000 sets out the strict timetable to be followed when a prisoner is recalled to prison, in terms of disclosing the reasons for recall to the prisoner (in the form of a recall dossier) and referring the matter to the parole board. It is important to check the correct procedure has been followed. In *Haynes v Secretary of State for Justice*[192] the respondent conceded that the claimant's Article 5(2)[193] rights had been infringed when he was arrested for breach of licence conditions and recalled to prison without being given the recall dossier, which should have been received shortly (within 24 hours of the prisoner's recall being notified to the PPCS) after his return to prison. In this case the PPCS was notified on a Friday, and so the recall dossier should have been provided to the claimant the following Monday; however, due to an 'administrative error' it was not provided until nine days after that.

---

187 CJA 2003, s 255A(3).
188 ibid s 255B.
189 ibid s 254(2). In *Jorgensen* (n 184) [24], the words of Lord Brown in *South Bucks DC v Porter (No 2)* [2004] 1 WLR 1953 [36], are quoted as a summary of what is required in terms of reasons: '[They] must be intelligible and they must be adequate. They must enable the reader to understand why the matter was decided as it was and what conclusions were reached on the principal important and controversial issues.'
190 ibid s 254(2B).
191 ibid s 255B(5).
192 *Haynes v Secretary of State for Justice* [2012] EWHC 2481 (Admin).
193 Art 5(2) reads: 'Everyone who is arrested shall be informed promptly, in a language which he understands, of the reasons for his arrest and the charge against him.'

Florence Iveson

Prisoners should be issued with a 'representations pack' regarding representations to the board along with the recall dossier to enable them to put representations in writing to the Board. In *Haynes* the delay in providing the dossier and representations pack meant the claimant did not have the opportunity to make representations to the Board about the reasons for recall and whether he should be re-released before it made its decision, which saw him being released nearly two months after he was recalled. The court was satisfied that his inability to make representations to the Board meant the procedure followed was unfair and therefore in breach of the claimant's Article 5(4) rights. The claimant was awarded £1,500 in damages for the breach of his Article 5(2) rights, the court considering that a declaration was just satisfaction of the Article 5(4) claim.[194]

With regard to the approach that should be taken by the Parole Board, the Secretary of State issued directions to the Board on the recall of determinate sentenced prisoners in December 2009.[195] These state that the Parole Board may do one of three things: **8-72**

   i.   recommend immediate release on licence;
   ii.   fix a future date for release within one year of the present hearing; or,
   iii. make no recommendation as to release.

The Parole Board, when considering release after recall, is not reviewing the decision taken by the Secretary of State to recall the prisoner, rather they must assess for themselves whether there is any risk posed by the prisoner if re-released and whether this can be managed in the community.[196] The 2009 directions require that the Parole Board must take into account factors such as the extent to which the prisoner has complied with supervision requirements previously and is likely to do so in the future, as well as the availability of suitable accommodation and relevant offending behaviour interventions.

There is no statutory test for release following recall of prisoners serving determinate sentences. In 'Guidance for Members on LASPO 2012', the Board recommends that the public protection test is applied, meaning that the same test is applied on release following recall as on initial release.[197]

As to whether Article 6 applies in the context of a Parole Board hearing to consider release after recall, the House of Lords found in *Smith and West* that recall on licence was not a punishment, and therefore the decision did not determine a criminal charge.[198] Their Lordships also considered the civil limb of Article 6. Lord Bingham stated that even if Article 6 was applicable (which he declined to determine), this would not necessarily afford greater protection than the common law duty of procedural fairness. More recently in *King*, the Court of Appeal held that the availability of judicial review was a just satisfaction of Article 6 in matters of release and recall. **8-73**

Therefore in *Haynes* when the claimant sought to claim that Article 6 was engaged, on the basis that determination of release following recall constitutes the determination of a civil right, he was unsuccessful. The High Court considered *Smith and West* and found that the claimant did not have a civil right to the liberty as asserted because the sentence imposed was not being altered, it was simply being administered.

---

[194] Compare this to the cases regarding Art 5(4) at 8-67 above.
[195] www.justice.gov.uk/offenders/parole-board/sos-directions/dec2009.
[196] *R v Parole Board, ex parte Watson* [1996] 1 WLR 906.
[197] The Parole Board 'must not [direct the release of a prisoner] unless the Board is satisfied that it is no longer necessary for the protection of the public for them to be confined'.
[198] *Smith and West* (n 20) [44] (Lord Bingham).

9

Other Statutory Bodies

The Legal Aid Agency, The Criminal Cases Review Commission, The Independent Police Complaints Commission and The Criminal Injuries Compensation Authority

DAVID BALL

A. Introduction

9-1   This chapter is concerned with such potential judicial claims against:

   i.   the Legal Aid Agency;
   ii.   the Criminal Cases Review Commission;
   iii. the Independent Police Complaints Commission; and
   iv.   the First Tier Tribunal (in respect of appeals from the Criminal Injuries Compensation Authority).

These claims often arise from a variety of issues with a range of individuals in criminal litigation, such as i) defendants seeking legal aid or wishing to challenge their conviction, ii) complainants against police conduct, or iii) victims who have suffered loss or injury from criminal conduct. In each case the decision taken by the public body in question may give rise to a claim for judicial review.

B. The Legal Aid Agency

(1) Introduction

9-2   The Legal Aid Agency (LAA) was established further to the Legal Aid, Sentencing and Punishment of Offenders Act (LASPO) 2012. Section 38 of LASPO 2012 abolished the predecessor to the LAA, the Legal Services Commission (LSC). The LAA is an executive agency of the Ministry of Justice. This is to be compared with the LSC, which was previously an arm's-length body.[1] As it is put in the explanatory notes to LASPO 2012, this means that decisions on legal aid in individual cases will ultimately be taken by a statutory office holder: a civil servant designated by the Lord Chancellor as the Director of Legal Aid Casework. The Lord Chancellor will have no power to direct or issue guidance to the Director in relation to individual cases. It is undoubtedly the case that previous judicial reviews involving LAA predecessor bodies, the Legal Aid Board (LAB), and the LSC will continue to be relevant.

(2) Decisions Subject to Challenge by Judicial Review

9-3   Judicial reviews of the LAB, LSC and LAA are many and varied. They can best be viewed grouped around certain themes:

   i.   Decisions relating to tenders.
   ii.   Decisions relating to grants of public funding relating to:
         a.   standing;
         b.   inquests;
         c.   Article 6;

---

[1] V Lang and S Pugh (eds), *Legal Aid Handbook 2013/14* (London, LAG, 2013) 17.

     d. exceptional funding;

     e. assessment of means.

  iii. Decisions relating to discharges of public funding certificates.

  iv. Decisions relating to costs and expenses.

(i) Decisions Relating to Tenders

There has been a raft of decisions looking at the process under which the then LSC   **9-4**
awarded contracts for the provision of publicly funded legal services:[2]

    i.   *R (Law Society) v LSC*[3] was a successful application relating to a tender for publicly funded family law services. The court found that the tendering process had been unfair and arbitrary. In a robust judgment the court went on to find that the failures identified in the process affected not only solicitors but also the wider public. Good administration demanded a fair competitive process.

    ii.   In *R (Public Interest Lawyers) v LSC*[4] a claim was brought by a number of firms who had previously held contracts to provide services in public law and mental health law. The application was granted in part. It was found that the LSC's verification of quality standards had been flawed. This meant that organisations might have gained contracts despite not meeting the supervision criteria (and vice versa). Importantly, as in many cases involving tender decisions, a challenge was made further to the equality duty. Here it was argued that the LSC failed to comply with the general disability equality duty contained in section 49A of the Disability Discrimination Act 1995. It was argued that the LSC had failed to assess the impact on patients in high-security hospitals who might now not be able to instruct their existing solicitors. It was found that the LSC had had regard to this, by considering the balance between continuity and quality of advice, and it had struck the balance in favour of continuity. In the same case the applicants applied for an injunction stopping the LSC entering into the contracts it had awarded until the outcome of the judicial review. This application for interim relief was rejected. Law firms who had been awarded contracts would suffer loss, having taken on premises and hired staff, but unable to open any cases. Notably, a protective costs order was made to ensure the lawfulness of the LSC's actions could be properly tested.

    iii. In *Hereward & Foster Ltd v LSC*[5] the applicants relied on the general equality duty under section 76A of the Sex Discrimination Act 1975. The firm applied for permission to judicially review the LSC's refusal to award it a contract for immigration new matter starts. The firm's sole immigration work supervisor was a woman who worked part-time. The tender awarded maximum points where the supervisor was in the office 100 per cent of the time. The firm argued the criterion was indirect sexual discrimination. Permission was refused. Bidders had almost a year between publication of the criteria and the deadline

---

[2] See also *R (Law Society) v LSC* [2007] EWCA Civ 1264, [2008] QB 737.
[3] *R (Law Society) v LSC* [2010] EWHC 2550 (Admin).
[4] *R (Public Interest Lawyers) v LSC* [2010] EWHC 3277 (Admin).
[5] *Hereward & Foster Ltd v LSC* [2010] EWHC 3370 (Admin).

to make arrangements and make good any deficit. There was nothing to show that the supervisor availability criterion had more of an effect on women as opposed to men, even if there were more women working part-time than men. In any event, ensuring high-quality supervision at all times was a proportionate means of achieving a legitimate aim.

iv.   In *R (Harrow Solicitors and Advocates) v LSC*[6] a firm challenged the decision not to award it an immigration contract. The firm had answered a question mistakenly, saying it did not carry out a drop-in session, when in reality it did. The firm followed the LSC's appeal procedure and corrected the error. The appeal was rejected and the firm sought judicial review, on the basis this was unreasonable and disproportionate. The application was unsuccessful. The court adopted a hard line. It held there was a need to maintain firm rules for the tendering process, and that correction of the error would have amounted to an impermissible change in the bid. In addition, when considering proportionality, a review was not to focus exclusively on the particular consequences for the failed tenderer, however severe.

v.   In *R (All About Rights Law Practice) v LSC*[7] a similar hard-line approach was endorsed. Here the firm accidentally submitted one blank form electronically. The accident was only spotted after the deadline when the LSC rejected the tender. The court confirmed that LSC's decision to reject the tender was a rational and proper one.

vi.   A similar issue arose in *R (Hoole and Co) v LSC*.[8] There, the firm had submitted the tender through an internet-based electronic portal, and some of the information had not saved properly. The question was whether the LSC was under a duty to tell the tenderer the application had arrived incomplete. It was held, on the evidence, that the failure was not a technical failure or inadequacy for which the LSC was responsible. It did not have a duty to inquire into other data held by the LSC or to alert the tenderer to defects in its submission.

vii.   In *R (Hossacks) v LSC*[9] a firm applied to judicially review the LSC's rejection of its tender. Bidders had to have an office in each area where services were to be delivered. The applicant firm did not. The court found the LSC were right to reject the tender accordingly.

(ii) Decisions Relating to Grants of Legal Aid

9-5 Once a firm has been awarded a contract to carry out publicly funded work, the next decision which logically falls to be considered is when should work actually be authorised.[10] Such challenges can again be considered thematically.

---

[6] *R (Harrow Solicitors and Advocates) v LSC* [2011] EWHC 1087 (Admin).
[7] *R (All About Rights Law Practice) v LSC* [2011] EWHC 964 (Admin).
[8] *R (Hoole and Co) v LSC* [2011] EWHC 886 (Admin).
[9] *R (Hossacks) v LSC* [2012] EWCA Civ 1203.
[10] For a recent challenge to a refusal of legal aid under the LASPO scheme in the context of immigration, see *R (Rrapaj) v Director of Legal Aid Casework* [2013] EWHC 1837 (Admin). An applicant should clearly identify, on the application form, the decision under challenge.

Standing (Challenges Concerning Grants of Legal Aid)

A fundamental question which has vexed the courts is the question of standing and its   **9-6**
interrelation with funding. In *R (Anderson) v LSC*[11] a group of claimants were looking to judicially review a planning decision. The LSC granted the claimants funding,
but conditional on the group providing a 50 per cent contribution to the legal costs.[12]
The group challenged the legality of this, arguing that it had not properly applied the
Funding Code criteria. The court found that applying the Funding Code, the following
'structured decision-taking process' applied. The following points emerge from the case.

i.   Having regard to the nature of the public interest, the LSC must decide whether
     there exists a reasonably ascertainable group of people who can reasonably be
     expected to contribute. If there is not such a group then it is obliged to fund. The
     greater the public interest the greater the constituency likely to be affected. It is
     important that the LSC correctly identify a group. This is a necessary prerequi-
     site in assessing contribution correctly.
ii. If there exists such a group which potentially might provide funding, the pre-
     sumption is that a broad starting point for that group's funding will be half the
     likely costs. However that will be varied in any given case, taking into account
     all the circumstances. These include the general financial resources of the
     ascertained group, and the nature of the benefits the group would gain from
     the action. The LSC will consider any information which is available on the
     ascertained group's general level of resources. Usually, it will not be necessary or
     practicable to assess each group member's means in detail.
iii. The LSC is likely to expect more private funding than half, where the group
     contains a significant number of people with substantial assets or where the
     litigation will produce direct financial benefit for the members of that group. It
     may accept less than half where the ascertained group is small or its members
     predominantly have limited means. The more intangible the benefit to the mem-
     bers of the group, the less substantial the contributions which can reasonably be
     expected. Lower levels of private funding could reasonably be expected in envi-
     ronmental challenges. Here the ascertained group was small. Its members were
     of limited means. The benefits were, to a great extent, intangible.
iv. The amount of contribution will normally be fixed at the beginning of the case,
     if possible by agreement, between the LSC and the solicitor. It is for the solicitor
     and clients to arrange the most appropriate method in time in which to raise the
     funds. Here, this did not happen. Instead, as proceedings progressed, the LSC
     embarked upon what was described as a 'highly detailed and intrusive' consider-
     ation of the means of each member of the group. The court found that the LSC's
     approach had been flawed. Whilst it could carry out such a detailed approach,
     this was the exception to the rule and it had not provided an adequate explana-
     tion or proper basis as to why it was necessary here. The claim for judicial review
     against the LSC was successful.

---

[11] *R (Anderson) v LSC* [2006] EWHC (Admin).
[12] See also *R (Burrows) v LSC* [2001] 2 FLR 998, [2001] EWCA Civ 205 where the Court of Appeal held
that the Legal Aid Act 1988 s 15(4) authorised financial limitations just as much as it authorised limitations
in scope.

A similar group litigation challenge arose in *R (Williams) v LSC*.[13] This concerned group litigation in relation to the MMR vaccine. The court had to consider when a party could be said to be 'directly affected' by a decision (*R (Muldoon) v Liverpool City Council*[14]). It was held on the facts that the applicant was not directly affected, and could not usefully contribute to the judicial review hearing. The applicant's public funding certificate had therefore been discharged lawfully.

Inquests (Challenges Concerning Grants of Legal Aid)

9-7   There is a long line of cases looking at where a refusal to grant legal aid might be said to be unlawful, and many of these have involved the state's obligation under Article 2 to proactively conduct an effective investigation into a death in custody.

   R (Humberstone) v LSC[15] concerned the LSC's refusal to recommend public funding for the mother of a 10-year-old boy. He had died in the care of health professionals following an asthma attack. She wanted representation to attend an inquest. The coroner supported the mother's application for funding. It was anticipated health professionals would blame her for her son's death. She had limited intellectual ability. The High Court quashed the LSC's refusal, and the LSC appealed to the Court of Appeal. The Court of Appeal dismissed the LSC's appeal. The court held that in relation to Article 2 inquests, the Lord Chancellor's guidance on funding was less than satisfactory since it focused on the needs of the coroner, not the family; and there seemed to be a presumption against representation and an overlooking of the right of the family to question witnesses.

   The decision can be contrasted with the earlier case of *R (Jones) v LSC*.[16] Here again the coroner had indicated that he considered it essential in the interests of justice that the applicant, a parent of the deceased, was represented. The court considered *R (Khan) v Secretary of State for Health*[17] and held it was clear the test was whether there were exceptional circumstances. It was held that here there were not exceptional factual or legal issues, the coroner's view was not determinative, and there was nothing irrational in the LSC's approach.

   In *R (Challender) v LSC*[18] the family sought representation at an inquest. They feared that the deceased had been unlawfully killed by an injection of heroin administered by a third party. The court held that the LSC's refusal had been appropriate. The death had been before the Human Rights Act (HRA) 1998 came into force. But in any event, there had been no error in the LSC's approach.

---

[13] *R (Williams) v LSC* [2004] EWHC 163 (Admin).
[14] *R (Muldoon) v Liverpool City Council* [1996] 1 WLR 1103.
[15] *R (Humberstone) v LSC* [2011] 1 WLR 1460, [2010] EWCA Civ 1479.
[16] *R (Jones) v LSC* [2007] EWHC 2106 (Admin), [2007] Inquest LR 197.
[17] *R (Khan) v Secretary of State for Health* [2004] 1 WLR 971, [2003] EWCA Civ 1129.
[18] *R (Challender) v LSC* [2004] EWHC 925 (Admin), [2004] Inquest LR 58.

Article 6 (Challenges Concerning Grants of Legal Aid)

Article 6 of ECHR (the right to a fair trial) has also frequently featured in challenges **9-8**
to refusals of public funding.[19] In *R (Jarrett) v LSC*[20] the court considered *X v United
Kingdom*,[21] which held:

> Only in exceptional circumstances, namely where the withholding of legal aid would make the
> assertion of a civil claim practically impossible, or where it would lead to an obvious unfairness
> of the proceedings, can such a right be invoked by virtue of Article 6(1) of the Convention.

Accordingly, it was held that the Lord Chancellor's guidance would only be lawful if it
complied with this. This led to the inclusion of an exceptionality provision within the
LSC's guidance.

This test of practical impossibility or obvious unfairness set out in *X v UK* has been
the subject of some controversy. For whatever reason *X v UK* has not been cited with
approval by the European Court of Human Rights (ECtHR) itself in a number of
subsequent cases.

In *PC & S v UK*[22] the court observed that when considering whether or not there
has been an interference with Article 8 (the right to respect to private and family life) it
was important to bear in mind there is an implicit procedural requirement to any such
interference. The 'decision making process involved in measures of interference must be
fair.' The case concerned the removal of a child from its mother who had been adjudged
to suffer from Munchhausen's syndrome.

In the long running so called McLibel case of *Steel and Morris v UK*[23] the court held
that the right of access to a court was 'not absolute' and 'may be subject to restrictions'
but it did not endorse the restrictions suggested by *X v UK*.

In *AK & L v Croatia*[24] the court again affirmed that a decision making process in an
Article 8 interference must be fair. There a breach of Article 8 was found after a mother
with a mild mental disability, speech impediment and limited vocabulary had to attend
unrepresented in a hearing to divest her of her parental rights to her son.

Conversely there have been a number of domestic authorities which , at least implicitly, appear to have endorsed the approach of *X v UK*.[25] This tension has recently been
considered by the High Court.[26] In light of the foregoing, it is submitted it would appear
that if a party is not able to present all necessary evidence and engage with the process
such that a court cannot do what is required of it, there will be obvious unfairness and
a breach of Article 6 without legal aid.

---

[19] It is outside the scope of this chapter to provide a comprehensive survey of the jurisprudence on legal
aid and Art 6 of the ECHR and Art 47 (right to an effective remedy and a fair trial) of the EU Charter of
Fundamental Rights.

[20] *R (Jarrett) v LSC* [2001] EWHC Admin 389, [2002] ACD 25.

[21] *X v United Kingdom* [1984] 6 EHRR 136.

[22] *PC & S v UK* (2002) 35 EHRR 1075, at para 119 (1107).

[23] *Steel and Morris v UK* [2005] 41 EHRR 22 at para 62 (428).

[24] *AK & L v Croatia* (App No 37965/11) (Judgment 8 January 2013).

[25] *R (Jarrett) v Legal Services Commission* [2001] EWHC Admin 389; *Pine v Law Society* [2001] EWCA Civ
154; *Holder v Law Society* [2003] 1 WLR 1059.

[26] See *Gudanaviciene and others v Director of Legal Aid Casework* [2014] EWHC 1840 (Admin)—judgment
handed down after the law cut off date for the purposes of this edition.

In *R (Chaney) v LSC*[27] it was argued that the levels of funding for representation by counsel in confiscation proceedings were so low that they effectively denied the right of access to justice provided for by Article 6. The applicant applied for a declaration of incompatibility in relation to Schedule 4 of the Criminal Defence Service (Funding) Order 2001 (SI 2001/855). The court refused. It was held that it would be premature to make any such declaration where the proceedings before the Crown Court had not even happened. The Crown Court stayed the proceedings until representation was obtained, and the matter could then be revisited.

In *R (Taylor) v Westminster Magistrates' Court*[28] the claimant applied to challenge the decision of a district judge in the magistrates' court. The applicant wanted the district judge to extend a representation order to include representation by an advocate in confiscation proceedings. The district judge held that he did not have jurisdiction to so extend the representation order. The High Court agreed. In relation to Article 6 the court considered in detail the jurisprudence on the equality of arms principle in *Croissant v Germany*[29] and *Re Attorney General's Reference (No 82a of 2000)*[30] and held that, in short, the state did not have to write a blank cheque.

Exceptional Funding (Challenges Concerning Grants of Legal Aid)[31]

9-9 In *R (Viggers) v LSC*[32] the High Court held that the LSC had acted unlawfully in refusing to recommend exceptional funding for an appeal to the First Tier Tribunal of the War Pensions and Armed Forces Compensation Chamber. This was a complex case following a remittal from the Court of Appeal. The LSC said the remittal did not make it complicated, but in fact made it more simple, because the tribunal had now been directed on the legal issues. The High Court disagreed. The Tribunal's decision had already been quashed twice on essentially the same reasoning, which was highly unusual, and the litigation was complex. The case provides an interesting illustration of what is required for litigation to be sufficiently complex to constitute exceptional funding.

In *R (G) v LSC*[33] the LSC refused public funding for a proposed action in negligence against a public authority. The applicant was 15 and had been remanded into the care of the local authority. Despite repeated requests from professionals and the applicant's mother, the local authority failed to place him in secure accommodation. He was seriously injured whilst driving a stolen car. Under the guidance then in force the LSC was authorised to provide funding where a public authority had allegedly i) committed a serious wrongdoing, ii) breached a duty or power, or iii) significantly breached human rights. The LSC did not consider that there was 'serious wrongdoing', because the local authority had not acted deliberately, maliciously or dishonestly. The High Court rejected this approach. A dereliction of duty could be inadvertent yet still grossly negligent.

---

[27] *R (Chaney) v LSC* [2008] EWHC 3239 (Admin).
[28] *R (Taylor) v Westminster Magistrates' Court* [2009] EWHC 1498 (Admin), (2009) 173 JP 405.
[29] *Croissant v Germany* (1993) 16 EHRR 135.
[30] *Re Attorney General's Reference (No 82a of 2000)*, [2002] EWCA Crim 215, [2002] 2 Cr App R 24.
[31] As above, the most recent, and noteworthy, challenge to the refusal to grant exceptional funding is the case of *Gudanaviciene* (n 26)—judgment handed down after the law cut off date for the purposes of this edition.
[32] *R (Viggers) v LSC* [2011] EWHC 2221 (Admin).
[33] *R (G) v LSC* [2004] PIQR P26, [2004] EWHC 276 (Admin).

David Ball

Assessment of Means (Challenges Concerning Grants of Legal Aid)

There is a further line of authorities challenging refusals not based on the merits, but on the assessment of means. In *R (Southwark Law Centre) v LSC*[34] the court considered in detail the provisions governing determination of disposable income. Disposable income is calculated by looking at an applicant's gross income and then subtracting any 'net rent payable' in respect of their main dwelling. The LSC argued that they could take into account any sums that were actually paid. This would have meant that the applicants had more disposable income, and would have been ineligible for public funding. The High Court disagreed with the LSC's approach. The draftsman was alive to the difference between payable and paid, and it would be tantamount to rewriting the regulation if it applied only to rent paid.

9-10

(iii) Decisions Relating to Discharge of Public Funding

There have been considerably less challenges relating to discharging a public funding certificate, as opposed to a refusal to grant in the first place. However, the authorities do provide some helpful principles. For example in *R (Toth) v LSC*[35] it was held that the LSC's Funding Review Committee can apply a matrix requirement of the ratio of likely damages to costs when considering whether to discharge a certificate.

9-11

R (Batemen) v LSC[36] was a successful challenge. Here the LSC had decided not merely to discharge a certificate, but actually to revoke it.[37] Even though the applicant had failed to disclose material changes in his income it was held that the LSC's decision was flawed because it had failed to provide adequate reasons, particularly given the absence of any proof of dishonesty.

In *R (Alliss) v LSC*[38] it was found that the LSC had acted unlawfully by withdrawing funding very close to trial. In particular, the court found that there was a breach of Article 6(1):

> I do not believe it is realistic to suggest that this claimant, even aided by a McKenzie friend, and even with the benefit of bundles and so forth having been prepared, would be able to conduct the proposed trial. I reach this conclusion by applying the principles which the European Court of Human Rights stated in *Airey v Ireland* [(1979) 2 EHRR 305] and *P, C and S v United Kingdom* [(56547/00); (2002) 35 EHRR 31].

The background to the case was a very serious neighbour dispute. The claimant's father was killed and the claimant ended up being seriously injured. The claimant brought civil proceedings against the defendants for unlawfully killing his father and for injuring him. Two weeks before the trial the LSC sent letters to the claimant's solicitors inviting them to show cause why the legal aid certificate should not be discharged. The LSC highlighted that the prospects of success were moderate, costs were substantially higher than the

---

[34] *R (Southwark Law Centre) v LSC* [2008] 1 WLR 1368, [2007] EWHC 1715 (Admin).
[35] *R (Toth) v LSC* [2002] EWHC 5 (Admin).
[36] *R (Batemen) v LSC* [2001] EWHC Admin 682.
[37] See *R (Machi) v LSC* [2002] 1 WLR 983, [2001] EWCA Civ 2010 on the distinction between embargo, revocation and discharge. The Court of Appeal found the LSC had no power to embargo a full legal aid certificate where revocation or discharge was being considered.
[38] *R (Alliss) v LSC* [2002] EWHC 2079 (Admin), [2003] ACD 16.

likely damages, and there was doubt about the defendants' ability to meet any judgment. The court found there was a breach of Article 6(1) having regard to the facts that:

  i.   the claimant was a young man with psychiatric problems, apparently brought on by the horrific circumstances in which his father was killed;

 ii.   he had limited education, having left school at the age of 15;

iii.   he faced representing himself at a three-week trial involving leading counsel paid by the LSC for one of the defendants; and

 iv.   where there was expert evidence and complex issues of fact and law.

(iv) Decisions Relating to Costs and Disbursements

9-12   In *R (Law Society of England and Wales) v Lord Chancellor*[39] the Law Society sought to judicially review the Lord Chancellor's decision to abolish the fee paid for committal proceedings. The application was unsuccessful. It was found that the work was still remunerated by virtue of other work in the magistrates' court and Crown Court in any such committal proceedings. It was not made out that the Lord Chancellor had failed to take into account any relevant factors such as the need to secure the provision of legal representation.

In *R (T) v Legal Aid Agency*[40] the High Court held that it was unreasonable for the LAA to refuse to grant prior authority for an expert report that a district judge had considered necessary, in particular given the LAA's failure to provide any reasons.

C. The Criminal Cases Review Commission

(1) Introduction

9-13   The Criminal Cases Review Commission (CCRC) became operative in March 1997. It was established by section 8 of the Criminal Appeal Act 1995. In the words of its website, its purpose is to 'review possible miscarriages of justice in the criminal courts of England, Wales and Northern Ireland and refer appropriate cases to the appeal courts'.

The CCRC consists of a minimum of 11 members. At least a third of these must be legally qualified and at least two-thirds must have knowledge or experience of the criminal justice system. There are currently 11 members, or commissioners.

Broadly speaking, since the CCRC was established it has considered in the region of 15,000 applications for referrals to the Court of Appeal. Of those 15,000, the CCRC has rejected approximately 14,500 as ineligible. The CCRC has so far referred 512 cases to the Court of Appeal, of which:

  i.   466 cases were heard by the Court of Appeal;

 ii.   328 convictions/sentences were quashed by the Court of Appeal; and

iii.   138 convictions/sentences were upheld by the Court of Appeal.[41]

---

[39] *R (Law Society of England and Wales) v Lord Chancellor* [2012] EWHC 794 (Admin), [2012] 3 Costs LR 558.

[40] *R (T) v Legal Aid Agency* [2013] EWHC 960 (Admin), [2013] Fam Law 805.

[41] www.justice.gov.uk/about/criminal-cases-review-commission.

David Ball

There have been approximately 18 reported judicial reviews of decisions of the CCRC. Invariably it is the CCRC's refusal to refer a matter to the Court of Appeal which becomes the subject of a challenge by way of judicial review.

(2) General Principles

Under section 9(1) of the Criminal Appeal Act 1995 (the 1995 Act), where a person has **9-14** been convicted of an offence on indictment in England and Wales, then the CCRC may at any time refer the conviction to the Court of Appeal. Equally, they may at any time refer to the Court of Appeal any sentence (other than one which has been fixed by law), which relates to a conviction.

The criteria for making any such reference are set out in section 13 of the 1995 Act. Section 13 prescribes the following conditions:

(1)—(a) the Commission consider that there is a real possibility that the conviction, verdict, finding or sentence would not be upheld were the reference to be made,
(b) the Commission so consider—
(i) in the case of a conviction, verdict or finding, because of an argument, or evidence, not raised in the proceedings which led to it or on any appeal or application for leave to appeal against it, or
(ii) in the case of a sentence, because of an argument on a point of law, or information, not so raised, and
(c) an appeal against the conviction, verdict, finding or sentence has been determined or leave to appeal against it has been refused.

(2) Nothing in subsection (1)(b)(i) or (c) shall prevent the making of a reference if it appears to the Commission that there are exceptional circumstances which justify making it.

In summary, if the CCRC considers that there is a 'real possibility' the Court of Appeal would not uphold a conviction or sentence, then they make a reference to the Court of Appeal.

In *R v Criminal Cases Review Commission, ex parte Pearson* Lord Bingham LCJ held: **9-15**

The exercise of the power to refer accordingly depends on the judgment of the Commission, and it cannot be too strongly emphasised that this is a judgment entrusted to the Commission and to no one else. Save in exceptional circumstances, the judgment must be made by the Commission, in a conviction case, on the ground of an argument or evidence which has not been before the court before, whether at trial, on application for leave to appeal or on appeal. In the absence of such exceptional circumstances, the Commission cannot therefore invite the court to review issues or evidence upon which there has already been a ruling. Resort to the Commission must ordinarily follow and not precede resort to the Court of Appeal.[42]

(3) Principles on Challenging Refusal of CCRC: *Ex p Pearson*

Ex p Pearson is the leading case on principles relating to judicial review challenges of a **9-16** CCRC refusal to refer a case to the Court of Appeal.[43]

---

[42] *R v Criminal Cases Review Commission, ex parte Pearson* [1999] 3 All ER 498, [2000] 1 Cr App R 141, 149.
[43] See also in Chapter 1 at 1-6.

Ms Pearson had been found guilty of murder. The victim was her ex-husband's new partner. At trial, her defence had been that she had not done it and it must have been her ex-husband. After conviction she admitted the murder. She relied upon a detailed psychiatric report as fresh evidence. This report suggested that at the time of the killing her responsibility was impaired by an underlying personality disorder, and aggravated by 'battered woman' syndrome. The CCRC refused to refer the case to the Court of Appeal. The CCRC decided that there was no likelihood the Court of Appeal would receive the fresh evidence and that it was unlikely the Court of Appeal would conclude the applicant was suffering from diminished responsibility at the time of the offence. The applicant judicially reviewed the refusal to refer the case to the Court of Appeal.

Lord Bingham LCJ gave the judgment. First, he considered section 23 of the Criminal Appeal Act 1968 on admitting fresh evidence:

(1)   For the purposes of this Part of this Act the Court of Appeal may, if they think it necessary or expedient in the interests of justice—
   (a)   ...
   (b)   ...
   (c)   receive any evidence which was not adduced in the proceedings from which the appeal lies.
(2)   The Court of Appeal shall, in considering whether to receive any evidence, have regard in particular to—
   (a)   whether the evidence appears to the court to be capable of belief;
   (b)   whether it appears to the court that the evidence may afford any ground for allowing the appeal;
   (c)   whether the evidence would have been admissible in the proceedings from which the appeal lies on an issue which is the subject of the appeal; and,
   (d)   whether there is a reasonable explanation for the failure to adduce the evidence in those proceedings.

Ms Pearson argued that if the job of the CCRC was to decide what evidence the Court of Appeal would accept, then they had usurped the function of the Court of Appeal. She argued that the CCRC had inappropriately applied the section 13 test as to whether there was a 'real possibility' of the Court of Appeal quashing the decision. The Divisional Court disagreed.

Lord Bingham LCJ said that:

The judgment required of the Commission is a very unusual one, because it inevitably involves a prediction of the view which another body (the Court of Appeal) may take. In a case which is likely to turn on the willingness of the Court of Appeal to receive fresh evidence, the Commission must also make a judgment how, on all the facts of a given case, the Court of Appeal is likely to resolve an application to adduce that evidence under section 23, because there could in such a case be no real possibility that the conviction would not be upheld were the reference to be made unless there were also a real possibility that the Court of Appeal would receive the evidence in question.[44]

---

[44]   *Ex p Pearson* (n 42) 150.

Thus, in a conviction case where fresh evidence is being relied upon, the CCRC has to ask itself two questions:

i.   Is there a real possibility that the Court of Appeal will receive the fresh evidence?
ii. If so, is there a real possibility that the Court of Appeal will not uphold the conviction?

In considering the nature of the 'real possibility' threshold, the court held that it 'plainly denotes a contingency which, in the Commission's judgment, is more than an outside chance or a bare possibility, but which may be less than a probability or a likelihood or a racing certainty'.[45] The court commented that it is not for the CCRC to 'mechanically' refer 'all but the most obviously threadbare cases'. This would overburden the Court of Appeal. But equally it was not for the CCRC to only refer cases 'assured' of success. This could potentially deprive deserving applicants of a potential appeal, and would render the purpose of the CCRC redundant. The CCRC is there to act as a meaningful filter. The CCRC simply have to decide whether there is a real possibility of fresh evidence being admitted and/or a conviction quashed.

On the question of whether the CCRC had usurped the role of the Court of Appeal, the court commented as follows:

> If one wants to predict what a reasonable person, on given facts and subject to a measure of guidance, would decide, there is no rational way to approach that task otherwise than by considering what, on the same facts and subject to the same guidance, one would decide oneself. That is not to usurp the decision of that other person but to set about predicting his decision in a rational way. In our view the Commission stated and also applied the right test, fully conscious of the respective roles of the Commission and the Court of Appeal.[46]

It is quite right for the CCRC to ask itself whether it thinks there is a realistic possibility that a conviction would be quashed. Provided the CCRC applies the same guidance as the Court of Appeal would, there is no problem with this approach. It follows that a considerable degree of deference is given to a decision of the CCRC when it comes to any challenge by way of judicial review. Far from the CCRC usurping the role of the Court of Appeal, the court said that it would be usurping the role of the CCRC if it decided to substitute its own decision just because it did not agree with it. The situation has a potential analogue with a line of cases in the immigration context considering the proper approach to consideration of a fresh claim. In *R (YH) v Secretary of State for the Home Department*[47] the Court of Appeal held that the Secretary of State, much like the CCRC under section 13, is 'acting simply as the gate-keeper to a process leading to a possible appeal'.[48] The Secretary of State, like the CCRC is quite properly, simply, 'standing in his or her own shoes in deciding this threshold question'.

The judgment in *Ex p Pearson* concludes:

> If this court were to hold that a decision one way or the other was objectively right or objectively wrong, it would be exceeding its function. The Divisional Court will ensure that the Commission acts lawfully. That is its only role.[49]

9-17

9-18

---

[45] ibid, 149.
[46] ibid, 168.
[47] *R (YH) v Secretary of State for the Home Department* [2010] EWCA Civ 116, [2010] 4 All ER 448.
[48] ibid [16].
[49] *Ex p Pearson* (n 42) 171.

This is the test the Divisional Court will adopt on a challenge to a decision of the CCRC. The court commented that it was not for the Divisional Court to subject the CCRC's decision to a 'rigorous audit' to establish whether they were open to legal criticism. Instead:

> The real test must be to ask whether the reasons given by the Commission betray, to a significant extent, any of the defects which entitle a court of review to interfere.[50]

Ex p Pearson has therefore set the bar for judicial review challenges to CCRC decisions. It is a bar which has been subsequently considered on a number of occasions.

(4) Developments in CCRC Challenges

9-19 Subsequent decisions of the Administrative Court have emphasised that there is a high bar for a successful application to judicially review a refusal of the CCRC. *R (Cleeland) v Criminal Cases Review Commission*[51] stated that there is a 'very high threshold that has to be crossed' to quash a decision of the CCRC.[52]

In *R v Criminal Cases Review Commission, ex parte Hunt*[53] the Administrative Court indicated that the courts should not allow the CCRC to be 'sucked into judicial review proceedings':

> It is to be remembered that the Commission only becomes involved after the exercise by an applicant to the Commission of his rights in the court below and, if he seeks this, on appeal. It is a residual, but a very important jurisdiction which the Commission exercises. It imposes a heavy burden on the Commission. It is a jurisdiction which was previously exercised by the Home Secretary. It is a jurisdiction which requires the Commission carefully to exercise the discretion which it is given by Parliament. In these circumstances it is important that the courts should not in inappropriate cases allow the Commission to be sucked into judicial review proceedings which are bound to distract it from fulfilling its statutory role.[54]

Hunt concerned a conviction for conspiring to cheat the Inland Revenue. The CCRC refused to refer the matter to the Court of Appeal. The claimant challenged that decision on the basis that the prosecution was a nullity, because the Revenue had brought it without the consent of the Attorney General. His challenge was unsuccessful.

9-20 It should be recalled that in the event of a refusal of permission for judicial review, following an oral hearing, there is no right of appeal against that refusal to the Court of Appeal. This is because of section 18(1)(a) of the Senior Courts Act 1981. This provides that the Court of Appeal has no jurisdiction to hear an appeal from the Divisional Court in 'any criminal cause or matter'. An appeal from a decision of the Divisional Court

---

[50] ibid, 169.

[51] *R (Cleeland) v Criminal Cases Review Commission* [2009] EWHC 474.

[52] The court noted that granting permission on paper was likely to raise the hopes of a defendant, and that an alternative might be to adjourn the permission decision to an oral hearing. However, note that these cases are treated as criminal causes or matters meaning that there is no further remedy to a refusal of permission. Because of this, applicants may wish to retain their two chances to persuade a judge (ie on the papers and, if unsuccessful, at an oral hearing) rather than relying only on the oral hearing. See the permission stage explained above at 2-30.

[53] *R v Criminal Cases Review Commission, ex parte Hunt* [2001] QB 1108, [2001] 2 WLR 319.

[54] ibid, 1114.

David Ball

refusing to grant permission against a CCRC refusal to refer is an appeal relating to a 'criminal cause or matter'.[55]

R (Mills) v Criminal Cases Review Commission[56] was an unsuccessful judicial review. **9-21** Yet exceptionally it still resulted in a recommendation that the Court of Appeal might find the conviction unsafe. There was an attempt to argue that it would be wrong for the Court of Appeal to be overly deferential to the CCRC. It was suggested that unlike challenges to other public bodies, here the Divisional Court were reviewing a decision about how the Court of Appeal itself would actually act in any given case. It was argued that the court would be particularly well placed, over and above any public body, to decide any such decision. This challenge was rejected. It was held to be 'not consistent with the proper approach to judicial review'.[57] It was reiterated that it was not for the court to 'fall into the trap' of deciding for itself what the Court of Appeal would do, and whether the CCRC's decision was right or wrong.

Mills concerned a case of murder. Following a libel trial the second officer in charge was found (on the balance of probabilities) to have perverted the course of justice, or committed perjury, or both. The CCRC refused a reference because, in summary, the matters sought to be relied on had already been considered by the Court of Appeal. The Divisional Court found that the CCRC had, 'given this case the most exhaustive and detailed consideration and have come to their conclusion having properly directed themselves as to the relevant considerations'. The court found the decision was 'perfectly logical' and was not legally flawed.[58] The court therefore refused the application for judicial review. However, it took the rare and exceptional course nonetheless of expressing the view that this was a case where the Court of Appeal could have a doubt about the safety of the convictions. The court left it to the CCRC to decide what weight if any to attach to this view.

R (Farnell) v Criminal Cases Review Commission[59] was a successful application for **9-22** judicial review. The case concerned a conviction for murder and the judge's direction on provocation. The claimant relied on a development in the law on provocation following *R v Smith (Morgan)*.[60] There was also fresh evidence from three of the four psychiatrists who had given evidence at the trial. The case provides one of the relatively rare examples where the Divisional Court found that 'the Commission has misunderstood the role of the Court of Appeal'.[61] The Divisional Court commented that in fresh evidence cases it was not for the Court of Appeal to 'fall into the temptation of converting itself into a jury'. The court found that the CCRC had fallen into this trap. The court also found that the jury would have received a very different direction as a result of *Smith*. The case was remitted back to the CCRC to make a fresh decision in light of the directions of the Divisional Court.

---

[55] *R (Saxon) v Criminal Cases Review Commission* [2001] EWCA Civ 1384. See above at 1-168.
[56] *R (Mills) v Criminal Cases Review Commission* [2001] EWHC Admin 1153.
[57] ibid, [14].
[58] ibid [110].
[59] *R (Farnell) v Criminal Cases Review Commission* [2003] EWHC 835 (Admin).
[60] *R v Smith (Morgan)* [2001] 1 AC 146.
[61] *Farnell* (n 59) [38].

R (Westlake) v Criminal Cases Review Commission[62] was an unusual case. The defendant had been found guilty of the death of his daughter, and sentenced to the death penalty in 1950. His wife had also been murdered, and this count had been ordered to lie on his file. After his execution, the defendant's neighbour confessed to the killing of the wife. The defendant was therefore posthumously granted a free pardon for both offences. After his death and posthumous pardon, his half sister applied to the CCRC seeking a referral to the Court of Appeal 'to correct the slur on his character'. The CCRC refused. The subsequent judicial review was unsuccessful. The Divisional Court commented that the CCRC had to take into account relevant consideration, and that considerations of cost were relevant in relation to posthumous cases.

9-23   In *Dowsett v Criminal Cases Review Commission*[63] the Divisional Court held and applied that not every breach of Article 6 of ECHR meant that there would be doubts about the safety of a conviction.

D. The Independent Police Complaints Commission

(1) Introduction

9-24   The Independent Police Complaints Commission (IPCC) started work in April 2004. It was established by the Police Reform Act 2002 (the 2002 Act). Before the IPCC was established, the Police Complaints Authority dealt with complaints about the police. The Police Complaints Authority had been created out of the Police and Criminal Evidence Act (PACE) 1984. There had been longstanding criticism of the Police Complaints Authority and the regime dealing with police complaints. In September 1997 the European Committee for the Prevention of Torture or Degrading Treatment or Punishment published a report with fairly damning conclusions. It described how under the Police Complaints Authority the police maintained a 'firm grip upon the handling of complaints against them', and retained 'substantial' influence over whether criminal or disciplinary proceedings would be initiated against them.[64] It was against this background that the IPCC was eventually established.

The IPCC is currently made up of a chair (technically appointed by the Queen) and at least five other members (technically appointed by the Secretary of State). Subsection 9(3) of the 2002 Act provides in effect that a person cannot be appointed a chair or member of the IPCC if they have previously worked for the police.

---

[62] *R (Westlake) v Criminal Cases Review Commission* [2004] EWHC 2779 (Admin).

[63] *Dowsett v Criminal Cases Review Commission* [2007] EWHC 1923 (Admin).

[64] Report to the United Kingdom Government on the visit to the United Kingdom and the Isle of Man carried out by the European Committee for the Prevention of Torture and Inhuman or Degrading Treatment or Punishment (CPT) from 8 to 17 September 1997, paras 48–49.

(2) General Principles

The key provisions setting out the powers and role of the IPCC are contained in Part 2   **9-25**
and Schedule 3 of the 2002 Act. Section 10 sets out the general functions of the IPCC.
These include at subsection 10(1)(d): 'to secure that public confidence is established and
maintained in the existence of suitable arrangements with respect to [its duties as set
out in section 10(2)]'. Schedule 3 sets out in detail the applicable rules for the handling
of complaints and conduct matters. The starting point is that there is a duty to preserve
evidence relating to complaints:

1   Duties to preserve evidence relating to complaints

(1)   Where a complaint is made about the conduct of a chief officer, it shall be the duty of the
       local policing body maintaining his force to secure that all such steps as are appropriate
       for the purposes of Part 2 of this Act are taken, both initially and from time to time after
       that, for obtaining and preserving evidence relating to the conduct complained of.

At the same time as dealing with complaints, the IPCC has a statutory duty to potentially investigate certain types of incident which are referred to it. These incidents are
known as 'recordable conduct matters' and include, for example when someone has died
or been seriously injured following direct or indirect contact with the police or similar
body exercising police-like powers (Schedule 3, Parts 2 and 2A and following).
    The Police and Social Responsibility Act 2011 introduced further changes to the
police complaints system. For interaction with complaints against the police, see above
at 4-2.

(3) Decisions Subject to Challenge

The sorts of IPCC decision that have been the subject of challenge are: **9-26**

i.   decisions not to carry out an investigation;
ii.   decisions not to record a complaint;
iii.   decisions refusing to direct or recommend disciplinary proceedings; and
iv.   decisions refusing to direct a chief officer to prevent collusion.

(4) Exhausting Alternative Remedies

As far as these various types of decision are concerned, regard must be had to the Police   **9-27**
(Complaints and Misconduct) Regulations 2012 (SI 2012/1204). Of essential importance is regulation 11, which provides for a right of appeal against certain decisions.
This appeal right will need to be exhausted before any judicial review can be contemplated against such a decision. The right of appeal attaches to the following decisions
(contained within Schedule 3 of the Police Reform Act 2002):

i.   Appeal against a failure to notify or record a complaint (paragraph 3(3)).
ii.   Appeal against a decision to handle a complaint otherwise than in accordance
       with the Schedule or take no action in relation to it (paragraph 7(8)).

iii.   Appeal against the outcome of a complaint subjected to local resolution or handled otherwise than in accordance with the Schedule (paragraph 8A(1)).

iv.   Appeal against a decision to discontinue an investigation (paragraph 21(7)).

v.   Appeal in relation to an investigation (paragraph 25(2)).

A claimant has 28 days after the date of the letter notifying them of their right to appeal. Importantly, this 28-day time limit does not run from the date of receipt or even the deemed receipt. It actually runs from the date of the letter itself. But time can still be extended where it is just. In *R (Burke) v IPCC* Richards LJ said this:

> If the complainant acted promptly once notification was received I would expect it normally to be a decisive factor, sufficient to establish that in the special circumstances of the case it is just to extend time (to use the language of regulation 10(8).[65]

Once any such appeal or alternative remedy has been exhausted, it is open to a claimant to apply for judicial review.

(5)   Grounds of Review[66]

9-28   There have been approximately 40 reported judgments involving the IPCC. The normal judicial review principles apply, of illegality, irrationality and procedural impropriety and associated heads of claim.

(i)   Illegality

9-29   As in any public law context, a decision by the IPCC will be amenable to judicial review if it is unlawful.

Of particular relevance in the context of decisions of the IPCC is the existence of the local resolution process. This procedure is only available for certain complaints. These are complaints which have been recorded and which are not of such a kind that they need to be automatically or voluntarily referred to the IPCC.[67] In broad overview, the local resolution process is designed for less serious complaints. It cannot result in disciplinary proceedings, but it may result in management action (for example under unsatisfactory performance procedures or capability procedures). In order to be suitable for the local resolution process the appropriate authority must be satisfied that:

i.   the conduct that is being complained about (even if it were proved) would not justify bringing criminal or disciplinary proceedings against the person whose conduct is complained about; and

ii.   the conduct complained about (even if it were proved) would not involve the infringement of a person's rights under Article 2 or 3 of ECHR.

---

[65]   *R (Burke) v IPCC* [2011] EWCA Civ 1665 [31].

[66]   Grounds of review more generally are analysed in detail in Chapter 1. See specific examples of challenges to the IPCC in that chapter at 1-101.

[67]   See the Police Reform Act 2002, Sch 3, paras 6–9.

This assessment should be made taking the complaint at face value.[68] There is a right of appeal to the IPCC against the outcome of a decision through the local resolution process.

Importantly, under paragraph 8(3) of Schedule 3 of the 2002 Act a statement made by any person for the purposes of a local resolution process is not admissible in any subsequent disciplinary proceedings. This is to encourage frankness. The issue which arose in *R (M) v IPCC*[69] was whether a statement that was made before a decision to embark on the local resolution process, would also be inadmissible in disciplinary proceedings. Her judicial review claim was dismissed. However, Bean J commented obiter that statements made before or after the local resolution process can and should be considered by the IPCC.[70] It follows that a decision of the IPCC may be unlawful if it relies on a statement made during a local resolution process. Equally, a decision may be unlawful if it fails to rely on a statement made before the process has begun or once it has concluded.

9-30

A further illustration of the illegality principle is *R (North Yorkshire Police Authority) v IPCC*.[71] Somewhat unusually, this was an application for judicial review by the police authority against the IPCC. The question was whether a refusal by a chief police officer to investigate a matter was a complaint about the chief police officer's 'conduct' or about the chief police officer's 'direction and control' of the force. If it was a complaint about his conduct then it had to be recorded, but it did not have to be recorded if it was considered a complaint about his direction and control. The court held that it did amount to a complaint about the chief police officer's conduct. Conduct did not just mean bad conduct. The IPCC had not acted unlawfully by considering this was a recordable conduct matter.

9-31

In *R (Reynolds) v IPCC*[72] the question of the power and legality of the IPCC's decision was directly in issue. The case concerned a death in custody, and a question as to whether this was caused by something which happened whilst in police custody or before. The IPCC argued that they did not have the power to investigate matters that might have happened before the police became involved. The Court of Appeal rejected this submission. They held that the IPCC had to also look at what happened before the conduct of the police, in order to be able to rule in or out whether or not the police conduct caused the death. It is not that it would have been unlawful for the IPCC to investigate what happened before because they had insufficient power. It would have been unlawful for them not to investigate what happened before.

In *R (Salimi) v Secretary of State for the Home Department*[73] the Court of Appeal stated that the IPCC did not have jurisdiction to investigate complaints of assault by a failed asylum-seeker against escorts exercising functions under the Immigration and Asylum Act 1999. The claimant had the alternative remedy of referring the matter to the Prisons Ombudsman.

In *R (Chief Constable of West Yorkshire) v Independent Police Complaints Commission*[74] the legality of the language used in a report by the IPCC was itself the subject of challenge. A police officer stopped an individual he suspected of speeding. The driver

9-32

---

68 IPCC Statutory Guidance 2013, para 5.11
69 *R (M) v IPCC* [2012] EWHC 2071 (Admin).
70 ibid [32].
71 *R (North Yorkshire Police Authority) v IPCC* [2010] EWHC 1690 (Admin), [2011] 3 All ER 106.
72 *R (Reynolds) v IPCC* [2008] EWCA Civ 1160, [2009] 3 All ER 237.
73 *R (Salimi) v Secretary of State for the Home Department* [2012] EWCA Civ 422.
74 *R (Chief Constable of West Yorkshire) v Independent Police Complaints Commission* [2013] EWHC 2698 (Admin).

and officer then got into an argument. The officer used his baton (causing a permanent injury to the driver's thumb) and CS spray. He arrested the driver for a public order offence, but the CPS subsequently dropped the charge. The driver complained to the IPCC that the officer's conduct had been oppressive. The IPCC completed a report which upheld the driver's complaint. Importantly, the IPCC also set out that in their view the arrest of the driver had been unlawful. The report concludes:

> Based on the fact the arrest was unlawful, the use of CS spray was not necessary or reasonable in these circumstances. Therefore, on the balance of probabilities the use of force used by PC Armstrong amounts to an assault.[75]

The case was referred to the CPS to consider prosecuting the officer for assault. In the event the CPS decided there was insufficient evidence for such a prosecution. However, the claimant challenged the legality of the report.

It was argued the IPCC had overstepped the mark. The High Court agreed. HHJ Richardson QC, sitting as a Deputy High Court Judge, identified 12 propositions:

1. The primary function of the IPCC in this context is to investigate a complaint against the police under the 2002 Act.
2. Such a complaint must be investigated with rigour and determination in order to maintain public confidence in such enquiries and to comply with Convention jurisprudence.
3. The function of the investigation is to record matters which may constitute a crime or breach of discipline. The investigative ambit must be confined to that important but limited role.
4. It is no part of the function of the IPCC to make definitive finding or rulings upon any issue but to gather evidence and establish facts to enable those who have the lawful authority to decide whether to commence disciplinary charges or institute criminal proceedings (the decision maker).
5. As a critical by-product (if appropriate) the report may go so far as to assist the decision maker to establish whether there is a case to answer in respect of misconduct or a criminal charge.
6. In this regard the high water mark is the report may give an opinion as to whether there is a case to answer.
7. The report is not permitted to be determinative or purport to be determinative of such matters.
8. It is for the criminal courts to determine the guilt or otherwise of any individual; it is for the civil courts to determine civil liability of any person or body; and it is for the police disciplinary body (in any given constabulary) to institute and resolve disciplinary issues of a police officer.
9. The IPCC must remain within the four corners of the 2002 Act which demands investigation and gathering of evidence to enable the decision maker to make a decision.
10. If there is a critical need to offer a view as to the lawfulness of conduct it must be couched in the language of an indication of opinion on the matter.
11. It is permissible to evaluate evidence and competing accounts. A report is not an arid distillation or summary of all that has been gleaned.
12. In viewing reports of the IPCC it is vital to remember to whom they are addressed and approach each one with a sense of realism. They are not judgments, nor lawyer-crafted contracts.[76]

---

[75] ibid [27].
[76] ibid [47].

David Ball

Applying these propositions, the court was of the clear view that the report had gone too far: 'Quite apart from anything else the report purports to find (not suggest) unlawful conduct—both criminal and civil. That far exceeds the lawful ambit of such reports'.[77] Yet at the same time the High Court granted permission to appeal to the Court of Appeal. At the time of writing, the appeal is still pending.

(ii) Irrationality

As with many areas of public law irrationality and reasons challenges often give rise to latent issues about the degree of deference that will be accorded to the decision maker. Given the role and functions of the IPCC, there is arguably a particular question mark about how intrusive courts may be prepared to be. In *Muldoon v IPCC*[78] the court held that:

9-33

> The IPCC is an independent statutory appeal body to whom Parliament has entrusted the function of reviewing the findings of investigations into police complaints if that is what an appellant requests. The IPCC's decisions are likely to involve matters of judgment. For these reasons this court will allow the IPCC a discretionary area of judgment and will not intervene unless satisfied that the IPCC has gone beyond that permissible area to reach a conclusion not fairly and reasonably open to it. This function of the court is important because an appellant is (and I quote from Saunders J in the case of *Dennis* [*R (Dennis) v IPCC* [2008] EWHC 1158 (Admin)] to which I have referred) entitled to have a proper review because it is important that the functions of the IPCC are carried out properly to maintain public confidence in the system and the police force and to ensure that if there are lessons to be learnt, that that happens: see paragraph 34.

Some commentators have suggested that the cases of *Dennis* and *Muldoon* support a proposition of a slightly more intrusive form of review in the context of decisions by the IPCC.[79] This may be a rather generous reading of the principles. *Muldoon* simply rehearses the standard *Wednesbury* test, that the court 'will not intervene unless satisfied that the IPCC has gone beyond that permissible area to reach a conclusion not fairly and reasonably open to it'. However, as a matter of practice it would appear that there may be more willingness to intervene in the context of decisions of the IPCC than in the context of charging decisions by the CPS (on which see Chapter 5 above). As above, the IPCC is under a statutory duty to secure that 'public confidence is established and maintained' in the process of investigating complaints. Arguably, a court might implicitly or explicitly afford less deference to a decision of the IPCC on the basis that a more intense review is consistent with the IPCC's own function of maintaining public confidence.

Where rights under the ECHR are in issue it would appear that a slightly different approach is required. This was considered by Underhill J in *R (Saunders) v IPCC*:[80]

9-34

> Mr Owen and Ms Kaufmann reminded me that, even if the Commission's position was defensible on a *Wednesbury* basis, that was not the test. It was for me, and not the Commission, to

[77] ibid [53].
[78] *Muldoon v IPCC* [2009] EWHC 3633 (Admin).
[79] A Straw, 'Judicial Review and the Independent Police Complaints Commission: An Update', www.tooks.co.uk/library/ipcc_judicial_review_seminar_notes.pdf.
[80] *R (Saunders) v IPCC* [2008] EWHC 2372 (Admin), [2009] 1 All ER 379.

judge whether in the circumstances of these cases the failure to take steps to prohibit conferring or collaboration was incompatible with the obligation under art. 2. I was referred to *Huang v Secretary of State for the Home Department* [2007] 2 AC 167 ([2007] UKHL 11), esp. *per* Lord Bingham at para 13 (p 185). Though I am not in fact sure that that passage from *Huang* is precisely in point, I accept the Claimants' submission. But in making my decision I am entitled to give full weight to the Commission's own judgment. Adopting that approach, it is my conclusion that in not giving a direction of the kind contended for by the Claimants the Commission was not acting incompatibly with their art. 2 rights.

If it is suggested that the IPCC's refusal to investigate is a potential breach of Article 2 or 3 then the court will decide this for itself, at the same time as giving weight to the IPCC's own judgment of the matter.

9-35   An illustration of the tension that exists in the court's approach to the intensity of review can be found in its analysis of the extent of reasons required. In *R (Dennis) v IPCC*,[81] Saunders J held that:

> It is right that I should not expect or look in the appeal decision for the sort of tightly argued judgment that might be expected of a Chancery Judge. What is important and necessary is that the conclusions should be clear and the reasons for those conclusions can be readily understood by the complainant, the police officers concerned, and the relevant police authority who may need to review their procedures in the light of the decision.

Extensive reasons are not required. They need only be adequate. There are various examples of unsuccessful reasons challenges, for example *R (Crosby) v IPCC*[82] and *R (Erenbilge) v IPCC*.[83]

9-36   However, by the same token, an IPCC decision will be flawed for inadequate reasons if it failed to deal with all of the separate strands of a complaint (*R (Herd) v IPCC*[84]). The facts of *Herd* are illustrative. The claimant had been convicted of criminal damage when he was younger. He applied to have his conviction stepped down, so that only the police, and not third parties, could have access to it. After a period of delay the police wrote back, but mistakenly said another offence would remain on record. They immediately corrected their mistake. The claimant complained about delay, the mistake and a third issue. The police said that they did not consider his letter constituted a complaint against them and the IPCC agreed. The claimant appealed against this classification to the IPCC. The judge accepted that 'considerable latitude has to be given to the [IPCC] case worker to interpret the complaint made and reach a decision accordingly'. Notwithstanding this the judge found that the IPCC's response was flawed because it did not deal with each aspect of the delay or mistake complaints. The case is an interesting illustration of how even with considerable latitude, where brief appeal findings were found to be acceptable, and the complaint had not been very clearly articulated, a decision can be found to be void for insufficient reasons.

---

[81] *R (Dennis) v IPCC* [2008] EWHC 1158 (Admin) [20].
[82] *R (Crosby) v IPCC* [2009] EWHC 2515 (Admin).
[83] *R (Erenbilge v IPCC* [2013] EWHC 1397 (Admin).
[84] *R (Herd) v IPCC* [2009] EWHC 3134.

(iii) Procedural Impropriety

Procedural impropriety is a frequent feature of challenges to IPCC decisions. In   **9-37**
Morrison v IPCC[85] the claimant applied for judicial review of the IPCC's decision to
allow the same police force to investigate a complaint which was the subject of the complaint. The claimant alleged that the police had pulled him from his car with excessive
force. (He received several cuts and bruises, including a wound which required stitches).
It was accepted that it was arguable he had suffered ill-treatment contrary to Article 3.
The issue was whether the obligation to investigate this could only be discharged if the
investigation was independent. The IPCC submitted that a possibility of an appeal to
the IPCC following a local investigation, together with the possibility of criminal and
civil proceedings, was such that there was no breach of the investigatory requirement
incumbent under Article 3. The court agreed. The court expressly relied on a 'flood-
gates'-type argument. Saunders J stated that:

> if the present claim is upheld then a very significant proportion of those complaints would
> have to be investigated by the Commission itself. That would put an impossible strain on the
> Commission's budget.[86]

It was held that the existence of the possibility of civil proceedings did not advance matters. However, the right of appeal to the IPCC and the possibility of criminal proceedings meant that the investigation even by the same force could be Article 3 compliant.

In *Saunders*[87] the claimant attacked the IPCC's failure to prevent officers involved in a
fatal shooting from conferring before they gave their first accounts. It was accepted such
collaboration had occurred. The challenge was unsuccessful. The court held that the risk
of evidence being contaminated by conferring could be guarded against by training and
guidance. The court held:

> a ban on 'mere' conferring not only would be difficult to enforce in practice but would in many
> cases have serious operational disadvantages: prompt exchange of information between officers
> in the immediate aftermath of an incident is often essential.[88]

The court considered in detail the jurisprudence of the ECtHR on Article 2, in particular, *Ramsahai v The Netherlands*.[89] The court considered that *Ramsahai* only affirmed
an investigation must be independent and adequate; on the facts of this investigation,
this was satisfied.

R (IPCC) v Chief Constable of West Midlands[90] was a judicial review brought by
the IPCC itself. A meeting was being held by the police to review the sanctions being
imposed on two police officers. The police refused to allow the IPCC to attend the meeting. The application was granted. It was generally desirable that such litigation took
place in public. The regulations did not expressly make the review meeting private so it
could be inferred it should be in public.

---

[85] *Morrison v IPCC* [2009] EWHC 2589 (Admin).
[86] ibid [45].
[87] *Saunders* (n 80).
[88] ibid [16].
[89] *Ramsahai v The Netherlands* (2007) 46 EHRR 983.
[90] *R (IPCC) v Chief Constable of West Midlands* [2007] EWHC 2715 (Admin).

(iv) Delay

9-38 It should be recalled that as with any judicial review, the claimant is seeking a prerogative order, which is a discretionary remedy. Delay will always be a factor when considering what the appropriate remedy might be.

In *R (D) v IPCC*[91] the claimant had been raped when aged 15. The existence of call
data was relevant to disproving the defendant's account. The claimant complained that
she had been repeatedly been told by the officer assigned to them that the call data had
been obtained. It had not, and the defendant was acquitted.

The IPCC carried out an investigation and found it was not possible to conclude the
officer had been dishonest, and did not submit a report for consideration of disciplinary
action. The claimant issued judicial review proceedings against this decision. The court
allowed the claim for judicial review, alleging that the IPCC's decision was not supported by sufficient reasons. However, here the incident complained of was now some
five years ago. In those circumstances it was considered that it would not be appropriate
for the officer to be faced with possible disciplinary proceedings. The conclusion that
the IPCC should have its report for consideration of disciplinary action was therefore
considered a sufficient remedy in the circumstances.

E. Criminal Injuries Compensations Authority

(1) Introduction

9-39 The First Tier Tribunal (Criminal Injuries Compensation) (the FTT) now hears appeals
against decisions taken by the Criminal Injuries Compensation Authority (CICA).
Previously these appeals were heard by the Criminal Injuries Compensation Appeals
Panel. This changed when the Tribunal Courts and Enforcement Act 2007 came into
effect.

The FTT (Criminal Injuries Compensation) is part of the Social Entitlement
Chamber. It is subject to the Tribunal Procedure (First Tier Tribunal) (Health,
Education and Social Care Chamber) Rules 2008 (SI 2008/2699).

It is beyond the ambit of this chapter to set out in detail the various tariff-based
schemes which govern determination of criminal injuries compensation appeals. The
reader should refer to the Criminal Injuries Compensation Scheme 2012 ('the 2012
Scheme').[92] The 2012 Scheme also sets out the process for applications for compensation and appeals.

The High Court retains jurisdiction over the CICA. However, there is a significant
range of alternative remedies available to an individual in respect of a CICA decision.

---

[91] *R (D) v IPCC* [2011] EWHC 1595 (Admin).
[92] The Criminal Injuries Compensation Scheme 2012 along with the various practice statements, protocols
and tribunal procedure can be found at www.justice.gov.uk/tribunals/criminal-injuries-compensation/rules-
and-legislation. For a guide to the former (2008) Scheme, see L Begley, A Downey and C Padley, *Criminal
Injuries Compensation Scheme 2008* (London, The Law Society 2010).

David Ball

These fall under either i) a reopening of that determination or ii) a review. The circumstances in which a determination may be reopened or a decision reviewed are set out in paragraphs 114 and 117 of the 2012 Scheme. An applicant has a right of appeal to the FTT only in respect of decisions taken on reopening and review. The UT has jurisdiction for claims for judicial review of decisions of the FTT. It is submitted that there may be decisions of CICA that fall outside paragraphs 114 and 117; for example, a failure to reach a decision within a reasonable time, as in *R (M) v Criminal Injuries Compensation Authority*[93] discussed above at 1-93. This does not fall within paragraphs 114 or 117, and so an applicant will not have a right to reopen or review and thereby no right of appeal in respect of such alleged failures. Therefore, it is submitted that such a complaint may found a claim for judicial review direct to the High Court.

(2) General Principles

When matters were considered by the Criminal Injuries Compensation Appeals Panel, in the event of an adverse decision, an appellant could consider judicially reviewing the decision of the Panel. The same applied with decisions of the Criminal Injuries Compensation Board which existed before it.   **9-40**

In essence, this is still the case. The Practice and Guidance Statement (CI-6) sets out that none of the tariff-based schemes provide that a final decision of the FTT can be reviewed, amended or otherwise interfered with, apart from:[94]

i.   The right to apply for reinstatement (a) where proceedings, or part of them, have been struck out (rule 8(5)–(7)) or (b) where proceedings or part of them have been withdrawn (rule 17(4)).

ii. The right to apply for a decision to be reconsidered at a hearing where the Tribunal makes a decision which disposes of proceedings without a hearing, other than decisions to which rule 27(5) apply (rule 27(4)).

iii. The right to apply for a rehearing where the tribunal proceeded with a hearing in a party's absence (rule 31).

iv. The correction of a clerical or other accidental slip or omission in a decision (rule 36).

v.   The right to apply for a decision, or part of a decision, to be set aside subject to certain conditions (rule 37).

Apart from these above exceptions, the only remedy to an appellant who wants to challenge a final decision of the FTT in this jurisdiction is to apply to bring judicial review proceedings of that decision. The Guidance sets out a number of steps such an appellant should consider taking in such circumstances. These include: requesting any written reasons within one month of notification of a final decision; providing written details without delay of the alleged error of law to the Tribunal, so that it can consider correcting or setting aside the decision further to rules 36 and 37.

---

[93] *R (M) v Criminal Injuries Compensation Authority* [2002] EWHC 2646 (Admin).
[94] FTT, Practice and Guidance Statement CI-6, www.justice.gov.uk/downloads/tribunals/criminal-injuries-compensation/FTT_CI_6_ PracticeStatement_JRs210509.pdf.

In the ordinary course, these proceedings are to be made on a form JR1 to the Upper Tribunal (Administrative Appeals Chamber).[95] The time limit is three months after the date of the decision, or one month after the date the written reasons were given or the applicant was notified that an application for setting aside the decision was unsuccessful, whichever period ends the latest. The application must be made in accordance with rule 27 of the Tribunal Procedure (Upper Tribunal) Rules 2008 (SI 2008/2698).

It follows from this that the previous jurisprudence relating to judicial reviews of the Criminal Injuries Compensation Appeals Panel is directly relevant when considering a judicial review to the Upper Tribunal against the FTT.

(3) Previous Judicial Reviews of Criminal Injuries Compensation Appeals Panel

9-41   Consideration of the decisions prior to the Tribunal Courts and Enforcement Act 2007 indicates that one of the most common grounds for successful judicial reviews of decisions of the Criminal Injuries Compensation Panel or Criminal Injuries Compensation Board was insufficient reasons.[96]

The general requirement for sufficient reasons is well established and was set out by Megaw J in *Re Poyser and Mills Arbitration*:[97]

> The whole purpose ... was to enable persons whose property, or whose interests, were being affected by some administrative decision or some statutory arbitration to know, if the decision was against them, what the reasons for it were. Up to then, people's property and other interests might be gravely affected by a decision of some official. The decision might be perfectly right, but the person against whom it was made was left with the real grievance that he was not told why the decision has been made ... proper, adequate reasons must be given. The reasons that are set out must be reasons which will not only be intelligible, but which deal with the substantial points that have been raised.

This was cited with approval by Hobhouse LJ in *R v Criminal Injuries Compensation Board, ex parte Cook*.[98] In the same case Aldous LJ circumscribed the duty on the decision-maker as follows:

> I believe it is clear that the board's reasons should contain sufficient detail to enable the reader to know what conclusion has been reached on the principal important issue or issues, but it is not a requirement that they should deal with every material consideration to which they have had regard. If the reasons given are sufficient, they cannot be reviewed in judicial review proceedings unless the board misconstrued their mandate or the decision is *Wednesbury* unreasonable: see *Ex parte Thompstone* [1984] 1 WLR 1234 at p1238.[99]

---

[95] Available from www.justice.gov.uk/tribunals/aa.
[96] See also C Padley and L Begley, *Criminal Injuries Compensation Claims* (London, The Law Society, 2005) 310; see also the subsequent edition, C Padley and L Begley, *Criminal Injuries Compensation Claims 2008* (London, The Law Society, 2008).
[97] *Re Poyser and Mills Arbitration* [1964] 2 QB 467, 477. See above at 1-121.
[98] *R v Criminal Injuries Compensation Board, ex parte Cook* [1996] 1 WLR 1037.
[99] ibid 1043.

The sufficient reasons test therefore does not require dealing with 'every material consideration', but it does require dealing with 'the substantial points which have been raised'.[100]

There have been a number of successful judicial reviews challenging the adequacy of reasons given. In *R v Criminal Injuries Compensation Appeals Panel, ex parte Leatherland*[101] it was held, 'there is a duty to give reasons which are proper sufficient and intelligible'.

In *R v Criminal Injuries Compensation Appeals Panel, ex parte M*,[102] Hooper J considered how reasons challenges should be approached. He explained that the court should be careful 'not to seize on occasional omissions and infelicities' as a ground for granting judicial review or allowing an appeal.[103] He concluded: **9-42**

> The need to give proper reasons accompanying the decision concentrates the mind of the decision maker at the time of making the decision (see *Flannery v Halifax Estate Agencies* cited above [2000] 1 WLR 377] and *R v Higher Education Funding Council, ex parte Institute of Dental Surgery* [1994] 1 WLR 241).

> Given the history of these proceedings and the fact that the Panel awarded the same sum (£2,000) as had been awarded on review by deducting 2/3rds, there was a particular need for proper sufficient and intelligible reasons. Justice to this claimant, who has suffered so much, required it. ibid, [46]–[47].[104]

The case concerned a 17-year-old applicant who alleged she had been sexually abused by her stepfather between the ages of five and 11; her application was supported by the local authority. She claimed damages for psychiatric injuries and loss of earnings. There was one sentence in which the Panel set out that they did not consider the applicant had a permanently disabling mental disorder attributable to sex abuse. In the circumstances of the case this was inadequate. The decision was quashed, and remitted to a differently constituted panel. Hooper J commented that inadequate reasons might not be fatal if the conclusion reached was the only possible conclusion:

> I shall assume, for the purposes of argument, that the failure to give proper reasons should not lead to the quashing of the decision if the conclusion reached by the Panel was the only possible conclusion on the evidence.[105]

It remains open to debate as to whether wholly inadequate reasons could ever quash a decision which is the only possible conclusion on the evidence.

Finally, it should be noted that the ECtHR has determined that Article 8 does not include a right to receive compensation for criminal injuries.[106]

---

[100] See respectively ibid 1043 and *Re Poyser* (n 97) 477. See also discussion above in Chapter 1 at 1-85.

[101] *R v Criminal Injuries Compensation Appeals Panel, ex parte Leatherland* [2001] ACD 13, The Times, 12 October 2000 [79].

[102] *R v Criminal Injuries Compensation Appeals Panel, ex parte M* [2001] EWHC Admin 720 [44]–[47].

[103] See also *R v Parole Board ex parte Oyston* (1 March 2000, CA) [46] (Lord Bingham LCJ) citing with approval Lord Mustil in *R v Secretary of State for the Home Department, ex parte Doody* [1994] 1 AC 531 (HL), 565.

[104] ibid, [46]–[47].

[105] *R v Criminal Injuries Compensation Appeals Panel, ex parte M* [2001] EWHC Admin 720 [72].

[106] *August v UK* (2003) 36 EHRR CD115.

(4) Judicial Reviews to Upper Tier

9-43   There have been approximately 40 decisions before the Upper Tier at time of writing. A considerable proportion of these decisions have granted the claim for judicial review.

YR v First-tier Tribunal[107] was a case in which the judicial review of the FTT decision was granted arising out of the FTT's failure to grant an adjournment. An issue arose before the FTT as to whether the applicant had ever made a statement to the police on a particular issue. The police officer before the FTT said there was such a statement, and the applicant denied it and requested an adjournment. The FTT refused. The Upper Tier quashed the FTT's decision. HHJ David Pearl sitting as a Judge of the Upper Tribunal commented as follows:

> It would seem to me that the correct approach to be taken by a Court or Tribunal when faced with a judicial review of a decision not to adjourn is that it should ask itself the question: 'was the decision of the tribunal not to adjourn within the legitimate scope of the Tribunal's judicial discretion in dealing with procedural applications and was it not unfair?' (Laws LJ in *Carpenter v Secretary of State* reported as R(IB)6/03).

> This Tribunal considered the question in *MA v Secretary of State for Work and Pensions* [2009] UKUT 211 (AAC) where the Tribunal said that the consideration of an adjournment should focus on three questions (a) what would be the benefit of an adjournment? (b) why was the party not ready to proceed? and (c) what impact will an adjournment have on the other party and the operation of the Tribunal system?

The Upper Tier agreed that the FTT was right to ask itself the *MA* questions, but it found that an adjournment should have been ordered. First, the benefits of an adjournment were obvious, allowing the question of whether a statement had been made to be clarified. Secondly, it was not the applicant's fault, because this issue only came to light during the hearing. Thirdly, a short adjournment would not have prejudiced either party. It therefore concluded the FTT's decision was vitiated by an error of law, 'in that it was a decision that fell outside the legitimate scope of its judicial discretion and was unfair'.

9-44   In *R (SB) v First-tier Tribunal*[108] the Upper Tier had to again deal with the issue of sufficiency of reasons. The Upper Tier considered in detail the Court of Appeal's decision in *Cook*. Interestingly, the Upper Tier appeared to subject it to some criticism: 'I find some of what was said in [*R v Criminal Injuries Compensation Board, ex parte Cook*] rather troubling'.[109] The Upper Tier went on to cite the test of sufficient reasons expounded by Lord Brown in *South Bucks District Council v Porter (No 2)*.[110] There, Lord Brown held how the reasoning, 'must not give rise to a substantial doubt as to whether the decision maker erred in law' while noting that 'such adverse inference will not readily be drawn'.[111] Applying this, the Upper Tier held as follows:

> 35 ... In my judgment the tribunal's reasons here did not come up to the standard required by those general principles as re-stated in *Porter*. The reasons left substantial doubt whether the

---

[107]   *YR v First-tier Tribunal (SEC) (CICA)* [2010] UKUT 204 (AAC).
[108]   *R (SB) v First-tier Tribunal (CIC)* [2010] UKUT 250 (AAC).
[109]   ibid [33].
[110]   *South Bucks District Council v Porter (No 2)* [2004] UKHL 33, [2004] 1 WLR 1953.
[111]   ibid [36].

tribunal had erred in law by asking itself the wrong question and fettering its discretion, but if (contrary to my conclusion above) that was not material to the outcome, any inadequacy of reasons would not in itself have justified quashing the tribunal's decision. However, in order for the claimant and her representative to understand why they had lost the appeal, there needed to be some further explanation of in what way the tribunal found the claimant's behaviour provocative, in the sense explained above of giving rise to some expectation of a violent reaction. The finding that the claimant had caused the incident did not in itself explain why the claimant lost ... In these particular circumstances there needed to be some further explanation of why the nature of the claimant's conduct made it inappropriate for something less than a full award (if the other conditions for qualification were met) to be made. The reference to provocative and disruptive behaviour was not enough by implication to provide an explanation. That was not put in terms of the proper test of inappropriateness or of whether or not any reasonable person could have expected a violent reaction to the behaviour.

... Claimants are entitled not to have to read between the lines on the decisive issue in their cases.

The case is authority for a further interesting proposition for all those appeals to the Upper Tier under the Tribunal Courts and Enforcement Act 2007. In this application for judicial review to the Upper Tier, the President of the Administrative Appeals Chamber granted permission. In granting it he drew attention to a number of points, including whether the tribunal had failed to ask the right question. In so doing he said this was 'without limiting the grounds that may arise'. It was part of CICA's submission that that ground should not be considered, as it had not formed an express part of the case made for the claimant.

The Upper Tier disagreed. They held that the mere identification of a number of grounds on which permission is granted or on which submissions are directed, without a formal limitation of the giving of permission to those specific grounds, does not exclude the consideration of any issue that is relevant to the question of whether one of the orders specified in section 15(1) of the Tribunals, Courts and Enforcement Act 2007 should be made. They concluded that in order to ensure that the correct result in law is reached, issues may be raised by the Administrative Appeals Chamber itself at any stage, subject always to the principles of natural justice.[112]

Jones (by Caldwell) v FTT[113] was a Supreme Court decision arising out of a judicial **9-45** review of the FTT. Mr Jones had been hit by a lorry after it was forced to swerve because of someone jumping in front of it. Mr Jones sought compensation. He argued that the person trying to commit suicide had inflicted grievous bodily harm on him. CICA held that there was no power to award compensation because there had not been a 'crime of violence'. Mr Jones appealed to the FTT, which agreed with CICA and found that no crime of violence had been committed. Mr Jones then judicially reviewed the FTT's decision to the Upper Tier. This also was unsuccessful. But he succeeded in the Court of Appeal and so CICA appealed to the Supreme Court, which reversed the Court of Appeal's decision and upheld the FTT. The importance of the case lies in its approach to the distinction between an unimpeachable finding of fact, and an amenable error of law. The FTT had found that there was no crime of violence because they did not consider

---

[112] *SB* (n 108) [15].
[113] *Jones (by Caldwell) v FTT* [2013] 2 AC 48, [2013] UKSC 19.

that the person who committed suicide intended to cause harm or was reckless as to whether any harm might be caused. It was this finding in relation to recklessness that was challenged in the Upper Tier and Court of Appeal.

In considering the definition of a crime of violence, the Supreme Court approved what Lawton LJ said in *R v Criminal Injuries Compensation Board, ex parte Webb*.[114] There he commented that what mattered was the nature of the crime, not its likely consequences: 'It is for the board to decide whether unlawful conduct, because of its nature, not its consequence, amounts to a crime of violence.' He continued:

> Most crimes of violence will involve the infliction or threat of force, but some may not. I do not think it prudent to attempt a definition of words of ordinary usage in English which the board, as a fact finding body, have to apply to the case before them. They will recognise a crime of violence when they hear about it, even though as a matter of semantics it may be difficult to produce a definition which is not too narrow or so wide as to produce absurd consequences ...

Arising out of this background the issue was whether the Court of Appeal was right to characterise the FTT's decision as disclosing an error of law. The Supreme Court found that the Court of Appeal had been wrong to find an error of law. In effect, it was said that, as a specialist tribunal, the Upper Tier retain a pragmatic flexibility as to the characterisation of an error of fact or an error of law, which a non-specialist appellate court should be wary of disturbing. Lord Hope held:

> A pragmatic approach should be taken to the dividing line between law and fact, so that the expertise of tribunals at the first tier and that of the Upper Tribunal can be used to best effect. An appeal court should not venture too readily into this area by classifying issues as issues of law which are really best left for determination by the specialist appellate tribunals.[115]

This point was affirmed in detail by Lord Carnwath. It remains to be seen how, in the words of Lord Carnwath, 'such a tribunal, even though its jurisdiction is limited to 'errors of law', should be permitted to venture more freely into the 'grey area' separating fact from law'.[116]

---

[114] *R v Criminal Injuries Compensation Board, ex parte Webb* [1987] QB 74, 79.
[115] *Jones (by Caldwell)* (n 113) [16].
[116] ibid [46] quoting from Carnwath, 'Tribunal Justice—A New Start' [2009] *Public Law* 48, 63–64.

David Ball

10

Coroners

GEOFFREY SULLIVAN

A. General Principles

(1) Introduction

The coronial jurisdiction stands outside the criminal justice system, therefore this **10-1** chapter does not form part of the core subject matter of this book. The intention of this chapter is to provide the practitioner, who may be unfamiliar with the jurisdiction, with a short introduction to this related area and outline some examples of the varied avenues it presents for challenge by way of judicial review.

Coroners occupy both an administrative and judicial position. They are a public body which can be subject to judicial review. In practice they hold office under the Crown and are appointed and paid by a local authority. Their central function is the investigation of deaths. There are a myriad of other functions and roles, but the focus of this chapter is challenges by way of judicial review to the manner in which coroners exercise their duty to investigate deaths.[1]

The most common ground of review is that an error has been made by the coroner in the decision-making process. The test is whether any reasonable coroner could have made the decision, or if the decision is in any other way irrational or perverse (this is discussed below at 10-8). Coroners can also be challenged on other heads of review described above in section G of Chapter 1. The most common remedies in the context of coronial law are a quashing order, quashing the decision, followed by a mandatory

---

[1] A useful guide to the law on coroners is Matthews (ed), *Jervis on the Office and Duties of Coroners*, 12th edn (London, Sweet & Maxwell, 2002).

order, compelling the decision to be made or inquest held afresh. Declarations may also be useful if a coroner has acted outside of his jurisdiction, for example, if issues of criminal or civil liability are touched on.

Finally, the potential claimants should note the particular differences on the law on costs against coroners in judicial review (see below at 16-1) and the case law on challenging refusals of grants of legal aid at inquests (see above at 9-7).

(2) Legal Framework

10-2   The main sources of law are set out in the Coroners and Justice Act (CJA) 2009,[2] the Coroners (Inquests) Rules 2013 (SI 2013/1616) and the Coroners (Investigations) Regulations 2013 (SI 2013/1629).[3] A coroner has a statutory duty to investigate the death of a person if he has reason to suspect that the deceased died a violent or unnatural death, the cause of death is unknown, or the deceased died while in custody or otherwise in state detention. A senior coroner, who is made aware that the body of a deceased person is within that coroner's area, must as soon as practicable conduct an investigation into that person's death.[4] This investigation may result in an inquest being held, with or without a jury, or in certain circumstances be discontinued if an inquest is no longer deemed necessary.

10-3   The purpose of any such investigation is set out in section 5 of CJA 2009:

> 5. Matters to be ascertained
> (1)   The purpose of an investigation under this Part into a person's death is to ascertain—
>   (a)   who the deceased was;
>   (b)   how, when and where the deceased came by his or her death;
>   (c)   the particulars (if any) required by the 1953 Act to be registered concerning the death.
> (2)   Where necessary in order to avoid a breach of any Convention rights (within the meaning of the Human Rights Act 1998 (c. 42)), the purpose mentioned in subsection (1)(b) is to be read as including the purpose of ascertaining in what circumstances the deceased came by his or her death'.

It is important to note that a coroner cannot determine any question of criminal liability on the part of a named person or civil liability.[5]

10-4   In addition to this duty, the coroner has a number of other duties as part of his investigation:

   i.   He must discontinue an investigation if an examination reveals the cause of death before an inquest has begun and he thinks it unnecessary to continue the investigation (although this does not apply if there was a violent or unnatural death, or the person died in custody or state detention).[6]
   ii.   He must suspend an investigation if requested to do so by a prosecuting body on grounds that a person is charged with offences relating to the death.[7]

---

[2] The CJA 2009 has brought about significant changes to both terminology and procedure in the coronial jurisdiction. These changes are only just being felt, so there will inevitably be references made to matters decided under the Coroners Act 1988 and using the terminology applicable to it.

[3] Note the Coroners (Inquests) Rules 2013 took effect from 25 July 2013.

[4] Coroners and Justice Act 2009 (CJA) 2009, s 1(1),

[5] ibid s 10(2).

[6] ibid s 4(1) and (2).

[7] ibid Sch 1, para 1.

iii. He must resume an investigation if he thinks there is sufficient reason for doing so providing that any proceedings in respect of an offence involving the death are not continuing.[8]

iv. At the conclusion of an inquest, he must make a determination as to the questions set out in section 5 (see above) that is the identity of the deceased, and how, when and where they died.[9]

v. He must report any matter where anything revealed in the investigation 'gives rise to a concern that circumstances creating a risk of other deaths will occur, or will continue to exist, in the future' and 'action should be taken to prevent the occurrence or continuation of such circumstances, or to eliminate or reduce the risk of death created by such circumstances'.[10]

(3) The Role of Judicial Review

There are no statutory appeals from inquests, in the sense of an opportunity for a rehearing on the merits and the potential for a fresh decision to be substituted for the original. There are, however, two established routes for properly interested persons to seek redress if they are dissatisfied with the outcome of an inquest or the conduct of a coroner: **10-5**

i. judicial review; and
ii. Attorney General's fiat.

The coroner's activities are defined by statute and involve the exercise of discretion in the performance of a wide range of public functions. The coroner therefore performs a public duty that is subject to the supervisory jurisdiction of the High Court. This chapter will outline the wide scope this provides for challenging coronial decisions in the Administrative Court.

The second avenue for redress is to seek the Attorney General's fiat by virtue of section 13 of the Coroners Act 1988. Section 13 has been preserved and amended to reflect the terminology of CJA 2009. This power is restricted to i) ordering investigations or inquests where the coroner has either neglected to hold one, or refused to do so in circumstances where he should, or ii) quashing investigations or inquests that are in some way deficient and ordering that a new one be held. This avenue for redress is narrower than judicial review and falls outside the scope of this chapter.

(4) Standing (Who Can Bring a Claim)

As explained above (see above at 1-45), a claimant must be able to demonstrate that they have sufficient interest (or standing) to bring a claim in judicial review. An applicant who is directly affected by the decision of a coroner or the outcome of an inquest will have standing. This could include a spouse, civil partner or close family member, but   **10-6**

---

[8] ibid Sch 1, para 8.
[9] Note in inquests that engage Art 2, 'how' is interpreted as 'by what means and in what circumstances'. See below at 10-12 *R v HM Coroner for West Somerset, ex parte Middleton* [2004] UKHL 10, [2004] 2 AC 182 [35] (Lord Bingham).
[10] CJA 2009, Sch 5, para 7.

also any one of the other 'interested persons' listed under section 47 of CJA 2009. This is a highly diverse group of individuals (see especially section 47(2)(m)):

> (2) 'Interested person', in relation to a deceased person or an investigation or inquest under this Part into a person's death, means—
>
>> (a) a spouse, civil partner, partner, parent, child, brother, sister, grandparent, grandchild, child of a brother or sister, stepfather, stepmother, half-brother or half-sister;
>> (b) a personal representative of the deceased;
>> (c) a medical examiner exercising functions in relation to the death of the deceased;
>> (d) a beneficiary under a policy of insurance issued on the life of the deceased;
>> (e) the insurer who issued such a policy of insurance;
>> (f) a person who may by any act or omission have caused or contributed to the death of the deceased, or whose employee or agent may have done so;
>> (g) in a case where the death may have been caused by—
>>> (i) an injury received in the course of an employment, or
>>> (ii) a disease prescribed under section 108 of the Social Security Contributions and Benefits Act 1992 (c. 4) (benefit in respect of prescribed industrial diseases, etc),
>
> a representative of a trade union of which the deceased was a member at the time of death;
>
>> (h) a person appointed by, or representative of, an enforcing authority;
>> (i) where subsection (3) applies, a chief constable;
>> (j) where subsection (4) applies, a Provost Marshal;
>> (k) where subsection (5) applies, the Independent Police Complaints Commission;
>> (l) a person appointed by a Government department to attend an inquest into the death or to assist in, or provide evidence for the purposes of, an investigation into the death under this Part;
>> (m) any other person who the senior coroner thinks has a sufficient interest'.

10-7 A person whose conduct may be called into question by an inquest verdict has standing to challenge that verdict,[11] and a person who may be charged with causing a person's death would have standing in respect of a decision as to whether a body may be released for disposal or removal out of the country.[12] Unsurprisingly, a person punished by a coroner for contempt—whether a witness or someone in the public gallery—has standing to challenge the coroner's decision to impose such a punishment.[13]

B. Challenges to Coronial Decisions

(1) Grounds for Judicial Review

10-8 The Administrative Court is unlikely to interfere with a coroner's decision unless it can be challenged on one of the following grounds:[14]

   i.   illegality;

---

[11] *R v Walthamstow Coroner, ex parte Rubenstein* [1982] Crim LR 509.
[12] *R v Bristol Coroner, ex parte Kerr* [1974] QB 652 (DC); *R v Bristol Coroner, ex parte Atkinson*, 5 May 1983.
[13] *R v West Yorkshire Coroner, ex parte Smith (No 2)* [1985] QB 1096 (DC).
[14] For detailed discussion of these grounds see Ch 1.

Geoffrey Sullivan

ii.   irrationality and proportionality; and/or

iii.   procedural impropriety.

The coroner holds a unique position amongst the judiciary of England and Wales. A large number of decisions are made by the coroner prior to an inquest taking place, relating to the disposal of the body and issues such as organ donation. It is often the coroner's decision as to whether there needs to be an investigation at all, let alone an inquest. Some of these decisions are strictly governed by statute; others will rely on the individual coroner's discretion.

If there is to be an inquest, the coroner gathers the evidence and he decides which witnesses to call and which evidence is to be read. The disclosure of evidence to interested parties used to be at the discretion of the coroner; under the CJA 2009 this is now a duty prescribed by statute. At the conclusion of an inquest, if the coroner is sitting without a jury, he will sum up the evidence, direct himself as to the relevant law and possible verdicts (now 'conclusions' under CJA 2009), before reaching his own conclusion.

Given the breadth of the coroner's public law role, judicial review is available across almost the entire scope of the coroner's decision-making.

In relation to any challenge by way of judicial review it is necessary to identify under which statutory power the coroner is acting and ask whether he is acting within those powers. If the coroner is exercising his discretion, it must be asked whether that discretion is being exercised in a way that is fair, reasonable and rational. Any decision made by a coroner must be based on proper consideration of the available relevant facts and disregarding those facts that are not relevant. Whether the coroner has discharged the UK's obligations under Article 2 of ECHR is also a key area for challenge.

There must be some fundamental unfairness to the applicant in either the investigation stage or inquest process, in order to have proper grounds for review. It is the coroner's decision-making process that is under review. The decision, then, is looked at on the basis of the evidence available to him at the time, not in the light of any new evidence that may present itself later, bringing the verdict or decision into question. If there is something amiss with the decision or verdict, but no clear fault on the part of the coroner, then the appropriate way for an interested party to proceed would be under the statutory power to quash, not by way of judicial review.[15]

The Administrative Court will generally only intervene if the decision or conclusion under review would be different if the decision were to be taken, or the inquest held, again.[16] In *R (Anderson) v Inner North London Coroner*[17] and *R (P) v Avon Coroner*[18] the Administrative Court found that the coroner had misdirected the jury, but on both occasions refused to order fresh inquests, as the court could identify no benefit from so doing.

Where there may have been a breach of Article 2, through insufficient investigation or a failure to summon a jury, however, the possibility of their being a different conclusion will not be a determining factor.[19]

---

[15] *R v Central Cleveland Coroner, ex parte Dent* (1986) 150 JP 251.

[16] *Re Davis* [1968] 1 QB 72, *Re Williams*, The Times, December 10,1968, DC and *R v Portsmouth Coroner, Ex p Keane* (1989) 153 JP 658, DC.

[17] *R (Anderson) v Inner North London Coroner* [2004] EWHC 2729.

[18] *R (P) v Avon Coroner* [2009] EWCA Civ 1367.

[19] *R v Brighton and Hove Coroner, ex parte Aineto* [2003] EWHC 1896 Admin and *R v HM Coroner for West Yorkshire, ex parte Sacker* [2004] 1 WLR 796.

Recent case law[20] has also re-affirmed that it is not always necessary to establish that a conclusion would be different to satisfy the interests of justice test in applications under section 13 of the Coroners Act 1988 to quash inquest conclusions. Those seeking to challenge a coronial decision should therefore consider carefully whether the statutory provision or an application for judicial review is the appropriate avenue to take.

(2) Types of Coronial Decisions that may be Challenged

10-9   Review of the coronial jurisdiction goes further than simply challenging the outcome of an inquest; the list below is not exhaustive, but illustrates potential areas for challenge.

(i) Pre-Inquest Decisions

10-10   There are several decisions taken by a coroner prior to an inquest that are susceptible to judicial review:

    i.   whether to release a body for burial;[21]
    ii.   refusal to hold an inquest[22] or whether one should be held at all;[23]
    iii. wrongfully carrying out a post-mortem, failure to allow family to attend, or failure to allow family arrange their own;[24]
    iv. where an inquest should be held[25] and whether it should be in camera; or[26]
    v.   refusal to sit with a jury.[27]

The CJA 2009 has introduced a distinct investigation and pre-investigation stage conferring certain duties upon the coroner. At the time of writing, no challenges have been made with reference to this particular aspect of the new legislation, but avenues for challenge clearly exist. One likely area for challenge will be the coroner's decision either not to open an investigation or to discontinue an investigation at an early stage.

(ii) The Inquest Hearing

10-11   There are many decisions taken during the conduct of an inquest hearing that can be challenged by way of judicial review, including:

    i.   wrongly limiting the scope of an inquest, omission or refusal to call a relevant witness;[28]

---

[20] *AG v HM Coroner of South Yorkshire (West)* [2012] EWHC 3783 (Admin) (the Hillsborough inquests) and *Brown v HM Coroner for Norfolk* [2014] EWHC 187 (Admin).
[21] *R v Hampshire Coroner, ex parte Horscroft* The Times, 3 October 1985.
[22] *R v Inner North London Coroner, ex parte Touche* [2001] QB 1206; and *R v Birmingham/Solihull Coroner, ex parte Bicknell* [2007] EWHC 2547 (Admin).
[23] *R v West Yorkshire Coroner, ex parte Smith* [1983] QB 335, CA.
[24] *R v South London Coroner, ex parte Ripley* [1985] 1 WLR 1347. See also *R (Kasperowicz) v Plymouth Coroner* [2005] EWCA Civ 44, which touched on invasive procedures and the feelings of the surviving family.
[25] *R v Inner North London Coroner, ex parte Greater London Council*, The Times, 30 April 1983.
[26] *R v McHugh, ex parte Trelford* (22 March 1984, DC).
[27] *R v Hammersmith Coroner, ex parte Peach* [1980] QB 211; *Paul v Deputy Coroner of the Queen's Household* [2007] 3 WLR 503.
[28] *R v HM Coroner for Inner North London, ex parte Takoushis* [2006] 1 WLR 461 and *R v Avon Coroner, ex parte Bentley* [2002] 166 JP 297.

ii.   refusal to obtain evidence from a relevant expert;[29]
iii.   failure to recognise someone as a properly interested person;[30]
iv.   admission of evidence not on oath or otherwise inadmissible;[31]
i.   omitting or refusing to obtain independent expert evidence;[32]
ii.   refusal to disclose evidence or unfair disclosure of evidence;[33]
iii.   refusal to hear legal submissions;[34]
iv.   failure to conduct a sufficient enquiry; [35]
v.   failure to sum up the evidence to a jury;[36]
vi.   the choice of questions to ask a jury;[37]
vii.   misdirecting the jury;[38]
viii.   omission or refusal to leave a particular verdict;[39]
ix.   leaving a verdict that ought not have been left;
x.   failure to act in accordance with the Human Rights Act (HRA) 1998.[40]

With inquests under greater scrutiny, there is now a greater emphasis on coroners hold-ing Pre-Inquest Reviews (PIRs), which if conducted properly may have the effect of reducing the number of challenges brought on the grounds set out above. In *Brown v HM Coroner for Norfolk*,[41] the Chief Coroner gave guidance as to both the content and conduct of PIRs. This guidance, inter alia, proposed that coroners provide a written agenda for PIRs. This agenda should address matters such as: the scope of the inquest, witness requirements, the need for a jury, Article 2 engagement, disclosure, the proposed hearing date and the time estimate. Interested persons or their representatives should now be in a position to make submissions to the coroner either orally or in writing at an early stage, leading to a more consensual approach at the final hearing. The guid-ance further advised that interested persons required sufficient notice and disclosure to properly take part in such proceedings.

The importance of coroners not giving any appearance of bias or giving the impres-sion that matters to be decided at the final hearing had been pre-determined was also emphasised by the Chief Coroner.

Practitioners should note that an inquest is an inquisitorial rather than adversarial process, it is not a trial, there are no parties and no person may address the coroner as to the facts.[42] Submissions may be made on the law, but it is the coroner's duty, sitting with or without a jury, to investigate the facts 'fully, fairly and fearlessly'.[43]

---

[29] *Goodson v HM Coroner for Bedfordshire and Luton* [2004] EWHC 2931 (Admin), [2006] 1 WLR 432.
[30] *R v Greater London South District Coroner, ex parte Driscoll* [1995] 159 JP 45.
[31] *R v Graham* (1905) 93 LT 371; *R v City of London Coroner, ex parte Calvi* The Times, 2 April 1983 (DC).
[32] *R v Secretary of State for the Home Department, ex parte Wright and Bennet* [2002] HRLR 1.
[33] *Ex p Bentley* (n 28).
[34] *R v East Berkshire Coroner, ex parte Buckley* (1992) 157 JP 425 (DC).
[35] *R v Avon Deputy Coroner, ex parte Lambourne* (29 July 2002, DC).
[36] *R v Antrim Coroner* [1980] NI 123.
[37] *R (D) v Inner South London Assistant Deputy Coroner* [2008] EWHC 3356 (Admin).
[38] *R v Inner London Coroner, ex parte Anderson* [2004] EWHC 2729 (Admin).
[39] *Ex p Middleton* (n 9) and *R v HM Coroner for Northamptonshire, ex parte Cash* [2007] EWHC 1354 (Admin).
[40] *Ex p Middleton* (n 9).
[41] *Brown v HM Coroner for Norfolk* (n 20)
[42] Rule 27, The Coroners (Inquests) Rules 2013
[43] *R v HM Coroner for North Humberside and Scunthorpe, ex parte Jamieson* [1995] QB 1, CA.

At the conclusion of the evidence, submissions are often made to the coroner as to which conclusions or jury questions can properly be left. Interested persons at inquests often have opposing aims and priorities and this is likely to remain a common area of challenge. If judicial review is to be sought, the question of when to make the application arises: wait until the objectionable decision is incorporated into an objectionable conclusion and then apply for review; or make a pre-emptive application in an attempt to prevent that decision being adopted and possibly prevent the need for a new inquest. The High Court recently considered two applications for judicial review that were made during the course of an inquest and prior to the jury's determination: in *Chief Constable of Devon and Cornwall v HM Coroner for Plymouth, Torbay and South Devon*[44] the application was granted, in *R (Cooper) v HM Coroner for North East Kent*[45] the application refused. What is clear from both cases is that it will only be in exceptional cases that the court will intervene in inquests that are still proceeding.

(3) Sufficiency of Inquiry and Article 2 ECHR

10-12 In cases where Article 2 of ECHR is engaged, the question of 'how' the person died is treated more broadly and is to be read as including the purpose of ascertaining 'in what circumstances' the person came by his or her death.[46] Under Article 2 the State has both substantive and procedural obligations. The substantive obligation is to have laws that protect the right and allow for full investigation of deaths. The procedural obligation is to implement a proper and independent public investigation in cases where the rights may have been breached and an arm of the state is implicated. Such an inquest is called for when the state's obligations to its citizens under the Convention are, or may be, called into question: such as deaths in any form of state detention, police shootings, or where there is a recognition of an immediate threat to life.[47]

In such cases an enhanced investigation is required, often called a *Middleton*[48] inquest, and certain criteria apply.[49] These criteria require that the investigation be initiated by the state, be effective and be carried out by someone genuinely independent. In addition, the hearing must have sufficient public scrutiny and the next of kin must have the opportunity to participate effectively in the hearing.

A standard inquest, often called a *Jamieson* inquest,[50] properly conducted should conform to these standards in any event. The increasing emphasis placed on family involvement in inquests and the new rule 13 mandating disclosure,[51] have brought the two types of inquest even closer.

---

[44] *Chief Constable of Devon and Cornwall v HM Coroner for Plymouth, Torbay and South Devon* [2013] EWHC 3729 (Admin).

[45] *R (Cooper) v HM Coroner for North East Kent* [2014] EWHC 586 (Admin).

[46] CJA 2009, s 5(2).

[47] *Osman v UK* (1998) 29 EHRR 245 (also mentioned above at 4-14).

[48] *Ex p Middleton* (n 9).

[49] *Jordan v UK* (2001) 37 EHRR 52.

[50] *R v HM Coroner for North Humberside and Scunthorpe, ex parte Jamieson* [1995] QB 1, CA. It should be noted that the state's obligations under the Convention also apply to *Jamieson* inquests.

[51] Coroners (Inquests) Rules 2013.

Geoffrey Sullivan

In a *Middleton* inquest, however, the scope of potential verdicts is wider, as is the role of the jury in providing them; for example, there must be a consideration of any defects in the system that contributed to the death, not simply a conclusion as to the course of events that directly led to and caused the death. The verdict must include the coroner's or the jury's conclusions on disputed factual issues in an expanded or narrative form.[52] It is important to remember in such inquests that it is for the coroner to determine the scope of such issues, and the coroner need not look into every peripheral matter.[53] Such a verdict must be careful not to trespass into giving opinions on matters of criminal or civil liability, and must be confined to matters of fact.[54] It is therefore likely that the way in which a coroner discharges his duties in a *Middleton* inquest, and how he applies the law and the rules of procedure, will be placed under greater scrutiny.

---

[52] *Ex p Middleton* (n 9) [36].

[53] *R (Allen) v HM Coroner for Inner North London* [2009] EWCA Civ 623, [2009] All ER (D) 287 and *R (D) v Inner South London Assistant Deputy Coroner* [2008] EWHC 3356 (Admin), [2008] All ER (D) 138.

[54] *Ex p Middleton* (n 9) [37]. However, this does not prevent it from being judgmental—see *R (Lewis) v Inner North London Coroner* [2009] EWHC 661 (Admin).

Part III
Specialist Areas—Youths, Mental Health, Extradition and European Union Law

11

Children, Young Persons and Juveniles

PIERS VON BERG

A. General Principles

(1) Introduction

11-1   Judicial review concerning children and young persons can arise in many different contexts. This chapter deals with the issues involved in applications for judicial review by young suspects, young defendants, young witnesses or young victims of crime. By way of example, the two most common instances are the charging or cautioning of young offenders and the sending of young defendants to the Crown Court for trial. The most common grounds of review in this area are that a public body has failed to fulfil a statutory duty, has unlawfully breached a child's rights under the European Convention of Human Rights (ECHR) or failed to follow mandatory guidance or policy. Practitioners considering judicial reviews involving a person aged under 18 need to be aware of the statutory framework, the way in which Convention rights operate in relation to children and the wide array of guidance and policies. This chapter attempts to chart this context and then identify where points of challenge lie.

The context is described in two parts. First, there are overarching principles that inform the way in which public bodies must act (described in Section A below). These are derived from statute and from international law and affect the way in which the ECHR is interpreted. For example, a public body must consider first the best interests of a child in all actions in regard to them. Secondly, there is a complex mesh of special procedural rules accorded to those under 18 throughout the criminal process, derived from many different sources. These are set out in the table in Section B.

In the subsequent two sections (C and D), the chapter explores five areas in which judicial review has been found to be a useful remedy. These are decisions relating to custody, out-of-court disposals, decisions to charge, trials and sentencing.

Readers should note that not all types of judicial review involving children are dealt with in this chapter. There is considerable overlap with other chapters:

i.   Children with mental health disorders are mentioned above at 12-37 and 12-43 with some discussion below at 11-37 in relation to rights of fair trial and special measures.[1]

ii.   Judicial review concerning decisions made by the police is dealt with above concerning stop and search (above at 4-16–4-38) search warrants (above at 4-39–4-49) arrest (above at 4-50–4-58) and protest (above at 4-59–4-72) (few of these challenges are age-specific).

iii. Challenges to decisions to prosecute children are dealt with above at 5-22 with more specific offences and guidance addressed below at 11-34.

iv.   Sending cases involving young defendants to the Crown Court is touched on below, but dealt with in detail in the sections concerning challenges to decisions by Youth Courts at 6-60–6-66.

---

[1] See also the section on Youths with Mental Disorders, including Learning Disabilities, in the CPS Legal Guidance on Young Offenders at www.cps.gov.uk/legal/v_to_z/youth_offenders/#a17. The CPS also has policies on 'Supporting victims and witnesses who have learning disabilities', www.cps.gov.uk/publications/docs/supporting_victims_and_witnesses_with_a_learning _disability.pdf, July 2009.

Piers von Berg

(2) Principles in Domestic and International Law

This chapter concerns those aged 18 and under. As will be seen below, persons aged **11-2** under 18 have a 'special position within the criminal justice system'.[2]

The first general point is that there is a 'youth justice system'. This is the system of criminal justice insofar as it applies to children and young persons.[3] The principal aim of the youth justice system is to prevent offending or reoffending by those aged under 18.[4] It is the duty of all persons and bodies carrying out functions in relation to the system to have regard to that aim.[5]

There are five provisions or categories that cut across many areas, which are specific to children that can provide grounds for review or inform the approach of the court in a criminal judicial review concerning youths:

  i. section 44(1) of the Children and Young Persons Act (CYPA) 1933;
  ii. section 11 of the Children Act 2004;
  iii. international law, including the following United Nations conventions, guidelines and rules:
    (a) the United Nations Convention on the Rights of the Child (UNCRC);
    (b) the United Nations Standard Minimum Rules for the Administration of Juvenile Justice (the 'Beijing Rules') 1985; and
    (c) the United Nations Guidelines for the Prevention of Juvenile Delinquency ('the Riyadh Guidelines') 1990.
  iv. Article 6 and Article 8 of ECHR as interpreted under the UNCRC; and
  v. section 149 of the Equality Act 2010.

The first three introduce a duty to have regard for a child's welfare, or a duty to place the child's welfare as a primary consideration. The United Nations instruments can influence the way in which rights under the ECHR and domestic law are interpreted. There is very little case law on section 149 of the Equality Act 2010 in this context.

Section 44(1) of CYPA 1933 requires every court to have regard to the welfare of a **11-3** child brought before it, whether as an offender or otherwise:[6]

> (1) Every court in dealing with a child or young person who is brought before it, either as an offender or otherwise, shall have regard to the welfare of the child or young person and shall in proper case take steps for removing him from undesirable surroundings, and for securing that proper provision is made for his education and training.

Section 44 has been applied in a variety of contexts in criminal judicial reviews. It has been held to be relevant when a court decides whether to impose a reporting restriction under sections 39 or 49(1) of CYPA 1933 (see the discussion below at 11-44).[7] It has also been held to be a necessary consideration when a court considers a fresh

---

[2] *R v G* [2003] UKHL 50, [2004] 1 AC 1034 [53] (Lady Hale).
[3] CDA 1998, s 42(1).
[4] ibid, s 37(1).
[5] ibid, s 37(2).
[6] See *R (R) v Durham Constabulary* [2005] UKHL 21 [2005] 1 WLR 1184 [25] (Lady Hale). All agencies working within the system have a duty to have regard to that aim. This case is discussed further below at 11-30.
[7] *R (Y) v Aylesbury Crown Court* [2012] EWHC 1140 (Admin) [41]; *T v DPP* [2003] EWHC 2408 (Admin); *R (T) v St Albans Crown Court* [2002] EWHC 1129 (Admin) [18].

application for bail by a youth.[8] It was a central consideration in challenges to the review of the tariff fixed for a young offender sentenced to detention at Her Majesty's pleasure under section 53(1) of CYPA 1933.[9] It has been cited and referred to in cases concerning remand of children charged with murder to local authority accommodation and the cautioning of young offenders, but without any noticeable impact on the outcome of those decisions.[10]

11-4   Section 11 of the Children Act 2004 requires bodies such as local authorities, a chief officer of police, a local probation board and youth offending teams to make arrangements to ensure that:

(a)   their functions are discharged having regard to the need to safeguard and promote the welfare of children; and

(b)   any services provided by another person pursuant to arrangements made by the person or body in the discharge of their functions are provided having regard to that need.

Such bodies must also have regard to any guidance provided by the Secretary of State in discharging their duty. A key document is the *Working Together to Safeguard Children: A guide to inter-agency working to safeguard and promote the welfare of Children*.[11] There is a vast range of guidance issued by several government departments.[12]

Section 11 has been relied on in criminal judicial reviews and is worth considering, as it imposes a specific duty. For example, *R (Alan Castle, Rosie Castle, Sam Eton) v Commissioner of Police for the Metropolis*[13] discussed above at 4-71 shows how section 11 is interpreted. This was a challenge to the lawfulness of a detention of three children (one aged 14 and two aged 16) in a police cordon during a protest from midday to between 7.00 and 8.30pm. The Divisional Court said that section 11 did not redefine the duties and functions of the police. Instead, Pitchford LJ said it had the following effect on those duties and functions:

> The impact which the duty will have upon the performance of a function will depend to a significant degree upon the function being performed and the circumstances in which it is being performed. The responsibility will take on its sharpest focus when a police officer encounters a child who needs protection, for example in circumstances such as those anticipated by the statutory guidance concerning police investigations during which an unprotected child or a child at risk comes to their attention. A police officer will not be deterred from performing his

---

[8] See *R (B) v Brent Youth Court* [2010] EWHC 1893 (Admin), discussed above at 6-49.

[9] *R (Smith) v Secretary of State for the Home Department* [2004] EWCA Civ 99, [2004] QB 1341 and *R (Smith) v Secretary of State for the Home Department* [2003] EWHC 692 (Admin), [2003] 1 WLR 2176. See also *R v Secretary of State, ex parte Venables and Thompson* [1997] 3 WLR 23, [1998] AC 407, 502 (Lord Browne-Wilkinson).

[10] See respectively *R (A) v Lewisham Youth Court* [2011] EWHC 1193 (Admin), [2012] 1 WLR 34 [20], and *D v Commissioner of Police of the Metropolis* [2008] EWHC 442 (Admin).

[11] This replaced *Working Together to Safeguard Children* (2010); *The Framework for the Assessment of Children in Need and their Families* (2000); and *Statutory guidance on making arrangements to safeguard and promote the welfare of children under section 11 of the Children Act 2004* (2007). See the Home Office website— http://media.education.gov.uk/assets/files/pdf/w/working %20together.pdf.

[12] A list of the guidance that sits alongside the above can be found at Appendix C of *Working Together to Safeguard Children: A guide to inter-agency working to safeguard and promote the welfare of Children*, 15 April 2013.

[13] *R (Alan Castle, Rosie Castle, Sam Eton) v Commissioner of Police for the Metropolis* [2011] EWHC 2317 (Admin).

public duty to detect or prevent crime just because a child is affected but when he does perform that duty he must, as the circumstances require, have *regard* to the statutory need.[14]

The Divisional Court applied the following test to the police decision:

The section 11 statutory duty required that planning, either in advance or at the time the decision to contain was made, should, where appropriate, have embraced the need to safeguard children and promote their welfare. If the decision-maker is unable to show that he could not, by taking reasonable steps, have avoided the need to use containment, or have mitigated the consequences to innocent third parties, in particular children, then he will have acted unlawfully towards them in breach of his public duty.[15]

It held that the police conformed to their duty. The children were lawfully contained and the police had plans in place for the release of vulnerable persons.

In *Castle* the court considered the UNCRC. The UNCRC is part of a range of interna-   **11-5**
tional instruments that may be drawn upon as an aid to interpreting domestic law and the ECHR. These also include the Beijing Rules and the Riyadh Guidelines. Although none have been incorporated into domestic law and the Beijing Rules and Riyadh Guidelines are not intended to be binding, they have on occasion been utilised by the courts.

A key provision of the UNCRC is Article 3(1):

In all actions concerning children, whether undertaken by public or private social welfare institutions, courts of law, administrative authorities or legislative bodies, the best interests of the child shall be a primary consideration.[16]

This was considered in *ZH (Tanzania) v Secretary of State for the Home Department*,[17] where the Supreme Court expressed the obiter view that the purpose of section 11 of the Children Act 2004 was to incorporate the spirit of Article 3(1). This was interpreted in the context of immigration and asylum law as follows:

This did not mean (as it would do in other contexts) that identifying their best interests would lead inexorably to a decision in conformity with those interests. Provided that the Tribunal did not treat any other consideration as inherently more significant than the best interests of the children, it could conclude that the strength of the other considerations outweighed them. The important thing, therefore, is to consider those best interests first.[18]

The Divisional Court in *Castle* relied on this principle in its assessment of the effect of section 11 of the Children Act 2004.

---

[14] ibid [51]. Emphasis contained in the judgment. The same was applied in *R (HC) v Secretary of State for the Home Department* [2013] EWHC 982 (Admin)—discussed below at 11-16.

[15] ibid [60].

[16] In October 2008, the United Nations Committee on the Rights of the Child issued 118 recommendations on the improvement of children's rights in the United Kingdom. For a report on progress, see the United Nation's Committee on the Rights of the Child's report: www2.ohchr.org/english/bodies/crc/docs/AdvanceVersions/CRC.C.OPAC.GBR.CO.1.pdf and the Children's Rights Alliance for England, *State of Children's Rights in England*, covering December 2012 to November 2013 (www.crae.org.uk/publications-resources/state-of-childrens-rights-in-england-2013/).

[17] *ZH (Tanzania) v Secretary of State for the Home Department* [2011] UKSC 4, [2011] 2 AC 166.

[18] ibid [23] (Lady Hale). See also [33].

In *R v G*[19] a well-known case on the issue of recklessness in criminal law, the House of Lords considered the culpability of two boys, aged 11 and 12, who threw lit newspapers under a bin which then caused £1m of damage to a shop. It was agreed that the boys did not think there was a risk of the fire spreading in the way it did. The old law in *R v Caldwell* [1982] AC 341, HL(E) compelled the judge to direct the jury that they could make no allowance for the boys' age, lack of maturity or inability to assess the situation. Lord Steyn referred to Article 40(1) of the UNCRC:

> States parties recognise the right of every child alleged as, accused of, or recognised as having infringed the penal law to be treated in a manner consistent with the promotion of the child's sense of dignity and worth, which reinforces the child's respect for the human rights and fundamental freedoms of others and which takes into account the child's age and the desirability of promoting the child's reintegration and the child's assuming a constructive role in society.[20]

His Lordship said that 'This provision imposes both procedural and substantive obligations on state parties to protect the special position of children in the criminal justice system'. This meant that it would be contrary to Article 40(1) to set the age of responsibility at 5 years or to ignore the age of a child in assessing whether a mental element was satisfied where the offence carried a maximum sentence of life imprisonment. His Lordship went on to say: 'the House cannot ignore the norm created by the Convention. This factor on its own justified a reappraisal of *R v Caldwell*'.[21]

11-6   In other cases the UNCRC has been brought to bear as an aid to interpreting the ECHR. The ECtHR has used the UNCRC, the Beijing Rules and the Riyadh Guidelines as an aid to interpreting the Convention. Lady Hale said in *R (R) v Durham Constabulary*[22] that 'it [the UNCRC] must be taken into account in the interpretation and application of those rights [under the ECHR] in our national law'.[23] In that case, all three international instruments informed the House of Lords' approach to the use of out-of-court disposals (see discussion below at 11-30).[24] The UNCRC and Beijing Rules have been used to interpret Article 6, and the Beijing Rules in cases of delay.[25] Under Article 6, the right to a trial within a reasonable time should be interpreted in light of Article 40(2)(b)(iii) of the UNCRC, which entitles a child (a person aged under 18) to a trial 'without delay'; rule 20.1 of the Beijing Rules requires criminal proceedings against a child to be handled expeditiously from the outset and without unnecessary delay.[26] In *Dyer v Watson* [2002] UKPC D1, [2004] 1 AC 379 the defendant was charged at age 13 and faced trial at age 16. There was a clear risk that with the passage

---

[19] *R v G* [2003] UKHL 50, [2004] 1 AC 1034.

[20] ibid, [53].

[21] ibid, [53]. Lord Hutton agreed with the speech of Lord Steyn. Note that Lord Bingham gave the lead judgment with whom the other members agreed. His Lordship did not rely on the UNCRC and see in particular his comments at [37] regarding modifications to the law to take account of age.

[22] *R (R) v Durham Constabulary* (n 6).

[23] ibid [26]. Reference was made to *V v United Kingdom* [1999] 30 EHRR 121, discussed below at 11-37.

[24] 'There can be no doubt, therefore, that constructive diversion policies and practices are thoroughly consistent with the fundamental principles of all these international instruments', ibid [24]–[29] (Lady Hale).

[25] *Dyer v Watson* [2002] UKPC D1, [2004] 1 AC 379 (discussed below at 11-41). See also and *V v United Kingdom* (1999) 30 EHRR 121 [76] (see below at 11-37).

[26] *Dyer v Watson* (n 25) [23], [104].

of time, the defendant would find it impossible to relate to procedure and disposition of the offence.[27]

Article 8 has also been interpreted in conjunction with the UNCRC in judicial reviews concerning children. In *R (SR) v Nottingham Magistrates' Court*,[28] Brooke LJ held that every public authority concerned with the care and management of children in custody must take their interests as a primary consideration.[29] This was a challenge to a decision of a District Judge to remand in custody prior to sentencing, and also that section 98 of the Crime and Disorder Act (CDA) 1998 was incompatible with the Human Rights Act (HRA) 1998 because it discriminated against boys aged 15–16. The Secretary of State accepted that where children are in custody, the UNCRC informs the content of Article 8.[30] This was applied in *R (HC) v Secretary of State for the Home Department*.[31] The claimant relied on Article 8 to challenge the provisions of Code C of the Police and Criminal Evidence Act (PACE) 1984 that provided that 17-year-olds should be treated as adults in police custody, and so restricted their access to help from their parents acting as appropriate adults (see discussion below at 11-16). Moses LJ held that: 'To afford a 17-year-old detainee no more than the rights and protections afforded to an adult is not consistent with the principle that Article 8 is to be interpreted in harmony with the UNCRC.'[32]

The above-mentioned international instruments have also aided the interpretation of other statutes and policies. In *McKerry v Teesdale and Wear Valley Justices*[33] Lord Bingham LCJ held that the CYPA 1933 should be read 'against the background' of international instruments including the UNCRC, the Beijing Rules and the recommendations of the Council of Europe[34] (the case concerned reporting restrictions—see below at 11-44). In addition, the UNCRC has been incorporated into the Code for Crown Prosecutors.[35] It

11-7

---

[27] ibid [181] (Lord Rodger), citing the commentary to the Beijing Rules, r 20: 'As time passes, the juvenile will find it increasingly difficult, if not impossible, to relate the procedure and disposition to the offence, both intellectually and psychologically.'

[28] *R (SR) v Nottingham Magistrates' Court* [2001] EWHC Admin 802. See also *R(HH) v Westminster City Magistrates' Court* [2012] UKSC 25, [33].

[29] In ibid [66], Brooke LJ found that they are entitled to the following rights drawn from the UNCRC, so far as these are consistent with their custodial status: i) the entitlement of such protection and care as is necessary for their well-being; ii) the right to maintain personal relations and direct contact with both their parents on a regular basis; iii) the right to a standard of living adequate for their physical, mental, spiritual, moral and social development; iv) the right to insist that any period of imprisonment must be in conformity with the law and used as a measure of last resort and for the shortest appropriate period of time; v) the entitlement, when deprived of liberty, to be treated with humanity and respect for the inherent dignity of the human person and in a manner which takes into account the needs of persons of their age; vi) the entitlement, when deprived of liberty, to be separated from adults unless it is considered in their best interests not to be so separated; vii) the entitlement, when deprived of liberty, to maintain contact with their family through correspondence and visits, save in exceptional circumstances; viii) when it is alleged or recognised that they have infringed the penal law, the right to be treated in a manner consistent with the promotion of their dignity and worth.

[30] ibid [65]. See also *Neulinger v Switzerland* [2010] 54 EHRR 1087 [31], [131], [135].

[31] *HC* (n 14).

[32] ibid [84]. The judgment at [13]–[21] contains a helpful analysis of the way in which 17-year-olds are treated under the legal framework set out in the table below at 11-14.

[33] *McKerry v Teesdale and Wear Valley Justices* (2000) 164 JP 355.

[34] Specifically, Recommendation R(87)20 of the Committee of Ministers of the Council of Europe on Social Reactions to Juvenile Delinquency and the European Convention on Human Rights.

[35] When considering whether it is in the public interest to prosecute a person under the age of 18, 'Prosecutors must also have regard to the obligations arising under the United Nations 1989 Convention on the Rights of the Child', the Crown Prosecution Service, 'The Code for Crown Prosecutors', January 2013, p 12. Note that 'international conventions' are also referred to in the sentencing guidelines for youths, para 1.3.

is notable that the courts have on occasion refrained from utilising these international instruments when the ECHR is not in issue. For example, in *R (T) v The Secretary of State for Justice and Birmingham Magistrates' Court*[36] the Divisional Court resisted an attempt to use the UNCRC and the Beijing Rules as an aid to interpreting section 33 of the CYPA 1933 concerning the treatment of children in custody. The court held that the case did not involve a Convention right and the UNCRC and Beijing Rules had not been incorporated into domestic law. This decision was recently approved by Sir Brian Leveson P in *R (JC and RT) v Central Criminal Court*[37] where the President deprecated 'direct reference to them [the Beijing Rules and other unspecified 'international instruments'], outside of the use made by the European Court ... the courts are concerned with binding and persuasive authorities' and they were 'certainly not authoritative' on the issue before that court on the construction of section 39(1) of the CYPA 1933.[38]

11-8   Section 149(7) defines age as a 'protected characteristic' under the Equality Act 2010. Section 149(1) of the Equality Act 2010 provides what is known as the Public Sector Equality Duty (PSED):

> (1)   A public authority must, in the exercise of its functions, have due regard to the need to—
>   (a)   eliminate discrimination, harassment, victimisation and any other conduct that is prohibited by or under this Act;
>   (b)   advance equality of opportunity between persons who share a relevant protected characteristic and persons who do not share it;
>   (c)   foster good relations between persons who share a relevant protected characteristic and persons who do not share it.

Under section 149(3) a public body must have due regard to the need to:

> (a)   remove or minimise disadvantages suffered by persons who share a relevant protected characteristic that are connected to that characteristic;
> (b)   take steps to meet the needs of persons who share a relevant protected characteristic that are different from the needs of persons who do not share it;

There are very few examples of this section being advanced as a ground of judicial review in respect of children.[39] It was relied on in *T*[40] a case concerning an alleged failure to prevent youths in custody associating with adults. This submission failed on the facts in that case, but it is notable that it was considered. It was summarised as:

> In carrying out its function of detaining defendants and deciding to accommodate children such as the claimant in the same cell block as adults, the Ministry of Justice was obliged to have due regard to the particular needs of children in such circumstances and to take steps to meet them. There was no evidence it had carried out its due regard duty rigorously ... or asked whether the detention, with its potential impact, would be consistent with the need to pay due regard to the principle of equality.[41]

---

[36] *R (T) v The Secretary of State for Justice and Birmingham Magistrates' Court* [2013] EWHC 1119 (Admin) [32].
[37] *R (JC and RT) v Central Criminal Court* [2014] EWHC 1041 (Admin).
[38] ibid [33].
[39] For an example outside of the criminal sphere see *R (Hunt) v North Somerset Council* [2013] EWCA Civ 1320 concerning a local authority's reduction in its budget for youth services.
[40] *T* (n 36).
[41] ibid [52]. See also discussion above at principle of non-discrimination and ECHR law at 1-139.

These cross-cutting provisions sit amongst a vast array of Acts of Parliament, statu- **11-9**
tory instruments, EU law,[42] agency policies and statements of guidance governing the
treatment of children or young persons in the criminal justice system. For example,
there are five different and overlapping definitions for a person aged under 18 arising
from at least six different Acts of Parliament, one statutory instrument and the CPR
that apply in separate circumstances and according to various ages (see table below
at 11-14).

A full account of the youth justice system and its services is outside the scope of
this chapter. As suggested above, the law is complex and extensive in this area. A summary of the most common provisions that require children and young persons to be
treated differently to adults is set out below at 11-14. The remainder of the chapter
focuses on areas where judicial review has been an appropriate remedy. As stated above,
readers should cross-refer where necessary to chapters on the substantive law regarding
particular public law defendants.

(3) Age

Since the law varies between the ages of 10–17, an important preliminary issue might be **11-10**
determining the age of a defendant, if this is unclear. In those circumstances, section 99
of the CYPA 1933 applies. This allows the court to inquire into the matter, consider any
relevant evidence and make a determination. Where a defendant attains the age of 18
after proceedings have begun, a Youth Court can continue to deal with him under section 29 of the Children Act 1989.[43] The Divisional Court has held that section 29 permits
the sentencing court to deal with the defendant as if he is a youth.[44]

(4) Party Status (Ability to Bring Proceedings) and Litigation Friends

A preliminary point is that whilst a person aged between 10 and 17 can be a party to **11-11**
criminal proceedings as a defendant,[45] they cannot conduct civil proceedings without a
litigation friend. In civil proceedings a child is under 18 (CPR 21.1(2)(a)). A child must
have a litigation friend in order to conduct civil proceedings, unless the court grants

---

[42] Art 24 of the Charter of Fundamental Rights and Freedoms of the European Union mirrors the obligations contained in Art 3(1) of the UNCRC (for discussion of EU law, see Chapter 14 below). There are no
reported cases on how Art 24 has been applied in criminal judicial reviews. Conceivably, it may have application in the context of two EU Directives: on combating the sexual abuse and sexual exploitation of children
and child pornography (Directive 2011/93), and on establishing minimum standards on the rights, support
and protection of victims of crime (Directive 2012/29).

[43] Therefore any remission of the case to the adult magistrates' court is unlawful. *R v Uxbridge Magistrates'
Court, ex parte H* (1998) 162 JP 327.

[44] *A v DPP* [2002] EWHC 403 (Admin), [2002] 2 Cr App R (S) 88. The court clarified that s 29 was not
impliedly repealed by PCC(S)A, s 100.

[45] Note the European Court of Human Rights (ECtHR) rejected the argument that the trial of two boys
for offences committed when they were 10 was a breach of Art 3, in *T v United Kingdom, V v United Kingdom*
App no 24724/94 [2000] 2 All ER 1024 (Note), (2000) 30 EHRR 121.

permission otherwise (CPR 21.2(3)).[46] The court will only grant such permission where the child has sufficient maturity and understanding.[47] In all other circumstances, a child cannot take any step in the proceedings without a litigation friend except to issue and serve the claim form or apply for the appointment of a litigation friend (CPR 21.3(2) (b)(i) and (ii)).

A person can become a litigation friend for a child either by filing a certificate of suitability[48] with the claim form, or by applying to the court to be appointed.[49] Importantly, a litigation friend must undertake to pay any costs which the claimant may be ordered to pay (CPR 21.4(3)). They are under a duty to take all decisions in the claim for the benefit of the child (PD, para 2.1).

As far as children are concerned, a litigation friend can be a person appointed by the court or a person who can fairly and competently conduct proceedings on behalf of a child and have no interests adverse to that of the child (CPR 21.4(2) and 21.6).

Any settlement, compromise, payment or acceptance of money paid into court in a judicial review claim on behalf of child is not valid without the approval of the court (CPR 21.10(1)).[50]

A child and their litigation friend should not be named in a claim form, but identified by their initials, eg John Smith and his litigation friend, Richard Smith, becomes '*JS (a child, by his litigation friend RS)*'.

(5) Taking Instructions

11-12   The above must be taken into consideration when taking instructions, in particular the contrasting position of children in criminal proceedings, where they do not require an adult in order to conduct their defence. For example, the Note for Guidance 1E of Code C of PACE 1984 allows for a solicitor to advise a juvenile (and a 17-year-old) suspect without an appropriate adult present. This is not to say an appropriate adult (defined below at 11-15) is merely an observer. They may also instruct a solicitor on behalf of a juvenile or instruct him to advise on their role.[51] Furthermore, an appropriate adult may instruct a solicitor against a juvenile's wishes providing it is in their best interests.[52] Clearly, both

---

[46] A litigation friend's appointment ceases when the child reaches 18 (CPR 21.9(1)). A notice must be served on the other parties stating that the appointment has ceased, give his address for service and stating whether he intends to continue the proceedings (CPR 21.9(4)). Importantly, if he does not do so within 28 days, the claim may be struck out (CPR 21.9(5)). The notice also acts to terminate any liability the litigation friend had for costs (CPR 21.9(6)). See also PD21 paras 5.1–5.8.

[47] *Gillick v West Norfolk and Wisbech Area Heath Authority* [1986] AC 112.

[48] Form N235. The certificate must set out that the litigation friend consents to act as such, they know or believe the claimant to be a child, they can fairly and competently conduct the proceedings for the child and have no interest adverse to that of the child, and, that they undertake to pay any costs which the child may be ordered to pay (see PD 21, para 2.3(2)a–f). The certificate must be filed on behalf of one of the child's parents or guardians, or if there are none, on the person with whom the child resides or in whose care the child is.

[49] See PD 21, paras 3.1–3.6.

[50] This means the other party may renege on it (*Drinkall v Whitwood* [2003] EWCA Civ 1547, [2004] 1 WLR 462). See also CPR 21.11 and PD 21, paras 8.1–8.5 for control of any money recovered and CPR 21.11A and PD 21, paras 8A.1–8A.2 for the ability of a litigation friend to recover expenses incurred. See also PD 21, paras 6.1–6.9.

[51] PACE, Code C, paras 3.19 and 6.5A.

[52] PACE, Code C, para 6.5A. However, a juvenile cannot be compelled to see a solicitor if they do not wish to.

in criminal proceedings and any subsequent civil proceedings arising from them (such as judicial review), practitioners will need to bear the above in mind, whilst steering a course that is sensitive to the needs of the client and the involvement of any others, including family who may be acting as appropriate adults and/or litigation friends.

B. The Statutory Framework

(1) Definitions and Age

Persons aged between 10 and 17 are variously defined as: **11-13**

   i.   children—those aged 10–13 or 10–17;
   ii.   young persons—those aged 14–17;
   iii. juveniles—those aged 10–16;
   iv. relevant minors—those aged 10–16;[53] and
   v.   young offenders—those aged 10–20 who have been convicted of an offence.

(2) Overview of Criminal Law Affecting those Aged Under 18

Generally speaking, those under 18 years are afforded additional protection with special   **11-14**
rules governing their passage through the youth justice system. Whilst they are subject to many of the same provisions applicable to adults, there are various provisions applicable only to their particular age groups. To a great degree, age determines the level of protection an individual can be provided in the youth justice system (see table below). For example:

   i.   Those aged between 10, 11 or 12 are treated differently to those aged 14 to 16 in areas of electronic tagging, taking of intimate samples and remand.
   ii.   Those aged 10 to 16 are treated differently to those aged 17 in certain areas of pre-trial investigation, out-of-court disposals and remand.

These distinctions have led to judicial reviews of the legal framework itself. The fact that 17-year-olds are not treated as juveniles under PACE 1984 has led to judicial reviews of Code C (see below at 11-16). Although Code C has been recently amended as a result of one such challenge to allow 17-year-olds the same protection as those aged 16, the statutory provisions in PACE 1984 remain unchanged.[54] For example, section 37(15) defines an 'arrested juvenile' as a person who appears under 17 for the purposes of Part IV of PACE 1984, which means that 17-year-olds are not accorded the same treatment as other children for detention after charge (section 38(6) of PACE 1984). Other areas also remain unchanged, such as the giving of 'appropriate consent' (section 65(1) of PACE 1984). Similarly, other statutes such as the Bail Act 1976 and Legal Aid, Sentencing and Punishment of Offenders Act (LASPO) 2012 maintain the distinction between

---

[53] Magistrates' Courts (Children and Young Persons) Rules 1992, r 4(1).
[54] *HC* and see PACE 1984, Code C, paras 1.5A a) and b). See below at 11-16 (n 14).

17-year-olds and other children and young persons. This exempts 17-year-olds from certain special treatment in areas such as bail and out-of-court disposals. It remains to be seen whether any of these provisions will be the subject of challenge on grounds of their incompatibility with the HRA 1998 following the successful review of Code C.

Another ground of judicial review is where police or local authorities have failed to comply with their duties to children and young persons, or juveniles as set out below. The relevant authorities are footnoted after each provision and then explored in more detail in Sections C and D of this chapter. Practitioners should bear in mind that the table below does not set out all the relevant law, as there are many additional provisions that apply to adults and children alike. It serves to summarise the special provisions or guidance for those aged under 18, and to highlight where differences in age are important and where 17-year-olds are treated as adults.

	Aged 10–13 years[55]	Aged 14–16 years	Aged 17 years
Definitions	In civil proceedings—a child (CPR 21.1(2)(a)). In proceedings under the Children Act 1989—a child.		
	Police powers including detention, interviewing and custody (PACE 1984 and Codes of Practice)—a juvenile.[56]		Note provisions of Codes of Practice that apply to juveniles also apply to 17 year olds (Code C para 1.5A)
	A relevant minor under the Magistrates' Courts (Children and Young Persons) Rules 1992, r 4(1).		
	Under CYPA 1933 and 1969—a child.[57]	Under CYPA 1933 and CYPA 1969—a young person[58]	
	Under the Bail Act 1976—a child.[59]	Under the Bail Act 1976—a young person.[60]	
	Under the Crime and Disorder Act (CDA) 1998 (out-of-court disposals)—a child.[61]	Under the CDA 1998 (out-of-court disposals)—a young person.[62]	
	Under LASPO 2012 (remands otherwise than on bail)—a child (note that amendments to the CDA 1998 for out-of-court disposals will use the definitions in that Act).[63]		

[55] Children aged under 10 may be subject to a child safety order if they have committed an act that might constitute a criminal offence had they been aged 10 or over (the Crime and Disorder Act (CDA) 1998, s 11). They may also be taken into police protection under the Children Act 1989, s 46. There is a conclusive presumption that they cannot be guilty of an offence (the Children and Young Persons Act (CYPA) 1933, s 50).

[56] PACE 1984, s 37(15) and Code C, para 1.5—a person who appears to be under 17.

[57] CYPA 1933, s 107(1). The Children and Young Persons Act (CYPA) 1969, s 70(1) but note s 29(2) excludes 17-year-olds in relation to recognisances for release under s 29(1).

[58] CYPA 1933, s 107(1) and CYPA 1969, s 70(1). Note this does not apply to CYPA 1933, s 34 as per the Criminal Justice Act 1991 (Commencement No 3 Order) 1992 (SI 1992/331), s 2(4).

[59] Bail Act 1976, s 2(2).

[60] Bail Act 1976, s 2(2) as amended by LASPO 2012 from 3 December 2012.

[61] CDA 1998, s 117(1).

[62] ibid.

[63] LASPO 2012, s 91(6).

	Aged 10–13 years[55]	Aged 14–16 years	Aged 17 years
Duty to have regard for welfare	Every court has a duty to have regard to welfare of any child or young person brought before it[64] and it is the duty of all persons carrying out functions in relation to the youth justice system to have regard to this aim.[65] See also Children Act 2004, s 11 discussed above at 11-4.		
Reporting restrictions during a criminal investigation	Where a criminal investigation has begun, no matter relating to any person involved in the offence shall while he is under 18 be included in any publication if it likely to lead to his identification.[66]		
Arrest	Where the police wish to interview a child who is a ward of court an application must be made for permission. The application must be on notice to all parties unless it is considered necessary for the child to be interviewed without a party knowing. There are exceptions to seeking permission where it is appropriate, if not essential, to take urgent action (e.g. in cases of serious offences against a child where collection of forensic evidence ought to be done promptly, where the police wish to interview a child on suspicion of committing an offence or as a potential witness). In such cases the police should notify the parent or foster parent, or another appropriate adult, and if practicable, the children's guardian.[67]		
	It is preferable that a juvenile is not arrested at his place of education unless it is unavoidable. Where he is so arrested, the principal or his nominee should be informed.[68]		
	Children and young persons arrested pursuant to a warrant cannot be released unless their parent or guardian provides a recognisance.[69]		
Informing parents and guardians of arrest and detention	The custody officer must, if it is practicable, ascertain the identity of a person responsible for their welfare. That person must be informed as soon as practicable that the juvenile has been arrested, the reasons for the arrest and where they are detained.[70] The custody officer must also inform the appropriate adult as soon as practicable of the grounds for any detention, their whereabouts and to ask the adult to attend to see the detainee. The procedure for detained persons, whether at a police station or elsewhere, as set out in paras 3.1–3.5 of Code C must be complied with in the presence of an appropriate adult.[71]		

---

[64] CYPA 1933, s 44.

[65] Cm 3809, para 2.5. This will include police, social services, the Probation Service, those working in youth offending teams, the CPS, defence solicitors and the Prison Service. Arguably, it would include those to whom contracts are awarded to perform services in the youth justice system.

[66] Youth Justice and Criminal Evidence Act (YJCEA) 1999, s 44.

[67] See Practice Direction 12D Inherent Jurisdiction (Including Wardship) Proceedings.

[68] PACE 1984, Code C, Note for Guidance 11C.

[69] CYPA 1969, s 29(1) and (2). The amount is determined by the custody officer in order to secure the child or young person's attendance at a future hearing. It may also be made conditional on the attendance of the parent.

[70] PACE 1984, Code C paras 3.13–3.15. The person may be the parent or guardian, or if they are a Looked After Child (see below at 11-15) a person appointed by that authority with responsibility for their welfare or any other person who for the time being has assumed responsibility for their welfare.

[71] PACE 1984, Code C, para 3.17.

	Aged 10–13 years[55]	Aged 14–16 years	Aged 17 years
Appropriate adults and legal advice	The detainee shall be advised that the duties of an appropriate adult include giving advice and assistance and that they may consult with the appropriate adult in private at any time.[72] If the detainee or appropriate adult on their behalf ask for a solicitor to attend section 6 of PACE 1984 shall apply. An appropriate adult should consider whether legal advice is required. They may ask for a solicitor to attend even if the detainee indicates they do not wish for legal advice, if this is in the best interests of the detainee. The detainee cannot be compelled to see a solicitor if they do not wish to.[73] Note the provision of legal advice in the absence of an appropriate adult (Note for Guidance 1E of Code C).		
Police bail	For street bail, the arresting officer must assess the level of risk to the safety and welfare of a juvenile and telephone contact must be made with parent or guardian as soon as practicable to inform them of the details of the arrest.[74] A constable may impose conditions on a child or young person for their own interest or welfare.[75]		
	A parent or guardian may consent to the surety of a child or young person. They may be required to secure that the child or young person complies with any requirement imposed on him. Such a requirement cannot be imposed if the child or young person will reach the age of 17 when they surrender to custody.[76]		
	The rights of a juvenile must be confirmed to allow them to use them immediately without waiting for an appropriate adult to arrive and in the presence of an appropriate adult once they have arrived. A detainee should not be placed in a police cell unless no other secure accommodation is available and the custody officer considers that it is not practicable to supervise them whilst they are not placed in a cell, or a cell provides more comfortable accommodation than other secure accommodation at the station. They may not be put in a cell with an adult prisoner.[77] Whenever possible, detainees should be visited more frequently.[78]		

---

[72] PACE 1984, Code C, para 3.18.
[73] PACE 1984, Code C, para 6.5A.
[74] Home Office, *Street Bail Guidance*, Home Office Circular 061/2003, pp 3–4.
[75] Bail Act 1976, s 3A(5)(d).
[76] ibid, s 3(7).
[77] PACE 1984, Code C, para 8.8.
[78] PACE 1984, Code C, para 9B, Note For Guidance.

Piers von Berg

	Aged 10–13 years[55]	Aged 14–16 years	Aged 17 years
Detention	There shall be arrangements to prevent a child or young person whilst in detention at a police station, in transit to or from any criminal court, or waiting at a criminal court, from associating with an adult (excluding relatives). This does not include those jointly charged. Girls shall be under the care of a woman at the above stages.[79] An officer should consider the fact that a juvenile is under 18 and their age when deciding whether to conduct a review by telephone or in person.[80] Detention of a juvenile for longer than 24 hours will be dependent on the circumstances of the case with reference to the person's special vulnerability, the obligation to provide an opportunity for representations to be made prior to a decision, the need to consult and consider the views of an appropriate adult and any alternatives to police custody.[81]		
Interviews	A juvenile must not be interviewed or asked to sign a written statement under caution or record of interview in the absence of an appropriate adult. They may be interviewed in the absence of an appropriate adult if an officer of the rank of superintendent or above considers that any consequent delay will lead to interference or harm to evidence, interference or physical harm to other persons or serious loss or damage to property, and, they are satisfied that the interview would not significantly harm their physical or mental state.[82] A juvenile can only be interviewed at their place of education in exceptional circumstances and if their principal or nominee agrees. Every effort must be made to inform the parent(s) or responsible person and appropriate adult. The interview may be conducted in their absence, if the offence is not against the educational institution, and waiting for the appropriate adult may cause unreasonable delay. In such circumstances, their principal or their nominee may act as the appropriate adult.[83] Regarding drawing of adverse inferences, the information that should be provided before any inference can be drawn (concerning the offence investigated etc), must be provided in the presence of an appropriate adult.[84] Special care should be taken when interviewing a juvenile, as they may 'without knowing or wishing to do so, be particularly prone in certain circumstances to provide information that may be unreliable, misleading or self-incriminating'.[85] It is important to obtain corroborating evidence wherever possible.[86]		

---

[79] CYPA 1933, s 31. A failure to provide such arrangements was successfully challenged in *T* (n 36)—see below at 11-18.

[80] PACE 1984, Code C para 15.3C.

[81] PACE 1984, Code C, paras 15.2A and 15.3. See PACE, s 42(1) for the extension of periods of detention.

[82] PACE 1984, Code C, paras 11.15, 11.18 and 11.1(a)–(c). Both parents can perform the role of an appropriate adult and be present in the interview—see *H and M v DPP* [1998] Crim LR 653 (QB). See below at 11-15 for further discussion of appropriate adults.

[83] PACE 1984 Code C, 11.16.

[84] PACE 1984, Code C, para 10.12. The information that must be provided first is at para 10.11.

[85] PACE 1984 1984, Code C, para 11C, Note for Guidance. Article 6 may be engaged—see *Panovits v Cyprus* 27 BHRC 464.

[86] ibid.

	Aged 10–13 years[55]	**Aged 14–16 years**	**Aged 17 years**
	An interpreter should be called if a juvenile is interviewed and their appropriate adult appears to have a hearing or speech impediment unless the interview is urgent.[87]		
Interviews of child witnesses and victims	There is guidance in 'Achieving Best Evidence in Criminal Proceedings: Guidance on interviewing victims and witnesses, and guidance on using special measures March 2011'.[88] Where a parent refuses consent for the police to interview, a family court has a jurisdiction to make a specific issue order or declaration. The test is a balance of interests between the rights of the child and the administration of justice and interests of others.[89] If a youth is cautioned in the absence of an appropriate adult, the caution must be repeated in their presence.[90] The appropriate adult must be given an opportunity to read and sign the interview record or any written statement.[91]		
Administering of cautions or youth conditional cautions	No caution other than a youth caution or a youth conditional caution may be given to a child or young person.[92] Youth cautions may be given if a constable decides there is sufficient evidence to charge a person with an offence, the person admits that he committed the offence and the constable does not think the person should be prosecuted or given a youth conditional caution.[93] Youth conditional cautions may be administered if an authorised person has evidence the person has committed an offence, the relevant prosecutor decides there is sufficient evidence and a conditional caution should be given. In addition, the offender must have admitted the offence, the authorised person explains the effect of the caution and warns him of the consequences of failure to comply, and, the offender signs a document containing details of the above.[94] The conditions may aim to facilitate rehabilitation, ensure reparation or punish.[95]		
	A youth caution must be given in the presence of an appropriate adult.[96] The warning and explanation accompanying a conditional caution must also be given in the presence of an appropriate adult.[97] A constable must explain the effect of that caution to the child or young person and the appropriate adult.		

---

[87] PACE 1984, Code C, para 13.6 and paras 11.1 or 11.18(c) in cases of urgency.

[88] CPS, Department for Education, Department for Health and Welsh Assembly Government, March 2011, see in particular pp 14–27 on child witnesses. It is arguable this applies to suspects—see *R(M) v Leicestershire Constabulary* [2009] EWHC 3640 (Admin).

[89] *Chief Constable of Greater Manchester v I* [2007] EWHC 1837 (Fam), [2008] 1 FLR 504.

[90] PACE 1984, Code C para 10.12.

[91] PACE 1984, Code C, para 11.12.

[92] CDA 1998, s 66ZA(6).

[93] ibid, ss 66ZA and 66ZB. Note that under the old system of warnings and reprimands a failure to notify a person that a warning for indecent assault would require him to register as a sex offender did not breach Art 6—see *R (R) v Durham Constabulary* (n 6). See discussion at 11-30.

[94] ibid, s 66B.

[95] ibid, s 66A(3).

[96] ibid, s 66ZA(2).

[97] ibid, s 66B(5).

	Aged 10–13 years[55]	Aged 14–16 years	Aged 17 years
'Appropriate consent' for identification, photographs and samples[98]	The consent of that person's parent or guardian.	The consent of that person and his/her parent or guardian.	The consent of that person.[99]
Taking of intimate samples[100]	Appropriate consent must be given (see above) otherwise the same procedure for adults applies including authorisation by an officer with reasonable grounds, informing the person in advance of certain matters and recording information afterwards.[101]		
Non-intimate samples[102]	The same provisions that apply to adults apply to children and young persons. These include the power to take a non-intimate sample without appropriate consent but subject to the conditions set out in PACE 1984, s 63.		
Testing for Class A drugs	The arrest condition or charge condition must be met. Both the age and request condition must be met. The notification condition must be met in relation to arrest, charge or age condition. The arrest condition is that the offence is a trigger offence[103] or an officer of least rank of inspector has reasonable grounds for suspecting that misuse of Class A drugs has caused or contributed to the commission of the alleged offence and he authorises the test. The charge condition is that the person has been charged with a trigger offence, or the person has been charged with an offence and the above condition concerning an officer of at least rank of inspector applies. The request condition is that an officer has requested the person to give a sample. The notification condition concerns a notice provided by the Secretary of State to that particular police area as defined in s 63B(4A). The making of a request, the giving of a warning and the taking of a sample may not take place in the absence of an appropriate adult.[104] If the arrest condition is met, the age condition is that the person has attained at least 18 years.		

[98] PACE 1984, s 65. An appropriate adult cannot give the appropriate consent. Photographs may be taken without appropriate consent, if it is withheld or it is not practical to obtain it. Fingerprints may be taken without appropriate consent and prior to arrest if the requirements of PACE 1984, s 61(6A) are met. These relate to reasonable suspicion and lack of knowledge of a person's name. Non-intimate samples may be taken without appropriate consent if the requirements of PACE 1984, ss 63(2), 63(3) and 63(3B) are met. Appropriate consent is mandatory for taking of intimate samples (s 62(1)).

[99] PACE 1984, s 65(1). It applies to intimate searches, X-ray and ultrasound, identification (Code D) and taking of fingerprints, samples, footwear impressions, photographs and evidential searches and examinations. An appropriate adult must be present when the warning is given regarding drug searches and consent is sought. PACE 1984, Annex A, para 2B.

[100] An intimate sample is defined as either a sample of blood, semen or any other tissue fluid, urine or pubic hair; a dental impression; a swab taken from any part of a person's genitals (including pubic hair) or from a person's body orifice other than the mouth (PACE 1984, s 65).

[101] See PACE 1984, s 62.

[102] A 'non-intimate sample' is either a sample of hair other than pubic hair; a sample taken from a nail on from under a nail; a swab taken from any part of a person's body other than a part from which a swab taken would be an intimate sample; saliva; or, a skin impression (PACE 1984, s 65).

[103] Listed in Code C, Notes for Guidance, para 17E.

[104] PACE 1984, Code C, para 17.7

	Aged 10–13 years[55]	Aged 14–16 years	Aged 17 years
		If the charge condition is met, the age condition is that the person has attained at least 14 years.	
		A request, warning and taking of the sample must be done in the presence of an appropriate adult.[105]	
	If the test is positive, an officer may only impose a requirement that a person attend an Initial Assessment if that person is aged at least 18 years.[106]		
Searches and examination to ascertain identity	Appropriate consent is required unless it is not practicable to obtain it. Otherwise children and young persons are subject to the same provisions as adults.[107]		
Intimate search[108]	Appropriate consent is required. An appropriate adult of the same sex must be present for the search. There is an exception if a juvenile objects to this in the presence of an appropriate adult. A record shall be made of the decision and signed by both.[109] An appropriate adult must be present when the person is informed of the grounds and authority for the search.[110] Appropriate consent is required in writing for a search for a Class A drug which the suspect intends for supply or export. Note that a court may draw such inferences from a refusal to provide appropriate consent to a drug search 'as appear proper'.[111]		
Strip search	An appropriate adult must be present except in urgent cases. The provisions on consent are as above. As above a juvenile may object to this in their presence and a record made.[112] The presence of more than two people other than the appropriate adult is only allowed in the 'most exceptional case'.[113]		
Photographing of suspects	Appropriate consent is required or, if it is withheld or it is not practicable to obtain it, without it.[114]		
Fingerprinting	Fingerprints may not be taken without the appropriate consent. Consent must be in writing if it is given when a person is in a police station. There is a range of scenarios when appropriate consent can be dispensed with. For example, they may be taken without the appropriate consent if the person is detained in consequence of an arrest for a recordable offence and he has not had his fingerprint taken during the investigation or if he answers bail to a police station or court and the court or an officer of at least rank of inspector authorises it.[115]		

---

[105] PACE 1984, Code C, para 17.7. Note this is inconsistent with PACE 1984, s 63B(5A).
[106] PACE 1984, Code C, para 17.17 (see Part 3 of the Drugs Act 2005).
[107] PACE 1984, s 54A(2).
[108] An 'intimate search' is a search which consists of the physical examination of a person's body orifices other than the mouth (PACE 1984, s 65).
[109] PACE 1984, Code C, Annex A, paras 2A, 2B and 5.
[110] PACE 1984, Code C, Annex A, para 2A.
[111] PACE 1984, ss 55 (3A) and (17).
[112] PACE 1984, Code C, Annex A, para 11(c).
[113] PACE 1984, Code C, Annex A, para 11.
[114] PACE 1984, s 64(A)(1).
[115] PACE 1984, ss 61(1), (2), (3), (4) and (4A). Other exemptions exist in ss 61(5A)—(6G).

Piers von Berg

	Aged 10–13 years[55]	Aged 14–16 years	Aged 17 years
Impressions of footwear	These may not be taken without the appropriate consent.[116]		
Identification procedure	An appropriate adult must be present unless the juvenile states they wish them to be absent and they agree.[117]		
Administering a breath test	An appropriate adult must be present although this is not rigidly applied as time is of the essence in drink drive procedures.[118]		A test applied without the benefit of legal advice is admissible (same treatment as adults).[119]
Decisions to charge	There is a range of policy and guidance for these decisions in the Code for Crown Prosecutors, CPS Legal Guidance and the DPP's policy. See below at 11-33.		
	An appropriate adult must be present for the charging procedure and should receive a copy of the charge sheet.[120] This includes administering of a caution on charge or being informed they may be prosecuted, provision of a written notice showing particulars of the offence (which they should receive a copy of), informing the detainee and handing them a copy of any written statement or interview of another person relating to such an offence.[121]		
	Note the substantive criminal law on sexual offences committed by those aged under 14.		Note the substantive criminal law on offences of cruelty to persons aged under 16 can only be committed by those who have reached the age of 16.
Decisions not to charge	Note the Victim's Right of Review (see above at 5-36) and the EU Directive on victims sexual offences (see below at 11-42).		
Detention after charge	A juvenile may be detained if the custody officer has reasonable grounds for believing it is in his interests.[122] If a custody officer authorises the detention of a juvenile, he must be transferred to local authority accommodation unless it is impracticable or,		The provisions for adults apply—the defendant can be detained if any of the criteria in PACE 1984, s 38(1)

---

[116] ibid, s 61A. Again there are exceptions to the rule—see s 61A(3).

[117] PACE 1984, Code D para 1.14. A record should be made of the decision and signed by the appropriate adult.

[118] See *R (DPP) v BE* [2002] EWHC 2976 (Admin), (2003) 167 JP 144. This principle was applied in *R (DPP) v Preston* [2003] EWHC 729 (Admin).

[119] *R v DPP, ex parte Ward (Jack)* [1999] RTR 11, Times, 24 March 1997. See also *DPP v Billington* [1988] 1 WLR 535.

[120] PACE 1984, Code C paras 16.1 and 16.3.

[121] See PACE 1984, Code C, paras 16.2–16.4 and 16.6.

[122] This is an alternative ground for the ones that exist for adults. PACE 1984, s 38(1)(b)(ii).

	Aged 10–13 years[55]	Aged 14–16 years	Aged 17 years
	for juveniles aged 12 or more, no secure accommodation is available and local authority accommodation would not be adequate to protect the public from harm from him.[123]		(a)(i)–(vi) are satisfied. They are excluded from s 38(b)(ii).
Commencement of proceedings	Any person who commences proceedings against a child or young person is under a duty to inform the local authority.[124]		
		In the case of someone aged 13 or over no proceedings can be commenced before a Probation Officer is informed.[125]	
Attendance at court of the defendant	Arrangements shall be made to keep children and young persons separate from adult prisoners whilst at court or in transit and for girls to be in care of a female.[126]		
	The court may require the attendance of a parent or guardian at all stages for any person aged under 15.[127]		
Court bail[128]	For children or young persons accused or convicted of imprisonable offences, a court can impose bail conditions if it appears necessary for welfare or interests.[129] A court can refuse bail on welfare grounds.[130] The defendant may have to comply with such requirements that appear necessary for his own interest and welfare.[131] Where a court refuses bail section 23 of the Children Act 1989 takes effect (remand to local authority care).[132]		

---

[123] PACE 1984, s 38(6). As a result this is not affected by the changes to PACE after *HC*. The duty is imposed on the Local Authority by Children Act 1989, s 21(2). See *R (M) v Gateshead Council* [2006] EWCA Civ 221, [2006] QB 650 discussed below at 11-19.

[124] CYPA 1969, s 5(8). See *DPP v Cottier* [1996] 3 All ER 126 [1996] 1 WLR 826.

[125] ibid, s 34(2).

[126] CYPA 1933, s 31. *T* (n 36). See below at 11-18.

[127] ibid, s 34A(1).

[128] Note that the Youth Court does not have jurisdiction to deal with an offender who is brought before it for a breach of bail if he has attained the age of 18 since being charged and bailed—*R v Uxbridge Youth Court, ex parte Howard* (1998) 162 JP 327, DC. Note the provisions for those aged under 18 in the Bail Act 1976, Sch 1, paras 6 and 6B.

[129] Bail Act 1976, Part 1, Sch 1, para 8.

[130] ibid, Part 1, Sch 1, para 3.

[131] ibid, s 3(6)(ca).

[132] ibid, s 7(6). This applies for youths charged with murder in a Youth Court which may decide the form of custody in which they are committed to the Crown Court for a decision on bail. See *R (A) Lewisham Youth Court* [2011] EWHC 1193 (Admin).

	Aged 10–13 years[55]	Aged 14–16 years	Aged 17 years
Electronically monitored bail	A court cannot impose a tag on a child aged 10 or 11.[133]	The conditions for children and young persons are set out in section 3AA(2)–(5) of the Bail Act 1976.	The conditions for 17-year-olds are contained in section 3AB of the Bail Act 1976.
Remand into local authority accommodation	The court designates a local authority that should receive the child and provide accommodation. The court may impose conditions that could be imposed under section 3(6) of the Bail Act 1976.[134]		
Secure accommodation	A child under 13 shall be not placed in secure accommodation without approval of the Secretary of State.[135]		Alternatively the court can remand a child into youth detention accommodation if they have reached the age of 12[136] and such a child is designated as a Looked After Child (LAC).[137]
Reporting restrictions in court	A court may direct that no newspaper report shall reveal the name, address, school or any particulars that may lead to the identification of a child or young person who is a defendant or witness.[138] The Youth Court has a power under CYPA 1933, s 49 to dispense with the anonymity of the defendant once convicted but this power must be used with great caution, care and circumspection.[139]		
Allocation and sending[140]	All those aged under 18 should be tried in the Youth Court unless: • they are charged with homicide; • they are charged with jointly with an adult and it is necessary in the interests of justice;[141] • the person is aged 16 or 17 and charged with offences under the Firearms Act 1968, s 5; • the offence is a grave crime and defendant should be sentenced under section 91 of the Powers of Criminal Courts (Sentencing) Act 2000; or,		

---

[133] ibid, s 3AA(1)–(2).

[134] LASPO 2012, ss 91–93.

[135] This includes such conditions as he/she sees fit. The Children (Secure Accommodation) Regulations 1991, SI 1991/1505, r 4.

[136] LASPO 2012, ss 91, 98, 99 and 102.

[137] ibid, s 104. Therefore, the designated local authority is under the duties in Children Act 1989, ss 22–23.

[138] CYPA 1933, s 39(1)(a). CYPA 1933, s 49, automatically imposes similar restrictions on proceedings in the Youth Court or appeals therefrom. In an adult magistrates' court or an appeal court it is the duty of that court to announce that that section applies or it will not apply (ss (10)).

[139] *McKerry v Teesdale and Wear Valley Justices* (n 33) mentioned below at 11-46.

[140] Committal hearings have been abolished and the new procedures for the Youth Court are discussed above at 6-58.

[141] CYPA 1933, s 46.

	Aged 10–13 years[55]	Aged 14–16 years	Aged 17 years
	– the offence is a 'specified offence' under section 224 of the Criminal Justice Act 2003 and if convicted, the criteria for a sentence of indeterminate detention for public protection or an extended sentence is met.[142]		
	First-time offenders charged alone aged under 15 and all offenders under 12 rarely receive a custodial sentence and should rarely be tried in the Crown Court.[143]		
Trial—defendants	A defendant aged under 18 may give evidence by live link if his ability to participate is compromised by his intellectual ability or social functioning and use of a live link would improve his ability to participate effectively.[144] Note the *Practice Direction (Criminal Proceedings)*[145] set out ground rules for questioning of a vulnerable defendant and guidance for hearings involving vulnerable defendants at G1–14. In a trial in the Youth Court, no person may attend except officers and members of the court, the parties, their legal representatives, witnesses and other persons with a direct concern in the case.[146] The court may authorise the attendance of bona fide representatives of the media and other persons.[147] Defendants aged under 18 are eligible for special measures only insofar as giving evidence by live link if their ability to participate effectively as a witness is compromised by their intellectual or social functioning and a live link would enable them to give evidence more effectively.[148] The lack of a statutory framework has not prevented judges from allowing the use of intermediaries (see below 11-40).[149] A conviction is called 'finding of guilty' and sentence 'order made on finding of guilty'.		

---

[142] The court must ask whether there is a real prospect of the defendant in light of their age receiving a sentence in excess of two years or whether there is some unusual aspect of the case. See *CPS v South East Surrey Youth Court and MG* [2005] EWHC 2929 (Admin) and *R (H, A, and O) v Southampton Youth Court* [2004] EWHC 2912 (Admin) [35]. For a discussions of these authorities see above at 6-64. See also Sentencing Guidelines Council, *Definitive Guideline: Overarching Principles Sentencing Youths*, para 12.11.

[143] ibid, para 34.

[144] YJCEA 1999, s 33A. See also the CPR, Pt 29, as amended on 7 October 2013. Note ss 33BA and 33BB, which are not yet in force, contain provisions allowing the court to give a direction permitting the defendant to give evidence through an intermediary. At present the courts have held that they have an inherent power to allow such special measures absent any statutory underpinning (these are discussed below at 11-40).

[145] *Practice Direction (Criminal Proceedings)* 3E1–6.

[146] In *R v Southwark Juvenile Court, ex parte J* [1973] 1 WLR 1300 (DC) the decision to exclude a welfare officer was quashed as she had a right as a person directly concern to attend and justice had to be seen to be done. See also *R v Willesden Justices, ex parte Brent LBC* [1988] 2 FLR 95.

[147] CYPA 1933, s 47(2).

[148] YJCEA 1999, s 33A(4).

[149] See the *Practice Direction (Criminal Proceedings)* (n 145) 3F1–6.

	Aged 10–13 years[55]	Aged 14–16 years	Aged 17 years
Trial – witnesses (special measures)	The court has an inherent power to alter the physical arrangements in court, eg to ask the defendant to step down from the dock so a child witness does not see him, and to clear the court (CYPA 1933, s 37).[150] The key provisions are in YJCEA 1999, Part II, Chapter 1, sections 16–30: a person aged under 18 is a 'child witness' and is automatically entitled to special measures.[151] The approach of the court under the Criminal Procedure Rules is summarised and relevant authorities cited in the *Practice Direction (Criminal Proceedings)* regarding vulnerable persons at 3D1–8, questioning of a vulnerable witness 3E1–6.		
	A child aged under 14 may give their evidence unsworn.		
Other provisions for victims and witnesses	The Code for Crown Prosecutors requires prosecutors to consider the welfare and interests of the victim. Where the victim is a child they must take into account the views of his family. See below at 11-43 on special measures for which those under 18 qualify as of right under the YJCEA 1999.[152] Various other considerations may apply including the Victim's Code, the CPS policy on Violence Against Women and Girls and in identifying whether children and young persons are defendants or victims (e.g. see below at 11-34 on human trafficking).		
Sentencing	In general, defendants should be remitted to the Youth Court for sentencing unless it is undesirable to do so.[153] A range of different disposals is available but it is extremely rare for a sentencing decision to be subject to challenge by way of judicial review. In cases before the magistrates' or Youth Courts see above at 6-83. For the Crown Court the jurisdiction resides with the Court of Appeal. Note section 89(1) of the Powers of Criminal Courts (Sentencing) Act (PCC(S)A) 2000 has a general prohibition on sentencing persons under 21 to imprisonment.		

---

[150] *R v Smellie* (1919) 14 Cr App R 128. Both these measures are contained in YJCEA 1999, ss 23 and 25.

[151] Eligibility is governed by YJCEA 1999, s 16(1)(a). 'Child witnesses' are defined in YJCEA 1999, s 21. Note the provision in s 21 for witnesses who turn 18 years of age after giving video-recorded evidence. It states that the 'primary rule' is that any video-recorded evidence (in chief) shall be admitted by s 27 and any other evidence given by live link under s 24. Special measures include use of screens, a live link, evidence in private, removal of wigs and gowns, an intermediary and video-recorded evidence-in-chief. These are discussed below at 11-40.

[152] The Government has commenced piloting of YJCEA 1999, s 28, which allows the cross-examination of vulnerable witnesses to be pre-recorded before trial. The Youth Justice and Criminal Evidence Act 1999 (Commencement No 13) Order 2013 (SI 2013/3236). See below at 11-42.

[153] PCC(S)A 2000, ss 8(1) and (2).

C. Pre Trial Matters

(1) Custody

(i) Appropriate Adults

11-15 Appropriate adults are defined in paragraph 1.7 of Code C in cases of a juvenile or 17-year-old as a parent, guardian, or if the juvenile or 17-year-old is in the care of the local authority or voluntary organisation, a person representing that organisation.[154] It can also be a social worker from a local authority or a 'responsible adult' aged 18 or over, who is not a police officer or employed by the police. A person is barred from acting as an appropriate adult if they are:

i. suspected of involvement in the offence;
ii. the victim;
iii. a witness;
iv. involved in the investigation; or
v. privy to admissions prior to attending.

A social worker or member of the youth offending team cannot act as an appropriate adult if the person has made admissions to them prior to their appointment as an appropriate adult.

The role of an appropriate adult is crucial for those aged under 18. They provide a 'gateway to a young person's access to justice' without which 'he cannot effectively make his voice heard whilst in police detention or in police interview'.[155] This goes to the constitutional duty of the state not to impede access to justice.[156] A juvenile, which now includes 17 year olds for the purposes of Code C of PACE 1984, is entitled to have an appropriate adult informed of his detention and to have an appropriate adult present at interview.[157]

At an interview, the police should inform an appropriate adult that they are not expected to act simply as an observer, and, that the purpose of their presence is to advise the person being interviewed, observe whether the interview is conducted fairly and properly, and, facilitate communication with the interviewee.[158] The Divisional Court has held that the mere presence of an adult who fulfills the definitions above but with whom the detainee has no empathy is not sufficient to comply with the aims of Code C. These facts arose in the case of *DPP v Blake* [1989] 1 WLR 432 where a detainee's estranged father attended. She had firmly refused to provide his contact details and did not want him to attend. When he arrived they had no conversation about the alleged offence or the reasons for her arrest and detention.[159] Where an appropriate

---

[154] PACE 1984, Code C, para 1.7.

[155] *HC* (n 14) [63].

[156] ibid [63], citing *R (The Children's Rights Alliance for England (CRAE)) v Secretary of State for Justice* [2013] EWCA Civ 34) [34]–[38] (Laws LJ).

[157] PACE 1984, Code C, paras 3.13, 3.15 and 11.15. Note that there are exceptions to this rule if any of the circumstances in paras 11.1, 11.18-11.20 apply. See table above for more detail.

[158] PACE 1984, Code C, para 11.17.

[159] See PACE 1984, Code C, Notes for Guidance paras 1B.

Piers von Berg

adult attends and robustly intervenes in the interview to contradict the detainee and encourage them to tell the truth this did not mean he had failed to carry out his role as an appropriate adult.[160]

When considering judicial review challenges to the availability and role of appropriate adults, practitioners should be aware that remedies may be sought within the trial process. For example, evidence obtained in the absence of an appropriate adult may be vulnerable to an application to exclude it under sections 76 or 78 of PACE 1984, depending on what was said and the circumstances of the case.[161] Breaches of Code C will have to be shown to be significant and substantial in order to persuade a court to exercise its discretion under section 78;[162] the age and maturity of the defendant, and the behaviour and health of the appropriate adult, may be relevant considerations in this respect.[163] It may also bring into question the fairness of the proceedings, if it can be said that the juvenile did not appreciate the need for legal advice for example.[164] In *DPP v Blake* the Divisional Court dismissed the prosecution's appeal against the justices' ruling that the confession obtained in the interview was inadmissible under section 76(2)(b) of PACE 1984 as they had been right to hold that the detainee's father was not an appropriate adult. However, the justices would not have been right to exclude the confession on the basis of other breaches of Code C such as a failure to record all visits to the detainee in the custody record. Another example of the approach to breaches of PACE Code C is *H and M v DPP*.[165] The Divisional Court held that a 'technical' breach did not invalidate magistrates' decision not to exclude the evidence of the interview. Here an officer had not explained to an adult the role of an appropriate adult as required by Code C. But the court found that there was evidence from which the magistrates could infer that the adults present acted to protect the child and no substantial unfairness had arisen.[166]

There are exceptions, for example, in *R (DPP) v BE*[167] the court held that it was unreasonable to exercise the discretion under section 78 of PACE 1984 to exclude evidence of a breath specimen where an appropriate adult had not been requested to attend. It was contrary to the authorities to delay the process in order to allow a juvenile to elect for a different test. It is submitted that it is questionable whether this approach might be followed in light of the decision in *HC* discussed below.

---

[160] *R v Jefferson* [1994] 1 All ER 270, (1994) 99 Cr App R 13, distinguishing *DPP v Blake*.

[161] *R v Fogah* [1989] Crim LR 141, *R v Maguire (Jason)* (1990) 90 Cr App R 115 (CA) and *R v Weekes* (1993) 97 Cr App R 227, which preceded the definition of an interview in Code C at para 11.1A. See also *R (DPP) v Stratford Youth Court* [2001] EWHC Admin 615.

[162] See *R v Keenan* (1989) 90 Cr App Rep 1 and *R v Walsh* (1989) 91 Cr App Rep 161, 163.

[163] See M Ashford, A Chard and N Redhouse, *Defending Young People in the criminal justice system*, 3rd edn (London, Legal Action Group, 2006) para 15.32. This is corroborated by Criminal Justice Joint Inspection, *Who's looking out for the children* (December 2011) pp 8–9. See *R v W* [1994] Crim LR 130 where a detainee's mother, who was mentally handicapped, acted as an appropriate adult. The Court of Appeal refused to interfere with a judge's ruling on s 76(2)(b) as the mother was capable of dealing rationally with issues concerning her family and current events.

[164] See *HC* (n 14) [94]. See also *R v Aspinall* [1999] 2 Cr App R 115.

[165] *H and M v DPP* (n 82).

[166] The court (May and Astill LJJ) also said that there was force in argument that unless a single person was designated to act as an appropriate adult there may be confusion leading to a result where neither performed the role of an appropriate adult. There were occasions, such as the instant case, where it may be appropriate for more than one adult to be present e.g. if one acted as an interpreter for another.

[167] *R (DPP) v BE* [2002] EWHC 2976 (Admin).

11-16   This area has been subject of an important recent challenge on the issue of the avail-ability of appropriate adults to 17-year-olds in custody. In *HC* a 17-year-old boy was arrested on suspicion of robbery of a mobile phone. He was taken to a police station and his request that his mother be informed was not acted on for four and a half hours. He was subsequently released on bail and no charges were preferred. The police refused to act on his request, because as a 17-year-old he did not have an unqualified right to have an adult informed immediately of his arrest and detention. He brought a challenge to the lawfulness of the Home Secretary's refusal to amend Code C in that it permitted the police to treat him in the same manner as an adult.

Under section 56(1) of PACE 1984, HC was subject to the same treatment as any adult when it came to informing another person of his detention. The effect of this provision was that the detainee's right to inform any such persons could be delayed by the police if any of the conditions in section 56(5) were made out (for example, alerting others, physical injury or loss of property).[168] In this case HC was suspected of an indictable offence for which property had not been recovered, and when he requested that his mother be informed, an inspector was entitled under Annex B of Code C to delay the implementation of that request.

Of particular importance were the vulnerability of a 17-year-old in custody and the purpose of the criminal justice system in relation to adolescents:

> This case demonstrates how vulnerable a 17-year-old may be. Treated as an adult, he receives no explanation as to how important it is to obtain the assistance of a lawyer ... If, at the heart of any policy in relation to 17-year-olds, lie the objectives of reinforcing strength of family ties, and development into a responsible adult with the assistance of a responsible parent, it is hard to see what Code C, in its treatment of 17-year-olds as adults, achieves other than to undermine such objectives.[169]

11-17   The judgment identifies what is arguably an anomaly in the law, that 17-year-olds are not defined as juveniles (under 17), even though they are defined as young persons (under 18). This 'anomaly' was documented in several reports on the youth justice system.[170] This was found to be inconsistent with domestic law and international law. For example, in respect of the former, the general principle underlying the youth justice system and the family justice system is to accord special protection to those under 18 to safeguard their welfare. Indeed, the police are specifically required to do the same under section 11 of the Children Act 2004. Moses LJ found an 'uncomfortable dissonance' between this requirement and PACE 1984 and Code C.[171] The court also noted the 'broad consensus' of all relevant international conventions that 17-year-olds should be regarded as children. This was also contained in the Government's own understanding

---

[168] Note other rights of a person in custody under Code C, para 5 can also be delayed.

[169] *HC* (n 14) [94]. Code C, Guidance Notes, para 11C recognises that juveniles are liable to give incrimi-nating, misleading or unreliable evidence. They are also less likely to ask for legal advice (V Kemp, P Pleasence and NJ Balmer, 'Children Young People and Requests for Police Station Legal Advice: 25 years on from PACE' (2011) 11 *Youth Justice* 28, cited in K Gooch, 'Case Comment, Treating 17-year-olds in police custody as chil-dren, not adults', *Journal of Criminal Law* 281.

[170] For example the judgment refers to reports by HM Inspectorates of Prisons and Constabulary and *Who's Looking Out for Children*, [52]. Both recommended that, in effect, 17-year-olds should be brought within the definition of 'juvenile' or the definition of 'child' in the Children Act 2004.

[171] *HC* (n 14) [37].

Piers von Berg

of how the principles of the UNCRC applied where it defined juveniles as 'under 18' for the purposes of Code C.[172]

The court found the Secretary of State's refusal to amend Code C unlawful on the grounds that it was an unjustified breach of Article 8.[173] It interpreted Article 8 in accordance with the UNCRC in that the best interests of the child must be a primary consideration:[174]

> It is difficult to imagine a more striking case where the rights of both child and parent under Article 8 are engaged than when a child is in custody on suspicion of committing a serious offence and needs help from someone with whom he is familiar and whom he trusts, in redressing the imbalance between child and authority. The wish of a 17 year-old in trouble to seek the support of a parent and of a parent to be available to give that help must surely lie at the heart of family life which, quite apart from Article 8, the government seeks to maintain and encourage.[175]

It is submitted that the approach in *HC* not only opens a door to challenging the way in which 17-year-olds are treated in police custody, but also provides a valuable illustration of how principles of domestic and international law can be relied upon in this area. On this latter point, practitioners should note the approach in *T* below at 11-18.

In response to the judgment the Home Secretary amended Code C to allow for 17-year-olds to be treated as juveniles under Code C (paragraph 1.5A). This excluded the definitions in the statute, which were not amended (and were not under challenge). The Home Office conceded that 17-year-olds are still treated as adults under section 38 of PACE 1984 (grounds for detention after charge) and requirements to transfer to local authority accommodation; and also under section 65(1) of PACE 1984, the provision of appropriate consent for taking of samples. This does not paint the full picture of the anomalous treatment of 17-year-olds that remains throughout the criminal law. For example, the Crime and Disorder Act 1998, the Bail Act 1976 and the Children and Young Persons Acts of 1933 and 1969 all provide special treatment to those aged under 17, which are set out in the table above at 11-14. It will be interesting to see if there are further judicial review challenges to this anomalous treatment of 17-year-olds.

(ii) Association with Adult Detainees

Section 31 of the CYPA 1933 requires that children and young persons are not allowed **11-18** to associate with adult detainees, and that girls are under the care of a woman. The duty attaches to the police and to any responsible for conveyance to and from court. The definition also applies to those who are witnesses or at court on bail:

> Arrangements shall be made for preventing a child or young person while detained in a police station, or while being conveyed to or from any criminal court, or while awaiting before or after

---

[172] Department for Children, Schools and Families, *The UNCRC: How Legislation Underpins Implementation in England*, March 2010, para 8.178, cited at [44], ibid.

[173] The claim was also brought on the basis of the Art 6. Moses LJ's comments on the applicability of Art 6 at the pre-charge stage are mentioned in the sections on police cautions at 11-31.

[174] As in *Castle* (n 13) the court relied on *R v Durham Constabulary* and *ZH Tanzania* (discussed above at 11-5) as well as *HH* (n 28). See *HC* (n 14) [81]–[84].

[175] ibid [85].

attendance in any criminal court, from associating with an adult (not being a relative) who is charged with any offence other than an offence with which the child or young person is jointly charged, and for ensuring that a girl (being a child or young person) shall while so detained, being conveyed, or waiting, be under the care of a woman.

This section was considered in *T* (n 36). This case concerned arrangements at court. It defined 'associating' as not simply interacting in some form with adult defendants, but covering 'risks of other types of contact' even if transitory or in physical proximity. Hence, the issues are highly fact-specific. It concerned a 13-year-old child with a long-standing diagnosis of autism and Attention Deficit Hyperactivity Disorder (ADHD), who was kept in a cell for three hours. He heard adult prisoners in other cells shouting at him or at other prisoners, and he had 'transitory contact' with two prisoners.

The court rejected the submissions on a breach of Article 8, as the detention was justified, and on section 149 of the Equality Act 2010, in that due regard was had in the Ministry's arrangements with its contractors. But it found that the defendant had breached section 31(1) of the Children and Young Persons Act 1933 and thereby unlawfully detained him.[176] Despite being referred to *ZH (Tanzania)* and *(R) v Durham Constabulary,* the court rejected the use of the UNCRC or the Beijing Rules in interpreting section 31, on the basis that i) they were not binding in international law, ii) had not been translated into domestic law, and iii) no right under ECHR was in contention.[177]

(iii) Transfer to Local Authority Accommodation

11-19   If a custody officer denies an arrested juvenile bail, he must make a request to the local authority for the juvenile to be placed in local authority accommodation.[178] This obligation is found in section 38(6) of PACE 1984. A juvenile can be placed in either accommodation or 'secure accommodation'. Secure accommodation is defined by section 38(6A) of PACE 1984 and section 25(1) of the Children Act 1989 as 'accommodation provided for the purpose of restricting liberty'. A juvenile should be placed in secure accommodation if local authority accommodation is not adequate to protect the public from serious harm.[179] A custody officer does not have to secure that the juvenile is transferred if it is impracticable. Impracticability, does not include consideration of the juvenile's behaviour or the offence, but refers to transport and travel requirements.[180] He also does not have to secure a transfer if no secure accommodation is available.[181] As set out in the table above, this section does not apply to 17-year-olds, and children

---

[176] Research has indicated in the past (December 2011) that little adjustment is made in police custody suites for juveniles to treat them separately to adults—see *Who's Looking Out for Children* (n 163) paras 3.31–3.36.

[177] *T* (n 36) [32] (Cranston J), with whom Sir John Thomas P agreed.

[178] Local authority accommodation is accommodation provided by a local authority within the meaning of the Children Act 1989 (PACE 1984, s 38(6A)). See the Children Act 1989, ss 20–21.

[179] 'Serious harm' is defined in relation to a juvenile charged with a violent or sexual offence as 'death or serious personal injury, whether physical or psychological, occasioned by further such offences committed by him'. PACE 1984, s 38(6A).

[180] PACE 1984, Code C, Note for Guidance 16D.

[181] This does not apply to 17-year-olds. See Code C Note for Guidance 16.7 (as amended).

Piers von Berg

younger than 13 cannot be placed in secure accommodation. Otherwise, the position is set out in sections 38(6)(a) or (b) of PACE 1984:

> (6) Where a custody officer authorises an arrested juvenile to be kept in police detention under subsection (1) above, the custody officer shall, unless he certifies—
>
> (a) that, by reason of such circumstances as are specified in the certificate, it is imprac- ticable for him to do so; or
>
> (b) in the case of an arrested juvenile who has attained the age of 12 years, that no secure accommodation is available and that keeping him in other local authority accom- modation would not be adequate to protect the public from serious harm from him,
>
> secure that the arrested juvenile is moved to local authority accommodation.

A child who is in local authority accommodation or is cared for by the state is called a 'looked after child' (LAC) (see further below at 11-24).[182] Such a child may not be trans- ferred to or kept in secure accommodation unless either of the two criteria in section 25(1)(a) or (b) are met:

> (a) that—
> (i) he has a history of absconding and is likely to abscond from any other description of accommodation; and
> (ii) if he absconds, he is likely to suffer significant harm; or
> (b) that if he is kept in any other description of accommodation he is likely to injure himself or other persons.[183]

The reality is that it is very rare for a child to be transferred to local authority accom- modation where they are not already in the care of a local authority. Practitioners in the field state that they find considerable police resistance, large demands on the provision of secure accommodation and failures by local authorities to provide accommodation where the child is not a LAC.[184] This leads to detention of children in police stations, sometimes overnight, with all the risks to a child or young person's welfare that entails; research indicates this is a very common occurrence.[185]

One attempted challenge was *R (M) v Gateshead Council*.[186] The claimant challenged **11-20** the refusal of a local authority to provide secure accommodation that led to her being detained overnight in a police station. The Court of Appeal interpreted section 38(6) of PACE 1984 and the relevant provisions in the Children Act 1989. Several important principles emerged:

> i. There is an obligation on the police to make a request to a local authority for a transfer of a youth held in custody but there is no absolute duty on the police to transfer the youth to local authority accommodation.

---

[182] Children Act 1989, s 22(1). Note a child must be in local authority accommodation continuously for at least 24 hours (s 22(2)).

[183] Subject to certain limited exceptions an application can only be made by a local authority looking after the child. The Children (Secure Accommodation) Regulations 1991, SI 1991/1505, r 8.

[184] See Ashford, Chard and Redhouse (n 163), para 7.333. They argue that if a child can be successfully accommodated within the community, this can affect potential disposals.

[185] See research commissioned by the Howard League. L Skinns, *The overnight detention of children in police cells: Summary* (London, Howard League, 2011) and *Who's Looking Out for Children* (n 163), paras 4.27–28.

[186] *R (M) v Gateshead Council* (n 123).

ii.   There is no absolute duty on a local authority to place a youth referred to them by the police under section 38(6) of PACE 1984 in secure accommodation but the local authority must have a reasonable system in place to enable them to respond to such requests.

iii.   There is an absolute duty on a local authority, which receives a request under section 38(6) to provide accommodation.

The facts were that a 16-year-old girl (the claimant) was arrested on suspicion of wounding. She was living at a hostel at the time. She was detained at a police station. A social worker, acting as her appropriate adult, asked his local authority if they could accommodate her in secure accommodation until she appeared before the court the next morning. The authority said it could only provide a bail address. The custody officer took the view that secure accommodation was necessary to protect the public from serious harm. This provided him with grounds to detain the claimant in a police station overnight.

The claimant brought a claim against the local authority on the grounds that it had breached its duty under section 21(1)(b) of the Children Act 1989 to receive and provide secure accommodation to her. The claim was refused permission but the Court of Appeal granted permission and heard the case in full. The court held that section 21(2)(b) granted a discretionary power to local authorities to provide secure accommodation on request by the police so far as it was practicable to do so. It did not impose an absolute duty on a local authority to accommodate a juvenile in secure accommodation from police custody whenever it was requested under section 38(6) of PACE 1984.

Evidence in the case showed the scarcity of secure accommodation places. Allied to this was that section 38(6) of PACE 1984 appears to contemplate that the police may not be able to transfer children to secure accommodation. On this basis, Dyson LJ preferred a limited duty on the part of the police:

> It is to be noted that the only obligation on the custody officer under section 38(6) is to 'secure [ie request] that the arrested juvenile is moved to local authority accommodation'. There is no obligation to secure, or use best endeavours to secure accommodation that is secure in those cases where the custody officer is of the opinion that keeping the juvenile in non-secure accommodation 'would not be adequate to protect the public from serious harm from him'. Section 38(6) is structured differently. It exempts the custody officer from the duty to secure accommodation where he or she certifies that no secure accommodation is available and that secure accommodation is necessary in order to protect the public from serious harm. The section, therefore, expressly contemplates that the custody officer may not be able to secure accommodation that is secure.[187]

As far as the local authority is concerned, it had a discretionary power which should be used on receipt of the request 'in so far as it was practicable for it to do so to further the policy objective of preventing children from being detained in police cells'.[188] A discretionary power should be exercised with regard to the policy aims of the statute, namely under Part III of the Children Act 1989, to support children and families. The duty is that it is 'incumbent' on the local authority to have 'a reasonable system to enable them

---

187   ibid [40]. Thorpe LJ and Moore-Bick LJ agreed.
188   ibid [42].

to respond to requests under section 38(6) for secure accommodation'.[189] The criteria for finding such arrangements as unlawful are where:

an authority has made no arrangements at all, so that they can never provide secure accommodation when it is requested, or where the arrangements that have been made are ones that could not have been made by a reasonable authority, mindful of the need to avoid having children detained in police cells if at all possible.[190]

As far as requests for mere accommodation, as distinct from secure accommodation, are concerned, a local authority is under an absolute duty under section 21(2)(b) of the Children Act 1989 to receive the child and provide accommodation.[191] This is subject to the question of 'impracticability'—a police officer does not have to secure that a juvenile is transferred if it is impracticable because of transport or travel requirements.

It remains to be seen if a challenge could be made against a local authority's failure to respond to a request to place a juvenile in accommodation, given this absolute duty. Secondly, it is submitted that following *HC*, one might also query if there may be situations where a 17-year-old's rights under the ECHR may be engaged by detention in a police station overnight, especially as 17-year-olds are defined as children under the Children Act 1989.

For practitioners considering potential claims against a local authority, the following guidance under the Children Act 1989 was cited in the judgment in *M v Gateshead* and may be of assistance (note it applies equally to the discrete section on secure accommodation below):

restricting the liberty of children is a serious step which must be taken only when there is no appropriate alternative. It must be a 'last resort' in the sense that all else must first have been comprehensively considered and rejected-never because no other placement was available at the relevant time, because of inadequacies in staffing, because the child is simply being a nuisance or runs away from his accommodation and is not likely to suffer significant harm in doing so, and never as a form of punishment. It is important, in considering the possibility of a secure placement, that there is a clear view of the aims and objectives of such a placement and that those providing the accommodation can fully meet those aims and objectives. Secure placements, once made, should be only for so long as is necessary and unavoidable.[192]

(iv) Secure Accommodation

Secure accommodation and the conditions for placing a child in such accommoda- **11-21**
tion are explained above at 11-19.[193] As is evident by the content in section 25, a child may also be placed in 'secure accommodation' on application to a court, which must also apply the criteria in that section. As a preliminary note, section 25 has been held

---

[189] ibid [43].
[190] ibid [48].
[191] See also the *National Standards for Youth Justice Services* (2004), para 2.10.
[192] *M* (n 123) [40]. Department of Health, *The Children Act Guidance and Regulations*, Vol 4 (Residential Care) (1991), para 8.5.
[193] Note the exclusions in the Children (Secure Accommodation) Regulations 1991, SI 1991/1505, r 5. There are a number of other important provisions in those Regulations regulating the effect on children of s 25. The Children Act Guidance and Regulations issued under the Local Authority Social Services Act 1970, s 7 state that secure placement 'should be for only so long as is necessary and unavoidable' (Vol 1, para 5).

not to be incompatible with Article 5 of ECHR (right to liberty).[194] This is because Article 5(1)(d) allows detention 'by lawful order for the purpose of educational supervision', and a local authority is obliged by statute to provide as much.

Proceedings for an application for a secure accommodation order are not criminal proceedings within the meaning of Article 6, but a child should be allowed a right to a fair trial.[195] The grant of an order is a judicial decision, and the first remedy often will be one of appeal rather than judicial review. However, the High Court has stated that where the continued legality of the order and role of the local authority is in issue, judicial review may be the appropriate means:[196]

> In my view, the role that a local authority has during the currency of a secure accommodation order, and in particular its duties to review the continued legality of a placement of a child in reliance on the authority provided by a secure accommodation order, are ones that are amenable to judicial review. Indeed, I would go further and say that it seems to me that judicial review is likely, in most cases, to be the most appropriate remedy because it can naturally be, and is regularly, combined with points made under the Human Rights Act.[197]

That case concerned a challenge to the lawfulness of a secure accommodation order on the basis of a change in circumstances. It also challenged the lawfulness of the local authority's decision to maintain the placement. It drew on the earlier decision of *LM v Essex County Council*,[198] which stated that once the criteria under section 25 ceased to apply, a detainee could challenge their continued detention by judicial review, or habeas corpus, as in *LM* (on the latter remedy, see the note of caution above at 3-31).

(v) Local Authorities' Statutory Duties Towards Children

11-22   A comprehensive account of local authorities' duties to children is outside the scope of this chapter. As far as the youth justice system is concerned, local authorities are under various statutory duties to provide youth justice services as appropriate in their area.[199] These services are wide-ranging, including:

i.   the provision of appropriate adults;

ii.   the supervision and rehabilitation of persons who receive cautions, the provision of support to those remanded on bail;

iii. the placement of children in local authority accommodation;

iv.   the performance of youth offending teams;

v.   the provision of responsible persons for youth rehabilitation orders, individual support orders and reparation orders, the supervision of children and young persons under detention and training orders and post-release, and the implementation of referral orders.

---

[194] *Re K (A Child) (Secure Accommodation Order: Right to Liberty)* [2001] Fam 377, [2001] 2 WLR 1141.

[195] *Re C (A Child) (Secure Accommodation Order: Representation)* [2001] EWCA Civ 458, [2001] 2 FLR 169.

[196] *S (A Child) v Knowsley BC* [2004] EWHC 491 (Fam), [2004] 2 FLR 716 (Charles J).

[197] ibid [72].

[198] *LM v Essex County Council* [1999] 1 FLR 988, [1999] 1 FCR 673.

[199] See CDA 1998, s 38(1). There is a range of different guidance issued by the Secretary of State to local authorities in respect of their duties towards children in this area. Eg 'Local authority responsibilities towards former looked after children in custody', November 2010, Department for Education. See n 207 below.

A key body is the youth offending team, whose role is to coordinate the provision of youth justice services within the authority's area.[200] This is not an area that has seen much activity in terms of judicial review challenges to local authority decisions.

In contrast, a more contested area in terms of public law is the provision of services under the Children Act 1989. Local authorities are under a duty to provide specific services to 'children in need' (defined in section 17(10) of the Children Act 1989) and disabled children (defined in section 17(11)).[201] These definitions will often encompass children who find their way into and out of the criminal justice system. For example, local authorities' duties to children, set out below, will continue to apply to children when they are in custody.[202] Local authorities also have duties to 'safeguard and promote' the welfare of any child who is in their care or provided with accommodation by them (section 22(3)(a)). Section 17(1) states that the services must safeguard and promote the welfare of the child, and so far as is consistent with the duty, promote their upbringing. This is not an absolute duty to meet needs of every individual child's needs once assessed.[203] For example, this does not constitute a duty to provide residential accommodation.[204]

11-23

An example of how these duties can be relevant in proceedings in criminal courts is *R (AB and SB) v Nottingham City Council*.[205] A local authority applied for an Anti-Social Behaviour Order (ASBO) against a child with learning disabilities and behavioural problems.[206] Part of the defence was that the local authority had failed to conduct an assessment of SB's needs and should consider dealing with him in other ways. The claimants succeeded on this point and a mandatory order was granted that an assessment be conducted.[207]

Following *AB and SB* above, a local authority must take reasonable steps to ascertain what a child's needs are, if they appear in need. This requires a proper assessment that considers the child's immediate and current circumstances and any imminent changes.[208]

---

[200] See CDA 1998, s 39.

[201] Section 17(10) provides that a child is 'in need' if '(a) he is unlikely to achieve or maintain, or to have the opportunity of achieving or maintaining, a reasonable standard of health or development without the provision for him of services by a local authority under this Part; (b) his health or development is likely to be significantly impaired, or further impaired, without the provision for him of such services; or (c) he is disabled.' A child is disabled under section 17(11) if 'he is blind, deaf or dumb or suffers from mental disorder of any kind or is substantially and permanently handicapped by illness, injury or congenital deformity or such other disability as may be prescribed'.

[202] *R (Howard League for Penal Reform) v Secretary of State for the Home Department* [2002] EWHC 2497 (Admin) [136] (Munby J). Whilst His Lordship held that these duties do not attach to the Prison Service or the Home Secretary (ibid [65]–[69]), those bodies will be bound by considerations under the HRA 1998. Eg see *R (BP) v Secretary of State for the Home Department* [2003] EWHC 1963 Admin.

[203] *R (G) v Barnet LBC* [2003] UKHL 57, [2003] 3 WLR 1194, [30].

[204] ibid.

[205] *R (AB and SB) v Nottingham City Council* [2001] EWHC 235 (Admin).

[206] Other examples of this conflict between the interests of the applicant local authority and the fulfilment of its statutory duties toward children occurred in *R (M) v Sheffield Magistrates' Court* [2004] EWHC 1830 (Admin), [2005] 1 FLR 81 where the child concerned was in the local authority's care.

[207] There are other examples of this approach, eg *R (J) v Newham LBC* [2001] EWHC (Admin) 992.

[208] *R (K) v Manchester City Council* [2006] EWHC 3164 (Admin). Local authorities should seek to comply with guidance issued by the Secretary of State unless local circumstances indicate exceptional reasons to justify a variation (ibid, [18]). See 'Framework for assessing children in need and their families', Department of Health, Department for Education and Employment and Home Office (2000). There is also practice guidance—Department of Health, 'Assessing children in need and their families: practice guidance', (2000).

It is then under a duty to provide a range of services appropriate to those needs. This was described as a target duty rather than a specific law duty.[209] This should be contained in a care plan.

11-24   If a child presents himself to a local authority and fulfils the criteria under section 20(1) of the Children Act 1989, there is a duty to provide him with accommodation.[210] These types of children are those for whom:

(a)   there being no person who has parental responsibility for him;

(b)   his being lost or having been abandoned; or,

(c)   the person who has been caring for him being prevented (whether or not permanently, and for whatever reason) from providing him with suitable accommodation or care.[211]

Local authorities also have duties to support children who have been accommodated. An 'eligible child' is a LAC (looked after child), aged 16–17, looked after by a local authority for 13 weeks or periods amounting to that, beginning after he reached 14 and ending before 16.[212] A 'relevant child' is not looked after, aged 16–17, either before ceasing to be looked after or when 16, was detained, and before then was looked after by the local authority for 13 weeks after aged 14.[213] Local authorities must assess both categories, prepare a pathway plan and keep it under regular review and appoint a personal advisor.[214] They must also take reasonable steps to stay in touch and safeguard and promote the welfare (including maintenance and accommodation) of a 'relevant child'. Similar duties exist towards children who are a 'former relevant child' (who is aged 18 and above, has been a relevant child and immediately before he ceased to be looked after was an eligible child), a 'former relevant child' or a 'person qualifying for advice and assistance'.[215]

There is scope for judicial review challenges to alleged failures by local authorities to fulfil their obligations under the above, although the examples in the case law do not derive from a criminal context.[216] Claimants should be careful to identify the exact nature of the duties owed. The courts have divided the duties under Part III of the Children Act 1989 into 'general' and 'specific' duties.[217] General duties concern duties

---

[209]   See *G v Barnet*, (n 203) [91]. See also the application in *R (T, D and B) v Haringey LBC* [2005] EWHC 2235 (Admin), (2006) 9 CCLR 500.

[210]   *R (G) v Southwark LBC* [2009] UKHL 26, [2009] 1 WLR 1299.

[211]   Children Act 1989, s 20(1).

[212]   The Children Act 1989, Sch 2, para 19B and the Care Planning, Placement and Case Review (England) Regulations SI 2010/959, r 40 (Care Planning Regulations).

[213]   The Children Act 1989, s 23A(2).

[214]   The Children Act 1989, ss 23B(1)–(2), 23B(3)(A), 23B(8), 23E(1D) and Sch 2, paras 19B(4) and (5) and the Care Planning Regulations, rr 4–9 and 42–44.

[215]   See respectively the Children Act 1989, s 23C, the Children Act 1989 (Higher Education Bursary) (England) Regulations 2009/2274 and the Care Leavers (England) Regulations 2010/2571 (the Care Leavers Regulations); the Children Act 1989, s 23CA and the Care Leavers Regulations; and the Children Act 1989, s 24.

[216]   Eg *R (P) v Newham LBC* [2004] EWHC 2210 (Admin), (2004) CCLR 553 concerning a failure to construct a satisfactory pathway plans and *R (J) v Caerphilly CBC* [2005] EWHC 586 (Admin), (2005) 8 CCLR 255 involving issues around the preparation of care plans, independence of personal advisors and the involvement of the child.

[217]   See *G v Barnet* (n 203) [91] applying *R v Barnet London Borough Council, Ex p B* [1994] ELR 357, 360–61 (Auld J).

to the public as a whole and are not governed by an individual's circumstances. An example is from the Guidance to sections 17 and 18 of the Children Act 1989, as cited in *R (G) v Barnet LBC*:[218]

> Local authorities are not expected to meet every individual need, but they are asked to identify the extent of need and then make decisions on the priorities for service provision in their area in the context of that information and their statutory duties.

As the House of Lords said in *G v Barnet*, which concerned section 17(1), a person can have sufficient standing to enforce this general type of duty by judicial review. This is quite different to a 'particular' duty, which can be enforced by a person when a local authority fails to discharge it.

(vi) Secure Remand by a Court

Where a court remands a child otherwise than on bail it must remand him/her to local authority accommodation.[219] The court must state that such a remand is necessary and explain to the defendant in open court in ordinary language the reasons for its decision, which should then be entered on the warrant of commitment and the register.[220] Alternatively, the court has an option to remand children aged 12 or more to youth detention accommodation.[221]   **11-25**

In relation to Youth Detention Accommodation (YDA), the responsible local authority is required to prepare a plan that addresses all matters in Schedule 2A of the Care Planning, Placement and Care Review (England) Regulations 2010 (SI 2010/959). This includes ascertaining the child's wishes and feelings and giving due consideration to where the child was looked after immediately prior to remand.

If a child or young person is remanded into local authority accommodation with a requirement they are placed into secure accommodation, even if they are not so placed, they remain in the lawful custody of the authority.[222] The question of when a child is in 'lawful custody' has been subsequently considered as one of fact and so a young person remanded simply into local authority accommodation without any security requirements can also be in lawful custody.[223] However, this does not mean that such periods spent in non-secure accommodation can be automatically counted to reduce any subsequent sentence.[224] A young person charged with murder cannot be remanded

---

[218] *G v Barnet* (n 203).

[219] LASPO 2012, ss 91–92. Note that LASPO 2012 has repealed many of the previous provisions relating to secure remand in CYPA 1969. Therefore, previous case law that interpreted those provisions, eg *R (M) v Inner London Crown Court* [2006] EWHC 2497 (QB), [2006] 1 WLR 3406, is of limited relevance as it concerns specific sections of CYPA 1969.

[220] ibid, ss 106(6) and (7).

[221] ibid, ss 91(4)(a), 98, 99, 102 and 104.

[222] *E (A Juvenile) v DPP* [2002] EWHC 433 (Admin), [2002] Crim LR 737 (appeal by way of case stated).

[223] *R (H) v DPP* [2003] EWHC 878 (Admin), (2003) 167 JP 486 applying *E (A Juvenile) v DPP*.

[224] *R v Secretary of State for the Home Department, ex parte A (A Juvenile)* [2000] 2 AC 276, [2000] 2 WLR 293. The House of Lords interpreted the Criminal Justice Act 2003, s 67(1)A(c) as imposing a requirement that a person is remanded to such a place that restricts their liberty as to amount to a form of custody.

into custody in a prison but instead a court must apply the provisions of section 23 of CYPA 1969 to remand into local authority accommodation.[225]

(2) Out-of-Court Disposals

(i) Introduction

11-26 Practitioners should note the general approach to judicial review of police cautions described above at 4-87. There is also considerable overlap with challenges to decisions by the CPS to prosecute where a claimant contends that an out-of-court disposal should have been administered instead (see above at 5-22). There are several challenges to the failure to administer a youth with a caution discussed above in Chapter 5 on the Crown Prosecution Service. The main ground relied upon is that the CPS failed to abide it guidelines in relation to youths:

> unless it could be demonstrated, in the case of a juvenile, that there had been either a total disregard of the policy or, contrary to it, a lack of enquiry into the circumstances and background of that person, previous offences and general character and so on, by the prosecutor and later by the CPS. But here too I envisage the possibility of showing that such disregard had happened as unlikely.[226]

This section predominantly deals with the new system introduced for youths and how that system may itself be vulnerable to challenge on various points.

(ii) Legal Framework

11-27 There is a separate and different system for dealing with out-of-court disposals for children and young persons (as defined by the Crime and Disorder Act (CDA) 1998). LASPO 2012 has simplified this system from 8 April 2013 into youth cautions and youth conditional cautions and abolished the Final Warning Scheme of warnings and reprimands and Penalty Notices for Disorder.[227] LASPO 2012 amended CDA 1998 and preserved its requirement for the presence of an appropriate adult for persons under 17 when giving youth cautions—the key provisions are sub-sections 66ZA(1), (2) and (3):

> (1) A constable may give a child or young person ('Y') a caution under this section (a 'youth caution') if—
>
>   (a)   the constable decides that there is sufficient evidence to charge Y with an offence,
>
>   (b)   Y admits to the constable that Y committed the offence, and
>
>   (c)   the constable does not consider that Y should be prosecuted or given a youth conditional caution in respect of the offence.

---

[225] Post 3 December 2012, LASPO 2012, ss 92–93. *R (A) v Lewisham Youth Court* [2011] EWHC 1193 (Admin), [2012] 1 WLR 34. This judgment interprets the apparent conflict between Coroner's and Justice Act 2009, s 115(1) which deals with grants of bail to those accused of murder, and the law requiring a court to remand a child or young person into local authority care. See also *R v Home Office, ex parte A (A Juvenile)* [2000] 2 AC 276, [2000] 2 WLR 293.

[226] *R v Chief Constable of Kent ex parte L; R v DPP, ex parte B* [1991] 93 Cr App R 416, 428. See above at 5-22.

[227] LASPO 2012, s 135 replaced CDA 1998, ss 65–66 and inserted new clauses into it. Penalty notices for disorder are also abolished.

(2) A youth caution given to a person under the age of 17 must be given in the presence of an appropriate adult.

(3) If a constable gives a youth caution to a person, the constable must explain the matters referred to in subsection (4) in ordinary language to—

(a) that person, and

(b) where that person is under the age of 17, the appropriate adult.

The matter referred to subsection (4) is in summary that a constable must explain the 'effect of' the following:

i. a referral to the Youth Offending Team (YOT);

ii. that the YOT may assess them and recommend them for a rehabilitation programme;

iii. that a court may be unable to order a conditional discharge in certain circumstances; and

iv. any guidance issued by the Secretary of State as to what is included in a rehabilitation programme.[228]

The new system is accompanied by fresh guidelines.[229]

The provisions governing youth conditional cautions can be found in sections 66A– **11-28** 66H of CDA 1998. Sections 66A(2)–(3) describe the core features of a youth conditional caution:

(2) In this Chapter, 'youth conditional caution' means a caution which is given in respect of an offence committed by the offender and which has conditions attached to it with which the offender must comply.

(3) The conditions which may be attached to such a caution are those which have one or more of the following objects—

(a) facilitating the rehabilitation of the offender;

(b) ensuring that the offender makes reparation for the offence;

(c) punishing the offender.

Section 66A(1)(b) requires that each five requirements set out in section 66B is satisfied before an authorised person may administer a youth conditional caution. These are:

(1) The first requirement is that the authorised person has evidence that the offender has committed an offence.

(2) The second requirement is that a relevant prosecutor or the authorised person decides—

(a) that there is sufficient evidence to charge the offender with the offence, and

(b) that a youth conditional caution should be given to the offender in respect of the offence.

---

[228] See CDA 1998, s 66ZA(4).

[229] Ministry of Justice and Youth Justice Board, 'Youth Cautions, Guidelines for Police and Youth Offending Teams', effective from 8 April 2013, www.justice.gov.uk/downloads/oocd/youth-cautions-guidance-police-yots-oocd.pdf. Director of Public Prosecutions, *The Director's Guidance on Youth Conditional Cautions, Guidance to Police Officers and Crown Prosecutors Issued by the Director of Public Prosecutions under PACE 1984*, s 37A. See also guidelines issued by ACPO, which include a Youth Offender Case Disposal Gravity Matrix; for an example see the Guidelines on the Investigation, Cautioning and Charging of Knife Crime Offences, ACPO, October 2012. Available from the ACPO website—www.acpo.police.uk/documents/crime/2012/2012 10CBAGuidInvKnfeCrime.pdf.

(3) The third requirement is that the offender admits to the authorised person that he committed the offence.

(4) The fourth requirement is that the authorised person explains the effect of the youth conditional caution to the offender and warns him that failure to comply with any of the conditions attached to the caution may result in his being prosecuted for the offence.

(5) If the offender is aged 16 or under, the explanation and warning mentioned in subsection (4) must be given in the presence of an appropriate adult.

(6) The fifth requirement is that the offender signs a document which contains—

(a) details of the offence,

(b) an admission by him that he committed the offence,

(c) his consent to being given the youth conditional caution, and

(d) the conditions attached to the caution.

A Code of Practice has been issued for youth conditional cautions.[230]

11-29 It is submitted that similar if not the same considerations will apply in judicial review challenges as before, which were for example brought on the basis of a lack of a clear and unqualified admission[231] and that a departure from the established guidelines for which there is no rational explanation was unlawful (for a fuller discussion of the authorities on challenging cautions on these grounds see above section I in Chapter 4).[232]

Practitioners should be mindful of the court's reluctance to intervene once criminal proceedings are underway. For example, other pre-LASPO 2012 authorities state that it will not be an unlawful exercise of discretion for the CPS to decline to re-interview a juvenile and consider a caution, who admits his guilt after charge and attends at court in the context of previous denials (see below at 11-32).[233] In any event, issues of fairness and Article 6 could be raised within the proceedings on common law grounds of abuse of process and under the HRA 1998. Moreover, there is much narrower scope for review of CPS decisions to prosecute (see above at 5-12).

It is submitted that a failure to satisfy the three requirements for a youth caution or the five requirements for a youth conditional caution set out above, would mean a lack of a statutory basis for the disposal and hence that it was unlawful. Whether those tests are made out may be a factual dispute between the parties. It is submitted that the new guidelines combined with the requirements set out in the CDA 1998 are a complicated process for either youth cautions or youth conditional cautions. To what extent the 'margin of appreciation' mentioned in *Ex p P* (see above at 4-88) will apply to this more detailed system remains to be seen.

---

[230] This is available online at http://www.justice.gov.uk/downloads/oocd/code-practice-youth-conditional-cautions-oocd.pdf.

[231] *Ex p P* and *Ex p Thompson* above at 4-88. This requirement is part of a three-part test under CDA 1998, s 66ZA(1) including sufficiency of evidence to obtain a reasonable prospect of conviction ('Youth Cautions, Guidelines for Police and Youth Offending Teams' (n 229) para 4.4).

[232] Even if this is proved, the intervention of the court is discretionary. See above *Ex p Thompson* at [1521B]–[1521D] at 4-88 and *R (A) v South Yorkshire Police and the Crown Prosecution Service* [2007] EWHC 1261 (Admin) above at 4-88.

[233] *R (F) v Crown Prosecution Service* [2003] EWHC 3266 (Admin), (2004) 168 JP 93 and *R v Chief Constable of Kent ex parte L* [1993] 1 All ER 756, (1991) 93 Cr App R 416, see above at 5-22 in the context of challenges to decisions to prosecute.

(iii) Challenges to the New System for Cautioning

One issue that may emerge concerns the requirement that a constable is required to   **11-30**
explain to the child or young person that a youth caution or youth conditional caution
may be disclosed to certain employers and organisations.[234] In *R (T) v Chief Constable of*
Greater Manchester Police[235] the Court of Appeal held that such disclosures may breach
Article 8 (see discussion above at 4-112 on disclosure of personal data). In the case of
adults, it has been held that it is crucial that such explanations are given, especially to
those whose employment may be affected, because informed consent is required.[236] It is
notable that the young person's consent is not a pre-requisite for a youth caution but it
is for a youth conditional caution.[237] The duty on the constable is to make the child or
young person and their appropriate adult (if under 17) aware of those consequences that
he is required to mention, but not with a purpose of securing their agreement to accept
the caution in light of that knowledge. For example, at first instance in *R (R) v Durham*
Constabulary,[238] the Divisional Court held that the failure to warn of the consequences
of administering a caution, namely in that case notification on the register of sex offenders, did not make the warning unlawful.[239] When *R (R) v Durham Constabulary* reached
the House of Lords, the House disagreed with the Divisional Court that the entry on
the Police National Computer and the sex offenders register were 'public declarations of
guilt' and so engaged Article 6 because only a limited number of persons had access to
them.[240] The court was not asked to consider the potential disclosure to future employers. Although no point was taken on Article 8, Lord Bingham said obiter that Article 8
was engaged but any interference was justified.[241] It will be interesting to see if this position is tenable in light of case law on informed consent, personal data and Article 8 that
has emerged since *R (R) v Durham Constabulary* (see discussion above at 4-99).

Another potential issue is that an appropriate adult does not have to be present when   **11-31**
an authorised person explains the effect of a youth conditional caution to 17 year olds.
One of the explicit statutory purposes of the conditional caution is punitive (section
66A(3)(c)). These punitive conditions can include a fine, unpaid work or attendance
at a specified place.[242] In *R (R) v Durham Constabulary* the central question on appeal
was whether a warning given to a child or young person was a determination of a
criminal charge and hence engaged Article 6. The appellant argued that if Article 6
was engaged, i) it required a determination by an impartial tribunal, which ii) a police

---

[234] 'Youth Cautions, Guidelines for Police and Youth Offending Teams' (n 229), para 9.10 and Code of
Practice for Youth Conditional Cautions, para 16.1.
[235] *R (T) v Chief Constable of Greater Manchester Police* [2013] 1 G App R 27. Note at time of writing judgment was awaited from the Supreme Court on appeal.
[236] See the case of *Stratton* above at 4-87 and 4-99.
[237] 'Youth Cautions, Guidelines for Police and Youth Offending Teams' (n 228) para 4.7.
[238] *R (R) v Durham Constabulary* (n 6).
[239] This part of the decision was not challenged on appeal before the House of Lords. The Guidance was
changed in 2002 to include requirements that certain information be provided in advance of any admissions
including the potential for notification on the sex offenders register. This has been included in the new guidance 'Youth Cautions, Guidelines for Police and Youth Offending Teams', (n 229) para 4.9.
[240] ibid [17].
[241] ibid [20].
[242] Code of Practice for Youth Conditional Cautions, para 7.4.

officer was not, unless iii) he consented to such a procedure, which he had not. The House held that it was not a determination of a criminal charge. Lord Bingham said this:

> the determination of a criminal charge, to be properly so regarded, must expose the subject of the charge to the possibility of punishment, whether in the event punishment is imposed or not. A process which can only culminate in measures of a preventative, curative, rehabilitative or welfare-promoting kind will not ordinarily be the determination of a criminal charge.[243]

It is submitted that fines, for example, cannot be construed as 'preventative, curative, rehabilitative or welfare-promoting'. It is also arguable that unpaid work, whose purpose is punitive, also cannot fulfil these criteria. If Article 6 is engaged, it is arguable that it may be breached due to the absence an appropriate adult. In *HC*, although Article 6 was not in issue, the Divisional Court commented on the question of the absence of an appropriate adult when an out of court disposal is administered:

> It merely reinforces the 17-year-old's vulnerability in the face of an intimidating criminal justice system. It undermines the very purpose the youth criminal justice system is designed to achieve.[244]

This point has been recognised and is addressed in the Criminal Justice and Courts Bill 2014.[245] But for the meantime it is questionable whether section 66B(5) of CDA 1998 is compatible with the HRA 1998.

(3) Decisions to Charge

11-32   As set out above at 5-22 judicial reviews can be mounted on the basis that the CPS has not adhered to its own policy. This is likely to be 'highly exceptional', given the nature of the discretion conferred.[246] In cases concerning youths, the courts have held that it requires a decision that is made regardless of or clearly contrary to the DPP's settled policy[247] or a departure from the statutory guidance for which there is no rational explanation (see above at 5-20 and 5-22).[248] In the former case this might also involve a failure to enquire into the background, circumstances and past record of the person. In the latter case this means that even where the decision-making process was deficient, if the final decision is defensible on public interest grounds, it cannot be challenged.[249]

These cases often involve offences that might merit an out-of-court disposal (see cases mentioned above at 5-22 in relation to the CPS). One example is *R (F) v Crown*

---

[243] *R v Durham Constabulary* (n 238) [14].

[244] *HC* (n 54) [93]. See in addition *Attorney-General's Reference No 2 of 2001* [26]-[29], see above at 6-40 and *Panovits v Cyprus* (n 85).

[245] Note that the Criminal Justice and Courts Bill 2014, laid before Parliament on 5 February 2014, contains clauses to amend the CDA 1998 to require a youth cautions to be administered and the explanation and warning for youth conditional cautions to be given in the presence of an appropriate adult for 16 and 17-year-olds.

[246] *R (Corner House Research) v Director of the Serious Fraud Office (JUSTICE intervening)* [2008] UKHL 60, [2009] AC 756 [30] (Lord Bingham) discussed above at 5-8.

[247] *R v Chief Constable of Kent, ex parte L* [1993] 1 All ER 756, (1991) 93 Cr App R 416. The decision is cited in the CPS's Legal Guidance.

[248] *R (A) v South Yorkshire Police and the Crown Prosecution Service* [2007] EWHC 1261 (Admin) [65].

[249] See *R (D) v Commissioner of Police for the Metropolis* [2008] EWHC 442 (Admin), [2008] ACD 47 applying *A* (n 248). In that case the officer had incorrectly graded the seriousness of the offence. However, he was justified in referring the matter to the CPS, given the aggravating factors.

Piers von Berg

Prosecution Service[250] where a youth refused to admit an offence in interview.[251] He was then charged. His solicitor said in court that he might be prepared to admit the offence and so should be considered for a warning or reprimand. The police refused to re-interview him or follow this course. The decision was upheld. The defendant had refused to change his position until he had reached court, thereby delaying matters. Furthermore, the police had given consideration to his best interests and the public interest.

(i) The Code for Crown Prosecutors

These types of decision require careful consideration of the applicable policies and guidance, which can be various and extensive.[252] A key starting point is the public interest test of the CPS Code for Crown Prosecutors (explained above at 5-8), which has a specific provision relating to charging of those under 18. This requires prosecutors to: **11-33**

i.   consider the best interests and welfare of the child or young person including whether any prosecution will have 'an adverse impact on his or her future prospects that is disproportionate to the seriousness of the offending';[253]

ii.   have regard to the principal aim of the youth justice system to prevent offending by children and young persons;

iii.   have regard to obligations under the UNCRC;

iv.   as a 'starting point, the younger the suspect, the less likely it is that a prosecution is required'; and

v.   a prosecution is in the public interest where the offence is serious, the suspect's past record 'suggests that there are no suitable alternatives to prosecution', or because of an 'absence of an admission' an out-of-court disposal is not available.[254]

In addition to the Code, the CPS legal guidance[255] states other 'key considerations' are that courts must have regard to the welfare of the child.[256] Prosecutors must have 'regard' for the principles set out in the ECHR, UNCRC and the Beijing Rules. All cases must be dealt with expeditiously.

An unusual but helpful authority is *R (E, S and R) v DPP*[257] (see above at 5-23). This was a challenge to the lawfulness of prosecutorial policy in not according special status

---

[250] *R (F) v Crown Prosecution Service* [2003] EWHC 3266 (Admin), (2004) 168 JP 93.

[251] ibid applying *Ex p L*. See also *R (C (A Child)) v DPP* (2001) 165 JP 102, Independent, 27 November 2000.

[252] The CPS Legal Guidance, which can be found on its website at www.cps.gov.uk/legal/v_to_z/youth_offenders/, covers matters relevant to charging such as out-of-court disposals, hate crime, looked after children (LAC) and children's homes, school bullying, motoring offences, sex offences and youths with mental disorders. There is overarching guidance—DPP, *The Director's Guidance On Charging 2013*, 5th edn, May 2013 (revised arrangements), Guidance to Police Officers and Crown Prosecutors Issued by the Director of Public Prosecution under PACE 1984, s 37A.

[253] An example of a successful review of a decision to prosecute where the best interests of both the defendant and the victims were not adequately considered was *R (E, S and R) v DPP* [2011] EWHC 1465 (Admin), [2012] 1 Cr App R 6 discussed above at 5-23.

[254] Code for Crown Prosecutors, January 2013, para 4.12(d).

[255] www.cps.gov.uk/legal/v_to_z/youth_offenders/.

[256] CYPA 1933, s 44.

[257] *E, S and R* (n 253).

to a child who is both a defendant and a victim. It demonstrates several of the above points, including that the CPS must take into account:

i.   the best interests of all the children involved, whether they are the defendant, victim or witness (these best interests include the impact of the decision to prosecute on the welfare of the child); and

ii. the views of other agencies involved in the lives of children.

This decision is a reminder of the principle that the courts should not formulate policy for which they lack the necessary expertise and competence (see discussion below in context of victims of crime at 11-42).[258]

As recognised by the CPS Legal Guidance, other considerations apply, such as whether it is proportionate to prosecute a minor offence,[259] and whether other forms of out-of-court disposal are available; for example, restorative justice, disciplinary measures in school, or Acceptable Behaviour Contracts.[260] This is particularly relevant for looked after children (LAC—see next section).

(ii) Decisions to Prosecute Vulnerable Children

11-34   The CPS has a specific policy on prosecuting LAC. These are children who are cared for in some capacity by the state, for example, under an order by a family court or on a planned basis.[261] It states that a criminal justice disposal (ie whether a prosecution or out-of-court):

> should not be regarded as an automatic response to offending behaviour by a looked after child, irrespective of their criminal history. This applies equally to persistent offenders and youths of good character.[262]

It will only be appropriate where 'clearly required'. Informal disposals may be 'sufficient to satisfy the public interest'. Prosecutors must consider the behaviour management policies of children's homes where offences are alleged to occur in those environments.

Regarding victims, in *R v N; R v Le (Vinh Cong)*,[263] Lord Judge LCJ said that the CPS should be able to exercise their discretion not to prosecute a defendant, who cannot advance the defence of duress, but falls within Article 26 of the European Convention on Action against Trafficking in Human Beings 2005. This requires States to 'provide for the possibility of not imposing penalties on victims for their involvement in unlawful activities, to the extent that they have been compelled to do so'. It is unlikely that judicial

---

[258] The court relied on the above decision of Lord Bingham in *Corner House* (n 246). Note that the CPS Legal Guidance states that a decision to prosecute should be not taken in order to 'secure access to the welfare powers of the court'.

[259] www.cps.gov.uk/legal/l_to_o/minor_offences/.

[260] An Acceptable Behaviour Contract (ABC) 'is a written agreement between a person who has been involved in antisocial behaviour and one or more local agencies whose role it is to prevent such behaviour'. The Home Office, *A Guide to Anti-Social Behaviour Orders and Acceptable Behaviour Contracts*.

[261] The Children Act 1989 defines these children as those provided with local authority accommodation (s 22(1)(b)). Typically, this will include children subject to orders made under the Children Act 1989 such as interim care orders and care orders.

[262] www.cps.gov.uk/legal/v_to_z/youth_offenders/.

[263] *R v N; R v Le (Vinh Cong)* [2012] EWCA Crim 189, [2013] QB 379 [21].

review is a remedy of last resort, as a criminal court could consider such a matter as an abuse of process, or could cater for such an outcome in its sentencing decision. To be clear, this does not mean that as a matter of principle a person should not be prosecuted for crimes committed as a result of being trafficked.[264]

Concerning child victims of trafficking, who are exploited to commit offences, the CPS guidance stresses that child trafficking is primarily a child protection issue.[265] Prosecutors should make proper allowance for their age, vulnerability and lack of maturity. This is an awkward area, as children's accounts may not appear credible because they may have been coached or coerced into giving false details.[266] In addition, it is not inconceivable that appropriate adults may be involved in trafficking.

(iii) Decisions to Prosecute Children for Sex Offences

The CPS has extensive guidance on how it takes decisions on charging and prosecuting youths for sexual offences.[266a] The case law on judicial review of CPS decisions on grounds of irrationality and/or failure to follow its own policy is likely to be relevant to challenges in this area and is considered separately above at 5-20, 11-33, and in particular the case of *E, S and R* discussed at 5-23. This section considers decisions to select particular charges.   **11-35**

The CPS Guidance is explicit that sexual offences committed by youths involving children aged under 13 cannot be charged under section 13 of the Sexual Offences Act 2003 but only sections 5-8.[267] This is a controversial area, as sections 5-8 are offences of strict liability and yet overlap with section 13, which carries a lesser penalty, less stigma and different notification requirements.[268]

The issue of whether a defendant should be charged with section 13 rather than section 5 where the victim consented divided the House of Lords in *R v G (Secretary of State for Home Department intervening)*.[269] The case is relevant to judicial reviews of decisions to prosecute and in particular the selection of charges. The claimant (aged 15) argued that section 5 was contrary to the presumption of innocence under Article 6(2), and the decision not to charge him under section 13 violated his right to privacy under Article 8. The facts were that the claimant accepted engaging in sexual intercourse with

---

[264] *R v M (L), B(M) and G(D)* [2010] EWCA Crim 2327 [2011] 1 Cr App R 12 [21]. This case was applied in *R v N* (n 263). See also the commentary on the case of *R v O* [2008] EWCA Crim 2835 in *R v M (L)* [20], where the defendant was aged 17.

[265] www.cps.gov.uk/legal/h_to_k/human_trafficking_and_smuggling/index.html#a30. Child victims of human trafficking may also be LAC. Note also there is a CPS policy on prosecuting cases where children are witnesses or victims (www.cps.gov.uk/victims_witnesses/ children_policy.pdf).

[266] Note also the Protocol to Prevent, Suppress and Punish Trafficking in Persons, Especially Women and Children (the Palermo Protocol), the Safeguarding Children Who May Have Been Trafficked guidance and the Safeguarding Children and Young People from Sexual Exploitation guidance (Department of Children Schools and Families, June 2009).

[266a] See the Guidance on 'Rape and Sexual Offences: Chapter 11: Youths' at http://www.cps.gov.uk/legal/p_ to_r/rape_and_sexual_offences/youths/ and on 'Youths' at http://www.cps.gov.uk/legal/v_to_z/youth_offenders/.

[267] www.cps.gov.uk/legal/v_to_z/youth_offenders/#a28 and http://www.cps.gov.uk/legal/p_to_r/rape_ and_sexual_offences/youths/.

[268] See Spencer, 'The Sexual Offences Act 2003: (2) Child and family offences' [2004] *Criminal Law Reports* 347. He argues that ss 5–8 should only be charged where there is mens rea. There is much debate over whether a child who engages in inappropriate behaviour is abusing or experimenting. See Home Office, *Setting the Boundaries: Reforming the law on sex offences* (July 2000), vol 1.

[269] *R v G (Secretary of State for Home Department intervening)* [2008] UKHL 37, [2009] 1 AC 92.

the complainant (aged 12), but asserted she had willingly taken part and he had reasonably believed her to be 15 years old. A basis of plea was accepted as the complainant said she had told the defendant she was 15 and she was unwilling to attend court to give evidence. Whilst the House agreed on Article 6 and dismissed the appeal, it was divided on Article 8. There was a wide spectrum of opinion from Lord Hoffman and Lady Hale, who said Article 8 was not engaged, to Lord Phillips LCJ, sitting in the Court of Appeal, who said it was.[270] The majority in the House of Lords held that in circumstances where there was an uncontested basis of plea that the complainant consented and the defendant reasonably believed she was over 13, it did not breach the defendant's Article 8 right to charge him with rape (section 5) rather than sexual activity with a child (section 13).[271] Lady Hale argued that in such cases the court can reflect the level of offending in the sentence—in this case a conditional discharge was substituted on appeal. Lord Hope disagreed, and said that where the offending fell within the scope of section 13, it would be disproportionate to prosecute under section 5.[272]

Whilst this authority suggests judicial review on these grounds will fail, the CPS Guidance appears closer to the view of Lord Hope, who stated that the lower the age, the less appropriate a prosecution will be.[273] For example, the Guidance states that if both defendant and complainant are under 13 and are consenting, a prosecution may not be appropriate:

> If the sexual act or activity was in fact genuinely consensual and the youth and the child under 13 concerned are fairly close in age and development, a prosecution is unlikely to be appropriate.[274]

Other factors are also important: it may not be appropriate to charge where there is little age difference, and the Guidance requires 'careful consideration' of the sexual and emotional maturity, any emotional or physical effects, whether the child under 13 freely consented, or a genuine mistake as to her age was in fact made. Understandably, it includes any aggravating features. It is submitted that a departure from this policy may instead provide a basis for challenge.

For example, after *R v G* a different outcome was reached in *R (S) v DPP*[275] where after proceedings were issued, the CPS substituted a charge under section 5 with one under sections 9 and 13. The facts in that case included a psychological assessment of the defendant, which suggested a very small gap in terms of development between the parties and that the effect of a decision to prosecute under section 5 would be profound.[276]

---

[270] ibid [9]–[10] (Lord Hoffmann), and [54] (Lady Hale). *R v G (Secretary of State for Home Department intervening)* [2006] EWCA Crim 82, [2006] 1 WLR 2052 [46] (Phillips LCJ). These views, along with the ECtHR's decision (see below), were considered in *SXH v Crown Prosecution Service* [2014] EWCA Civ 90 [71]—see above at 5-34. Pitchford LJ, with whom Gloster LJ specifically agreed with on this point, departed from Lord Hoffmann's view.

[271] Note that this view clashes to some degree with other commentators. See A Ashworth, 'Case Comment, Rape: rape of a child under 13—mental element—consent' [2006] *Criminal Law Reports* 930–34. *R v G* (n 269) has been recently followed on a slightly different point in *R v Brown* [2013] UKSC 43 (a Northern Ireland case).

[272] *R v G* (n 269) [39]. His Lordship noted that the Court of Appeal went so far as to say that the judge should have taken the view in light of the basis of plea that a prosecution under section 13 was more appropriate.

[273] ibid [39] (Lord Hope).

[274] www.cps.gov.uk/legal/v_to_z/youth_offenders/#a28.

[275] *R (S) v DPP* [2006] EWHC 2231 (Admin).

[276] *Rook & Ward on Sexual Offences—Law and Practice* 4th edn (London, Thomson Reuters (Legal) Limited, 2010), para 3.19, considers this case and *R v G* and states: 'Notwithstanding R v G, it is to be hoped that in future cases of underage sex, in which the public interest requires a prosecution, the CPS will be prepared to rely on s.13 rather than on s.5, unless there is a very clear element of exploitation or abuse.'

The potential for challenges based on Article 6, that the strict liability offence of section 5 infringes Article 6, and based on Article 8, have been dealt a blow by the ECtHR. The defendant in *R v G* failed to have his claim ruled admissible before the court in *G v United Kingdom*.[277] The ECtHR found that section 5 did not create presumptions of law or fact such that the burden of proof is reversed on the defendant so as to engage Article 6.[278] Whilst the court did find that the sexual activities in question fell within the definition of private life, and a prosecution, conviction and sentence of *G* constituted an interference with it, this was in accordance with the law and necessary. A key reason behind this was the wide margin of appreciation granted to domestic courts when protecting individuals from rape.[279]

In considering whether the CPS has properly applied its existing policy in any prosecutorial decisions, an important consideration in this area now is its Violence Against Women and Girls (VAWG) strategy. This incorporates policies on domestic violence, forced marriage, honour-based violence, female genital mutilation, rape and sexual offences, prostitution, trafficking, child abuse and pornography.[280]

(4) Sending to the Crown Court

The presumption is that all those aged under 18 are tried in the Youth Court unless **11-36** certain exceptions apply. These are set out in summary in the table above and are considered in detail above at 6-60–6-64 in the sections on challenges to the Youth Court where the changes to the law are also explained. Once a youth is committed with an adult to the Crown Court, they must be tried in the Crown Court even if the adult pleads guilty. This seems odd as the adult magistrates' court has a power under section 29 of the Magistrates' Court Act 1980 to remit a juvenile to the youth court where an adult with whom he is jointly charged pleads guilty or is sent to the Crown Court. This lacuna in the law was identified in *R (W) v Leeds Crown Court*[281] where Sir Anthony May P declined an invitation to read such a power into section 29. His Lordship expressed regret and said that he felt 'strongly' that this was a matter for which parliament should legislate as 'I am very conscious that the interests of children and young persons, although not in this sphere the only consideration, nevertheless are interests of huge importance'.[282] If the situation remains unchanged, it remains to be seen whether a challenge could be mounted on the grounds of the incompatibility of the current legislation with Article 6 given the concerns around the abilities of especially youths with learning disabilities to participate effectively in a trial (see the cases below at 11-38–11-40).

---

[277] In its judgment the ECtHR noted the decision of *R v Corran* [2005] EWCA Crim 192, [2005] 2 Cr App R (S) 73, 453, where the Court of Appeal said that in relation to sentencing for s 5, presence of consent and difference in age are likely to material factors. *G v United Kingdom* (2011) 53 EHRR SE25 [19].

[278] ibid [29].

[279] ibid [38].

[280] www.cps.gov.uk/publications/equality/vaw/.

[281] See *R (W) v Leeds Crown Court* [2011] EWHC 2326 (Admin), [2012] 1 WLR 2786.

[282] ibid [51]. Langstaff J agreed and wished 'emphatically to associate myself with the concluding remarks of Sir Anthony May P's judgment'.

D. Trial

(1) Trial

11-37   The issues of absence of the defendant, age and remittals to an adult court are dealt with above at 6-79. This section deals with all other matters that may found a claim for judicial review.

The treatment and questioning of vulnerable witnesses or defendants is addressed at 3D and 3E in the *Practice Direction (Criminal Proceedings)*. In the Crown Court, any claim for judicial review will be almost certainly precluded by section 29(3) of the Senior Courts Act (see above at 7-2–7-3).

The question of what is an appropriate venue to try young children for serious offences can affect the decision to commit the case to the Crown Court, procedures adopted in the Youth Court and the exercise of the prosecutor's discretion in selecting charges. Most importantly, whether a child or young person can participate effectively in the proceedings engages Article 6 of ECHR. The court has a continuing jurisdiction to stay the proceedings if a defendant cannot receive a fair trial (see above on applications concerning abuse of process at 6-34). If there are concerns relating to the defendant's fitness to plead, it is open to the court to proceed with a fact finding rather than a criminal trial (see above at 12-37).[283] All of these decisions by a Youth Court are susceptible to challenge by way of judicial review. The following commentary shall consider how the case law has developed and what avenues may exist for judicial review challenges.

11-38   The 2002 *Consolidated Criminal Practice Direction* (now replaced by the *Practice Direction (Criminal Proceedings)*) incorporated the Government's response to the ECtHR's findings on the fairness of the trial of the two boys who abducted and killed James Bulger in *T v United Kingdom, V v United Kingdom*.[284] The issue was how young children can effectively participate in trials in the Crown Court for the most serious offences. The defendants were tried in the Crown Court for murder aged 11. Both boys sat in full public view in a raised dock for three weeks in a packed court room. Expert assessments indicated that *T* was terrified and was unable to follow the evidence, whilst *V* needed 12 months to recover from the trauma. The ECtHR agreed that they were unable to participate effectively in the proceedings and so were denied a fair trial. It said it was:

> essential that a child charged with an offence is dealt with in a manner which takes full account of his age, level of maturity and intellectual and emotional capacities, and that steps are taken to promote his ability to understand and participate in the proceedings.[285]

---

[283] See the guidance in *R (P (A Juvenile)) v Barking Youth Court* [2002] EWHC 734 (Admin), [2002] 2 Cr App R 19 discussed at 12-43.

[284] *T v United Kingdom, V v United Kingdom* [2000] 2 All ER 1024, (2000) 30 EHRR 121.

[285] ibid [86]. This decision did not subsequently prevent very young children (11 years old) with evidence of learning difficulties and troubled childhood being committed to the Crown Court eg *R v C (A Juvenile)* The Times, 19 May 2000.

Piers von Berg

Since then, the law has moved on quite considerably with the introduction of intermediaries, live links for defendants and ground rules hearings—see the *Practice Direction (Criminal Proceedings)* discussed below.

After the introduction of the 2002 *Consolidated Criminal Practice Direction* the **11-39** ECtHR revisited the issue in *SC v United Kingdom*.[286] This case involved a defendant charged with attempted robbery during which an 87-year-old female complainant sustained a fractured arm. Expert evidence found his cognitive abilities to be between six and eight years. The defence argued that he would not receive a fair trial because he would not be able to follow the proceedings. The Court of Appeal rejected his appeal against conviction. However, the ECtHR said that in cases such as this:

> it is essential that he be tried in a specialist tribunal which is able to give full consideration to and make proper allowance for the handicaps under which he labours, and adapt its procedure accordingly.[287]

This was applied in *R (TP) v West London Youth Court*.[288] Where the Divisional Court found that the defendant, who had a mental age of eight, had failed to establish that there was no real possibility of having a fair trial given the following measures:

i.   Keeping the claimant's level of cognitive functioning in mind;
ii.   Using concise and simple language;
iii.   Having regular breaks;
iv.   Taking additional time to explain court proceedings;
v.   Being proactive in ensuring the claimant has access to support;
vi.   Explaining and ensuring the claimant understands the ingredients of the charge;
vii.   Explaining the possible outcomes and sentences;
viii.   Ensuring that cross-examination is carefully controlled so that questions are short and clear and frustration is minimised.[289]

As is evident from some of the authorities below, these issues often occur where a defendant suffers from a mental disorder or has difficulty participating in the trial process.

These considerations are reflected in the *Practice Direction (Criminal Proceedings)*,[290]   **11-40** where the approach to hearings involving vulnerable defendants is addressed. Importantly, special measures for defendants, in the form of live links are now available under a new section 33A of the YJCEA 1999 (inserted by the Police and Justice Act 2006).[291] Intermediaries are available only at common law and their availability has been a contested area in judicial review.[292]

---

[286] *SC v United Kingdom* [2004] 40 EHRR 10.

[287] ibid [35].

[288] *R (TP) v West London Youth Court* [2005] EWHC 2583 (Admin), [2006] 1 WLR 1219.

[289] ibid [26]. It is submitted that the same considerations of a 'specialist tribunal' must apply to the Crown Court when dealing with such vulnerable young defendants. However, due to the High Court's restricted jurisdiction in relation to matters relating to trial on indictment (see above at 7-2), such matters cannot be addressed by claims by way of judicial review.

[290] *Practice Direction (Criminal Proceedings)* G1–13.

[291] See also the Criminal Procedure Rules, Pt 29, as amended on 7 October 2013.

[292] Note that this issue was before the High Court at the time of writing in the case of *R (OP) v Secretary of State for Justice* and judgment handed down on 13 June 2014.

The previous unavailability of special measures for child defendants was found not to be a breach of Article 6 in *R (S) v Waltham Forest Youth Court*.[293] The defendant in that case was aged 13, had serious learning difficulties and was too frightened to give evidence in the presence of her co-defendants. However, in *R (C) v Sevenoaks Youth Court*,[294] Sullivan LJ said there was in nothing in that decision that prevented the use of an intermediary.[295] The Court of Appeal has also confirmed that there is no limit on a court's power when it concerns ensuring an accused's participation in his trial.[296] At the time of writing, section 33BA of YJCEA 1999 is not implemented, which allows for intermediaries for defendants. Intermediaries are communication specialists who facilitate communication between the witness and the court and advocates. At present, intermediaries for defendants have no statutory footing.

An example of the difficulties that can arise was in *R (AS) v Great Yarmouth Youth Court*[297] where a Youth Court refused to grant the claimant, S, an intermediary where he had Attention Deficit and Hyperactivity Disorder. Mitting J held that there was a right, which might in certain circumstances amount to a duty, to appoint a registered intermediary to assist the defendant to follow the proceedings and give evidence if without assistance he would not be able to have a fair trial. However, in *R v Cox*,[298] Lord Judge LCJ held that where a defendant's evidence may be improved by an intermediary, it did not follow that their involvement was mandatory, and any failure to find one would necessarily render the trial unfair. The judge had to make an assessment of whether a fair trial could be held in the absence of an intermediary. It would be most unusual for a properly brought prosecution to be stayed where a defendant was fit to plead.[299]

The current case law is reflected in the *Practice Direction (Criminal Proceedings)*, which recognises this position that whilst a judge may have a common law power to direct an intermediary for a defendant, it may be ineffective if none can be identified for whom funding is available.[300] It provides guidance on when an assessment should be considered and the role of an intermediary at a ground rules hearing.[301]

11-41   Child defendants should not experience unnecessary and excessive delay between charging and trial. As with any defendant they are entitled to a trial within a reasonable time under Article 6(1) of the ECHR (see above at 6-39). However, Article 6 is read in the context of the UNCRC (Article 40(2)(b)) and the Beijing Rules (r 20), the latter of which states there must not be any unnecessary delay. A defendant's young age can be a very important factor in determining whether any delay is inordinate or excessive.[302] In *Dyer v Watson* the defendant was aged 13 at the time of charge and 16 at the time of

---

[293] *R (S) v Waltham Forest Youth Court* [2004] EWHC 715 (Admin), [2004] 2 Cr App R 21. The fact that this may lead to an inequality of arms does not mean special measures for Crown witnesses can be excluded. See *R (D) v Camberwell Green Youth Court* [2005] UKHL 4, [2005] 1 WLR 393 (discussed above at 6-68).

[294] *R (C) v Sevenoaks Youth Court* [2009] EWHC 3088 (Admin), [2010] 1 All ER 735.

[295] YJCEA 1999, ss 33BA and 33BB, when implemented, contain provisions allowing for the use of intermediaries by defendants.

[296] *R v Ukpabio* [2008] 1 Cr App R 6, CA, a decision of Latham LJ. See also *R v Dixon* [2013] EWCA Crim 465.

[297] *R (AS) v Great Yarmouth Youth Court* [2011] EWHC 2059 (Admin).

[298] *R v Cox* [2012] EWCA Crim 549, [2012] 2 Cr App R 6.

[299] ibid [29]–[30] (Lord Judge LCJ).

[300] *Practice Direction (Criminal Proceedings)*, 3F.4.

[301] Ibid 3F.5 and 3E.2-3.

[302] *Dyer v Watson* (n 25) [103].

trial. This did not, on its own, make the trial unfair, but the court found the explanations given by the prosecuting authorities unsatisfactory:

> the explanations which the Crown have provided for the various periods of delay lack any indication that the lapse of time ever led the authorities to treat the case with increasing urgency as time went by.[303]

This issue may lead to judicial review challenges to prosecution decisions and decisions to adjourn in the lower courts.

(2) Children as Victims and Witnesses

The CPS has a policy for prosecuting cases involving children as victims and witness-es.[304] This covers many of the key decisions taken during the investigation and trial process. The key obligations of the CPS are to consider the best interests of the child and the views of the victim. The policy covers other sensitive topics such as parents' consent, consultation and therapy. It summarises other important documents that should be referred to directly, including guidance on interviewing children.[305] The CPS has more specific legal guidance on 'Safeguarding Children as Victims and Witnesses'.[306] Complainants against CPS conduct should be aware of the mechanism for complaints and the new scheme for Victim's Right of Review (see above at 5-37). In addition, a new Code of Practice for Victims of Crime was issued in October 2013 that sets out the position with respect to victims aged under 18. **11-42**

Judicial review challenges of CPS decisions surrounding the treatment of child victims and witnesses are rare. One example is *R v Highbury Corner Magistrates' Court, ex parte D*,[307] where the court granted an application to compel a magistrates' court to grant a witness summons against a child. But the Administrative Court is the only available forum if a victim seeks to quash a decision to prosecute. In *E, S and R* (discussed above at 5-23 and at 11-33) the court considered much of the guidance set out above and the international law, and said:

i.   It is not for the courts to consider whether the DPP's policy allegedly failed to accord proper status to children as defendants and victims.
ii. There is no obligation to obtain a victim's views only to consider them.
iii. The victim's interests are not given priority, but considered in the balance with other factors such as the interests of the defendant and the public.[308]

---

[303] ibid [107] (Lord Hope).
[304] www.cps.gov.uk/victims_witnesses/ children_policy.pdf.
[305] CPS, Department for Education, Department of Health and Welsh Assembly Government, *Achieving best evidence in criminal proceedings: Guidance on interviewing victims and witnesses, and using special measures*, and *Provision of therapy for child witnesses prior to a criminal trial—Practice guidance*, March 2011. There are also Codes of Practice for Victims of Crime ('Victim's Code') and Pre-Trial Witness Interviews, a CPS Public Policy Statement on the Delivery of Services to Victims ('Prosecutor's Pledge'), the Attorney General's Guidelines on the Acceptance of Pleas and the Prosecutor's Role in the Sentencing Exercise (revised 2009) and the CPS Core Quality Standards.
[306] www.cps.gov.uk/legal/v_to_z/safeguarding_children_as_victims_and_witnesses/.
[307] *R v Highbury Corner Magistrates' Court, ex parte D* (1997) 161 JP 138, [1997] 1 FLR 683.
[308] *E, S and R* (n 257) [50], [66] and [85].

It is submitted that this position might be reconsidered in light of the EU Directives on the treatment of the victims of sexual abuse (2011/92/EU) and for the support and protection of victims of crime (2012/29/EU).[309]

Another issue that may have to be revisited in light of the above Directives is the non-availability of lifelong anonymity orders for child victims or witnesses, who are not victims of sexual offences under section 1 of the Sexual Offences (Amendment) Act 1992. Adult witnesses have the availability of such protection under section 46 of YJCEA. Sir Brian Leveson P in *JC and RT* said that this 'requires to be addressed as a matter of real urgency'.[310]

(3) Special Measures for Children as Victims and Witnesses

11-43   As stated in the table above, witnesses aged under 18 are automatically entitled under the YJCEA 1999 to the special measures in sections 16–30. These include screens, evidence by live video-link, evidence given in private, removal of wigs and gowns, video recording of evidence-in-chief, examination of a witness through an intermediary and provision of aids to communication. There are no grounds in principle for objecting to justices hearing a case if they have heard and granted an application for screens unless there are particular circumstances that indicate that they cannot be fair-minded about the case.[311]

An example of a challenge to the use of this procedure is *R (Crown Prosecution Service) v Brentford Youth Court*.[312] The court rejected a challenge to a judge's decision to play parts of a video of a complainant's evidence-in-chief containing irrelevant information, as the evidence could not be understood without it.

There have been several criticisms made of the current system of special measures,[313] and calls for change.[314] It is submitted that the main problems are:

i.   The effect of the delay on a child's memory between the time a child discloses the allegation and when s/he attends court to be cross-examined,[315] and, the difficulties in accessing therapy, if required, during this waiting period;[316]

---

[309] For a discussion of the potential impact of the Directives on this area see Piers von Berg, 'Children's evidence and new EU Directives' (2013) 3 *Archbold Review*.

[310] *JC and RT*, see above (n 37) [38].

[311] *KL (A Juvenile) v DPP* [2001] EWHC Admin 1112, (2002) 166 JP 369. See above at 6-77.

[312] *R (Crown Prosecution Service) v Brentford Youth Court* [2003] EWHC 2409 (Admin).

[313] For example see Criminal Justice Joint Inspection, Her Majesty's Chief Inspectors of the Crown Prosecution Service, Constabulary and Court Administration, *Joint Inspection Report on the Experience of Young Victims and Witnesses in the Criminal Justice System* (2012), and J Plotnikoff and R Woolfson, 'Measuring up? Evaluating implementation of Government commitments to young witnesses in criminal proceedings', July 2009, www.nspcc.org.uk/inform.

[314] JR Spencer and MR Lamb, *Children and Cross-Examination, Time to Change the Rules?* (eds) (Oxford, Hart Publishing, 2012). See also Lord Judge, 'Half a Century of Change: The Evidence of Child Victims', Tomlin Lecture in Law and Psychiatry, 20 March 2013, www.judiciary.gov.uk/Resources/JCO/Documents/Speeches/lcj-speech-law-and-psychiatry.pdf and Lord Judge, 'The Evidence of Child Victims: the Next Stage', Bar Council Annual Law Reform Lecture, 21 November 2013.

[315] For example see *R v Powell* [2006] EWCA Crim 3. A three-and-a-half-year-old girl gave evidence nine months after an alleged sexual assault. Her responses to cross-examination were not intelligible and the conviction was overturned on appeal.

[316] The latter was a material consideration in *E, S and R* (n 253).

ii.   The potential for a child to be misled[317] or to be significantly traumatised by cross-examination in an adversarial setting;[318]

iii. The effect on a young child of attending a criminal court, in particular, when there are substantial periods spent waiting.[319]

These considerations may play a part in judicial review of decisions in the Youth Court to adjourn a trial or decisions on special measures. It might be said that these considerations could inform challenges to the current statutory regime in terms of its compatibility with the ECHR or the rights of the child under the EU Charter of Fundamental Rights. At present section 28 of the YJCEA, which allows for pre-recording of cross-examination, is being piloted.[320] It is submitted that this reform mostly targets the issue of delay, and not the manner of cross-examination and the need to attend a criminal court. The former problem is now addressed in the *Practice Direction (Criminal Proceedings)*, which states robustly that 'Over-rigorous or repetitive cross-examination of a child or vulnerable witness should be stopped'.[321]

(4) Reporting Restrictions

(i) General Principles

Section 39 of the CYPA 1933 provides: **11-44**

(1) In relation to any proceedings in any court, the court may direct that—

(a) no newspaper report of the proceedings shall reveal the name, address or school, or include any particulars calculated to lead to the identification, of any child or young person concerned in the proceedings, either as being the person by or against or in respect of whom the proceedings are taken, or as being a witness therein;

(b) no picture shall be published in any newspaper as being or including a picture of any child or young person so concerned in the proceedings as aforesaid;

except in so far (if at all) as may be permitted by the direction of the court.

(2) Any person who publishes any matter in contravention of any such direction shall on summary conviction be liable in respect of each offence to a fine not exceeding level 5 on the standard scale.[322]

---

[317] It should be noted that the Court of Appeal has already indicated its lack of tolerance for such questioning particularly with leading or 'tagged' questions. See *R v Wills* [2011] EWCA Crim 1938 and *R v E* [2011] EWCA Crim 3028.

[318] See the evidence cited in Plotnikoff and Woolfson (n 313), pp 8 and 127–28.

[319] An example is *R v B* [2010] EWCA Crim 4. The witness, a girl aged three, had to be got out of bed at 6.00 am to get to court on time. When she arrived, the court was not ready for her. She waited for a whole day at the Old Bailey and was sent home without giving evidence. She was then persuaded to return the next day, only for the experience to be repeated. She was cross-examined on the afternoon of that second day. She was exhausted and her minimal replies to defence counsel formed the basis of the appeal to the Court of Appeal. This account is contained in Spencer and Lamb (n 314), p 12.

[320] The pilots are at the Crown Court sitting in Kingston-upon-Thames, Leeds and Liverpool. Youth Justice and Criminal Evidence Act 1999 (Commencement No 13) Order 2013 (SI 2013/3236).

[321] *Practice Direction (Criminal Proceedings)* 3E.1-4. It also says that 'traditional cross-examination' may not enable a young witness to 'give the best evidence they can' and the court may impose restrictions on the advocate 'putting his case' where a young witness may fail to understand, become distressed or acquiesce to leading questions.

[322] Note that YJCEA 1999, s 45 is intended to replace CYPA 1933, s 39 but is not yet in force.

The general principles are that reports should be restricted unless there are good reasons to do so;[323] different principles apply in the Youth Court (as discussed below at 11-44). It is the duty of the prosecutor to remind the court of its power to impose reporting restrictions.[324] There is a balance to be struck with the public interest in fair and accurate reporting and in knowing the identity of offenders who may pose a threat.[325] The fact that the defendant is under 18 is usually a good reason. An order under section 39(1) cannot extend to reports of the proceedings after the subject of the order has reached the age of 18.[326] The welfare of the defendant as mandated by section 44(1) of the CYPA 1933 must be balanced with the public interest and Article 10 of ECHR.[327] A restriction may be more likely where the defendant is to serve a short period in custody for a minor offence than if a serious offence was committed resulting in a lengthy period. In the latter case there may be i) less prejudice to the defendant, ii) a deterrent effect and iii) the public interest would outweigh that prejudice.[328] But a court should not identify young defendants merely to publicise a sentencing principle without specifically allowing for the deterrent effect on the defendant and others.[329]

An order made under section 39 must be restricted to the specific words of the section, and cannot go beyond it.[330] In *Ex p Godwin* the court overturned an order prohibiting the publication of the names and addresses of the adult defendants. The court has a discretion to hear representations from those whom the judge considers have a legitimate interest in the making of the order.[331] The test to be applied is balancing the public interest in reporting of a crime against the need to protect the victim from further harm. The order handed down must be clear and precise in order that any person knows exactly what is prohibited.[332] An order can be made at any time, including in other proceedings.

It has been held that the Crown Court has no jurisdiction to grant an injunction preventing publication of a defendant's details in order to protect his children.[333] This concerned an order made under section 11 of the Contempt of Court Act 1981. Such an order is not incidental to the jurisdiction of the court, in that did not relate to trial,

---

[323] For a summary see Judicial Studies Board, *Reporting Restrictions in the Criminal Courts* (2009), section 4.2.
[324] *R v Crown Court at Southwark, ex parte Godwin* [1991] 3 All ER 818.
[325] *R v Leicester Crown Court, ex parte S (A Minor)* [1993] 1 WLR 111, [1992] 2 All ER 659 explained in *R v Central Criminal Court, ex parte S and P* (1999) 163 JP 776, [1999] 1 FLR 480.
[326] *JC and RT*, see above (n 37), [39].
[327] *R (Y) v Aylesbury Crown Court* [2012] EWHC 1140 (Admin).
[328] *R v Lee* [1993] 1 WLR 103, (1993) 96 Cr App R 188, CA.
[329] *Ex p S and P* (n 325).
[330] *Ex p Godwin* (n 324) applied in *R v Central Criminal Court, ex parte Crook* [1995] 1 WLR 139, [1995] 1 All ER 537 and in *R (Gazette Media Co Ltd) v Teesside Crown Court* [2005] EWCA Crim 1983, [2005] EMLR 34.
[331] *Ex p Crook* (n 330).
[332] *Briffett v Crown Prosecution Service* [2001] EWHC Admin 841, (2002) 166 JP 66.
[333] *R (Trinity Mirror Plc) v Croydon Crown Court* [2008] EWCA Crim 50, [2008] QB 770. The five-judge panel included Sir Igor Judge P and Sir Mark Potter P. See also *Re S (A Child) (Identification: Restrictions on Publication)* [2004] UKHL 47, [2005] 1 AC 593; *C v Crown Prosecution Service* [2008] EWHC 854 (Admin), 172 JP 273 and *R (A) v Lowestoft Magistrates' Court* [2013] EWHC 659 (Admin), [2013] EMLR 20. In the latter case it was held that proceedings concerned a child for the purposes of CYPA 1933, s 39 where the offence was being drunk in charge of a child aged under seven in a public place (Licensing Act 1902, s 2(1)).

Piers von Berg

conviction or sentence.[334] However, the High Court can make such an order.[335] Similarly, it has also been held that section 39 of CYPA 1933 does not apply to children who are not defendants, victims or witnesses.[336]

(ii) Jurisdiction of the High Court

There is conflicting authority on whether orders under section 39 of the CYPA 1933 can **11-45** be challenged by way of judicial review, as they may concern matters relating to trial on indictment (section 29(3) of the Senior Courts Act 1981).[337] The authorities appear to suggest that the issue is one of timing. An application made after conviction may present as one that is collateral rather than integral to the matters relating to trial on indictment. There are authorities on either side of the line:

i. It was said that it was outside the remit of the court in *R v Winchester Crown Court, ex parte B (A Minor)*.[338]

ii. The court entertained such applications in i) *R v Leicester Crown Court, ex parte S (A Minor)*,[339] ii) *R v Lee (Anthony William) (A Minor)*,[340] iii) *R v Harrow Crown Court, ex parte Perkins*,[341] iv) *R v Manchester Crown Court, ex parte H (A Juvenile)*[342] and in v) *R (Y) v Aylesbury Crown Court*.[343]

In *Ex p H (A Juvenile)*, Rose LJ considered the relevance of section 29(3) and the contrary authority in *Ex p B (A Minor)*.[344] He identified the timing of the challenge as an important factor:

The subject matter of the order sought to be challenged is obviously a very important factor when considering whether section 29(3) of the Supreme Court Act 1981 applies. But it is not, as it seems to me, the sole determinative factor ... there are other factors for consideration, including when in relation to the course of the trial or proceedings a section 39 order is made.[345]

For example, in *Ex p S (A Minor)*, *Ex p H (A Juvenile)* and *Y* the application was made post-conviction or post-sentence. In *Y* the court considered the case law and Hooper LJ said that 'Although there have been doubts expressed in the past, it seems clear that this court had jurisdiction to entertain an application for judicial review of the judge's

---

[334] Senior Courts Act 1981, s 45(4).

[335] *Re W (Children) (Identification: Restrictions on Publication)* [2005] EWHC 1564 (Fam), [2006] 1 FLR 1.

[336] *R v Jolleys* [2013] EWCA Crim 1135 [12]–[14]. This was also a case where a defendant sought to protect the identity of one of his children.

[337] This would not affect proceedings concerning Anti Social Behaviour Orders. *R (T) v St Albans Crown Court* [2002] EWHC 1129 (Admin). Note the decision in *R (Stanley) v Commissioner of Police of the Metropolis* [2004] EWHC 2229 (Admin), (2004) 168 JP 623 which concerned the distribution of posters with the names, photographs and partial addresses of those subject to ASBOs. A similar decision is the Northern Irish case of *Re JR38's Application for Judicial Review* [2013] NIQB 44.

[338] *R v Winchester Crown Court, ex parte B (A Minor)* [1999] 1 WLR 788, [1999] 4 All ER 53.

[339] *R v Leicester Crown Court, ex parte S (A Minor)* [1993] 1 WLR 111, [1992] 2 All ER 659.

[340] *R v Lee (Anthony William) (A Minor)* [1993] 1 WLR 103.

[341] *R v Harrow Crown Court, ex parte Perkins* (1998) 162 JP 527.

[342] *R v Manchester Crown Court, ex parte H (A Juvenile)* [2000] 1 WLR 760, [2000] 2 All ER 166.

[343] *Y* (n 327).

[344] See I Cram, 'To review or not to review' (1999) 149 *New Law Journal* 1468, 1470.

[345] *Ex p H (A Juvenile)* (n 342) 767.

order'.[346] Although this point was not argued before Sir Brian Leveson P in *JC and RT* the President referred to many of the above authorities and cited Hooper LJ's dicta saying that 'This court has, in fact, tended to consider that section 39 orders (and orders discharging such orders) are amenable to judicial review by the child affected'.[347] There are other examples of where defendants have brought challenges on conviction to the discharge of an order, for example, in *Ex p S and P*.[348]

(iii) Magistrates' Courts (Reporting Restrictions)

11-46 Section 29(3) of the Senior Courts Act 1980 does not apply to the magistrates' courts, which by definition include the Youth Court. In the Youth Court there is a presumption of privacy unless it is in the interests of the defendant or, in exceptional cases, in the public interest to publicise matters.[349] The decision to allow publicity must be taken with great care, after allowing for representations from the parties, and possibly from the media.[350] There may be exceptions where there is an application for an ASBO.[351] However, these may not apply until there is a finding of fact made.[352] The restrictions will cease if the defendant attains the age of 18 during the proceedings.[353]

(5) Sentencing[354]

11-47 Judicial reviews of sentencing decisions in the magistrates' and Youth Courts are extremely rare, as there is an appeal as of right to the Crown Court (see above at 6-8). Instances of judicial review are where the court has incorrectly applied the various statutory provisions regarding the proper venue for sentence. For example, sub-sections 8(1) and (2) of the PCC(S)A 2000, provide that any court other than the Youth Court by or before which a defendant is found guilty must remit the case to the Youth Court for sentence, unless it is satisfied that it would be undesirable to do so. On receipt, the sentencing court has all the powers from first instance, including accepting a change of plea and trying the case.[355] Another example is where a Youth Court remits a case to the adult magistrates' court for sentencing where a youth has been convicted of an

---

[346] *Y* (n 327) [21].

[347] *JC and RT*, see above (n 37), [41].

[348] *Ex p S and P* (n 325).

[349] S 49(4A) CYPA 1933. It also imposes restrictions on i) appeals from a Youth Court, ii) proceedings under the PCC(S)A 2000 Sch 7 (supervision orders) and iii) proceedings on appeal from the magistrates' courts relating to the PCC(S)A 2000.

[350] *McKerry v Teesdale and Wear Valley Justices* (n 33).

[351] See *Medway Council v BBC* [2002] 1 FLR 104 and *R v Crown at Winchester, ex parte B* [2000] 1 Cr App R 11 followed in *T* [2002] (n 337).

[352] *R (K) v Knowsley Metropolitan Borough Council* [2004] EWHC 1933 (Admin), 168 JP 461.

[353] *T v DPP* [2003] EWHC 2408 Admin, 168 JP 194.

[354] Note the Criminal Justice Act 2003, s 142A, when implemented, will require a sentencing court to have consideration for i) the welfare of the child, ii) the principal aim of the youth justice system and iii) the purposes of sentencing.

[355] *R v Stratford Youth Court, ex parte Conde* [1997] 1 WLR 113, [1997] 2 Cr App Rep 1.

indictable offence; such an unusual occurrence could be dealt with by the court rescinding the remittal under section 142 of MCA 1980.[356]

Judicial review will not be available for sentencing decisions in the Crown Court, as the Court of Appeal provides an avenue of redress. However, where the Crown Court sits in its appellate capacity, judicial review may be available (see above at 7-25). An example is *R (M) v Inner London Crown Court*,[357] which concerned an appeal against a parenting order.

(6) Anti-Social Behaviour Orders (ASBOs)[358]

Any child over 10 years may be subject to an ASBO if i) they have acted in a manner that **11-48** caused or was likely to cause harassment, alarm or distress to one or more persons not of the same household as himself, and ii) the order is necessary to protect those persons from further anti-social acts by him.[359] These are civil proceedings but the criminal standard of proof applies and there is no need to prove *mens rea*. Hearsay evidence can be admitted, although the criminal standard of proof must apply in proving anti-social behaviour but not to whether an order is necessary.[360]

The Divisional Court has set the bar very high in respect of judicial review challenges. The first obstacle is that there are alternative remedies by way of application to the magistrates' court to vary or discharge the order. Claimants who have not used this route have been criticised and had their claim refused on this ground.[361] A claimant must prove that the making of the order was so flawed that making of the order amounted to an excess of jurisdiction. This was the decision of the Divisional Court in *R (W) v Action Youth Court*.[362]

In making an order under section 1C of the Crime and Disorder Act 1998 a court must consider all the circumstances, which may include i) whether the court had declined to make an order on a previous occasion, and ii) whether there had been any change in circumstances since then.[363] Of relevance is the defendant's compliance with any orders passed since then. In such situations the court should provide clear reasons for its decision, especially where any order is wide in its application.[364] These principles were approved by the Lord Woolf LCJ in *R v P*.[365] In that case it was said that the terms of the order must be precise and capable of being understood,[366] and the supporting

---

[356] *R (Denny) v Acton Youth Court* [2004] EWHC 948 (Admin), [2004] 1 WLR 3051
[357] *R (M) v Inner London Crown Court* [2003] EWHC 301 (Admin), [2003] 1 FLR 994.
[358] Note that ASBOs are to be replaced with Injunctions to Prevent Nuisance and Disorder and Criminal Behaviour Orders under Parts 1 and 2 of the Anti-Social Behaviour, Crime and Policing Act 2014. At time of writing, the relevant provisions in the Act had not yet been brought into force. Section 15 provides for a right of appeal to the Crown Court from injunctions made against those under 18 by a Youth Court.
[359] CDA 1998, s 1(1).
[360] *R (McCann) v Manchester Crown Court* [2002] UKHL 39, [2003] 1 AC 787.
[361] *R (A (A Child)) v Leeds Magistrates Court* [2004] EWHC 554 (Admin), [29]–[37].
[362] *R (W) v Action Youth Court* [2005] EWHC 954 (Admin), (2006) 170 JP 31.
[363] *C v Sunderland Youth Court* [2003] EWHC 2385 (Admin), [2004] 1 Cr App R (S) 76.
[364] ibid.
[365] *R v P* [2004] EWCA Crim 287, [2004] 2 Cr App R (S) 63.
[366] Note that ambiguity of an order cannot be relied upon as a defence as the correct challenge is to appeal or apply to vary *Crown Prosecution Service v T* [2006] EWHC 728 (Admin), [2007] 1 WLR 209. This was applied in *Heron v Plymouth City Council* [2009] EWHC 3562 (Admin). Both challenges were by way of case stated.

facts must also be clear, with all proceedings conducted with the defendant present.[367] These authorities were followed in *R v Kirby*,[368] which stated that making an ASBO with a view to allowing higher sentencing in case of future offending 'was not a use of the power which should normally be exercised'.[369]

---

[367] *R v P* [2004] EWCA Crim 287, [2004] 2 Cr App R (S) 63. This approach has been subsequently applied in at least six other cases in the Court of Appeal. It was also said that the proper venue for challenging ASBO's made in the Crown Court was the Court of Appeal. However, note challenges by way of case stated—*Hills v Chief Constable of Essex* [2006] EWHC 2633 (Admin), (2007) 171 JP 14.

[368] *R v Kirby* [2005] EWCA Crim 1228, [2006] 1 Cr App R (S) 26.

[369] This was approved in *R v H* [2006] EWCA Crim 255, [2006] 2 Cr App R (S) 68, (Sir Igor Judge P).

Piers von Berg

12

Mental Health

JUSTIN LESLIE

A. General Principles

(1) General Principles

12-1   The position of mentally disordered persons in the criminal justice system can differ in terms of the procedures and outcomes that are available. For instance, a mentally disordered defendant can be detained in a psychiatric hospital for treatment if the court concludes that the defendant committed a particular offence.

This chapter considers the various ways in which such defendants are subject to a modified regime. The focus of this chapter is the procedure for a mentally disordered defendant within this regime, and the role of judicial review in relation to that procedure. Section A sets out the legislative framework. Sections B–H consider how this operates in more detail at various points during the criminal justice process with reference to potential challenges by way of judicial review. This chapter will i) identify the areas where judicial review may be an appropriate remedy and ii) the areas in which it has been relied on in the case law. Practitioners will find that these instances are limited. Nevertheless, it is submitted that there is room for development.

Justin Leslie

This chapter does not address in detail the substantive defences that mentally disordered defendants may rely on, which include: i) the defence of insanity and the *M'Naghten* rules; ii) diminished responsibility and the Homicide Act 1957; iii) *mens rea* and mistake of fact; iv) self-defence; and v) duress. The reason for not dealing with these matters is procedural: if a defendant is convicted of an offence, having relied on one of these defences, the way to challenge the conviction or sentence is by way of an appeal to the Crown Court or the Criminal Division of the Court of Appeal.

'Mental disorder' is widely defined in the Mental Health Act 1983 as 'any disorder or disability of the mind' (see below at 12-7). The diagnosis of a mental disorder is a matter for mental health professionals. However, lawyers should be aware of the key indicators of mental disorders. Mind, the mental health charity, has produced a toolkit to assist advocates identifying whether there may be unacknowledged mental health concerns, and how to respond in a court environment.[1] Indicators of mental distress can include where a person:

(i)   appears distressed, disturbed or distracted;
(ii)   talks incoherently or laughs incongruously;
(iii)   appears to have illogical thought processes;
(iv)   seems over-excited, euphoric, irritable or aggressive;
(v)   appears dazed, withdrawn or shut down;
(vi)   appears fidgety, restless or jumpy;
(vii)   repeats themselves or is obsessing;
(viii) appears not to be taking information in; and/or
(ix)   responds to experiences, sensations or people not observable by others.

It should be noted that mental health conditions fluctuate, and assumptions or generalisations should not be made.

If, and when, a mental health concern is sought or identified, it may be appropriate to seek expert advice from a psychiatrist or other relevant professionals, and to raise the matter with the police or Crown Prosecution Service and the court.

(2) Litigation Friends

Note that if a person lacks mental capacity, in order to bring judicial review proceedings a litigation friend may be required under Part 21 of the Civil Procedure Rules. This is because if a person lacks capacity to conduct proceedings, they are defined as a 'protected party' (CPR 21.1(2)) and as such are required to have a litigation friend to conduct proceedings on their behalf (CPR 21.2).

12-2

A litigation friend may be appointed by the court on the application of a prospective litigation friend or a party to proceedings (CPR 21.6), or a deputy may be appointed by the Court of Protection under the Mental Capacity Act 2005 to conduct proceedings (CPR 21.4). Alternatively, a litigation friend may simply submit a 'certificate of

---

[1] Mind, *Achieving Justice for victims and witnesses with mental distress: a mental health toolkit for prosecutors and advocates* (2010). See also: McConnell and Talbot, *Mental health and learning disabilities in the criminal courts* (2013).

suitability' (CPR 21.5(3)). This must satisfy the criteria that i) the prospective litigation friend can fairly and competently conduct the proceedings on behalf of the protected party, ii) they have no adverse interest to the protected party, and iii) they are willing to undertake paying any costs associated with bringing the proceedings (CPR 21.4(3)). The court retains a power to change a litigation friend or prevent a person acting as a litigation friend (CPR 21.7).

It is important to remember that a person can have a mental health condition but also retain mental capacity in relation to decisions to litigate. However, if a litigation friend has been appointed and the person regains or acquires capacity to litigate, the litigation friend's appointment continues until it is ended by court order (CPR 21.9(2)).

The person and their litigation friend should not be named in a claim form but identified by their initials, for example, Susan Rogers and her litigation friend, David Rodger, becomes '*SR (by her litigation friend DR)*'.

(3) The Availability of Judicial Review

12-3 The applicable legal framework for dealing with mentally disordered defendants depends on whether the offence is being dealt with in the magistrates' court or the Crown Court. Both the Crown Court and magistrates' court have powers under Part III of the Mental Health Act 1983. However, the powers that are available to each court vary; for instance, in relation to the range of disposals available to each court. Furthermore, the availability of judicial review is different between the two courts.

In the magistrates' court the relevant procedure is derived from a combination of section 37(3) of the Mental Health Act 1983 and section 11(1) of the Powers of Criminal Courts (Sentencing) Act (PCC(S)A) 2000 (for more detail, see below at 12-41). In contrast to the Crown Court, there are no jurisdictional bars in statutory law to a judicial review challenge against the magistrates' court, although it is important to note the availability of an appeal by way of case stated.[2]

12-4 In the Crown Court, the procedure for determining whether a person has a mental disorder such that they are unfit to stand trial is provided by section 4 of the Criminal Procedure (Insanity) Act 1964 (the '1964 Act'—for more detail, see below at 12-45).

In the Crown Court, if a matter relates 'to trial on indictment', section 29(3) of the Senior Courts Act 1981 excludes the availability of judicial review of the Crown Court (see above at 1-25 and 7-2). It has been held that an order made following a finding that a mentally disordered person did the act charged against him is a matter that relates to a trial on indictment.[3] Accordingly, judicial review of such a decision is excluded for that reason.[4]

But judicial review remains available in cases of jurisdictional error, notwithstanding section 29(3) of the Senior Court Act 1981. This was the decision of a three-judge

---

[2] See above at 6–8.
[3] This includes a hospital order (with or without a restriction order), a supervision order, or an order for absolute discharge (see Criminal Procedure (Insanity) Act 1964, s 5(2)).
[4] However, the court may intervene to correct errors of jurisdiction. See *R v Maidstone Crown Court, ex parte Harrow LBC* [2000] 1 Cr App R 117, 138–41.

Justin Leslie

Divisional Court in *R (Kenneally) v Snaresbrook Crown Court*.[5] In that case it was held that an order under section 51(5) of the Mental Health Act 1983 (making a hospital order in the absence of the defendant) is a matter that relates to a trial on indictment, and so judicial review of such a decision on that basis is excluded. Despite this, the High Court retained the power to quash an order if the Crown Court had made a jurisdictional error of the type so fundamental that it took the case outside the scope of the Crown Court's jurisdiction in matters relating to trial on indictment.[6] Tomlinson J explained the nature of the judge's jurisdictional error as an application of the wrong test:

> Mr Sales accepted, as I understood him, that if the proper test to be applied under section 51(5) relates to the practicability or appropriateness of bringing the detainee before the court at all, ie for any purpose, and if further this court is satisfied that the judge failed to apply that test but rather applied a different test, ie one which related to the practicability or appropriateness of conducting a trial in the presence of the detainee, then that is a misdirection of sufficient gravity to amount to a jurisdictional error of the type said by this court in *R v Maidstone Crown Court, Ex p Harrow London Borough Council* [2000] QB 719 to take the case outside the scope of the jurisdiction of the Crown Court in matters relating to trial on indictment.[7]

Another example of a fundamental error that can be challenged by judicial review is where a judge has no basis in law for an order. For example, in *R (A) v Harrow Crown Court*, an order was made under section 37 of the Mental Health Act 1983 on the mistaken basis that the defendant had been convicted when in fact he had been found unfit to plead. The High Court quashed that order. Stanley Burnton J held that sections 28(2) and 29(3) of the Senior Courts Act 1981 did not apply as the order:

> was one the Crown Court had no power to make. The appropriate remedy in a case such as the present is by way of judicial review. The order was not made on a trial on indictment.[8]

Furthermore, it is important to note that when a decision of the Crown Court is challenged by way of judicial review, the issue will be whether the decision is unlawful so as to render the decision 'irregular' rather than a 'nullity'. This is due to the Crown Court's status as a superior court of record. In *A* the court considered the authorities on this point and confirmed that an order by the Crown Court is legally effective until it is set aside.

B. Key Concepts in Mental Health Law

(1) The Statutory Framework

The two most significant pieces of legislation for those with a mental disorder are the Mental Health Act 1983 (the '1983 Act') and the Mental Capacity Act 2005 (the '2005 Act'). **12-5**

---

[5] *R (Kenneally) v Snaresbrook Crown Court* [2001] EWHC 968 (Admin), [2002] QB 1169.
[6] ibid [38] (Pill LJ). Rafferty J agreed with this 'second category' in Pill LJ's judgment, as did Tomlinson J. See also *R (Sullivan) v Crown Court at Maidstone* [2002] EWHC 967 (Admin), [2002] 1 WLR 2747 [6]–[8].
[7] ibid [47].
[8] *R (A) v Harrow Crown Court* [2003] EWHC 2020 (Admin) [9].

The 1983 Act is primarily concerned with the compulsory detention and treatment of those with a 'mental disorder' (defined in the next section). Part III contains the provisions relevant to those concerned with criminal proceedings. However, many of the other provisions of the 1983 Act are relevant to mentally disordered defendants and offenders.

In England, the First-Tier Tribunal (Health, Education and Social Care Chamber) deals with applications to review detention and treatment under the 1983 Act. In Wales, the Mental Health Review Tribunal hears such cases (see sections 65–79 of the 1983 Act). The Upper Tribunal (Administrative Appeals Chamber) hears appeals.[9] See below for more detail.

The 2005 Act provides a framework through which decisions can be made for those who lack capacity. Such decisions must be made in the best interests of person in question (defined by section 4 of the 2005 Act). The Act establishes the Court of Protection and the Office of the Public Guardian.[10]

(2) Mental Health Act 1983

12-6   The 1983 Act is the primary statute in relation to those with mental disorders. With regard to the criminal justice process, the 1983 Act has a key role concerning the disposal of cases where there has been a finding that the defendant did the act or made the omission as charged. This section describes the key provisions.

(i) What is 'a Mental Disorder'?

12-7   Section 1(2) of the 1983 Act defines a mental disorder as 'any disorder or disability of the mind'. This is a deliberately wide definition, and requires interpretation in both medical and legal terms.

In medical terms, mental disorders are most commonly defined in relation to two resources: first, the American Psychiatric Association's Diagnostic and Statistical Manual ('DSM-IV-TR'); second, the World Health Organisation's International Classification of Diseases ('ICD-10'). These resources provide medical practitioners with the diagnostic tools to identify mental disorders.

In legal terms, the case law of the European Court of Human Rights (ECtHR) has developed the concept of the 'unsound mind', in light of Article 5 of ECHR. This provides for the right to liberty, but gives an exception for the 'lawful detention ... of persons of unsound mind'. Article 5 is an absolute right, with exceptions.[11] By virtue of section 6 of the Human Rights Act (HRA) 1998, compliance with Article 5 is a pre-condition to

---

[9] Prior to the reorganisation of the tribunal system as a result of the Tribunals, Courts and Enforcement Act 2007, the only way to challenge a decision of the Mental Health Review Tribunal (as it was then titled) was by way of judicial review. The reconstitution of the tribunal as a First-Tier Tribunal and creation of the Upper Tribunal therefore reduced the number of instances where judicial review of a tribunal decision will be appropriate. See above at 9-39.

[10] See below at 12-15 for more detail on the 2005 Act.

[11] *Secretary of State for the Home Department v JJ* [2007] UKHL 45, [2008] AC 385 [35].

lawful detention under the 1983 Act. This has the practical effect that there is consider-able overlap in the definitions of a 'mental disorder' and an 'unsound mind'.

In *Winterwerp v Netherlands* the court held that:

[unsound mind] is a term whose meaning is continually evolving as research in psychiatry progresses, an increasing flexibility in treatment is developing and society's attitudes to mental illness change, in particular so that a greater understanding of the problems of mental patients is becoming more widespread.[12]

It also said:

The very nature of what has to be established before the competent national authority—that is, a true mental disorder—calls for objective medical expertise. Further, the mental disorder must be of a kind or degree warranting compulsory confinement. What is more, the validity of continued confinement depends upon the persistence of such a disorder.[13]

This links the legal definition of 'unsound mind' with the medical definition. The practical impact of this approach is to require a clinical opinion in order to determine whether an individual falls within the scope of section 1 of the 1983 Act. In the event that there is a conflict of medical opinion, a court will need to give reasons for why it preferred one opinion to another.[14]

Section 1 of the 1983 Act makes special provision for two categories of people. First, **12-8** there are those who have a learning disability. It states that a person with a learning disability will not be considered to be suffering from a mental disorder, unless 'that dis-ability is associated with abnormally aggressive or seriously irresponsible conduct on his part' (section 1(2A)). The term 'associated with' does not require causation.[15] The term 'seriously irresponsible' is subject to a restrictive interpretation.[16]

Secondly, dependence on alcohol or drugs is not considered to be disorder or dis-ability of the mind (section 1(2)).

It should be noted that simply because a person has a mental disorder within the meaning of section 1 of the 1983 Act, this does not necessarily mean that they are unfit to plead within the meaning of section 4 of the Criminal Procedure (Insanity) Act 1964, as defined in *R v Pritchard*[17] (see below at 12-46). However, coming within section 1, and hence the scope of the 1983 Act, does give the court jurisdiction to make various orders, once there has been a finding of unfitness to plead. Furthermore, the existence of a mental disorder does not automatically mean that the defendant will meet the criteria for a disposal under the 1983 Act, as this will ultimately depend on a further assessment of the defendant at the disposal stage.

(ii) The Civil Provisions (Part II of the Act)

Sections 2–34 of the 1983 Act provide the civil scheme for the detention and treatment **12-9** of those with a mental disorder. This is relevant to mentally disordered defendants

---

[12] *Winterwerp v Netherlands* (1979) 2 EHRR 387 [37].
[13] ibid [39].
[14] *Kiernan v Harrow Crown Court* [2003] EWCA Crim 1052.
[15] *R (P) v Mental Health Review Tribunal and Rampton Hospital* [2001] EWHC Admin 876 [26].
[16] *F (A Child) (Care order: sexual abuse)* [2000] 1 FLR 192.
[17] *R v Pritchard* (1836) 7 C&P 303.

in criminal proceedings because the policy of 'diversion' can mean a defendant may be liable to be detained even if no action is taken as a result of criminal proceedings. Furthermore, certain outcomes of criminal proceedings take effect as if the person is subject to the civil scheme; for instance, section 37 orders effectively put the defendant in the position of a person detained under the civil scheme.

Within the civil scheme, the key provisions are sections 2 and 3, which respectively deal with compulsory admission to hospital for assessment and compulsory admission to hospital for treatment. Note that informal admission to hospital is provided for by section 131 of the 1983 Act and emergency admissions are dealt with by section 4 of the 1983 Act.

Compulsory admission to hospital for assessment is provided by section 2 of the 1983 Act. In order to use this power, the following grounds must be satisfied:

(a) he is suffering from mental disorder of a nature or degree which warrants the detention of the patient in a hospital for assessment (or for assessment followed by medical treatment) for at least a limited period; and

(b) he ought to be so detained in the interests of his own health or safety or with a view to the protection of other persons.

12-10 The procedure for making an application under section 2 is provided in section 11 of the 1983 Act. This requires that the application is made either by the 'nearest relative' or by an 'approved mental health professional' (AMHP). In practice, AMHPs make most of the applications under section 2, and section 11 provides that the AMHP must notify the nearest relative (section 11(3)).

An application under section 2 must be accompanied by two medical recommendations that the criteria in section 2(2) are met (see section 2(3)). Section 12 provides detail about the requirements of the medical reports, such as that the doctors must have examined the patient no more than five days apart.

Once a section 2 application has been made, it provides authority to detain for up to 28 days (see section 2(4)). The detention must begin within 14 days of the final medical recommendation (see section 6(1)). The 28-day period can be extended if efforts are being made to admit the patient for treatment under section 3, but the nearest relative has objected to the section 3 application and steps are being taken to remove the nearest relative, as their objection is unreasonable (section 29). The effect of such an extension is to ensure that the patient is not at risk of being discharged because of difficulties associated with the section 3 application.

Discharge from a section 2 order can be done administratively by the hospital managers or the nearest relative via section 23 of the Act, or by way of an application to the tribunal under section 66 of the Act. The test for discharge is essentially whether the conditions for detention still apply (see paragraph 31.14 of the Code of Practice for the Mental Health Act 1983). Whilst the nearest relative is entitled to discharge an order under both section 2 and 3, if the responsible clinician (sometimes referred to as the 'RC') is of the view that a detention for treatment under section 3 is appropriate, an application can be made in the county court under section 29 to displace the nearest relative.

12-11 Admission to hospital for treatment is provided for by section 3 of the 1983 Act. Given the more intrusive nature of a section 3 application when compared to a section 2 application, there is a slightly different set of criteria and procedure.

Justin Leslie

The criteria for a section 3 application are:

(a)   he is suffering from a mental disorder of a nature or degree which makes it appropriate for him to receive medical treatment in a hospital;

...

(c)   it is necessary for the health or safety of the patient or for the protection of other persons that he should receive such treatment and it cannot be provided unless he is detained under this section; and

(d)   appropriate medical treatment is available for him.

Procedurally, a section 3 application requires two medical recommendations in the same format as a section 2 application (see above at 12-10). The nearest relative has a right to be notified in advance and a right to object (see section 11(4)).[18]

Discharge from section 3 treatment has the same format as discharge under section 2—it can be done i) administratively by the hospital managers, or ii) the nearest relative under section 23 of the Act, or iii) by way of an application to the tribunal under section 66 of the Act. The test for discharge is essentially whether the conditions for detention still apply.[19]

Detention under section 3 initially lasts for up to six months, but can be renewed under section 20 of the Act, assuming that the criteria for detention still apply. Frequently section 3 orders will be for much shorter periods, and six months is a maximum period.

(iii)   The Criminal Provisions (Part III of the Act)

Part III of the 1983 Act contains the key sections relevant to mentally disordered defen-   **12-12**
dants in criminal proceedings. It deals with the circumstances in which patients may be admitted or detained in hospital or received into guardianship on the order of the court, or transferred into hospital from prison. The powers available to the Crown Court are different to those available to the magistrates' court. Irregular or defective orders made by the Crown Court under these provisions may be the subject of a judicial review challenge.[20] Indeed, in *Mooren v Germany*,[21] the ECtHR held that defects in a detention order (such as those provided for by this part of the 1983 Act) may amount to unlawful detention under Article 5 if they amount to 'a gross and obvious irregularity'.[22]

The criminal powers available under the 1983 Act include the following:

i.   Section 35: the power to remand a person to hospital for the preparation of a medical report (both magistrates' and Crown Courts).

ii.   Section 36: the power to remand a person pre-trial or pre-sentence for treatment (Crown Court only).

iii.   Section 37: the power to make a hospital order, ie to admit a person to hospital for treatment. In the magistrates' courts, this can be made without a conviction

---

[18]   See *TW v Enfield Borough Council* [2014] EWCA Civ 362
[19]   See the Code of Practice for the Mental Health Act 1983, para 31.16.
[20]   See *R (A) v Harrow Crown Court* [2003] EWHC 2020 (Admin).
[21]   *Mooren v Germany* (2010) 50 EHRR 23.
[22]   ibid [84] and [86].

(although a finding that the defendant did the act charged is required); in the Crown Court, a conviction is required, save for the limited exceptions in section 51 or if there has been a finding of unfitness to plead (section 37 also allows a guardianship order to be made, as per section 7 of the civil scheme of the 1983 Act).

iv. Section 38: the power to make an interim hospital order, which is made with a view to assessing whether a hospital order under section 37 should be made (both magistrates' courts and the Crown Court).

v. Section 41: the power to make a restriction order to a hospital order, the effect of which is to impose special restrictions on an offender (Crown Court only).

vi. Sections 45A and 45B: the power to direct hospital admission subject to a hospital direction and limitation direction. The effect of this is to combine a criminal sentence with a hospital order such that an offender who recovers in hospital can be removed directly into a prison (Crown Court only).

vii. Sections 47 and 48: powers to transfer those in custody, both pre-sentence and post-sentence, to hospital if their mental health requires it (power of the Secretary of State).

Note also the powers under sections 135 and 136 (discussed below at 12-18 and 12-19), which are police powers. Section 135 provides a power to enter a private place with a warrant. Section 136 provides a power to detain a person in a public place who appears to be in immediate need of care and control on account of a mental disorder.

(iv) Comparing the Civil and Criminal Provisions of the 1983 Act

12-13   An individual who is being taken through the criminal process towards trial can be subject to both the civil and criminal provisions of the 1983 Act at the same time.[23] Furthermore, the general criteria under the civil and criminal provisions are similar: (i) existence of a mental disorder; (ii) the mental disorder is of a nature or degree that makes detention in hospital appropriate; and (iii) appropriate treatment is available.

A point of contrast is that a section 3 order requires that such an order is necessary for the protection of the patient or others that such treatment is given. Instead, the criminal provisions refer to other terms, such as whether orders are 'preferable' (such as an order for remand for treatment under section 36) or 'most suitable' (for a hospital order under section 37). However, in practice the tests are substantively similar and overlapping.

In terms of procedure, most orders under the criminal provisions require two medical recommendations in the same format as the civil provisions. However, there is no provision for the 'nearest relative' under the criminal provisions, nor is there necessarily a right to apply to the tribunal. For instance, those who are subject to orders made under sections 35, 36 and 38 do not have access to the tribunal, but do have access to the criminal court (see below 12-51 *et seq*). A section 37 hospital order can be subject to an application to the tribunal to discharge, but that the sections dealing with remand cannot.

Also, the effect of a hospital order or a guardianship order made under section 37 (discussed below at 12-52 and 12-53) is that the offender is treated as being detained

---

[23] *R v North West London Mental Health NHS Trust, ex parte Stewart* [1998] QB 628.

under section 3 or 7 the 1983 Act respectively, by virtue of section 40(5) of the Act. This means that most of the provisions of the civil scheme are engaged, such as in relation to discharge and renewal, with certain key modifications, dealt with below.

(v) The Code of Practice

Under section 118, the Secretary of State has issued statutory guidance, the Code of Practice for the Mental Health Act 1983. There is a separate Code for Wales. The Code should be followed unless there is good reason not to do so.[24]   **12-14**

The Code supplements the statutory provisions and gives details about how applications under the Act should be approach. Chapter 33 deals specifically with patients concerned with criminal proceedings. The Code is an important source of guidance, and failure by a medical professional to follow it without good reason can render a decision unlawful.

There is also a significant amount of non-statutory guidance in the mental health arena. Although this does not carry the weight of the Code, it forms a relevant consideration that ought to be taken into account.[25] This may inform any challenges on the basis of *Wednesbury* irrationality (see above at 1-82).

(3) Mental Capacity Act 2005

As noted above, the 2005 Act is primarily concerned with making decisions for those   **12-15**
who lack capacity. The relevance of the 2005 Act to criminal proceedings is indirect: decision-making on behalf of a suspect or offender will often be managed through the provisions of the 1983 Act. For instance, section 28 of the 1983 Act provides that treatment decisions in relation to mental disorder that are regulated by that Act, remain governed by that Act.

There will be times where it may be necessary for the police or prison authorities to undertake a 'best interests' assessment, in situations where a person's capacity is in issue.[26] A best interest assessment is made under section 4 of the 2005 Act, and should take into account the principles in section 1 of the Act.

C. Pre-Trial Matters

(1) Introduction

In this section, the various pre-trial matters in the criminal process are discussed in rela-   **12-16**
tion to mentally disordered suspects. Having set out these matters, including the various

---

[24] See *R (Munjaz) v Mersey Care NHS Trust* [2005] UKHL 58, [2006] 2 AC 148.
[25] For instance *R (Rixon) v London Borough of Islington* (1998) 1 CCLR 119.
[26] See *ZH v Commissioner of Police of the Metropolis* [2012] EWHC 604 (QB) [33]–[44], affd CA [2013] EWCA Civ 69 [39]–[42].

powers and duties exercised by the police, the applicable principles of judicial review are discussed. It is important to note that a failure to comply with the legal provisions set out can give rise to a claim for judicial review on the grounds of unlawful detention. However, it is also important to acknowledge that judicial review claims of decisions or actions at the pre-trial stage are comparatively rare, and represents an area of potential future development.

(2) Arrest

12-17 Powers to arrest mentally disordered persons are available from two sources: first, the general power of arrest under section 24 of the Police and Criminal Evidence Act 1984 (PACE) 1984; secondly, specific powers of arrest under the Mental Health Act 1983. This chapter focuses on the powers under the 1983 Act, as the powers under PACE 1984 are dealt with elsewhere in this book (see above at 4-50).

The powers of arrest under the 1983 Act arise in two circumstances: first, when an individual is not already subject to an order under the Act; secondly, when an individual is already subject to an order, but then, for instance, subsequently absconds.

The 1983 Act provides two powers of arrest of people not subject to an order under the 1983 Act:

  i.   under section 135 there is a power for magistrates to issue a warrant to search for and remove patients to a place of safety; and
  ii. under section 136 there is a power to remove mentally disordered persons found in public places to a place of safety.

In respect of both these categories, decisions by magistrates' courts are challengeable by way of judicial review on grounds set out in section G of Chapter 1. Practitioners should also cross-refer to section A of Chapter 6 on what are the most appropriate remedies for unlawful decisions made by magistrates' courts. Decisions by police officers are also amenable to judicial review. Section E of Chapter 4 deals with the potential remedies against police action and challenges to decisions to arrest.

(i) Magistrates' Court Warrant to Search for and Remove Patients to a Place of Safety

12-18 To exercise the power to issue a warrant to enter premise and remove an individual to a place of safety under section 135 of the 1983 Act, the magistrate must be satisfied that on the basis of the information on oath laid by an approved mental health professional there is reasonable cause to suspect that a person believed to be suffering from a mental disorder:

  (a) has been, or is being, ill-treated, neglected or kept otherwise than under proper control, in any place within the jurisdiction of the justice; or
  (b) being unable to care for himself, is living alone in any such place.

In executing the warrant, the police constable must be accompanied by an approved mental health professional (AMHP) and a registered medical practitioner (section 135(4)).

Justin Leslie

The magistrate has no power to impose conditions on the warrant, such as identifying the particular professionals that should attend—see *Ward v Commissioner of Police for the Metropolis* [2005] UKHL 3, [2006] 1 AC 23.

A 'place of safety' includes social services accommodation, a hospital, a police station, a care home or 'any other suitable place the occupier of which is willing temporarily to receive the patient' (section 135(6)). An individual can be held in a place of safety for up to 72 hours under a section 135 warrant (section 135(3)).[27] Although the point has not been tested, it is possible that the use of a police station as a place of safety may be unlawful in certain cases if a more suitable alternative existed in light of the duty to make reasonable adjustments (section 15 of the Equality Act 2010) or even that the threshold of Article 3 of ECHR had been crossed.[28]

The purpose of section 135 was explained by Baroness Hale in *Ward*:

> A crisis will arise in which there is good reason to suppose that a person ought to be admitted to hospital (or otherwise taken care of) but the necessary assessments cannot be made in advance because of problems in gaining access and speaking to the prospective patient. Section 135(1) of the Mental Health Act 1983 is designed to cater for that difficulty... this is a serious step which ought only to be taken when there is no other solution to the problem and with the greatest possible care to ensure that its criteria and requirements are observed.[29]

Note that in addition to the power of entry under section 135, section 17(1)(d) of PACE 1984 gives a power of entry to recapture a person who is 'unlawfully at large', although there is a requirement for a chase.[30]

(ii) Power to Remove Mentally Disordered Persons Found in Public Places to a Place of Safety

Section 136 of the 1983 Act provides that: **12-19**

> If a constable finds in a place to which the public have access a person who appears to him to be suffering from mental disorder and to be in immediate need of care or control, the constable may, if he thinks it necessary to do so in the interests of that person or for the protection of other persons, remove that person to a place of safety within the meaning of section 135.

Under section 136, an individual can only be held in a place of safety for up to 72 hours, and this must be for the purpose of: (i) enabling an examination by a medical practitioner; (ii) enabling an interview by an AMHP; and (iii) making arrangement for treatment or care. It was held in *Francis v DPP*[31] that whilst a person was detained under section 136, police officers were not precluded from administering a breath test in relation to a suspected drink driving offence. The reasoning of the court in *Francis* indicates that the police are not disempowered from conducting parallel investigations whilst an individual is detained under section 136.

---

[27] See House of Commons Health Select Committee, *Post-legislative scrutiny of the Mental Health Act 2007* (July 2013) para 66, which notes the use of police stations as 'places of safety'. This has been criticised by many commentators.

[28] By analogy, see *ZH v Commissioner of Police of the Metropolis* (n 26).

[29] *Ward v Commissioner of Police for the Metropolis* [2005] UKHL 3, [2006] 1 AC 23 [12]–[13].

[30] *R v D'Souza* [1992] 1 WLR 1073.

[31] *Francis v DPP* [1997] RTR 113.

The term 'a place to which the public have access' is not easily defined. For instance, in other contexts it has been held that a block of flats that restricted access by security systems and intercoms was not a public place.[32] However, a balcony in a block of flats that is freely accessible has been held to be a public place.[33] It is inevitable that the applicability of this term is highly case-specific.

Further, it was noted in *Ward* that section 136 precludes entering a premises, removing a person to outside and then using the section 136 power, because the person cannot have been 'found' in a public place.[34] It is important to note that a person cannot be deemed to have been lawfully removed and detained under section 136 if the detaining authority uses other provisions (such as sections 5 and 6 of the 2005 Act) 'for the purposes of section 136'.[35]

Concerning both sections 135 and 136, when a person is detained in a place of safety under sections 135 and 136, the person is deemed to be in 'legal custody' (section 137). If the person escapes from the place of safety, section 138 grants a power for that person to be taken back into custody.

(iii) Powers of Arrest under the 1983 Act

12-20   Where an individual is already subject to an order under the 1983 Act, but the individual subsequently absconds, the 1983 Act provides powers of arrest.

   i.   Section 18: patients held under sections 2, 3, 37 or 41 of the 1983 Act can be given leave by virtue of section 17. Section 17(4) enables this leave to be revoked and the patient to be recalled by the responsible clinician if it 'is necessary so to do in the interests of the patient's health or safety or for the protection of other persons'. If the patient fails to return, section 18 allows the patient to be taken into custody. This also applies to those who have absconded from their residence as part of a guardianship order (see section 18(3)).

   ii.   Section 35(10): if a patient who has been remanded to hospital for a report under section 35 of the 1983 Act absconds, section 35(10) provides for a power to arrest without a warrant and that the patient must be brought before the court as soon as reasonably practicable. This power also applies to those who have been remanded to hospital for treatment under section 36 (see section 36(8)).

   iii. Section 38(7): if a patient has been made subject of an interim hospital order, section 38(7) provides for a power to arrest without a warrant and that the patient must be brought before the court as soon as reasonably practicable.

   iv.   Section 138: pending admission under sections 35, 36 and 38, the patient may be detained in a place of safety. By virtue of sections 137 and 138 (see above), there is a power to take the patient into custody.

---

[32] *Williams v DPP* (1992) 95 Cr App R 415.
[33] *Knox v Anderton* (1983) 76 Cr App R 156.
[34] *Ward* (n 29) [60].
[35] See *R (Sessay) v South London and Maudsley NHS Foundation Trust* [2011] EWHC 2617 (QB), [2012] QB 760 [54].

(3) At a Police Station

The provisions of PACE 1984 regulate detention in a police station. PACE 1984 is   **12-21**
supplemented by Codes of Practice, the most relevant of which is Code C. Annex E of
Code C provides a summary of provisions relating to mentally disordered persons.

There are six important aspects to how mentally disordered defendants should be
treated at police stations: i) the importance of identifying a mental disorder; ii) the role
of the appropriate adult; iii) access to legal advice; iv) cautioning and interviewing;
v) identification parades; and vi) confessions.

A failure to comply with any of these criteria could amount to aggravating factors in
the context of an unlawful detention claim, as well as provide the basis for an abuse of
process argument in the criminal proceedings.

(i) Identifying a Mental Disorder

When a suspect arrives in a police station, paragraph 1.4 of Code C provides that if   **12-22**
the police officer has any suspicion, or is told in good faith, that a person is mentally
disordered, then he is to be treated as mentally disordered for the purposes of the Code.
Further, paragraph 3.5(c) requires the custody officer to determine whether a detainee
may need medical treatment or an appropriate adult. If detained under section 136,
paragraph 3.16 states that it is imperative that an assessment takes place as soon as possible. Note that sections 5 and 6 of the 2005 Act may be relevant at this point, as these
sections allow for restraint and treatment of a person who lacks capacity.

(ii) Appropriate Adults

A consequence of a suspect being treated as having a mental disorder is that an 'appro-   **12-23**
priate adult' should be appointed, and called to attend the police station. This applies
even if a doctor certifies that a mentally vulnerable person is fit for interview.[36]

The role of the appropriate adult is to advise the person with a mental disorder and
check on the propriety of what is happening. An appropriate adult can be a relative,
guardian or some other person who is responsible for the care of the individual, someone who is experienced in dealing with mentally vulnerable people or, failing these,
some other person over 18. The appropriate adult cannot be a police officer or someone
employed by the police (see paragraph 1.7(b) of Code C). In appointing an appropriate
adult, the wishes of the individual should be respected.[37]

There is a right for the mentally disordered person to talk to the appropriate adult in
private (paragraph 3.18), although such discussions are not protected by legal professional privilege (see Note for Guidance 1E).

Note that access to an appropriate adult has been the subject of successful judicial
review challenges in the area of children and young persons (see above at 11-16). A key
issue was the vulnerability of a person in need of the assistance of appropriate adult but

---

[36] See *R v Aspinall* [1999] MHLR 12.
[37] See *DPP v Blake* [1989] 1 WLR 432.

denied access to them. It is submitted that these considerations may apply by way of analogy and, perhaps, in the case of severe mental disorders, with greater force.

(iii) Access to Legal Advice

12-24 There is a right to have legal advice under section 58 of PACE 1984. Either the suspect or the appropriate adult can ask for it (paragraph 3.19 of Code C). The detainee has a right to require the appropriate adult not to be present at a discussion with his solicitor, so as to maintain client-lawyer privilege and privacy (see Note for Guidance 6J of Code C). Judicial review has been used in cases where access to legal advice by the police has been denied (see above at 4-82).

(iv) Cautioning and Interviewing

12-25 Any caution of a mentally vulnerable person must be given, or at least repeated, in the presence of an appropriate adult (paragraph 10.12 of Code C). Any interview must be in the presence of an appropriate adult, as required by paragraph 11.15 of Code C, save for an exception in relation to interviews conducted outside police stations, and urgent interviews in circumstances where there is a risk of serious consequences for not doing so (see paragraphs 11.1 and 11.18 of Code C). The role of the appropriate adult is likely to be in facilitating communication during the interview.

Paragraph 12.3 of Code C provides that an interview should not take place if it will cause significant harm to the mental state of the subject, and this can require consultation with the investigating officer and health professionals (see also Annex G of Code C). One of the themes of Annex G is that the interview process can be rendered more appropriate by making certain modifications, such as the length of the interview.

As regards potential judicial review challenges, potential claimants should be mindful of the alternative remedies that exist within the trial process. For example, section 76(2) of PACE 1984 imposes a duty on the court to exclude confessions obtained by means of oppression or in any circumstances where the evidence may be deemed unreliable. Section 77 of PACE 1984 allows a judge to direct a jury to be aware of 'a special need of caution' for those who are 'mentally handicapped' where the case against them depends wholly or substantially on a confession.

(v) Identification Parades

12-26 Code D requires that consent to an identification parade from a mentally vulnerable person must be made in the presence of the appropriate adult for the consent to be valid (paragraph 2.12) and that the person must be given notice of the special arrangements for mentally vulnerable people before the parade takes place (paragraph 3.17(viii)).

(vi) Charge

12-27 The decision to charge a mentally vulnerable individual is subject to what is commonly known as a 'policy of diversion'. This means that where there should be a presumption not to chose the criminal justice system where there is a choice about whether to proceed under mental health law and the provisions of the Mental Health Act 1983 or to proceed under the criminal law.[38]

Such a policy is given effect in the Code for Crown Prosecutors. This applies a two-stage test to the question whether to prosecute: the evidential stage, and the public interest stage (see above at 5-10).

At the evidential stage, a view must be taken about whether there is sufficient evidence to provide a realistic prospect of conviction. The special caution to confessions given by mentally handicapped persons (section 77 of PACE 1984) is relevant in this regard.

At the public interest stage, the issue of mental disorder can be relevant to the factors listed at paragraph 4.12 of the Code. For instance, question 'B' focuses on the culpability of the suspect. This makes specific reference to whether the suspect was suffering from any significant mental ill-health, as 'this may mean that it is less likely that a prosecution is required'. The Code is supplemented by the Crown Prosecution Service's (CPS) guidance which can be found on the CPS website.[39] This supports the overall policy of diversion.

If it is decided not to prosecute the suspect, other disposals are available. These include cautions, anti-social behaviour orders, and penalty notices for disorder.

If the CPS decides to charge a defendant without complying with these requirements, the decision will be vulnerable to challenge if the Code had been departed from without good and substantial reason.[40] The most appropriate route to challenge the decision will depend on timing: if the challenge is brought promptly and before the criminal proceedings have progressed, an application for judicial review seeking to quash the decision may be appropriate (see above at 7-5). If proceedings are already underway, potential claimants should be mindful of the different rules affecting challenges to prosecutions in the magistrates' courts (see above at 6-16) and the Crown Court (see above at 7-2).

For an interesting and unusual example of where a victim rather than a defendant with a mental disorder brought a successful challenge to a decision not to prosecute and obtained damages see *R (B) v DPP*[41] discussed above at 5-31.

(vii) Cautions

The practice for imposing cautions is set out in the Ministry of Justice's guidance on Simple Cautions for Adult Offenders (the 'MoJ guidance') and the Director for Public Prosecution's (DPP) Guidance on Charging. Cautions are typically aimed at 'low-level offending' (paragraph 5 of MoJ guidance). In cases where an offence would attract a high community order, exceptional circumstances are needed to justify imposing a caution. A factor includes the extent of culpability, to which a person's mental health is clearly relevant (paragraph 15 of MoJ guidance).

12-28

---

[38] At the time of writing, the National Health Service is trialing 'Liaison and Diversion services'. See: http://www.england.nhs.uk/ourwork/commissioning/health-just/liaison-and-diversion/.

[39] See: www.cps.gov.uk/legal/l_to_o/mentally_disordered_offenders.

[40] Applying the principle derived from *Munjaz* (n 24) in the context of the Code of Practice for the Mental Health Act 1983.

[41] *R (B) v DPP* [2009] EWHC 106 (Admin), [2009] 1 WLR 2072.

The MoJ guidance makes clear that an admission of guilt, which must be made before a caution can be issued, can be called into question if there is any doubt about the mental state of the offender (paragraph 50). The MoJ guidance also indicates that an appropriate adult might be required when administering the caution (paragraph 69).

Another species of caution is the conditional caution, which is provided by sections 22 and 23 of the Criminal Justice Act (CJA) 2003. Section 23 provides the conditions for a conditional caution, which include that there is sufficient evidence of the offence and it has been admitted. There is a relevant Code of Practice issued under section 25 (which does not specifically deal with mentally disordered offenders), and specific guidance from the CPS called 'Diverting offenders with mental health problems and/ or learning disabilities within the National Conditional Cautioning Framework'.[42] This provides guidance on the different kinds of conditions that might be imposed, including reparative, restrictive and rehabilitative conditions.

Note that cautions can be challenged if their consequences are not properly explained to the individual, as this prevents informed consent.[43] For instance, in *R (Stratton) v Thames Valley Police*[44] the court was unable to conclude that the claimant had been made fully aware of the implications of accepting a caution and so the caution was quashed (see above at 4-87 and 4-99). For a review of the case law applying to judicial review of cautions, see above section I in Chapter 4.

This would apply with particular force in relation to those with mental health problems where informed consent can be more difficult to obtain, and additional arguments arising from the duty to make reasonable argument could be raised (section 15 of the Equality Act 2010). Again, access to and the presence of an appropriate adult is vital. It is submitted that failure to allow for this could engage Article 6 (see by way of analogy similar concerns for children and young persons above at 11-30).

Similarly, cautions can be challenged if a misunderstanding of the facts of the case leads the police officer to overstate the public interest in administering a caution.[45]

(4) Anti-Social Behaviour Orders (ASBOs)[46]

12-29 Under sections 1 and 1C of the Crime and Disorder Act 1998, anti-social behaviour orders provide another alternative to prosecution. However, in *Cooke v DPP*[47] it was noted that if:

> by reason of mental incapacity an offender is incapable of complying with an order, then an order is incapable of protecting the public and cannot therefore be said to be necessary to protect the public.

---

[42] Available at: www.cps.gov.uk/legal/d_to_g/diverting_offenders_with_mental_health_problems_and_ or_learning_disabilities_within_the_national_/.

[43] See *R (Stratton) v Thames Valley Police* [2013] EWHC 1561 (Admin).

[44] ibid.

[45] See *Caetano v Commissioner of Police of the Metropolis* [2013] EWHC 375 (Admin).

[46] Note that ASBOs are to be replaced with Injunctions to Prevent Nuisance and Disorder and Criminal Behaviour Orders under Parts 1 and 2 of the Anti-Social Behaviour, Crime and Policing Act 2014. At time of writing, the relevant provisions in the Act had not yet been brought into force.

[47] *Cooke v DPP* [2008] EWHC 2703 (Admin) [10].

Justin Leslie

On this basis, a decision to impose an ASBO that a mentally disordered client will not be able to comply with may be challenged by way of judicial review as irrational or *Wednesbury* unreasonable. It has been held that an ASBO could be combined with a hospital order, although this may be considered artificial.[48]

(5) Penalty Notices for Disorder

Although penalty notices for disorder, which are on-the-spot fines, are an available disposal under Part 1 of the Criminal Justice and Police Act 2001, the relevant guidance states that this will not be appropriate where the person is unable to understand what is being given to them or there is any doubt about the person's ability to understand the procedure.[49] Accordingly, if a penalty notice is imposed on a defendant who cannot understand the process, this could be challenged by way of judicial review as *Wednesbury* unreasonable.   **12-30**

D. Interim Matters

(1) Introduction

If a decision to charge a mentally vulnerable suspect has been made, there are three interim issues that commonly arise: **12-31**

   i.   remand on bail;
  ii.   remand in custody; and
 iii.   transfer to hospital.

(2) Remand on Bail

The right to bail arises from section 4 of the Bail Act 1976. Although the Bail Act regime does not make specific provision for those with mental disorders, there are elements that are relevant.   **12-32**

Under section 1 of the Criminal Justice and Public Order Act 1994 (the 1994 Act), a person with previous convictions such as homicide or rape will only be granted bail in exceptional circumstances. The presence of a mental disorder can arguably amount to an exceptional circumstance. It is important to note that if a mental disorder is identified, it is highly likely that the court may seek to remand the defendant to hospital. Note that a finding of not guilty by reason of insanity or unfitness to stand trial is a 'conviction' under the 1994 Act (see section 25(5)).

---

[48] *R v Chaudhury* [2011] EWCA Crim 936 [17]–[18].
[49] See Ministry of Justice, *Penalty Notices for Disorder (PNDs)*, July 2013, para 3.50.

Under Schedule 1, Part 1, paragraph 2(1) of the Bail Act 1976, if there are substantial grounds for believing that the suspect will abscond, commit a further offence or obstruct justice, bail can be refused. The presence of a mental disorder may well be relevant here.

(3) Remand in Custody

12-33   A person with a mental disorder may be remanded under sections 35 or 36 of the 1983 Act.

Section 35 provides a power to remand an accused to hospital to produce a report on their mental condition. Both the Crown Court and magistrates' courts can exercise this power. The court requires written or oral evidence from a registered medical practitioner that there is reason to suspect that the person is suffering from a mental disorder, and the court must be of the opinion that producing such a report would be impractical if the person was on bail (section 35(3)). This second requirement goes to the proportionality of the remand, in light of Article 5 of ECHR.[50]

The court must be satisfied by evidence from the responsible clinician, who would make the report (or from a representative of the hospital managers), that arrangements had been made for the person's admission within seven days of the remand (section 35(4)). There is an overall time limit of 12 weeks (section 35(7)). Where there is no bed available, section 35 cannot be used. For example, in *R (Bitcon) v West Allerdale Magistrates' Court*[51] a defendant on remand challenged the lawfulness of a decision to revoking an order under section 35 that he be assessed after a NHS Trust had elected not to fund the treatment. On the facts of that case, Collins J held the order was lawful although the court should have adjourned to make enquiries and allowed the Trust to make representations.

Section 36 provides a power to remand an accused to hospital for treatment. This power is only available to the Crown Court. The court must be satisfied, on the oral or written evidence of two registered medical practitioners, that the accused is suffering from a mental disorder which makes detention in hospital appropriate, and that appropriate medical treatment is available (section 36(1)). The court must be satisfied by evidence from the approved clinician, who would make the report (or from a representative of the hospital managers), that arrangements had been made for the person's admission within seven days of the remand (section 36(3)). There is an overall time limit of 12 weeks (section 36(6)).

(4) Transfer to Hospital

12-34   If a court has not remanded a defendant to hospital under sections 35 and 36 of the 1983 Act (see above 12-33), and the defendant is being held in custody, it is possible to transfer the defendant to hospital under section 48 of the 1983 Act. This power

---

[50] *Litwa v Poland* [2000] MHLR 226.
[51] *R (Bitcon) v West Allerdale Magistrates' Court* [2003] EWHC 2460 (Admin).

can be used as a convoluted way of affecting a remand for those who were before the magistrates' court but were unable to be remanded for treatment because of the limitations of section 36.

Section 48 has to be read together with the requirements of section 47 (which is the transfer power for those serving sentences). The requirements for a section 48 transfer are that two reports from registered medical practitioners are required to satisfy the Secretary of State that the person is suffering from a mental disorder which makes it appropriate to detain the person for medical treatment, the person is in urgent need of treatment and the appropriate medical treatment is available (section 48(1)). The Secretary of State must be satisfied that it is in the public interest and it is expedient to make the transfer direction (section 47(1)). The transfer direction needs to be acted on within 14 days of it being made (section 47(3)).[52]

Note that a section 48 transfer is for the purpose of treatment, not for the purpose of assessing whether treatment is required. However, section 22(2) of the Prison Act 1962 can be used to fill this gap.

Three further issues are relevant under a section 48 transfer. First, the effect of a transfer is that the prisoner is treated as if a hospital order had been made (see sections 47(3) and 48(3)). This means that section 40 of the 1983 Act is applicable, and the consent to treatment of provisions Part IV of the 1983 Act is applicable.

Second, section 49 requires that a prisoner remanded by the Crown Court or a magistrates' court, who has been subject to a section 48 transfer direction, should also have a restriction direction imposed. The effect of this is that the leave and transfer provisions can only be exercised with the consent of the Secretary of State.

Thirdly, sections 51 and 52 provide when the transfer will come to an end. For Crown Court detainees, this will occur if the case is 'disposed of' (section 51(2)), if treatment is no longer required or no effective treatment can be given at the hospital where the detainee has been placed (section 51(3)). A direction under section 51(3) can be made by the Secretary of State or by the court, and this requires evidence from the responsible clinician (see section 51(4)). For magistrates' court detainees, section 52 applies. This provides a power for the court to decide that treatment is no longer necessary akin to section 51 (see section 52(5)), or if the underlying remand expires (see section 52(2)).

(5) Role of Judicial Review at the Interim Stage

At the interim stage, there are several sets of decision-makers or potential defendants. **12-35** These include mental health professionals, local authorities, the police, the CPS, the Secretary of State and the courts.

Some of these decision-makers are required to act on a mandatory basis under the Act. For instance, in executing a warrant under section 135 of the Act, the police officer 'shall' be accompanied by an AMHP and a registered practitioner. Failure to do so would be beyond the powers (*ultra vires*) of the statutory framework and hence vulnerable to a claim for judicial review. If this had led to identifiable loss, a claimant could seek a

---

[52] There is a good practice guide published by the Department of Health: *Good Practice Procedure Guide: The transfer and remission of adult prisoners under s 47 and s 48 of the Mental Health Act* (2011).

declaration of unlawful conduct accompanied by a claim for damages. Such a claim should not be an attempt to enforce private law rights by means of a judicial review claim (see the comparisons at 4-5).

Many of the decision-makers are allowed to act on a discretionary basis. For instance, the decision to charge or not to charge is a discretionary matter for the CPS taking into account the Code for Crown Prosecutors.[53] Such a decision could be challenged on the basis that the prosecutor had substantially departed from not only the Code but also the guidance in place for prosecuting persons with mental disorders.[54] A judicial review challenge could proceed on the basis of a *Wednesbury* unreasonableness (this ground is explained above at 1-81).[55]

If there has been a failure to follow a procedural or substantive requirement that 'bears on' the decision to detain this renders the detention unlawful and will lead to a finding of false imprisonment. If the detainee would have been detained in any event, this goes to the assessment of damages.[56] For an application in the mental health context see *R (Sessay) v South London and Maudsley NHS Foundation Trust*.[57] In that case the claimant challenged decisions to remove her from her home and detain her for up to 13 hours. The defendant NHS Trust was not saved by the fact that it could have lawfully detained the claimant under sections 2 and 4 of the 1983 Act.[58] This could also include a failure to follow the Code of Practice, where there was no good or cogent reason for doing so—this was the issue in *Munjaz*.[59]

It should be noted that, in relation to actions under the 1983 Act, there is a statutory defence afforded by section 139. This provides that liability can only be established if it was done in bad faith or without reasonable care. However, in *TTM v Hackney LBC*[60] it was held that because detention engages Article 5 of ECHR, it was possible to read down section 139 under section 3 of the HRA 1998 to allow a claim for compensation to proceed notwithstanding the lack of bad faith or unreasonable care.[61]

Further, section 139 provides that leave from the High Court is required to bring a civil claim. The test is whether the case warrants a 'fuller investigation'.[62] The failure to obtain leave renders the proceedings a nullity.[63] However, section 139 does not apply to judicial review proceedings.[64] Accordingly, a judicial review for unlawful detention would escape section 139, although a claim for damages for false imprisonment would not.

---

[53] See above 5-10.

[54] www.cps.gov.uk/legal/l_to_o/mentally_disordered_offenders/#a05. See discussion above on challenges to CPS decisions to prosecute at 5-20.

[55] See, for instance, *R (B) v DPP* [2009] EWHC 106 (Admin), [2009] 1 WLR 2072 where it was held that the CPS decision to stop a prosecution was irrational due to a misapplication of the Code. Note that costs in such claims are likely to only be available if there was bad faith. *R v P* [2011] EWCA Crim 1130.

[56] See *R (Lumba) v Secretary of State for the Home Department* [2012] AC 245, [2012] 1 AC 245 and *R (Kambadzi) v Secretary of State for the Home Department* [2011] UKSC 23, [2011] 1 WLR 1299.

[57] *Sessay* (n 35).

[58] ibid [54] (Supperstone J).

[59] *Munjaz* (n 24). See also *Munjaz v United Kingdom* App no 2913/06 ECHR 2012–1704 where the ECtHR held that Mr Munjaz's seclusion did not violate Arts 3, 5, 8 or 14.

[60] *TTM v Hackney LBC* [2011] EWCA Civ 4 [66].

[61] See *TW v Enfield LBC* [2013] EWHC 1180 (QB).

[62] *Winch v Jones* [1986] QB 296.

[63] *Seal v Chief Constable of South Wales* [2007] UKHL 31.

[64] *Re Waldron* [1986] QB 824.

E. Trial or Fact-Finding

(1) General Principles

After a mentally disordered suspect has been arrested and charged, and interim matters **12-36** have been dealt with, the next stage is the trial or fact-finding process. The term 'fact-finding' is used to refer to the process of determining whether the defendant 'did the act'. Strictly speaking, this is not a criminal process.[65] At this stage there is sharp distinction between the processes of the magistrates' courts and the Crown Court.

There are two preliminary issues to bear in mind: i) the first concerns the applicability of Article 6 of ECHR; and, ii) the second relates to pre-trial diversion under section 51 of the 1983 Act.

(2) Article 6 of ECHR

The right to a fair trial under Article 6 'guarantees the right of an accused to participate **12-37** effectively in a criminal trial'.[66] This means that a defendant needs to have some level of active involvement in his or her trial, which includes rights 'to defend himself in person', 'to examine or have examined witnesses', and 'to have the free assistance of an interpreter if he cannot understand or speak the language used in court'.[67] This particularly applies to vulnerable defendants.[68]

However, it should be noted that these protections of Article 6 do not necessarily apply in fact-finding hearings before the criminal courts; this is because such hearings are not 'trials' or a 'criminal' process'.[69] Accordingly, it has been held that because such hearings are not criminal in nature, an unfit accused is not entitled to claim the protection of the criminal elements of Article 6.[70]

(3) Pre-Trial Diversion under Section 51(5)

Where a defendant is the subject of a transfer direction under section 48 of the 1983 **12-38** Act, and the defendant remains too ill to be brought before the court, the court may nevertheless make a hospital order in respect of the defendant under section 51(5) of the 1983 Act if: (i) it is impracticable or inappropriate to bring the defendant before the court; and (ii) the court is satisfied on the evidence of two registered medical practitioners that the detainee is suffering from a mental disorder such that detention in hospital is appropriate, and that appropriate medical treatment is available.

---

[65] *R v H* [2003] UKHL 1, [2003] 1 WLR 411.
[66] *Stanford v United Kingdom* App no 16757/90 (ECtHR, 23 February 1994) [22].
[67] ibid [26].
[68] See *T and V v United Kingdom* (2000) 30 EHRR 121; and *SC v United Kingdom* (2005) 40 EHRR 10. In the domestic context, see *R (TP) v West London Youth Court* [2005] EWHC 2583 (Admin), [2006] 1 WLR 1219 [7] mentioned above at 11-39.
[69] See *Crown Prosecution Service v P* [2007] EWHC 946 (Admin), [2008] 1 WLR 1005.
[70] See *R v H* [2003] UKHL 1, [2003] 1 WLR 411.

Orders under section 51(5) should only be exercised by the Crown Court in exceptional circumstances. If the trial has begun, then a person's mental fitness to stand trial should be determined in accordance with the unfitness to plead procedure as provided by section 4 of the 1964 Act.[71]

(4) Evidence

12-39 In the mental health context it is important to recall that whether a person is 'competent' to give evidence is a relevant factor in criminal proceedings. The test of competence is given in sections 53–56 of the Youth Justice and Criminal Evidence Act (YJCEA) 1999, which provides that a person of unsound mind is not competent if it appears to the court that the defendant is unable to understand questions put to him or is unable to give answers that can be understood (see section 53 of YJCEA). Typically, the court will seek to adduce expert evidence on the point.[72]

Furthermore, it is important to note that the weight of evidence given by a person with a mental disorder is a relevant factor. For instance, when an individual pleads not guilty by reason of insanity, this is normally accompanied by a special warning to the jury. Blanket assumptions ought not to be made about the weight to be attached to the evidence of a mentally disordered person.[73] This point can also be relevant about the decision to prosecute. For instance in *R (B) v DPP* the victim had a mental illness (see above at 5-31). The Crown Prosecution Service took the view that this meant the victim could not be a reliable witness, and so no evidence was offered at trial. This was held to be irrational, contrary to section 49A(1)(c) of the Disability Discrimination Act 1995 (see now the Equality Act 2010), and a violation of Article 3 of the ECHR.

It is axiomatic that cross-examination is necessary to resolve disputes of fact. This is a requirement of Article 6, and applies both in criminal and civil proceedings: *R (Wilkinson) v Broadmoor Hospital.*[74] Where there are considerations of mental health, it is submitted that questioning should take this into account. Guidance produced by Mind suggests that special measures might be adopted, or that reasonable adjustments could be made.[75] This could include shorter sittings and taking regular breaks, allowing a carer to accompany the person, and making sure that the person is comfortable with court procedures.[76] Furthermore, an intermediary may be used.[77] However, it is important to note that a decision of a judge in ongoing proceedings in the Crown Court is a case where judicial review will not be the appropriate route of challenge, although failure to adopt appropriate procedures may well found an appeal against conviction.

---

[71] *Kenneally* (n 5).

[72] *R v Barratt* [1996] Crim LR 495.

[73] ibid.

[74] *R (Wilkinson) v Broadmoor Hospital* [2001] EWCA Civ 1545.

[75] Mind, *Achieving Justice for victims and witnesses with mental distress: a mental health toolkit for prosecutors and advocates* (2010) pp 30–32.

[76] It is of note that the special measures provisions contained in the YJCEA 1999 still do not apply to defendants, despite criticisms regarding this issue.

[77] See Practice Direction (Criminal Proceedings) 3E, *Ground Rules Hearings to plan the questioning of a vulnerable witness or defendant*; ibid 3F, *Intermediaries*; and Pt 29 ibid.

Justin Leslie

On the other hand, it can provide a ground for a challenge by judicial review for decisions in the Youth Court.[78]

(5) Experts

The need for expert evidence is interwoven with the orders and powers of the Mental Health Act 1983. For instance, hospital orders under section 37 require the written or oral evidence of two registered medical practitioners. However, further evidence from mental health experts is often required on specific issues raised in individual cases. Putting this evidence before the court is a matter for the parties.

    It was held in *G v DPP*[79] that where a judge is presented by several expert opinions and there is a conflict of between the experts, the judge must come to his or her own decision on the evidence. Note that the fact that the court may take the view that the accused is not capable of making decisions which are in his or her best interests is not enough to conclude that he or she is unfit to plead, as in *R v Robertson*.[80]

12-40

F. Court Procedure

(1) Magistrates' Court Procedure

The procedure applicable for mentally disordered defendants appearing in a magistrates' court is derived from two key sources: first, section 11(1) of the PCC(S)A and secondly, section 37(3) of the 1983 Act. This procedure is applicable to juveniles appearing in a Youth Court, as this is a magistrates' court (section 45 of the Children and Young Persons Act 1933).[81] As is apparent from the cases cited below, judicial review is more readily available as an appropriate remedy for decisions in the lower courts than against the Crown Court. This section should be read in conjunction to that concerning the trial of youths (see above section D in Chapter 11).

    Section 11(1) of the PCC(S)A provides that:

12-41

> If, on trial by a magistrates' court of an offence punishable on summary conviction with imprisonment the court:
> (a)   is satisfied that the accused did the act or made the omission charged, but
> (b)   is of the opinion that an inquiry ought to be made into his physical or mental condition before the method of dealing with him is determined,
> the court shall adjourn the case to enable a medical examination and report to be made, and shall remand him.

---

[78] Note the discussion on the use of intermediaries above at 11-40 for young defendants, especially *R (AS) v Great Yarmouth Youth Court* [2011] EWHC 2059 (Admin), where a defendant suffered from Attention Deficit and Hyperactivity Disorder.

[79] *G v DPP* [2012] EWHC 3174 (Admin).

[80] *R v Robertson* [1968] 3 All ER 557.

[81] See further, *CPS v P* [2007] EWHC 946 (Admin), [2008] 1 WLR 1005 which held that proceedings in a Youth Court can be stayed in exceptional cases where a juvenile has mental capacity issues.

Section 11(1) gives a magistrates' court a power to order a medical report on a defendant's physical or mental condition when i) he or she is being tried for a summary offence, and ii) the court is satisfied that he or she did the act or made the omission charged.

The power under section 11(1) presumes that a trial is in process, and then the mental disorder becomes apparent. However, it was suggested in *Crown Prosecution Service v P*[82] that the trial process can be switched into a fact-finding process to determine whether the defendant 'did the act or made the omission'. In that case, the role of a Youth Court in relation to mentally disordered juveniles was under consideration, but the general point was made that the court has a duty to keep under continuing review the question of whether the criminal trial should continue and that the court has a discretion about whether to switch to a fact-finding process.[83]

Section 37(3) of the 1983 Act provides that:

> Where a person is charged before a magistrates' court with any act or omission as an offence and the court would have power, on convicting him of that offence, to make an order (hospital or guardianship) under subsection (1) above in his case, then, if the court is satisfied that the accused did the act or made the omission charged, the court may, if it thinks fit, make such an order without convicting him.

Therefore, a magistrates' court can also impose hospital and guardianship orders without convicting the defendant, if the conditions of section 37(1) are satisfied.

The powers under section 11(1) and section 37(3) require the court to be satisfied that the defendant 'did the act'. This has been held to 'not import any question of *mens rea*'.[84] Accordingly, only the conduct element of the offence needs to be proved.[85]

12-42   Taken together, these provisions result in a three-stage procedure:

i.   Assuming a plea of not guilty has been entered, the court would hear the prosecution evidence.

ii.   If that evidence proves that the defendant 'did the act', it is open to the court under section 11(1) to adjourn for medical reports.

iii. If on the basis of the reports, the medical criteria are satisfied, the court may then go on to make a hospital order under section 37(3) of the 1983 Act without convicting the accused.

When this procedure should apply appears to be a matter for the court. In *R (Blouet) v Bath & Wansdyke Magistrates' Court*,[86] it was held that the section 11 procedure should only be adopted if a section 37 order was a possibility. As a result, if a section 37 order is not appropriate (i.e. in less serious cases of mental disorder) then the section 11 procedure will not be adopted. This can leave the mentally disordered defendant open to the full trial process. In *Blouet* the claimant had Asperger's Syndrome. In a factually similar case, *R (Varma) v Redbridge Magistrates' Court*,[87] the 'possibility' point made in *Blouet*

---

[82] *Crown Prosecution Service v P* [2007] EWHC 946 (Admin), [2008] 1 WLR 1005.
[83] ibid [54]–[56].
[84] *Bartram v Southend Magistrates' Court* [2004] EWHC 2691 (Admin), [2004] MHLR 319 [6].
[85] See also: *R v Antoine* [2000] UKHL 20, [2001] 1 AC 340.
[86] *R (Blouet) v Bath & Wansdyke Magistrates' Court* [2009] EWHC 759 (Admin).
[87] *R (Varma) v Redbridge Magistrates' Court* [2009] EWHC 836 (Admin).

was not a factor in the judgment, and it held that a trial should not have taken place. However, in *DPP v P*[88] it was said that there may be advantages to having a fact-finding hearing, even if it was unlikely that a hospital order would be imposed.

Raising the issue of insanity is likely to trigger a consideration of whether the section 11 procedure should apply. The defence of insanity is available in the magistrates' court.[89] However, note that the defence was not open to the accused on a summary-only charge where there was no mental element in the offence.[90]

12-43

In *R (P) v Barking Youth Court*[91] it was said that provisions of sections 11(1) and 37(3) amount to:

> A complete statutory framework for the determination by the magistrates' court ... of all the issues that arise in cases of defendants who are or may be mentally ill or suffering from severe mental impairment in the context of offences which are triable summarily only.

Although there was no statutory power for a magistrates' court to appoint an intermediary, the court had an inherent power to do so in order to achieve a fair trial.[92] The court can also adapt its procedures to ensure effective participation.[93]

This process is quite different to the 'fitness to plead' procedure found in the Crown Court. It has been held that the fitness to plead process is not available for summary offences.[94] In cases that are triable either way, it is of course possible that the case may be sent the Crown Court. The fitness to plead regime would then apply.

12-44

(2) Crown Court Procedure

The central procedural provisions for those defendants suffering from a mental disorder are sections 4, 4A and 5 of the Criminal Procedure (Insanity) Act 1964. This provides for a scheme whereby: first, the court determines that the defendant is suffering from a disability ('trial of the issue'); second, a jury then determines whether the defendant did the act ('trial of the facts'); and third, the court then considers what order (if any) should be used to dispose of the case.

12-45

First, in terms of the trial of the issue, section 4 of the 1964 Act provides as follows:

(1) This section applies where, on the trial of a person, the question arises (at the instance of the defence or otherwise) whether the accused is under a disability, that is to say, under any disability such that apart from this Act it would constitute a bar to his being tried.

(2) If, having regard to the nature of the supposed disability, the court are of opinion that it is expedient to do so and in the interests of the accused, they may postpone consideration

---

[88] *DPP v P* [2007] EWHC 946 (Admin), [2008] 1 WLR 1005 [56].

[89] See *R v Horseferry Road Magistrates' Court, ex parte K* [1997] QB 23, confirmed in *R (Singh) v Stratford Magistrates' Court* [2007] EWHC 1582 (Admin), [2007] 1 WLR 3119.

[90] See *Bartram* (n 84).

[91] *R (P) v Barking Youth Court* [2002] EWHC 734 (Admin), [2002] 2 Cr App R 19 [10].

[92] *C v Sevenoaks Youth Court* [2009] EWHC 3088 (Admin) discussed above at 11-40.

[93] See *R (P) v West London Youth Court* [2005] EWHC 2583 (Admin), [2006] 1 WLR 1219 [26] discussed above at 11-39.

[94] *R v Metropolitan Stipendiary Magistrate, ex parte Aniifowosi* (1985) 144 JP 752.

of the question of fitness to be tried until any time up to the opening of the case for the defence.

(3) If, before the question of fitness to be tried falls to be determined, the jury return a verdict of acquittal on the count or each of the counts on which the accused is being tried, that question shall not be determined.

(4) Subject to subsections (2) and (3) above, the question of fitness to be tried shall be determined as soon as it arises.

(5) The question of fitness to be tried shall be determined by the court without a jury.

(6) The court shall not make a determination under subsection (5) above except on the written or oral evidence of two or more registered medical practitioners at least one of whom is duly approved.

Accordingly, section 4 provides a scheme for the Crown Court to consider the fitness of an individual to be tried, taking into account the evidence of at least two registered medical practitioners.

12-46   The legal test for whether a person is unfit to plead is derived from the cases of *R v Pritchard*, and *R v Davies*.[95] They are known as the '*Pritchard* criteria' and, in short, they are as follows: i) whether the defendant has the ability to plead to the indictment, ii) to understand the course of the proceedings, iii) to instruct a lawyer, and iv) to challenge a juror and to understand the evidence.

Expert evidence required under section 4(6) is normally directed to these criteria; simply because a person is unable to make decisions in their best interests does not amount to unfitness to plead.[96] Furthermore, whilst medical evidence is important, it should be emphasised that the ultimate decision is for the court. This general principle was confirmed in *Masterman-Lister v Jewell*.[97]

Recent interpretations of the *Pritchard* criteria have sought to interpret the criteria in a way that is consistent with modern practice. Accordingly, in *R v M (John)*,[98] the trial judge's directions, which included reference to whether the defendant could follow the course of the proceedings and give evidence if he wishes in his own defence, were approved by the Court of Appeal. However, it is important to note that the *Pritchard* criteria create a relatively high hurdle for most mentally disordered defendants.

If the Crown Court falls into error regarding the trial of the issue, the appropriate remedy is likely to be an appeal to the Criminal Division of the Court of Appeal. This should be considered before any application for judicial review.

12-47   In terms of the trial of the facts, if it is found that the defendant is suffering from a disability under section 4 of the 1964 Act, then the procedure in section 4A applies. This provides that:

(1) This section applies where in accordance with section 4(5) above it is determined by a court that the accused is under a disability.

---

[95] *R v Davies* (1853) Car & Kir 328.
[96] *R v Robertson* [1968] 3 All ER 557.
[97] *Masterman-Lister v Jewell* [2002] EWHC 417 (QB), [2002] All ER (D) 247 [16].
[98] *R v M (John)* [2003] EWCA Crim 3452, [2003] All ER (D) 199 [21].

(2) The trial shall not proceed or further proceed but it shall be determined by a jury—
  (a) on the evidence (if any) already given in the trial; and
  (b) on such evidence as may be adduced or further adduced by the prosecution, or adduced by a person appointed by the court under this section to put the case for the defence, whether they are satisfied, as respects the count or each of the counts on which the accused was to be or was being tried, that he did the act or made the omission charged against him as the offence.
(3) If as respects that count or any of those counts the jury are satisfied as mentioned in subsection (2) above, they shall make a finding that the accused did the act or made the omission charged against him.
(4) If as respects that count or any of those counts the jury are not so satisfied, they shall return a verdict of acquittal as if on the count in question the trial had proceeded to a conclusion.
(5) Where the question of disability was determined after arraignment of the accused, the determination under subsection (2) is to be made by the jury by whom he was being tried.

Section 4A thereby provides for the jury to determine whether the defendant 'did the act'. The jury need only be concerned with the conduct element of the offence, the *actus reus*, and not the *mens rea*—see *R v Antoine*.[99]

Although these decisions of a Crown Court are almost always taken during the trial process, and so are not amenable to judicial review, there are occasions when judicial review can be a suitable remedy. For example, it should be noted that if, following a further section 4 hearing, it turns out that the defendant is fit to plead, then the machinery of section 4A does not apply. In *Hasani v Blackfriars Crown Court*[100] the defendant was found to be unfit to plead, but subsequently recovered before the trial of the facts occurred. It was held that it was not unlawful to arraign the defendant for trial, although a further section 4 hearing was required. **12-48**

Furthermore, if there is a second trial of the facts, section 4A(2) does not mean that prior findings can be relied upon. In *Ferris v DPP*,[101] the defendant was found to have killed her two children and was admitted to a psychiatric hospital. However, subsequent medical opinion was that she was fit to stand trial, so the matter returned to the Crown Court; but a new jury found the defendant unfit to stand trial. The prosecution position was that given the previous findings, there was no need to determine whether she had done the act. The Divisional Court disagreed and there was a further trial of the facts.

Section 4A(2) requires that a person is 'appointed by the court ... to put the case for the defence'. In *R v Norman*[102] it was held that this should normally be a specialist in mental health issues. However, a failure to appoint a representative will not amount to a material irregularity and will not jeopardise the ultimate finding of the court.[103] **12-49**

[99] *R v Antoine* (n 85).
[100] *Hasani v Blackfriars Crown Court* [2005] EWHC 3016 (Admin), [2006] 1 WLR 1992.
[101] *Ferris v DPP* [2004] EWHC 1221 (Admin).
[102] *R v Norman* [2008] EWCA Crim 1810, [2009] 1 Cr App R 192.
[103] *R v Egan* [1998] 1 Cr App R 121 (in practice, defence counsel would remain representing the defendant).

As noted above at 12-37, the House of Lords held in *R v H*[104] that a hearing under section 4A is not a 'trial'. This means that the criminal protections of Article 6 of ECHR do not apply. The process shares some but not all the characteristics of a criminal trial— *R (Ferris) v Director of Public Prosecutions*.[105]

(3) The Role of Judicial Review at the Trial/Fact-Finding Stage

12-50   As indicated above, the role of judicial review in relation to this phase is limited by three factors.

   i.   First, there is the availability of an alternative remedy, namely an appeal to the Crown Court or the Court of Appeal (in respect of the former see above at section A in Chapter 6).
   ii. Secondly, section 29(3) of the Senior Courts Act 1981 precludes judicial review proceedings with respect to 'matters relating to trial on indictment'. For instance, it was held in *R v Maidstone Crown Court, ex parte Harrow LBC*[106] that an order under section 5 of the 1964 Act comes within this definition (see below at 12-56).
   iii. Thirdly, in respect of the magistrates' courts, there is a reluctance to entertain judicial review challenges before a case has concluded (see above discussion at 6-16).

However, during the trial or fact-finding stage there are points that lend themselves to judicial review proceedings. These relate to when a third party is required to make a decision. These 'third parties' include local authorities, hospitals, the Secretary of State and the Crown Prosecution Service.

For instance, under section 37(6) of the 1983 Act, when the court is making a guardianship order, the local authority must be 'willing to receive the offender into guardianship'. There is no other manner of challenging whether the local authority is 'willing' and this decision would be open to challenge on ordinary public law principles.

It is not possible to give a comprehensive list of every scenario when a third party might be open to a judicial review challenge. However, it is important to be aware that the trial or fact-finding requires there to be interaction with other public authorities. Subject to the limitations outlined above, the decisions of these public authorities are susceptible to judicial review applications, if their decisions fall foul of public law principles.

G. Disposal

(1) Disposals in the Magistrates' Court

12-51   Under section 37(3), a magistrates' court has the option of two methods of disposing of a case where a person is mentally disordered: i) a hospital order, or ii) a guardianship

---

[104] *R v H* [2003] UKHL 1, [2003] 1 WLR 411.
[105] *R (Ferris) v Director of Public Prosecutions* [2004] EWHC 1221 (Admin) [18].
[106] *R v Maidstone Crown Court, ex parte Harrow LBC* [2000] QB 719, [2000] 2 WLR 237.

order. Section 38 also gives the magistrates' court the power to make interim hospital or guardianship orders. These powers are in addition to the ordinary sentencing powers that are available to the court when a person is convicted at the conclusion of a trial.[107]

There is a limited range of disposals under section 37(3), and they may not be appropriate for all cases. This can be problematic. As noted above, if a hospital order is not a 'possibility' the court may conclude that the section 11 procedure should not apply.[108] This is a matter that could be raised by way of judicial review.

(i) Hospital Orders

The requirements for the imposition of a hospital order under section 37 of the 1983 Act are that the court must be satisfied on the written or oral evidence of two medical practitioners that:

    12-52

i.   the mental disorder from which the offender is suffering is of a nature or degree which makes it appropriate for him or her to be detained in hospital; and
ii.   appropriate medical treatment is available.

The magistrates' court can make an order under section 37 if the accused is convicted of an offence punishable on summary conviction with imprisonment, or has been charged with such an offence and the court is satisfied that the accused did the act or made the omission. There must be evidence that arrangements have been made for the defendant's admission to hospital, and admission must take place within 28 days (section 37(4) of the 1983 Act). It was held in a judicial review of a NHS Trust in *R (X) v An NHS Trust*[109] that if the person is admitted later than the 28-day period, the detention is unlawful.

(ii) Guardianship Orders

Under a guardianship order, the offender is placed under the responsibility of a local authority or a person approved by the local authority (see section 37(1)). Like a hospital order, a magistrates' court can make this order either following conviction or without conviction, if the court is satisfied that the defendant did the act.

    12-53

A guardianship order shall not be made 'unless the court is satisfied that that authority or person is willing to receive the offender into guardianship' (section 37(6)). Magistrates' courts are entitled to revoke orders that they should not have made, such as in circumstances where it ordered placement in a private care home, and then the funding fell away, as happened in *R (Bitcon) v West Allerdale Magistrates' Court* (see above 12-33). In that case, the claimant had been remanded to a nursing home for an assessment under section 35 of the 1983 Act. However, the local hospital trust refused to fund the treatment of a placement at a nursing home and so the remand order became *ultra*

---

[107] Guidance on disposals has been provided by the government—see Ministry of Justice, *Mental Health Act 2007: Guidance for the courts on remand and sentencing powers for mentally disordered offenders* (2008), www.justice.gov.uk/downloads/offenders/mentally-disordered-offenders/guidance-for-the-courts-mha.pdf.
[108] See *Blouet* (n 86).
[109] *R (X) v An NHS Trust* [2008] EWCA Civ 1354, [2009] 2 All ER 792.

vires under section 35(4). It is submitted that this analysis would apply to guardianship orders in light of the similar wording of section 37(6).

(iii) Interim Hospital or Guardianship Orders

12-54   Under section 38 of the 1983 Act, the court also has the power to make an interim hospital order, prior to making a hospital order under section 37 or dealing with the convicted offender in some other way. The offender must be suffering from a mental disorder, and there must be reason to suppose that the mental disorder is such that it may be appropriate for a hospital order to be made. An interim hospital order can be made by a magistrates' court after conviction, when the court needs more time to decide whether to impose a hospital order or to use an alternative disposal.

(iv) Other Disposals

12-55   A further disposal for mentally disordered offenders is the 'mental health treatment requirement' which can form part of a community order or a suspended sentence order (see sections 177(1)(h) and 190(1)(h) of CJA 2003). But if the offender's mental health is 'such as to warrant the making of a hospital order or guardianship order', then a mental health treatment requirement is not appropriate (see section 207(3)(a)(ii) of CJA 2003).

(2) Disposals in the Crown Court

12-56   In terms of disposals by the Crown Court, these are provided for by section 5 of the 1964 Act,[110] which states that:

(1)   This section applies where—
   (a)   a special verdict is returned that the accused is not guilty by reason of insanity; or
   (b)   findings have been made that the accused is under a disability and that he did the act or made the omission charged against him.
(2)   The court shall make in respect of the accused—
   (a)   a hospital order (with or without a restriction order);
   (b)   a supervision order; or
   (c)   an order for his absolute discharge.
   ...
(4)   In this section—
   'hospital order' has the meaning given in section 37 of the Mental Health Act 1983;
   'restriction order' has the meaning given to it by section 41 of that Act;
   'supervision order' has the meaning given in Part 1 of Schedule 1A to this Act.

---

[110] Guidance on disposals has been provided by the government—see (n 107).

Accordingly, the Crown Court is able to impose four orders under section 5:

  i.   a hospital order;
  ii. a restriction order;
  iii. a supervision order; and
  iv. an order of absolute discharge.

Where relevant, these are explicitly linked to sections of the 1983 Act.

However, section 5A also provides that orders under sections 35, 36 and 38 of the 1983 Act can apply. Accordingly, before an order under section 5 is imposed, the court can remand the defendant for a report (section 35) or for treatment (section 36). On these matters, see above 12-33. The court can also impose an interim hospital order (section 38).

The following describes these various forms of disposal, as well as the possibility of remittal. This section does not consider hospital and limitation directions, as these only apply where a defendant has been convicted, ie he has relied on the defence of insanity but has been convicted. This does not arise in the context of fitness to plead procedure in the Crown Court, as the defendant is not 'convicted' under the fitness process.

(i) Hospital Orders in the Crown Court

Section 5 of the 1964 Act enables the Crown Court to impose a hospital order, as defined   12-57
by section 37 of the 1983 Act. Such an order allows for the detention of the individual in hospital or placed under the guardianship of the local social services authority (a 'guardianship order'—see below in this section).

For the court to make a hospital order, by virtue of section 37(2)(a)(i) of the 1983 Act, the court must be satisfied on the written or oral evidence of two medical practitioners that:

  i.   the mental disorder from which the offender is suffering is of a nature or degree which makes it appropriate for him or her to be detained in hospital; and
  ii. appropriate medical treatment is available.

There must be evidence that arrangements have been made for the defendant's admission to hospital, and admission must take place within 28 days (section 37(4)).

A person ought to be admitted within 28 days of making a section 37 hospital order. In *R (X) v An NHS Trust* (n 109) it was held that if the person is admitted later than the 28 days, the order ceased to have effect and the detention is unlawful. In that case a hospital order was made, but due to a mistake in the order, the defendant was not detained in a secure unit. The order was amended to change this, but admission to the secure unit did not occur within 28 days of the initial order. As a result, the subsequent detention was unlawful.

Under a guardianship order, the offender is placed under the responsibility of a local authority or a person approved by the local authority.

Section 5A makes certain adjustments to section 37 of the 1983 Act. These include that section 37 should be read as if the words after 'punishable with imprisonment' and before 'or is convicted' had been omitted (section 5A(1)(b)) and imposes a duty on the hospital to admit the defendant (section 5A(1)(c)).

(ii) Restriction Orders

12-58   Where the Crown Court makes a hospital order under section 37 of the 1983 Act, it may make 'further order that the offender shall be subject to special restrictions' set out in section 41 of the 1983 Act. This is known as a restriction order. A restriction order can also be given where an unfit accused, found to have done the act, is given a hospital order. The main effect of a restriction order is that the patient cannot be given leave of absence, transferred to another hospital or discharged without the approval of the Secretary of State (see section 41(3)).

In deciding whether to impose a restriction order, the court must consider whether, having regard to the nature of the offence, the antecedents of the offender and the risk of reoffending if set at large, it is necessary for the protection of the public from serious harm that the court restrict the offender's discharge from hospital (section 41(1)).

The Secretary of State can direct that the patient no longer be subject to a restriction order, or discharge the patient during the time a restriction order is in force, either absolutely or subject to conditions. Restriction orders imposed by the court will remain in force until the Secretary of State or the tribunal discharges them.

(iii) Supervision Orders

12-59   A supervision order is an order that requires the defendant to be under the supervision of a social worker, an officer of a local probation board, or an officer of a provider of probation services for a specified period of not more than two years. Such orders are made under Schedule 1A of the 1964 Act.

A supervision order may require the person to submit during the whole or part of that period to treatment by or under the direction of a registered medical practitioner; but only if the court is satisfied on the evidence of at least two registered medical practitioners that the defendant's mental condition is 'such as requires and may be susceptible to treatment; but is not such as to warrant the making of a hospital order'. This can include treatment as a non-resident at an institution specified in the order.

(iv) Interim Hospital Orders

12-60   Under section 38 of the 1983 Act, the court also has the power to make an interim hospital order, prior to making a hospital order under section 37 or dealing with the convicted offender in some other way. The offender must be suffering from mental disorder, and there must be reason to suppose that the mental disorder is such that it may be appropriate for a hospital order to be made. An interim hospital order may not last longer than 12 months.

An interim hospital order is not available in respect of a person who is convicted of 'an offence the sentence for which is fixed by law' (section 38(1) of the 1983 Act). The same restriction does not, however, apply where the person is found not guilty by reason of insanity or unfit to plead and to have done the act in respect of an offence the sentence for which is fixed by law (section 5A(2)(d) of the 1964 Act).

(v) Remittal

If a person has been found to be unfit and to have done the act or made the omission and consequently is detained by a hospital order with a restriction order under section 41 which has not ceased to have effect, then the Secretary of State may remit the person for trial (see section 5A(4) of the 1964 Act). This must follow a consultation with the person's responsible clinician. The Secretary of State would then consult the CPS who should review the case for prosecution. In coming to a discussion on this matter, the Secretary of State's decision is open to challenge by way of judicial review, for instance if there had been no consultation with the responsible clinician. **12-61**

Note that the legislation is silent on the matter of remission in respect of a person who has been made the subject of a hospital order without a restriction order, a supervision order or an absolute discharge under section 5 of the 1964 Act. Whether a prosecution can be resumed in these circumstances is far from clear. The CPS argues that 'the statutes [the 1964 Act, the 1991 Act and the 2004 Act] neither restrict nor reserve the trial of an offender who becomes fit to plead after an order is made'. It is unlikely that the CPS will be made aware when a person subject to an unrestricted hospital order or supervision order becomes fit again as the responsible clinician has no duty to advise the CPS if the person's mental condition improves. However, the CPS takes the view that a prosecution can still be resumed if such information does come to light.[111]

(vi) Absolute Discharge Order

Section 5A(6) of the 1964 Act provides that section 12(1) of the PCC(S)A (which provide for absolute and conditional discharges) shall have effect as if section 5 of the 1964 Act applies and as if section 12 included a reference to it thinking that an order for absolute discharge would be most suitable in all the circumstances of the case. **12-62**

Accordingly, under these provisions, the court has a discretion to impose an absolute discharge order on the defendant.

(3) Availability of Judicial Review at the Disposal Stage

As far as the magistrates' courts are concerned, the Administrative Court has discouraged judicial reviews of decisions to sentence (see *Allen v West Yorkshire Probation Service* above at 6-8). The considerations that prevailed in that judgment would apply with even more force in the case of a vulnerable defendant, in that appeal to the Crown Court may provide a more speedy remedy for a defendant who has lost his liberty. Judicial review or appeal by way of case stated will, however, be more appropriate for decisions made by the Crown Court in its appellate capacity (see above at 7-25). **12-63**

---

[111] See CPS, *Legal Guidance—Mentally Disordered Offenders* (revised December 2010), www.cps.gov.uk/legal/l_to_o/mentally_disordered_offenders/index.html.

As described above at 12-4 in the commentary on the decisions on *Kenneally* and *(A) v Harrow Crown Court* the scope for judicial review of decisions in the Crown Court at first instance is very limited. There are exceptions where the court's decision has made such a fundamental jurisdictional error that it can be said to not be a decision relating to a matter concerning trial on indictment.

H. Post-Disposal

(1) Introduction

12-64   This section concerns what may happen to a mentally disordered person after the conclusion of proceedings in the magistrates' court or the Crown Court. The topics covered are:

i.   treatment;
ii.   transfer from prison;
iii.   return to prison; and
iv.   discharge.

Examples of where judicial review may be used are included in the body of each section. Defendants in this area may include a responsible clinician and the Secretary of State. Grounds of challenge include *Wednesbury* irrationality and failure to perform statutory duties.

(2) Treatment

12-65   'Medical treatment' is defined in section 145 of the Mental Health Act 1983 thus:

'medical treatment' includes nursing, psychological intervention and specialist mental health rehabilitation, rehabilitation and care.

Subsection (4) provides that:

Any reference in this Act to medical treatment, in relation to mental disorder, shall be construed as a reference to medical treatment the purpose of which is to alleviate, or prevent a worsening of, the disorder or one or more of its symptoms or manifestations.

Accordingly, medical treatment is widely defined within the 1983 Act. The application of such medical treatment is provided for by Part IV of the 1983 Act (which includes sections 56–64), which focuses on consent to treatment. This provides a regime whereby treatment can be administered without consent. This will be relevant for those who have been detained by a hospital order under section 37, or remanded to hospital for treatment under section 36.

12-66   In short, Part IV of the 1983 Act provides as follows. First, treatment by or under the direction of the clinician in charge of treatment can be given without consent (section 63). This includes any mental disorder from which the patient is suffering, not only the particular mental disorder which caused the order authorising detention to be made.[112] Medication cannot be given without consent for more than three months without the approval of a second doctor (section 58).[113]

The following points are important (references are to the 1983 Act):

i. Capacity is not the critical factor in determining whether treatment can be administered without consent; rather, the patient's best interests and the necessity of the treatment is key, as in *S v B*.[114]

ii. Electro-convulsive therapy requires consent or, if the patient cannot consent, the approval of a second doctor (section 58A).

iii. Invasive treatments (such as psychosurgery) require consent and a second medical opinion and support from two non-medical reviewers (section 57)

iv. It is possible for the patient to withdraw their consent at any time before the completion of the treatment (section 60).

v. There is a requirement on the approved clinician in charge of the treatment to provide a report on the treatment and the patient's condition (section 61).

vi. Sections 57, 58 and 58A do not apply in urgent situations, such as when it is immediately necessary to save the patient's life (section 62).

A failure to follow these provisions, and to subsequently administer treatment, is likely to give rise to a claim for damages, although note that section 139 of the 1983 Act can provide a defence to such claims.

Judicial review proceedings can be brought against decisions to administer without consent. See, for instance, *R (B) v Haddock (Responsible Medical Officer)*[115] where a claimant challenged the lawfulness of his treatment under section 58. In that case it was established that to determine whether treatment without consent was a 'medical necessity' required the court to make a value judgment on the merits of the case, not simply limit itself to a review of the decisions involved.

(3) Transfer from Prison

If a person with a mental disorder is convicted before the magistrates' court or the Crown Court, the Secretary of State has a power under section 47 of the 1983 Act to transfer the offender from prison to hospital using a 'transfer direction'. This has the same effect as a hospital order made under section 37.   **12-67**

The Secretary of State may only make a direction under section 47 where he or she is satisfied, by reports from at least two registered medical practitioners (of which one is approved by the Secretary of State):

(1) that the said person is suffering from mental disorder; and

(2) that the mental disorder is of a nature or degree which makes it appropriate for him or her to be detained in a hospital for medical treatment;

---

[112] *B v Ashworth* [2005] UKHL 20.

[113] See further, *B v Haddock* [2006] EWCA Civ 961.

[114] *S v B* [2006] EWCA Civ 28. See also *PS v G* [2003] EWHC 2335 (Admin) where best interests trumped a decision made with capacity.

[115] *R (B) v Haddock (Responsible Medical Officer)* [2006] EWCA Civ 961.

(3)   that appropriate medical treatment is available; and that

(4)   having regard to the public interest and all the circumstances, that it is expedient so to do.

The Secretary of State may add a 'restriction direction' to the transfer direction (section 49 of the 1983 Act).

12-68   It has been held that a transfer is appropriate where the mental disorder develops after sentence; if the mental disorder at the time of sentence is such that a hospital order is appropriate, then that should be the order made at disposal, as in *R v Beatty*.[116]

If offenders have been transferred under section 47 but are detained in hospital after the release date, then they 'cease to be restricted patients but remain detained as if on a hospital order without restrictions'.[117]

In *R (Miah) v Secretary of State for the Home Department*[118] a transfer direction was challenged. In that case the prisoner had been transferred from prison to a mental hospital shortly before he was due to be released on licence. Whilst in hospital he was involved in an incident that amounted to a breach of his licence conditions, and on release from the hospital was arrested and returned to prison. It was held that the transfer decision did not prevent the licence conditions from continuing to run, nor did it interfere with the power to recall to prison.

(4) Return

12-69   If the Secretary of State makes a transfer direction and a restriction direction (see above at 12-34 and 12-58), he or she can later direct that the person be remitted to any prison or other institution in which he or she might have been detained if the prisoner had not been removed to hospital (section 50 of the 1983 Act).

Alternatively, the Secretary of State may release the person on licence or discharge him or her with supervision if such a power would have been available if he or she had been remitted to a prison or other institution (section 50(1)(b) of the 1983 Act).

In *R (IR) v Shetty*[119] a claimant sought judicial review of the Secretary of State's decision to return him to prison. The court held that a decision to return a mental patient to prison under section 50 is only subject to review by the court, albeit subject to heightened scrutiny. In that case, the prisoner argued that returning him to prison would risk a violation of his Article 3 and 5 rights. However, the court decided that the threshold for establishing the risk of such a violation was high, it being necessary for R to show that a return to prison 'will' bring about a violation.

The role of medical opinions is important in section 50 decisions. In *W v Larkin*[120] a prisoner challenged a notification by the responsible clinician under section 50 and the issue of a warrant by the Secretary of State to return him to prison. The issue was the appropriateness of his return to prison from hospital. Relying on the opinion of medical practitioners, the Secretary of State decided it was appropriate. In *W* it was held that this

---

116 *R v Beatty* [2006] EWCA Crim 2359.
117 See Department of Health, Code of Practice: Mental Health Act 1983 (2008) para 33.35.
118 *R (Miah) v Secretary of State for the Home Department* [2004] EWHC 2569 (Admin).
119 *R (IR) v Shetty* [2003] EWHC 3022 (Admin). See also: *R (Pendlebury) v Secretary of State for Justice* [2013] EWHC 3613 (Admin).
120 *W v Larkin* [2012] EWHC 556 (Admin).

reliance was legitimate and that there was no additional requirement to investigate what treatment other hospitals could offer. However, in *R (Morley) v Nottinghamshire Health Care NHS Trust*[121] it was held that the responsible medical officer had a limited duty of enquiry regarding section 50 decisions, and had to take an overall view about whether a prisoner's condition was treatable.

(5) Discharge

The routes of release available to a person detained in hospital are largely the same whether he or she is detained under the civil or the criminal sections of the 1983 Act. There are four principal routes to discharge: **12-70**

   i.   discharge by the responsible clinician or the hospital managers;
   ii.   discharge by the tribunal;
   iii.   discharge by a nearest relative (albeit in a significantly restricted means by comparison to civil admissions); and
   iv.   discharge by the Secretary of State.

These routes are more limited where a restriction order has been imposed. If a restriction order is attached to the hospital order, the responsible clinician or the hospital managers can only discharge him or her if the Secretary of State consents (see section 41(3)(c)(iii) of the 1983 Act).

(i) Discharge by the Responsible Clinician or the Hospital Managers

First, in relation to discharge by the responsible clinician or the hospital managers, the responsible clinician has a power to discharge most unrestricted patients from detention (section 23(2)(a) of the 1983 Act). This decision can be made at any time, and not necessarily at the termination of the detention period. This applies to i) hospital orders made under the civil sections of the 1983 Act and ii) hospital orders made by a court under section 37, or iii) following a transfer under section 47. It does not extend to patients 'remanded to hospital or under an interim hospital order'.   **12-71**
   The Code of Practice states that:

> if, at any time, responsible clinicians conclude that the criteria which would justify renewing a patient's detention ... are not met, they should exercise their power of discharge.[122]

There is no statutory guidance on what the responsible clinician needs to consider in the exercise of this discretion.
   The hospital managers—that is, 'the organisation or individual in charge of the hospital'—have a similar power to discharge unrestricted patients (see section 23(2)(a) of the 1983 Act). As with the responsible clinician, no statutory criteria are specified for the exercise of their discretion. However, the Code of Practice states that 'the

---

[121] *R (Morley) v Nottinghamshire Health Care NHS Trust* [2002] EWCA Civ 1728, [2003] 1 All ER 784.
[122] See Department of Health, Code of Practice: Mental Health Act 1983 (2008) para 29.16.

essential yardstick is whether the grounds for continued detention … under the Act are satisfied'.[123]

In *South West London and St George's Mental Health NHS Trust v W*,[124] it was suggested that it would be appropriate for the considerations to be taken by the responsible clinician or the hospital managers to be the same as those required of the tribunals. Therefore, in assessing the continued detention of a patient, the hospital managers and responsible clinician should consider whether:

i.   the patient is still suffering from mental disorder;
ii.   the disorder continues to be of a nature or degree which makes assessment or assessment followed by medical treatment (for section 2 patients) or treatment (for section 3 patients and section 37) in a hospital appropriate;
iii. for section 3 patients and section 37, the appropriate medical treatment test continues to be satisfied; and
iv.   detention in a hospital is still necessary in the interest of the patient's own health or safety for the protection of others.

The patient should be discharged if any of those questions can be answered in the negative. If the patient is not discharged on this basis, a judicial review challenge should be considered only after an application to the tribunal and then only if some defect in the reasoning of the tribunal making the decision as to discharge can be argued (see below 12-72).

It should be noted that the powers of discharge of the responsible clinician and the hospital managers are exercised independently: the hospital managers are not able to block the discharge of a patient if it is ordered by the responsible clinician, and equally, the responsible clinician cannot block the discharge of a patient if ordered by the hospital managers. Hospital managers also have a duty to refer cases of unrestricted patients detained under Part 3 of the 1983 Act to the relevant tribunal if three years have passed without their case being heard by the tribunal (section 68 of the 1983 Act).

(ii) Discharge by the Tribunal

12-72   The tribunal has the power to review a person's continued detention under the 1983 Act. The detained person can apply to the tribunal within the relevant period, which differs depending on the power under which the person is detained.

A person compulsorily detained under the civil section for treatment (section 3) is entitled to apply within the first six months of detention (section 66(2)(b) of the 1983 Act). Similarly, persons detained in hospital under section 5(1) of the 1964 Act following a special verdict or finding of unfitness to plead and prisoners transferred to hospital (with or without a restriction order) can apply within the first six months of detention (section 69(2) of the 1983 Act). A person subject to a section 37 hospital order can only apply to the tribunal in the second six months of detention.

---

[123] ibid para 31.14.
[124] *South West London and St George's Mental Health NHS Trust v W* [2002] EWHC 1770 (Admin) [81].

The role of the tribunal is to determine whether the grounds for continued detention exist. It has been held that it falls to the party seeking to continue detention to prove that the grounds are made out.[125]

Section 72 sets out the criteria to be applied by the tribunal in the consideration for unrestricted patients. In essence, this is whether treatment is still necessary and whether medical treatment is available.

The tribunal has similar powers in relation to restricted patients (section 70 of the 1983 Act). Patients under a restriction order have a right to apply to the tribunal within the second six months of detention and every year thereafter. The criteria to be applied by the tribunal in the determination of release of a restricted patient are set out in section 73.

The tribunal must order the discharge of a restricted patient if not satisfied that the criteria under section 72(1)(b) are made out, and further that 'it is not appropriate for the patient to remain liable to be recalled to hospital for further treatment' (section 73(1)(b) of the 1983 Act). If the tribunal is satisfied that it is not appropriate for the patient to remain liable to be recalled to hospital for further treatment, they must direct an absolute discharge. However, if the tribunal considers that it may be appropriate for a patient to be liable to recall, they must grant a conditional discharge. Conditions typically relate to the supervision, residence or medical treatment of the patient.

For the relevant procedural rules in the tribunal, see Part 4 of Tribunal Procedure (First-tier Tribunal) (Health, Education and Social Care Chamber) Rules 2008 (SI 2008/2699). Note that before judicial review proceedings are brought in relation to a failure to release, the possibility of bringing an application before the tribunal must be explored.

(iii) Discharge by a Nearest Relative

Thirdly, in relation to discharge by a nearest relative, in the context of a hospital order imposed as a result of criminal proceedings the nearest relative can only request the release of the detained person in an application to the relevant tribunal (section 69(1) of the 1983 Act). **12-73**

This is much narrower than where a person is detained under the civil provisions which provide that a person compulsorily admitted to hospital under the civil section can be discharged by their nearest relative (section 23(2) of the 1983 Act). Under the civil regime, the responsible clinician would only be able to block the discharge if he or she certifies that, if discharged, the patient 'would be likely to act in a manner dangerous to other persons or to himself' (section 25(1) of the 1983 Act).[126] This decision could be subject to a judicial review challenge. But the decision is unlikely to be a good target for judicial review before the hospital managers have been invited to review the detention subject to that certification.[127] Failure by the hospital managers to review the certification, or to do so inadequately, might by the subject of a judicial review.

---

[125] See *R (H) v Mental Health Review Tribunal For North and East London Region* [2001] EWCA Civ 415, [2002] QB 1.
[126] Note that the nearest relative provisions do not apply to restricted patients.
[127] *R v Riverside Mental Health Trust ex parte Huzzey* [1998] EWHC Admin 465, [1998] 43 BLMR 167.

The responsible clinician may also make an application to the county court to displace the nearest relative under section 29 of the 1983 Act if the nearest relative:

> has exercised without due regard to the welfare of the patient or the interests of the public his power to discharge the patient from hospital … or is likely to do so.

(iv) Discharge by the Secretary of State

12-74   Fourthly, and finally, the Secretary of State has the power to order the discharge (absolute or conditional) of a restricted patient under section 42(2) of the 1983 Act at any time. Unlike the tribunal's power of discharge, the Secretary of State is not bound by any statutory criteria in the exercise of this discretion. However, if satisfied that the patient is no longer suffering from mental disorder from the evidence on the patient's mental condition, the Secretary of State should discharge the patient.[128] This power would usually be exercised at the request of a patient's responsible clinician. Even though there are no statutory criteria to guide the Secretary of State's discretion, the ordinary principles of judicial review require the discretion cannot be exercised unreasonably in the *Wednesbury* sense; although this is also a matter which could be addressed first in an application to the tribunal.

---

[128] See *Kynaston v Secretary of State for Home Affairs* (1981) 73 Cr App R 281.

Justin Leslie

13

Extradition

SAOIRSE TOWNSHEND

A. General Principles

(1) Introduction

Extradition is the process by which a person who has been accused or convicted of a **13-1** crime in another country is returned to that country to face trial or serve a sentence of imprisonment. Extradition law is a highly specialised area in which there is a continuous overlap between crime and public law. It is outside the scope of this chapter to provide a complete description of the field, save for a description and analysis of key provisions that may be relevant to challenges by way of judicial review.

Extradition proceedings commence when a requested person is arrested and transported to the City of Westminster Magistrates' Court in London for their first appearance. The cases are heard by specialist district judges. There is a statutory right of appeal to the Administrative Court under sections 26, 28, 103, 105, 108 and 109 of the Extradition Act 2003 ('the 2003 Act') (see below at 13-3). This should not be confused with an application for judicial review, especially as they have some similar features.

This means that the first instance decision on the substantive issues will not be open to judicial review challenges as there is an alternative remedy.

This chapter considers the circumstances in which it is appropriate to issue judicial review proceedings, in place of, or in conjunction with a statutory appeal. The following are non-exhaustive examples of types of decisions for which judicial review may be an appropriate remedy:

i.   A refusal to discharge a defendant where delays in producing the defendant from custody has meant that they have not received a warrant as soon as practicable (see below at 13-7).

ii.   A decision on the identity of the defendant (see below at 13-11).

iii.   The refusal or grant of an adjournment in Part 2 cases (see below at 13-15).

iv.   Decisions to proceed in the absence of the defendant (see below at 13-19).

v.   Judgments showing basic procedural errors that are brought to the attention of the High Court immediately (see below at 13-20).

vi.   A refusal to issue a witness summonses (see below at 13-21).

vii.   An extension of the required time period to surrender (see below at 13-22).

The most common ground of judicial review that is utilised is *Wednesbury* unreasonableness (see Ouseley J in *R (Robert Slavik) v District Court of Nitra, Slovak Republic*[1] below at 13-16) A fuller discussion of the grounds of review is set out above at section G of Chapter 1.

The 2003 Act can be read sequentially in sections, and therefore the chapter follows the structure of the 2003 Act, considering decisions which can be challenged by way of judicial review. Finally, the chapter considers the effect of the new developments in extradition law, as implemented by the Crime and Courts Act 2013 ('the 2013 Act') and the Anti-Social Behaviour, Crime and Policing Act 2014, and the potential for applications for judicial review.

(2) Legal Framework

13-2   The extradition process was governed entirely until very recently by one Act of Parliament, the 2003 Act. This Act repealed the Extradition Act 1989, which itself was a consolidation of three earlier pieces of legislation. The 2003 Act was an attempt to modernise and streamline proceedings the extradition process where there is a renewed need for improved judicial cooperation. This need was based on the changing nature of crime, where crime is becoming increasingly international in nature and criminals can flee justice by crossing borders with increasing ease. The 2003 Act aimed to:

> provide a quick and effective framework to extradite a person to the country where he is accused or has been convicted of a serious crime, provided that this does not breach his fundamental human rights.[2]

The objective of this 'quick and effective framework' was to implement a single avenue of appeal for all extradition cases.

---

[1] *R (Robert Slavik) v District Court of Nitra, Slovak Republic* [2011] EWHC 265.
[2] Extradition Act 2003, Explanatory Notes, para 7.

     Saoirse Townshend

B. Appeals

(1) Category 1

Part 1 of the 2003 Act implements the framework decision on the European Arrest **13-3**
Warrant ('EAW').[3] EAW extradition partners are named 'Category 1 territories'.[4] There
is a statutory right of appeal in Category 1 cases to the Administrative Court against a
judge's decision following the extradition hearing. The right of appeal is granted to both
the defendant (section 26) and the requesting judicial authority (section 28), and the
defendant cannot be returned whilst such an appeal is outstanding.

Where a case involves a point of law of public importance, section 32 of 2003 Act
provides for a right of appeal for both parties with leave to the Supreme Court. Both
defence and prosecution appeals can be either on law or fact. In relation to defence
appeals, the High Court has the power to either allow the appeal or dismiss the appeal
(section 27(1)) and, if the appeal is allowed, the court must order the person's discharge
and quash the order for extradition (section 27(5)). The court may only allow the appeal
if the judge ought to have decided a question before him at the extradition hearing differently and, if he had decided it in the way that he ought to have done, he would be
been required to order the person's discharge (section 27(3)).

Similarly, in prosecution appeals, the court may only allow the appeal if the judge
ought to have decided a question before him at the extradition hearing differently and
if he had decided it in the way that he ought to have done, he would not have been
required to order the person's discharge (section 29(3)).

The High Court has the power to either allow the appeal or dismiss the appeal (section 29(1)) and, if the appeal is allowed, unlike in defence appeals, the court must quash
the order discharging the person, remit the case to the judge and direct him to proceed
as he would have been required to do if he had decided the question differently at the
extradition hearing.

An appeal of the High Court's decision under section 26 or 28 is only available to the
Supreme Court on a point of law of general public importance (section 32(4)).

(2) Category 2

There is also a statutory right of appeal in Category 2 cases to the Administrative Court **13-4**
against a judge's decision following the extradition hearing.[5] In Part 2 cases, an appeal

---

[3] Council Framework Decision of 13 June 2002 (2002/584/JHA).
[4] Austria, Belgium, Bulgaria, Cyprus, Czech Republic, Denmark, Estonia, Finland, France, Germany,
Gibraltar, Greece, Hungary, Ireland, Italy, Latvia, Lithuania, Luxembourg, Malta, the Netherlands, Poland,
Portugal, Romania, Slovakia, Slovenia, Spain and Sweden.
[5] Under Pt 2 of the Act. 'Category 2 territories' are: Albania, Algeria, Andorra, Antigua and Barbuda,
Argentina, Armenia, Australia, Azerbaijan, the Bahamas, Bangladesh, Barbados, Belize, Bolivia, Bosnia and
Herzegovina, Botswana, Brazil, Brunei, Canada, Chile, Colombia, Cook Islands, Croatia, Cuba, Dominica,
Ecuador, El Salvador, Fiji, the Gambia, Georgia, Ghana, Grenada, Guatemala, Guyana, Hong Kong Special
Administrative Region, Haiti, Iceland, India, Iraq, Israel, Jamaica, Kenya, Kiribati, Lesotho, Liberia, Libya,
Liechtenstein, Macedonia (FYR), Malawi, Malaysia, Maldives, Mauritius, Mexico, Moldova, Monaco,

may be brought by the requested person[6] against the judge's decision to send her case to the Secretary of State (section 103(1) and (3)). The appeal may be on a question of law or fact (section 103(4)) and the focus of such appeal is the questions decided by the district judge.[7] In a similar way to appeals under section 26, for the appellant to succeed he must satisfy the court that the judge below ought to have decided questions before him differently and had he done so, he would have been required to order discharge (section 104(3)). The Administrative Court may allow the appeal, or remit the case with a direction to decide again a question which was determined at the extradition hearing; or, dismiss the appeal (section 104(1)).

An appeal may also be brought by the requesting territory against the first instance judge's decision to discharge the requested person under sections 105(1) and (3). The appeal may be on a question of law or fact (section 105(4)). For the appellant to succeed, he must satisfy the court that the judge below ought to have decided questions before him differently and had he done so, he would not have been required to order discharge (section 106(4)).

Under section 108, an appeal may be brought by the requested person against the Secretary of State's decision to order his extradition. The appeal can be on law or fact (section 108(3)). For the appellant to succeed, he must satisfy the court that the Home Secretary ought to have decided the question before her differently, and had she done so, she would not have ordered extradition (section 109(3)).

The requesting territory may appeal against the Secretary of State's decision to discharge the person (section 110(1)). The appeal may be on a question of law and fact (section 110(4)).

For the appellant to succeed, the judge must be satisfied that the Home Secretary ought to have decided the question before her differently, and had she done so, she would not have ordered extradition (section 111(3)).

For both the requesting state and the requested person, there is then a right of appeal to the Supreme Court under section 114 of the 2003 Act.

C. Decisions Subject to Judicial Review

(1) General Principles

13-5   The appeal route is only appropriate when making a challenge to the decision to order or refuse extradition based on the merits of the case. Decisions which are dealt with

---

Montenegro, Nauru, New Zealand, Nicaragua, Nigeria, Norway, Panama, Papua New Guinea, Paraguay, Peru, Russian Federation, Saint Christopher and Nevis, Saint Lucia, Saint Vincent and the Grenadines, San Marino, Serbia, Seychelles, Sierra Leone, Singapore, Solomon Islands, South Africa, Sri Lanka, Swaziland, Switzerland, Tanzania, Thailand, Tonga, Trinidad and Tobago, Turkey, Tuvalu, Uganda, Ukraine, the United Arab Emirates, the United States of America, Uruguay, Vanuatu, Western Samoa, Zambia and Zimbabwe.

[6] The person requested by the judicial authority, ie he is subject to an EAW or arrest warrant under Pt 2 of the Act.

[7] *Vullnett Mucelli v The Government of Albania and others* [2007] EWHC 2632 (Admin).

at the 'initial hearing', such as decisions under sections 4 to 8 of the 2003 Act, are not subject to the statutory appeal provisions of sections 26 or 28. The only way of challenging an adverse decision under sections 4 to 8 is by way of judicial review or, if the person is in custody, applying for a writ of habeas corpus (see above at 3-31). This approach was approved by the High Court in the case of *Nikonovs v Governor of Brixton Prison.*[8]

In practice, if an appeal is lodged in a case where judicial review would have been a more appropriate route, the Administrative Court will 'reconstitute' itself and a judicial review hearing will take place in a 'rolled up' hearing. However, this is not to be relied upon because there are strict time limits to bringing judicial review proceedings. It is likely then that by the time an appeal is listed, more than three months will have passed since the district judge's decision.

The 'initial hearing' starts when the requested person is brought before the appropri- **13-6** ate judge at City of Westminster Magistrates' Court. In relation to Part 1 cases, at the initial hearing, the judge must decide whether:

i. Under section 4:[9]
    (a) the requested person has been served with a copy of the European Arrest Warrant (EAW) as soon as practicable after arrest (section 4(2)); and
    (b) the requested person has been produced before the appropriate judge as soon as practicable section 4(3).
ii. Under section 7[10]: the requested person has been brought before her is the person referred to in the EAW.
iii. Under section 8[11]: the judge must fix a date for the extradition hearing.

(2) Section 4 of the Extradition Act 2003

Section 4(2) states that a copy of the warrant must be given to the requested person as **13-7** soon as practicable after her arrest. The requested person may apply to be discharged if this section is not complied with. The judge then has a discretion and may order her discharge (section 4(4)). The arresting officer's statement usually states whether the EAW has been given to the requested person, and if it has, when it was given. The judge will usually take into consideration such factors as what prejudice has been caused by the EAW not being served on the requested person, the duration of the delay, and whether the requested person was shown a copy of the warrant by his lawyer before court. In practical terms, often the judge will remedy the problem by ensuring that a copy of the EAW is given to the requested person in the dock.

Section 4(3) states that the person must be brought as soon as practicable before a judge. The requested person may also apply to be discharged if this section is not complied with. If the judge is satisfied that the person has not been produced

---

[8] *Nikonovs v Governor of Brixton Prison* [2005] EWHC 2405 (Admin), [2006] 1 WLR 1518.
[9] There are identical provisions in relation to Part 2 cases in s 72 of the 2003 Act.
[10] The corresponding provisions in Part 2 cases are contained within s 78.
[11] In Part 2 cases, the principle is the same, save for the differing timetable.

before the court as soon as practicable and the requirements of this section are not met, the judge has no discretion and must order the requested person's discharge (section 4(4)).

The judge must make a factual determination as to what constitutes 'as soon as practicable'. The judge will ask the CPS to assist in providing a detailed chronology of events from the arrest to production at court. The judge will consider such factors as:

i.   time of arrest;
ii.   the time of arrival at the police station;
iii. arrangements made for the collection of the requested person to be taken to court, when those arrangements were made (for example by phone calls to GeoAmy[12]);
iv.   time of pick-up from police station to court;
v.   the distance between the police station and court;
vi.   whether there was there an intervening event when transporting the requested person to court which delayed production (for example, the requested person became ill or the prison van broke down); and
vii. whether there had been any request to the appropriate judge the previous day after the cut-off time.

13-8   The leading authority on production is *Nikonovs v Governor of Brixton Prison*. The facts of the case are briefly described at paragraph 4 of the judgment:

> At 5.45 on the morning of Saturday 17 September GSL Court Services, who were responsible for conveying Mr Nikonovs to court, telephoned the Boston Custody Suite to say that Mr Nikonovs would not be collected until Monday as Bow Street Magistrates' Court was not open over the weekend. In fact this was an error, the court was open on Saturday. In the event Mr Nikonovs was not brought before a judge at Bow Street until 14:00 hours on Monday 19 September, which was nearly 66 hours after his arrest at Boston police station and some 74 hours after his arrest at his home.

Two principles can be derived from this case in relation to the test of 'as soon as practicable', namely:

i.   'The criterion is practicable rather than the more elastic reasonably practicable'; and
ii.   'The draughtsmen has chosen the practicability rather than the more precise criterion of a specified period as, for example, 48 hours in section 6(3) [Part 1 provision arrests]. There will no doubt be cases at the margins where views could reasonably differ whether the applicant was indeed brought before the appropriate judge as soon as practicable.'[13]

Scott Baker LJ, having considered these principles, held that:

> The only reason why Mr Nikonovs was not brought before the court on Saturday 17 March was because GSL Court Services were under the mistaken impression that the Bow Street court was closed on that day. No one suggests it was not practicable to bring him to London that day. He could have been brought to Bow Street and the district judge was very unhappy that he was

---

[12] A private contractor which transports prisoners.
[13] *Nikonovs* (n 8) [21].

not. He was not, in the event, brought before District Judge Wickham at Bow Street until 14:00 hours on the Monday afternoon. In these circumstances I have no hesitation in concluding that the applicant was not brought before an appropriate judge as soon as practicable.[14]

This approach was followed in *Huczko v Governor of HMP Wandsworth*.[15] In this case, **13-9** the requested person was arrested on an EAW at 20.42 on 6 June, having been previously arrested the same day for handling stolen goods. The soonest that the requested person could have been brought before the City of Westminster Magistrates' Court was the following morning. He eventually was brought before the Court at 1pm on 7 June. The delay had been caused by the fact that he had been mistakenly taken to Hammersmith Magistrates' Court at 8.30 in the morning. He was picked up at the magistrates' court at 12.12 and was brought to the City of Westminster at 1pm. His case was not called on for the initial hearing until 4pm. This meant that he was brought to the court over 16 hours after his arrest.

The Divisional Court refused the application for habeas corpus, citing the following factors as decisive, whilst emphasising that each case turns on its own facts:

i.   Eight of the 16 hours between arrest and production were night-time and there-fore he could not produced.
ii. The four-hour delay in taking the Requested Person to the wrong court was nothing more than human error, and once realised, was immediately rectified.
iii. The further three hours waiting in court to be called on was due to listing and is not unusual.[16]

Toulson LJ added that the court must look at the cause and duration of the delay, in assessing whether the decision of the district judge was *Wednesbury* unreasonable.[17]

More recently, in *Komendant v Poland*[18] Mitting J refused a writ of habeas corpus **13-10** where the appellant had been produced at court two days after his initial arrest. Echoing Toulson LJ's judgment in *Huczko*, Mitting J held that the statutory test was practicability, and the test to be applied was whether the district judge had reached a decision which a judge correctly directing himself could reasonably have reached; a qualified *Wednesbury* test. The court found that the district judge's decision was not unlawful, the operative failure having been the judge's decision not to accept the case because it was behind an already lengthy queue of cases that day.

(3) Section 7 of the Extradition Act 2003

At the initial hearing, the district judge must decide whether the person before the court **13-11** is, on a balance of probabilities, the subject of the warrant. If the judge is not so satis-fied, he must discharge the person. The appropriate judge must determine identity on

---

[14] ibid [21].
[15] *Huczko v Governor of HMP Wandsworth* [2012] EWHC 4134 (Admin); followed in almost identical circumstances in *R (Jochemczk) v Poland* [2012] EWHC 3990 (Admin).
[16] ibid [15]–[18].
[17] ibid [18].
[18] *Komendant v Poland* [2013] EWHC 2712 (Admin).

the balance of probabilities (section 7(3)). The burden of proof lies on the requesting authority. The court may use the following sources in order to determine identity:

i.   comparing details of identity given in Box 'A' of the EAW to the details given by the person on arrest;

ii.   comparing a photograph in the EAW with the person before the court;

iii. admissions by the person at the time of arrest;

iv.   ID documents seized by police;

v.   PNC if the person has been subject to a livescan check; and

vi.   any fingerprints with the EAW.

A district judge does not have the power to review the decision on identity at the extradition hearing, and it must instead be challenged by way of judicial review.[19]

(4) Section 8 of the Extradition Act 2003

13-12   In relation to Part 1 cases, if the judge is satisfied on the question of identity, he must fix a date for the start of the extradition hearing. This must be within 21 days, starting with the date of arrest (section 8(1)(a)). Section 8, so far as is material, provides:

(1) If the judge is required to proceed under this section he must—

    (a) fix a date on which the extradition hearing is to begin;

    ....

(4) The date fixed under sub-section (1) must not be later than the end of the permitted period, which is 21 days starting with the date of the arrest referred to in Section 7 (1) (a) or (b).

(5) If before the date fixed under sub-section (1) (or this sub-section) a party to the proceedings applies to the judge for a later date to be fixed and the judge believes it to be in the interests of justice to do so, he may fix a later date; and this sub-section may apply more than once.

(6) Sub-sections (7) and (8) apply if the extradition hearing does not begin on or before the date fixed under this section.

(7) If the person applies to the judge to be discharged the judge must order his discharge, unless reasonable cause is shown for the delay.

(8) If no application is made under sub-section (7) the judge must order the person's discharge on the first occasion after the date fixed under this section when the person appears or is brought before the judge, unless reasonable cause is shown for the delay.

(i) Section 75 of the Extradition Act 2003

13-13   There is a similar provision in relation to Part 2 cases under section 75 of the Act, which reads as follows:

(1) When a person arrested under a warrant issued under section 71 first appears or is brought before the appropriate judge, the judge must fix a date on which the extradition hearing is to begin.

---

[19] *Hilali v The National Court, Madrid and Another* [2007] 1 WLR 768 [20] and more recently, *Ivanovs-Jeruhovics v Rezekne Court Latvia* [2014] EWHC 1913 (Admin).

Saoirse Townshend

(2) The date fixed under subsection (1) must not be later than the end of the permitted period, which is 2 months starting with the date on which the person first appears or is brought before the judge.

(3) If before the date fixed under subsection (1) (or this subsection) a party to the proceedings applies to the judge for a later date to be fixed and the judge believes it to be in the interests of justice to do so, he may fix a later date; and this subsection may apply more than once.

(4) If the extradition hearing does not begin on or before the date fixed under this section and the person applies to the judge to be discharged, the judge must order his discharge.

The most important difference between the two sections, aside from the amount of time in which the date for the extradition hearing must be fixed, is whether the judge has discretion to order that the person is discharged in the event that the hearing is not fixed in the time specified by the 2003 Act. In light of the authorities in relation to sections 8 and 75, this difference could to be significant when deciding whether to appeal or judicially review the district judge's decision to discharge.

In *Kozluk v Circuit Court in Lublin Poland*[20] the court entertained an appeal by determining that for the commencement of an extradition hearing, for the purposes of the time limit contained within section 8(4) of the 2003 Act, something had to be said or done to show that an extradition had been started; merely adjourning proceedings was not enough. In the instant appeal, the district judge was correct in his exercise of discretion in deciding that where such adjournment was to enable the individual sought to be returned to obtain legal representation, that would amount to a reasonable cause for delay, precluding discharge of the extradition proceedings under section 8(7).[21]   **13-14**

This is in contrast to the Divisional Court's approach in a Part 2 case, *R (Asliturk) v City of Westminster Magistrates' Court*.[22] Stanley Burnton LJ held as follows:

> 24 A statutory provision that purports to restrict the right to apply for judicial review or for a writ of habeas corpus is to be narrowly, but sensibly, construed. Section 116 [general appeal provision] does not purport to exclude recourse to the court: it restricts the manner of recourse to the court. However, in my judgment the refusal of the appropriate judge to order the discharge of a person under section 75(4) is not a decision for the purposes of section 116.

> 25 First, the kind of decision involved will not generally be typically judicial. The judge is not required to, and has no power to, exercise any judgment of the kind involved in, for example, the decision under sections 79 to 83 whether there is a bar to extradition. Under section 75(4) the judge has no choice and exercises no judgment: if the application is made at the appropriate time, whatever the other merits of the case for extradition, he must order the person's discharge.

> 26 Secondly, it is I think consistent with the difference in the nature of the judicial function, and in any event significant in the present context, that in sections 78 to 83, in contradistinction to section 75, the judge is expressly required to 'decide'. The same applies to sections 84 to 87, each of which uses the formula 'If the judge is required to proceed under this section he must decide …'. In my judgment, the difference in language is deliberate: decisions under sections 79 to 87 can only be questioned by appeal under section 116, which is expressly limited to decisions.

---

[20] *Kozluk v Circuit Court in Lublin Poland* [2009] EWHC 3523 (Admin).
[21] This approach was later followed in *Jeziorowski v Poland* [2010] EWHC 2112 (Admin).
[22] *R (Asliturk) v City of Westminster Magistrates' Court* [2010] EWHC 2148 (Admin).

Following these authorities, as a general rule, Part 1 cases should be challenged by way of appeal on the principle that the judge has discretion as to whether to discharge, whereas in Part 2 cases judicial review is the appropriate remedy as the judge 'must' discharge if the hearing is not fixed within the specific time period.

(5) Adjournments

13-15   The most common judicial review challenge in extradition proceedings is to a judge's decision to grant or refuse an adjournment. It is well established that the most appropriate way to challenge such a decision is by way of a judicial review application rather than a statutory appeal[23] The Criminal Procedure Rules apply insofar as they are relevant to extradition proceedings.[24] Rule 1.1(1) sets out the overriding objective 'that criminal cases be dealt with justly'. Rule 1.1(2) states that dealing with cases justly includes: '(e) dealing with the case efficiently and expeditiously'. Rule 1.2(1)(a) sets out that each party in a case must comply with the directions made by the court.

Part 3 of the Rules concerns the court's case management duties and powers. Rule 3.2, as far as relevant, sets out the court's duties in relation to case management in the following terms:

The duty of the court

3.2.—

(1)   The court must further the overriding objective by actively managing the case.
(2)   Active case management includes
    (a)   the early identification of the real issues;
    (b)   the early identification of the needs of witnesses;
    (c)   achieving certainty as to what must be done, by whom, and when, in particular by the early setting of a timetable for the progress of the case;
    (d)   monitoring the progress of the case and compliance with directions;
    (e)   ensuring that evidence, whether disputed or not, is presented in the shortest and clearest way;
    (f)   discouraging delay, dealing with as many aspects of the case as possible on the same occasion, and avoiding unnecessary hearings;

The court's case management powers are set out in rule 3.5. Rule 3.5(6) sets out the powers of the court when a party has failed to comply with a rule or direction in the following terms:

(6)   If a party fails to comply with a rule or a direction, the court may—
    (a)   fix, postpone, bring forward, extend, cancel or adjourn a hearing;
    (b)   exercise its powers to make a costs order; and
    (c)   impose such other sanction as may be appropriate.

13-16   Article 17(1) of the Framework Decision on the EAW provides that 'a European arrest warrant shall be dealt with and executed as a matter of urgency'.[25] In the case of *Stopyra v*

---

[23]   *Olah v Regional Court in Plzen, Czech Republic* [2008] EWHC 2701 (Admin) [7–9].
[24]   See *United States v Tollman* [2006] EWHC 2256 [77] (Lord Phillips LCJ).
[25]   2002/584/JHA.

Saoirse Townshend

District Court of Lublin, Poland; Debreceni v Hajda-Bihar County Court, Hungary,[26] Sir John Thomas P made the following observations concerning Article 17:

> Article 17 of the Framework Decision, to which District Judge Evans referred in his judgment in Stopyra, requires an EAW to be dealt with and executed as a matter of urgency. A final decision should be taken within 60 days after the arrest of the requested person; if the decision is not made within that timescale, then the executing judicial authority must inform the issuing judicial authority and give the reasons for the delay. The time limit is then extended by a further 30 days. If the time limits cannot be observed, then Eurojust must be informed.
>
> Although this Article was not given direct effect in the 2003 Act, it is clear that a UK court should interpret the 2003 Act so far as is possible consistently with the Framework Decision: see *Assange v Swedish Prosecution Authority* [2012] UKSC 22 at para 10. The time limits specified in the 2003 Act should, therefore, be read in the context of that obligation. Furthermore in view of the presumption that the domestic law of the UK should accord with its international obligations, a court as part of the judicial branch of the state should so far as possible discharge its functions under the 2003 Act so as to fulfil the obligations of the state undertaken under the Framework Decision.[27]

The President went on to make the following observations as to the proper approach to be adopted when a district judge considers an application for an adjournment in extradition proceedings:

> If a judge was to accede to every request made for an adjournment, that judge would be abdicating his case management responsibilities. There would be interminable delays at great cost to the state, there would be fishing expeditions and lawyers might commission expert reports to see if they could get the necessary clear and cogent evidence. A convicted person in the position of Mr Stopyra had every incentive to delay extradition so he could serve his sentence in the UK rather than in Poland; many such persons appealed as they had nothing to lose and everything to gain. He considered that, to obtain an adjournment, a requested person had to convince the court that there was a real issue and there was a realistic prospect of obtaining the necessary evidence. A court should probe and satisfy itself that there was a proper case for an adjournment.[28]

Regarding the time required to prepare a case and obtain evidence:

> In cases where more assistance is needed than can be provided under the duty solicitor scheme, once the means test has been completed, the court should endeavour to complete the extradition hearing in the time set out in the 2003 Act and in accordance with the obligations under the Framework Decision.
>
> If the legal adviser requests more time, it is for the court to consider whether it is in the interests of justice to grant it: s.8(5) of the 2003 Act. It is for the lawyer for the requested person to justify more time. The lawyer must demonstrate that there is an issue that can be properly argued and explain why time is needed. The lawyer can anticipate that the request will be the subject of robust and rigorous scrutiny by the judge.
>
> Each case must depend on its circumstances. For example, in an Article 3 case, if the case advanced does not meet the high threshold required of clear and cogent evidence in view of

---

[26] *Stopyra v District Court of Lublin, Poland; Debreceni v Hajda-Bihar County Court, Hungary* [2012] EWHC 1787 (Admin).

[27] *Stopyra* (n 21) [30]–[31].

[28] ibid [14].

the rebuttable presumption of compliance (to which we refer at paragraph 63 below), there will be no need to adjourn the case for evidence to be obtained. If a case is advanced in relation to matters that this court has already decided, then again, in the absence of the real prospect of credible fresh evidence, there is no need for an adjournment. But there will be other cases where justice requires an adjournment and delays in the grant of legal aid which are not attributable to the requested person must not be held against him.

The length of the adjournment should be as short as is required by the interests of justice. The legal advisers are under a duty to progress the obtaining of evidence with the utmost expedition; pressure of other commitments is no excuse.

District Judge Evans drew attention to the risk of creating 'an industry for lawyers to make money out of routine cases by allowing inappropriate adjournments so as to accommodate defence requests to seek evidence'. Counsel in the appeal and the LSC all denied that there was any such industry. A court must, however, be astute to such a risk. It can guard against it by a suitably rigorous examination of requests for adjournments as we have set out.[29]

In *R (Robert Slavik) v District Court of Nitra, Slovak Republic*, Ouseley J stated that, in effect, a *Wednesbury* test applied when considering an application for judicial review of adjournment decision:

> A decision refusing an adjournment can only be challenged if it is an unreasonable decision, so unreasonable that no District Judge, properly directing himself in law, could reach it or if it is has been reached on wrong principles or plainly did not taken into account a material consideration.[30]

13-17 This test was applied in *Olah v Regional Court in Plzen, Czech Republic*[31] when the Divisional Court considered the question of whether a district judge had been wrong to refuse the appellant an adjournment to obtain medical evidence to support an argument under section 25 of the 2013 Act. The appellant had made his initial appearance following his arrest two weeks before the hearing at which the adjournment was refused and his extradition ordered. The Divisional Court observed that:

> questions of adjournment are peculiarly for the tribunal before which the application is made. This court must be extremely reluctant and careful before it intervenes where a decision as to an adjournment has been made.[32]

The Divisional Court went on to conclude that the appellant had had 'no reasonable opportunity' to marshal the medical evidence. The district judge's decision was quashed and an order made that the matter be remitted to a district judge to be determined afresh, giving the appellant a 'fair opportunity' to produce such medical evidence as he was able.

---

[29] ibid [48]–[52]. The expression 'suitably rigorous' is similar to the 'rigorous scrutiny' test applied to adjournment decisions in substantive criminal proceedings in the magistrates' courts. Practitioners may wish to refer to the Administrative Court's approach to adjournment decisions in the magistrates' courts generally as discussed above at 6-69.

[30] *R (Robert Slavik) v District Court of Nitra, Slovak Republic* [2011] EWHC 265 [19].

[31] *Olah, op cit.*

[32] ibid [6]. This cautious approach is again similar to how the Administrative Court views interference with the exercise of a discretion to adjourn under ss 5, 10 and 18 of the MCA 1980. See above at 6-69.

In the recent decision of *R (Zmijewski) v Westminster Magistrates Court*,[33] the court **13-18** considered that the appellant had in fact had every opportunity to canvas the necessary evidence to contest his extradition. The appellant had thrice flouted directions to serve a proof of evidence, skeleton argument and evidence of his successful asylum application. The case had lasted almost six months and had been adjourned three times previously. The appellant appeared represented at the final extradition hearing without any evidence and without any documents. The judge refused an adjournment and did not allow the appellant to give evidence. By the time of the judicial review hearing, the appellant had produced a proof of evidence but no evidence of his asylum claim. It became apparent from this that even if he had applied for asylum, as a matter of law his right to humanitarian protection had since lapsed. The district judge had not made an 'unless order' warning the appellant of the effect of non-compliance with directions. Despite this omission, Mitting J found that the judge was entitled to take the step that he did in reference to the Criminal Procedure Rules r 3.5(6)(c).[34] And therefore 'committed no error or law or irrationality and his decision is not open to challenge in judicial review proceedings'.[35]

(6) Proceedings in the Involuntary Absence of the Requested Person

In the case of *R (Pasquetti) v Westminster Magistrates' Court*,[36] extradition was ordered **13-19** in the absence of the requested person and in the absence of his representative. The district judge was told that the requested person had refused to get on the prison van to go to court and, making no other enquiries, was satisfied that he had deliberately absented himself, and therefore continued with the extradition hearing culminating in an order for his extradition. In fact, the requested person had been ill and had signed a document to this effect at the prison. There was also further medical evidence to support this. However, these documents were only produced later at the Administrative Court and were not before the district judge. Although the requested person had both appealed under section 26 and sought to challenge the decision by way of judicial review, Dobbs J found that the most appropriate remedy was by way of judicial review and consequently remitted the case back to Westminster Magistrates' Court for a full extradition hearing.

This case gives helpful guidance for practitioners to distinguish when it is appropriate to appeal or apply for the judicial review of a decision. The judgment makes clear that appeals under that 2003 Act are on points of law or fact which relate to the merits of the case, because in each case if successful, the decision would have been to order the person's discharge.[37]

In the instant case, the decision to be challenged was to proceed in the requested person's absence. This was a decision before the order for extradition order was made and did not relate to the substantive challenge to extradition. In these circumstances, judicial review proceedings were the most appropriate means of challenging the judge's decision.

---

[33] *R (Zmijewski) v Westminster Magistrates Court* [2013] EWHC 368 (Admin) [11].
[34] ibid, [9].
[35] ibid, [11].
[36] *R (Pasquetti) v Westminster Magistrates' Court* [2010] EWHC 3139. (Admin).
[37] See ss 26(3) and 27(3) and (4).

(7) Failure to Consider Submissions

13-20   The Divisional Court in *R (Berners) v Council of the Criminal Matters Court Regional Court of Riga Latvia*[38] dismissed a judicial review application in which the claimant argued that the failure to consider written submissions in his case breached the principle of procedural fairness. The merit of the submissions were relevant to the judge's assessment of whether there had been a breach of Article 3. The Divisional Court dismissed the judicial review application, Pill LJ finding that:

> there is no real possibility that consideration of the written submissions would, or could properly, have achieved a different result in the terms of an alleged infringement of the appellant's rights under article 3 of the Convention.[39]

However, in principle, the court held that a judge might reconsider an order if a basic error, including a procedural error, which emerged from the terms of the judgment, was brought to his attention immediately after delivery of the judgment and pronouncement of the order.[40]

(8) Refusal to Issue a Witness Summons

13-21   A refusal by the district judge to issue a witness summons was the subject of judicial review proceedings in the case of *R (Kaupaitis) v Prosecutor General's Office (Lithuania)*.[41] The Administrative Court dismissed the application for judicial review, having decided that the district judge was justified in refusing the application to issue a witness summons in support of the claimant's argument that extradition should be barred due to the passage of time. The judge had refused the application, on the basis that the witness' evidence was not relevant and admissible in extradition proceedings in the UK. The question of the claimant's guilt or innocence was a matter for the Lithuanian trial court, not for the English extradition proceedings, following *Office of the King's Prosecutor (Brussels) v Cando Armas*.[42] The district judge had therefore been right to refuse to issue a witness summons having decided that the relevant documents were not material to the extradition proceedings.

(9) Wrongful Extension of the Required Period for Surrender (Section 35)

13-22   In *R (Szklanny) v City of Westminster Magistrates' Court*,[43] the Administrative Court held that the court's power under section 35(4)(b) of the 2003 Act to grant an extension of time for an extradition was not restricted to circumstances in which extradition within the normal time limit imposed under s 35(4)(a) had been prevented by circumstances beyond the control of the Member States.

---

[38] *R (Berners) v Council of the Criminal Matters Court Regional Court of Riga Latvia* [2010] EWHC 1010 (Admin).

[39] ibid [24].

[40] ibid, [19].

[41] *R (Kaupaitis) v Prosecutor General's Office (Lithuania)* [2006] EWHC 2185 (Admin).

[42] *Office of the King's Prosecutor (Brussels) v Cando Armas* [2005] UKHL 67, [2006] 2 AC 1.

[43] *R (Szklanny) v City of Westminster Magistrates' Court* [2007] EWHC 2646 (Admin). See above at 1-75.

Section 35(4) reads as follows:

(4) The required period is—
   (a) 10 days starting with the first day after the period permitted under section 26 for giving notice of appeal against the judge's order; or
   (b) if the judge and the authority which issued the Part 1 warrant agree a later date, 10 days starting with the later date.

Article 23, paragraph 3 of the Framework Decision 2002/584, states that:

1. The person requested shall be surrendered as soon as possible on a date agreed between the authorities concerned.
2. He or she shall be surrendered no later than ten days after the final decision on the execution of the European arrest warrant.
3. If the surrender of the requested person within the period laid down in paragraph 2 is prevented by circumstances beyond the control of any of the Member States, the executing and issuing judicial authorities shall immediately contact each other and agree on a new surrender date. In that event the surrender shall take place within ten days of the new date thus agreed.
4. The surrender may exceptionally be temporarily postponed for serious humanitarian reasons, for example if there are substantial grounds for believing that it would manifestly endanger the requested person's life or health. The execution of the European arrest warrant shall take place as soon as these grounds have ceased to exist. The executing judicial authority shall immediately inform the issuing judicial authority and agree on a new surrender date. In that event, the surrender shall take place within ten days of the new date thus agreed.
5. Upon expiry of the time limits referred to in paragraphs 2 to 4, if the person is still being held in custody he shall be released.

In the instant case, administrative errors on the part of the CPS led to delayed notification of the judicial authority after the time for appeal had expired. The district judge granted an extension of time. The Divisional Court dismissed the claimant's claim for judicial review of this decision considering Article 23 in conjunction with the Framework Decision's underlying purpose of facilitating extradition and enhancing extradition procedures based on a spirit of mutual cooperation. The Administrative Court held that the judge had exercised his discretion to extend time in a 'wholly unimpeachable' fashion.[44]

D. New Bars to Extradition and Use of Judicial Review Procedure and Principles

(1) The Crime and Courts Acts 2013

Schedule 20 of the Crime and Courts Act 2013 amends the 2003 Act by introducing a forum bar to extradition and removing the Home Secretary's obligation to consider human rights issues when making an extradition decision.

13-23

---

[44] Szklanny (n 43), [20].

Citing Parliamentary concerns that enhanced protections were needed with regards to extradition, particularly regarding requests from the United States, the Home Secretary announced her intention to legislate for a new forum bar that would 'better balance the safeguards for defendants and delays to the extradition process which were predicted by [the Scott Baker review 2011]'.[45] The Government also took the view that the discretion to consider final human rights representations in Part 2 extradition cases should be transferred from the Secretary of State to the courts. Section 50, and accompanying Schedule 20, were intended to give effect to these policy objectives. The Crime and Courts Act 2013 was given Royal Assent on 25 April 2013 and came in to force in its entirety on 14 October 2013.

First, the 2013 Act transfers the Home Secretary's powers to the High Court to consider late representations on human rights grounds against being sent abroad to stand trial. Paragraphs 10, 11, 12 and 13 of Part 2 of Schedule 20 amend the 2003 Act to provide that in Part 2 cases, human rights issues, including those raised after the end of the normal statutory process, must not be considered by the Secretary of State, but may be raised with the courts right up until the time of surrender.

Previously, the judge at an extradition hearing and any subsequent appeal hearings considered human rights matters in Part 2 cases. Once the appeal process was complete, but before the person's surrender had taken place, the person may have raised human rights issues with the Secretary of State, but only new representations that have not already been considered by the courts. Instead, now in cases where the requested person wishes to raise late human rights issues she will be able to give notice of appeal out of time. The High Court will consider the appeal if it is satisfied that:

i.   the appeal is necessary to avoid real injustice; and
ii. the circumstances are exceptional and make it appropriate to consider the appeal.

13-24   The 2013 Act also introduces a new bar to extradition under section 19B (for Part 1 cases) and section 83A (for Part 2 cases), which allows domestic courts to block an extradition request if they believe that it is in the interests of justice for the accused to stand trial in the United Kingdom rather than abroad. Paragraphs 3 and 6 also insert new sections 19C, 19D and 19E, and 83B, 83C and 83D into the 2003 Act, which provide that extradition cannot be barred on forum grounds if a designated prosecutor issues a certificate that he or she has:

i.   considered the offences for which the person could be prosecuted in the United Kingdom;
ii. decided that there are one or more such offences which correspond to the extradition offence; and
iii. decided that the person should not be prosecuted in the United Kingdom for a corresponding offence because the prosecutor:
     (a) believes that there is insufficient admissible evidence or it would not be in the public interest; or
     (b) believes that the person should not be prosecuted in the United Kingdom because of concerns about disclosure of sensitive material.

---

[45] www.official-documents.gov.uk/document/cm84/8458/8458.pdf.

Saoirse Townshend

A designated prosecutor may apply for an adjournment in the proceedings in order to consider whether to give a certificate. The inserted section 19E (Part 1 requests) and section 83D (Part 2 requests) of the 2013 Act expressly state that decisions in relation to a prosecutor's certificate can only be challenged by way of appeal under the usual statutory route, under section 26 for Part 1 requests and sections 103 and 108 for Part 2 requests of the 2003 Act. This challenge requires permission from the High Court and, interestingly, specifically states that the:

> High Court must apply the procedures and principles which would be applied by it on the application for judicial review.

The High Court may quash the prosecutor's certificate and decide the question of whether or not the extradition is barred by reason of forum afresh. This change in the law is likely to ensure that appeals in relation to prosecutor's certificates will lead to a 'hybrid' hearing which requires the judge to consider traditional judicial review principles, and not just mistakes in fact and law.

(2) Anti-Social Behaviour, Crime and Policing Act 2014

The Anti-Social Behaviour, Crime and Policing Act 2014 received Royal Assent on 13 March 2014. Part 12 of the Act makes significant amendments to the Extradition Act 2003. New bars to extradition will be introduced: trial readiness or 'absence of a prosecution decision' (Section 12A) and a stand alone 'proportionality' bar (Section 21A), as well as changing other procedures in extradition proceedings such as temporary transfer (Section 21B). At present, there is no date for implementation of Part 12.[46] This new legislation will open up further opportunities for judicial review. The most apparent opportunity arises out of new proportionality bar. It will read as follows:

13-25

21A 'Person not convicted: human rights and proportionality

(1) If the judge is required to proceed under this section (by virtue of section 11), the judge must decide both of the following questions in respect of the extradition of the person ("D")—
    (a) whether the extradition would be compatible with the Convention rights within the meaning of the Human Rights Act 1998;
    (b) whether the extradition would be disproportionate.
(2) In deciding whether the extradition would be disproportionate, the judge must take into account the specified matters relating to proportionality (so far as the judge thinks it appropriate to do so); but the judge must not take any other matters into account.
(3) These are the specified matters relating to proportionality—
    (a) the seriousness of the conduct alleged to constitute the extradition offence;
    (b) the likely penalty that would be imposed if D was found guilty of the extradition offence;

---

[46] Subsequent to the law cut-off date for this book, Statutory Instrument 2014 No. 1916 (C.87) was passed. The sections above came in to force on 21 July 2014.

> (c)   the possibility of the relevant foreign authorities taking measures that would be less coercive than the extradition of D.
>
> (4)   The judge must order D's discharge if the judge makes one or both of these decisions—
>   (a)   that the extradition would not be compatible with the Convention rights;
>   (b)   that the extradition would be disproportionate.
>
> (5)   The judge must order D to be extradited to the category 1 territory in which the warrant was issued if the judge makes both of these decisions—
>   (a)   that the extradition would be compatible with the Convention rights;
>   (b)   that the extradition would not be disproportionate.
>
> (6)   If the judge makes an order under subsection (5) he must remand the person in custody or on bail to wait for extradition to the category 1 territory.
>
> (7)   If the person is remanded in custody, the appropriate judge may later grant bail.
>
> (8)   In this section "relevant foreign authorities" means the authorities in the territory to which D would be extradited if the extradition went ahead.'

In section 2 of 2003 Act, the following will inserted:

> (7A) But in the case of a Part 1 warrant containing the statement referred to in subsection (3), the designated authority must not issue a certificate under this section if it is clear to the designated authority that a judge proceeding under section 21A would be required to order the person's discharge on the basis that extradition would be disproportionate.
>
> In deciding that question, the designated authority must apply any general guidance issued for the purposes of this subsection.
>
> (7B) Any guidance under subsection (7A) may be revised, withdrawn or replaced.
>
> (7C) The function of issuing guidance under subsection (7A), or of revising, withdrawing or replacing any such guidance, is exercisable by the Lord Chief Justice of England and Wales with the concurrence of—
>   (a)   the Lord Justice General of Scotland, and
>   (b)   the Lord Chief Justice of Northern Ireland.

The purpose of this insertion in to Section 2, as defined by the Home Office is to '*to reduce the potential burden on the criminal justice system, we will take a more pragmatic approach to our administrative processes when an EAW is received, to ensure that the most trivial requests are identified …*'.[47] Subsection 7A states that the designated authority, ie the National Crime Agency ('NCA') when deciding whether to certify the warrant must have regard to the Lord Chief Justice's guidance. This guidance is not yet available at the time of publication. There will be much scope to challenge the NCA's decision by way of judicial review. Grounds could include, for example, error of law if the NCA did not follow the LCJ's guidance, or failure to take account of relevant considerations as set out in the guidance, or under Section 21A.

---

[47] Para, 8, https://www.gov.uk/government/uploads/system/uploads/attachment_data/file/251333/14_Factsheet_extradition_-_updated_for_Lords.pdf

14

European Union Law

KATHRYN HOWARTH

A. General Principles

(1) Introduction

European Union (EU) law plays a very limited role in judicial reviews in the criminal **14-1**
justice system. This may be set to change. A large number of EU criminal justice measures are to become enforceable and applicable law in the United Kingdom over the next
few years, starting in 2014.

The purpose of this chapter is twofold. First, it seeks to inform the reader of what
those measures are and how they may affect domestic law (Sections B and C). This
should allow practitioners to spot when a point of EU law may be engaged. Secondly, it
explains how EU law may be relied upon in criminal judicial reviews (Section C). Due to

constraints of space it does not provide a detailed exposition of more general underlying principles of EU law such as supremacy and direct effect.[1]

(2) Applicability of European Union Law to Domestic Criminal Proceedings

14-2 EU law is applicable to domestic criminal proceedings and more widely to public bodies involved in the criminal justice system. There are a plethora of European Framework Decisions, Directives and other measures pertaining to policing and criminal justice.
It is to be recalled that:

    i.   Framework Decisions refer to legislative acts of the EU which require Member States to achieve a particular result, without dictating the means of achieving that result. Framework Decisions are distinguished from Directives because Framework Decisions are not enforceable.

    ii.   Directives are legislative acts of the EU which require Member States to achieve a particular result, without dictating the means of achieving that result. Directives are distinguished from Framework Decisions because they are enforceable. Member States must pass domestic legislation to implement directives.

    iii.   Regulations are those legislative acts of the EU that are immediately enforceable as law in all Member States. Regulations can be relied upon directly by an individual without the need for any domestic legislation implementing the Regulation.

(i) 'Pre-Lisbon' Measures

14-3 More than 130 Council police and criminal justice measures were passed by the EU prior to the Treaty of Lisbon, 2009. These measures, primarily Framework Decisions, relate to:

    i.   the definitions of substantive crimes and minimum penalties for those crimes;
    ii.   criminal procedure rules;
    iii.   policing and shared cooperation measures; and
    iv.   measures for the mutual recognition of legal judgments.

A familiar example of a Framework Decision is Council Framework Decision 2002/584/JHA of 13 June 2002 on the European Arrest Warrant and the surrender procedures between Member States, which was implemented into domestic law by the Extradition Act 2003. Another commonplace example is Council Framework Decision 2008/675/JHA of 24 July 2008 on taking account of convictions in the course of new criminal proceedings, which was implemented by section 144 and Schedule 17 of the Coroners and Justice Act 2009.

---

[1] See above for discussion of EU law and grounds of review at 1-72.

        Kathryn Howarth

These 130 measures will remain in force until 1 December 2014, by which date they will become Regulations or Directives. Under the much-hyped Protocol 36, Article 10 to the Treaty on the Functioning of the European Union (TFEU), the Government had to decide whether or not the United Kingdom should continue to be bound by these measures, which were adopted before the Treaty of Lisbon entered into force, or whether it would exercise its right to opt out of all of them. That decision had to be made at the latest by 31 May 2014. If the Government do not opt out, then those measures that become Regulations will become directly enforceable in the United Kingdom, whilst those measures that become Directives, if they have not already been implemented, will need to be implemented though domestic legislation. The United Kingdom will become subject to the jurisdiction of the Court of Justice of the European Union (CJEU) and the powers of enforcement of the European Commission in relation to those Regulations and Directives. If the Government decides to exercise the opt-out, these measures will cease to apply to the United Kingdom as a matter of EU law. The United Kingdom may later rejoin the measures, but only subject to the conditions set out in Protocol 36. At the time of writing, the indication was that the Government would exercise its opt-out power.

14-4

(ii) 'Post-Lisbon' Measures

In addition to these 130-plus measures since the Lisbon Treaty 2009, the United Kingdom has opted into a number of Directives in relation to criminal justice and policing. These Directives are not subject to the potential 'opt-out' decision. The United Kingdom is and will continue to be subject to the jurisdiction of the CJEU and the European Commission in relation to these post-Lisbon measures. The United Kingdom must therefore implement these post-Lisbon Directives (set out below at 14-14) through domestic legislation according to the timeframes mandated by the EU.

14-5

Just like the pre-Lisbon Framework Decisions, these post-Lisbon Directives relate to:

i.   the definitions of substantive crimes and minimum penalties for those crimes;
ii. criminal procedure rules;
iii. policing and shared cooperation measures; and,
iv. measures for the mutual recognition of legal judgments.

These measures cover diverse issues, ranging from:

i.   The right to interpretation and translation in criminal proceedings (see below at 14-5).
ii. Combating sexual abuse, sexual exploitation of children and child pornography (see below at 14-14).
iii. Establishing minimum standards on the rights, support and protection of victims of crimes (see below at 14-16).

This chapter will provide an overview of both the pre-Lisbon Framework Decisions and other measures, and the post-Lisbon Directives concerning policing and criminal justice. Having provided an overview of these measures, the chapter will consider whether judicial review proceedings might be used to enforce EU law rights in the field of police and criminal justice measures at the domestic level.

B. Pre-Lisbon Criminal Justice and Policing Measures

(1) Introduction

14-6 Recommended reading in relation to the pre-Lisbon criminal justice system and policing measures includes:

    i.   A working paper by the Centre for European Legal Studies, 'Opting out of EU
Criminal law: What is actually involved?'.[2]

    ii.   The 13th Report of Session 2012–13 of the House of Lords European Union
Committee, *EU police and criminal justice measures: The UK's 2014 opt-out
decision.*[3]

    iii. A Justice publication, *EU Criminal Procedure: A general defence practitioner's
guide.*[4]

This chapter will provide a summary of these 130-plus measures. A categorisation similar to that set out in the CELS Working Paper will be adopted. The pre-Lisbon measures
can be divided into the following categories:

    i.   Measures concerning substantive criminal law.
    ii.   Measures concerning criminal procedure.
    iii. Measures relating to police cooperation.
    iv. Measures concerning mutual recognition.

(2) Measures Concerning Substantive Criminal Law

14-7 This category comprises of 17 instruments that require all Member States to ensure that
their domestic criminal law prohibits certain kinds of conduct and provides sufficient
penalties for the commission of those crimes. These measures include Framework
Decisions on:

    i.   Terrorism (Council Framework Decision 2002/475/JHA of 13 June 2002 on
combating terrorism).

    ii.   Drug dealing (Council Framework Decision 2004/757/JHA of 25 October 2004
laying down minimum provisions on the constituent elements of criminal acts
and penalties in the field of drug trafficking).

    iii. Cybercrime (Council Framework Decision 2005/222/JHA of 25 February 2005
on attacks against information systems).[5]

    iv. Bribery (Council Framework Decision 2003/568/JHA on combating corruption
in the private sector).

---

  [2] A Hinarejos, JR Spencer and S Peers, 'Opting out of EU Criminal law: What is actually involved?' CELS
Working Paper No 1, September 2012.
  [3] House of Lords European Union Committee, 13th Report of Session 2012–13, *EU police and criminal
justice measures: The UK's 2014 opt-out decision* (HL 2013, 159) (HL EU Committee Report).
  [4] J Blackstock, *EU Criminal Procedure: A general defence practitioner's guide* (London, Justice, 2012).
  [5] But note that this instrument is likely to be replaced by a new Directive, the proposal for which the
United Kingdom has opted into.

v.   Money laundering (Council Framework Decision 2001/500/JHA of 26 June 2001 on money laundering, the identification, tracing, freezing, seizing and confiscation of instrumentalities and the proceeds of crime (repealing Articles 1, 3, 5(1) and 8(2) of Joint Action 98/699/JHA)).

vi.   People-smuggling (Council Framework Decision 2002/946/JHA of 28 November 2002 on the strengthening of the penal framework to prevent the facilitation of unauthorised entry, transit and residence).

vii.   Frauds in relation to electronic payments (Council Framework Decision 2001/413/JHA of 28 May 2001 combating fraud and counterfeiting of non-cash means of payment).

viii.   Counterfeiting the euro and other currencies (Council Act of 26 July 1995 drawing up the Convention on the protection of the European Communities' financial interests—notably this Convention will be replaced by a new Directive 2014/62/EU on Protection of the euro and other currencies against counterfeiting by criminal law).

Most of the offences referred to in these instruments were already criminal in the United Kingdom at the time the EU instruments were adopted, and the United Kingdom already had penalties in place that were at least as severe as the penalties the EU measures required. The only exception was bribery, where English law was questionably compliant with EU law at the time the Framework Decision was adopted, but has been comprehensively reformed by the Bribery Act 2010.

(3) Measures Concerning Criminal Procedure

This category comprises of three instruments: 14-8

i.   The first is in relation to the standing of victims in criminal proceedings—the 2001 Council Framework Decision 2001/220/JHA of 15 March 2001 on the standing of victims in criminal proceedings. This Framework Decision is now replaced by Directive 2012/29 of 14 November 2012 on establishing minimum standards on the rights, support and protection of victims of crime.[6] The United Kingdom has already opted into this Directive.

ii.   The second is in relation to the status of previous convictions from another Member State in national criminal proceedings (2008 Council Framework Decision 2008/675/JHA of 24 July 2008 on taking account of convictions in the Member States of the European Union in the course of new criminal proceedings). Section 144 and Schedule 17 of the Coroners and Justice Act 2009 implemented this Framework Decision.

iii.   Thirdly, Article 54 of the Schengen Convention deals with the issue of prosecutions for offences which have previously been the subject of criminal proceedings in another Member State. Section 76(4)(c) of the Criminal Justice Act 2003

---

[6] The well-known Case C-105/03 *Pupino* [2006] QB 83, [2005] 3 WLR 1102 concerned an application of the Framework Decision to special measures in a criminal trial, specifically the availability of pre-trial recording for young complainants to give their evidence and its impact on Art 6.

permits retrials following the discovery of fresh evidence of guilt provided there is no contravention of Article 54 of the Schengen Convention.

(4) Measures Relating to Police Cooperation

14-9   These constitute the majority of measures adopted pre-Lisbon. These instruments concern police cooperation in relation to the exchange of information, such as i) the Schengen Information System (SIS) and the Prüm system of information exchange; ii) cross-border operations, including special intervention units and joint investigation teams; and iii) measures which created third 'pillar' bodies and agencies, in particular Europol, Eurojust and CEPOL (the European Police College).

(5) Measures Relating to Mutual Recognition

14-10   This category comprises of 11 instruments. Mutual recognition has been defined as a:

> principle whereby the decisions and rulings of the courts and other competent authorities of one Member State are accepted by the courts and competent authorities of the other Member States and enforced on the same terms as their own.

This can entail 'passive' mutual recognition—whereby a decision or ruling of a criminal court in one Member State must be given the same effect by the legal system of another Member State as that state would give to an equivalent decision or ruling of its own. Alternatively, this can entail 'active' mutual recognition—whereby a Member State must both accept the validity of a decision or ruling of a criminal court in another Member State, and also take positive steps to give effect to, or enforce, that decision or ruling.

These mutual recognition instruments include:

i.   The 2008 Council Framework Decision 2008/675/JHA of 24 July 2008 on taking account of convictions in the Member States of the European Union in the course of new criminal proceedings (see above 14-3 and 14-8).

ii.   Article 54 of the Schengen Convention, which deals with the related but distinct issue of prosecutions for offences which have previously been the subject of criminal proceedings in another Member State (see above 14-8).

iii.   The 1998 Convention providing for the mutual recognition of disqualifications from driving (Council Act of 17 June 1998 drawing up the Convention on Driving Disqualifications).

iv.   Council Framework Decision 2002/584/JHA of 13 June 2002 on the European Arrest Warrant and the surrender procedures between Member States.

v.   Council Framework Decision 2008/978/JHA of 18 December 2008 on the European Evidence Warrant for the purpose of obtaining objects, documents and data for use in proceedings in criminal matters (European Evidence Warrant).[7]

---

[7] Note that the European Evidence Warrant will be replaced by the proposed Directive creating a European Investigation Order (see below at 14-16).

vi. Council Framework Decision 2003/577/JHA of 22 July 2003 on the execution in the European Union of orders freezing property or evidence.[8]

vii. Council Framework Decision 2009/829/JHA of 23 October 2009 on the application, between Member States of the European Union, of the principle of mutual recognition to decisions of supervision measures as an alternative to provisional detention (referred to as the European Supervision Order).

Instruments relating to sentences imposed after trial and conviction include: **14-11**

i. An instrument in relation to the mutual recognition of fines (Council Framework Decision 2005/214/JHA of 24 February 2005 on the application of the principle of mutual recognition to financial penalties).

ii. An instrument in relation to the mutual recognition of confiscation orders (Council Framework Decision 2006/783/JHA of 6 October 2006 on the application of the principle of the mutual recognition to confiscation orders).

iii. An instrument in relation to the mutual recognition of probation orders and other non-custodial penalties (Council Framework Decision 2008/947/JHA of 27 November 2008 on the application of the principle of mutual recognition to judgments and probation decisions with a view to the supervision of probation measures and alternative sanctions).

iv. An instrument concerning the mutual recognition of prison sentences (Council Framework Decision 2008/909/JHA of 27 November 2008 on the application of the principle of mutual recognition to judgments in criminal matters imposing custodial sentences or measures involving deprivation of liberty for the purposes of their enforcement in the European Union).

Of these 130 measures, the vast majority have been implemented by the United **14-12** Kingdom. However, some 15 measures have not been implemented in full; some of these are considered defunct, whilst others will be superseded once new post-Lisbon Directives enter into force.

Those 15 measures are:

i. Council Framework Decision 2003/577/JHA of 22 July 2013 on the execution in the EU of orders freezing property or evidence (which will be partially superseded by the European Investigation Order).

ii. Council Framework Decision 2005/211/JHA of 24 February 2005 concerning the introduction of some new functions for the Schengen Information System, including in the fight against terrorism.

iii. Council Framework Decisions 2006/228/JHA of 9 March 2006, 2006/229/JHA of 9 March 2006 and 2006/631/JHA of 24 July 2006 fixing the date of application of certain provisions of Council Framework Decision 2005/211/JHA of 24 February 2005.

---

[8] Note that if and when the proposed Directive for a European Investigation Order is adopted, it will replace those parts of this Framework Decision which deal with the freezing of evidence (but not property), and the United Kingdom has opted into this proposed Directive (see below at 14-16).

iv.   Council Framework Decision 2006/783/JHA of 6 October 2006 on the application of the principle of mutual recognition to confiscation orders (the European Confiscation Order).

v.   Council Framework Decision 2008/615/JHA of 23 June 2008 on stepping up of cross-border cooperation, particularly in combating terrorism and cross-border crime.

vi.   Council Decision 2008/616/JHA of 8 June 2008 on its implementation (the Prüm Decisions).

vii.   Council Framework Decision 2008/978/JHA of 18 December 2008 on the European evidence warrant for the purpose of obtaining objects, documents and data for use in proceedings in criminal matters (the European Evidence Warrant is to be superseded by the European Investigation Order).

viii.   Council Framework Decision 2009/905/JHA of 9 December 2009 on accreditation of forensic service providers carrying out laboratory activities.

ix.   Council Framework Decision 2009/829/JHA of 11 November 2009 on the application between Member States of the EU of the principle of mutual recognition to decisions on supervision measures as an alternative to provisional detention (the European Supervision Order).

x.   Council Framework Decision 2008/947/JHA of 27 November 2008 on the application of the principle of mutual recognition to judgments and probation decisions with a view to the supervision of probation measures and alternative sanctions (the European Probation Order).

xi.   Council Framework Decision 2009/948/JHA of 30 November 2009 on prevention and settlement of conflicts of exercise of jurisdiction in criminal proceedings.

xii.   Council Framework Decision 2009/299/JHA of 27 March 2009 amending Council Framework Decisions 2002/584/JHA, 2005/514/JHA, 2006/783/JHA, 2008/909/JHA and 2008/947/JHA, thereby enhancing the procedural rights of persons and fostering the application of the principle of mutual recognition to decisions rendered in the absence of the person concerned at the trial (an amendment to the European Arrest Warrant Framework Decision).

xiii.   Agreement on Cooperation in Proceedings for Road Traffic Offences and the Enforcement of Financial Penalties Imposed in Respect Thereof (SCH/III (96)25rev18) (considered to be defunct).

If the Government do not exercise the 'opt-out', then the United Kingdom will have to implement any outstanding measures that are neither defunct nor superseded, such as the European Supervision Order, and they will be subject to the CJEU and the European Commission's powers of enforcement should they fail to do so.

C. Post-Lisbon Criminal Justice and Policing Measures

(1) Introduction

14-13   Since the Lisbon Treaty a number of police and criminal justice measures have been passed as Directives and Regulations. The United Kingdom has opted into the majority of these measures. A number of Directives are also at the drafting stage. The United Kingdom and the other Member States will have to decide whether or not to adopt these Directives in the future where it has not already made that commitment. For the purposes of this chapter, the post-Lisbon measures will be divided into the same categories as the pre-Lisbon measures:

i.   measures concerning substantive criminal law;
ii.   measures concerning criminal procedure;
iii. measures relating to police co-operation; and
iv.   measures concerning mutual recognition.

Recommended reading in relation to the post-Lisbon criminal justice and policing measures includes the CELS Working Paper and the HL European Union Committee Report (referred to above at 14-6).

(2) Measures Concerning Substantive Criminal Law

This category comprises of three measures which the United Kingdom has already **14-14** opted into and which replace pre-Lisbon Framework Decisions:

i.   A proposal in relation to cyber-crime (proposal for a Directive on attacks against information systems, which will repeal Framework Decision 2005/222/JH).
ii.   A Directive in relation to trafficking (Directive 2011/36/EU of 5 April 2011 on preventing and combatting trafficking in human beings and protecting victims, replacing Council Framework Decision 2002/629/JHA of 5 April 2011).
iii. A Directive concerning sexual abuse and sexual exploitation of children and child pornography (Directive 2011/92/EU of 13 December 2011 on combating the sexual abuse and sexual exploitation of children and child pornography, replacing Framework Decision 2004/68/JHA).

In addition there is a proposal for a Directive on the protection of the euro and other currencies against counterfeiting by criminal law, replacing Framework Decision 2000/383/JHA—at the time of writing the opt-out period is still running in relation to this proposed Directive.

(3) Measures Concerning Criminal Procedure

There are a group of new post-Lisbon measures which the United Kingdom has adopted, **14-15** including two Directives which guarantee certain minimum rights to suspects during a police investigation. First, there is a Directive on the right to interpretation and translation in criminal proceedings (Directive 2010/64/EU of 20 October 2010 on the right to interpretation and translation in the framework of criminal proceedings). Notably, reference was made to this Directive in the case of *R v Applied Language Solutions Ltd (now known as Capita Translation and Interpreting Ltd)*,[9] in which the Court of Appeal

---

[9] *R v Applied Language Solutions Ltd (now known as Capita Translation and Interpreting Ltd)* [2013] EWCA Crim 326.

allowed an appeal by Capita Translation following a wasted costs order made by the Crown Court. Secondly, there is a Directive on the right to information in criminal proceedings (Directive 2012/13/EU of 10 March 2010). The United Kingdom has also opted into Directive 2012/13/EU on the European Protection Order, which is intended to provide trans-border protection to victims of domestic violence.

14-16   There are also a group of measures that will repeal and replace, or amend, pre-Lisbon measures that the United Kingdom has already opted into, including the European Investigation Order,[10] which will replace the European Evidence Warrant (Framework Decision 2008/978/JHA), and apply instead of the corresponding provisions of the Schengen Convention, Council of Europe Convention and Protocols on mutual assistance, and EU Convention and Protocol on mutual assistance. As noted above, Directive 2012/29/EU, establishing minimum standards on the rights, support and protection of victims of crime, replaces Council Framework Decision 2001/220/JHA.

(4) Measures Relating to Police Cooperation

14-17   This category currently comprises of:

    i.   A Regulation that will enable the United Kingdom to partake in Schengen Information System (SIS II) (Regulation 542/2010/EU of 3 June 2010 amending Decision 2008/839/JHA on migration from the SIS to SIS II).

    ii.   A proposal in relation to Europol (a proposal for a Regulation on the European Union Agency for Law Enforcement Cooperation and Training (Europol)) repealing Framework Decisions 2009/371/JHA and 2005/681/JHA.

    iii.   A proposal for a Directive on the use of passenger name record data for the prevention, detection, investigation and presentation of terrorist offences and crime.

    iv.   A proposal for a Directive on the protection of individuals with regard to the processing of personal data by competent authorities for the purpose of prevention, investigation, detection and prosecution of criminal offences or the execution of criminal penalties, and the free movement of such data, which would replace Framework Decision 2008/977/JHA.

(5) Measures Concerning Mutual Recognition

14-18   The principal measure in this category is the European Investigation Order.[11] This Directive will replace the European Evidence Warrant (Framework Decision 2008/978/JHA), and will apply instead of the corresponding provisions of the Schengen Convention, Council of Europe Convention and Protocols on mutual assistance. The United Kingdom has opted into the European Investigation Order. The European

---

[10] Initiative of the Kingdom of Belgium, the Republic of Bulgaria, the Republic of Estonia, the Kingdom of Spain, the Republic of Austria, the Republic of Slovenia and the Kingdom of Sweden for a Directive regarding the European Investigation Order in criminal matters.

[11] ibid.

Kathryn Howarth

Investigation Order will enable judicial authorities in Member States to issue search warrants, and other types of orders for the collection of evidence, which are enforceable across borders.

(6) The European Charter of Fundamental Rights

Thus far, this chapter has focused upon substantive EU law measures in the area of polic-   **14-19**
ing and criminal justice. An important additional instrument that practitioners should be aware of is the European Charter of Fundamental Rights (the Charter). The Charter sets out 50 substantive rights, and as such it is more expansive than the ECHR. The rights set out in the Charter can be relied upon by an individual where a public body is act-ing within the scope of EU law, in other words purporting to implement a Framework Decision, Directive or to apply a Regulation. *R (NS) v Secretary of State for the Home Department*,[12] a decision of the CJEU Grand Chamber, made plain that Protocol 30 to the Lisbon Treaty does not provide the United Kingdom with an 'opt out' from the Charter.[13]

In the context of judicial review and criminal justice, a claimant sought to rely upon the Charter in the case of *R (Sandiford) v Secretary of State for the Foreign & Commonwealth Affairs*.[14] The case concerned a United Kingdom national who had been sentenced to death in Indonesia on charges of drug trafficking. She sought to rely upon the Charter to challenge a refusal of legal aid to fund her case in the Indonesian Supreme Court. The Administrative Court dismissed her claim, on the basis that EU law was not sufficiently engaged so as to enable her to rely upon the Charter. This decision was upheld by the Court of Appeal,[15] and at the time of writing judgment from the Supreme Court is pending. Another case in which the courts have refused to find that a situation falls within the scope of EU law for the purposes of Charter protection is the prisoner voting rights case in the Supreme Court—*Chester v Ministry of Justice/McGeoch v Lord President of the Council*.[16] These cases demonstrate that there is scope to rely upon the fundamental rights protection provided in the Charter, but only where a material con-nection to EU law can be established.

At the EU rather than the domestic level, claimants have met with some success in using the Charter to challenge the lawfulness of EU measures on the basis of its incompatibility with fundamental rights. Although a review of the case law in this area is beyond the scope of this chapter, the cases of *Kadi v Council and Commission* (known as '*Kadi I*')[17] and *Commission, Council, United Kingdom v Yassin Abdullah Kadi*

---

[12] Case C-411/10 *R (NS) v Secretary of State for the Home Department* [2013] QB 102, [2012] 3 WLR 1374.

[13] This was applied in *R (AB) v Secretary of State for the Home Department* [2013] EWHC 3453 (Admin) [13]–[14]. Mostyn J observed: 'it would seem that the much wider Charter of Rights is now part of our domestic law'. Ibid [14].

[14] *R (Sandiford) v Secretary of State for the Foreign & Commonwealth Affairs* [2013] EWHC 168 (Admin).

[15] *R (Sandiford) v Secretary of State for Foreign & Commonwealth Affairs* [2013] EWCA Civ 581.

[16] *Chester v Ministry of Justice/McGeoch v Lord President of the Council* [2013] UKSC 63, [2013] 3 WLR 1076.

[17] Joined Cases C-402/05P and C-415/05P *Kadi v Council and Commission* [2009] 1 AC 1225, [2009] 3 WLR 872.

(known as '*Kadi II*')[18] warrant mention (see also discussion above at 1-77). These cases concerned EU Regulations implementing a UN Security Council resolution which required Member States to freeze the funds and financial resources of persons or entities associated with Usama bin Laden, Al-Qaeda and the Taliban. The facts of the cases are rehearsed above at 1-77. In summary, in the first instance K was not provided with any reasons or evidence for his inclusion on the list (*Kadi I*), and in the second instance K was provided with limited reasons and evidence (*Kadi II*). In *Kadi II*, the CJEU re-affirmed its reasoning in *Kadi I*; and through a careful analysis of the scope of the material disclosed in relation to K ensured that the protection of his fundamental rights was effective.

Ultimately, the CJEU annulled EU Regulations in *Kadi I* and *Kadi II*. As explained above at 1-77, the CJEU held that it must ensure the review of the lawfulness of all EU law acts, including those designed to implement UN Security Council resolutions, and that obligations imposed by an international agreement cannot prejudice the principle that EU measures must respect fundamental rights, including the rights of the defence and the rights to effective judicial protection.

The *Kadi* litigation demonstrates the central importance placed by the CJEU on fundamental rights as a touchstone for review, something which must inevitably inform the approach to be taken by our domestic courts when considering the Charter (see discussion above at 1-72). The *Kadi* litigation also demonstrates the possibility (albeit limited—see below) of challenging EU law measures directly before the CJEU.

D. Using European Union Law in Criminal Judicial Reviews

(1) Remedies in Judicial Review Proceedings for Breaches of European Union Law

14-20   The role of judicial review and the Administrative Court has been described as 'critical' to the effective enforcement of EU law. This is primarily because very few cases involving points of EU law will get as far as the CJEU. The first reason is because of the limited mandate of the CJEU. The mandate of the CJEU is limited to ensuring that 'in the interpretation and application of the Treaties, the law is observed'. The CJEU has jurisdiction:

  i.   to hear infringement actions against Member States by the Commission or other Member States for non-compliance with EU law;
  ii.   to hear preliminary references—providing interpretative judgments at the request of national courts and tribunals in order to help them decide a case with a EU law dimension; and
  iii. to review the legality of acts by the EU institutions (for example *Kadi I* and *Kadi II* (above)).

---

[18] Joined Cases C-584/10 P, C-593/10 P and C-595/10 P *Commission, Council, United Kingdom v Yassin Abdullah Kadi.*

Kathryn Howarth

It is important to understand that the CJEU does not deliver final rulings on cases before national courts. It merely interprets the applicable EU law, then remits the case to the Member State. Secondly, the CJEU has narrow rules on standing, which make it almost impossible for a member of the public to challenge an act of an EU institution. Thirdly, the decision whether to make a preliminary reference can only be made by the national court or tribunal, and not the litigant—this contrasts with the procedure before the ECtHR, via which complaints can be made directly by an individual once domestic remedies have been exhausted.

Given the limited role of the CJEU, it falls primarily to the domestic legal systems of the Member States to enforce EU law. Much of the enforcement of EU law is achieved through steps taken by various national public law administrative bodies. Therefore it is primarily by way of judicial review that any action or inaction by those public law administrative bodies is subjected to judicial supervision. Judicial review is therefore a procedure by which claimants can seek the effective enforcement of their rights under EU law.

In areas of law other than criminal justice and policing the Administrative Court is   **14-21** familiar with issues of EU law. For example, in planning and environment law, public procurement law, and immigration and asylum law, there have been numerous challenges by claimants against public law bodies implementing EU law including by way of judicial review. In these areas of law, legislation has for some time been passed by way of Regulations and Directives under the old three 'pillar' system. By contrast up until the Lisbon Treaty in 2009 most policing and criminal justice measures were not passed by way of Regulations or Directives but rather by unenforceable Framework Decisions.

(2) Potential Changes from 2014

Pre-Lisbon criminal justice and policing measures will become Regulations and   **14-22** Directives on 1 December 2014. Post-Lisbon criminal justice and policing measures already take the form of Regulations and Directives, although many of these measures do not require implementation by Member States until 2014 or 2015. The possibility for challenge by means of judicial review has not therefore been ripe in the area of criminal justice and policing, as compared to planning and environmental law, public procurement law and immigration and asylum law, in which the EU has long legislated by way of Regulations and Directives. However, once the pre-Lisbon measures become Regulations and Directives, and/or the time periods for the implementation of the various post-Lisbon Directives pass, the door for appropriate judicial review claims will open in the area of criminal justice and policing.

(3) Using European Union Law in Criminal Judicial Review

It is important for criminal law and public law practitioners to be aware of when a   **14-23** point concerning EU law arises in the context of criminal proceedings. This chapter has provided an overview of the many and varied EU measures in the area of criminal justice and policing with the aim of helping practitioners to spot when and where EU law is in operation.

In the criminal justice sphere, most EU legislation will now be passed in the form of Directives. These will usually be implemented through domestic legislation. When faced with domestic law purporting to implement Directives, reference should be made to the original text of the Directive. Consideration should then be given as to:

i.   whether the domestic legislation achieves what the Directive requires;
ii. whether there are any discrepancies, significant or otherwise, between the requirements of the Directive and the domestic legislation purporting to implement it; and
iii. cases in which the public body, perhaps a court, a prison, the police or probation services, are implementing the legislation in accordance with the intended result of the Directive.

In circumstances where a Regulation refers to criminal justice and policing measures, such Regulations can be relied upon directly by individuals. Reference should be made to the original text of the Regulation, and consideration given as to whether the public law body is properly applying the Regulation.

Where a point of EU law arises, criminal and public law practitioners will then have to consider the most appropriate forum to raise that point. This could be in the magistrates' court, the Crown Court, the Court of Appeal or by way of judicial review proceedings in the Administrative Court. In terms of proceedings in the Administrative Court a claimant might seek to challenge:

i.   a failure by the public law body to implement, or give effect to the result/s required by a Directive;
ii. a failure by a public law body to give effect to the requirements of a Regulation;
iii. a 'collateral challenge' to EU law by challenging the validity of the secondary EU legislation itself; or
iv. a failure to protect fundamental rights, including rights protected by the Charter provided the public law body is implementing EU law.

At the time of writing, the Administrative Court has seldom had reason to analyse EU measures in the area of police and criminal justice beyond extradition law. It is submitted that the door will open for appropriate challenges in the area of policing and criminal justice in the future.

Kathryn Howarth

Part IV
Public Funding and Costs

15

Legal Aid

DAVID BALL

A. General Principles

(1) Introduction

In summary, there are several important points to note, especially for criminal solicitors, **15-1** who may be new to the civil legal aid regime:

  i. Judicial reviews arising from a criminal matter fall within scope of the 2010 Standard Contract that governs criminal cases (this includes applications for habeas corpus and proceedings under the Human Rights Act (HRA) 1998), which means solicitors who do not hold a civil contract can obtain legal aid for judicial review applications of this kind (for a full discussion, see below at 15-8 to 15-11).

ii.   Legal aid is available for judicial reviews not arising out of criminal matters, but an applicant would need to hold a civil contract.

iii. Legal aid for judicial review operates under the rules for civil legal aid (see below at 15-12 for a fuller exposition)—a key difference for criminal practitioners is that there are several types of legal aid available that correspond to different stages of a case.

Section A of this chapter sets out the statutory framework including the incoming wave of reforms to legal aid. Section B explains the criteria, forms, timescales and other practical steps for obtaining the different types of civil legal aid. Section C deals with appeals.

(2) Statutory Framework

15-2   The framework for the provision of legal aid was significantly amended by the Legal Aid, Sentencing and Punishment of Offenders Act (LASPO) 2012. For the avoidance of doubt, this chapter, as with the rest of this work, states the law as it was on 1 May 2014.[1]

(i) The Old Framework

15-3   Before LASPO 2012 legal aid was governed by the Access to Justice Act 1999. This set up two separate funds for the provision of legal aid: the Community Legal Service (for civil legal aid), and the Criminal Defence Service (for criminal legal aid). The Legal Services Commission (LSC) administered the distribution of these funds. Under sections 8 and 9 of the Access to Justice Act 1999 the LSC published the Funding Code. This set out the criteria according to which a decision would be made as to whether to fund a funded service. Funding Code Guidance in turn supplemented the Funding Code.

(ii) The New Framework

15-4   Section 38 of LASPO 2012 abolished the LSC.[2] The Legal Aid Agency (LAA) now administers legal aid. This is an executive agency of the Ministry of Justice. The Director of Legal Aid Casework is the Chief Executive of the LAA. This is to be compared with the LSC, which was previously an arm's-length body.[3]

---

[1] See www.justice.gov.uk/legal-aid/newslatest-updates/legal-aid-reform.
[2] Instead, by s 1, LASPO 2012 provided that the Lord Chancellor 'must secure that legal aid is made available' in accordance with Pt 1 of the Act. S 4 then provides that the Lord Chancellor must designate a civil servant as the Director of Legal Aid Casework, and must provide the Director with appropriate assistance.
[3] V Lang and S Pugh (eds), *Legal Aid Handbook 2013/14* (London, LAG, 2013) 17. As it is put in the explanatory notes to LASPO 2012, this means that decisions on legal aid in individual cases will ultimately be taken by a statutory office holder: a civil servant designated by the Lord Chancellor as the Director of Legal Aid Casework. The Lord Chancellor will have no power to direct or issue guidance to the Director in relation to individual cases.

The Funding Code that previously existed under the Access to Justice Act 1999 has been abolished. It has been replaced by:

i.   Civil Legal Aid (Procedure) Regulations 2012 (SI 2012/3098);
ii.   Civil Legal Aid (Merits Criteria) Regulations 2013 (SI 2013/104); and
iii. Criminal Legal Aid (General) Regulations 2013 (as amended) (SI 2013/09).[4]

In turn, the Funding Code Guidance has been abolished. It has been replaced by the Lord Chancellor's Guidance.[5] There are currently four items of Lord Chancellor's Guidance:[6]

i.   Lord Chancellor's Guidance on Civil Legal Aid;
ii.   Lord Chancellor's Guidance Exceptional Funding;
iii. Lord Chancellor's Guidance on Exceptional Funding (Non-Inquests); and
iv. Lord Chancellor's Guidance on Exceptional Funding (Inquests).

(iii) Ongoing Reforms

On 1 November 2013 a number of changes were introduced further to the 'Legal Aid Transformation' change programme. For example, on 1 November 2013 a maximum disposable income cap of £37,500 was introduced into criminal legal aid.[7] From 2 December 2013 the controversial 30 per cent fee cut for litigators and advocates was introduced for all criminal Very High Cost Case work, except for those exempted by transitional provisions.[8] It is beyond the confines of this chapter to deal in full with the various changes to rates and requirements that have happened and are pending following the introduction of LASPO 2012.   **15-5**

On 22 April 2014 a further raft of reforms were introduced. For present purposes the most significant of these was as follows:

(iv) Payment and Permission

The Civil Legal Aid (Remuneration) (Amendment) (No 3) Regulations 2014 (SI 2014/607) took effect on 22 April 2014. They introduced a new section 5A to the Civil Legal Aid (Remuneration) Regulations 2013. This new section 5A provides that if you   **15-6**

---

[4] There are a host of statutory instruments governing the regulation of the LASPO 2012 regime, including: Civil Legal Aid (Costs) Regulations 2013 (SI 2013/611); Civil Legal Aid (Remuneration) Regulations 2013 (as amended) (SI 2013/422); Civil Legal Aid (Statutory Charge) Regulations 2013 (SI 2013/503); Criminal Legal Aid (Financial Resources) (Amendment) Regulations 2013 (SI 2013/2791); Criminal Legal Aid (Contribution Orders) Regulations 2013 (as amended) (SI 2013/483); Criminal Legal Aid (Remuneration) (Amendment) Regulations 2013 (as amended) (SI 2013/2803).

[5] www.justice.gov.uk/legal-aid/funding/funding-guidance.

[6] See also: 'Legal Aid Agency: Guidance for reporting Controlled Work & Controlled Work matters', issued 18 October 2013, www.justice.gov.uk/downloads/legal-aid/funding-code/guidance-reporting-controlled-work-matters.pdf. See also: 'Legal Aid Agency: Costs Assessment Guidance 2013: for use with the 2013 Standard Civil Contract', issued 30 April 2013, www.justice.gov.uk/downloads/legal-aid/funding-code/costs-assessment-guidance-2013-standard-contract.pdf.

[7] The Criminal Legal Aid (Financial Resources) (Amendment) Regulations 2013 (SI 2013/2791). Some aspects come into force on 2 December 2013 and others on 27 January 2014.

[8] The Criminal Legal Aid (Remuneration) (Amendment) Regulations 2013 (SI 2013/2803).

have issued an application for judicial review proceedings then the Lord Chancellor 'must not pay' you for these civil legal services unless either the court gives you permission, or the court neither gives or refuses permission but the Lord Chancellor considers it reasonable having regard to certain prescribed factors:

5A(1) Where an application for judicial review is issued, the Lord Chancellor must not pay remuneration for civil legal services consisting of making that application unless either the court—
  (a)   gives permission to bring judicial review proceedings; or
  (b)   considers that it is reasonable to pay remuneration in the circumstances of the case, taking into account, in particular—
     (i)   the reason why the provider did not obtain a costs order or costs agreement in favour of the legally aided person;
     (ii)   the extent to which, and the reason why, the legally aided person obtained the outcome sought in the proceedings; and
     (iii) the strength of the application for permission at the time it was filed, based on the law and on the facts which the provider knew or ought to have known at that time.

The effect of this is that if permission is refused then a provider will not be able to recover from the LAA. If there is a Consent Order before there is a decision on permission then the Lord Chancellor will look very closely at why the claimant was not able to obtain any costs agreement. The Regulations as they currently stand are silent on the position where work is done after the issue of a legal representation certificate but the matter settles prior to issue. Equally, the Regulations relate to 'an application for judicial review'. They do not deal with applications for interim relief made under Part 25 of the Civil Procedure Rules. It is reported in Hansard that the Government has given a commitment to fund interim applications in all circumstances.[9]

The procedure is to fill in a pro-forma document setting out the factors under section 5A(1) that apply in your case and explaining why you consider it reasonable for the Lord Chancellor to remunerate the work.[10]

(iv) Residence Test

15-7   It should be noted the controversial residence test is also due to be implemented on 22 August 2014. The Regulations (the Legal Aid, Sentencing and Punishment of Offenders Act 2012 (Amendment of Schedule 1) Order 2014) and Guidance are still only in draft. It should be noted the controversial residence test was also due to be implemented on 22 August 2014. The Regulations (the Legal Aid, Sentencing and Punishment of Offenders Act 2012 (Amendment of Schedule 1) Order 2014) and Guidance are still only in draft. Regard should be had to the case of *R (Public Law Project) v Secretary of State for Justice* considered after the law cut-off date for this edition in which the proposed amendment was found to be unlawful.

---

[9] Column 527, Public Bill Committee, Tuesday 1 April 2014.
[10] The current pro forma can be found on the LAA website at: http://www.justice.gov.uk/downloads/forms/legal-aid/civil-forms/judicial-review-discretion-pro-forma-completion-guidance.pdf.
When LAA Online is introduced and it is all done electronically then such an application for an exercise of discretion will be reported through the LAA's Client and Cost Management System (see 15-18 below).

For judicial review matters the residence test applies in part. It only does not apply where services are provided in relation to a judicial review in respect of the lawfulness of detention (or various other immigration related matters not relevant to criminal judicial reviews).[11] For all other judicial reviews the residence test will apply. This is because it will be recalled that associated civil work arising out of a matter within the Crime Category is subject to the civil legal aid regulations.[12]

In summary, to satisfy the residence test a client must on the date of application:

— Be lawfully resident in the United Kingdom (UK), Channel Islands, Isle of Man or a British overseas territory (BOT); and
— Have been, at any time in the past, lawfully resident in the UK, Channel Islands, Isle of Man or a BOT for a period of 12 consecutive months and have not been absent for more than a total of 30 days in that 12 month period.

This test generally does not apply if the:

— Client is a child less than 12 months old;
— Client is an asylum seeker;
— Client is a recent successful asylum seeker;
— Client is a recent resettled refugee; or
— Client is a serving member of Her Majesty's (HM) United Kingdom Armed forces or their immediate family.

It is beyond the confines of this Chapter, which states the law as at 1 May 2014 to set out in any further detail the requirements to be met to satisfy the residence test, whilst both the Regulations and the Guidance are still in draft form.

(3) Contract

In order to provide any legal aid work, it is necessary for a provider to have a con-   **15-8**
tract with the LAA. There are two Standard Contracts in existence: the 2010 Standard Contract and the 2013 Standard Contract.

The 2010 Standard Contract governs criminal cases, while the 2013 Standard Contract applies to Family, Immigration and Asylum, and Housing and Debt. The 2013 Standard Contract governs all other civil areas that remain in scope. There are three main sections to each contract:

i.   the standard terms setting out the contract between the firm and the LAA;
ii. the schedule setting out the type of work the firm can do;
iii. the specification setting out the rules of conduct for individual cases.

---

[11] These immigration related judicial reviews which are exempted from the residence requirement are where services are provided in relation to proceedings before the Special Immigration Appeals Commission, judicial review of a negative decision in relation to an asylum application where there is no right of appeal to the First-tier Tribunal against the decision, or judicial review of certification under sections 94 or 96 of the Nationality, Immigration and Asylum Act 2002 (certificate preventing or restricting appeal of immigration decision).
[12] Standard Crime Contract 2010 Specification Part B, para 13.2.

(4) Definition of Criminal Proceedings

15-9   Section 14 of LASPO 2012 defines criminal proceedings as follows:

> 14 Criminal proceedings
>
> In this Part 'criminal proceedings' means—
>
> (a)   proceedings before a court for dealing with an individual accused of an offence,
>
> (b)   proceedings before a court for dealing with an individual convicted of an offence, including proceedings in respect of a sentence or order,
>
> (c)   proceedings for dealing with an individual under the Extradition Act 2003,
>
> (d)   proceedings for binding an individual over to keep the peace or to be of good behaviour under section 115 of the Magistrates' Courts Act 1980 and for dealing with an individual who fails to comply with an order under that section,
>
> (e)   proceedings on an appeal brought by an individual under section 44A of the Criminal Appeal Act 1968 (appeal in case of death of appellant),
>
> (f)   proceedings on a reference under section 36 of the Criminal Justice Act 1972 on a point of law following the acquittal of an individual on indictment,
>
> (g)   proceedings for contempt committed, or alleged to have been committed, by an individual in the face of a court, and
>
> (h)   such other proceedings, before any court, tribunal or other person, as may be prescribed.

Regulation 9 of the Criminal Legal Aid (General) Regulations 2013 (as amended) goes on to prescribe a number of other matters as criminal proceedings.[13]

(i) Judicial Reviews Arising from Criminal Matters

15-10   Importantly, for the purposes of legal aid, judicial review arising from a criminal matter constitutes 'associated civil work'. Standard Crime Contract 2010 Specification Part A para 1.13 sets out as follows:

> 'Associated Civil Work' means Legal Help and civil Legal Representation in actual or proposed proceedings:
>
> i.   for judicial review (including proceedings under the Human Rights Act 1998) or proceedings for habeas corpus, provided those proceedings arise from a Matter or Case within the Crime Category; or
>
> ii.   proceedings under the Proceeds of Crime Act 2002;

A person with a criminal contract therefore has authority to undertake units of work concerning:

> actual or proposed proceedings concerning public law challenges to the acts, omissions or decisions of public bodies by way of judicial review (including under the Human Rights Act 1998).[14]

---

[13] See *King's Lynn and West Norfolk Council v Bunning and Legal Aid Agency* [2013] EWHC 3390: committal proceedings for breach of an order at court (Queen's Bench Division) are criminal proceedings. This is further to the Criminal Legal Aid (General) Regulations 2013, 9(v): 'proceedings that involve the determination of a criminal charge for the purpose of Article 6(1) of the European Convention on Human Rights'.

[14] Standard Crime Contract 2010 Specification Part B, para 13.2.

There is no limit to the number of such matters starts. The work should be carried out in accordance with the Standard Civil Contract and the relevant civil legal aid regulations. The relevant Standard Civil Contract will be the one in force on the date the associated civil work is commenced.

Associated Civil Work arising out of a matter within the Crime Category is therefore covered by criminal legal aid but subject to the civil legal aid regulations.[15] For the avoidance of doubt, the Crime Category definitions are: **15-11**

Crime

7. Representation in all proceedings defined as criminal proceedings under section 14 of the Legal Aid, Sentencing Punishment of Offenders Act 2012 and regulations made under that section.

8. All criminal Advice and Assistance as defined in section 13 and 15 of the Legal Aid, Sentencing Punishment of Offenders Act 2012 and regulations made under those sections.

9. All appeals in relation to criminal proceedings including applications for case stated arising out of criminal proceedings.

10. The Crime Category also includes Advice and Assistance and Representation in the following areas (as defined in the 2010 Standard Crime Contract):
    (a) Prison Law;
    (b) Associated Civil Work.

11. The undertaking of civil proceedings is excluded from the Crime Category unless falling within the definitions given above. Proceedings brought under the Environmental Protection Act 1990 for a statutory nuisance where the client is the complainant are excluded from the Crime Category as are proceedings under the Animal Welfare Act 2006 for the destruction of animals.[16]

To put this in very broad terms, where the defendant is the magistrates' court or the CPS, this will almost inevitably be a judicial review arising from a crime category. As above, such a matter would be funded as criminal legal aid subject to the relevant civil legal aid regulations. If the defendant is the police, the prison service, the Legal Aid Agency, the Criminal Cases Review Commission, Criminal Injuries Compensation Authority, the Independent Police Complaints Commission, or a coroner, then it will depend whether the initial matter was started within the Crime Category. In many instances this may be satisfied, but each case will turn on its own facts. The fundamental difference is that if the judicial review arises from a criminal matter (ie something in the Crime Category), a civil contract is not needed. If it does not arise from a criminal matter then a civil contract is needed. However, if the earlier matter was conducted on civil legal aid, then a case holder should have a civil contract anyway.

---

[15] ibid paras B 13.2.
[16] www.justice.gov.uk/downloads/legal-aid/civil-contracts/category-definitions-2010.pdf.

B. Types of Legal Aid

(1) Definitions

15-12 Section 1(2) of LASPO 2012 sets out that there are two types of legal aid. There are 'civil legal services' which are 'civil legal aid', and 'criminal legal aid'. As above, judicial review arising out of criminal proceedings constitutes associated civil work.

Civil legal services are then broken down into three categories:

    i.   Controlled Work;
    ii. Licensed Work;
    iii. Special Case Work.

Controlled work is defined by regulation 21 of the Civil Legal Aid (Procedure) Regulations 2012 (Part 3). It is made up of:

    i.   Legal Help;
    ii. Help with family mediation;
    iii. Help at court;
    iv. Family help (lower); or
    v.   Legal representation for proceedings in various tribunals.

For present purposes the most relevant category of Controlled Work is Legal Help.

Licensed Work is defined by regulation 29(2) of the Civil Legal Aid (Procedure) Regulations 2012 (Part 4). It is made up of:

    i.   Family help (higher); or
    ii. Legal representation that is not Controlled Work or Special Case Work.

The effect of this is that Legal Representation is technically known as a form of Licensed Work.

15-13 Special Case Work is dealt with in Part 6 of the Civil Legal Aid (Procedure) Regulations 2012. As the name suggests, it is for a small minority of cases deemed special. It applies where for example the Director of Legal Aid Casework has reasonable grounds to believe that the actual or likely costs of the case exceed £25,000.

Advisors should also bear in mind exceptional funding. This is governed by section 10 of LASPO 2012, and is designed to provide potential funding to cases which are out of scope of legal aid (that is they are not listed in Part 1 of Schedule 1 of LASPO 2012). As matters within the Crime Category and any judicial review arising from a matter within the Crime Category are in scope, it shall not be considered further here.[17]

---

[17] See above at 9-8, n 26, and *Gudanaviciene (and others) v Director of Legal Aid Casework and the Lord Chancellor* [2014] EWHC 1840 (Admin)—(judgment handed down after the law cut off date for the purposes of this edition).

David Ball

(2) Legal Help

It is beyond the scope of this chapter to provide a comprehensive account of every single   **15-14**
step necessary in the legal aid process to ensure full compliance with a LAA audit. What
follows is a succinct overview of the key steps.[18]

Legal Help is available to provide advice and assistance for a specific matter. It covers
all work up to the issue of proceedings and advocacy. It is to cover correspondence, general advice and any letter before action. It can also cover reasonable costs for completing
the funding forms.

There are two significant hurdles in the provision of Legal Help: the means test and
the merits test.

(i) The Means Test

As regards the means test, it is imperative that a client's means are assessed at the outset.   **15-15**
Satisfactory evidence must be obtained in support 'as soon as practicable'. This 'as soon
as practicable requirement' and the exceptions contained in paragraphs 3.24–3.25 of the
2013 Standard Civil Contract Specification are narrowly construed by the LAA. Every
effort should be made to obtain satisfactory evidence at the outset, to avoid the file
being 'nil assessed', and the serious consequences that can otherwise flow from this. The
Civil Legal Aid (Financial Resources and Payment for Services) Regulations 2013 (as
amended) (SI 2013/480) set out the thresholds for capital, gross income and disposable
benefit. They are amended regularly. Reference should be made to the civil eligibility
calculator to determine a client's eligibility to legal aid.[19]

(ii) The Merits Test

As regards the merits test, this sets out that Legal Help can only be provided where   **15-16**
'there is sufficient benefit to the client, having regard to the circumstances of the matter, including the circumstances of the individual, to justify the cost of the provision of
legal help'.[20] As the Lord Chancellor's Guidance suggests, this sufficient benefit test is:
'primarily a test of whether a reasonable private paying individual of moderate means
would pay for the legal advice and assistance'.[21]

(iii) Other Criteria

Further matters that will need to be considered, over and above the means and merits   **15-17**
test, include whether the client has received previous advice. The client will have to
certify on the Legal Help form that they have not previously received advice on the
same matter. If they have done so in the last six months, then the advisor must explain

---

[18] See *Legal Aid Handbook 2013/14* (n 3) for more detailed guidance.
[19] Http://civil-eligibility-calculator.justice.gov.uk/.
[20] The Civil Legal Aid (Merits Criteria) Regulations 2013, reg 32(b).
[21] Lord Chancellor's Guidance on Civil Legal Aid, para 4.2.13.

and justify why the case has been taken on. Regard must also be had to other sources of funding.[22] An advisor should always check with a potential client whether they have legal expense insurance or are a member of a trade union that might cover the legal costs of the proposed matter.

(iv) Forms

15-18 The relevant form that needs to be completed is a CW1. A signed copy should be kept on file. It will ultimately need to be reported through the application within LAA Online (this is the Contracted Work and Administration application, or CWA). This is the portal through which providers report information regarding their contracted work and manage all their LAA Online users.[23]

(v) Fees and Disbursements

15-19 Legal Help provides for a standard fee, currently set at £259. It is possible to apply for a matter to be considered an exceptional case outside the standard fee regime. Such cases are now known as 'escape fee cases'. These are instead paid at hourly rates. A provider must apply to the LAA to have their case considered as an escape fee case.[24]

Disbursements can be claimed in addition to the fixed fee. In order to do this the disbursement must meet the requirements set out in the contract, namely:

    i.   It is in the best interests of the Client to do so;

    ii. It is reasonable for you to incur the disbursement for the purpose of providing Controlled Work to the Client;

    iii. The amount of the disbursement is reasonable; and,

    iv. Incurring the disbursement is not prohibited.[25]

Further to paragraph 3.59 of the Standard Civil Contract 2013, counsel's fees under Legal Help do not count as a disbursement. The only exception is if the case escapes from the standard fee regime. In this case counsel's fees are treated as a disbursement.

(vi) Cases Where the Merits are Unclear

15-20 Therefore, there are three potential options available if an advisor is unclear as to whether there is sufficient merit to send a Letter Before Action under the Pre-Action Protocol (see above at 2-9 and Annex 1).

---

[22] Civil Legal Aid (Merits Criteria) Regulations 2013, reg 32.

[23] See section N: Legal Aid Agency: Guidance for reporting Controlled Work & Controlled Work matters, issued 18 October 2013, www.justice.gov.uk/downloads/legal-aid/funding-code/guidance-reporting-controlled-work-matters.pdf.

[24] EC-CLAIM 1; www.justice.gov.uk/downloads/forms/legal-aid/civil-forms/ec-claim1-civil-version-5-april-2013.pdf. See also Standard Contract Specification 2013, para 4.11–4.17. The current threshold for applying to be considered an escape fee case is £777 for public law actions (£717 for actions against the police). See the Civil Legal Aid (Remuneration) Regulations 2013.

[25] Standard Contract Specification 2013, para 4.21.

i.   the advisor could obtain a short advice on the merits from counsel which would come out of the £259 fixed amount;
ii. the advisor could seek to obtain an advice from counsel which counsel could not recover for under the legal aid regime; or
iii. the advisor could consider obtaining a formal advice from counsel through Investigative Representation. This will be considered next.

(3) Legal Representation

Legal Representation is the provision of legal services to someone who is contemplating issuing proceedings (or is already a party or wishes to be joined to proceedings).[26] It can be provided in one of two ways:

i.   As Investigative Representation; or
ii. As Full Representation.

(i) Investigative Representation: Criteria

Investigative Representation is a form of Legal Representation which is limited to investigating the strength of some contemplated proceedings. The criteria for a grant of Investigative Representation are set out in regulation 40 of the Civil Legal Aid (Merits Criteria) Regulations 2013 (SI 2013/104). The standard criteria for determinations of Legal Representation must be met. These are that:[27]

(a) The individual does not have access to other potential sources of funding;
(b) The case is unsuitable for a conditional fee agreement;
(c) There is no person other than the individual, including a person who might benefit from the proceedings, who can reasonably be expected to bring the proceedings;
(d) The individual has exhausted all reasonable alternatives to bringing proceedings;
(e) There is a need for representation in all the circumstances of the case including—
   i.   the nature and complexity of the issues;
   ii. the existence of other proceedings; and
   iii. the interests of other parties to the proceedings; and
(f) The proceedings are not likely to be allocated to the small claims track.

In addition to these standard criteria, an advisor will need to show that:[28]

(a) The prospects of success of the case are unclear and substantial investigative work is required before those prospects can be determined;
(b) The Director has reasonable grounds for believing that, once the investigative work to be carried out under investigative representation is completed, the case will satisfy the criteria for full representation and, in particular, will meet the cost benefit criteria in regulation 42 and the prospects of success criterion in regulation 43; and

15-21

15-22

15-23

---

[26] It is a form of Licensed Work (see 15-12 above). It is defined by r 9(2) of the Civil Legal Aid (Procedure) Regulations 2012 (SI 2012/3098).
[27] Civil Legal Aid (Merits Criteria) Regulations 2013 (SI 2013/104), r 39.
[28] ibid, r 40.

(c) Subject to paragraph (2) [re multi-party actions], if the individual's claim is primarily a claim for damages or other sum of money in which the likely damages do not exceed £5,000, the case must be of significant wider public interest.

15-24 Investigative Representation may therefore be appropriate where there is particular concern about a limitation period having expired, or where the prospects of success are genuinely unclear. In such circumstances it may well be appropriate for an advice from counsel to be obtained. The Lord Chancellor's Guidance on Civil Legal Aid sets out that:

> investigative representation may only be granted where substantial investigative work is required before prospects can be determined. In deciding whether substantial investigative work is required, it is appropriate to consider disbursements (including for this purpose any counsel's fees) separately from profit costs. For these purposes substantial investigative work will be where:
>
> i) the solicitor will reasonably need to carry out at least six hours of fee earner investigative work; or,
> ii) disbursements together with any counsel's fees would cost £400 or more excluding VAT.[29]

It should also be noted that in relation to Investigative Representation for a judicial review, an applicant will need to show that the specific criteria for public law claims are satisfied (see regulation 53 below: a decision is susceptible to challenge and there is no alternative remedy). Importantly, in addition, under regulation 54 such an applicant will need to show one of two things: either i) that they have notified the proposed defendant of the potential challenge (giving a reasonable time to respond); or ii) that doing so would be impracticable. It may well be that where the merits are unclear, an applicant can show that it would be unreasonable to threaten proceedings through a Letter Before Action under the Pre-Action Protocol (or equivalent, see above at 2-9 and Annex 1) because it is not clear that such an application for judicial review could ever be issued.

(ii) Investigative Representation: Forms

15-25 Investigative Representation is obtained by completing a Form CIV APP 1 and submitting it to the LAA. It will need to be accompanied by the appropriate evidence of means (for example, a MEANS 1 for an applicant not receiving income support; MEANS 1A for self-employed applicants etc). It is imperative that the form is completed correctly, with the appropriate supporting evidence of means. A particularly important section is the Statement of Case (on page 10). This is the opportunity to set out in detail the cause of action and justification that the merits criteria are met. It is often advisable to provide direct reference to the cost benefit and prospects of success criteria to assist the Legal Aid Agency Caseworker.[30] It is also generally a case of the more information the better, including any advices or attendance notes on merit, and setting out any background that may have been already detailed in any earlier correspondence.

---

[29] Lord Chancellor's Guidance on Civil Legal Aid, para 6.11.
[30] Civil Legal Aid (Merits Criteria) Regulations 2013 (SI 2013/104), rr 42 and 43, respectively.

(iii) Investigative Representation: Timescales

The Ministry of Justice website sets out that the timescales the Legal Aid Agency will aim   **15-26**
to work to when processing an application for civil legal aid are to decide 85 per cent of
applications in 20 working days (four weeks).[31]
    Once Investigative Representation has been granted, and the work has been carried
out, if the conclusion is that there is merit, then it will be necessary to apply to amend
to Full Representation.[32]

(iv) Full Representation

As with Legal Help, there are in essence two requirements for being granted Legal   **15-27**
Representation (whether this is Investigative Representation or Full Representation).
First, an applicant must meet the means test. Secondly, they meet the merits test.

(v) Full Representation: the Means and Merits Tests

As regards the means test, the same principles apply as with Legal Help and Controlled   **15-28**
Work.
    As regards the merits test, regulation 41 sets out that the following criteria need to be
established for a grant of Full Representation:

   i.   the standard criteria (regulation 39);
   ii.   the cost benefit test (regulation 42);
   iii.   the prospects of success test (regulation 43);
   iv.   a test for multi-party actions primarily for damages (regulation 44).

In addition to the requirements set out in regulation 41 there is:

   v.   a test specific to public law claims (regulation 53).

    First, the standard criteria are as set out above (at 15-22). Full Representation will only   **15-29**
be granted where the standard criteria contained in regulation 39 of the Civil Legal Aid
(Merits Criteria) Regulations 2013 (SI 2013/104) are met. These are in essence that there
are no other alternative sources of funding, all reasonable alternatives have been exhausted,
and representation is necessary having regard to the complexity of the issues etc.
    Secondly, there is the cost benefit test. This is set out in regulation 42 of the Civil
Legal Aid (Merits Criteria) Regulations 2013 (SI 2013/104). If the case is primarily a
claim for damages and is not of significant wider public interest, then the damages must
exceed the costs in various ratios, depending on the merits of the case. In the majority
of judicial reviews, for example of decisions of the magistrates' courts, this is unlikely
to apply. Such judicial reviews are unlikely to include a claim for damages. However,
if the claim is not primarily a claim for damages, and also is not a case of significant
wider public interest (as may be the case in many judicial reviews of magistrates' court
decisions), further criteria apply. As with Legal Help, the Director must be satisfied

---

[31] www.justice.gov.uk/legal-aid/financial-statements-bacs-dates/civil-payment-dates.
[32] CIV APP 8 form.

that the reasonable private paying test would be met. If there is significant wider public interest, then the only question is whether the likely benefits to the individual and others justify the likely costs, having regard to the merits and all the circumstances of the case. This is the proportionality test.[33]

15-30   Thirdly, there is the prospects of success test. This is set out in regulation 5 of the Civil Legal Aid (Merits Criteria) Regulations 2013 (SI 2013/104). The prospects of success test refers to the chances of a successful outcome at trial. A successful outcome is itself defined as 'the outcome a reasonable individual would intend to achieve in the proceedings in all the circumstances of the case'.[34] Therefore in terms of a judicial review it is not the prospect of permission being granted, but of the relief being sought being granted, which is the critical issue. The prospects are categorised as follows:[35]

'very good'   = 80% or more chance of success.
'good'   = 60% or more chance, but less than an 80% chance;
'moderate'   = 50% or more chance, but less than a 60% chance;
'borderline'   = not 'unclear' but that it is not possible because of disputed law, fact or expert evidence, to decide that the chance of obtaining a successful outcome is 50% or more; or to classify the prospects as poor;
'poor'   = unlikely to obtain a successful outcome;
'unclear'   = there are identifiable investigations which could be carried out, after which it should be possible for the Director to make a reliable estimate of the prospects of success.

The relevant threshold will depend on the nature of the claim. A claim needs to be moderate or above in order to pass the prospects of success test.[36]

15-31   Fourthly, there is a test for multi-party actions primarily for damages. This will not be considered further here, on the basis it is unlikely to be of much relevance to the majority of judicial reviews arising in the criminal context.

Fifthly, public law claims (defined in regulation 2 as including claims for judicial review and habeas corpus) must meet the criteria set out in regulation 53. In addition to the standard criteria, the applicant needs to satisfy the Director that:

(a)   the act, omission or other matter complained of in the proposed proceedings appears to be susceptible to challenge; and

(b)   there are no alternative proceedings before a court or tribunal which are available to challenge the act, omission or other matter, except where the Director considers that such proceedings would not be effective in providing the remedy that the individual requires.[37]

Once all of the criteria have been met, the merits test should be satisfied.

---

[33] Civil Legal Aid (Merits Criteria) Regulations 2013 (SI 2013/104), r 8.
[34] ibid, r 4(4).
[35] ibid, r 5.
[36] ibid, r 43(a). Previously a public law claim assessed with borderline merits could pass the merits test if it was of significant public interest or overwhelming importance to the individual. By virtue of regulation 2(4) of the Civil Legal Aid (Merits Criteria) (Amendment) Regulations 2014 (SI 2014/131), which came into force on 27 January 2014, this no longer applies. Further to regulation 56(3) of the Civil Legal Aid (Merits Criteria) Regulations 2013 (SI 2013/104) in order to be granted legal aid you must show that the prospects of successfully obtaining the substantive order sought in the proceedings are very good, good or moderate.
[37] Reg 53(b) inserted by the Civil Legal Aid (Merits Criteria) (Amendment) Regulations 2013.

(vi) Full Representation: Forms

Applications should be made on a form CIV APP 1 accompanied by the necessary **15-32** means form and evidence of means (e.g. a MEANS 1 for an applicant not receiving income support, MEANS 1A for self-employed applicants etc).

As with an application for Investigative Representation it is vital that the form is completed correctly, with the appropriate supporting evidence of means. It is advisable in the Statement of Case to fully detail the cause of action and how the merits criteria are met, with direct reference to the requirements of the Civil Legal Aid (Merits Criteria) Regulations 2013 (SI 2013/104) and the Lord Chancellor's Guidance on Civil Legal Aid, as appropriate. Again, the Ministry of Justice website sets out that the LAA will aim to process 85 per cent of applications for civil legal aid in 20 working days (four weeks).[38]

(4) Legal Representation Certificate

If an application for Legal Representation is successful, a funding certificate will be **15-33** issued. This will be subject to limitations.[39] First, it is generally granted up to a particular step in proceedings, such as all steps up to a decision on permission. Secondly, it is generally granted with a costs limitation, often £2,250. This figure covers profit costs, disbursements and counsel's fees, but is exclusive of VAT. It is obviously important that work is only carried out in accordance with the limitations of the certificate. If it is necessary to apply for an amendment to the certificate, then this should be done on a Form CIV APP 8. The same form is used if applying for prior authority.[40]

(5) Emergency Funding

As set out above, the published timescales that the LAA aim to work to when processing **15-34** an application for civil legal aid are to decide 85 per cent of applications in 20 working days (four weeks).[41] In many cases a delay of four weeks (or often longer) can be seriously prejudicial.

(i) Criteria

Regulation 46 of the Legal Aid (Merits Criteria) Regulations 2013 (as amended) (SI **15-35** 2013/104) sets out the criteria to be met for legal representation provided as emergency representation. Such representation is also governed by regulations 50–53 of the Civil Legal Aid (Procedure) Regulations 2012 (SI 2012/3098). The criteria are straightforward. First, the Director must be satisfied that the merits criteria which apply to that application are met. Secondly the Director must be satisfied that it is 'in the interests of justice to provide emergency representation'.

---

[38] www.justice.gov.uk/legal-aid/financial-statements-bacs-dates/civil-payment-dates.
[39] Civil Legal Aid (Procedure) Regulations 2012 (SI 2012/3098), r 35.
[40] See Standard Civil Contract 2013, para 5.11.
[41] www.justice.gov.uk/legal-aid/financial-statements-bacs-dates/civil-payment-dates.

The Lord Chancellor's Guidance on the interests of justice test is important. At paragraphs 7.28–7.29 it sets out that the test 'essentially involves consideration to two questions':

(i)   Whether the services sought need to need to [sic] be provided before there would be time for the Director to make a determination in relation to a substantive application (ie non-emergency) in order for those services to be effective; and

(ii) The seriousness of the consequences of those services not being made available on an emergency basis, having regard to the fact that emergency representation is provided before the applicant has been determined as qualifying for services under financial regulations; for example whether:

   (a)   There will be a risk to the life, liberty or physical safety of the applicant or his or her family or the roof over their heads; or

   (b)   The delay will cause a significant risk of miscarriage of justice, or unreasonable hardship to the applicant, or irretrievable problems in handling the case;

and in either case ((a) and (b)) there are no other appropriate options available to deal with the risk.

7.29. It may, however, be considered not to be appropriate, pursuant to regulation 11(6) of the merits regulations [general and specific merits criteria], to provide emergency representation where it is the conduct of the applicant that has created the alleged urgency, and in particular where it would have been reasonable to have made an earlier substantive application.

It follows from this that in any application for emergency funding it is strongly advisable to set out:

i.   whether a non-emergency application would be too late, ie why the services would not be effective if they were provided on a non-emergency basis;

ii.   the 'serious consequences' if those services were not provided on an emergency basis, eg risk to liberty or serious risk of miscarriage of justice;

iii. why there are no other options to deal with the above risk other than through an emergency application;

iv.   if possible, explaining why it is not the conduct of the applicant which has given rise to the urgency, or why it would not have been reasonable to have made an earlier substantive application. It is often helpful to include a brief chronology setting out how it has arisen that the application is being made on an emergency basis.

(ii) Forms

15-36   The form for making an application for emergency representation is Form CIV APP 6. However, under regulation 51(1) of the Civil Legal Aid (Procedure) Regulations 2012 (SI 2012/3098) an application can be made by such method (including by fax, telephone or email) as the Director has agreed to accept, given the urgency of the particular circumstances. (This of course is on the assumption one is able to speak to an appropriate representative of the Legal Aid Agency to reach such agreement in advance). In the absence of any alternative method, the standard procedure for emergency applications is set out in Legal Aid Agency: Applications for emergency funding in judicial review cases—processes and procedures from 1 April 2013.[42] This sets out that where a supplier seeks a grant of an emergency certificate and requests to undertake work in less than 48 hours, they should apply via an emailed application CLS APP 6 to the following email address (for non-immigration work): emergency-apps@legalaid.gsi.gov.uk.

C. Appeals

(1) Challenging a Refusal to Grant a Certificate

The procedure for an appeal against a refusal to grant a Legal Representation certifi-   **15-37** cate is set out in regulation 44 of the Civil Legal Aid (Procedure) Regulations 2012 (SI 2012/3098). In summary a person can apply for a review by the Director of Legal Aid Casework and then on to an independent adjudicator. There is a need to apply for the review within 14 days of receipt of the notice of the decision subject to challenge. It should be noted that there is a Director's review of a refusal on financial grounds, but there is not an appeal to an independent adjudicator on such a point. Instead a fresh application can be made if there is a change of circumstances.[43] (See above in section B of Chapter 9 for judicial reviews of decisions of the LAA.)

---

[42] www.justice.gov.uk/downloads/legal-aid/funding-code/judicial-review-emergency-funding-process.pdf.

[43] It should be noted that under Practice Direction 54C it is open to the Legal Services Commission (the 2014 White Book and Ministry of Justice website have not yet amended references to the Legal Services Commission to the Legal Aid Agency) can refer to the High Court a question that arises on review of a decision about an individual's financial eligibility for a representation order in criminal proceedings under the Criminal Defence Service (Financial Eligibility) Regulations 2006. The question will be decided by the High Court on the papers unless the court directs otherwise. See Chapter 2, n 5.

16

Costs

JAMES PACKER

Section	Para

A. General Principles and Powers

(1) General Principles and Powers

16-1   To an even greater extent than in substantive proceedings, courts will decide questions of costs in public law cases in the interests of justice. No practice, no matter how hallowed, will be allowed to harden into a rule that can prevent the court from making an order on that basis.[1] Through a series of reports, lectures, rule changes and guideline judgments, the senior judiciary have asserted that the 'interests of justice' are broader than securing a just result in an individual case. The 'wider public interest of ensuring that other litigants can obtain justice efficiently and proportionately' is now seen to require heavy sanctions, especially in costs, for breaches of court rules and directions.[2]

Costs in judicial review proceedings in the Administrative Court[3] are governed by CPR 44, which underlines that the court has discretion as to whether, to what extent, when and on what basis costs are payable by one party to another.[4] Costs are always ultimately discretionary, but the court is guided by rules, practice and principle.[5]

16-2   Save as to the basis of assessment, which will be on the standard basis unless the indemnity basis is explicitly ordered (and cannot be on any other basis) by CPR 44.3(4) the court can make any order requiring a party to pay the costs of the judicial review proceedings. This applies not only to claimants and defendants, but also to interested parties, and even in rare cases a non-party.[6] Regrettably, with minor exceptions in criminal matters considered below, the court cannot order that a party's legal costs are to be paid out of central funds.[7]

Specific power is given to make costs orders under CPR 44.2(6) that a party must pay:

(a)   A proportion of another party's costs.
(b)   A stated amount in respect of another party's costs.
(c)   Costs from or until a certain date only.
(d)   Costs incurred before proceedings have begun.
(e)   Costs relating to particular steps taken in the proceedings.

---

[1] *Bolton MDC v Secretary of State for the Environment* [1995] 1 WLR 1176, 1178: where costs are concerned, 'the fundamental rule is that there are no rules'.

[2] Jackson LJ was tasked with conducting a review into the costs of civil litigation. His report has led to series of changes to the CPR called the 'Jackson reforms'. The quote is from the 18th 'Implementation lecture' by the Master of the Rolls, in March 2013, giving guidance to the judiciary on the intentions and philosophy of the rule changes: www.judiciary.gov.uk/Resources/JCO/Documents/Speeches/mr-speech-judicial-college-lecture-2013.pdf, cited in *Mitchell MP v News Group Newspapers* [2013] EWCA Civ 1537 [38].

[3] Some judicial reviews are conducted in the Upper Tribunal; see Section E below.

[4] CPR 44.2(1)(a)–(c) and CPR 44.3(1) respectively.

[5] 'The discretion … must be exercised in accordance with the rules of court and established principles', *McDonald v Horn* [1995] 1 ALL ER 961, 969 (Hoffmann LJ). See also *M v LB Croydon* [2012] EWCA Civ 595 [44]. Note that the Criminal Justice and Courts Bill 2014 was laid before Parliament on 5 February 2014. Cll 51–56 propose changes to the rules on provision of financial information, costs in respect of interveners and protective costs orders.

[6] For a discussion of the relevant principles in relation to non-parties, see *Ewing v Deputy Prime Minister* [2005] EWCA Civ 1583, [2006] 1 WLR 1260 [28]–[31], and see CPR 46.2.

[7] One example of many such laments is in *R (Touche) v Inner London North Coroner* [2001] EWCA Civ 383, [2001] QB 1206 [55]: 'Parliament [has] chosen not to heed repeated pleas by the court that there be power in this sort of case to order costs out of public funds.'

(f)   Costs relating only to a distinct part of the proceedings.
(g)   Interest on costs from or until a certain date, including a date before judgment.

B. Interim and Special Costs Orders

(1) Interim Costs Orders

A court can award costs to date, or in respect of a sub-issue to a party (though a later order   **16-3**
in the same issue supersedes the earlier). 'Costs in any event' and 'Costs of and occasioned
by' are examples of orders whereby a party will receive their costs in respect of that issue—
for example, the costs thrown away by an unjustifiably late submission of new material necessitating the adjournment of a hearing at the eleventh hour—regardless of the
eventual outcome. 'Costs in the application' is a similar order—for example, a potentially
meritorious application to rely upon new material which is resisted, leading to an interim
hearing: the costs of the sub-issue will be awarded to the party successful on that issue.

More usually, the court at an interim stage will defer the question until final determination, either through leaving the whole question open through a 'costs reserved' order,
or indicating that they should be awarded to the party that succeeds in the main action
through orders such as, 'costs in the case' and 'costs in the cause'.

'No order as to costs' means that neither party will recover costs for the interim issue.
Silence as to costs is to the same effect, save that where the court makes any order or direction sought by a party on an application without notice, if the order is silent as to costs it
will be deemed to include an order for the applicant's costs in the case—CPR 44(10)(2)(c).

Representatives should note CPR 44.8:

Where—
(a)   the court makes a costs order against a legally represented party; and
(b)   the party is not present when the order is made, the party's legal representative must
notify that party in writing of the costs order no later than 7 days after the legal representative receives notice of the order.

CPR 44 PD 10 further specifies that this should include the reasons why the order was made.

(2) Protective Costs Orders

(i) The Basis for Making Protective Costs Orders (PCOs)

A PCO is an order that limits or removes a party's liability to pay the costs of another   **16-4**
party. The basis for their award was set out in *R (Corner House Research) v Trade and
Industry Secretary*: 'It is for the court, in its discretion, to decide whether it is fair and
just to make the order in the light of the [governing principles]'.[8]

---

[8]   *R (Corner House Research) v Trade and Industry Secretary* [2005] EWCA Civ 192, [2005] 1 WLR 2600
[74] (Lord Phillips MR).

These principles are that:

    i)   the issues raised are of general public importance;

    ii)   the public interest requires that those issues should be resolved;

    iii) the applicant has no private interest in the outcome of the case;

    iv) having regard to the financial resources of the applicant and the respondent(s) and to the amount of costs that are likely to be involved it is fair and just to make the order; and

    v)   if the order is not made the applicant will probably discontinue the proceedings and will be acting reasonably in so doing…

       … If those acting for the applicant are doing so pro bono this will be likely to enhance the merits of the application for a PCO.[9]

Later authorities make clear that the governing principles are to be approached 'flexibly'.[10] The paragraphs in the *Corner House* case are 'not … to be read as statutory provisions, nor to be read in an over-restrictive way'.[11] Whether an issue is of 'general public importance' is a matter for the judge in the case to decide, and the phrase does not denote that it affects the public nationally.[12]

The 'elusive' requirement that the applicant should have no private interest has been 'diluted', and a private interest now amounts to no more than an element of the 'weight and importance' of which the Court considers when deciding the application.[13] The utility of this test has been doubted and its ambit is now uncertain.[14]

(ii) The Application for a Protective Costs Order

16-5   A party may apply for a PCO at any time (though in normal circumstances it should be sought on the face of the initiating Claim Form). *Corner House* held that the applicant (i) should have a modest exposure to costs should the application be resisted and refused, and (ii) should then have a further modest exposure to the defendant's costs should the claimant then request a hearing of the application. The principles are designed to ensure that claimants are not tempted to make inappropriate applications due to the advantages if they are granted, and defendants should not be able to defeat the purpose of PCOs by putting the applicant at the risk of substantial costs if the application is defeated. If the defendant challenges a PCO granted following a paper application, he must seek an oral hearing in the High Court and show a compelling reason.

The applicant should set out his anticipated future costs, though these should be 'modest'. His costs are liable to be capped in total, by item, by reduced rates, or a combination of these with reference to both how clearly the case merits a PCO and the likely

---

[9] ibid, [74].

[10] *Morgan & Baker v Hinton Organics (Wessex) Ltd* [2009] EWCA Civ 107, [47] (per Carnwath LJ).

[11] *R (Compton) v Wiltshire PCT* [2008] EWCA Civ 749, [2009] 1 WLR 1436 [23] (Waller LJ), approved by Sir Anthony Clarke MR in *R (Buglife) v Thurrock Gateway Development Corp and another* [2008] EWCA Civ 1209 [19], and followed in *Morgan & Baker v Hinton Organics (Wessex) Ltd* [33]. See Carnwath LJ's drawing together of the threads at [47]—applied in *R (Garner) v Elmbridge BC* [2010] EWCA Civ 1006 [22].

[12] *R (Bullmore) v West Hertfordshire Hospitals NHS Trust* [2007] EWHC 1350 (Admin).

[13] *Wilkinson v Kitzinger* [2006] 2 FLR 397.

[14] See *Morgan & Baker v Hinton Organics (Wessex) Ltd* (n 10) [37]–[39].

costs, his remaining liability and the resources of the parties.[15] There is a recent overview of the application of these principles in *R (The Plantagenet Alliance) v Secretary of State for Justice and Anor*.[16]

(3) Wasted Costs Orders

In an exceptional case, where the actions of one party's representatives cannot be justi- **16-6** fied and have caused loss, the court may direct that they bear those costs themselves. The court will be 'slow' to initiate a wasted costs enquiry of its own motion; and a party seeking the order should normally do so only at the conclusion of the case, to the trial judge. The judge will normally first consider whether the representative should be invited to 'show cause' why the order should not be made (see now CPR 46 PD 5.6–5.9), and it is unlikely to be appropriate to do so where a lengthy enquiry would result. The order should only be made 'in a clear case'.[17]

The court will only make an order on this basis if there is no possible reasonable explanation where the client's refusal to waive privilege prevents a representative explaining himself.[18]

C. The Award of Costs

(1) General Principles

The general rule is that the unsuccessful party will be ordered to pay the costs of the **16-7** successful party (CPR 44.2(2)(a)). The court is specifically enjoined to consider under CPR 44.2(4):

(a) the conduct of all the parties;
(b) whether a party has succeeded on part of its case, even if that party has not been wholly successful; and

any admissible offer to settle made by a party which is drawn to the Court's attention, and which is not an offer to which costs consequences under Part 36 apply. Liability for costs is usually decided at the time judgment is handed down, though it may be deferred to a later oral hearing or after written submissions. Particularly in the latter case, lengthy delays can ensue between the substantive and costs decisions; new facts or case law can dramatically alter the complexion of a case in the interim. The court does not close its eyes to later developments: 'it is the date at which the application for costs is determined that is the relevant date for assessment'.[19]

---

[15] ibid, [87].
[16] *R (The Plantagenet Alliance) v Secretary of State for Justice and Anor* [2013] EWHC 3164 (Admin), [58]–[67].
[17] *Ridehalgh v Horsefield* [1994] EWCA Civ 40, [1994] 3 All ER 848.
[18] For a helpful illustration of the breadth of this principle and its operation in practice, see *Sharma & Anor v Hunters* [2011] EWHC 2546 (COP).
[19] *Bahta & Ors v Secretary of State for the Home Department* [2011] EWCA Civ 895 [58].

(2) Pre-Action Costs

16-8   Pre-action costs cannot be recovered (other than by agreement) unless proceedings are commenced.[20] A claimant should be aware that the sometimes extensive costs of preparing a claim (where, for example medical reports need to be commissioned, or an extensive file considered before a detailed pre-action letter can be composed) are unlikely ever to be recovered if the demands in that letter are acceded to.

A claimant is nonetheless well advised to carefully prepare and draft a detailed letter before action. Failure to do so can sound later in costs as the clarity with which an issue is raised pre-action, and the degree to which the claim is based on the same issues, can be decisive as to the award of both relief and costs.

Should a claim be issued, a claimant's pre-action costs are in principle recoverable from the defendant.[21] The very purpose of the Pre-Action Protocol is to narrow the issues between the parties before a claim is commenced. It follows that, absent exceptional circumstances, a claimant will face no penalty in costs for abandoning some of the issues raised pre-action and bringing a claim on a more limited basis.[22]

(3) Permission Costs

16-9   Special considerations apply to the costs of applying for and resisting permission; these are best dealt with by the permission judge.[23] If awarding costs against the claimant, the judge should consider whether preparation costs are to be included in addition to acknowledgement costs.[24] Generally a party that goes further than settling mere summary grounds at the permission stage should do so at its own expense.[25] Whether or not Administrative Court judges follow this rule in practice is debatable,[26] and an experienced judge has commented that:

> nowadays it often seems to be the case—and it is understandable why it should be—that the Acknowledgement of Service effectively will stand as the grounds of defence.[27]

If the permission judge makes an undifferentiated order for costs in a defendant's favour, the order has to be regarded as including any reasonably incurred preparation costs, but not the costs of preparing for or attending an oral permission hearing.[28] Those costs should only be awarded to a defendant in an exceptional case.[29]

---

[20] *Callery v Gray* 2001 [EWCA] Civ 1117 [54]. [2012] EWHC 764 (QB)
[21] *Citation plc v Ellis Whittam Ltd.*
[22] *McGlinn v Waltham Contractors Ltd & Ors* [2005] EWHC 1419 (TCC) [10]–[18].
[23] *Roudham & Anor v Breckland Council* [2008] EWCA Civ 714 [29] (Buxton LJ).
[24] *Davey v Aylesbury Vale DC* [2007] EWCA Civ 1166 [2008] 1 WLR 878.
[25] See *Ewing v Office of the Deputy Prime Minister* [2005] EWCA Civ 1583 [2005] All ER (D) 315 [53] (per Brooke LJ).
[26] *Roudham* (n 23) [26]–[27] gives insight into the divergence of views between the Administrative Court and the Court of Appeal on this point.
[27] *R (Ministry of Defence) v HM Coroner for Wiltshire and Swindon* [2005] EWHC 889 (Admin) [44] (Collins J).
[28] *Davey* (n 32). See also *R (Raphael) v Highbury Corner Magistrates' Court* [2011] EWCA Civ 462 [61].
[29] See *R (Mount Cook Land Ltd) v Westminster City Council* [2003] EWCA Civ 1346, [2004] 2 Costs LR 211 [76]. *R (Payne) v Caerphilly County Borough Council* [2004] EWCA Civ 433 and *Ewing* (n 32) provide examples of the principle in action.

James Packer

Where the court makes an order granting permission to apply for judicial review and its order does not mention costs, it will be deemed to include an order for applicant's costs in the case (CPR 44.10(2)(b)).

(4) Where a Claim Settles by Agreement Before a Final Hearing

It is not unusual in judicial review matters for the parties to agree that there is no need   **16-10**
for the matter to continue to a final hearing. This could be because, for example, a change in case law or information coming to light shows that the claim is hopeless or irresistible, or the grant of interim relief or intervening events render the claim academic.

The parties should attempt to agree where costs lie, but can seek a determination of that sole issue if necessary. This is usually achieved through a consent order that disposes of the claim on the basis that the issue of costs is to be settled by written submissions.

It is desirable that the parties first outline their positions for seeking and resisting costs in correspondence, to allow submissions to be short and to the point. Minimal further papers should be adduced. In an ordinary case the letter before action, the claim form and acknowledgement with their grounds, and the costs correspondence should suffice.[30] The Administrative Court is in the process of transition and determination of written submissions will increasingly be done by masters rather than judges of the High Court.

The issue will be decided on the basis of the guidelines set down in *Boxall v Waltham Forest LBC* and *Bahta & Ors v Secretary of State for the Home Department*:

> The overriding objective is to do justice between the parties without incurring unnecessary court time and consequently additional cost; [where it is not clear which party would have succeeded] [h]ow far the court will be prepared to look into the previously unresolved substantive issues will depend on the circumstances of the particular case, not least the amount of costs at stake and the conduct of the parties, ... the fall back is to make no order as to costs.[31]

The court, however, 'must not be tempted too readily to adopt the fall back position of no order for costs'.[32]

The introduction of the Pre-Action Protocol has altered the focus of the search for the successful party:

> What is not acceptable is a state of mind in which the issues are not addressed by a defendant once an adequately formulated letter of claim is received by the defendant. In the absence of an adequate response, a claimant is entitled to proceed to institute proceedings. If the claimant then obtains the relief sought, or substantially similar relief, the claimant can expect to be awarded costs against the defendant.[33]

---

[30] Master Gidden, Administrative Court Users Group meeting, June 2013. Formal guidance has now been given: www.justice.gov.uk/downloads/courts/administrative-court/aco-costs-guidance-dec-13.pdf.
[31] *Boxall v Waltham Forest LBC* (2001) 4 CCL Rep 258 [22].
[32] *R (Scott) v London Borough of Hackney* [2009] EWCA Civ 217 [51].
[33] *Bahta* (n 19) [59].

It is the grant of relief, rather than the prospect of success had the claim continued, that identifies the successful party.[34]

It was also said in *Bahta* that while:

> [t]here may be cases in which relief may be granted for reasons entirely unconnected with the claim made ... A clear explanation is required, and can expect to be analysed, so that [the court can be satisfied that it] is not used as a device for avoiding an order for costs that ought to be made.[35]

M v LB Croydon divides cases into three categories: where the claimant has been 'wholly successful',[36] where there has been partial success, and where the settlement does not reflect the basis of claim. The court held that in cases of 'partial success':

> the court will normally determine questions such as how reasonable the claimant was in pursuing the unsuccessful claim, how important it was compared with the successful claim, and how much the costs were increased as a result of the claimant pursuing the unsuccessful claim. ... In many such cases, the court will be able to form a view as to the appropriate costs order based on such issues; in other cases, it will be much more difficult. I would accept the argument that, where the parties have settled the claimant's substantive claims on the basis that he succeeds in part, but only in part, there is often much to be said for concluding that there is no order for costs. ... However, where there is not a clear winner, so much would depend on the particular facts. In some such cases, it may help to consider who would have won if the matter had proceeded to trial, as, if it is tolerably clear, it may, for instance support or undermine the contention that one of the two claims was stronger than the other.[37]

Where the parties have settled on a basis other than the basis of claim:

> the court is often unable to gauge whether there is a successful party in any respect, and, if so, who it is. In such cases, therefore, there is an even more powerful argument that the default position should be no order for costs. However, in some such cases, it may well be sensible to look at the underlying claims and inquire whether it was tolerably clear who would have won if the matter had not settled. If it is, then that may well strongly support the contention that the party who would have won did better out of the settlement, and therefore did win.[38]

(5) Discontinuance

16-11   CPR 38.6(1) deals with discontinuance and provides that, unless the court orders otherwise, a claimant who discontinues is liable for the defendant's costs to the date of the discontinuance. The claimant bears the burden of justifying a departure from the presumption.

---

[34] Though cf *Naureen & Anor (R oao) v Salford City Council* [2012] EWCA Civ 1795. Interim relief may not suffice.

[35] *Bahta* (n 19) [63].

[36] *M v LB Croydon* (n 5) [61]. It is submitted that later cases establish that this should be read as 'substantially successful' and, in particular, that a claimant is not to be regarded as only 'partially successful' on the basis that minor or peripheral elements of his claim were abandoned or unsuccessful.

[37] ibid, [62].

[38] ibid [63].

(6) Partial Success

Difficult issues can arise when each side can claim a measure of success. The court can   **16-12**
offset an award of costs to a party on one issue against the costs incurred on the other,
or make a reduced global award to reflect the partial success of a party, but '[t]here is
no automatic rule requiring reduction of a successful party's costs if he loses on one
or more issues'.[39] There are competing priorities: an issue-based approach is generally
fairer to the individual litigant and discourages a 'no stone unturned' approach, but it
has also been considered to risk satellite litigation.

Taken as a whole, the authorities suggest that the more substantial and the more
severable the issue, the less reasonably it was pursued and the more important its
defeat (especially if it amounted to allegations of criminal conduct), the more likely
it is that it will be taken account of in costs.[40] *R (Mousa) and Others v Secretary of
State for Defence*[41] is a recent example of an issue-based order, notwithstanding the
understandable preference shown in the rules for percentage reductions shown at CPR
44.2(7). *HE v Secretary of State for the Home Department*[42] provides a counter example,
and demonstrates the importance of identifying success on the main issue in the claim.

(7) Challenges to the Decisions of Judicial Bodies (Criminal Courts and Coroners' Courts)

On the authority of *Davies v HM Deputy Coroner for Birmingham (No 2)*,[43] the 'general   **16-13**
rule' at CPR 44.2(2)(a) is insufficient to justify an order that such a defendant should
pay the costs of the successful claimant; it is only if there is a good reason that costs
should be awarded.[44]

Where the court wishes to show 'strong disapproval' of the proceedings below, where
there has been 'perversity' or a 'flagrant instance' of 'improper behaviour' or 'disregard for the
elementary principles which every court ought to obey', an award of costs may be justified.

Likewise, where the position of the defendant has increased costs unnecessarily, such
as when the inferior court or tribunal unreasonably declined or neglected to sign a consent order disposing of the proceedings, or by attending court when a simple statement
of their position was all that was required, a costs order may be made. Further, where
the defendant resists:

> actively by way of argument in such a way that it made itself an active party to the litigation, as
> if it was such a party ... in the normal course of things costs would follow the event.[45]

There is no special protection for an interested party who defends a claim in these cases
(as the CPS frequently do in claims by criminal defendants against the magistrates'
courts and Crown Court).

---

[39] *HLB Kidsons (a firm) v Lloyd's Underwriters and Ors* [2007] EWHC 2699 (Comm) [11].
[40] See ibid [10]–[16] for a discussion and application of the principles.
[41] *R (Mousa) and Others v Secretary of State for Defence* [2013] EWHC 2941(Admin) [52]–[54].
[42] *HE v Secretary of state for the Home Department* [2013] EWCA Civ 1846.
[43] *Davies v HM Deputy Coroner for Birmingham (No 2)* [2004] EWCA Civ 207.
[44] The conclusions are at ibid [47]–[49].
[45] ibid [47].

It should be noted that where the defendant does take an active role in unsuccessfully resisting the claim, then the additional presence of active interested parties, plainly vulnerable in costs, is not a shield against an award of costs against the defendant. In *R (Pounder) v HM Coroner for the North and South Districts of Durham and Darlington*,[46] in which the coroner was an active defendant, two of the three interested parties made submissions at the inquest that materially influenced the coroner to (wrongly) decline to give a ruling on the legality of their actions before directing the jury. Both then unsuccessfully defended the subsequent judicial review of the coroner on the bases that (i) that issue had been immaterial to the outcome, and (ii) that on the facts, a further inquest was unnecessary in any event. Further, their conduct as uncovered in the inquest showed the practice of one was systematically unlawful, whilst there had been a 'gross failure' by the other to discharge their responsibility of oversight. By contrast the court had 'some sympathy ... [for] the Coroner'.[47] Nonetheless, the coroner was ordered to meet 40 per cent of the costs of the claim,[48] and it was also stated that:

> the fact that the Coroner was ordered to pay a contribution towards the Claimant's costs says nothing about his conduct beyond the fact that he took an adversarial role in proceedings.[49]

Otherwise if the civil defendant takes no part in the claim, or adopts a studiously neutral position, such as restricting itself to setting out the facts or by assisting the court on the implications of the case or on points of law that the defendant is more familiar with, then a successful claimant will neither generally recover his costs from them, nor be liable for their costs.

Other 'important considerations', however, may warrant an award of costs against even a neutral defendant of this type, where the successful claimant is not in receipt of legal aid and there is no appropriate third party to bear liability.[50] It is suggested that the factors will include i) whether the claim was necessary to remedy a breach of the ECHR, and ii) whether there had been any involvement in the case by the defendant worthy of some blame or straying away from strict neutrality.

It is submitted that the position in relation to claimants' costs may now be more favourable than the statements of principle in *Davies* (discussed below at 16-17). However, first it is convenient to consider the additional costs implications where the judicial review arises from criminal proceedings, and other occasions in which the applicability of the general rule can be questioned.

(8) A Criminal Cause or Matter

16-14   The question as to whether particular proceedings are a 'criminal cause or matter' is not always clear (see discussion above at 1-168 and at 2-44). It is to be determined by the

---

[46] *R (Pounder) v HM Coroner for the North and South Districts of Durham and Darlington* [2009] EWHC 76 (Admin).

[47] ibid [60].

[48] This was disclosed in a subsequent claim *R (Pounder) (No 2) v HM Coroner for North and South Districts of Durham and Darlington* [2010] EWHC 328 (Admin), which referred to the costs awarded against the coroner in the earlier claim at [36].

[49] ibid [37].

[50] *Davies* (n 43) [47(iv)].

character of the proceedings rather than by direct reference to whether the immediate proceedings under review are a criminal prosecution.[51]

The result is that ostensibly civil proceedings can amount to a 'criminal matter', while ancillary applications in criminal proceedings can fall outside of the definition. For example, following *Amand,* an application for habeas corpus arising out of a charge to be heard before a military tribunal is a criminal matter, as are extradition proceedings.[52] But an application for disclosure of documents produced in extradition proceedings by a third party is not: *R (Guardian News and Media Ltd) v City of Westminster Magistrates' Court & Anor.*[53] The *Guardian* case contains a thorough review of the authorities, the difficulty of reconciling them, and a somewhat uncertain attempt by the Master of the Rolls to resolve the issues.[54]

(9) Defence Costs Orders or 'RDCOs' (Recovery of Defence Costs Orders)

Until recently, where the judicial review was of a court by an accused in a 'criminal cause **16-15** or matter', section 16 of the Prosecution of Offences Act 1985 ameliorated the approach to costs in *Davies.* Such judicial reviews are usually dealt with by the Divisional Court, which had the power to award costs out of public funds, as section 16(5)(a) and 16(6) provide that where:

(a)   any proceedings in a criminal cause or matter are determined before a Divisional Court of the Queen's Bench Division;

...

the court may make a defendant's costs order in favour of the accused.

(6)   A defendant's costs order shall, subject to the following provisions of this section, be for the payment out of central funds, to the person in whose favour the order is made, of such amount as the court considers reasonably sufficient to compensate him for any expenses properly incurred by him in the proceedings.

However, the position has changed since October 2012, when Schedule 7 of LASPO 2012 came into force. This inserted section 16A into the Prosecution of Offences Act 1985, which emasculates defendant's costs orders made in the Divisional Court. These are renamed 'Recovery of Defence Costs Orders' (RCDOs). They now exclude the accused's legal costs in the Divisional Court. 'Legal costs' are defined in section 16A(10) as 'fees, charges, disbursements and other amounts payable in respect of advocacy services or litigation services including, in particular, expert witness costs'. It appears that 'out of pocket expenses, travelling expenses and subsistence allowance', which were defined as separate to 'legal costs' in the Costs in Criminal Cases (General) Regulations 1986 (SI 1986/1335), remain included.

---

[51]   *Amand v Home Secretary* [1943] AC 147, 156, 160.

[52]   *R (Government of the United States of America) v Bow Street Magistrates' Court* [2006] EWHC 2256 (Admin).

[53]   *R (Guardian News and Media Ltd) v City of Westminster Magistrates' Court & Anor* [2011] EWCA Civ 1188.

[54]   'I accept that this conclusion may be said to fall foul of the wide principle ... in *Amand* ... I am far from saying that, in the absence of any authority, I would have reached the same conclusion, or that I would be confident that, if they were called on to clarify the law in this area, the Supreme Court would reach the same conclusion ... [T]he competing arguments ... appear finely balanced'. Ibid [37]–[40],

An RDCO made by the Divisional Court may however provide for the recovery of legal costs incurred below in the magistrates' court or in the Crown Court on appeal under section 108 of MCA 1980.

(10) Other 'Special Parties' and Claims

16-16 It is inherent in claims for judicial review that the defendant will be a public body. Public bodies, especially those exercising regulatory functions, are accustomed to costs protection from the courts on the basis of the principles in *Bradford MDC v Booth*.[55] Other than as noted above, such principles do not however apply in proceedings (such as judicial review) where the costs regime is governed by the CPR.[56]

The fact that a party is legally aided is normally irrelevant to the principles upon which costs are awarded as established in *Boxall* and *Bahta*. It is however a factor that encourages detailed examination of the merits of a claim and militates against a 'fall back order' of no order as to costs; see *Re appeals by Governing Body of JFS*[57] as analysed in *Bahta*.

The reasons for the claim are also relevant:

> On the conclusion of full judicial review proceedings in a defendant's favour, the nature and purpose of the particular claim is relevant to the exercise of the judge's discretion as to costs. In contrast to a judicial review claim brought wholly or mainly for commercial or proprietary reasons, a claim brought partly or wholly in the public interest, albeit unsuccessful, may properly result in a restricted or no order for costs.[58]

(11) Implications for *Davies*

16-17 It will be noted that the cases cited above post-date *Davies*, as do the changes to RDCOs. In particular, the Supreme Court's decision in *JFS* casts doubt on the suggestion in *Davies*[59] that whether a lawyer recovers from a party at commercial rates or directly from the LAA is not a relevant consideration:

> It is one thing for solicitors who do a substantial amount of publicly funded work, and who have to fund the substantial overheads that sustaining a legal practice involves, to take the risk of being paid at lower rates if a publicly funded case turns out to be unsuccessful. It is quite another for them to be unable to recover remuneration at inter partes rates in the event that their case is successful. If that were to become the practice, their businesses would very soon become financially unsustainable. The system of public funding would be gravely disadvantaged in its turn, as it depends upon there being a pool of reputable solicitors who are willing to undertake this work …[60]

---

[55] *Bradford MDC v Booth* [2000] EWHC Admin 444.
[56] See *Peripanathan v City of Westminster Magistrates' Court (1) and the Metropolitan Police Commissioner (2)* [2010] EWCA Civ 40 [40].
[57] *Re appeals by Governing Body of JFS* [2009] UKSC 1 [24]–[25].
[58] *Davey v Aylesbury Vale DC* (n 24) [21].
[59] *Davies* (n 43) [46.7].
[60] *JFS* (n 57) [25].

It is submitted that the savage cuts made subsequently to the legal aid scheme both add force to this reasoning, and underline the importance of a further substantial benefit it entails. Where costs are awarded to a publicly funded solicitor it results in a great saving to the LAA, who are left bearing only nominal costs. In *Bahta*, *JFS* was held to be 'of general application'.[61]

It is also hard to reconcile the reference in *Davies* to the relevance of a lack of public funding,[62] with the forthright rejection of basing any order for costs on such considerations in *Mousa*. In that case the Divisional Court held that it was bound by section 22(4) of the Access of Justice Act 1999[63] to find as it did, notwithstanding its 'enormous sympathy and greatest respect' for the claimant's (successful in part) legal team who had acted with 'industry ... great skill and very considerable restraint and economy'.[64]

Further, given that both courts are now ostensibly governed by the same costs regime, notwithstanding the pre-CPR authorities cited in *Davies*, it might be thought that Simon Brown LJ's observation in *Touche* (considered in *Davies*) retains considerable force that:

> [h]aving appealed ... the coroner is to be treated like any other appellant: if he wins, he recovers his costs; if he loses, he pays the respondent's costs. Why then should the position be different [on judicial review]?[65]

Similarly, it is not immediately apparent that the interests of justice require the protection in costs given in *Davies* to magistrates and others, when it is accepted that other elements of the justice system, such as the CPS, the police, the Legal Aid Agency and the Ministry of Justice are treated as ordinary litigants.

D. Basis and Method of Assessment

(1) General Principles

Costs are only recoverable where they were reasonably incurred and reasonable in **16-18** amount. Any doubts are resolved in favour of the paying party where costs are assessed on the standard basis CPR 44.3(2), or the receiving party if on the indemnity basis CPR 43(3).

Costs are only recoverable on the 'indemnity principle'. 'Indemnity' here has an entirely different meaning: it means that the successful party cannot recover more from the unsuccessful party than he would have been required to pay his own lawyers. Costs are a recompense of the expense the successful party has been put to; not a punishment.

---

61 *Bahta* (n 19) [49].
62 *Davies* (n 43) [47.4].
63 See now LASPO, s 30 which has identical terms
64 *Mousa* (n 41) [63]–[64].
65 *Touche* (n 7) [54].

(2) Conduct

16-19   The court will have regard to 'all of the factors' when deciding costs issues, but conduct is of paramount importance.

CPR 44.2(5) provides that conduct' includes:

(a)   conduct before as well as during the proceedings, and in particular, the extent to which the parties followed the Practice Direction—Pre-Action Conduct or any relevant pre-action protocol;

(b)   whether it was reasonable for a party to raise, pursue or contest a particular allegation or issue;

(c)   the manner in which a party has pursued or defended its case or a particular allegation or issue; and

(d)   whether a claimant who has succeeded in the claim, in whole or in part, exaggerated its claim.

The extent to which a party has conducted the litigation in an appropriate manner (or otherwise) by, for example appropriately limiting the points taken, maintaining a consistent line in the litigation and suitably and promptly applying to amend to reflect a changed case can in themselves have a major bearing on the award of costs.[66] The recent amendments to CPR 1 and CPR 3, part of the Jackson reforms, give increased emphasis to adherence to the court timetable and directions generally. A 'stricter approach' to these issues is now appropriate.[67] *Mitchell MP v News Group Newspapers*[68] is an example of that approach in a costs context, including an express acceptance that this can amount to a 'windfall' for a party.[69] The lead authority on the new approach is currently the Court of Appeal's judgment in *Mitchell,*[70] though given the controversy that the application of the principles as there enunciated has led to it seems likely that these will, at the least, be refined further shortly. At the time of writing judgment is awaited from the Court of Appeal on a number of linked cases that were expected to give further guidance.

The principles derived from *Mitchell* can be summarised as follows:

—   For every breach of a court order, direction or provision of the CPR, the starting point is that the sanctions there set out (i.e. in the CPR or contained in the Order) are proportionate.[71]

—   A breach that is 'trivial', for example where in substance the direction etc. was complied with albeit with minor technical defects, or where a court deadline was missed by a matter of hours rather than days, will not attract sanctions.[72]

---

[66] *R (Srinivasans Solicitors) v Croydon County Court & Anor* [2013] EWCA Civ 249 provides an object lesson in the costs consequences of failing to heed these principles. The successful claimant sought over £40, 000 on summary assessment. The Court of Appeal upheld the judge's refusal to make any order as to costs. Although this is in part based on the fact that the claimant was only partially successful, that in itself reflected a scatter-gun approach by the claimant, who was described as 'the author of its own misfortune'. It is perhaps worth noting, given the focus of the rest of this section, that there was no suggestion that the order was based on any of the *Mitchell* principles.

[67] *Fons HF v Corporal Ltd and Anor* [2013] EWHC 1278 (Ch) [10].

[68] *Mitchell MP v News Group Newspapers* [2013] EWHC 2355 [25]–[31].

[69] ibid [46].

[70] *Mitchell MP v News Group Newspapers* [2013] EWCA Civ 1537.

[71] ibid [45].

[72] ibid [41].

— Where the breach is not trivial, a 'good reason' will need to be shown to avoid the imposition of the sanction.[73]
— That an appropriate 'sanction' can be derived from a similar rule of the CPR and need not explicitly cover the exact scenario before the court.[74]
— Where it becomes apparent that there will be a breach, an application to extend time should be made before the time for compliance, rather than for relief from sanctions after the event.[75]

The Court of Appeal stressed repeatedly that the increased emphasis on compliance with court rules and directions in the CPR was in the interests of justice generally, albeit that they may appear disproportionate in an individual case. It appears inevitable that timeliness throughout the claim will be an increasingly weighty factor when 'conduct' is assessed.

Much judicial consideration has been given to, and much ink spilled in analysis of, **16-20** the question of how these principles should be applied to a range of factual scenarios and provisions of the CPR. While it is outside the scope of this chapter to consider the ramifications in detail it should be noted that the new approach has led to decisions to deny parties the opportunity to rely upon witness evidence,[76] an expert report,[77] or even to maintain certain aspects of their case.[78]

The draconian and rigid approach to compliance has tempted parties to make applications on the basis of *Mitchell*, seeking to persuade a court that they have been too lenient about a breach by the other side. These have generally been disparaged, with the court making the point that sanctions for non-compliance in the broader interests of justice are a matter for the court and not the other party. For a party to seek an advantage on the basis of these principles can lead to unnecessary further expense and court time, precisely the evil the reforms were aimed at discouraging. Opportunistic applications have been rejected, and the non-defaulting party ordered to bear the whole of both parties' costs.[79]

(i) The Application to Judicial Review Cases

The extent to which the interests of justice, in their new formulation, would be served **16-21** by the *Mitchell* approach in judicial review matters is questionable. The paradigm civil claim is a private matter between two parties and the interests of the pubic generally are at least arguably upheld through a philosophy that elevates the justice system and the interests of litigants as a whole above the individual parties. By contrast a claim for judicial review is an allegation that a public body has acted unlawfully, and there is a greater public interest in ensuring that individual decisions are arrived after full consideration of the matter, rather than on an artificial basis where one party is prevented

---

[73] ibid [41].
[74] ibid [27].
[75] ibid [41]
[76] ibid.
[77] See *Boyle v Commissioner of Police for the Metropolis* [2013] EWCA Civ 1477.
[78] *M A Lloyd & Sons Ltd. (t/a KPM Marine) v PCC International Ltd. (t/a Professional Powercraft)* [2014] EWHC 41 (QB).
[79] *Summit Navigation Ltd & Anor. v Generali Romania Asigurare Reasigurare SA Ardaf SA & Anor* EWHC 398 (Comm) [63].

from putting its full case due to, for example, a delay in preparing its case. The court is particularly reluctant to find that a public body has acted unlawfully without full argument and materials, and these defendants often find that they are unable to comply with the deadlines in CPR 54. There has been little sign that these failings have attracted the severe approach in *Mitchell*, and presumably in the interests of the principle of equality of arms, claimants' failings also seem to receive some indulgence.

The judgment in *R (Singh & Ors) v Secretary of State for the Home Department* [2013] EWHC 2873 (Admin) is a case in point. There is no mention of *Mitchell* at all, though the court stated 'Although its manifestation may be different, the spirit of the Jackson reforms apply to public law cases as much as to private law claims'.[80] The court even expresses sympathy for the defendant[81] and despite some tough words the judgment effectively removed the requirement for compliance with some of the rules for the defendant for an interim period.[82] In many judicial reviews in the criminal context there will be an even greater public interest in ensuring that the final decision is arrived at on the merits, and a corresponding reluctance to impose *Mitchell* style sanctions.[83] This should not be taken to mean that there will not be severe consequences in costs for the defaulting party.

The above considerations do not imply that all aspects of a judicial review claim will be treated in a like manner. Some claims for judicial review include a claim for damages, and there is no reason why those elements should not attract a *Mitchell* approach—see for example *Singh* [33]–[34]. The court has sent a very clear signal that the rules relating to summary assessment must be complied with in judicial review matters.[84] Likewise, there have been some very 'robust' decisions about non-compliance with the CPR where the detailed assessment procedure is concerned;[85] there is no reason to think that a different approach is due where the costs in question arise from a judicial review.

(3) Basis for Indemnity Costs Awards

16-22   The courts have refused to trammel the discretion to award costs on the indemnity basis. It is an exceptional award, and requires 'some conduct or … some circumstance which takes the case out of the norm'.[86] The conduct of the party applying for the order is also relevant.[87]

The more significant the underlying wrong requiring remedy, the greater the affront to justice, the less acceptable the conduct of the paying party in the general sense, and the less reasonably the litigation has been conducted, the more likely the court is

---

[80]   *R (Singh & Ors) v Secretary of State for the Home Department* [2013] EWHC 2873 (Admin), [27].
[81]   ibid, [15].
[82]   ibid, [21]–[24], [28].
[83]   Though see *Durrant v Chief Constable of Somerset & Avon Constabulary* EWCA Civ [2013] 1624, where similar arguments were given short shrift, albeit in the context of a claim for damages.
[84]   *R (Chu) v Secretary of State for the Home Department* EWHC 1610 (Admin) [58].
[85]   See *Mount Eden Land Ltd v Speechly Bircham LLP* [2014] EWHC 169 QB [18]. Cf *Hallam Estates Ltd & Anor v Baker* [2014] EWCA Civ 66.
[86]   *Excelsior Commercial and Industrial Holdings Ltd v Salisbury Ham Johnson and Others* [2002] EWCA Civ 879 [19] (Lord Woolf).
[87]   *Bank of Tokyo LCJ Mitsubishi & Anor v Baskan Gida Sanayi Ve Pazarlama AS & Ors* [2009] EWHC 1696 [28]–[29].

James Packer

to make the award (*R (Rawlinson and Hunter Trustees SA) v Central Criminal Court (Costs), R (Tchenguiz) v Serious Fraud Office (Costs)*).[88] In that case costs were awarded on the indemnity basis to both sets of claimants but each receiving party was restricted to the costs of one leading counsel (each having two), illustrating that the award is not a blank cheque.

(4) Standard Basis—Proportionality

Where costs are assessed on the standard basis they must also be proportionately **16-23** incurred and proportionate in amount, with doubt to be resolved in favour of the paying party. Costs which are disproportionate in amount may be disallowed or reduced even if they were reasonably or necessarily incurred CPR 44.3(2)(a).[89] Costs must be proportionate to the matters in issue.

Judicial review litigation is unpredictable and it is not unusual in the life of the case for the facts or the law to develop as:

i. Many claims must be brought on an urgent basis before the whole picture is available.
ii. The consequences of any relief granted or the ongoing impact of the underlying alleged breach are often relevant to the case.
iii. It is common for cases to be brought where the law is uncertain and they are liable to be stayed pending a lead judgment.

This can make the application of the proportionality principle problematic. In recognition of factors of this sort the rules mandating costs budgets in multi-track litigation have not been applied to claims for judicial review. Similarly, there is no reported case in which a costs capping order has been sought under CPR 3.19 rather than as a part of a PCO.

(5) Summary and Detailed Assessment

Judicial reviews, even in the criminal context, are civil proceedings, and it is open to the **16-24** court to conduct an immediate summary assessment of the costs of the whole of the claim in accordance with CPR 44 PD 9.2 where a trial lasts less than one day; this is a common procedure where a case is dismissed at the permission stage. CPR 44 PD 9.5 gives detailed guidance to the preparation the court expects the parties to undertake where summary assessment is anticipated, which includes the service of a schedule of costs before the date of the hearing. As noted above at 16-19 and note 85 the increased emphasis upon compliance with the CPR makes adherence to these rules vital.

---

[88] [2012] EWHC 3218 (Admin).
[89] This is a tightening, as of April 2013, of the previous principle laid down in *Lowndes v Home Office* [2002] EWCA Civ 365, [31], that costs necessarily incurred were recoverable on the standard basis even where the overall total was disproportionate.

Where detailed assessment is ordered the parties may (and should attempt to) agree the amount to be paid as *inter partes* costs. If agreement cannot be reached, then a bill will need to be drawn and served by the receiving party. CPR 47 sets out the procedure to be followed, which should clarify the points in dispute between the parties and any concessions made by either side. If the parties remain unable to reach agreement the court will make a provisional assessment on the papers, which is subject to a fixed costs regime CPR 47.15(5).

A party which remains dissatisfied and persists to an oral hearing must generally pay the whole of the costs of that hearing (of both parties) unless it achieves an adjustment in its own favour by 20 per cent or more of the sum provisionally assessed CPR 47.15(10)(b).

(6) Where the Claimant is Legally Aided

16-25   The costs to be received by a party who has been funded by legal aid must be subject to detailed assessment, though the costs awarded against that party could be summarily assessed. If the parties can agree the amount of costs to be paid as between themselves, the 'legal aid only costs' will still require detailed assessment.

As noted above, the court will generally make an order for costs against a party without regard to the fact that it is receipt of public funding. That party will however have 'costs protection' in respect of costs incurred whilst the public funding is in place. The court can only make an order that he pays an amount that is reasonable having regard to his resources (and to those of the other parties to the litigation) and his conduct.[90] This will usually require a yet further assessment by the court and, given the meagre resources of those who qualify for public funding, it is rare in practice that such orders are sought.

The effect of the Civil Legal Aid (Costs) Regulations 2013 (SI 2013/611) is to prevent a public body from seeking its costs in the Administrative Court from the Lord Chancellor (ie the LAA). This does not however operate so as to prevent the public body setting off costs it was awarded on one issue against those it is to pay on another.

E. Costs in the Upper Tribunal

(1) Costs in Principle

16-26   Some categories of claims judicial review must now be brought in, and others must or may be transferred to, the Upper Tribunal ('UT'). As one of the limiting conditions on the ability of the UT to hear claims is that they 'must not call in to question anything done by the Crown Court' (section 18(5) of the Tribunals, Courts and Enforcement

---

[90] LASPO 2012 s 26.

Act 2007), their relevance to this book is in respect of criminal injuries compensation matters (see above at section E in Chapter 9).

Appeals against CICA review decisions are heard in the First-Tier Tribunal (Social Entitlement Chamber). There is no right of further appeal to the Upper Tribunal, but the UT has jurisdiction over applications for judicial review of these decisions of the First-Tier Tribunal (FTT).

Judicial review in the UT is something of a novelty, and currently there is uncertainty as to the correct approach to costs. The sole authority on the point to date is *R (LR) v FTT (HESC) and Hertfordshire CC*.[91] In this case the UT held that:

> We acknowledge that the relevant principles may be different in categories of judicial review which are not before us, but as regards those where it is the First tier Tribunal whose decision is being challenged, rather than an initial decision-maker, and where the case is of a category where the Upper Tribunal has exclusive jurisdiction, we conclude that, as a general rule ... the appropriate basis for applying the Upper Tribunal's discretion under section 29 is that it should not do so to make an award of costs where the tribunal below would have had no power to do so.[92]

The Social Entitlement Chamber of the FTT having no power to award costs, it appears that the general rule in CICA cases is that there will be no award of costs.[93] The Upper Tribunal does, however, have a residual power to award wasted costs, though the case suggests that even these may be refused if, as in Social Entitlement Chamber cases, the First-Tier had no power to award costs.[94]

It should be noted that rule 10 of the UT Procedure Rules sets out in detail how and when an application for costs must be made, how it is to be decided, and provision for assessment in the High Court.

F. Costs on Appeal

(1) Summary

There are a number of additional costs elements to consider on appeal from the High   **16-27** Court. The following is a short summary.

    i.   The appeal court may amend orders as to costs made in the court below (CPR 44.10(4)). Generally, the party successful on appeal will be awarded the costs of the case below.

---

[91] *R (LR) v FTT (HESC) and Hertfordshire CC* [2013] UKUT 294 (AAC).

[92] ibid [34]. A review of a decision of the Health, Education and Social Care Chamber (HESC).

[93] Tribunal Procedure (First-Tier Tribunal) (Social entitlement Chamber) Rules, r 10.

[94] *LR* (n 71) [27]: 'Mr Newton submits that it would be odd to adopt the principle ... in that it would, for instance, preclude the Upper Tribunal from making a wasted costs order in judicial review cases originating from tribunals whose rules do not ... allow them to do so. While there may be unexplored issues around the interaction between section 29(4) and the rules of some of chambers, we do not feel the need to explore them here. Whatever the position is with regard to judicial review cases coming to the Upper Tribunal from such chambers, it is also the case in relation to the far more numerous category of statutory appeals and does not appear to cause difficulty, thus we attach little weight to the point.'

ii.   The protection afforded to judicial officers (for example magistrates and coroners) does not apply on appeal, following *Davies* (although that does not indicate that the costs order below ought to be disturbed for this class of defendant).

iii.   Appeals from the Upper Tribunal exercising its judicial review functions are to the Court of Appeal. It remains to be seen how costs will be dealt with in those circumstances, but logically the principles in (ii) above should apply.

iv.   Even where multiple representation was suitable below, where for example many cases raised the same issue, it will not usually be appropriate on appeal (see for example *Rawlinson and Hunter* discussed above at 16-22).[95]

v.   The High Court or Court of Appeal can impose conditions upon a grant of permission to appeal (CPR 52.3(7)(b) and CPR 52.9(1)(c)). These can include prohibiting the appellant from recovering any costs consequent upon the appeal, ordering that it shall meet the costs of the respondent in any event, and even that the costs ordered below shall not be disturbed. These orders have received some judicial encouragement, especially where it is the public body appealing in its own interests on a point of general concern.[96]

vi.   Where the court grants permission to appeal, and the order is silent as to costs, it is deemed to include the applicant's costs in the case (CPR 44.10(2)(c)).

vii.   Where a claimant was successful at first instance, and was the beneficiary of a PCO, they will ordinarily be granted a PCO in the Court of Appeal (see *Compton* above at 16-4).

viii.   If a public body defendant is successful on appeal, where the claimant was publically funded, it may make an application that the LAA meets its costs directly (of the appeal only). (The barrier to such applications applies to 'first instance' proceedings.)

ix.   An appeal does not bar the successful party below proceeding with his application for costs while the appeal is considered unless the court so orders (CPR 47.2).

x.   Where a Divisional Court in a criminal cause or matter is appealed to the Supreme Court, that court may make an RDCO in respect of 'legal costs' of both the application for permission and the appeal itself (see discussion above at 16-15).[97]

---

95   *Rawlinson and Hunter Trustees* (n 88) [17].
96   *Weaver v London & Quadrant Housing Trust* [2009] EWCA Civ 235.
97   POA 1985 ss 16A(2) and 16A(5).

Annexes

Annex 1

Pre-Action Protocol for Judicial Review

Introduction

This protocol applies to proceedings within England and Wales only. It does not affect the time limit specified by Rule 54.5(1) of the Civil Procedure Rules which requires that any claim form in an application for judicial review must be filed promptly and in any event not later than 3 months after the grounds to make the claim first arose or the shorter time limits specified by Rules 54.5(5) and (6) which set out that a claim form for certain planning judicial reviews must be filed within 6 weeks and the claim form for certain procurement judicial reviews must be filed within 30 days.[1]

1

Judicial review allows people with a sufficient interest in a decision or action by a public body to ask a judge to review the lawfulness of:

— an enactment; or
— a decision, action or failure to act in relation to the exercise of a public function[2]

2

Judicial review may be used where there is no right of appeal or where all avenues of appeal have been exhausted.

Alternative Dispute Resolution

3.1

The parties should consider whether some form of alternative dispute resolution procedure would be more suitable than litigation, and if so, endeavour to agree which form to adopt. Both the Claimant and Defendant may be required by the Court to provide evidence that alternative means of resolving their dispute were considered. The Courts take the view that litigation should be a last resort, and that claims should not be issued prematurely when a settlement is still actively being explored. Parties are warned that if the protocol is not followed (including this paragraph) then the Court must have regard to such conduct when determining costs. However, parties should also note that a claim for judicial review 'must be filed promptly and in any event not later than 3 months after the grounds to make the claim first arose'.

---

[1] While the court does have the discretion under r 3.1(2)(a) of the Civil Procedure Rules to allow a late claim, this is only used in exceptional circumstances. Compliance with the protocol alone is unlikely to be sufficient to persuade the court to allow a late claim.
[2] Civil Procedure Rule 54.1(2).

3.2

It is not practicable in this protocol to address in detail how the parties might decide which method to adopt to resolve their particular dispute. However, summarised below are some of the options for resolving disputes without litigation:

— Discussion and negotiation.
— Ombudsmen—the Parliamentary and Health Service and the Local Government Ombudsmen have discretion to deal with complaints relating to maladministration. The British and Irish Ombudsman Association provide information about Ombudsman schemes and other complaint handling bodies and this is available from their website at www.bioa.org.uk . Parties may wish to note that the Ombudsmen are not able to look into a complaint once court action has been commenced.
— Early neutral evaluation by an independent third party (for example, a lawyer experienced in the field of administrative law or an individual experienced in the subject matter of the claim).
— Mediation—a form of facilitated negotiation assisted by an independent neutral party.

3.3

The Legal Services Commission has published a booklet on 'Alternatives to Court', CLS Direct Information Leaflet 23 (www.clsdirect.org.uk), which lists a number of organisations that provide alternative dispute resolution services.

3.4

It is expressly recognised that no party can or should be forced to mediate or enter into any form of ADR.
Back to top

4

Judicial review may not be appropriate in every instance.

Claimants are strongly advised to seek appropriate legal advice when considering such proceedings and, in particular, before adopting this protocol or making a claim. Although the Legal Services Commission will not normally grant full representation before a letter before claim has been sent and the proposed defendant given a reasonable time to respond, initial funding may be available, for eligible claimants, to cover the work necessary to write this. (See Annex C for more information.)

5

This protocol sets out a code of good practice and contains the steps which parties should generally follow before making a claim for judicial review.

6

This protocol does not impose a greater obligation on a public body to disclose documents or give reasons for its decision than that already provided for in statute or common law. However, where the court considers that a public body should have provided relevant documents and/or information, particularly where this failure is a breach of a statutory or common law requirement, it may impose sanctions.

This protocol will not be appropriate where the defendant does not have the legal power to change the decision being challenged, for example decisions issued by tribunals such as the Asylum and Immigration Tribunal.

This protocol will not be appropriate in urgent cases, for example, when directions have been set, or are in force, for the claimant's removal from the UK, or where there is an urgent need for an interim order to compel a public body to act where it has unlawfully refused to do so (for example, the failure of a local housing authority to secure interim accommodation for a homeless claimant) a claim should be made immediately. A letter before claim will not stop the implementation of a disputed decision in all instances.

This protocol may not be appropriate in cases where one of the shorter time limits in Rules 54.5(5) or (6) applies. In those cases, the parties should still attempt to comply with this protocol but the court will not apply normal cost sanctions where the court is satisfied that it has not been possible to comply because of the shorter time limits.

7

All claimants will need to satisfy themselves whether they should follow the protocol, depending upon the circumstances of his or her case. Where the use of the protocol is appropriate, the court will normally expect all parties to have complied with it and will take into account compliance or non-compliance when giving directions for case management of proceedings or when making orders for costs.[3] However, even in emergency cases, it is good practice to fax to the defendant the draft Claim Form which the claimant intends to issue. A claimant is also normally required to notify a defendant when an interim mandatory order is being sought.

The Letter Before Claim

8

Before making a claim, the claimant should send a letter to the defendant. The purpose of this letter is to identify the issues in dispute and establish whether litigation can be avoided.

9

Claimants should normally use the suggested standard format for the letter outlined at Annex A.

10

The letter should contain the date and details of the decision, act or omission being challenged and a clear summary of the facts on which the claim is based. It should

---

[3] Civil Procedure Rules Costs Practice Direction.

also contain the details of any relevant information that the claimant is seeking and an explanation of why this is considered relevant. If the claim is considered to be an Aarhus Convention claim, the letter should state this clearly and explain the reasons, since specific rules as to costs apply to such claims.

11

The letter should normally contain the details of any interested parties[4] known to the claimant. They should be sent a copy of the letter before claim for information. Claimants are strongly advised to seek appropriate legal advice when considering such proceedings and, in particular, before sending the letter before claim to other interested parties or making a claim.

12

A claim should not normally be made until the proposed reply date given in the letter before claim has passed, unless the circumstances of the case require more immediate action to be taken.

The Letter of Response

13

Defendants should normally respond within 14 days using the standard format at Annex B. Failure to do so will be taken into account by the court and sanctions may be imposed unless there are good reasons.[5]

14

Where it is not possible to reply within the proposed time limit the defendant should send an interim reply and propose a reasonable extension. Where an extension is sought, reasons should be given and, where required, additional information requested. This will not affect the time limit for making a claim for judicial review[6] nor will it bind the claimant where he or she considers this to be unreasonable. However, where the court considers that a subsequent claim is made prematurely it may impose sanctions.

15

If the claim is being conceded in full, the reply should say so in clear and unambiguous terms.

---

[4] See Civil Procedure Rule 54.1(2)(f).
[5] See Civil Procedure Rules Pre-action Protocol Practice Direction paragraphs 2–3.
[6] See Civil Procedure Rule 54.5(1).

16

If the claim is being conceded in part or not being conceded at all, the reply should say so in clear and unambiguous terms, and:

    (a)   where appropriate, contain a new decision, clearly identifying what aspects of the claim are being conceded and what are not, or, give a clear timescale within which the new decision will be issued;

    (b)   provide a fuller explanation for the decision, if considered appropriate to do so;

    (c)   address any points of dispute, or explain why they cannot be addressed;

    (d)   enclose any relevant documentation requested by the claimant, or explain why the documents are not being enclosed; and

    (e)   where appropriate, confirm whether or not they will oppose any application for an interim remedy.

If the letter before claim has stated that the claim is an Aarhus Convention claim but the defendant does not accept this, the reply should state this clearly and explain the reasons.

17

The response should be sent to all interested parties[7] identified by the claimant and contain details of any other parties who the defendant considers also have an interest.

A. Letter Before Claim

Section 1. Information Required in a Letter Before Claim

Proposed Claim for Judicial Review

1

To
(Insert the name and address of the proposed defendant—see details in section 2)

2

The claimant
(Insert the title, first and last name and the address of the claimant)

3

Reference details
(When dealing with large organisations it is important to understand that the information relating to any particular individual's previous dealings with it may not be immediately

---

[7] See Civil Procedure Rule 54.1(2)(f).

available, therefore it is important to set out the relevant reference numbers for the matter in dispute and/or the identity of those within the public body who have been handling the particular matter in dispute—see details in section 3)

4

The details of the matter being challenged
(Set out clearly the matter being challenged, particularly if there has been more than one decision)

5

The issue
(Set out the date and details of the decision, or act or omission being challenged, a brief summary of the facts and why it is contented to be wrong)

6

The details of the action that the defendant is expected to take
(Set out the details of the remedy sought, including whether a review or any interim remedy are being requested)

7

The details of the legal advisers, if any, dealing with this claim
(Set out the name, address and reference details of any legal advisers dealing with the claim)

8

The details of any interested parties
(Set out the details of any interested parties and confirm that they have been sent a copy of this letter)

9

The details of any information sought
(Set out the details of any information that is sought. This may include a request for a fuller explanation of the reasons for the decision that is being challenged)

10

The details of any documents that are considered relevant and necessary
(Set out the details of any documentation or policy in respect of which the disclosure is sought and explain why these are relevant. If you rely on a statutory duty to disclose, this should be specified)

11

The address for reply and service of court documents
(Insert the address for the reply)

12

Proposed reply date
(The precise time will depend upon the circumstances of the individual case. However, although a shorter or longer time may be appropriate in a particular case, 14 days is a reasonable time to allow in most circumstances)

Section 2. Address for sending the Letter Before Claim

Public bodies have requested that, for certain types of cases, in order to ensure a prompt response, letters before claim could be sent to specific addresses.

Where the claim concerns a decision in an Immigration, Asylum or Nationality case:

The claim may be sent electronically to the following UK Border Agency email address: UKBAPAP@UKBA.gsi.gov.uk
Alternatively the claim may be sent by post to the following UK Border Agency postal address:
Judicial Review Unit
UK Border Agency
Lunar House
40 Wellesley Rd
Croydon CR9 2BY

Where the claim concerns a decision by the Legal Services Commission:

The address on the decision letter/notification;
Legal Director
Corporate Legal Team
Legal Services Commission
102 Petty France
London SW1H 9AJ

Where the claim concerns a decision by a local authority:

The address on the decision letter/notification; and
Their legal department[8]

Where the claim concerns a decision by a department or body for whom Treasury Solicitor acts and Treasury Solicitor has already been involved in the case a copy should also be sent, quoting the Treasury Solicitor's reference, to:

The Treasury Solicitor,
One Kemble Street,
London WC2B 4TS

In all other circumstances, the letter should be sent to the address on the letter notifying the decision.

---

[8] The relevant address should be available from a range of sources such as the Phone Book; Business and Services Directory, Thomson's Local Directory, CAB, etc.

Section 3. Specific Reference Details Required

Public bodies have requested that the following information should be provided in order to ensure prompt response.

Where the claim concerns an Immigration, Asylum or Nationality case, dependent upon the nature of the case:

The Home Office reference number
The Port reference number
The Asylum and Immigration Tribunal reference number
The National Asylum Support Service reference number

Or, if these are unavailable:

The full name, nationality and date of birth of the claimant.

Where the claim concerns a decision by the Legal Services Commission:

The certificate reference number.

B. Response to a Letter Before Claim

Information Required in a Response to a Letter Before Claim

Proposed Claim for Judicial Review

1

The claimant
(Insert the title, first and last names and the address to which any reply should be sent)

2

From
(Insert the name and address of the defendant)

3

Reference details
(Set out the relevant reference numbers for the matter in dispute and the identity of those within the public body who have been handling the issue)

4

The details of the matter being challenged
(Set out details of the matter being challenged, providing a fuller explanation of the decision, where this is considered appropriate)

5

Response to the proposed claim
(Set out whether the issue in question is conceded in part, or in full, or will be contested. Where it is not proposed to disclose any information that has been requested, explain the reason for this. Where an interim reply is being sent and there is a realistic prospect of settlement, details should be included)

6

Details of any other interested parties
(Identify any other parties who you consider have an interest who have not already been sent a letter by the claimant)

7

Address for further correspondence and service of court documents
(Set out the address for any future correspondence on this matter)

C. Notes on Public Funding for Legal Costs in Judicial Review

Public funding for legal costs in judicial review is available from legal professionals and advice agencies which have contracts with the Legal Services Commission as part of the Community Legal Service. Funding may be provided for:

Legal Help to provide initial advice and assistance with any legal problem; or

Legal Representation to allow you to be represented in court if you are taking or defending court proceedings. This is available in two forms:

— Investigative Help is limited to funding to investigate the strength of the proposed claim. It includes the issue and conduct of proceedings only so far as is necessary to obtain disclosure of relevant information or to protect the client's position in relation to any urgent hearing or time limit for the issue of proceedings. This includes the work necessary to write a letter before claim to the body potentially under challenge, setting out the grounds of challenge, and giving that body a reasonable opportunity, typically 14 days, in which to respond.

— Full Representation is provided to represent you in legal proceedings and includes litigation services, advocacy services, and all such help as is usually given by a person providing representation in proceedings, including steps preliminary or incidental to proceedings, and/or arriving at or giving effect to a compromise to avoid or bring to an end any proceedings. Except in emergency cases, a proper letter before claim must be sent and the other side must be given an opportunity to respond before Full Representation is granted.

Further information on the type(s) of help available and the criteria for receiving that help may be found in the Legal Service Manual Volume 3: "The Funding Code". This may be found on the Legal Services Commission website at:

www.legalservices.gov.uk

A list of contracted firms and Advice Agencies may be found on the Community Legal Services website at:

www.justask.org.uk

Annex 2

| Click here to reset form | Click here to print form |

Judicial Review
Claim Form

| In the High Court of Justice |
| Administrative Court |

Notes for guidance are available which explain how to complete the judicial review claim form. Please read them carefully before you complete the form.

For Court use only	
Administrative Court Reference No.	
Date filed	

Seal

SECTION 1 Details of the claimant(s) and defendant(s)

Claimant(s) name and address(es)

name

address

Telephone no.   Fax no.

E-mail address

Claimant's or claimant's solicitors' address to which documents should be sent.

name

address

Telephone no.   Fax no.

E-mail address

Claimant's Counsel's details

name

address

Telephone no.   Fax no.

E-mail address

1st Defendant

name

Defendant's or (where known) Defendant's solicitors' address to which documents should be sent.

name

address

Telephone no.   Fax no.

E-mail address

2nd Defendant

name

Defendant's or (where known) Defendant's solicitors' address to which documents should be sent.

name

address

Telephone no.   Fax no.

E-mail address

SECTION 2 Details of other interested parties

Include name and address and, if appropriate, details of DX, telephone or fax numbers and e-mail

name

address

Telephone no.   Fax no.

E-mail address

name

address

Telephone no.   Fax no.

E-mail address

SECTION 3 Details of the decision to be judicially reviewed

Decision:

Date of decision:

Name and address of the court, tribunal, person or body who made the decision to be reviewed.

name

address

SECTION 4 Permission to proceed with a claim for judicial review

I am seeking permission to proceed with my claim for Judicial Review.

Is this application being made under the terms of Section 18 Practice Direction 54 (Challenging removal)? ☐ Yes ☐ No

Are you making any other applications? If Yes, complete Section 8. ☐ Yes ☐ No

Is the claimant in receipt of a Community Legal Service Fund (CLSF) certificate? ☐ Yes ☐ No

Are you claiming exceptional urgency, or do you need this application determined within a certain time scale? If Yes, complete Form N463 and file this with your application. ☐ Yes ☐ No

Have you complied with the pre-action protocol? If No, give reasons for non-compliance in the box below. ☐ Yes ☐ No

Have you issued this claim in the region with which you have the closest connection? (Give any additional reasons for wanting it to be dealt with in this region in the box below). If No, give reasons in the box below. ☐ Yes ☐ No

Does the claim include any issues arising from the Human Rights Act 1998?
If Yes, state the articles which you contend have been breached in the box below. ☐ Yes ☐ No

---

SECTION 5 Detailed statement of grounds

☐ set out below   ☐ attached

SECTION 6 Aarhus Convention claim

I contend that this claim is an Aarhus Convention claim ☐ Yes ☐ No

If Yes, indicate in the following box if you do not wish the costs limits
under CPR 45.43 to apply.

If you have indicated that the claim is an Aarhus claim set out the grounds below

---

SECTION 7 Details of remedy (including any interim remedy) being sought

---

SECTION 8 Other applications

I wish to make an application for:-

SECTION 9 Statement of facts relied on

Statement of Truth

I believe (The claimant believes) that the facts stated in this claim form are true.

Full name_____

Name of claimant's solicitor's firm _____

Signed _____ Position or office held_____

           Claimant ('s solicitor)   (if signing on behalf of firm or company)

SECTION 10 Supporting documents

If you do not have a document that you intend to use to support your claim, identify it, give the date when you expect it to be available and give reasons why it is not currently available in the box below.

Please tick the papers you are filing with this claim form and any you will be filing later.

☐ Statement of grounds

☐ included   ☐ attached

☐ Statement of the facts relied on

☐ included   ☐ attached

☐ Application to extend the time limit for filing the claim form

☐ included   ☐ attached

☐ Application for directions

☐ included   ☐ attached

☐ Any written evidence in support of the claim or
application to extend time

☐ Where the claim for judicial review relates to a decision of
a court or tribunal, an approved copy of the reasons for
reaching that decision

☐ Copies of any documents on which the claimant
proposes to rely

☐ A copy of the legal aid or CSLF certificate *(if legally represented)*

☐ Copies of any relevant statutory material

☐ A list of essential documents for advance reading by
the court *(with page references to the passages relied upon)*

If Section 18 Practice Direction 54 applies, please tick the relevant box(es) below to indicate which papers you are filing with this claim form:

☐ a copy of the removal directions and the decision to which
the application relates

☐ included   ☐ attached

☐ a copy of the documents served with the removal directions
including any documents which contains the Immigration and
Nationality Directorate's factual summary of the case

☐ included   ☐ attached

☐ a detailed statement of the grounds

☐ included   ☐ attached

Reasons why you have not supplied a document and date when you expect it to be available:-

Signed _____ Claimant ('s Solicitor)_____

Click here to print form

Annex 3

Click here to reset form | Click here to print form

Judicial Review
Application for urgent consideration

In the High Court of Justice	
Administrative Court	

This form must be completed by the Claimant or the Claimant's advocate if exceptional urgency is being claimed and the application needs to be determined within a certain time scale.

The claimant, or the claimant's solicitors must serve this form on the defendant(s) and any interested parties with the N461 Judicial review claim form.

To the Defendant(s) and Interested Party(ies)
Representations as to the urgency of the claim may be made by defendants or interested parties to the relevant Administrative Court Office by fax or email:-

For cases proceeding in

Claim No.	
Claimant(s) *(including ref.)*	
Defendant(s)	
Interested Party(ies)	

London
Fax: 020 7947 6802   **email:** administrativecourtoffice.generaloffice@hmcts.x.gsi.gov.uk

Birmingham
Fax: 0121 250 6730   **email:** administrativecourtoffice.birmingham@hmcts.x.gsi.gov.uk

Cardiff
Fax: 02920 376461   **email:** administrativecourtoffice.cardiff@hmcts.x.gsi.gov.uk

Leeds
Fax: 0113 306 2581   **email:** administrativecourtoffice.leeds@hmcts.x.gsi.gov.uk

Manchester
Fax: 0161 240 5315   **email:** administrativecourtoffice.manchester@hmcts.x.gsi.gov.uk

SECTION 1 Reasons for urgency

SECTION 2 Proposed timetable *(tick the boxes and complete the following statements that apply)*

☐ a) The N461 application for permission should be considered within _____ hours/days

   If consideration is sought within 48 hours, you must complete Section 3 below

☐ b) Abridgement of time is sought for the lodging of acknowledgments of service

☐ c) If permission for judicial review is granted, a substantive hearing is sought by _____ (date)

SECTION 3 Justification for request for immediate consideration

Date and time when it was first appreciated that an immediate application might be necessary.

Date	Time

Please provide reasons for any delay in making the application.

What efforts have been made to put the defendant and any interested party on notice of the application?

SECTION 4 Interim relief *(state what interim relief is sought and why in the box below)*

A draft order must be attached.

SECTION 5 Service

A copy of this form of application was served on the defendant(s) and interested parties as follows:

Defendant

☐ by fax machine to   time sent
Fax no. / time

☐ by handing it to or leaving it with
name

☐ by e-mail to
e-mail address

Date served
Date

Interested party

☐ by fax machine to   time sent
Fax no. / time

☐ by handing it to or leaving it with
name

☐ by e-mail to
e-mail address

Date served
Date

I confirm that all relevant facts have been disclosed in this application

Name of claimant's advocate
name

Claimant (claimant's advocate)
Signed

Annex 4

Judicial Review
Acknowledgment of Service

Name and address of person to be served

name	

address	

In the High Court of Justice	
Administrative Court	

Claim No.	
Claimant(s) (including ref.)	
Defendant(s)	
Interested Parties	

SECTION A

Tick the appropriate box

1. I intend to contest all of the claim ☐ ⎫
2. I intend to contest part of the claim ☐ ⎬ complete sections B, C, D and F
3. I do not intend to contest the claim ☐ complete section F
4. The defendant (interested party) is a court or tribunal and **intends** to make a submission. ☐ complete sections B, C and F
5. The defendant (interested party) is a court or tribunal and **does not intend** to make a submission. ☐ complete sections B and F
6. The applicant has indicated that this is a claim to which the Aarhus Convention applies. ☐ complete sections E and F

Note: If the application seeks to judicially review the decision of a court or tribunal, the court or tribunal need only provide the Administrative Court with as much evidence as it can about the decision to help the Administrative Court perform its judicial function.

SECTION B

Insert the name and address of any person you consider should be added as an interested party.

name		name	

address		address	

Telephone no.	Fax no.	Telephone no.	Fax no.

E-mail address		E-mail address	

633

SECTION C

Summary of grounds for contesting the claim. If you are contesting only part of the claim, set out which part before you give your grounds for contesting it. If you are a court or tribunal filing a submission, please indicate that this is the case.

SECTION D

Give details of any directions you will be asking the court to make, or tick the box to indicate that a separate application notice is attached.

> If you are seeking a direction that this matter be heard at an Administrative Court venue other than that at which this claim was issued, you should complete, lodge and serve on all other parties Form N464 with this acknowledgment of service.

SECTION E

Response to the claimant's contention that the claim is an Aarhus claim

Do you deny that the claim is an Aarhus Convention claim?   ☐ Yes   ☐ No

If Yes, please set out your grounds for denial in the box below.

SECTION F

| *delete as appropriate | *(I believe)(The defendant believes) that the facts stated in this form are true. | (if signing on behalf of firm or company, court or tribunal) | Position or office held |
| | *I am duly authorised by the defendant to sign this statement. | | |

(To be signed by you or by your solicitor or litigation friend)

Signed _____   Date _____

Give an address to which notices about this case can be sent to you

name _____

address _____

Telephone no. _____ Fax no. _____

E-mail address _____

If you have instructed counsel, please give their name address and contact details below.

name _____

address _____

Telephone no. _____ Fax no. _____

E-mail address _____

Completed forms, together with a copy, should be lodged with the Administrative Court Office (court address, over the page), at which this claim was issued within 21 days of service of the claim upon you, and further copies should be served on the Claimant(s), any other Defendant(s) and any interested parties within 7 days of lodgement with the Court.

Click here to print form

Administrative Court addresses

- Administrative Court in **London**

  Administrative Court Office, Room C315, Royal Courts of Justice, Strand, London, WC2A 2LL.

- Administrative Court in **Birmingham**

  Administrative Court Office, Birmingham Civil Justice Centre, Priory Courts, 33 Bull Street, Birmingham B4 6DS.

- Administrative Court in **Wales**

  Administrative Court Office, Cardiff Civil Justice Centre, 2 Park Street, Cardiff, CF10 1ET.

- Administrative Court in **Leeds**

  Administrative Court Office, Leeds Combined Court Centre, 1 Oxford Row, Leeds, LS1 3BG.

- Administrative Court in **Manchester**

  Administrative Court Office, Manchester Civil Justice Centre, 1 Bridge Street West, Manchester, M3 3FX.

Annex 5

Schedule 1 of the Human Rights Act 1998

Schedule 1

The Articles

Section 1(3)

Part I

The Convention Rights And Freedoms

Right To Life

Article 2

1. Everyone's right to life shall be protected by law. No one shall be deprived of his life intentionally save in the execution of a sentence of a court following his conviction of a crime for which this penalty is provided by law.
2. Deprivation of life shall not be regarded as inflicted in contravention of this Article when it results from the use of force which is no more than absolutely necessary:
   (a) in defence of any person from unlawful violence;
   (b) in order to effect a lawful arrest or to prevent the escape of a person lawfully detained;
   (c) in action lawfully taken for the purpose of quelling a riot or insurrection.

Prohibition of torture

Article 3

No one shall be subjected to torture or to inhuman or degrading treatment or punishment.

Prohibition of slavery and forced labour

Article 4

1. No one shall be held in slavery or servitude.
2. No one shall be required to perform forced or compulsory labour.

3. For the purpose of this Article the term "forced or compulsory labour" shall not include:
   (a) any work required to be done in the ordinary course of detention imposed according to the provisions of Article 5 of this Convention or during conditional release from such detention;
   (b) any service of a military character or, in case of conscientious objectors in countries where they are recognised, service exacted instead of compulsory military service;
   (c) any service exacted in case of an emergency or calamity threatening the life or well-being of the community;
   (d) any work or service which forms part of normal civic obligations.

Right to liberty and security

Article 5

1. Everyone has the right to liberty and security of person. No one shall be deprived of his liberty save in the following cases and in accordance with a procedure prescribed by law:
   (a) the lawful detention of a person after conviction by a competent court;
   (b) the lawful arrest or detention of a person for non-compliance with the lawful order of a court or in order to secure the fulfilment of any obligation prescribed by law;
   (c) the lawful arrest or detention of a person effected for the purpose of bringing him before the competent legal authority on reasonable suspicion of having committed an offence or when it is reasonably considered necessary to prevent his committing an offence or fleeing after having done so;
   (d) the detention of a minor by lawful order for the purpose of educational supervision or his lawful detention for the purpose of bringing him before the competent legal authority;
   (e) the lawful detention of persons for the prevention of the spreading of infectious diseases, of persons of unsound mind, alcoholics or drug addicts or vagrants;
   (f) the lawful arrest or detention of a person to prevent his effecting an unauthorised entry into the country or of a person against whom action is being taken with a view to deportation or extradition.
2. Everyone who is arrested shall be informed promptly, in a language which he understands, of the reasons for his arrest and of any charge against him.
3. Everyone arrested or detained in accordance with the provisions of paragraph 1(c) of this Article shall be brought promptly before a judge or other officer authorised by law to exercise judicial power and shall be entitled to trial within a reasonable time or to release pending trial. Release may be conditioned by guarantees to appear for trial.
4. Everyone who is deprived of his liberty by arrest or detention shall be entitled to take proceedings by which the lawfulness of his detention shall be decided speedily by a court and his release ordered if the detention is not lawful.
5. Everyone who has been the victim of arrest or detention in contravention of the provisions of this Article shall have an enforceable right to compensation.

Right to a fair trial

Article 6

1. In the determination of his civil rights and obligations or of any criminal charge against him, everyone is entitled to a fair and public hearing within a reasonable time by an independent and impartial tribunal established by law. Judgment shall be pronounced publicly but the press and public may be excluded from all or part of the trial in the interest of morals, public order or national security in a democratic society, where the interests of juveniles or the protection of the private life of the parties so require, or to the extent strictly necessary in the opinion of the court in special circumstances where publicity would prejudice the interests of justice.
2. Everyone charged with a criminal offence shall be presumed innocent until proved guilty according to law.
3. Everyone charged with a criminal offence has the following minimum rights:
    (a) to be informed promptly, in a language which he understands and in detail, of the nature and cause of the accusation against him;
    (b) to have adequate time and facilities for the preparation of his defence;
    (c) to defend himself in person or through legal assistance of his own choosing or, if he has not sufficient means to pay for legal assistance, to be given it free when the interests of justice so require;
    (d) to examine or have examined witnesses against him and to obtain the attendance and examination of witnesses on his behalf under the same conditions as witnesses against him;
    (e) to have the free assistance of an interpreter if he cannot understand or speak the language used in court.

No punishment without law

Article 7

1. No one shall be held guilty of any criminal offence on account of any act or omission which did not constitute a criminal offence under national or international law at the time when it was committed. Nor shall a heavier penalty be imposed than the one that was applicable at the time the criminal offence was committed.
2. This Article shall not prejudice the trial and punishment of any person for any act or omission which, at the time when it was committed, was criminal according to the general principles of law recognised by civilised nations.

Right to respect for private and family life

Article 8

1. Everyone has the right to respect for his private and family life, his home and his correspondence.
2. There shall be no interference by a public authority with the exercise of this right except such as is in accordance with the law and is necessary in a democratic

society in the interests of national security, public safety or the economic well-being of the country, for the prevention of disorder or crime, for the protection of health or morals, or for the protection of the rights and freedoms of others.

Freedom of thought, conscience and religion

Article 9

1. Everyone has the right to freedom of thought, conscience and religion; this right includes freedom to change his religion or belief and freedom, either alone or in community with others and in public or private, to manifest his religion or belief, in worship, teaching, practice and observance.
2. Freedom to manifest one's religion or beliefs shall be subject only to such limitations as are prescribed by law and are necessary in a democratic society in the interests of public safety, for the protection of public order, health or morals, or for the protection of the rights and freedoms of others.

Freedom of expression

Article 10

1. Everyone has the right to freedom of expression. This right shall include freedom to hold opinions and to receive and impart information and ideas without interference by public authority and regardless of frontiers. This Article shall not prevent States from requiring the licensing of broadcasting, television or cinema enterprises.
2. The exercise of these freedoms, since it carries with it duties and responsibilities, may be subject to such formalities, conditions, restrictions or penalties as are pre-scribed by law and are necessary in a democratic society, in the interests of national security, territorial integrity or public safety, for the prevention of disorder or crime, for the protection of health or morals, for the protection of the reputation or rights of others, for preventing the disclosure of information received in confidence, or for maintaining the authority and impartiality of the judiciary.

Freedom of assembly and association

Article 11

1. Everyone has the right to freedom of peaceful assembly and to freedom of asso-ciation with others, including the right to form and to join trade unions for the protection of his interests.
2. No restrictions shall be placed on the exercise of these rights other than such as are prescribed by law and are necessary in a democratic society in the interests of national security or public safety, for the prevention of disorder or crime, for the protection of health or morals or for the protection of the rights and freedoms of others. This Article shall not prevent the imposition of lawful restrictions on the exercise of these rights by members of the armed forces, of the police or of the administration of the State.

Right to marry

Article 12

Men and women of marriageable age have the right to marry and to found a family, according to the national laws governing the exercise of this right.

Prohibition of discrimination

Article 14

The enjoyment of the rights and freedoms set forth in this Convention shall be secured without discrimination on any ground such as sex, race, colour, language, religion, political or other opinion, national or social origin, association with a national minority, property, birth or other status.

Restrictions on political activity of aliens

Article 16

Nothing in Articles 10, 11 and 14 shall be regarded as preventing the High Contracting Parties from imposing restrictions on the political activity of aliens.

Prohibition of abuse of rights

Article 17

Nothing in this Convention may be interpreted as implying for any State, group or person any right to engage in any activity or perform any act aimed at the destruction of any of the rights and freedoms set forth herein or at their limitation to a greater extent than is provided for in the Convention.

Limitation on use of restrictions on rights

Article 18

The restrictions permitted under this Convention to the said rights and freedoms shall not be applied for any purpose other than those for which they have been prescribed.

Part II

The First Protocol

Protection of property

Article 1

Every natural or legal person is entitled to the peaceful enjoyment of his possessions. No one shall be deprived of his possessions except in the public interest and subject to the conditions provided for by law and by the general principles of international law.

The preceding provisions shall not, however, in any way impair the right of a State to enforce such laws as it deems necessary to control the use of property in accordance with the general interest or to secure the payment of taxes or other contributions or penalties.

Right to education

Article 2

No person shall be denied the right to education. In the exercise of any functions which it assumes in relation to education and to teaching, the State shall respect the right of parents to ensure such education and teaching in conformity with their own religious and philosophical convictions.

Right to free elections

Article 3

The High Contracting Parties undertake to hold free elections at reasonable intervals by secret ballot, under conditions which will ensure the free expression of the opinion of the people in the choice of the legislature.

Part III

Article 1 of The Thirteenth Protocol

Abolition of the death penalty

The death penalty shall be abolished. No one shall be condemned to such penalty or executed.

Table of Statutes

Table of Statutory Instruments

Table of Cases

Court of Justice of the European Union (formerly European Court of Justice)

European Commission and Court of Human Rights

General Court (EU) (formerly Court of First Instance (CFI)

Germany

Republic of Ireland

United Kingdom

Table of Practice Directions

Table of International and European Legislation, Treaties and Conventions

717

Table of Codes of Practice, Policy and Guidance

Index